READING AMERICAN INDIAN LAW

The study of American Indian law and policy usually focuses on federal statutes and court decisions, with these sources forming the basis for most textbooks. Virtually ignored is the robust and growing body of scholarly literature analyzing and contextualizing these primary sources. *Reading American Indian Law* is designed to fill that void. Organized into four parts, this book presents 16 of the most impactful law review articles written during the last three decades. Collectively, these articles explore the core concepts underlying the field: the range of voices including those of tribal governments and tribal courts, the role property has played in federal Indian law, and the misunderstandings between both people and sovereigns that have shaped changes in the law. Structured with flexibility in mind, this book may be used in a wide variety of classroom settings including law schools, tribal colleges, and both graduate and undergraduate programs.

GRANT CHRISTENSEN is an Associate Professor of Law at the University of North Dakota, an Affiliated Professor of American Indian Studies, and an Associate Justice on the Supreme Court of the Standing Rock Sioux Tribe. He is the author of *American Indians: Historical and Contemporary Perspectives* (2017).

MELISSA L. TATUM is Research Professor of Law at the University of Arizona. She has served on the Southwest Intertribal Court of Appeals and has edited multiple volumes of tribal court opinions including for the Navajo Nation and the Muscogee (Creek) Nation. She is the author of *Indigenous Justice: New Tools, Approaches, and Spaces* (2018), *Law, Culture & Environment* (2014), and *Structuring Sovereignty: Constitutions and Native Nations* (2014).

Reading American Indian Law

FOUNDATIONAL PRINCIPLES

Edited by

GRANT CHRISTENSEN
University of North Dakota

MELISSA L. TATUM
University of Arizona

CAMBRIDGE
UNIVERSITY PRESS

CAMBRIDGE
UNIVERSITY PRESS

University Printing House, Cambridge CB2 8BS, United Kingdom

One Liberty Plaza, 20th Floor, New York, NY 10006, USA

477 Williamstown Road, Port Melbourne, VIC 3207, Australia

314–321, 3rd Floor, Plot 3, Splendor Forum, Jasola District Centre, New Delhi – 110025, India

79 Anson Road, #06–04/06, Singapore 079906

Cambridge University Press is part of the University of Cambridge.

It furthers the University's mission by disseminating knowledge in the pursuit of education, learning, and research at the highest international levels of excellence.

www.cambridge.org
Information on this title: www.cambridge.org/9781108488532
DOI: 10.1017/9781108770804

© Grant Christensen and Melissa L. Tatum 2020

First published 2020

Printed and bound in Great Britain by Clays Ltd, Elcograf S.p.A.

A catalogue record for this publication is available from the British Library.

Library of Congress Cataloging-in-Publication Data
NAMES: Christensen, Grant, 1982- editor. | Tatum, Melissa L., editor.
TITLE: Reading American Indian law : foundational principles / [edited by]
Grant Christensen, Melissa L. Tatum.
DESCRIPTION: New York : Cambridge University Press, 2019. |
Includes bibliographical references and index.
IDENTIFIERS: LCCN 2019038212 (print) | LCCN 2019038213 (ebook) |
ISBN 9781108488532 (hardback) | ISBN 9781108726481 (paperback) |
ISBN 9781108770804 (epub)
SUBJECTS: LCSH: Indians of North America–Legal status, laws, etc. |
Indians of North America–Civil rights.
CLASSIFICATION: LCC KF8205 .R43 2019 (print) | LCC KF8205 (ebook) | DDC 342.7308/72–dc23
LC record available at https://lccn.loc.gov/2019038212
LC ebook record available at https://lccn.loc.gov/2019038213

ISBN 978-1-108-48853-2 Hardback
ISBN 978-1-108-72648-1 Paperback

We dedicate this book to the authors whose work made it possible and to all those who have devoted their lives and careers to the field of federal Indian law.

Contents

Editors and Contributors

EDITORS

Grant Christensen is an Associate Professor of Law, Director of the Indian Law Certificate Program, and Affiliated Professor of American Indian Studies at the University of North Dakota. He is the Co-Chair of the American Bar Association Business Law Section's Committee on Tribal Litigation, a peer reviewer for the American Indian Law Review, and an Associate Justice on the Standing Rock Sioux Tribe's Supreme Court. Professor Christensen earned his JD from Ohio State and his LLM in Indigenous Peoples Law and Policy from the University of Arizona. Before accepting his position at North Dakota he was a visiting professor at the University of Oregon, an adjunct professor at the University of Toledo, and a Fulbright Scholar exploring issues of treaty law and interpretation at Vilnius University in Lithuania.

Professor Christensen has both published and spoken widely on questions of Indian law. He is the author of American Indians: Historical and Contemporary Perspectives which has been widely adopted in undergraduate programs, as well as a number of law review articles and a collection of book chapters published by both Cambridge University Press and the American Bar Association. His work has been cited by Judge Posner on the Seventh Circuit, in Cohen's Handbook of Federal Indian Law, and extensively in the US Code Annotated. Professor Christensen has been asked to speak about Indian law issues on four continents to a wide variety of forums including tribal courts, legal practitioners, and fellow scholars.

Melissa L. Tatum is a Research Professor of Law and former Chair of the American Indian Studies Graduate Interdisciplinary Program at the University of Arizona, where she also holds affiliated faculty appointments with the Indigenous Peoples Law and Policy Program, the Native Nations Institute, and with Gender and Women's Studies. She has also served as Director of postgraduate Indian law programs at both the University of Arizona and the University of Tulsa. She has served on the Southwest Intertribal Court of Appeals, edited multiple volumes of tribal court opinions including for the Navajo Nation and the Muscogee (Creek) Nation, and has trained law enforcement and court personnel across the nation in issues relating to the Violence Against Women Acts. Professor Tatum earned her JD from the University of Michigan. Before taking her position at the University of Arizona she taught at the University of Tulsa, as a visiting professor at Michigan State and Wayne State Universities, and as an adjunct at the University of Detroit Mercy.

Professor Tatum is the author or co-author of seventeen law review articles and four books, including two textbooks which have been adopted by a variety of law, Indian Studies, and tribal governance programs. She has contributed chapters to the leading treatise on federal Indian law, as well as to three books exploring various aspects of comparative Indigenous peoples law. She has guest lectured at universities and conferences in six countries on three continents.

CONTRIBUTORS

Bethany Berger is the Wallace Stevens Professor of Law at the University of Connecticut. She is a graduate of Yale Law School and is a co-author and member of the Editorial Board of *Cohen's Handbook of Federal Indian Law*, the foundational treatise in the field. She is also the co-author of casebooks in both property law and American Indian law. Before joining the academy she was the Director of the Native American Youth Law Project of DNA-People's Legal Services on the Navajo and Hopi Nations and then became Managing Attorney of Advocates for Children of New York. She has also served as a judge for the Southwest Intertribal Court of Appeals.

Kristen Carpenter is the Council Tree Professor of Law, Director of the American Indian Law Program at the University of Colorado Law School, and a Faculty Affiliate with the Department of Ethnic Studies and the Center for the American West. Professor Carpenter also serves on the United Nations Expert Mechanism on the Rights of Indigenous Peoples as its member from North America. She is a graduate of Harvard Law School. Professor Carpenter was a founding member of the campus-wide Center for Native American and Indigenous Studies at University of Colorado Boulder and in 2016 she was the Oneida Indian Nation Visiting Professor of Law at Harvard Law School.

Robert N. Clinton is a Professor Emeritus at Arizona State University, where he is the Foundation Professor of Law. He is a graduate of the University of Chicago Law School and serves as Chief Justice of the Hopi Appellate Court and the Winnebago Supreme Court; as a justice for the Colorado River Indian Tribes Court of Appeal and the Hualapai Court of Appeals; and as a judge pro tem for the San Manuel Band of Serrano Mission Indians Tribal Court. Before joining the faculty at Arizona State, Professor Clinton taught at the University of Iowa where he was a founder and affiliated faculty member of the American Indian and Native Studies Program. Professor Clinton teaches and writes about federal Indian law and policy, constitutional law, and federal jurisdiction.

Matthew L. M. Fletcher is Professor of Law at Michigan State University College of Law, where he also serves as Director of the Indigenous Law and Policy Center. He is a graduate of the University of Michigan Law School and he sits as the Chief Justice of the Poarch Band of Creek Indians Supreme Court and as an appellate judge for the Grand Traverse Band of Ottawa and Chippewa Indians, the Mashpee Wampanoag Tribe, the Match-E-Be-Nash-She-Wish Band of Pottawatomi Indians, the Pokagon Band of Potawatomi Indians, the Hoopa Valley Tribe, the Nottawa-seppi Huron Band of Potawatomi Indians, the Tulalip Tribes, and the Santee Sioux Tribe of Nebraska. He is a member of the Grand Traverse Band. He is also the primary editor and author of Turtle Talk, the leading law blog on American Indian law and policy.

Philip Frickey was a member of the law faculty at Berkeley from 2000 until his death in 2010. Before joining the Berkeley faculty, he spent seventeen years as a member of the law faculty at the University of Minnesota. Professor Frickey was a graduate of the University of Michigan School of Law and began his legal career as a judicial clerk for US Supreme Court Justice Thurgood Marshall. He is widely considered a leading scholar in constitutional law, statutory interpretation, and Indian law. For his dedication to Indian law Professor Frickey was awarded the Lawrence R. Baca Lifetime Achievement Award from the Federal Bar Association's Indian Law section.

David H. Getches was Dean and Raphael J. Moses Professor of Natural Resources Law at the University of Colorado Law School. He taught on the faculty from 1979 until his death in 2011, taking two leaves of absence to serve as the Executive Director of the Colorado Department of Natural Resources and as a special consultant to the US Department of Interior. He was a graduate of the University of Southern California Law School and a prominent scholar in federal Indian law. Before entering academia, he founded and served as Executive Director of the Native American Rights Fund (NARF), a nonprofit law firm specializing in Native American legal issues. Upon his death the National Congress of American Indians unanimously voted to award him its Lifetime Achievement Award.

Sonia Katyal is the Distinguished Haas Professor and Chancellor's Professor of Law at Berkeley, where she is also the Co-Director of the Berkeley Center for Law & Technology. She is also an affiliate scholar at Stanford Law's Center for Internet and Society, and serves on the Executive Committee for the Berkeley Center for New

Media. She is a graduate of the University of Chicago Law School. Her scholarly work focuses on the intersection of technology, intellectual property, and civil rights. Professor Katyal's work is published with a variety of law reviews, as well as in other publications, including the *New York Times, Washington Post*, CNN, and the *Los Angeles Times*.

Sarah Krakoff is the Moses Lasky Professor of Law and Associate Dean for Faculty Affairs and Research at the University of Colorado (CU). She is a graduate of the University of California at Berkeley, Boalt Hall. Her areas of expertise include American Indian law, natural resources and public land law, and environmental justice. Professor Krakoff started her legal career at DNA-People's Legal Services on the Navajo Nation, where she initiated DNA's Youth Law Project. Before joining the Colorado Law tenure-track faculty, Professor Krakoff directed CU's American Indian Law Clinic.

Nell Jessup Newton is the Joseph A. Matson Dean and Professor of Law at Notre Dame Law School. She has previously served as Dean at the University of Connecticut School of Law and the Hastings College of the Law at the University of California. She is a graduate of the University of California, Hastings College of Law and is a prominent scholar of Indian law, authoring more than fifty articles and book chapters on Indian legal issues. She is also the editor-in-chief of *Cohen's Handbook of Federal Indian Law*, the leading treatise in the field. She has also previously served as an Associate Justice on the Yurok Tribal Supreme Court.

Judith Resnik is the Arthur Liman Professor of Law at Yale Law School and the founding director of the Liman Center for Public Interest Law. Her scholarship focuses on the impact of democracy on government services, the relationships of governments to their populations, and the roles of the federal, state, and tribal courts in a federalist system. She is the co-author of *Representing Justice: Invention, Controversy, and Rights in City-States and Democratic Courtrooms* (Yale University Press 2011) and many books and essays. A graduate of New York University School of Law, in 2018 Professor Resnik received an Honorary Doctorate from University College London and a two-year Andrew Carnegie Fellowship to write a book, *Impermissible Punishments*. She is also an occasional litigator. She has argued cases involving the exclusion of women from the Rotary Club and the role of appellate courts in the US Supreme Court.

Angela R. Riley is Professor of Law at University of California, Los Angeles, the Director of UCLA's Native Nations Law and Policy Center, and the director of the JD/MA joint degree program in Law and American Indian Studies. She is a graduate of Harvard Law School and she is a member of the Citizen Potawatomi Nation of Oklahoma where she serves as Chief Justice. Professor Riley's research focuses on Indigenous peoples' rights, with a particular emphasis on cultural property and Native governance. She is the Co-Chair for the United Nations–Indigenous

Peoples' Partnership Policy Board, an Evidentiary Hearing Officer for the Morongo Band of Mission Indians, and a co-editor of *Cohen's Handbook of Federal Indian Law*. In 2015 she served as the Oneida Indian Nation Visiting Professor of Law at Harvard Law School.

Judith V. Royster is Professor of Law at the University of Tulsa. She is a graduate of the University of Wisconsin Law School and her scholarly interests are in the field of American Indian law, with an emphasis on water rights, energy and mineral issues, and jurisdictional matters. She is on the Editorial Board for *Cohen's Handbook of Federal Indian Law*, is co-author of *Native American Natural Resources Law: Cases and Materials* (now in its fourth edition), and has published widely in law reviews and edited collections.

Joseph William Singer is the Bussey Professor of Law at Harvard Law School. He teaches and writes about property law, conflict of laws, and federal Indian law. He is also a graduate of Harvard Law School, and has published more than eighty law review articles and seven books on topics ranging from federal Indian law to the subprime mortgage crisis. Professor Singer has distinguished himself as one of the executive editors of the 2012 edition of *Cohen's Handbook of Federal Indian Law* (with 2015 Supplement). His work has been published in the *Yale Law Journal*, *Stanford Law Review*, *Northwestern Law Review*, and the *New York Times*.

Kevin Washburn is the N. William Hines Dean and Professor of Law at the University of Iowa. Dean Washburn is a citizen of the Chickasaw Nation of Oklahoma and a graduate of Yale Law School. He previously served as the Assistant Secretary of Indian Affairs in the Obama Administration and as general counsel of the National Indian Gaming Commission, an independent federal regulatory agency in Washington, DC. Before arriving at Iowa, Dean Washburn served as Dean of the University of New Mexico School of Law and had taught on the faculties of both the University of Arizona and the University of Minnesota. He also taught as the Oneida Indian Nation Visiting Professor of Law at Harvard Law School. His scholarship focuses on criminal law in Indian country and Indian gaming.

Robert A. Williams, Jr. is the Regents' Professor, E. Thomas Sullivan Professor of Law, and Faculty Co-Chair of the University of Arizona Indigenous Peoples Law and Policy Program. He is a graduate of Harvard Law School and was named the first Oneida Indian Nation Visiting Professor of Law at Harvard. Professor Williams is a member of the Lumbee Nation. He has served as Chief Justice for the Court of Appeals, Pascua Yaqui Indian Reservation, and as a Justice for the Court of Appeals and trial judge pro tem for the Tohono O'odham Nation. He has represented tribal groups and members before the Inter-American Court of Human Rights, the Inter-American Commission on Human Rights, the United Nations Working Group on Indigenous Peoples, the United States Supreme Court, and the Supreme Court of Canada.

Robert Yazzie is a citizen of, and Chief Justice Emeritus of, the Navajo Nation. He served as Chief Justice from 1992 through 2003. Before being called to the bench, CJ Yazzie was the Director of the Diné Policy Institute of Diné College, where he worked on developing policy using authentic Navajo thinking. He is a graduate of the University of New Mexico School of Law and the author of articles and book chapters on Navajo Peacemaking, traditional Indian law, and international human rights law. He has lectured and taught traditional Indigenous law at various venues throughout the world, including as a visiting professor at the University of New Mexico, an adjunct professor of the Department of Criminal Justice of Northern Arizona University, and a visiting member of the faculty of the National Judicial College. Since 2013 he also teaches Navajo law as an Associate Professor of Law Advocate at Navajo Technical University in Crownpoint, New Mexico.

Preface

This book is designed for use in a wide variety of undergraduate, graduate, and law classes. It can be used as a standalone text or as a supplemental reader in virtually any class where federal Indian law and policy plays a role. The book is structured so it can be used in its entirety or the instructor can pick and choose among the chapters.

The book starts with an introductory chapter providing a brief history of federal Indian law scholarship, explaining the methodology behind our ranking system, and the manner in which we selected the sixteen law review articles excerpted in this volume. Those sixteen articles are divided into four parts, each of which is organized around a particular theme. Each part begins with a short introduction presenting the theme and providing an overview of each of the four articles contained in that part of the book.

Each article is presented in a separate chapter. The chapters begin with a few scene-setting paragraphs to establish the context and central argument of the featured article and conclude with Notes & Questions designed to help guide discussion of the material. A list of recommended further reading is also included in each chapter.

Editing the articles presented in each chapter was quite challenging. Because we were editing each article not only in and of itself, but also in light of the other three articles presented in each part, we did not provide the authors of the original articles with an opportunity to review the edits. Any editing errors are ours and ours alone.

Some of the law review articles were 75–100 pages long in their original published form. This necessitated deep cuts to some of the pieces when editing for this volume. In making those cuts, we sought to distill the article down to its central contribution. Most of the articles contained more than one central contribution, and in deciding which contribution to highlight, we were guided by the theme of the section in which the article is included, as well as by the arguments in those chapters. Readers are strongly encouraged to seek out and read the articles in their full, original version.

A word about our editing conventions. In editing each article, we let the words of the original article speak for themselves – we deleted but did not summarize or add text. We kept the numbering and the wording of the headings as in the original, but we did impose a uniform format – all roman numeral headings are capitalized and all major subsection headings are italicized. Deletions are indicated with three asterisks, with the following exceptions: all introductory quotations have been deleted, and with very few exceptions we deleted all footnotes. Where we did retain a footnote, we have kept the footnote numbering as it was in the original.

Finally, we have included three appendices to assist the reader: a glossary containing specialized terms and definitions, a brief summary of the US Supreme Court decisions discussed in the volume, and a master list of additional sources used in the volume. Given the structure and nature of the book, we have opted to forgo an index, as the Contents list should provide the necessary guidance in navigating the volume.

We have thoroughly enjoyed the process of preparing this book. Reading through articles both new and familiar has given us a renewed appreciation for the work of our colleagues. We hope you find it as useful and interesting as we have.

Acknowledgments

We wish to express our appreciation to Marty Two Bulls for his wonderful cover art, as well as acknowledge and thank the copyright holders who provided permission to reprint portions of the articles included in this volume:

Philip Frickey, *Marshalling Past and Present: Colonization, Constitutionalism, and Interpretation in Federal Indian Law* © Harvard Law Review

Robert A. Williams, Jr., *The Algebra of Federal Indian Law: The Hard Trail of Decolonizing and Americanizing the White Man's Jurisprudence* © Wisconsin Law Review

Bethany Berger, *Red: Racism and the American Indian* © Bethany Berger

Angela Riley, *(Tribal) Sovereignty and Illiberalism* © California Law Review

Robert Yazzie, *"Life Comes from It": Navajo Justice Concepts* © Robert Yazzie

Nell Jessup Newton, *Tribal Court Praxis: One Year in the Life of Twenty Indian Tribal Courts* © Nell Jessup Newton

David Getches, *Beyond Indian Law: The Rehnquist Court's Pursuit of States' Rights, Color-Blind Justice and Mainstream Values* © Minnesota Law Review

Sarah Krakoff, *A Narrative of Sovereignty: Illuminating the Paradox of the Domestic Dependent Nation* © Sarah Krakoff

Joseph Singer, *Sovereignty and Property* © Joseph Singer

Judith V. Royster, *The Legacy of Allotment* © Arizona State Law Journal

Philip Frickey, *A Common Law for Our Age of Colonialism: The Judicial Divestiture of Indian Tribal Authority over Nonmembers* © Yale Law Journal

Kristen Carpenter, Sonia Katyal, & Angela Riley, *In Defense of Property* © Yale Law Journal

Judith Resnik, *Dependent Sovereigns: Indian Tribes, States, and the Federal Courts* © University of Chicago Law Review

Robert Clinton, *There Is No Federal Supremacy Clause for Indian Tribes* © Robert Clinton

Kevin Washburn, *American Indians, Crime, and the Law* © Kevin Washburn

Matthew Fletcher, *Factbound and Splitless: The Certiorari Process As Barrier to Justice for Indian Tribes* © Arizona Law Review

Introduction

Responding to a Changing Field

Grant Christensen and Melissa L. Tatum

Thirty years ago the Indian law community was small enough that it was possible for even a scholar new to the field to keep up with most of the Indian law scholarship published annually. However, as our field has proliferated, it has also fragmented, and today more than two hundred pieces of new legal scholarship are published annually in law reviews alone.* These law reviews are not just ivory tower musings; there are now some scholarly contributions which are as fundamental for the study of Indian law as many cases or statutes. These articles help to contextualize the changing doctrines announced by the Court, reconcile contradictory authority, challenge assumptions of race/place/power, and push for courts, tribal leaders, legislators, lawyers, educators, and students to adopt new ways of thinking about our fundamental doctrine. However, with so many new contributions we realized that new scholars may miss some of the most impactful articles, and even the progenitors of the field will have forgotten about some of the best ideas put forward by colleagues over the years. While several federal Indian law textbooks exist to preserve judicial doctrine, there is no definitive collection of related legal scholarship.

This text attempts to remedy this omission by selecting sixteen of the most impactful law review articles published between 1985 and 2015. We divided the selected articles into four equal parts, each centered amid an ongoing critical scholarly debate that is fundamental to the development of Indian law but beyond the scope of judicial analysis. Part I explores the legal fictions and political realities inherent in addressing colonialism, including questions of sovereignty, legal pluralism, and race. Part II questions the legitimacy of federal courts to make decisions

---

* Parts of the material below, including the ranking of the 100 most impactful pieces of Indian law scholarship, were taken from our law review article, Grant Christensen & Melissa L. Tatum, *Reading Indian Law: Evaluating Thirty Years of Indian Law Scholarship*, 54 Tulsa L. Rev. 81 (2018).

involving a sovereign people without respect for their voices and traditions. Part III engages with the struggle to define the nature of property and ownership of both tangible and intangible assets, including allotments, cultural property, and traditional knowledge. Finally, Part IV concludes by looking at the structure of law itself and inquires whether the rules of the system justly allocate power between competing sovereigns.

The remainder of this introduction serves several purposes. It starts by providing a short narrative of the history of federal Indian policy and its impact on federal Indian law. Building upon this history, it proceeds to lay a foundation for the creation of federal Indian legal scholarship and articulates the emergence of different voices in the field. This multiplicity of voices raised questions about identifying and defining the foundations of Indian law precipitating the research upon which this text is based. The introduction continues with a discussion of our methodology for the selection of these incorporated texts and finishes with both a few short concluding remarks from the authors and a ranking of the 100 most impactful Indian law pieces from 1985 to 2015.

HISTORY OF INDIAN LAW AND POLICY

The foundations of federal Indian law are inextricably intertwined with the history of the United States and with the history of federal Indian policy. It is thus impossible to assemble a book exploring those foundations without discussing the relevant history.

When Europeans began exploring the "New World," they often chose to negotiate agreements or treaties with the Indigenous governments. The earliest treaties were negotiated as between equals and were often favorable to the tribes. These agreements were occasionally mutual aid or military alliances. Indeed, one of the grievances enumerated in the Declaration of Independence was that the king had "excited domestic insurrections amongst us, and has endeavoured to bring on the inhabitants of our frontiers, the merciless Indian Savages, whose known rule of warfare, is an undistinguished destruction of all ages, sexes and conditions." Despite the unconscionable rhetoric of "Indian Savages," the placement of Indians in the Declaration is proof that the relationship between tribal governments and the United States can trace its origins back to the very founding of our government.

The newly formed United States of America chose to continue the practice of dealing with Indians through treaties. The Articles of Confederation reserved to the federal government "the sole and exclusive right and power of *** regulating the trade and managing all affairs with the Indians" (Article IX). When it became clear that the Articles of Confederation were not working and needed to be replaced, the new Constitution reserved to Congress the power to "regulate Commerce with foreign Nations, and among the several States, and with the Indian Tribes" (Article I, Section 8), and provided that representation in the legislature "shall be apportioned among the several States which may be included within this Union, according to their respective Numbers, which shall be determined by adding to the whole Number of free Persons, including those bound to Service for a Term of Years, and excluding Indians not taxed, three fifths of all other Persons" (Article I, Section 2).

Tribal governments were thus not considered part of the United States, at least not initially, and the practice of negotiating treaties continued until ended by Congress in 1871, when treaties were replaced by the more euphemistic "Agreements." As time progressed and treaties became agreements, the relationship between Indian tribes and the United States became less focused on securing mutual aid and alliance and more focused, at least from the perspective of the federal government, on acquiring land. To keep a separation between settlers and Indians, the United States first sought to remove and resettle tribes west of the Mississippi River. However, as the boundaries of the new nation advanced ever westward, the focus shifted to negotiating agreements that confined Indians to reservations.

In 1849, the federal government moved its office of Indian Affairs from the Department of War to the Department of Interior, and the process of incorporating tribes into the United States began. In the late 1800s, federal Indian policy officially shifted to one of allotment and assimilation, with the intention of eliminating tribal governments and incorporating Indians into the larger US population. This policy proceeded along two parallel paths. Indian Agents were assigned to administer reservations, eradicating traditional religions and cultural practices by enforcing the newly promulgated Code of Indian Offenses. Indian Agents also facilitated the process of removing Indian children from their families and placing them in Christian-run boarding schools. These schools sought to eradicate traditional religious and cultural practices.

Congress "allotted" reservations, dividing the land into parcels and assigning a set number of acres to individual members of the tribe. The extra, or "surplus," land was then sold to non-Indians. The title to these individually assigned parcels was held in trust by the federal government for a set period of years, after which the restrictions on alienation were released. Not all reservations were allotted, but a significant portion of the reservations suffered this fate. A great deal of fraud, corruption, and mismanagement grew out of the allotment process, with approximately two-thirds of the land initially reserved for tribes flowing out of tribal hands. The "checkerboard" nature of landownership on these allotted reservations has caused, and continues to cause, problems for tribal governments seeking to exercise governmental authority over the lands within their territorial boundaries.

In the late 1920s, a study commissioned by the federal government resulted in what has become known as the Meriam Report. This report contained a detailed examination of the dismal social and economic conditions on reservations and concluded that the allotment policy had been a failure. In response to this report, Congress enacted the Indian Reorganization Act (IRA) in 1934. The IRA officially repudiated the allotment policy and encouraged tribes to reorganize their tribal governments. The IRA provided a mechanism by which tribes could adopt a constitution, although they were not required to do so, and created the foundation for tribal courts. In recognition of the fact that governments need revenue to operate, and the allotment policy had destroyed the tax base on most reservations, the IRA also encouraged tribes to establish businesses and develop their local economies.

Congress changed direction again in the 1950s, adopting a policy of "terminating" not the tribal government, but the official relationship between tribes and the United States. Congress also enacted two key laws during this time. One, which became known as Public Law 280, transferred some federal responsibilities to states. Six states were ultimately given no choice about accepting these transferred powers, while other states had the option to select what, if any, authority they would assume. The second law, the Indian Relocation Act, created a process for relocating individual Indians from reservations to large cities, resulting in the creation of an urban Indian population.

The termination process was not applied to all tribes, but most of those who were terminated suffered hardship. Some tribes have successfully sought to reestablish official relationships with the United States. Others are still seeking to revoke their terminated status.

The Termination Era was short-lived and officially ended when President Nixon announced the launch of a new era of federal Indian policy in 1970. This new era would again encourage tribal self-determination, and the federal government would deal with tribal governments on a government-to-government basis. Emblematic of this change was the enactment in 1975 of the Indian Self-Determination and Education Assistance Act. The ISDEAA established a mechanism through which tribes could contract to administer services previously provided by the federal government. Known as 638 contracting, this process enabled tribal governments to run services including schools, police departments, and hospitals, in a manner which was culturally appropriate to each tribal community.

From its beginning and through most of the 1970s, a consistent narrative flowed through federal Indian law. While the policies changed, the principles of federal Indian law did not. Those principles stated that tribes were sovereign, although their sovereignty had been diminished upon incorporation into the United States, and that the federal government retained primary authority over Indian affairs. Until the 1970s the Supreme Court continuously deferred to Congress in the area of federal Indian policy. The specific policies changed from assimilation to reorganization to termination to self-determination, but the Supreme Court's deference to Congress did not. This clear narrative of deference ended in the 1970s at the same time that federal Indian law emerged as a discrete academic discipline. The confluence of these events would dramatically change the field.

AN EMERGENCE OF VOICES

The 1970s saw an emergence of voices in federal Indian law, not just in the legal academy, but also in the judicial and political worlds. While the political branches of government continued to implement the announced policy of tribal self-determination, culminating in tribal courts prosecuting non-Indian persons, tribal governments levying taxes on non-Indians and non-Indian businesses, and demanding recognition of treaty-protected rights to hunt, fish, and gather both on and off the reservation, the Court pushed back. No longer wedded to the original Indian law canons, including deference to Congress, the Court took a more active role in rewriting federal Indian law and redefining the power of tribal governments.

These changes in the Supreme Court coincided with the rise of federal Indian law as a discrete academic discipline, with two textbooks being published in the 1970s and a growth in the number of schools hiring faculty to teach and write in the area. The first scholars predominantly came from the public interest world, thereby cementing a close relationship between the legal academy and the practicing bar. The scholarship that emerged from these first faculty was rooted in the historic principles of federal Indian law and the canons of construction, which provide that ambiguities in treaties and statutes should (1) be resolved in favor of the Indian tribal interest and (2) be interpreted as Indians would have understood them.

These scholars spoke with a consistent voice that there was one narrative underlying federal Indian law. They drew upon a series of three cases decided by Chief Justice Marshall in the early 1800s that established the basic principles governing the relationship between tribes, states, and federal government. In explaining the Court's behavior, these first scholars returned consistently to the foundational ideas established a century earlier. They may have argued among themselves about the application of those ideas, but the ideas themselves were not in question.

By the end of the 1970s the Supreme Court began to depart radically from this shared history and the principles laid out in the Marshall Trilogy. Tribal court jurisdiction provides a good contextual example. In *Williams v. Lee* (1959) a pair of Navajo Indians challenged the authority of the State of Arizona to hear a claim for repayment of a debt incurred when a non-Indian shopkeeper extended the tribal members' credit at a store located on the reservation. The Supreme Court held that Arizona had no authority to hear the case; "absent governing Acts of Congress, the question has always been whether the state action infringed on the right of reservation Indians to make their own laws and be ruled by them." Two decades later the Court had suddenly become much more protective of non-Indians. In *Montana v. United States* (1981) the Crow Tribe sought to require non-Indians to comply with Crow rules banning non-Indians from fishing on the Crow reservation. The Court held that the Tribe could not regulate the non-Indian conduct while on non-Indian land within the reservation: "exercise of tribal power beyond what is necessary to protect tribal self-government or to control internal relations is inconsistent with the dependent status of the tribes, and so cannot survive without express congressional delegation." As it became clear that the Supreme Court was not interested in remaining faithful to the foundational principles, the legal academy began to search for alternative explanations for the Court's behavior. It is at this point that the voice of the legal academy ceased to be unified, and a search for new perspectives precipitated an emergence of different voices.

At this juncture Indian law scholars in the academy began to bifurcate their approaches to the development of legal scholarship. Some held fast to the traditional approach rooted in history, while others sought new and different ways to conceptualize the emerging doctrines. Even within these alternative approaches, there was no one unified voice but rather competing ideas to explain the Court's behavior and to question the origins of the field.

Rooted in history, one group focused on rethinking the approach taken by practitioners in litigating Indian law cases. This scholarship re-centered itself from a focus on the principles laid out in the Marshall Trilogy to an attempt to reconcile the new reality of an unbounded Supreme Court. It sought out the practical, attempting to show a way forward for practitioners to use more traditional areas of law to advocate for tribal clients. For example in *United States v. White Mountain Apache* (2003), instead of focusing on the historical or treaty relationship between the Tribe and the United States, advocates returned to trust law, something with which the Court was comfortably familiar. In *White Mountain* the Tribe argued that Fort Apache, located on the reservation, had been permitted to fall into disrepair. It sought compensation from the United States to restore the Fort to working condition. The Court agreed, recognizing that the property in question was held by the United States as trustee for the tribal beneficiary, and accordingly found for the Tribe; holding that the United States had breached its trust responsibility.

Other scholars looked farther afield in seeking to explain and confront the Court's departure from the traditional approach to Indian law. These scholars were less interested in technical niceties of the law, and more interested in philosophical and jurisprudential explanations – rethinking the relationship between tribes, states, and the United States. Critical perspectives flourished among this group, finding a basis in Critical Legal Studies, Critical Race Theory, American Indian Studies, and related disciplines. Rather than speaking to practitioners, much of this scholarship looked for alternative solutions to the problems created by the Court's changing jurisprudence. The solutions offered by this group were varied; some encouraging the development of tribal voices and strengthening tribal governance while others critiqued even the ability of the existing power relationship to reach an effective solution. These scholars collectively offered new voices and perspectives from which to approach the discipline of federal Indian law.

This diversity of approaches meant there was no longer a unified foundation; it has made the field more exciting and challenging, but at the same time it has also made it more difficult to succinctly articulate the foundations of the field. Who owns federal Indian law? Does it belong to those who continue to ground the approach in nineteenth-century cases, territorial boundaries, and competing conceptions of individual rights; or does it more properly belong to those critical scholars who have encouraged a reexamination of judicial doctrine and the involvement of tribal government? Is there space for multiple voices and perspectives within the field of Indian law?

SEARCHING FOR THE FOUNDATIONS OF INDIAN LAW

These questions arose for us during a conversation about the role of Indian legal scholarship in the law school curriculum. We first met in 2009 at the University of Arizona, where Melissa was on the faculty and Grant had enrolled in the Indigenous Peoples Law and Policy LLM program. After graduation, Grant was immediately hired as an adjunct professor in Indian law at the University of Toledo and then a visiting professor at the University of Oregon before accepting his first tenure track appointment. Melissa had joined the academy almost two decades earlier. We therefore became Indian law professors at two very different points in the history of the field, and brought with us different perspectives.

Melissa graduated from the University of Michigan in 1992. During her time there, no federal Indian law course was offered. She became interested in the topic through her service as a member of the *Michigan Law Review*. While she received some guidance from interested faculty, there was no formal training available to her in law school. Therefore her knowledge of Indian law was built by studying the existing tradition and history-bound scholarship that existed at that time, and her first contributions built upon that narrative.

In contrast, by the time Grant got to law school in 2004 he was able to join the Indian Law Summer Program offered by Lewis & Clark – where he spent an entire summer semester studying federal Indian law, several advanced Indian law electives, and an externship placement working with tribes through the Department of Energy's Bonneville Power Authority. He was able to continue his study of Indian law in a dedicated year-long graduate program at the University of Arizona in 2010. Through the culmination of these courses Grant was exposed to different narratives in Indian law, exploring the diverse voices and perspectives in the field. As a result of this more comprehensive experience as a student, Grant's first scholarship was more conversant with the different perspectives that had further developed by the time he entered the academy.

This book grew out of a conversation we initiated during the Federal Bar Association's annual Indian Law Conference in 2014. Now colleagues, we began discussing the difference between using legal scholarship and black letter case law when teaching Indian law to students. We realized that while we often refer to cases with students, we rarely if ever discuss scholars. Yet, in our own scholarship, much of what we read and write is influenced by the voices of other scholars and their interpretations of history, philosophy, law, and culture. Was it possible to design materials that would correct for this omission and bring these important voices expressing foundational ideas back into the classroom?

To answer this question we would have to identify what scholarship would be included. While we each had personal favorites, we endeavored to apply a rigorous approach to identifying the most important Indian law scholarship. Perhaps in this way we, too, could add something important to the field.

HOW THE PIECES WERE SELECTED: MEASURING ARTICLE IMPACT

We wanted to ensure that the pieces we included in this text were not just pieces that we qualitatively thought to be exceptional, but rather that our selection would be informed by a more rigorous methodological approach. We began by using the *Index to Legal Periodicals* and the National Indian Law Library's annual bibliography to identify the 3,334 law review articles dealing with Indian law and published in academic journals between 1985 and 2015.

There are two principal electronic databases for legal materials in the United States: Lexis and Westlaw. To help measure the relative impact of each article, we started by putting each citation into Lexis. A preliminary score was then created for each article by totaling the number of citations by courts, in law reviews, and in treatises that Lexis recorded. This preliminary score treated every citation identically and did not attempt to weight any one citation higher than any other. To correct for the element of time, because articles decided thirty years ago will have more citations than those decided two years ago, we then divided the number of citations by the number of years the article had been in print. The denominator was determined by subtracting the year of publication from 2017. This created a citations-per-year metric for each article which allowed us to compare articles directly against each other.

We are aware that it is possible that Lexis and Westlaw may record slightly different citation counts because they index slightly different lists of journals and treatises. To correct for this we took all articles that had an average of 2.0 citations per year in the preliminary Lexis score and used Westlaw's KeyCite feature to verify their citations. For each of these articles we recorded the number of court citations identified by KeyCite. Encouragingly, these counts were virtually identical. We also recorded the number of citations in "Secondary Sources" in order to mirror the analysis used in Lexis.

To create a final impact score we added the number of case, law review, and treatise citations from Lexis with the number of case and secondary source citations from Westlaw. We then divided that total citation count by the number of years since the article was published. This created a score which is roughly twice the number of citations per article per year. It gives equal weight to both Lexis and

Westlaw citations. It essentially double counts a citation that was indexed by both search engines while still giving an article full credit when it was identified in a source captured by only one search tool.

The result was a single score that allowed direct comparisons between articles. By sorting articles by their combined score, a ranking of Indian law scholarship emerged that was exact enough to identify the top 100 Indian law articles when measured by their relative citation count. We have included a complete list of the 100 most impactful articles at the end of this introduction.

An important caveat: we recognize that the topic of an article will have an important effect on its citation count. The articles that are the most cited tend to deal with observations that affect the entire field or that have applications in many different Indian law contexts, like sovereignty, tribal property, or federal–tribal relations. Alternatively, some of the most cited pieces deal with singular topics that exist throughout Indian country and are regularly the subject of observation or critique, like the Indian Child Welfare Act or the status of tribal attorneys. Articles that cover these universal issues are much more likely to be widely cited and therefore be elevated in the ranking system. We also recognize that there are some very important articles in our field that, because they deal with niche issues that may affect only one tribe or region, are not cited enough to make their way into the top 100 articles listed here. Their omission certainly does not take away from their importance or say anything about the merits of their scholarship, they were simply not considered for inclusion in this volume.

QUALITATIVE SELECTION

We decided to limit our selection of articles for this volume to sixteen of the 100 most impactful pieces of scholarship, but have qualitatively chosen those sixteen contributions from that list. There are many reasons we did not simply select the first sixteen. First, any ranking system has inherent limitations and sometimes a couple of citations could dramatically alter an article's relative ranking. Additionally, because the purpose of this volume is to explore contributions that are foundational to the field, simply taking the top sixteen would not provide the rich diversity of ideas that exists in legal scholarship. Finally, we wanted to ensure a diversity of authors and perspectives so that this contribution is as comprehensive as possible.

Our qualitative selection should not be taken to imply that scholarly pieces in the top 100, but not included in this volume, are of any less importance to the field. When compiling a volume of this nature, inevitably some lines must be drawn and some articles selected over others. We have included the entire list of articles at the end of this introduction, and incorporated many of them by reference throughout this volume, precisely because each makes an important contribution to Indian law scholarship.

CONCLUDING REMARKS

The field of Indian law has evolved tremendously over the last thirty years. Helping courts, practitioners, tribal governments, scholars, congresspersons, and students make sense of these changes and critique them has been the primary work of tremendous contributions to Indian law scholarship. The sixteen articles highlighted here, and hundreds more, deserve to be celebrated and even more widely read by all audiences.

It is our hope that readers will not use the rankings below to quarrel over whether Professor Clinton's work on plenary power is really five places more important than Professor Resnik's work on the federal courts. In many ways a direct comparison of the substantive ideas embedded in these works is truly impossible. Instead we hope to celebrate all of these pieces as making foundational contributions to our field. This selection, excerpting sixteen of these works, is our first attempt to highlight and celebrate the incredible scholarly contributions of our friends, colleagues, mentors, and peers.

When we started this project, we knew our field had grown but we never expected to find more than 3,000 Indian law articles. At times we were haunted by the collective works of legends in our field who have walked on: Bill Rice, David Getches, Philip Frickey, and so many others. After cataloging three decades' worth of Indian law scholarship, we have both rediscovered old favorites and come across new pieces that have challenged and informed our own understanding of what 'Indian law' really is. We hope this book ultimately sparks some of those same feelings of rediscovery and excitement in every reader.

THE RANKINGS

The top 100 Indian law articles as determined by the ranking system are reported here, ranked by their score. When an article had multiple authors, the authors' names are reported in the order they appeared in the article. Citation abbreviation for each journal conforms with the Bluebook rules for journal citation. When two or more articles had an identical score, they have been given an identical rank and listed in alphabetical order by the first author's surname. The next number is then skipped to ensure that only 100 articles are listed. For example, there are two articles with a score of 8.43 and thus tied for 54th place. Each of those articles is ranked 54th and the next article is ranked 56th.

Represented among these top 100 articles are professors who authored the first wave of Indian law legal scholarship like Philip Frickey and David Getches, the first indigenous voices like Robert Williams and Gloria Valencia-Weber, as well as newer members of the academy like Matthew L. M. Fletcher, Angela Riley, and Bethany Berger.

RANK	AUTHOR	ARTICLE TITLE	CITATION	SCORE
1	Philip Frickey	A Common Law for Our Age of Colonialism: The Judicial Divestiture of Indian Tribal Authority over Nonmembers	109 Yale L.J. 1 (1999)	21.50
2	David Getches	Beyond Indian Law: The Rehnquist Court's Pursuit of States' Rights, Color-Blind Justice and Mainstream Values	86 Minn. L. Rev. 267 (2001)	20.94
3	Judith Royster	The Legacy of Allotment	27 Ariz. St. L.J. 1 (1995)	20.09
4	Robert Clinton	There Is No Federal Supremacy Clause for Indian Tribes	34 Ariz. St. L.J. 113 (2002)	19.80
5	Philip Frickey	Marshalling Past and Present: Colonization, Constitutionalism, and Interpretation in Federal Indian Law	107 Harv. L. Rev. 381 (1993)	19.29
6	Kristen Carpenter, Sonia Katyal, & Angela Riley	In Defense of Property	118 Yale L.J. 1022 (2009)	17.88
7	Philip Frickey	(Native) American Exceptionalism in Federal Public Law	119 Harv. L. Rev. 431 (2006)	17.64
8	David Getches	Conquering the Cultural Frontier: The New Subjectivism of the Supreme Court in Indian Law	84 Cal. L. Rev. 1573 (1996)	17.29
9	Judith Resnik	Dependent Sovereigns: Indian Tribes, States, and the Federal Courts	56 U. Chi. L. Rev. 671 (1989)	16.32
10	Robert A. Williams, Jr.	The Algebra of Federal Indian Law: The Hard Trail of Decolonizing and Americanizing the White Man's Jurisprudence	1986 Wisc. L. Rev. 219 (1986)	15.94
11	Angela Riley	(Tribal) Sovereignty and Illiberalism	95 Cal. L. Rev. 799 (2007)	15.70
12	Kevin Washburn	American Indians, Crime, and the Law	104 Mich. L. Rev. 709 (2006)	14.82

(continued)

(continued)

RANK	AUTHOR	ARTICLE TITLE	CITATION	SCORE
13	Daniel Meltzer	The *Seminole* Decision and State Sovereign Immunity	1996 Sup. Ct. Rev. 1 (1996)	14.14
14	Siegfried Wiessner	Rights and Status of Indigenous Peoples: A Global Comparative and International Legal Analysis	12 Harv. Hum. Rts. J. 57 (1999)	13.83
15	Joseph Singer	Sovereignty and Property	86 Nw. U. L. Rev. 1 (1991)	13.54
16	Bethany Berger	Red: Racism and the American Indian	56 UCLA L. Rev. 591 (2009)	13.13
17	Mary Wood	Indian Land and the Promise of Native Sovereignty: The Trust Doctrine Revisited	1994 Utah L. Rev. 1471 (1994)	12.61
18	Kevin Washburn	Federal Criminal Law and Tribal Self-Determination	84 N.C. L. Rev. 779 (2006)	12.36
19	Vicki Jackson	*Seminole Tribe*, the Eleventh Amendment and the Potential Evisceration of *Ex Parte Young*	72 N.Y.U. L. Rev. 495 (1997)	12.10
20	Sarah Krakoff	A Narrative of Sovereignty: Illuminating the Paradox of the Domestic Dependent Nation	83 Or. L. Rev. 1109 (2005)	11.92
21	Angela Riley	Good (Native) Governance	107 Colum. L. Rev. 1049 (2006)	11.91
22	Philip Frickey	Congressional Intent, Practical Reasoning, and the Dynamic Nature of Federal Indian Law	78 Cal. L. Rev. 1137 (1990)	11.74
23	Addie Rolnick	The Promise of *Mancari*: Indian Political Rights As Racial Remedy	86 N.Y.U. L. Rev. 958 (2011)	11.50
24	Gregory Ablavsky	The Savage Constitution	63 Duke L.J. 999 (2014)	11.33
25	Angela Riley	Straight Stealing: Towards an Indigenous System of Cultural Property Protection	80 Wash. L. Rev. 69 (2005)	11.00
26	Nell Jessup Newton	Tribal Court Praxis: One Year in the Life of Twenty Indian Tribal Courts	22 Am. Indian L. Rev. 285 (1998)	10.79
27	Bethany Berger	Justice and the Outsider: Jurisdiction over Nonmembers in Tribal Legal Systems	37 Ariz. St. L.J. 1047 (2005)	10.75

RANK	AUTHOR	ARTICLE TITLE	CITATION	SCORE
28	William Bradford	"With a Very Great Blame on Our Hearts": Reparations, Reconciliation, and an American Indian Plea for Peace with Justice	27 Am. Indian L. Rev 1 (2003)	10.64
29	L. Scott Gould	The Consent Paradigm: Tribal Sovereignty at the Millennium	96 Colum. L. Rev. 809 (1996)	10.57
30	Philip Frickey	Adjudication and Its Discontents: Coherence and Conciliation in Federal Indian Law	110 Harv. L. Rev. 1754 (1997)	10.45
31	Angela Riley	Indians and Guns	100 Geo. L.J. 1675 (2012)	10.40
32	Robert Clinton	Redressing the Legacy of Conquest: A Vision Quest for a Decolonized Federal Indian Law	46 Ark. L. Rev. 77 (1993)	10.33
33	Donna Coker	Enhancing Autonomy for Battered Women: Lessons from Navajo Peacemaking	47 UCLA L. Rev. 1 (1999)	10.28
34	Robert A. Williams, Jr.	Encounters on the Frontiers of International Human Rights Law: Redefining the Terms of Indigenous Peoples' Survival in the World	1990 Duke L.J. 660 (1990)	10.04
35	Barbara Atwood	Flashpoints under the Indian Child Welfare Act: Toward a New Understanding of State Court Resistance	51 Emory L.J. 587 (2002)	10.00
36	Holly Doremus & A. Dan Tarlock	Fish, Farms, and the Clash of Cultures in the Klamath Basin	30 Ecology L.Q. 279 (2003)	9.79
37	Zachary Price	Dividing Sovereignty in Tribal and Territorial Criminal Jurisdiction	113 Colum. L. Rev. 657 (2013)	9.75
38	Matthew Fletcher	The Supreme Court's Indian Problem	59 Hastings L.J. 579 (2008)	9.67
39	Bethany Berger	In the Name of the Child: Race, Gender, and Economics in *Adoptive Couple v. Baby Girl*	67 Fla. L. Rev. 295 (2015)	9.50
40	Philip Frickey	Domesticating Federal Indian Law	81 Minn. L. Rev. 31 (1996)	9.48

(continued)

(continued)

RANK	AUTHOR	ARTICLE TITLE	CITATION	SCORE
41	Angela Riley	Recovering Collectivity: Group Rights to Intellectual Property in Indigenous Communities	18 Cardozo Arts & Ent. L.J. 175 (2000)	9.47
42	Nathalie Martin & Joshua Schwartz	The Alliance between Payday Lenders and Tribes: Are Both Tribal Sovereignty and Consumer Protection at Risk?	69 Wash. & Lee L. Rev. 751 (2012)	9.40
43	Gloria Valencia-Weber	Tribal Courts: Custom and Innovative Law	24 N.M. L. Rev. 225 (1994)	9.30
44	Jack Trope & Walter Echo-Hawk	The Native American Graves Protection and Repatriation Act: Background and Legislative History	24 Ariz. St. L.J. 35 (1992)	9.28
45	Gerald Torres & Kathryn Milun	Translating Yonnondio by Precedent and Evidence: The Mashpee Indian Case	1990 Duke L.J. 625 (1990)	9.22
46	Patty Gerstenblith	Identity and Cultural Property: The Protection of Cultural Property in the United States	75 B.U. L. Rev. 559 (1995)	9.14
47	Saikrishna Prakash	Against Tribal Fungibility	89 Cornell L. Rev. 1069 (2004)	9.08
48	Sarah Krakoff	Inextricably Political: Race, Membership, and Tribal Sovereignty	87 Wash. L. Rev. 1041 (2012)	9.00
48	Elizabeth Kronk Warner	Tribes as Innovative Environmental "Laboratories"	86 U. Colo. L. Rev. 789 (2015)	9.00
50	Carole Goldberg & Duane Champagne	Is Public Law 280 Fit for the Twenty-First Century? Some Data at Last	38 Conn. L. Rev. 697 (2006)	8.82
51	Matthew Fletcher	Indian Courts and Fundamental Fairness: "Indian Courts and the Future" Revisited	84 U. Colo. L. Rev. 59 (2013)	8.75
52	Allison Dussias	Ghost Dance and Holy Ghost: The Echoes of the Nineteenth-Century Christianization Policy in Twentieth-Century Native American Free Exercise Cases	49 Stan. L. Rev. 773 (1997)	8.70

RANK	AUTHOR	ARTICLE TITLE	CITATION	SCORE
53	Allison Dussias	Geographically-Based and Membership-Based Views of Indian Tribal Sovereignty: The Supreme Court's Changing Vision	55 U. Pitt. L. Rev. 1 (1993)	8.63
54	Katherine Florey	Indian Country's Borders: Territoriality, Immunity, and the Construction of Tribal Sovereignty	51 B.C. L. Rev. 595 (2010)	8.43
54	Joseph Singer	Canons of Conquest: The Supreme Court's Attack on Tribal Sovereignty	37 New Eng. L. Rev. 641 (2003)	8.43
56	Ann Tweedy	Connecting the Dots between the Constitution, the Marshall Trilogy, and *United States v. Lara*: Notes toward a Blueprint for the Next Legislative Restoration of Tribal Sovereignty	42 U. Mich. J.L. Ref. 651 (2009)	8.38
57	Sandra Day O'Connor	Lessons from the Third Sovereign: Indian Tribal Courts	33 Tulsa L.J. 1 (1997)	8.35
58	Paul Spruhan	A Legal History of Blood Quantum in Federal Indian Law to 1935	51 S.D. L. Rev. 1 (2006)	8.27
59	Graham Dutfield	TRIPS-Related Aspects of Traditional Knowledge	33 Case W. Res. J. Int'l. L. 233 (2001)	8.25
59	Samuel Ennis	Reaffirming Indian Tribal Court Criminal Jurisdiction over Non-Indians: An Argument for a Statutory Abrogation of *Oliphant*	57 UCLA L. Rev. 553 (2009)	8.25
61	Kenneth Bobroff	Retelling Allotment: Indian Property Rights and the Myth of Common Ownership	54 Vand. L. Rev. 1559 (2001)	8.19
61	Sarah Krakoff	Undoing Indian Law One Case at a Time: Judicial Minimalism and Tribal Sovereignty	50 Am. U.L. Rev. 1177 (2001)	8.19
63	Christine Farley	Protecting Folklore of Indigenous Peoples: Is Intellectual Property the Answer?	30 Conn. L. Rev. 1 (1997)	8.15

(continued)

(continued)

RANK	AUTHOR	ARTICLE TITLE	CITATION	SCORE
64	Gabe Galanda & Ryan Dreveskracht	Curing the Tribal Disenrollment Epidemic: In Search of a Remedy	57 Ariz. L. Rev. 383 (2015)	8.00
64	Christine Zuni Cruz	(On the) Road Back In: Community Lawyering in Indigenous Communities	5 Clinical L. Rev. 557 (1999)	8.00
64	Unsigned Note	Indian Law – Tribal Courts – Congress Recognizes and Affirms Tribal Courts' Special Domestic Violence Jurisdiction over Non-Indian Defendants – The Violence against Women Reauthorization Act of 2013	127 Harv. L. Rev. 1509 (2014)	8.00
67	Matthew Fletcher	The Supreme Court and Federal Indian Policy	85 Neb. L. Rev. 121 (2006)	7.91
68	Matthew Fletcher	Tribal Consent	8 Stan. J. C.R. & C.L. 45 (2012)	7.80
69	Kristen Carpenter	A Property Rights Approach to Sacred Sites Cases: Asserting a Place for Indians As Non-Owners	52 UCLA L. Rev. 1061 (2005)	7.75
70	Robert Yazzie	"Life Comes from It": Navajo Justice Concepts	24 N.M. L. Rev. 175 (1994)	7.74
71	Wenona Singel	Indian Tribes and Human Rights Accountability	49 San Diego L. Rev. 567 (2012)	7.60
72	Robert Clinton	The Dormant Indian Commerce Clause	27 Conn. L. Rev. 1055 (1995)	7.59
73	Sanford Levinson	"Who Counts?" "Sez Who?"	58 St. Louis U. L.J. 937 (2014)	7.33
74	Milner Ball	Stories of Origin and Constitutional Possibilities	87 Mich. L. Rev. 2280 (1989)	7.29
75	Matthew Fletcher	Tribal Membership and Indian Nationhood	37 Am. Indian L. Rev. 1 (2013)	7.25
76	Mark Rosen	Multiple Authoritative Interpreters of Quasi-Constitutional Federal Law:	69 Fordham L. Rev. 479 (2000)	7.24

RANK	AUTHOR	ARTICLE TITLE	CITATION	SCORE
77	Bethany Berger	Of Tribal Courts and the Indian Civil Rights Act "Power over This Unfortunate Race": Race, Politics and Indian Law in *United States v. Rogers*	45 Wm. & Mary L. Rev. 1957 (2004)	7.23
78	Carole Goldberg	American Indians and "Preferential" Treatment	49 UCLA L. Rev. 943 (2002)	7.13
79	David Williams	The Borders of the Equal Protection Clause: Indians as Peoples	38 UCLA L. Rev. 759 (1991)	7.12
80	L. Scott Gould	Mixing Bodies and Beliefs: The Predicament of Tribes	101 Colum. L. Rev. 702 (2001)	7.06
81	Robert Anderson	Water Rights, Water Quality, and Regulatory Jurisdiction in Indian Country	34 Stan. Envtl. L.J. 195 (2015)	7.00
81	Matthew Fletcher	Factbound and Splitless: The Certiorari Process As Barrier to Justice for Indian Tribes	51 Ariz. L. Rev. 933 (2009)	7.00
81	Steven Quesenberry, Timothy Seward, & Adam Bailey	Tribal Strategies for Protecting and Preserving Groundwater	41 Wm. Mitchell L. Rev. 431 (2015)	7.00
81	Wenona Singel	The First Federalists	62 Drake L. Rev. 775 (2014)	7.00
85	Naomi Mezey	The Paradoxes of Cultural Property	107 Colum. L. Rev. 2004 (2007)	6.90
86	Judith Royster	Practical Sovereignty, Political Sovereignty, and the Indian Tribal Energy Development and Self-Determination Act	12 Lewis & Clark L. Rev. 1065 (2008)	6.89
87	Russel Barsh	Indigenous Peoples in the 1990s: From Object to Subject of International Law?	7 Harv. Hum. Rts. J. 33 (1994)	6.83
88	Rebecca Hart	Honoring Sovereignty: Aiding Tribal Efforts to Protect Native American Women from Domestic Violence	96 Cal. L. Rev. 185 (2008)	6.78
88	Siegfried Wiessner	Indigenous Sovereignty: A Reassessment in Light of the	41 Vand. J. Transnat'l. L. 1141 (2008)	6.78

(continued)

(continued)

RANK	AUTHOR	ARTICLE TITLE	CITATION	SCORE
90	Mary Wood	UN Declaration on the Rights of Indigenous Peoples Protecting the Attributes of Native Sovereignty: A New Trust Paradigm for Federal Actions Affecting Tribal Lands and Resources	1995 Utah L. Rev. 109 (1995)	6.77
91	Eric Kades	The Dark Side of Efficiency: *Johnson v. M'Intosh* and the Expropriation of American Indian Lands	148 U Penn. L. Rev. 1065 (2000)	6.76
91	Nell Jessup Newton	Indian Claims in the Courts of the Conqueror	41 Am. U.L. Rev. 753 (1992)	6.76
93	Kristen Carpenter & Eli Wald	Lawyering for Groups: The Case of American Indian Tribal Attorneys	81 Fordham L. Rev. 3085 (2013)	6.75
94	Kevin Washburn	Tribal Self-Determination at the Crossroads	38 Conn. L. Rev. 777 (2006)	6.73
95	Robert Anderson	Indian Water Rights, Practical Reasoning, and Negotiated Settlements	98 Cal. L. Rev. 1133 (2010)	6.71
95	Matthew Fletcher	Resisting Federal Courts on Tribal Jurisdiction	81 U. Colo. L. Rev. 973 (2010)	6.71
97	Robert Natelson	The Original Understanding of the Indian Commerce Clause	85 Denv. U.L. Rev. 201 (2007)	6.60
97	Rebecca Tsosie	Reclaiming Native Stories: An Essay on Cultural Appropriation and Cultural Rights	34 Ariz. St. L.J. 299 (2002)	6.60
99	Randall Abate	Public Nuisance Suits for the Climate Justice Movement: The Right Thing and the Right Time	85 Wash. L. Rev. 197 (2010)	6.57
100	Robert Porter	Strengthening Tribal Sovereignty through Peacemaking: How the Anglo-American Legal Tradition Destroys Indigenous Societies	28 Colum. Human Rights L. Rev. 235 (1997)	6.55

Core Concepts

There are some ideas and doctrines within Indian law that are so fundamental that conversations within the field cannot take place without them. Concepts like "jurisdiction," "colonialism," "race," and "self-government" speak to the heart of most conversations about federal Indian law. These terms may be sufficiently broad that different scholars have their own articulations of what each term means, creating situations where the concept itself becomes a flashpoint for scholarly debate.

Part I of this text thus attempts to lay a foundation for readers to familiarize themselves with some of these core concepts. The section intentionally includes pieces that speak to different conceptualizations of the field so as to provide both more traditional and pragmatic scholarship as well as more critical and philosophical engagement. Each piece touches in some way on the construction of race, on tribal sovereignty, and upon the relationship between states and tribes – however, no two pieces bring exactly the same perspective. The goal is that together these pieces provoke questions, and spark conversations, about these core concepts. It is not our intention that all readers will come away with the same understanding of the law; rather each reader will have immersed themselves in some of the scholarly debates that control the core concepts of federal Indian law and will decide for themselves where they stand.

There are so many quality pieces that speak to the fundamental ideas that underlie our field that it was difficult to select just a handful from among the many qualified scholarly works which emerged as among the 100 most cited Indian law articles of the last three decades. We have selected four that highlight very different aspects of Indian law, but at the same time speak to each other. Their order was selected intentionally to promote a progressive discussion of the evolution of core concepts within the field.

Philip Frickey's *Marshalling Past and Present* (rank 5/100) provides an introduction to the Marshall Trilogy, the foundational set of Indian law Supreme Court opinions. These cases announced a presumption that while Congress has plenary power in the area of Indian affairs, that which it has never taken away remains among the inherent powers of tribes. Frickey questions whether the modern court is remaining faithful to these principles and explores the implications for Indian country should the presumption of inherent tribal power be eroded.

Written in 1993, Frickey's piece emerged at a commonly accepted turning point in Indian law. With the emergence of the federalism bent of the Rehnquist Court, the evolution of Indian gaming, and the retirement of justices who helped bolster the civil rights movement like Thurgood Marshall, William Brennan, and Harry Blackmun, the Court was changing. Frickey's piece nicely captures the consensus view of Indian law that prevailed through the 1980s; that a largely territorial conception of jurisdiction existed between states and tribes and that ambiguities in this area of the law were to be resolved in the Indians' favor. He presciently identifies that the Court is changing and that many of the original principles and canons of Indian law are going to be tested by a new Supreme Court more hostile to tribal independence.

Robert Williams' *The Algebra of Federal Indian Law* (rank 10/100) does not respond to Frickey by name, but directly confronts many of the assumptions about the Marshall Trilogy endemic in Frickey's writing. Williams suggests that legal discourse inherited from a European perspective has helped to justify colonialism and perpetuate the ongoing subordination of Indian tribes. Because the common law was inherited from a system that treated non-Christian, non-White, Indigenous peoples as inferior, judicial treatment of Indians can never reconcile competing worldviews. Instead, Williams argues for a rejection of European legal norms and the creation of an "Americanized" approach to Indian law that reconsiders the origins of the power dynamic between Indian and European peoples to synthesize a new worldview.

In many ways Williams is writing at the vanguard of a new movement within Indian law that brings critical perspectives rooted in other disciplines into the principled study of the relationship between Indian tribes and the federal government. He approaches the assumptions made by the Marshall Trilogy and, not content to concede that Indian tribes lost any of their inherent powers at the moment of "discovery," challenges the teleological foundations upon which the Court has based almost two centuries of federal power over Indian tribes. Williams is among the first scholars to call for resistance to the changing direction of Supreme Court jurisprudence, and his meticulous work documenting the origins of some of the Court's assumptions directly challenges the narrative that federal power in the area of Indian affairs is benign.

Bethany Berger's *Red: Racism and the American Indian* (rank 16/100) builds upon much of the critical work done by Williams in exploring the racist underpinnings of modern Indian law doctrine. She explores how racial attitudes toward Indians changed throughout American history and were reflected in American law. In the nineteenth century, American Indians were targeted not for their labor but for control of their land and resources. Berger suggests the different origins of racism have manifested in a modern movement to make Indians "equal" that is really a twenty-first-century attempt to treat tribes as racial groups instead of recognizing them as sovereign entities.

Berger provides context to fundamental questions like "who is an Indian?," "are Indians citizens?," and "what is an Indian tribe?" Rather than provide normative answers to these questions, she provides historical context to show that the answers are not static. Her work highlights how the United States has suggested different answers at different times based upon political expediency, populist support, and regional demographics. At its core, Berger offers a critique that while policymakers are focused on treating Indian tribes as groups of racially Indian people, they miss the point that Indian tribes are sovereign governments that manage populations which are themselves diverse.

Finally, Angela Riley's *(Tribal) Sovereignty and Illiberalism* (rank 11/100) makes a compelling argument for tribal sovereignty and self-government. Accepting as true Berger's premise that Indian tribal governments are more than merely collections of Indian people, Riley suggests that these governments have the right as sovereigns to organize themselves in illiberal ways. This means that tribal conceptions of justice, gender, and even religion will play a role in the construction of governance structures which will not always comply with the constraints placed upon state and local governments by the US Constitution.

Riley engages meaningfully with the idea of illiberalism, suggesting that individual rights commonly protected in other jurisdictions may not be protected by tribes, or may be protected in different ways, depending on the cultural traditions in each community. She explains that the US Constitution does not bind tribal governments. This means that tribes may use their inherent sovereignty to do things that appear to intrude on the legal protections of their members. Riley's piece confronts this tension directly by exploring competing sympathies – tribal sovereignty and civil rights – to make a compelling argument in favor of tribal self-government free from excessive federal regulation.

As you read the following four pieces consider the role each has played in articulating core concepts that underlie much of federal Indian law including colonialism, sovereignty, legal pluralism, and race. Try to connect the pieces together. Can you see how Williams' critique of the Marshall Trilogy is in tension with Frickey's call for the Court to return to the Trilogy's central tenets? In what ways does Berger build upon the colonialist observations Williams makes regarding assumptions about plenary power or colonialism? How does Riley bolster Berger's central contention that Indian tribes are sovereign governments and not merely collections of racial Indians? Would Williams or Frickey support the illiberal nature of tribal governments defended by Riley? Collectively these four pieces not only engage with many of the core concepts of Indian law but they have a conversation with each other.

1

Marshalling Past and Present: Colonialism, Constitutionalism, and Interpretation in Federal Indian Law

Philip P. Frickey

107 Harv. L. Rev. 381 (1993)

After the United States won its independence the new Republic struggled operationally to implement a system that respected the powers of its three constituent sovereigns: tribes, states, and the federal government. The Supreme Court, led by Chief Justice John Marshall, ultimately issued a trio of opinions that established a basic framework for these relationships. Known as the "Marshall Trilogy," these cases have come to define the theoretical and constitutional origins of the federal judiciary's treatment of Indians. Virtually every comprehensive examination of federal Indian law and policy recognizes the Trilogy as the starting point for exploring the federal–tribal relationship, and no collection of Indian law scholarship would be complete without the Trilogy's inclusion.

This piece by Philip Frickey argues that one of the most important tenets of the Marshall Trilogy was a recognition that while the courts would not undo the effects of colonialism on American Indians, they would not continue to assist in its promulgation. Frickey argues that Chief Justice Marshall established important presumptions, grounded in the Constitution itself, that recognized the enduring sovereignty of tribes and required clear language from Congress to intrude into Indian self-governance. Despite these fundamental presumptions, Frickey concludes that recently courts have forgotten the constitutional precepts of Marshall's conception of the federal–tribal relationship and, as a consequence of this selective memory, have begun to wrongfully permit states to interfere on Indian lands and with Indian policy.

As you read the following piece pay careful attention to Frickey's summary of each of the cases in the Marshall Trilogy. Try to articulate what separates the first case from the other two and what constitutional presumptions the author believes courts are required to apply when states attempt to assert themselves into tribal affairs. Why does the author believe that courts are beginning to depart from Marshall's vision of the federal–tribal relationship and what challenges do courts face in trying to return to Marshall's original conception of the jurisdictional lines between states and tribes? Finally, form your own opinion about the Marshall Trilogy. Would there have been a better way for the Court to decide the original cases that might have resolved some of the problems that the author exposes today?

I INTRODUCTION

In 1987, the American legal community celebrated the bicentennial of the Constitution. Five years later, few of the same people paid much attention to the quincentennial of Christopher Columbus' contact with the western hemisphere. If that event had any current significance, it seemed largely social or cultural, not legal. The Constitution and Columbus do not conjoin in contemporary thought. ***

The purpose of this Article is to suggest that it does not have to be that way. *** Federal Indian law is *** rooted in the fundamental contradiction between the historical fact and continuing realities of colonization, on the one hand, and the constitutional themes of limited government, democracy, inclusion, and fairness that, on the other hand, constitute part of our "civil religion." It is the one area of law in which the (constitutional) bicentennial and the (Columbian) quincentennial meet. My claim in this Article is that, although the federal Indian law crafted in the early-nineteenth century by Chief Justice John Marshall assisted the implementation of colonization in a variety of ways, it did not abandon the civil religion entirely. Further, I will argue that, when properly understood, the method by which Chief Justice Marshall accommodated colonialism and constitutionalism is of both theoretical interest and current practical significance. ***

II EMBRACING COLONIALISM: *JOHNSON V. MCINTOSH*

Johnson v. McIntosh was the first significant federal Indian law case in the Supreme Court. It involved a dispute between two non-Indians to the title of a parcel of land. One party traced his title back to a conveyance from a tribe to a non-Indian; the other established that his title flowed from a later transaction in which the tribe sold the land to the United States, which then patented the land in fee simple. On these facts, the Supreme Court found good title in the party whose title ultimately flowed from the United States. In explaining the basis for this conclusion, Chief Justice Marshall constructed the initial legal framework for federal Indian law.

Chief Justice Marshall first examined the justifications for European colonization of the "new world":

> On the discovery of this immense continent, the great nations of Europe were eager to appropriate to themselves so much of it as they could respectively acquire. Its vast extent offered an ample field to the ambition and enterprise of all; and the character and religion of its inhabitants afforded an apology for considering them as a people over whom the superior genius of Europe might claim an ascendancy. The potentates of the old world found no difficulty in convincing themselves that they made ample compensation to the inhabitants of the new, by bestowing on them civilization and Christianity, in exchange for unlimited independence.

Because these competing European sovereigns were all after the same thing, it became necessary to develop a rule to avoid conflicts among them. "This principle,"

Chief Justice Marshall explained, "was, that discovery gave title to the government by whose subjects, or by whose authority, it was made, against all other European governments, which title might be consummated by possession." Under this scheme, for purposes of Anglo-American law the Indians held their lands under what amounted to only a tenancy at sufferance, which could be acquired only by the European discovering sovereign, not by any private party or other government. That sovereign could extinguish Indian title "either by purchase or by conquest."

In *Johnson*, Chief Justice Marshall did not engage in a full legal, much less normative, defense of the theory of discovery and conquest. Instead, he asserted that the Court was compelled to embrace the theory for institutional reasons. The non-Indian portions of the country had been settled based on this theory, he stressed, which rendered it impossible for the Court to undo by law what had already occurred in fact. Moreover, he acknowledged that the Court was hardly situated to serve as an impartial umpire of this dispute. In a remarkable passage, he wrote that "[c]onquest gives a title which the Courts of the conqueror cannot deny, whatever the private and speculative opinions of individuals may be, respecting the original justice of the claim which has been successfully asserted." The message was simple: in order to claim a land title enforceable in the Supreme Court of the United States, one must demonstrate that the title flows from that government or its predecessor.

* * *

This summary clearly demonstrates that, in its first extended exposure to federal Indian law, the Court in *Johnson* did not mediate the tension between colonialism and constitutional government as much as it simply preferred the former. Chief Justice Marshall relied in part upon two starkly colonial visions. One was *cultural superiority* – the Christian nature and "superior genius" of the Europeans, who would exploit the resources of the continent efficiently, as compared to the primitive economic system and savagery of the natives, who thus were incapable of assimilation into the "superior" culture. The other was *judicial inferiority*, based on the situatedness of the judges themselves. United States courts simply could not adjudicate the most basic questions about the way that non-Indians had colonized and converted aboriginal lands into fee-simple lands for their own use. Chief Justice Marshall cleverly played both of these themes against each other. Ultimately, he never directly addressed whether the outcome in *Johnson* could be justified normatively under visions of cultural superiority. Instead, he based the decision upon judicial incompetency to resolve the underlying normative questions. But even though he refused to address colonialism in general – "[w]e will not enter into the controversy, whether agriculturists, merchants, and manufacturers, have a right, on abstract principles, to expel hunters from the territory they possess, or to contract their limits" – and more particularly did "not mean to engage in the defence of those principles which Europeans have applied to Indian title," his opinion immunized both broad questions of colonialism and narrower questions concerning its implementation from any sober second thought of judicial review.

To put the matter most starkly, by denying that full Indian property rights could be recognized and enforced in "the Courts of the conqueror," and by suggesting that legally enforceable title must flow from the United States government standing as successor to the colonies, *Johnson* seemed to establish a rigid dichotomy between power and law.

Colonialism, *Johnson* seemed to say, raises almost exclusively nonjusticiable, *normative* questions beyond judicial authority and competence. Colonialism was thus prior to, and the antithesis of, constitutionalism, which involves justiciable, *legal* questions about judicially enforceable limits on governmental action traceable to the founding of the United States. In short, a legal claim was defined as one found within the legal system of the colonizing government.

***

Even though all these themes were present in *Johnson*, however, that case was an unlikely vehicle for cementing them into American law. Recall that no tribe or Indian was even a party to the case. Non-Indian litigants sought a definitive resolution of a claim to non-Indian land from United States courts, and the party who traced his title to a grant from the United States prevailed. In short, *Johnson* can be read much more narrowly: instead of definitively privileging the colonial to the constitutional regime, perhaps *Johnson* merely concluded that the rights of members of the colonizing community must flow from their own government. On this understanding, *Johnson* leaves room for later adjudication that more precisely addressed the rights, if any, tribes and Indians might claim in United States courts. Indeed, the opinion was not entirely silent on whether tribes retained sovereignty despite colonization. Chief Justice Marshall wrote that, upon discovery, the tribes' "rights to complete sovereignty, as independent nations, were necessarily *diminished*," not destroyed. ***

III ABANDONING UNILATERAL COLONIAL ASSUMPTIONS: THE CHEROKEE CASES

A *Laying the Foundation:* Cherokee Nation v. Georgia

In *Cherokee Nation v. Georgia*, the tribe brought an original action in the Supreme Court to seek injunctive relief against a series of draconian Georgia laws that purported to apply to its reservation. Unlike in *Johnson*, in *Cherokee Nation* there was an Indian party in the case and Indian sovereignty was a central aspect of the controversy. Moreover, rather than challenge the very premises of colonization, the Cherokee crafted their position to fall on the "law" side of Chief Justice Marshall's power–law dichotomy, by positing the issue as whether the Georgia legislature had acted outside of its authority under United States constitutional structures.

In dismissing the case, Chief Justice Marshall held that it did not come within the Court's original jurisdiction, because the Cherokee Nation was not a "foreign state." But this was no ordinary dismissal. Chief Justice Marshall could have prepared a simple and short opinion to justify this outcome, reasoning that, whatever might be the sovereign status of the Cherokee Nation, it exists within the boundaries of the United States, and therefore is in no sense "foreign." *** That was not, however, what Chief Justice Marshall chose to do.

Chief Justice Marshall's opinion in *Cherokee Nation* began in a starkly normative vein and assumed the truth of the underlying facts and legal conclusions alleged by the Cherokee, even though Georgia had never appeared in the case either to admit or to deny them and had never formally been declared to be in default. ***

> This bill is brought by the Cherokee nation, praying an injunction to restrain the State of Georgia from the execution of certain laws of that state, which, *as is alleged,* go directly to annihilate the Cherokees as a political society, and to seize, for the use of Georgia, the lands of the nation which have been assured to them by the United States in solemn treaties repeatedly made and still in force.

> If courts were permitted to indulge their sympathies, a case better calculated to excite them can scarcely be imagined. A people once numerous, powerful, and truly independent, found by our ancestors in the quiet and uncontrolled possession of an ample domain, gradually sinking beneath our superior policy, our arts and our arms, have yielded their lands by successive treaties, each of which contains a solemn guarantee of the residue, until they retain no more of their formerly extensive territory than is deemed necessary to their comfortable subsistence. To preserve this remnant, the present application is made.

*** It may be tempting to dismiss these discussions by Chief Justice Marshall as mere musings about platonic notions of sovereignty, rather than about sovereignty under United States law – in other words, dictum that fell on the normative (nonjusticiable) side of the dichotomy suggested in *Johnson*. Later in *Cherokee Nation*, however, Chief Justice Marshall tied his conclusion that tribes were sovereigns directly to the Constitution itself. He quoted the Commerce Clause in full – Congress may "regulate commerce with foreign nations, and among the several states, and with the Indian tribes" – not merely to demonstrate that tribes are different from "foreign nations," but also to confirm the sovereign status of tribes. Chief Justice Marshall wrote: "We perceive plainly that the constitution in this article does not comprehend Indian tribes in the general term 'foreign nations;' not we presume, because a tribe may not be a nation, but because it is not foreign to the United States."

B *Mediating Colonialism through Interpretation:* Worcester v. Georgia

Although the Cherokee Nation itself failed to obtain Supreme Court assistance in its dispute with Georgia, a non-Indian litigant soon sought the aid of that forum in a case that raised essentially the same issues as *Cherokee Nation*. In *Worcester v. Georgia*, the state imprisoned a non-Indian missionary for refusing to comply with state laws that required him to have state permission to be on the reservation and to swear a loyalty oath to the state. As in *Cherokee Nation*, the issue was therefore whether Georgia law applied on the Cherokee reservation. Chief Justice Marshall held that the Georgia law was preempted by the exclusive sovereign-to-sovereign relationship that existed between the tribe and the federal government. In so holding, the Chief Justice had to rebuff arguments that the tribe had lost its sovereignty, either through the legally operative effects of discovery and conquest or by ceding it in a treaty, and had therefore become legally indistinct from other residents of Georgia. In considering these arguments, Chief Justice Marshall translated the dictum on tribal sovereignty in *Cherokee Nation* into a full-fledged holding that defined the sovereign status of Indian tribes.

After *Johnson*, the normative questions surrounding colonization might have seemed beyond the scope of judicial comment. Nonetheless, Chief Justice Marshall revisited them in *Worcester*. He began the substantive portion of the opinion with three remarkable paragraphs in which he seemed to express serious qualms about colonization. Then, in the fourth paragraph, in a move of extraordinary cleverness, Chief Justice Marshall simultaneously acknowledged and partially deflated the "judicial incompetency" theme of *Johnson*:

> But power, war, conquest, give rights, which, after possession, are conceded by the world; and which can never be controverted by those on whom they descend. We proceed, then, to the actual state of things, having glanced at their origin; because holding it in our recollection might shed some light on existing pretensions.

*** To be sure, opening the door to normative considerations could not fundamentally alter all aspects of the judicial role. As *Johnson* indicated, the judiciary was simply powerless to review the *historical* aspects of colonization. American courts were the "Courts of the conqueror" and could not turn against the government and people from which they derived their authority. It follows in *Worcester* that courts could not invalidate the root assumptions of colonization. Chief Justice Marshall thus implicitly endorsed the plenary power of Congress to implement colonization, a notion later squarely embraced by the Court. Moreover, any effort to undo the settled aspects of colonization would be futile. American courts could not annul the effects of the theories of discovery and original Indian title, upon which all Euro-American land titles were based.

These prudential concerns about judicial restraint, Chief Justice Marshall suggested, matter far less when indigenous peoples are challenging *current* efforts to destroy whatever rights they still possess. To return to Chief Justice Marshall's language in *Worcester*, "existing pretensions" are subject to judicial scrutiny, and their lawfulness must be informed by "holding" an honest assessment of colonization "in our recollection." Thus, the appropriateness of state regulation of tribal autonomy was open to judicial scrutiny in *Worcester*. Moreover, although the *existence* of congressional plenary power over tribes was probably settled, *Worcester* left open the possibility that an *exercise* of that power could be subjected to some kind of judicial evaluation. The dichotomy drawn in *Johnson* between power and law, between the normative and the justiciable, was thus reshaped into a distinction between historical wrongs, whose adjudication would too seriously threaten settled Euro-American rights and expectations, and current "pretensions."

Under this revised vision of federal Indian law, it was crucial to determine exactly what the history of colonization had conclusively settled for purposes of American law. *Worcester*, unlike *Johnson*, provided Chief Justice Marshall with a salient context in which to reflect upon this question. For although *Worcester* nominally involved the rights of a non-Indian, it required the resolution of a controversy between the Cherokee Nation and the State of Georgia concerning whether the tribe possessed current rights rooted in positive American law: a treaty with the United States. *Worcester*, then, involved a situation far removed from a Euro-American land claimant challenging the long-ago-settled patterns of establishing Euro-American land title. This context, combined with an admitted concern about the normative questions surrounding colonization, seemed to sharpen Chief Justice Marshall's focus on the relevant colonial history. Indeed, in this context, Chief Justice Marshall imaginatively rewrote the historical assumptions upon which *Johnson* had seemingly been premised. ***

C *The Interpretive Strategies of Worcester*

Chief Justice Marshall's interpretive method in *Worcester* is not self-evidently correct, however. Indeed, its elements are highly controversial. The identification of the debatable moves and an assessment of their validity are worthy tasks for both Indian law scholars and practicing lawyers and judges. These inquiries probe fundamental aspects of federal Indian law – not just as issues of historical or scholarly curiosity, but also as matters relevant to current practice.

***

Recall Chief Justice Marshall's general presumptions that, prior to discovery, tribes possessed complete, inherent sovereignty; that discovery had reduced their sovereignty only with respect to external sovereign relations; and that in the treaty-making process neither Great Britain nor the United States had sought to interfere with internal tribal governance. These presumptions, left unchallenged in *Worcester*, made it rather simple to counter the apparent force of some of the provisions of the foundational treaty with the Cherokee, the Treaty of Hopewell of 1785, in which the tribe arguably surrendered its autonomy.

For example, the treaty began as follows: "The Commissioners Plenipotentiary of the United States, in Congress assembled, give peace to all the Cherokees, and receive them into the favour and protection of the United States of America, on the following conditions." As Justice Johnson argued in *Cherokee Nation,* this language appears to embody a Cherokee surrender to superior power – an abandonment of sovereignty in return for whatever protections the United States might wish to bestow on the tribe. Chief Justice Marshall quickly dismissed this argument. He pointed out that, because peace was a bilateral bargain sought by both parties, and because the United States actually went to Hopewell to make the treaty, "[t]he word 'give,' ... has no real importance attached to it."

But two of the provisions of this treaty were not so easily overcome, as evidenced by Chief Justice Marshall's elaborate discussion of them in *Worcester* even in the absence of any counterargument by a party or a dissenting Justice. To construe them to preserve tribal authority, Chief Justice Marshall had to develop a more elaborate theory of Indian treaty-making and its interpretive consequences.

The fourth article set forth the "boundary allotted to the Cherokees for their hunting grounds." As Justice Johnson argued in *Cherokee Nation,* this language strongly suggests that the Cherokee had granted all their land and whatever sovereign power they possessed to the federal government, which had then "allotted to" the Cherokee the use of certain of those now-public lands for hunting. This interpretation is supported by the fact that, in the treaty, the Cherokee had yielded extensive territory to the United States. Moreover, this interpretation would promote the purposes of colonization, as understood in *Johnson,* for it would lodge in non-Indian hands the conclusive power over future development of the land from its status as "hunting grounds" into use by "agriculturalists and manufacturers." It would consider the tribe to have at most a property interest in land, rather than any sovereign power, again consistent with the major thrust of *Johnson.*

Chief Justice Marshall provided two justifications for rejecting this interpretation of the fourth article. Each has become a central feature of federal Indian law interpretation.

First, Chief Justice Marshall stressed that the treaty was negotiated and written in English, a language foreign to the tribal negotiators. They should not have been expected, therefore, to "distinguish the word 'allotted' from the words 'marked out.'" Nor would the words "hunting ground" have suggested any limitation to the tribe, because "[h]unting was at that time the principal occupation of the Indians, and their land was more used for that purpose than for any other." In other words, the term "hunting ground" should be construed as the Indians would have understood it – complete land possession and control – rather than as non-Indians would have – at most an exclusive license to hunt.

*** In essence, Chief Justice Marshall placed the responsibility upon the federal treaty negotiators to ensure that tribes understood what they were abandoning through the treaty. This duty was especially important because it applied retroactively to existing treaties as well as prospectively to future negotiations. Whereas in *Johnson* Chief Justice Marshall understood the Court to have some responsibility for rationalizing the *historical* and settled components of colonization, in *Worcester* he signaled that *further* encroachments upon tribes – the ongoing process of colon-ization – would receive no special assistance from the judiciary. The executive branch, when it negotiated treaties, and the Senate, when it ratified them, were the only institutions appropriate to do the problematic work of further colonization. The judiciary would not enforce their work unless it was compelled to do so.

Second, Chief Justice Marshall concluded that to give the fourth article the plain meaning of its text – particularly the word "allotted" – would be inconsistent with the fundamental nature of the transactions at the heart of Indian treaties. ***

Chief Justice Marshall *** conceptualized an Indian treaty as a grant of rights from a tribe to the United States, rather than a cession of all tribal rights to the United States, which then granted back certain concessions to the tribe. Chief Justice Marshall reasoned that Indian treaties were not acts of complete tribal surrender to the conquering government. Instead, they were reservations by the tribe of all rights not clearly granted to the United States – hence the term "reserva-tion" for the lands retained by the tribe. Although this "reserved rights doctrine" is usually associated with later cases in which the Supreme Court squarely embraced it, this doctrine is rooted in a subtle Marshallian move in *Worcester*. ***

IV QUASI-CONSTITUTIONALISM BY INTERPRETATION: THE POTENTIAL LEGACY OF *WORCESTER*

A *Understanding Chief Justice Marshall's Methodology*

Although the interpretive techniques Chief Justice Marshall used in *Worcester* are fascinating, their precise nature and justification are rather obscure, and they may at first appear largely ad hoc. Careful examination of his approach, however, reveals a systematic and attractive theory of Indian treaty interpretation that is consistent with Chief Justice Marshall's overall approach to the interpretation of certain kinds of public law documents.

***

2. *Indian Treaties as Constitutive Documents.* – In *Cherokee Nation* and *Worces-ter*, Chief Justice Marshall repeatedly stressed the sovereign-to-sovereign relationship between tribes and the British crown and its successor, the United States. He rightly understood that this relationship extended far beyond anything like a contractual model. Rather, it involved a mixture of brute force – *Johnson's* assumptions of conquest and colonization, which are literally matters of war and peace – and territorial sovereignty – cessions of land from the tribe to the United States, with remaining land reserved for the tribe. In this context the treaty became, in essence, the piece of positive law that reflected the *constitutive* relationship between two sovereigns. This linkage between the tribe and the United States, as a matter of law rather than sheer power, was the element missing in *Johnson v. McIntosh*.

That this connection was made in the form of a "treaty" between sovereigns does not defeat the constitutional analogy. Because the treaty involved the relation of a domestic dependent nation and the larger government to which it was inextricably tied and by which it was geographically surrounded, the treaty stood less as a matter of international law than of domestic law. ***

Chief Justice Marshall's most famous efforts to establish principles of constitutional interpretation are found, of course, in *Marbury v. Madison* and *McCulloch v. Maryland.* In these cases, he emphasized that the very nature – or "spirit," to use his language in *Worcester* – of a written constitution is to provide enforceable limits on lawgivers and simultaneously to give them the flexibility necessary to govern in a functional manner. Chief Justice Marshall's famous words in *McCulloch,* which warned that judges "must never forget, that it is *a constitution* we are expounding," posit an essentialist view of a constitution as the constitutive document of a complex government in an ever-evolving society; if the document that provides the undergirding and framework for that government cannot serve functional ends over time, the society will founder.

In *Worcester,* Chief Justice Marshall attributed a similar nature to an Indian treaty. It was the constitutive document providing the undergirding and framework for an ongoing (tribal) government–(federal) government relationship. It was, if you will, the joinder of two sets of "We the People," and it therefore resonated with *Marbury's* notion that constitutional authority flows from the people themselves. The treaty was a sovereign act of law rather than of sheer power – that is, of conquest. ***

3. *Quasi-Constitutional Clear-Statement Rules.* – In both *McCulloch* and *Worcester,* Chief Justice Marshall went to great lengths to immunize a constitutive document from a construction that would violate its underlying nature and purposes. As explained below, he essentially created a clear-statement rule of interpretation, under which only crystal-clear text could trump the spirit of the document under construction. In *McCulloch,* he concluded that, "unless [its] words imperiously require it," the Constitution should not be interpreted to forbid the exercise of Congress's enumerated powers through all feasible means. *Worcester* contains a similar passage in which Chief Justice Marshall refused to read the ninth article of the Treaty of Hopewell to "convert a treaty of peace covertly into an act, annihilating the political existence of one of the parties." "Had such a result been intended," Chief Justice Marshall wrote, "it would have been openly avowed."

***

Clear-statement rules are policy-based canons of a different order of magnitude. They go beyond end-game tiebreakers, and even beyond initial rebuttable presumptions, to require that a document be interpreted a certain way unless unambiguous statutory text or, perhaps, absolutely compelling legislative history requires a contrary conclusion. In *McCulloch* and *Worcester,* Chief Justice Marshall approached interpretation with this degree of vigor. Because no clear constitutional text denied Congress the discretion to use all feasible means to implement its enumerated powers, *McCulloch* held that Congress had that discretion. Because the Treaty of Hopewell nowhere contained language that terminated the sovereignty of the Cherokee Nation in so many words, that sovereignty survived.

Clear-statement rules, because they can radically bend documents away from their apparent meaning, are used sparingly. Their primary justification today is to guard against the erosion of constitutional structures that are difficult to protect by more direct forms of judicial review. ***

This approach has significant institutional implications both for the Court and for Congress. It provides the Court with a structural lodestar to cut through the complexities of a difficult statutory case. The state gets the benefit of a strong presumption in favor of its sovereignty, and the opposing party bears the burden of marshalling the legal complexities and finding clear evidence of congressional support for its position. If, as is often the case, state sovereignty survives the challenge, the burden of combatting inertia and seeking legal change lies with the party who sought to intrude upon state authority. ***

These rationales for employing clear-statement rules in the federalism and separation of powers contexts fit Chief Justice Marshall's methodology in *Worcester* well. The "Courts of the conqueror" cannot realistically be expected to invalidate even harsh colonial measures in the name of the very constitution established by the colonizers. How can such courts determine when Congress or the executive "goes too far" to promote colonization? How could a decree that made such a judgment be enforced, in any event? These concerns do not mean, however, that the courts must slavishly enforce colonial measures to the limits of their plausible meanings. By centralizing the power over Indian affairs in the federal government, by conceptualizing the relationship of tribes with the federal government as a sovereign-to-sovereign one, by envisioning an Indian treaty as the constitutive document of that sovereignty and structure, and by protecting treaty-recognized sovereignty and structure from erosion by all but crystal-clear treaty text, Chief Justice Marshall built a complex, institutionally sensitive interpretive scheme. His approach to the problems of colonization, then, parallels the current Court's efforts to domesticate important but essentially nonjusticiable questions of governmental structure by creating clear-statement rules. Both techniques have been justified by the centrality to these disputes of a constitutive document of sovereignty – an Indian treaty in the first instance, and the American Constitution in the second.

Because of this parallel, it is not surprising that the Supreme Court has long applied a clear-statement requirement to congressional acts that appear to invade tribal sovereignty. The clearest example is the principle that, absent compelling evidence, a court should not hold that a federal statute has abrogated an Indian treaty. Unilateral federal treaty abrogation, one of the starkest acts of colonization, is within the discretion of Congress, the Court has held, and thus injunctive relief is unavailable to prevent the abrogation. That the counterpoint to this deference in judicial review has been some vigilance in statutory interpretation – if plausible, to interpret the statute not to abrogate the treaty – is a natural extension of Chief Justice Marshall's work in *Worcester*. Just as contemporary decisions protect against all but express repeals of values rooted in the Constitution, the Indian treaty abrogation doctrine protects against all but clear repeals of values rooted in the spirit of Indian treaties.

B *The Court and Federal Indian Law: Losing Touch with Chief Justice Marshall*

My argument thus far has suggested considerable similarity between Chief Justice Marshall's method in *Worcester* and the current Court's use of clear-statement rules. Unfortunately, these parallels break down where the overlap is greatest: in contemporary federal Indian law. As we shall see, the current Court's approach to federal Indian law is in great tension with Marshall's model.

A century and a half has passed since Chief Justice Marshall generated his approach. In that period, at least three developments might appear to undercut Chief Justice Marshall's method and to defeat the parallelism between canonical protection of tribal and state sovereignty. Yet ultimately none of these developments explains the current Court's sharp deviation from Chief Justice Marshall's approach.

First, respect for tribal sovereignty may be harder to generate when the Court has confidently declared for a century that congressional power over tribes is plenary. These decisions, in line with Chief Justice Marshall's basic assumptions in *Worcester*, view the *existence* of plenary congressional power over tribes as part of the sovereign-to-sovereign relationship settled at the point of colonization. Nonetheless, consistent with Chief Justice Marshall's approach, the current Court has held that the *exercise* of that power is still subject to limitation by clear-statement interpretive requirements. Tribal sovereignty is thus similar to state sovereignty, another beneficiary of clear-statement interpretive protection, for the Court allows Congress essentially plenary authority to subject states to federal judicial jurisdiction and regulation.

Second, states today look much more like sovereigns than do some tribes. For example, unlike the Cherokee Reservation in *Worcester*, some Indian areas today have lost much of their distinctive character and contain many non-Indian residents. Some of the Court's relatively recent cases have involved this difficult context, which arose from the allotment process of the late nineteenth and early twentieth centuries, in which a portion of the reservation was divided into individual parcels for tribal members and the remainder opened for homesteading by non-Indians.

To apply Chief Justice Marshall's legacy in this context is no simple matter. To bring his method to bear in these cases would require, at a minimum, that the Court confront this situation directly. An evaluation of the level of residual tribal sovereignty in each case would parallel Chief Justice Marshall's inquiry in *Worcester* into whether the inherent sovereignty of the Cherokee Nation survived the Treaty of

Hopewell. By acknowledging the conflicting interests at play, the Court could require Congress to authorize any substantial change clearly. In any event, not all federal Indian law cases will be shaped by allotment. Many cases still involve unallotted reservations or other contexts in which tribal sovereignty has retained significant contextual support, and the Court has not even clearly signaled a methodological shift in the context of allotment. Whatever its complexities, then, the allotment process poses no insurmountable barrier to the modern application of Chief Justice Marshall's approach.

Third, many federal Indian law decisions, especially those dealing with developments since the mid-nineteenth century, turn not on treaty language, but on the text of seemingly more mundane instruments of law, such as statutes, executive orders, and federal regulations. For example, millions of acres of Indian lands are located on reservations established by executive order. This difference in form should not, however, substantially alter judicial methodology. Some of these non-treaty enactments embody agreements with tribes that would have been handled by treaty in former eras. *** Consistent with this notion, the Court has drawn no fundamental interpretive distinction between reservations established by statute or executive order and those protected by treaty.

Nonetheless, the current Supreme Court has recently moved away from Chief Justice Marshall's model in dramatic fashion. It has not justified this shift by reference to any longstanding historical, doctrinal, or contextual development. Indeed, the Court has supported this switch more by ipse dixit than explanation. But whatever the motivating rationale, the Court has simultaneously deflated the power of the Indian law canon and privileged other values, in particular federalism.

In its most important recent decision, *Cotton Petroleum Corp. v. New Mexico*, the Court held that a state could impose its severance tax upon oil and gas extracted by a non-Indian company from tribal lands on an Indian reservation. The extraordinary tension between this case and *Worcester* is patent. Recall that, in *Worcester*, Chief Justice Marshall concluded that, absent clear tribal or congressional authorization, an Indian reservation remains "a distinct community occupying its own territory, with boundaries accurately described, in which the laws of [the state] can have no force." *Cotton Petroleum* instead stated, apparently as a general proposition, that "[s]tates and tribes have concurrent jurisdiction over the same territory." Turning Chief Justice Marshall's clear-statement approach almost completely on its head, the Court in *Cotton Petroleum* then concluded that the state could tax because Congress had failed to prohibit it from exercising that power.

What happened in *Cotton Petroleum* to Chief Justice Marshall's clear-statement rule? In its only allusion to the canon, the Court in *Cotton Petroleum* wrote that, "although state interests must be given weight and courts should be careful not to make legislative decisions in the absence of congressional action, ambiguities in federal law are, as a rule, resolved in favor of tribal independence." This language reveals much about the extent to which the Indian law canon has been degraded:

here it appears to be something approximating only a weak end-of-the-game tie-breaker. Moreover, the passage demonstrates a strong preference for state authority, consistent with the current Court's federalism-protecting clear-statement rules discussed earlier.

* * *

The primary explanation for the Court's language in *Cotton Petroleum*, I believe, is that the quasi-constitutional, structural nature of Chief Justice Marshall's approach is lost on the current Court. The canon has little bite because it seems so blatantly normative – "you should help those poor Indians" – and normative in a fuzzy, liberal direction at that. If I am right that the Justices perceive the canon as designed to promote a public value that favors Indians as a down-trodden minority, the Justices are not alone. The two principal recent commentaries on the substantive canons treat the Indian law canon the same way. William Eskridge categorizes that canon as part of a cluster of canons that protect discrete and insular minorities – "*Carolene* groups" – against legislative oppression. Similarly, Cass Sunstein calls the Indian canon "the most conspicuous example" of an interpretive principle that favors "disadvantaged groups."

In the hands of sympathetic commentators, this conceptualization might seem innocuous. In truth, though, by masking the essential differences between the legal and cultural situations of Native Americans and of America's racial minorities, this conceptualization is antagonistic to the most basic claim put forward by American Indians: the claim to be free from assimilative forces and to make and be governed by their own laws. It is not a conceptualization, then, that Native American leaders would likely embrace even if it could produce a few judicial victories along the way. In any event, in the hands of the current Court, this conceptualization of the canon has quite the opposite effect. Its patently value-laden nature renders it easily trumped by federalism principles.

With all due respect, the commentators are wrong to categorize the Indian law canon as designed to protect disadvantaged minorities. They overlook that the Indian law canon is essentially structural and institutional and was not established to promote equality or to combat political powerlessness. Much more important, the Court has committed the same error, and its error threatens to destroy much of the force of the Indian law canon. There is nothing "neutral" or "value-free" about the Court's preference for structural principles, involving federalism and the separation of powers, over nonstructural principles such as individual rights or interpretive protections for "disadvantaged groups." But even if values rooted in the Constitution somehow automatically deserve heightened interpretive protection, the Court has articulated no neutral reason to prefer federalism to Indian sovereignty, as Chief Justice Marshall conceptualized it. Of course, the Supreme Court has the power to prefer the former to the latter, but such a decision warrants intense scrutiny and discussion, which have not occurred. * * *

C *Reviving Chief Justice Marshall's Approach: Some Exploratory Thoughts*

How much, if anything, can be retrieved of Chief Justice Marshall's legacy? Maybe no one should even try to exhume his perspective. The history of federal Indian law since Chief Justice Marshall has been filled with tragedy, a story in which the rule of law often has become a vehicle to rationalize what can only be understood as crimes against humanity. More basically, any effort to retrieve Chief Justice Marshall's approach will strike some critics as wrong, not because it comes far too late, but because his vision is irredeemably tainted by the poison of colonization. The conclusion that federal Indian law cannot be reconstructed and thus is worthy only of critique is understandable. Nonetheless, my own judgment is that room remains for scholarly work that criticizes federal Indian law from the inside and that assumes that the legal interpretive community is not closed to arguments in this field.

*** The most important result of a revival of Chief Justice Marshall's legacy would be that judges would be compelled to view Indian law afresh in today's context. The issues would be structural, involving conflicts among sovereigns, and not contests between sovereigns and disadvantaged groups who seek judicial solicitude with hat in hand. Tribes would not win every new case, and situations in which congressional actions have radically eroded the Indian social context would still prove particularly troublesome. But the spirit of the structural, constitutive approach would force judges to do the hard work exemplified by John Marshall in *Worcester* – to challenge rather than to accept blindly assumptions rooted in colonialism, of which there are many today; to interpret documents of positive law flexibly in order to promote the ongoing sovereign-to-sovereign relationship of the tribe and the federal government; to keep the judiciary out of the business of imposing new forms of colonialism; and to refuse to relieve Congress of the responsibility to determine expressly whether future exercises of colonialism should occur.

In this way, *Worcester* stands as the preeminent, paradigmatic case for what "doing federal Indian law" should be all about. In federal Indian law, as elsewhere, paradigmatic cases teach us more than the formulation of any rule. To be sure, to implement Chief Justice Marshall's model would require a fair measure of nuance and subtlety, and all the practical implications of doing so cannot be identified with complete specificity. Nonetheless, it should be valuable to explore some paradigmatic cases that shed light on the practical implications of the approach. I have selected two cases: one, a Burger Court case in which the Court performed remarkably consistently with the model, and the other the Rehnquist Court decision that seems most starkly in conflict with it.

1. *Embracing the Model: Bryan v. Itasca County.* – In 1953, Congress adopted Public Law 280, one of the most assimilationist laws in the history of federal Indian policy. The current version of this law delegates to six specified states criminal law

enforcement responsibility for Indian country within their borders. The statute also grants the states wide-ranging civil jurisdiction. ***

Nonetheless, in *Bryan v. Itasca County*, the Court held that the statute did not confer upon the states any power to tax Indians in Indian country. The opinion for the Court was not an artful one. It asserted that the conclusion that the statute delegates to states this power to tax "is foreclosed by the legislative history of Pub. L. 280 and the application of canons of construction." But the legislative history of Public Law 280 is essentially silent on the question. Similarly, the formulation of the canon that the Court quoted was hopelessly inapplicable to the context before it. If its canonical underpinnings are uprooted in this way, *Bryan* seems wrongly decided. ***

What drove the Court's result in *Bryan* seems to have been an appreciation of the structural values at stake. Any federal delegation to states of power to intervene in Indian country would, of course, under *Worcester* constitute an abrogation of any Indian treaty that is silent with respect to state jurisdiction over Indian tribes. The Court in *Bryan* feared that tribal government would be undermined, even destroyed, and tribes would become "little more than 'private, voluntary organizations,' . . . if tribal governments and reservation Indians were subordinated to the full panoply of civil regulatory powers, including taxation, of state and local governments." In a footnote, the Court elaborated on the destructive effects of conferring on states general civil regulatory power over reservation Indians. The Court noted that current federal Indian policy favored tribal self-government and quoted a lower court decision that "courts 'are not obliged in ambiguous instances to strain to implement [an assimilationist] policy Congress has now rejected, particularly where to do so will interfere with the present congressional approach to what is, after all, an ongoing relationship.'" Finally, the Court stressed that the same Congress that had adopted Public Law 280 had enacted several statutes that terminated the federal status of certain tribes. Congress therefore had shown itself capable of clearly subjecting reservation Indians to the full scope of state law, but it had apparently chosen a narrower compass in Public Law 280. "[W]e conclude," the Court wrote, "that construing Pub. L. 280 *in pari materia* with these [termination statutes] shows that if Congress in enacting Pub. L. 280 had intended to confer upon the States general civil regulatory powers, including taxation, over reservation Indians, it would have expressly said so."

***

Unartful drafting aside, *Bryan* represents as close an instinctive approximation of Chief Justice Marshall's methodology in *Worcester* as is found in any modern case. Both Courts saw the conflicts to be structural and rooted in sovereignty, rather than to involve the regulation of a disadvantaged minority group. Both Courts assumed a baseline of ongoing tribal sovereignty that should be judicially protected against all but clear congressional intrusion. Both resolved the disputes in a way that left the burden to seek change upon those who would promote colonization. Illustratively, in *Bryan* the choice was whether to leave the burden of legislative inertia – that is, the burden of seeking congressional action – on the states or on the tribes. The notions of a baseline of tribal sovereignty and an ongoing federal–tribal relationship, coupled with the states' superior access to Congress, fully support the resolution of this issue in *Bryan*. Moreover, the interpretive strategy used in each case to domesticate expansive language that seems destructive of tribal sovereignty is essentially identical. Both cases limited the intrusion upon tribal prerogatives to the specific subject of the provision in question – state court jurisdiction in *Bryan*, trade in *Worcester*. *Bryan*, a unanimous opinion, demonstrates that the Court in the modern era remains able to apply Chief Justice Marshall's basic approach, at least for disputes in which there is no significant non-Indian interest at stake.

    2. *Mangling the Model: Cotton Petroleum Corp. v. New Mexico.* – In 1924, Congress expressly empowered states to tax mineral production on Indian lands. Fourteen years later, in the Indian Mineral Leasing Act of 1938, Congress adopted comprehensive legislation to govern mineral leasing in Indian country. The 1938 Act contained no provision authorizing state taxation. It did not expressly repeal the provision of the 1924 Act that allowed state taxation, but it did contain a general repealer clause that proclaimed that all Acts "or parts of Acts inconsistent herewith are hereby repealed." * * *

    I have already identified the second case, *Cotton Petroleum Corp. v. New Mexico*, as perhaps the Rehnquist Court's prime offender of the Marshall legacy. As discussed earlier, this case expressed the general proposition, completely contrary to *Worcester*, that an Indian reservation is within the territorial jurisdiction of three sovereigns: the state, the tribe, and the federal government. At a minimum, a revival of the Marshall legacy requires rejection of that dictum. Once that is done, a complex, but factually doubtful, case remains.

    In *Cotton Petroleum*, the question was whether the state could tax the production of oil and gas by a non-Indian company that held a mineral lease to reservation lands under the 1938 Act. * * * In several earlier cases in which the governing federal statutes were unclear, the Court ultimately denied the state this kind of taxing authority over non-Indian contractors on the ground that the federal and tribal interests in freedom from state interference outweighed any state concerns. In those cases, however, it was clear that the state tax, if imposed on the non-Indian contractor, would ultimately redound to the economic detriment of the tribe. In contrast, in *Cotton Petroleum* – an action brought by the non-Indian contractor for a tax refund in which the tribe was neither a party nor an active participant in structuring the case – the record failed to demonstrate that payment of the tax would harm the tribe, either by effectively imposing the practical incidence of the tax on the tribe or by interfering with the tribe's ability to impose a severance tax on the contractor. The earlier cases also involved situations in which states provided no services in Indian country linked to the activity that they sought to tax. Again in contrast, in *Cotton Petroleum* the state had demonstrated that it provided services of value related to the oil and gas production at issue.

Thus, *Cotton Petroleum* was a poor vehicle to resolve the general issue of the state power to tax non-Indian mineral contractors. The record is devoid of evidence of the tribe's interests, and the arguments against the imposition of the state tax were crafted to serve the interests of the contractor, not the tribe. To accept the record in this case at face value, one must assume that the imposition of the tax had no effect upon the tribe's revenue, which simply seems implausible. Even if the tax was not passed back to the tribe, surely the presence of the state tax placed an otherwise artificial ceiling on the level of the tribe's taxation of the contractor. Yet the state courts concluded to the contrary. This case demonstrates the peril that arises when the Indians are taken out of Indian law.

It seems odd to attempt to apply the Marshall legacy in this setting, in which tribal interests have been artificially depreciated. In brief, an attempt to do so would start with a presumption against the state power to tax, because state taxation represents both an invasion of tribal sovereignty and an intrusion on the exclusive federal–tribal relationship. Under Chief Justice Marshall's approach that presumption should be overcome only on a showing of clear evidence that the federal statute in question delegates taxing authority to the states.

*** Recall that *Worcester* conclusively ousted state law from Indian country. Rearrangement of this jurisdictional barrier is within Congress's plenary power, but the canonical approach requires Congress to speak clearly if it wishes to do so. Absent clear congressional direction, even a modern-day dilution of *Worcester* still suggests that states should have no role in Indian country unless significant non-Indian interests are involved and no legitimate tribal interest is present to counterbalance them. Again, the virtue of Chief Justice Marshall's approach is that it makes the argument for reservation immunity from state regulation straightforward and presumptively correct, and it forces the state to bear the burden of presenting the complex side of the case in a highly persuasive fashion.

Such clear congressional consent to redesign the jurisdictional barriers in Indian country is simply absent in *Cotton Petroleum*. As [*Montana v.*] *Blackfeet Tribe* indicated, the relationship between the 1938 Act, which contains no congressional consent to state taxation, and the prior law that did is hardly a model of clarity. Even if the canon in *Cotton Petroleum* should not be as stringent as the one involved in *Blackfeet Tribe*, because the former case involved non-Indians and a clearer state interest in taxation, there seems to be no reason to find that the presumption against state taxation was overcome. Moreover, counterbalancing the state's interests in the case is a significant tribal sovereignty interest; surely in reality, if not in the record in that case, the tribe's practical ability to tax the non-Indian contractor is inversely related to the state's power to tax that entity.

3. *Retrieving the Model.* – *** The case for reviving Chief Justice Marshall's legacy thus has significant power as a theoretical matter and is hardly foreclosed

by the Court's current doctrinal situation. Candor requires, however, an acknowledgment that the prospects of a revival of Chief Justice Marshall's legacy are
questionable. ***

As I have stated, most of the doctrinal shift in *Cotton Petroleum* is in dicta, and the
odd record in that case should make it distinguishable from future controversies.
Whether the judicial will exists to limit *Cotton Petroleum* to its facts is another
matter. One of the most vital questions in contemporary federal Indian law is
whether the methodology suggested in *Cotton Petroleum* will prove to be ephemeral.
As the treatment of prior cases in *Cotton Petroleum* itself demonstrates, the prece-
dential effect of federal Indian law decisions is often weak. *** In a future case,
then, a majority should feel free to return to the soundest, and obviously the most
longstanding, approach taken to federal Indian law: that of Chief Justice Marshall.
And that majority should feel equally free to say, if "the dissent accuses [them] of
repeating what it announces as Chief Justice Marshall's misunderstanding," three
words in reply: "We are honored."

V CONCLUSION

To emulate Chief Justice Marshall in *Worcester* requires many things, including
judicial courage. Chief Justice Marshall's *Worcester* decision outraged not only the
State of Georgia, but President Andrew Jackson as well. It produced what was, up to
that point, the most serious conflict between the Supreme Court and another federal
branch in American constitutional history.

It is too much, I suppose, to ask the current Justices to risk the institutional
survival of the Supreme Court on the outcomes of federal Indian law cases. But it is
not too much to ask them to recognize that federal Indian law is about institutional
survival as well – the perpetuation of the oldest continuous sovereigns on this
continent. The Court's current structural clear-statement rules concerning federalism and the separation of powers serve much the same function as would a properly
conceptualized and revitalized Indian law canon. Indeed, the Indian law canon has
a much longer and much more venerable heritage than the Court's current canons
of preference. Recognizing this fact might help the Justices and their professional
audience to see that federal Indian law disputes are not "crud" or "peewee" cases,
but structural, quasi-constitutional cases of the first rank, opportunities for revisiting –
after all these centuries – the ongoing, and probably never-ending, dilemmas of
constitutionalism in a colonial society.

NOTES & QUESTIONS

1. *Reading Indian Law*:
   • Frickey suggests that American courts cannot turn their back on the
     government from which they derive their power and thus federal

courts are "courts of the Conqueror." How can tribal interests work within this system to advocate for favorable interpretations of the law for Indians?

- Frickey talks about Indian law being "quasi-constitutional" and traces that origin to Chief Justice Marshall's opinion in *Worcester*. What justifications exist to interpret treaties as quasi-constitutional documents and how does that reasoning change as the Supreme Court has moved from interpreting treaties to interpreting statutes?
- Try to articulate the clear-statement rule for yourself. What does Frickey mean when he says that *Cotton Petroleum* turned Marshall's conception of Indian law on its head? If the Supreme Court in *Cotton Petroleum* had been true to Marshall's conception of Indian law and applied the clear-statement presumption how would the case have turned out differently?

2. *The Marshall Trilogy*: Chief Justice Marshall and the constitutional presumptions laid out in the Marshall Trilogy are referenced several times in other pieces throughout this volume and have captivated courts and commentators for generations. The Trilogy established a framework for federal Indian law that treats tribes as sovereign, that justifies congressional control in the area of Indian affairs, that recognizes that tribes have use and occupancy rights over their lands, and that created a presumption against state interference in tribal affairs. As you consider the fifteen other pieces in this volume see if you can identify moments when the authors are referring back to these first principles.

3. *Before the Trilogy*: Chief Justice Marshall's rejection of earlier notions of both the nonjusticiable nature of Indian land claims and the lack of the power of the judiciary to resolve those questions, discussed at length in the Frickey piece, is perhaps even more remarkable given earlier Supreme Court authority. Before the Trilogy cases were decided the Supreme Court had deferred to the ability of states to appropriate and sell tribal lands.

In *Fletcher v. Peck*, 10 U.S. 87 (1810) the Supreme Court issued its first opinion on the question of state authority over Indian country. In 1795 Georgia had simply assumed jurisdiction over the Yazoo lands – lands encompassing a roughly 35 million acre Indian reserve west of the agreed Georgia boundary line. Georgia proceeded to sell those lands at below market rates in exchange for significant bribes paid to state legislators. After new elections that resulted in many legislators losing their seats, Georgia attempted to invalidate those sales.

Writing for the majority, Chief Justice Marshall declared that the repeal of the land sale was unconstitutional because it violated a provision of the Constitution protecting contracts. The opinion merely glossed over how Georgia had attempted to obtain title to the lands originally, suggesting that it was proper for states to simply declare their ownership of Indian lands:

> The question, whether the vacant lands within the United States became a joint property, or belonged to the separate states, was a momentous question which, at one time, threatened to shake the American confederacy to its foundation. This important and dangerous contest has been compromised, and the compromise is not now to be disturbed.

> It is the opinion of the court, that the particular land stated in the declaration appears, from this special verdict, to lie within the state of Georgia, and that the state of Georgia had power to grant it.

> Some difficulty was produced by the language of the covenant, and of the pleadings. It was doubted whether a state can be seized in fee of lands, subject to the Indian title, and whether a decision that they were seized in fee, might not be construed to amount to a decision that their grantee might maintain an ejectment for them, notwithstanding that title.

> The majority of the court is of opinion that the nature of the Indian title, which is certainly to be respected by all courts, until it be legitimately extinguished, is not such as to be absolutely repugnant to seizing in fee on the part of the state.

Fletcher v. Peck, 10 U.S. at 142–143. The Marshall Trilogy challenged many of the presumptions made by the Court in *Fletcher*. Apply Frickey's discussion to the *Fletcher* case. How has the Court evolved its understanding of the nature of Indian tribes and the proper relationship between tribes and their constituent states? Can *Fletcher*'s decision allowing Georgia to simply claim the fee interest in Indian lands be reconciled with *Worcester*'s decision that Georgia could not extend its laws requiring non-Indian missionaries to obtain a license in order to be on Indian lands?

4. *Doctrine of Discovery*: Frickey, in his discussion of *Johnson v. McIntosh*, touches on the development of the discovery doctrine. Essentially Chief Justice Marshall traced the Indians' loss of fee simple interest in their lands to the arrival of European powers. While the Frickey piece focuses on the presumptions against state interference on tribal lands that are deeply embedded in the Marshall opinions, other commentators have been less forgiving. Frickey's piece calls for a return to Supreme Court jurisprudence that remains faithful to Marshall's vision of Indian law. What are the implications of continuing to adopt the discovery doctrine along with the clear-statement rule?

5. *Return to Justice Marshall*: Despite Frickey's call for a return to the clear-statement language of *Worcester*, his concerns about *Cotton*

Petroleum have proved more prophetic. Since the publication of
Marshalling Past and Present the Supreme Court has not returned
wholeheartedly to the presumption against state authority, but neither
has it entirely embraced *Cotton Petroleum's* suggestion that states may
regulate conduct on the reservation unless Congress explicitly prohibits
them from doing so.

Consider the following two recent examples. In *Jicarilla Apache* the
Court denied the Tribe a right regularly conferred upon other fiduciaries because Congress had not clearly enacted a statute conferring upon
tribes the relevant exception; while in *Parker* the Court reaffirmed that a
clear and unambiguous statement from Congress was necessary to deny
the tribe the ability to impose its alcohol tax over non-member businesses located on the reservation.

(A): In *United States v. Jicarilla Apache Nation*, 564 U.S. 162 (2011)
Justice Alito issued an opinion that the fiduciary exception to
attorney–client privilege does not apply to Indian tribes, although
it applies to other fiduciaries, because Congress had not passed a
statute expressly recognizing the government's obligation. In language reminiscent of *Cotton Petroleum* the Court appears to have
reversed Marshall's understanding of the relationship between
Indians and the United States articulated in the Trilogy and moved
dramatically away from the clear-statement rule.

> When "the Tribe cannot identify a specific, applicable, trust-
> creating statute or regulation that the Government violated, ...
> neither the Government's 'control' over [Indian assets] nor
> common-law trust principles matter." The Government assumes
> Indian trust responsibilities only to the extent it expressly accepts
> those responsibilities by statute. *** Over the years, we have
> described the federal relationship with the Indian tribes using vari-
> ous formulations. The Indian tribes have been called "domestic
> dependent nations," under the "tutelage" of the United States, and
> subject to "the exercise of the Government's guardianship over ...
> their affairs." These concepts do not necessarily correspond to a
> common-law trust relationship. That is because Congress has
> chosen to structure the Indian trust relationship in different ways.
> We will apply common-law trust principles where Congress has
> indicated it is appropriate to do so. For that reason, the Tribe must
> point to a right conferred by statute or regulation in order to obtain
> otherwise privileged information from the Government against its
> wishes.

Id. at 177–178 (internal citations omitted).

(B): In contrast, in *Nebraska v. Parker*, 136 S. Ct. 1072 (2016) Justice Thomas issued an opinion for a unanimous Court that comes close to embracing Frickey's call for a return to the clear-statement rule. In *Parker* the Court had to determine whether the Omaha Tribe could impose its liquor tax and licensure requirements upon non-Indians located on a part of the reservation that had been opened to non-Indian settlement more than 100 years before.

> More illuminating than cherry-picked statements by individual legislators would be historical evidence of "the manner in which the transaction was negotiated" with the Omaha Tribe. *** No such unambiguous evidence exists in the record of these negotiations. In particular, petitioners' reliance on the remarks of Representative Edward Valentine of Nebraska, who stated, "You cannot find one of those Indians that does not want the western portion sold," and that the Tribe wished to sell the land to those who would "'reside upon it and cultivate it'" so that the Tribe members could "benefit of these improvements," falls short. Nothing about this statement or other similar statements unequivocally supports a finding that the existing boundaries of the reservation would be diminished.

Id. at 1081. What are the implications for Indian law if the Court fails to wholeheartedly embrace the principles articulated in the Marshall Trilogy, resulting in divided opinions like the ones above? Do you understand the importance of Frickey's call for a return to the Marshall principles any differently given the movement of the Court since the piece was written?

6. *Beyond the Law*: Precisely because the Marshall Trilogy forms the basis of the relationship between tribes and states, its shadows loom large throughout Indian studies. Consider the role of the reservation; it was in *Worcester* that the Supreme Court articulated the principle of territorial jurisdiction, whereby states could not assert their power in Indian country. This motif is explored in contexts well beyond the law. Consider the classic movie *Smoke Signals*, written by Sherman Alexie, where in an early scene Thomas and Victor, the young protagonists, are asked "do you guys have your passports?" after they suggest that they are going to leave the reservation.

The reservation boundary is really a construct created by the Marshall Trilogy. That boundary, described in a treaty and enforced by the Court, becomes part of the identity of people living on both sides. David Johnson and Scott Michaelson describe, engage, and critique this identity in their book *Border Theory: The Limits of Cultural Politics* (University of Minnesota Press, 1997). In their chapter "Resketching Anglo-Amerindian Identity Politics" they suggest that "Contact changes everything. The very possibility, for example, of sites of translation and communication *between* cultures implies that the cultural situation is always already shaped in such a way that something more than cultural translation or cultural crossing takes place." The Marshall Trilogy is the embodiment of the change that resulted from contact between Indigenous people and the first Europeans. Consider all the changes that resulted from this interaction of cultures.

FURTHER READING

- Milner Ball, *John Marshall and Indian Nations in the Beginning and Now*, 33 J. Marshall L. Rev. 1183 (2000).
- Robert Clinton, *Redressing the Legacy of Conquest: A Vision Quest for a Decolonized Federal Indian Law*, 46 Ark. L. Rev. 77 (1993).
- Allison Dussias, *Geographically-Based and Membership-Based Views of Indian Tribal Sovereignty: The Supreme Court's Changing Vision*, 55 U. Pitt. L. Rev. 1 (1993).
- Matthew L. M. Fletcher, *The Iron Cold of the Marshall Trilogy*, 82 N.D. L. Rev. 627 (2006).
- Eric Kades, *The Dark Side of Efficiency: Johnson v M'Intosh and the Expropriation of American Indian Lands*, 148 U. Penn. L. Rev. 1065 (2000).
- Robert Miller, *The Doctrine of Discovery in American Indian Law*, 42 Idaho L. Rev. 1 (2006).
- Robert Miller & Jacinta Ruru, *Discovery Indigenous Lands: The Doctrine of Discovery in the English Colonies* (Oxford University Press 2012).
- Nell Jessup Newton, *Indian Claims in the Courts of the Conqueror*, 41 Am. U. L. Rev. 753 (1992).
- Wenona T. Singel, *The First Federalists*, 62 Drake L. Rev. 775 (2014).
- Alex Tallchief Skibine, *Redefining the Status of Indian Tribes within "Our Federalism": Beyond the Dependency Paradigm*, 38 Conn. L. Rev. 667 (2006).
- Ann Tweedy, *Connecting the Dots between the Constitution, the Marshall Trilogy, and United States v. Lara: Notes toward a Blueprint for the Next Legislative Restoration of Tribal Sovereignty*, 42 U. Mich. J.L. Ref. 651 (2009).
- Robert A. Williams, Jr., *The American Indian in Western Legal Thought* (Oxford University Press 1990).

2

The Algebra of Federal Indian Law: The Hard Trail of Decolonizing and Americanizing the White Man's Jurisprudence

Robert A. Williams, Jr.

1986 Wisc. L. Rev. 219 (1986)

Much of federal Indian law comes not from statutes or regulations but emerges instead from federal common law – legal principles articulated by courts of equity that define the relationship between constituent sovereigns. After securing its independence the United States largely left to the judiciary the task of articulating the metes and bounds of tribal power, for it assumed that there must naturally be limits. The Supreme Court has built on its approach, first articulated in the Marshall Trilogy, to develop a framework through which to evaluate the limits of tribal sovereignty. Even a student only casually acquainted with the fraught relationship between tribes, states, and the United States could predict that such a framework exists, at least in part, to benefit the existing non-Indian majority. It is therefore not surprising that the current rules adopt an approach firmly rooted in the common law tradition inherited from Europe and developed at a time when Indigenous peoples were mistakenly viewed as an "uncivilized" other.

In the earliest piece chosen for inclusion in this volume, Robert A. Williams, Jr. directly confronts the European legacy that continues to play a role in constructing federal Indian law at the highest levels. Williams traces the origins of American jurisprudential thinking back to the Crusades and meticulously shows, through the analysis of three recent cases, how American legal thinking is complicit in a colonizer's attitude that rewards tribes that attempt to assimilate while rejecting tribal attempts to assume powers and develop systems which are traditional (autochthonous) if those attempts challenge the overriding sovereignty of the United States. This piece was profoundly impactful for laying bare, in a clarion manner, the ugly legacy implicit in the Court's treatment of Indian law and for suggesting that tribes should consciously embrace traditional notions of justice and governance instead of accommodating the White Man's jurisprudence.

As you read the following piece pay careful attention to the way Williams traces the origins of American Indian law back through the British common law and into the Crusades. Are you persuaded by Williams' argument that the modern version of Indian law used by the American Supreme Court embodies the principles of colonization? Merrion and Kerr-McGee are both opinions which reaffirm the right of the Jicarilla Apache and Navajo tribes to levy taxes, and thus achieve a result which appears to recognize tribal power. Why does Williams nonetheless claim both opinions reaffirm the colonial mindset embodied in his critique? Finally, put yourself in the position of a tribal leader. Would you recommend trying to assimilate your tribal systems in order to obtain greater recognition of tribal power from the courts?

I INTRODUCTION TO AN AMERICANIZED SCHOLARSHIP OF THE WHITE MAN'S LAW

A *Goals*

Following World War II, the United States government decided the time had come once again to "Americanize" the American Indian. So called "friends of the Indian" raised the familiar argument that to accomplish the Indian's "complete integration" into the mass of the population as "full, tax paying citizens," America's first Americans had to be freed from the oppressive control of the United States government itself. Thus, policymakers in Washington concluded that to emancipate the Indian the United States had to terminate its treaty-pledged trust responsibility to Indian Nations.

The liberative discourse associated with this newly urged policy fused harmoniously with an emergent, liberalized racial consciousness in United States society. In the United States' post-war odyssey for racial equality, words such as "emancipation" and "integration" provided convenient reference points for whites unfamiliar with the treacherous historical terrain of federal Indian policy. The freedom road was not to be detoured around Indian Country.

Many Indians, however, doubted the sincerity of efforts to "Americanize" them by terminating their federally recognized status as sovereign, self-defining peoples. Some went so far as to interpret the new termination policy as the last step in a genocidal process of cultural liquidation; the final cleanup campaign in the United States' conquest and colonization of Indian Nations. And indeed, Indian people had legitimate reasons for such dark thoughts. The man chosen to carry out the federal government's termination plan, Dillon S. Myer, had served previously as director of the War Relocation Authority, the federal government's euphemistic moniker for its Japanese-American detention camp program of World War II.

Despite Myer's previous success in carrying out a sensitive mission with dark moral overtones, many Indians balked at the bill of goods the new Commissioner-designate of Indian Affairs had been assigned to sell. At one gathering of Indian people, for instance, Myer had been preaching about the potential benefits of the Indian's "complete integration" into the mainstream of political, economic, and social life in the United States, when he asked the rhetorical question of the day: "What can we do to Americanize the Indian?" An Indian elder rose and answered Mr. Myer as follows:

You will forgive me if I tell you that my people were Americans for thousands of years before your people were. The question is not how you can Americanize us but how we can Americanize you. We have been working at that for a long time. Sometimes we are discouraged at the results, but we will keep trying.

And the first thing we want to teach you is that, in the American way of life, each man has respect for his brother's vision. Because each of us respected his brother's dream, we enjoyed freedom here in America while you people were busy killing and enslaving each other across the water.

The relatives you left behind ... are still trying to kill each other and enslave each other because they have not learned there that freedom is built on my respect for my brother's vision and his respect for mine. We have a hard trail ahead of us in trying to Americanize you and your white brothers. But we are not afraid of hard trails.

This Article pursues the same hard trail described by that wise grandfather; a trail which Indian people have been traveling for nearly half a millennium. The Article argues that the white man's law denies respect to the vision of the American Indian, and thus stands as an intractable barrier to the white man's own Americanization. ***

B *Methods*

A central argument of an Americanized scholarship is that law and legal discourse played, and continue to play, both a legitimating, and an energizing role in the dynastic activities of European colonizing nation-states and the establishment of their New World hegemony. An Americanized scholarship painfully recognizes that power in its most brutal and naked forms has determined to a large degree the past and present collective fates of American Indian Nations. Obviously, it could be forcefully argued that what "caused" or "led to" the establishment of European hegemony in the New World had far more to do with superior destructive technologies and a consumption-oriented worldview than with theoretical formulations of the legal status and rights of Indian tribes. As our explorations into the neglected doctrinal archives of European legal thought will clearly reveal, however, the white man's theoretical engine of colonialism had built a five-hundred year head of steam prior to reaching the station of its destiny in the virgin forests of America. ***

An Americanized scholarship, therefore, asserts that law and legal discourse affect the exercise of power; at times arguing effectively for its restraint, and at times arguing persuasively for its unleashing. Particularly with respect to a colonized people, the conqueror's law and legal doctrine permit him to peacefully and in good conscience pursue the same goals that he formerly accomplished by the sword with imperialistic fury. Further, as this Article will argue, the conqueror's law quite often achieves a highly efficient, hegemonic function. The territorial, social,

economic, ideological and other forms of colonization facilitated by that law come
to appear as inevitable historical necessities, rather than deliberate acts of genocide,
to the subjugated peoples.

An Americanized scholarship seeks to demonstrate that the white man's legal
vision of the Indian obscures more diverse constructions and interpretations of a
vision of life which might permit both peoples to pursue their separate paths in
peace and without resort to power. An Americanized scholarship is practiced in
the optimistic (and one hopes not vain) belief that once directly confronted by the
primitive and barbaric myths underlying his legal vision of the Indian, the white
man will accept the challenge of reinterpreting and reconstructing the vision of life
he has maintained for the past half millennium at the expense of his Indian brother's
own differently-oriented worldview. Thus, as in the tradition of all Indian gift-giving,
the ultimate goal of an Americanized scholarship is to enrich both the receiver and
the giver of the gift – to cement an alliance built not on power and enforced
inequality, but on trust and mutual respect.

II INFIDELS, HEATHENS AND CHRISTIAN PRINCES; THE MYTHOLOGICAL STRUCTURE OF EUROPEAN LEGAL THEORY AND DISCOURSE RESPECTING THE INDIAN

*** For nearly one thousand years, European-derived legal thought has steadfastly
adhered to a highly systematized mythological structure in confronting its experience of normatively divergent peoples. The foundational premises of this structure
have always assumed first, the immanence of the European's worldview, and
second, the rightness and necessity of subjugating and assimilating other peoples
to that worldview. Admittedly, the first premise has been shared in varying forms by
all great cultures. Only the European, however, has sought to enable himself to
actualize the second premise on a world scale. ***

Before the Crusades, few Church legal theorists had devoted extensive study
toward developing a systematized legal theory of relations between Christian and
non-Christian societies. Pre-Crusade era canonists were only concerned about the
effects that pagans, heretics and schismatics might have on Christians. The canon
lawyers' primary interest was in the right ordering of Christian society, not the
development of theories of international law or relations. When papally authorized
Christian armies began engaging in frequent and violent confrontations throughout
the Holy Lands, however, a more precise refinement of the legal status and rights of
these reluctant sheep of God's flock was required. Pope Innocent IV *** subtly
manipulated the elasticized matrix of knowledge provided by medieval Church
legal theory to mediate this apparent conflict in the universal Christian common-
wealth. His theorizations on the rights and status of normatively divergent peoples
provided the necessary regulating principles for the conquest of these unregenerate
infidel and heathen nations.

*** Innocent was the first great medieval legal theorist who attempted to systematically address the question of the legal rules that might govern Christian relations with non-Christians. Numerous legal theorists would subsequently embellish upon his influential work. Innocent, however, was the first great European legal theorist to articulate systematically the legal status and rights of non-Christian societies. In an extended commentary upon an earlier papal decretal, Innocent asked: "[I]s it licit to invade a land that infidels possess, or which belongs to them?"

*** According to Innocent, these people "belong to Christ's flock by virtue of their creation, although the infidels do not belong to the sheepfold of the flock of Church." Therefore, "the Pope has jurisdiction over all men and power over them in law but not in fact."

Innocent limited his supra-jurisdictional authority to instances where it was clearly necessary for the Pope to intervene to protect the spiritual well-being of non-Christians. Such instances included situations where infidels clearly violated natural law but their rulers refused to punish them as required by God's divine law. While Innocent did not identify the content of these natural law dictates in detail, he indicated that sexual perversion, for example, would necessitate papal intervention. The worship of idols if left unchecked, would similarly require papal intervention because "it is natural for man to worship the one and only God." ***

To Innocent, God's divine will, interpreted through the pontifical office, expressed a far more perfect rationality than that possessed by imperfect man. Those who refused to recognize God's papally-revealed plan were irrational and in error. According to Innocent: "There is only one right way of life for mankind, and . . . the papal monopoly of this knowledge makes obedience to the Pope the only means of salvation." The manifest irrationality of heathens and infidels who rejected the Pope's message patently demonstrated the need for papal remediation. According to Innocent his office required him to call upon Christian princes to raise armies to punish serious violations of natural law, and to order those armies to accompany missionaries to heathen lands for purposes of conversion. "[I]f the infidels do not obey, they ought to be compelled by the secular arm and war may be declared against them by the Pope and not by anybody else." Once more relying on the certitude of his Eurocentric conception of reason and truth, Innocent was careful to point out that an infidel, such as a Moslem missionary, could not be accorded reciprocal rights to proselytize in Europe, "because they are in error and we are on a righteous path." ***

1 Against the Law of God and of Nature

By the late sixteenth century, legal theorists throughout Europe were freely borrowing from the universalized, hierarchical structures of medieval thought to articulate a secularized, rationally conceived Law of Nations binding upon all civilized societies. In doing so, these more secularly-oriented theorists abandoned certain explicit theologically oriented aspects of European legal discourse. ***

Even a cursory examination of the works of any of the major writers of the post-Reformation period indicates the extent to which the principles of unity and hierarchy central to medieval consciousness have been resuscitated in service of this secularized normative discourse on the Law of Nations. For instance, Lord Coke's opinion in Calvin's Case reveals the secularized spirit of post-Reformation English jurisprudence distilled from the heritage of Christian medieval legal mythology. *** According to Coke, as long as other Christian Europeans remained in league with the King of England as "alien friends," they were granted certain important rights under the common law. In this mercantile age, these rights related principally to commerce (regarded as a "natural law" right under the European's evolving Law of Nations). Friendly aliens could maintain a right of action for personal property acquired by gift, trade, or other lawful means; "for if they should be disabled to acquire and maintain these things," Coke argued, "it were in effect to deny unto them trade and traffic, which is the life of every island." Infidels, however, because of the remote possibility of their conversion, were presumed under the common law to be at perpetual war with the King. They were, therefore, without rights in the King's realm.

The implications of this perpetual enemy status extended beyond the boundaries of English domestic law and into the realm of international law. According to Coke:

> [U]pon this ground, there is a diversity between a conquest of a kingdom of a Christian king and the conquest of a kingdom of an infidel; for if a king came to a Christian kingdom by conquest ... until he does make an alteration the ancient laws of that kingdom remain. But if a Christian king should conquer a kingdom of an infidel, and bring them under his subjection, there *ipso facto* the laws of the infidel are abrogated, for that they be not only against Christianity, but against the law of God and of nature.

Thus, the infidel's laws were presumed *ipso facto* to be against Christianity, as well as against the law of God and nature. As with Innocent, Coke's conception of reason was grounded in Eurocentrically-derived value structures ("the law of God and nature"). This vision of reason determined ultimate rights. The radical difference presented by the infidel's non-belief in the European's God established an inability to conform to natural law. Therefore, non-believers were not accorded any rights under that law, and other forms of law subordinate to it, such as the common law. ***

A year after his decision, Coke as attorney general to James I applied his jurisprudential views on infidel status and rights to England's colonial enterprise in the New World. In 1609, Coke drew up the Second Charter of Virginia. This Charter confirmed the rights of the Virginia Company, the corporate colonizers of Jamestown, to an extensive portion of the North American continent. The new Charter also rearranged the inefficient governing structure of the colony. The opening lines of the Second Charter recited the Company's original 1606 grant of Virginia by King James which led to the eventual settlement of Jamestown. Coke simply reincorporated the familiar refrain of numerous other contemporary European royal documents authorizing discovery and conquest of non-Christian territory. Written in the royal "We," the Charter granted the Company a license to "deduce a colony" in territories in "America, appertaining unto us, of which are not now actually possessed by any Christian Prince or People." *** The mission to colonize lands not "possessed by any Christian Prince or People" is legitimated by the desire to spread Christianity to those who live "in Darkness and miserable Ignorance of the true Knowledge and Worship of God." Coke's presumption in Calvin's Case of the inherent defects in the infidel's laws is here restated as a mandate for remediation through conquest and colonization. Knowledge not only justified, but compelled the exercise of brute power in the New World. Conquest it was hoped, would "bring the infidels and savages" of America "to human civility, and to a settled and quiet Government." Even with the passage of nearly half a millennium, the iconography of European legal mythology has remained largely undisturbed. *** All that has changed in this somewhat more secularized form of legal consciousness is that the secular king has assumed the hierarchical function formerly held by the Pope to license the spread of the Christian message into an infidel world of darkness and ignorance at perpetual war with Christianity. ***

3 An Invasion of Our Territory and an Act of Hostility

As Europe entered its period of most intense and rapid colonization, which not coincidentally paralleled its so-called age of "enlightenment," European monarchs came to recognize that some secularly derived principle was needed to resolve their conflicting claims to infidel-occupied territory in the New World. Given the vast, untapped wealth of the two continents of the New World, it was in the self-interest of European monarchs with dynastic aspirations to tacitly agree upon some simple but expedient principle to regulate their conquests in the Americas.

The principle which was gradually accepted was based upon the concept of priority of occupation, a notion traceable to the ancient and revered Roman *ius gentium* (law of nations). Practical and effective occupation of discovered lands, defended by the sword if necessary, became recognized as an evident and undeniable source of title and sovereignty to territory inhabited by indigenous peoples. But as for those indigenous peoples, however, European legal theory rejected classical teachings about their legal status and rights. The legal position of Indian tribes in their own territory was settled by the medievally-derived principle that by virtue of their normative divergence from Europe's ethnocentrically conceived "Law of Nations," the heathen and infidel populations of the New World required Europe's hierarchical subjugation and remediation. Only by conquest would the natives be brought from darkness to light; a light discoverable only within the European's universalized vision of reason.

Thus it was that European legal conceptions of the status and rights of American Indian Nations became defined by the aptly named Doctrine of Discovery, the paradigmatic tenet informing and determining contemporary European legal discourse respecting relations with Western tribal societies. ***

The acceptance of the Discovery principle into United States law had profound implications for future relations between the white man and his Indian brother. The underlying medievally-derived ideology – that normatively divergent "savage" peoples could be denied equal rights and status accorded to the civilized nations of Europe – had become an integral part of the fabric of United States law. The architects of an idealized European vision of life in the Indian's America had successfully transplanted an Old World form of legal discourse which denied all respect to the Indian's Americanized vision of life. While the task of conquest and colonization had not yet been fully actualized, the legal rules set down by Marshall assured that future acts of genocide proceeded upon a rationalized basis. The familiar mythic categories of unity and hierarchy central to European legal discourse had become embodied in a totalizing ideology that presupposed the rightful subjugation of Indian Nations, and subsumed their radical difference within the overriding superior sovereignty of their "conqueror," the United States. ***

III THE REASON OF THE STRONGEST IS ALWAYS THE BEST

Marshall's early nineteenth century articulation of diminished tribal status derived from the Doctrine of Discovery provided an important legitimating doctrinal foundation for the refinement of European-derived colonial theory. This ideology was most successfully applied in the United States' final imposition of the reservation system upon American tribal nations during the latter part of the nineteenth century. A somewhat misplaced and delayed realization of Innocent's thirteenth century proselytizing mission to the heathen and infidel, the reservation existed solely for the total colonization and assimilation of the Indian into European Christianity's vision of "civilization." ***

Numerous late nineteenth and early twentieth century Supreme Court opinions freely extended Marshall's original limited recognition of an overriding sovereignty of the federal government in Indian affairs to entail a superior and unquestionable power on the part of Congress unrestrained by normal constitutional limitations. In case after case, the Court simply refused to check Congress' free reign in matters where it was thought that broad discretionary powers were vital to the solution of the immensely difficult "Indian problem." In *Lonewolf v. Hitchcock*, the Court held that treaties with American Indian Nations could be unilaterally abrogated by act of Congress, "particularly if consistent with perfect good faith toward the

Indians." In upholding the Senate's breach of a treaty between the Kiowa and Comanche Nations and the United States, the Court stated:

> We must presume that Congress acted in perfect good faith in its dealings with the Indians of which complaint is made, and that the legislative branch of the government exercised its best judgment in the premises. In any event, as Congress possessed full power in the matter, the judiciary cannot question or inquire into the motives which prompted the enactment of this legislation.

This refusal to question Congress' actions concerning treaty-guaranteed Indian property rights sounded the death knell for any prior notion that Indian treaties vested property and other rights that might be entitled to judicially enforced Constitutional protection.

***

Besides justifying unquestioned abrogation and unilateral determination of tribal treaty and property rights, the plenary power paradigm has been interpreted to permit the denial of other fundamental human rights of Indian people in the United States. Violent suppression of Indian religious practices and traditional forms of government, separation of Indian children from their homes, wholesale spoliation of treaty-guaranteed resources, forced assimilative programs and involuntary sterilization of Indian women, represent but a few of the practical extensions of a false and un-Americanized legal consciousness that at its core regards tribal peoples as normatively deficient and culturally, politically and morally inferior to Europeans. *** Animated by a central orienting myth of its own universalized, hierarchical position among all other discourses, the white man's archaic, European-derived law respecting the Indian is ultimately genocidal in both its practice and intent. This un-Americanized collection of legal rules and principles seeks to silence a radically-opposed teaching that in the American way of life, freedom is built on respect for my brother's vision and his respect for mine.

1 Those Powers Inconsistent with Their Status

The archaic, medievally derived myths animating European-derived legal discourse regarding the Indian continue to exercise a critical impact upon contemporary legal thought on the rights and status of American Tribal Nations. Today, a crucial concern to Indian Nations is their ability to control their national homelands, and to maintain peaceful, prosperous and well-regulated communities according to Indian preferences. This Part analyzes two of the most important cases decided by the Burger Court that involve this crucial concern, *Oliphant v. Suquamish Indian Tribe* and *Merrion v. Jicarilla Apache Tribe,* as well as one of its most recent cases, *Kerr-McGee Corporation v. Navajo Tribe.* An analysis of these cases from an Americanized scholarly angle of vision indicates the extent to which reliance by the Court on European-derived legal myths such as the Doctrine of Discovery inevitably generates a form of legal discourse that undermines and threatens with extinction any truly indigenous expression of an Indian vision.

A OLIPHANT *** Decisions of the Supreme Court during the past decade have severely hampered recent tribal efforts to build the social, economic, and political infrastructure needed for effective self-government according to an Indian vision. By far the most threatening and serious of these decisions is *Oliphant v. Suquamish Tribe of Indians. Oliphant* represents a critical anamnesis for United States' colonial legal theory. Its anachronistic and rigid adherence to principles derived from the Doctrine of Discovery has revived the tradition of denying respect to the Indian's vision which had begun to dissolve with the dramatic shift of federal policy in recent years toward encouraging tribal self-governing initiatives.

The question that confronted the Court in *Oliphant* was whether an Indian tribe, as part of its inherent powers of self-determination, retained the right to try and punish non-Indians for minor crimes committed in Indian communities. Justice Rehnquist, writing for the majority, stated that "Indian tribes are proscribed from exercising both those powers of autonomous states that are expressly terminated by Congress and those powers inconsistent with their status." In effect, *Oliphant* denies the Suquamish tribe, and all other Indian Nations, "the power to preserve order on the reservation ... *a sine qua non* of the sovereignty that the Suquamish originally possessed."

Rehnquist's opinion in *Oliphant* has been frequently and fiercely criticized as an aberration in Federal Indian law jurisprudence. Upon closer analysis, however, *Oliphant* cannot be so easily exorcised from the heritage of European-derived legal discourse on the rights of normatively divergent peoples, of which contemporary United States colonial legal theory is so clearly a part. An Americanized scholarly analysis of *Oliphant* reveals a close affinity with discursive practices nearly one thousand years old.

Like all texts in their initiation, *Oliphant* confronts a familiar problem, that of a beginning. *** In *Oliphant*, the problem of beginnings is made particularly acute in that Rehnquist must frankly concede that no formally binding precedent guides the Court in its decision. "The effort by Indian tribal courts to exercise criminal jurisdiction over non-Indians, however, is a relatively new phenomenon ... it is therefore not surprising to find no specific discussion of the problem before us in the volumes of the United States Reports." As Rehnquist's text confronts this lack of an authoritative presence, it simultaneously immerses itself in numerous operations of discriminating difference between the Suquamish and society at large. As we have seen, the discursive practice of discrimination, derived from European legal myth-ology, seizes upon the radical difference presented by the Indian to initiate processes of reason by which the Indian's normative divergence is identified and judged. It is from these normative judgments of reason that Rehnquist's text, as well as the entire corpus of the white man's legal thought respecting the Indian, derives its beginnings.

In his first footnote Rehnquist is careful to point out the minority status of the Suquamish Indians on their own reservation. Non-Indians owned sixty-three percent of all land and outnumbered tribal members 2928 to fifty in terms of total population. In the same paragraph containing this footnote, Rehnquist also notes that the Suquamish Tribe's Law and Order Code, which "purports to extend the tribe's criminal jurisdiction over both Indians and non-Indians," excludes non-Indians from Suquamish tribal court juries. These notations of the antimajoritarian nature involved in the exercise of tribal criminal jurisdiction over non-Indians are combined with another footnote in the same paragraph recognizing that "the Bill of Rights does not apply to Indian tribal governments." The text thus expresses strong normative implications of difference. A sense of trepidation and urgency is thereby added to the fact that defendants in tribal court proceedings are not entitled to the "identical" due process protections "accorded to defendants in federal or state criminal proceedings."

Rehnquist explains the genesis of this contemporary difference through a two paragraph gloss of two centuries' worth of tribal history and culture, concluding that until "the middle of this century, few Indian tribes maintained any semblance of a formal court system. Offenses by one Indian against another were usually handled by social and religious pressure and not by formal judicial processes; emphasis was on restitution rather than on punishment." Not only does this deficient history explain the differences presented by contemporary tribal criminal court proceedings, it also explains what might otherwise be an embarrassing lack of authoritative legal precedent. "For (these) reasons . . ., there was little reason to be concerned with assertions of tribal court jurisdiction over non-Indians because of the absence of formal tribal judicial systems." ***

This textual strategy of discrimination, in effect, provides the rationalized and legitimated normative foundation for *Oliphant's* structural subordination of tribal autonomy claims within the federalized matrices of United States political and legal theory. In a key passage, Rehnquist declares: "[T]he tribes retained powers are not such that they are limited only by specific restrictions in treaties or congressional actions ... Indian tribes are prohibited from exercising both those powers of autonomous states that are expressly terminated by Congress and those powers 'inconsistent with their status.'" This status is derived directly from the Doctrine of Discovery, which, as has been seen, subordinates Indian Nations to the status of dependent colonized peoples possessing diminished rights in relation to their superior sovereign, the United States. Citing directly to Chief Justice Marshall's famous formulation in *Johnson v. McIntosh*, Rehnquist states:

> Upon incorporation into the territory of the United States, the Indian tribes thereby come under the territorial sovereignty of the United States and their exercise of separate power is constrained so as not to conflict with the interests of the overriding sovereignty. "Their rights to complete sovereignty, as independent nations [are] necessarily diminished." (citing *Johnson v. McIntosh*)

The crucial test in *Oliphant*, therefore, is to determine whether the exercise of tribal criminal jurisdiction powers over non-Indians "conflicts" with the sovereign interests of the United States. If there is a conflict, then the exercise by tribes of such powers is "inconsistent with their status" as dependent, colonized peoples. Rehnquist admitted the absence of any authoritative text expressly delineating the sovereign interests of the United States on this issue. *Oliphant's* numerous operations of discrimination focusing upon the geopolitical features of the reservation to identify the deficient nature of tribal criminal jurisdiction now begin to assume a critical role in his analysis. Difference evidences conflict, a divergence of interests between the tribes and the United States. Rehnquist states that along with protection of territory within its borders as central to its sovereign interests, "the United States has manifested an equally great solicitude that its citizens be protected from unwarranted intrusions on their personal liberty." As colonized, dependent peoples, Indian tribes' divergent exercises of criminal jurisdiction amount to "unwarranted," and, in essence, unreasonable intrusions on the personal liberty of non-Indians. European legal theory's familiar rage for unity, attained through hierarchical subordination of radical difference, manifests itself in Oliphant's express holding: ". . . By submitting to the overriding sovereignty of the United States, Indian tribes therefore necessarily give up their power to try non-Indians except in a manner acceptable to Congress."

One cannot help but be reminded here of the pedantic form of Lord Coke's famous declaration in Calvin's Case that "if a Christian king should conquer a kingdom of an infidel . . . there *ipso facto* the laws of the infidel are abrogated for that they be not only against Christianity but against the law of God and nature." Despite recognizing that "some Indian tribal court systems have become increasingly sophisticated and resemble in many respects their state counterparts," and that subsequent congressional legislation has eliminated "many of the dangers that might have accompanied the exercise by tribal courts of criminal jurisdiction over non-Indians," Oliphant has nevertheless located a still too-radical difference. Not even the Court's awareness of "the prevalence of non-Indian crime on today's reservations," which necessitated the Suquamish tribe's attempt to exercise authority, can overcome the greater need to deny this difference. Only with the superior sovereign's express permission may tribes be permitted to maintain peaceful communities according to their own preferences. In the absence of a clear congressional directive to the contrary, the Court will define "the inherent limitations on tribal powers," derived from the tribe's diminished status in United States Indian law jurisprudence.

***

B MERRION While *Oliphant* perhaps shows most clearly the determining impact of this archaic form of legal discourse on contemporary conceptions of Indian status and rights, other major cases decided by the Burger Court also reflect a similar inaugurating genesis from within the mythic structures of European-derived legal thought. In *Merrion v. Jicarilla Apache Tribe* one of its more important recent decisions, the Court drew upon European-derived legal discourse on Indian rights to delimit tribal taxing authority over non-Indians. The manner in which the Court defined the scope of tribal taxing jurisdiction in *Merrion* effectively constrains, and thereby seriously threatens the ability of tribes to control the course of Indian Country economic development independently and according to their own autochthonous vision.

In *Merrion*, a case interpreted by many commentators as a victory for Indian Nations, the Burger Court upheld the "sovereign" power of tribal governments to impose severance taxes within their jurisdictions on non-Indian mineral extraction activities. As stated by the Court, the "power to tax is an essential attribute of Indian sovereignty because it is a necessary instrument of self-government and territorial management." However, Justice Thurgood Marshall, writing for the majority, qualified this "essential" tribal taxing power:

> [T]he Tribes' authority to tax non-members is subject to constraints not imposed on other governmental entities: the federal government can take away this power, and the Tribe must obtain the approval of the Secretary [of Interior] before any tax on non-members can take effect. These additional constraints minimize potential concern that Indian tribes will exercise the power to tax in an unfair or unprincipled manner, and ensure that any exercise of the tribal power to tax will be consistent with national policies.

Thus, *Merrion* can be interpreted as a victory for Indian tribes only from a thoroughly myopic, un-Americanized perspective. The Court balanced the concern that tribes might act in an "unfair or unprincipled manner" with the comforting fact that secretarial approval ensures "that any exercise of the tribal power to tax will be consistent with national policies." "Congress," reminded the Court, "has affirmatively acted by providing a series of federal check-points that must be cleared before a tribal tax can take effect."

Supported by a long line of precedents generated from the Marshallian Discovery paradigm, *Merrion*'s text engages in all the familiar operations determined by a discourse grounded in the initiating premise of Indian normative deficiency. Numerous operations of discrimination identify difference and similarity, which in turn inaugurate *Merrion*'s analysis of the extent of home rule powers for tribal governments in the United States insular colonial empire. The court begins by focusing on the geopolitical topography of the Jicarilla Apache Nation, noting that the entire reservation is held as tribal trust property. The tribe's majoritarian status, an important legitimating factor in the exercise of political power in United States legal and political theory, thus distinguishes *Merrion* from *Oliphant*, where non-Indians constituted an unrepresented racial and landholding majority.

This critical issue of suspect divergence from European-derived norms of representational legitimacy arises frequently in federal Indian law. *** Fortuitously for the Jicarillas in *Merrion*, the Court did not even confront such questions. The tribe's majoritarian status on its own reservation lent substantial legitimacy to its claim of taxing jurisdiction.

The Court noted other aspects of similarity between Jicarilla and non-Indian institutions throughout its opinion. The Jicarilla government organized itself under the Indian Reorganization Act of 1934 (IRA), a congressionally-sanctioned scheme to streamline and decentralize the administration of the United States' Indian colonies. Created by the social engineers of the Roosevelt Administration in an attempt to modify disastrous assimilationist policies of the past, the IRA permitted tribes to adopt Anglo-style constitutions and by-laws in a mimetic effort toward civilized "self-government." In virtually every case, of course, these "self-governing" articles of government were drafted by the Bureau of Indian Affairs in the Department of Interior, which in turn coerced the tribes into adopting Anglicized structures of government.

*** The Court's analysis has identified a governmental entity, founded upon an Anglicized constitution, enjoying majoritarian land ownership status within its borders, providing "the advantages of a civilized society," and adopting secretarially-approved taxing ordinances "similar" to that of other governmental entities. The cumulative impact of this form of analysis is compellingly clear. The Court's own conclusion on its extended operation of discrimination states: "Under these circumstances, there is nothing exceptional in requiring petitioners to contribute through taxes to the general cost of tribal government."

The ad hoc nature of the Court's particularistic form of discriminatory analysis of tribal sovereignty exercised over non-Indians is amply demonstrated by the simple phrase, "under these circumstances." The Court confronts comforting similarity in the *Merrion* tribe's exercise of jurisdiction rather than the threatening difference it encountered in *Oliphant*. The "civilized" Jicarillas operate under the same set of normative criteria as their governmental counterparts in the non-Indian world. Even more importantly, the exercise of this tribal taxing power is totally contained by the governing supervisory apparatus of the colonial sovereign which possesses the unquestioned right to condition or "take away this power." ***

C KERR-MCGEE At first glance, the preceding analysis of *Merrion* appears substantially undermined by the Burger Court's latest pronouncement in the field of Indian taxing jurisdiction, *Kerr-McGee v. Navajo Tribe.* Yet in this opinion also, another apparent victory for Indian Nations draws upon a form of analysis which ultimately undermines the integrity of any truly indigenous tribal vision. Further, an Americanized analysis of Chief Justice Burger's opinion in *Kerr-McGee* clearly indicates what was only intimated in cases such as *Oliphant* and *Merrion*; the winning strategy in this discursive game of European-derived legal thought compels the Indian himself to validate the superior sovereign's alien vision by adopting its order of reason as his own.

In *Kerr-McGee*, a non-Indian energy company challenged the authority of the Navajo tribe to impose a mineral severance tax in the absence of approval by the Secretary of Interior. The Navajos had never adopted an IRA constitution or any by-law which required the Secretary's approval of Tribal Council actions. The tribe, however, "uncertain whether federal approval was required," had submitted its tax ordinances to the Bureau of Indian Affairs in the Department of Interior. The Bureau, however, informed the tribe that no federal statute or regulation expressly required either Interior's approval or disapproval. The tribe therefore sought to impose its tax on Kerr-McGee without federal sanction. The company promptly filed suit in federal court. Chief Justice Burger, writing for a unanimous court, held federal law did not require secretarial approval of the Navajo tax.

The issue in *Kerr-McGee* differed substantially from that posed in *Merrion*. The Navajo tax had not "traveled" through the precise channels established by Congress, but was a unilateral, essentially unconstrained exercise of tribal sovereignty over non-Indians. The Court thus initiated its analysis in *Kerr-McGee* as follows:

> In *Merrion v. Jicarilla Apache Tribe*, we held that the 'power to tax is an essential attribute of Indian sovereignty because it is a necessary instrument of self-government and territorial management.' Congress, of course, may erect "check-points that must be cleared before a Tribal Tax can take effect." The issue in this case is whether Congress has enacted legislation requiring Secretarial approval of Navajo tax laws. (citations omitted)

Kerr-McGee's frame of analytical reference is thus the plenary power doctrine, which vests in the superior sovereign an unquestioned authority to privilege its own normative vision over that of the Indian. Regardless of the Court's particular holding, therefore, *Merrion*'s circumscription of tribal taxing power still applies to the Navajos. As stated in *Merrion*, "Congress is well aware that Indian Tribes impose mineral severance taxes . . . Congress, of course, retains plenary power to limit tribal taxing authority."

As the Court's analysis of the Navajo taxing scheme clearly indicates, however, there would be no need for Congress to limit the particular exercise of tribal power here. Even lacking congressional or secretarial sanction, the Navajo levy is every bit as sophisticated and rationalized as consistent with national policies as that approved in *Merrion*. According to the Court, the tribe's complicated taxing scheme applies in a non-discriminatory manner to both Indian and non-Indian business, with dissatisfied taxpayers enjoying the right of appeal to the Navajo Tax Commission and the Navajo Court of Appeals. The sophisticated, complimentary nature of the taxing scheme and the contemporary Navajo governing structure is thus indicated by the existence, not only of a Tax Commission, but also by a Court of Appeals. ***

The Court's numerous notations of similarity indicate that in *Kerr-McGee*, the strategy of discriminating difference and similarity which pervades United States

Indian law jurisprudence is clearly working in the Navajo's favor. The Navajos have assumed the essential trappings of a "civilized" government that lend to their actions a legitimacy no longer requiring, perhaps, the closely monitored federal supervision present in *Merrion*. They vote like the white man, they elect their representatives like the white man, they tax like the white man. They even provide the same type bureaucratic judicial morass to dissatisfied taxpayers as the white man. Therefore, they must be possessed of a similar normative vision as the white man.

Thus, while the Navajos lack an authoritative text sanctioning their independent exercise of power over non-Indians, the situation in *Kerr-McGee* differs substantially from that in *Oliphant*. Unlike the Navajo Nation, the Suquamish's non-congressionally sanctioned criminal jurisdiction over non-Indians was exercised in a normatively divergent manner, and was thus in conflict with the United States sovereign interest. In *Kerr-McGee*, the Court is untroubled by doubts about the consanguinity of the Navajo taxing scheme and the United States sovereign interest. In fact, the Navajo financing of essential governmental services through taxation of mineral development perfectly supplements the federal government's current policies (dictated by pressing fiscal and national security interests) of reducing its financial support in Indian Country and encouraging increased production of domestic energy supplies. As the Court recognizes in *Kerr-McGee*: "The power to tax members and non-Indians alike is surely an essential attribute of such self-government; the Navajos can gain independence from the Federal Government only by financing their own police force, schools, and social programs."

2 The Algebra of Federal Indian Law: The Wolf's Game

Kerr-McGee's text and its deployment of strategies identifying the supplementarity of the Navajo tax and governing structures with United States interests and norms permits the discernment of a more precise understanding of the discursive game-space defined by contemporary United States Indian law jurisprudence. We arrive at this understanding only indirectly, by examining the winning strategies dictated by this game-space. It is clear, however, once we arrive at this understanding that the discursive practices engendered by European-derived legal theory, expressed and refined in contemporary United States federal Indian law, rely upon the acceptance of a certain ordered political and legal structure as a factual necessity. *** To illustrate, this ordered structure, its elements, and its law are clearly indicated in *Oliphant*: "[T]here exists in the broad domain of sovereignty only the United States government, or the States of the Union. There may be cities, counties and other organized bodies with limited legislative functions, but they ... exist in subordination to one or the other of these."

Both *Merrion* and *Kerr-McGee* refer and pay obeisance to this same, totalizing structure, whose order of reason posits as its absolute limit the superior sovereignty of the United States' non-Indian governments. The vertiginous, metaphysical nature of this absolute limit is obscured by the myth, central to European-derived legal and political theory, that the interests of the sovereign can be divined by scientific application of the tools of legal discourse. An ancient game-space, generated from European mythological legal discourse, thereby comes to be defined. The Indian is confined in a totalizing structure of thought which hierarchically subordinates all divergent, potentially decentering visions to its own universalized norms and values.

The principles of unity and hierarchy which are at the core of this European-derived and defined game-space thus reveal a strategy and a succession of moves that might escape the relative nature of the relationships within the game. To dominate all the relations within the game, one must supplement the embarrassing lack of plentitude and full presence of the structure's absolute limit, the sovereign interests of the United States. One must, in short, insinuate oneself into European legal discourse's epistemological project of maximization which has sought for a millennium to dominate all discourses.

Thus, we know the rule of the game determined by this game-space, and the winning strategies to be employed. The Court presides as neutral arbiter in a "search for a maximum which determines the ultimate winner in a game of power." The game of federal Indian law is won by the player who successfully appropriates the position of the absolute limit, signified by the United States as superior sovereign. The player who occupies this maximum position as one's own cannot be succeeded in the ordered relations of the game-space. ***

Thus, in *Oliphant*, the tribe's radical attempt to exercise criminal jurisdiction assured its defeat before the game had really begun. Absent an authorizing congressional legislative text, the tribe could not be permitted to appropriate the maximum position in a game which treats as suspect any aberrant, uncontained exercise of power. The non-Indian's interest in being tried according to his own culture's norms therefore stood unopposed. At this point, the generative capacity of European derived legal discourse to dissimulate its non-presence comes into full play. European-derived norms substantiate a transcendent presence for the superior sovereign's will. So reified and infused with life, the sovereign's will in turn inscribes a subordinated supplementary status for the tribe's desire to maintain law and order according to its own vision.

In *Kerr-McGee*, as in *Oliphant*, the maximum position is similarly open for appropriation, due to the absence of a clear authorizing text. Yet, in *Kerr-McGee*, the Navajos had at hand the elements necessary to employ the winning strategy of similarity first indicated in *Merrion*: a sophisticated, anglicized taxing scheme, and a sophisticated, anglicized bureaucratic governing structure to administer the tax in a "fair" and "principled" manner. In short, for the Navajos and Jicarillas elaborateness equaled legitimacy: "The Navajo government has been called 'probably the most elaborate' among tribes. The legitimacy of the Navajo Tribal council, the freely elected governing body of the Navajos, is beyond question." Elaborateness, a clear normative standard totally at odds with traditional Indian governmental values, allows the Navajos access to the maximum position and indicates that the Indian has learned an important lesson. As in the La Fontaine fable of the Wolf and the Lamb, "the reason of the strongest is always the best." In a game in which the Court always searches for the reason of the strongest – that of the superior sovereign – the tribes' similarity to the sovereign's expression of rationality permits the claim that the tribe's reason is also the "reason of the strongest." No longer infidels and savages, the tribe and its members have begun to assume the trappings of a "civilized society." Such a reasonable expression of the tribe's self-defining vision cannot possibly conflict with the interests of the superior sovereign. The winning strategy requires a metamorphosis: the lamb must become a wolf.

Increasingly, both Indian and non-Indian "leaders" are preaching the necessity of aggressively pursuing this strategy of accommodating tribal sovereignty and governmental decisions to forms similar to those of the dominant sovereign. Tribes such as the Navajo and Jicarilla Apache, who have pursued this strategy through a long series of conscious decisions made by and for their people over the years, demonstrate clearly the important victories to be won in this game of federal Indian law. It is an inevitable and necessary trail, they argue, which the first Americans must follow if they are to express any type of self defining vision at all, even if it is a vision which they would not have chosen were they truly free.

Many of the most "traditional" of Indian people pay little attention to their "leaders" who have helped implement such strategies. For them, the game is not worth playing. As our Americanized analysis of cases such as *Oliphant, Merrion,* and *Kerr-McGee* clearly indicates, this is a game of knowledge and power which confines its players in an episteme totally alien to an Americanized vision, one which denies freedom and respect to differently oriented worldviews. They fear that to play this game, Indian people must surrender those self-defining aspects of their vision which diverge too radically from the superior sovereign's interest. Their response to those who argue the contemporary necessity of this game is that the only result of the white man's vision after 500 years has been the continual extinction of hundreds of distinct American tribal visions. Why, they ask, should joining in this game assure the Indian's survival when to win, the Indian must act like a white man, cheating himself of his own identity. They argue that in this game "the more one cheats, the less one knows." The reason of the strongest is always the best. Unless one has the courage to break out of this game, recognizing its relative nature, the reason of the strongest will eventually exterminate all other visions of reason. Today, many Indian people seek to play a different game, one played by Americanized rules, which would permit the free play of many different visions in the political and legal discourses of the world.

IV AMERICANIZING THE WHITE MAN: IDEAS TO BOW DOWN TO

***

B *The Two Row Wampum*

The principles embodied in the Gus-Wen-Tah, the Two Row Wampum, were the basis for all treaties and agreements between the great nations of the Haudenosaunee Confederacy and the great nations of Europe. These basic principles were the covenant chain linking these two different peoples by which each agreed to respect the other's vision.

When the Haudenosaunee first came into contact with the European nations, treaties of peace and friendship were made. Each was symbolized by the Gus-Wen-Tah, or Two Row Wampum. There is a bed of white wampum which symbolizes the purity of the agreement. There are two rows of purple, and those two rows have the spirit of your ancestors and mine. There are three beads of wampum separating the two rows and they symbolize peace, friendship, and respect. These two rows will symbolize two paths or two vessels, travelling down the same river together. One, a birch bark canoe, will be for the Indian people, their laws, their customs and their ways. The other, a ship, will be for the white people and their laws, their customs and their ways. We shall each travel the river together, side by side, but in our own boat. Neither of us will try to steer the other's vessel.

The vision signified by the Gus-Wen-Tah has been articulated throughout the corpus of American Indian legal and political thought and discourse. Even the wise grandfather who spoke to Commissioner-designate Dillon Myer of an American way of life was espousing a simple, basic principle. At the core of an Americanized vision of law is the idea that freedom requires different peoples to respect each other's vision of how their respective vessels should be steered.

What steps must be taken, therefore, to strike up the Gus-Wen-Tah between us once again, so that our two peoples may go our own ways, side by side, in peace, friendship, and respect? First the Doctrine of Discovery, as well as the guardianship responsibility by which individual European colonizers arrogated to themselves an unquestioned authority over Indian Nations, must be surrendered. What was originally justified in European colonial theory as a sacred duty of trust and protection has become transformed into a hemisphere-wide unquestioned privilege of spoliation and imprudent control. The white man must give up his unilateral power over the Indian's vessel, and offer meaningful reparations sufficient to enable the Indian to resume his own path.

Further, given that two peoples with radically divergent worldviews have been irredeemably fated to share the same river, it is inevitable that disputes arise between them. The white man, however, has required that the Indian resolve any disputes only according to the white man's law. Since the Discovery era, in fact, post-colonial

European-derived governments in the Western Hemisphere have been able to shield their abuses and exploitation of indigenous populations from world scrutiny by asserting that the legal status and rights accorded colonized Indian Nations raise questions of exclusive domestic concern, and are not matters of international legal or political debate. Thus, this principle of exclusive domestic jurisdiction central to European legal discourse on the Indian, has conveniently operated to force tribal nations to litigate their disputes with the conqueror's subjects, or the conqueror itself, under the eurocentric vision of justice dispensed by the conqueror's courts.
***

Like the white man's guardianship exercised over Indian Nations, the principle of exclusive jurisdiction over Indian legal controversies in the white man's own courts violates the most basic principles of justice signified by the Gus-Wen-Tah. Under a principle of exclusive jurisdiction, the white man reserves for himself final judgment on how the Indian's vessel will be steered. The white man must surrender this principle of exclusive jurisdiction because it denies respect to the Indian's vision. *** Legal doctrines whose un-American premises, once revealed, would shame those who cite them, continue to be asserted today to deny respect to the Indian's vision and to assert its truths in a world which has not yet learned that freedom is built on my respect for my brother's vision and his respect for mine.

NOTES & QUESTIONS

1. *Reading Indian Law*:
   - Williams traces the origins of modern Indian law back to the development of legal principles first articulated by the Catholic Church in order to prevent conflict among European states engaging in the process of colonization. How did those principles take root in American jurisprudence? What traces of them continue to exist in modern decisions regarding the power of Indian tribes? What might this mean for tribal sovereignty?
   - Williams argues that when Indian tribes choose to develop law in "traditional" or autochthonous ways that are noticeably different from the Western common law system, their attempts are more likely to be struck down by the courts as improper challenges to the overarching federal sovereign. What differentiates between those powers American courts appear willing to allow tribes to exercise, and those which are "inconsistent" with tribal status? What are some examples of tribal powers likely to be struck down under Williams' theory?
   - Explain what Williams means when he suggests that "[t]he winning strategy requires a metamorphosis: the lamb must become a wolf." Is it possible for tribes to "win" without succumbing to the "White Man's Jurisprudence"?

2. *The Marshall Trilogy*: Like the Frickey piece in Chapter 1, Williams' argument builds off the foundational arrangement of powers established by the Marshall Trilogy. However, where Frickey finds comfort in the Trilogy's articulation that tribes ought to retain all rights and powers not explicitly taken by Congress, Williams criticizes even the Marshall Trilogy for being based in colonial thinking. Compare these authors' arguments. Are you more persuaded by Frickey or Williams? For a further critique of the origins and use of plenary power see Robert Clinton's article *There Is No Federal Supremacy Clause for Indian Tribes* in Chapter 14.

3. *In Response to Professor Williams*: The Algebra of Federal Indian Law is among those rare pieces of legal writing to have attracted additional scholarship directly in response to its central tenets. In fact a scholarly dialog emerged between Professor Williams and Professor Robert Laurence centered around the critique of plenary power offered by the original Williams piece. See Robert Laurence, *Learning to Live with the Plenary Power of Congress over the Indian Nations: An Essay in Reaction to Professor Williams'* Algebra, 30 Ariz. L. Rev. 413 (1988); Robert A. Williams, Jr., *Learning Not to Live with Eurocentric Myopia: A Reply to Professor Laurence*, 30 Ariz. L. Rev. 439 (1988); Robert Laurence, *On Eurocentric Myopia, the Designated Hitter Rule and "The Actual State of Things,"* 30 Ariz. L. Rev. 459 (1988).

While the articles clash on many points and provide decidedly varied perspectives/approaches to the law which are worth reading in full, consider just the following short exchange on plenary power. Professor Laurence writes:

> Professor Williams, in the *Algebra*, finds that the plenary power is an unprincipled embodiment of the Discovery Doctrine and urges the uncontradicted recognition of tribal sovereignty. In the first place, I am not sure that such a system is achievable in today's legal and political world. Even if it is, I am not sure it is the wisest system. In my view, the most serious deviations from principles have come when one of those contradictory forces has seriously out-weighed the other. Allotment and termination resulted when the principle of tribal sovereignty was neglected. For the United States to cut the Turtle Mountain Chippewa Tribe loose to sink or swim as an independent sovereign would be just as neglectful.
>
> The better position, I think, lies between the two; stability and strength lie in the counterbalancing of contradictory forces. The plenary power may be lived with, but the recognition of tribal sovereignty must be made an equal tenet of federal Indian law. The necessary tension between inherent tribal sovereignty and

Congress's plenary power will give federal Indian law the strength it
needs to face the next century, even as it means that neither the
power nor the sovereignty will carry the full force it might were the
other not recognized.

Professor Williams rejoins:

Professor Laurence places faith in a federal judiciary populated
during the last few years with ideologues possessed by a rationalizing
philosophy committed to eradicating the types of inefficient contra-
dictions Professor Laurence so "relish[es]." Further, given the
United States Supreme Court's recent reaffirmations of the core
threat to tribal existence contained in the plenary power doctrine,
in other words, that "all aspects of Indian sovereignty are subject to
defeasance by Congress," I am not sure that such a system as he
proposes for Federal Indian law is achievable in today's legal and
political world. Given the Court's views on the ephemeral nature of
asserted tribal sovereignty, it is either preposterous or disingenuous
to talk about the theoretically-postulated sovereignty of Indian tribes
ever possessing the "potential to destroy" the plenary power of
Congress. Tribal sovereignty as the Supreme Court understands that
term today (as the Supreme Court has always understood that term)
does not conflict with congressional plenary power, for Congress can
unilaterally and whimsically destroy the ability of tribes to exercise
self-governing powers Congress finds inconvenient or unwise.

The conversation between Professors Williams and Laurence has
continued to play out among Indian law scholars in the decades since
Algebra was published. As Professor Laurence readily admits, *Algebra*
broke new ground by approaching Indian law from a Critical Legal
Studies perspective (what the article calls an "Americanized" legal
scholarship) which had been almost entirely lacking in Indian law. This
critical approach, whereby Professor Williams encourages a rethinking
not just of the place of Indians in the law but of the foundations of the
law itself, is one of the reasons *Algebra* has remained so important to the
Indian law canon. It has inspired generations of lawyers to think about
the interaction between history, power, law, and colonialism in new
ways and has found a cadre of dedicated junior scholars who continue to
advance the critical perspectives first articulated by Professor Williams in
this piece.

4. *Autochthonous*: As part of its critical perspective, *Algebra* contrasts tribes'
   "autochthonous visions" with legal traditions and practices developed by
   Western courts. "Autochthonous" or "chthonic" law has been broadly
   defined by H. Patrick Glenn to describe a legal tradition in juxtaposition
   to common law or civil law and encompassing a legal order that emerges

from custom, ceremony, practice, and oral tradition. *See Legal Traditions of the World* (Oxford University Press 2010). Professor Williams suggests that tribal self-governance emerges as tribes embrace and develop their autochthonous/chthonic legal traditions, but he also cautions that the further these traditions appear from Western legal approaches, the more often they will be rejected by American courts. In Chapter 5 Robert Yazzie, the former Chief Justice of the Navajo Nation Supreme Court, adds his voice to this conversation, arguing forcefully that tribes cannot ignore their autochthonous traditions.

Think about what you know already about American Indian customs and practices. While each tribe has different traditions, there are customs in every indigenous community that are different from the legal norms practiced in the states. Do you agree with Professor Williams that these autochthonous visions are essential to tribal governance? How can a tribe reconcile remaining faithful to its cultural practices but not risk having those values overturned by federal courts for looking too "foreign" and thereby infringing on the liberty interests of individuals?

5. *The Wolf's Game*: Are you persuaded by Professor Williams' conclusion that tribes are more likely to be successful in litigation when they mirror the governance and structures of states which are more familiar to the Court? (Note that he also critiques tribal attempts to assimilate as being dangerous to tribal sovereignty on many levels.) Consider the Jicarilla Apache Tribe at the center of *Merrion*. Professor Williams postulates that the Tribe may benefit from its "geopolitical topography" in that it owns most of its land and that it has organized itself under the IRA with a government structure that echoes the checks and balances endemic in most state systems. However, none of these attempts to assimilate aided the Jicarilla upon their return to the Court. In *United States v. Jicarilla Apache*, 564 U.S. 162 (2011) the Court sided with the United States against the Tribe in an 8-1 opinion, holding that the fiduciary exception to the attorney–client privilege rule does not apply to the general trust relationship between Indian tribes and the United States.

What makes this *Jicarilla Apache* case different than *Merrion*? After all, the Tribe's territorial integrity and governance system had not appreciably changed. It could be that, unlike in *Merrion*, the opposing party was the United States. If Professor Williams is right that the Court is looking for Indian tribes to assimilate, any legal divergence from the interests of the federal government would be immediately suspect. Yet, in *Jicarilla* the Tribe was asking the Court to apply a common law exception generally available to non-Indian beneficiaries in order to secure access to information the United States had commissioned. In an opinion authored by Justice Alito, an almost unanimous Court relied upon plenary power and contrary federal interests to deny to the Jicarilla the protection of the fiduciary exception:

> Although the Government's responsibilities with respect to the management of funds belonging to Indian tribes bear some resemblance to those of a private trustee, this analogy cannot be taken too far. The trust obligations of the United States to the Indian tribes are established and governed by statute rather than the common law, and in fulfilling its statutory duties, the Government acts not as a private trustee but pursuant to its sovereign interest in the execution of federal law.

Does *Jicarilla* reaffirm or call into question the central thesis of Williams' *Algebra*? If the Tribe had assimilated even more completely might the outcome have been different?

6. *Beyond the Law*: Williams ends his piece with a call for a return to the principles of the Two Row Wampum whereby American legal tradition sets aside the doctrine of discovery and the assumption of plenary power to engage openly and equally with Indian people, customs, and traditions. Such a call has mirrored reverberations throughout Indian studies through the restorative justice movement. Restorative justice is a broad term that critiques the traditional criminal justice system for its emphasis on punishment and concomitant failure to rehabilitate those who have broken society's trust. Drawing inspiration from indigenous values of community healing, and the foreignness to many Indian communities of incarceration, it suggests reconceptualizing the justice system in an attempt to rehabilitate individuals and communities. *See* Carol Hand, Judith Hankes, & Toni House, *Restorative Justice: The Indigenous Justice System*, 15 J. Contemporary Justice Review 4 (2012); Donna Coker, *Restorative Justice, Navajo Peacemaking and Domestic Violence*, 10 Theoretical Criminology 1 (2006); Jon'a F. Meyer, *History Repeats Itself: Restorative Justice in Native American Communities*, 14 J. Contemporary Criminal Justice 1 (1998).

FURTHER READING

- William Bradford, *"With a Very Great Blame in Our Hearts": Reparations, Reconciliation, and an American Indian Plea for Peace with Justice*, 27 Am. Indian L. Rev. 1 (2002).
- Robert Clinton, *Redressing the Legacy of Conquest: A Vision Quest for a Decolonized Federal Indian Law*, 46 Ark. L. Rev. 77 (1993).
- Kimberle Crenshaw & Neil Gotanda, *Critical Race Theory: The Key Writings That Formed the Movement* (The New Press 1996).

- N. Bruce Duthu, *The Thurgood Marshall Papers and the Quest for a Principled Theory of Tribal Sovereignty: Fueling the Fires of Tribal/State Conflict*, 21 Vt. L. Rev. 47 (1996).
- Philip Frickey, *A Common Law for Our Age of Colonialism: The Judicial Divestiture of Indian Tribal Authority over Nonmembers*, 109 Yale L.J. 1 (1999).
- Philip Frickey, *Domesticating Federal Indian Law*, 81 Minn. L. Rev. 31 (1996).
- Robert Porter, *A Proposal to the Hanodaganyas to Decolonize Federal Indian Control Law*, 31 U. Mich. J.L. Ref. 899 (1998).
- Robert A. Williams, Jr., *Documents of Barbarism: The Contemporary Legacy of European Racism and Colonialism in the Narrative Traditions of Federal Indian Law*, 31 Ariz. L. Rev. 237 (1989).
- Robert A. Williams, Jr., *The American Indian in Western Legal Thought* (Oxford University Press 1990).

3

Red: Racism and the American Indian

Bethany R. Berger

56 UCLA L. Rev. 591 (2009)

Race is a complicated construct in America. Too often disparate minority communities are grouped together, the narrative of their relationship with the United States conflated by those who assume that each group has a shared experience of oppression. In reality the various communities that comprise the American "other" each have their own distinct narrative, and even similarly situated subgroups may have differentiated histories and experiences. Consider the juxtaposition between different Indian tribes and slavery. While a few American Indians may have been valued for their labor – particularly in the American Southwest – other Indian tribes themselves owned Black slaves. While the apportionment clause of the Constitution treated slaves as three-fifths of a person, by "excluding Indians not taxed" the founding document refused to treat Indians as people at all. The result of these constructs has raised questions about the role of the Indian – are Indian tribes merely groups of racial Indians or does a tribe have a status and position greater than the racial composition of its members? What is the role of the modern Indian tribe?

This piece by Bethany Berger tackles the issue of race and racism in American law and history. Berger argues that the United States has engaged in a centuries-long project to treat Indian tribes as racial groups in an attempt to deny them the status of sovereign governments. Her piece embarks on an ambitious and comprehensive narrative that documents the evolution of the racial status of Indians in America. It lays bare the often contradictory attitudes of policymakers while collecting rich and textured examples to demonstrate that the racial narrative surrounding Indians and tribes is troubled and inconsistent. Her project concludes by arguing that the narrative she has collected does not permit Indian tribal governments to be relegated to racial groups, but that Indian people are citizens of tribal governments which are empowered to act for themselves and their members. As sovereign nations, Indian tribes play a larger role than merely collections of Indian people.

As you read the following piece pay careful attention to Berger's discussion of the interaction between race and Indian-ness. Try to differentiate the "racial" Indian from the tribal "government." Berger arranges much of her discussion chronologically. What are some important and notable differences between the treatment of American Indians and other racial groups in each period covered by the chronology? Can you trace the evolution of policymaking regarding Indians from colonialization through present day? What trends emerge as the idea of the "Indian" evolves in American policy?

INTRODUCTION

What is the role of race, and particularly of racism, in American Indian law and policy? This question is particularly pressing today, as national attention focuses on the efforts of the Cherokee to limit their membership to those with Cherokee or Delaware blood, the US Supreme Court continues to reduce tribal jurisdiction over non-Indians, and the recent Bush Administration has blocked recognition of Native Hawaiian sovereignty on the grounds that it is impermissibly race based. Although the federal government has wide constitutional discretion to implement its obligations to native people, in these and other places, questions of race continue to haunt Indian policy.

These questions become more difficult to answer because of the American tendency to measure racism according to its particular manifestations with respect to African Americans: slavery, control of labor, and the social segregation and classification of individuals according to descent. Although this paradigm obscures even the realities of black–white racism, it is particularly inadequate with respect to Indian–white relations, which since colonial days have not focused on the control of Indian labor, and have, at their most coercive, announced a goal of Indian assimilation. This paradigm also creates unease with federal Indian law and policy, which to a great extent focus on the rights of tribes whose membership depends in part on descent.

***

European Americans were not primarily concerned with using Indian people as a source of labor, and so did not have to theorize Indians as inferior individuals to justify the unfair terms of that labor. Rather, colonists' primary concern with respect to Indians was to obtain tribal resources and use tribes as a flattering foil for American society and culture. It was therefore necessary to theorize tribal societies as fatally and racially inferior while emphasizing the ability of Indian individuals to leave their societies and join non-Indian ones. Throughout the most oppressive periods of Indian policy (and at the height of violent segregation of African Americans), policymakers continued to emphasize the need to encourage Indians to leave their tribes and assimilate with white society. At the same time, Indian tribes, regardless of their degree of actual conformity to non-Indian ideals, as well as Indians who followed the supposedly inborn urge to cling to tribal ways, were viewed as being fixed in the backward patterns of blood and habit, and doomed to disappear or to be destroyed.

There are of course situations in which discrimination against American Indians accords with classical paradigms of racism. Indians have been denied the right to vote, attend schools with or marry whites, eat at restaurants, stay at hotels, or get jobs because of their race. Like African Americans, native people have been lynched, raped, and had their homes burnt out from under them because of their race. In some parts of the country, Indian people are "timber niggers" or "prairie niggas," the necessarily inferior economic and social group.

Throughout the United States, moreover, Native Americans fall at the bottom of assessments of education, health status, and income, and at the top of assessments of crime victimization and incarceration. But if one identifies racism only by the appearance of such paradigmatic manifestations, one would elide some of the most important ways that notions of Indian inferiority have been constructed and used. ***

But other aspects of the treatment of Indians during this period could result in the opposite conclusion, that Indian people were not the victims of racism at all. In the same period that sexual contact between blacks and whites was the surest way to raise a lynch mob to fury, intermarriage between Indians and whites was advocated by prominent policy makers and even rewarded by Congress under certain circumstances. And while the segregationist Jim Crow era closed its iron grip around African Americans, graduates of federal Indian boarding schools received university scholarships, Indian artists ran movie studios and starred in operas at Carnegie Hall, and Indian ballplayers played on both teams in the 1911 World Series. Throughout this period, moreover, much of the starkest oppression suffered by Indian people was publicly justified by the supposed need to integrate them. ***

A few clarifications are in order. Most important, this Article should not be understood to argue that tribes are at heart racial groups. The reverse is true: I argue that the basic racist move at work in Indian law and policy is to racialize the tribe, defining tribes as racial groups in order to deny tribes the rights of governments. Second, this Article does not argue that racism defines all of Indian law and policy. Perhaps even more than for other racial groups, important currents in Indian law and policy have supported a notion of tribal equality and self-government. Moreover, as any theory arguing that material interests importantly contribute to racial oppression must acknowledge, many interests and impulses other than racism affected Indian policy. Finally, this Article does not attempt to establish some kind of equivalency of oppression between Indians and African Americans or the many other victims of racism in the United States. Not only is there enough heartache for all to share, but a premise of this Article is that we have obscured a complete understanding of the way race works in America by trying to measure it against the experience of a single group. ***

II FOUNDING AND RACING THE NATION

In the century beginning with the Revolutionary War, Americans were transformed from a collection of British colonies to a single American nation. In the same period, ideas of innate racial hierarchy gained greater hold on science, law, and popular thought. Not surprisingly, the two movements influenced each other, as America came to think of itself as a white nation, and national and cultural differences – Mexican and Chinese as well as Indian – became linked with, and understood as, expressions of innate racial differences. Assimilation of Indian individuals was a symbol of this racial triumph, and was aggressively pursued by federal policymakers and occasionally celebrated in popular culture. At the same time, tribes were increasingly understood not as governments, but as "unfortunate races" under federal control. ***

A 1776–1871: Revolution to Reservation

In the years between the founding of the American republic and the declaration of the end of treatymaking in 1871, the racial role of American Indians became more fixed and defined. Individual Indians, particularly for communities far removed from native populations, became a symbol of the potential and duty of the American republic. Through civilization and incorporation of the Indian, the white race could both fulfill the sacred obligations that came with Manifest Destiny and partake of the romance of the natural world. Tribes, however, were increasingly treated not as nations or governments, but as collections of individuals joined only by race. Within this divide between the assimilable individual and the racialized tribe, the greatest innate defect of the Indian was the unfathomable insistence on clinging to the barbarous tribe.

The US Constitution reflected the divergent legal places of Africans and Indians in the racial schema of the new nation. Although the constitutional terms relating to these groups are largely intended to allocate power among American states and the branches of the federal government, they provide an apt metaphor for their divergent roles. African American slaves would be inferior individuals, three-fifths of a person, incorporated within American communities. Indians, however, were mentioned in the Commerce Clause as "Indian tribes," alongside "foreign nations" and the "several states." This enumeration with states and foreign countries helps to establish tribes as sovereigns, with important legal rights. Still, as both Indian and tribe, these sovereigns were clearly other, a form of government defined in part, and limited by its racial origin. ***

Ultimately, the nationalism that grew during and after the Revolution only increased notions of American superiority over Indian tribes and the justice of Anglo-American claims to the continent. *** This is evident in George Washington's 1783 letter insisting on "the propriety of purchasing [Indian] Lands in preference to attempting to drive them by force," an expediency justified as "the gradual extension of our Settlements will as certainly cause the Savage as the Wolf to retire; both being beasts of prey tho' they differ in shape." If these beasts of the forests chose not to disappear or assimilate voluntarily, the new nation would help them along. By 1819, Congress had created a permanent fund for civilization of the Indians, stating that: "In the present state of our country one of two things seems to be necessary. Either that those sons of the forest should be moralized or exterminated."

These opinions do not, in themselves, prove that the limitations placed on Indian tribes were considered innate or racial. They leave open the possibility that an Indian tribe might, by adopting an Anglo-American government and economy, win the right to maintain its existence. The Removal Crisis of the 1820s and 1830s, however, demonstrated that it was only by assimilating as individuals, not members of tribes, that Indians could win a place in American society. Federal policy between 1812 and 1850 concentrated on moving tribes west of the Mississippi, where the tribes could "pursue their plan of civilization" without interfering with "the natural superiority allowed to the claims of civilized communities over those of savage tribes." But the Cherokee Nation, which refused to sign removal treaties, had all of the characteristics policymakers had designated as those of a civilized community: Its members farmed, engaged in manufacturing, established a common school system, trial and appellate courts, and a constitution, and even held African slaves, perhaps the ultimate symbol of civilization at the time. Despite this, because the Cherokee Nation refused to give up its tribal status and dissolve into the American populace, the tribe was damned for misusing the gifts of Anglo-American teaching and was ultimately forced across the Mississippi. ***

Over the next decades, the Court would emphasize the status of tribes as racial rather than political groups. In 1846 in *United States v. Rogers,* the Court held that the benefits of tribal membership were limited by race, holding that a white man naturalized as a Cherokee citizen was not an Indian under statutes exempting crimes between Indians from federal jurisdiction. Tribes, the decision affirmed, were not governments entitled to naturalize citizens of any race, but instead themselves a race subject to federal power. Although the United States had "exercised its power over this unfortunate race in the spirit of humanity and justice," tribes had "never been acknowledged or treated as independent nations by the European governments . . ."

Yet individual Indian rights continued to be affirmed by the Supreme Court. Justice Taney even used them as a foil for the African American absence of rights in *Dred Scott v. Stanford,* carefully distinguishing between the racial limitations on the rights of Indian tribes and the ability of individual Indians to become naturalized American citizens. Indian tribes, the Court opined, were "under subjection to the white race; and it has been found necessary, for their sake as well as our own, to regard them as in a state of pupilage, and to legislate to a certain extent over them and the territory they occupy." Nevertheless, unlike African Americans, Indians could become naturalized citizens by the authority of Congress; indeed, "if an individual should leave his nation or tribe, and take up his abode among the white population, he would be entitled to all the rights and privileges which would belong to an emigrant from any other foreign people." ***

This simultaneous condemnation of the incurable barbarity of the tribe and affirmation of the potential of the Indian individual produced the Reservation Policy that dominated federal policy between the 1850s and 1870s. Where Removal sought to transport tribes to unpopulated lands, where (federal negotiators promised) native people could escape intrusion by grasping whites, the Reservation Policy sought to confine them on reservations where they could be forcibly trained to disdain their tribes and emulate Anglo Americans. Tribes, formerly removed to an ill-defined Indian territory, were now confined on smaller plots of land where they could be "controlled, and finally compelled by stern necessity to resort to agricultural labor or starve." Federal agents were dispatched to the reservations to replace tribal govern-ments and culture with white institutions. ***

B 1871–1928: Assimilation and Oppression

The Jim Crow Era for African Americans was the Allotment and Assimilation Era for Native Americans. During the 1870s and 1880s, the military confined the last independent tribes on reservations, and in 1890, Wounded Knee marked the end of the Indian wars. With the waning of a significant military threat, policymakers would regulate tribes and Indian individuals more forcefully than ever before in the quest to separate the Indian from the tribe. Courts obliged by eliding the limitations that tribal sovereignty and treaties had placed on federal action. Histor-ians self-consciously designated the triumph over Indian tribes as the formative experience of the white American race. Although assimilating Indians frequently confronted color prejudice, individual examples of Indian assimilation were cele-brated in academic and cultural arenas, opening doors wholly closed to other races.

Federal Indian policy, which previously vacillated between sovereign and racia-lized views of tribes, moved decisively toward the latter. The 1887 Dawes Allotment Act was the defining legislation of the era. The Act authorized the federal govern-ment to divide remaining tribal territories among individual Indian households, with land not divided declared surplus and free for white acquisition. Although the policy was supported as a means to open reservation land to white settlement, it was also "inspired by the highest motives" and "regarded as a panacea which would make restitution to the Indian for all that the white man had done to him in the past." The law was "a mighty pulverizing engine for breaking up the tribal mass" and separating the individual from the tribe.

This direct intrusion on tribal economies was accompanied by coercive efforts directed toward the "ultimate absorption of the Indian race into the body politic of the nation." Federal agents created tribal police forces and courts staffed with trusted Indians for the same purpose, to establish "a power entirely independent of the chiefs" and thereby "finally destroy, the power of tribes and bands." Indian children were taken from their families and placed in boarding schools to enable the individual to overcome the fatal allure of the tribal community. Captain Richard Pratt, founder of the Carlisle Indian School, described the goal of the schools: "All the Indian there is in the race should be dead. Kill the Indian in him and save the man." The way to kill the "Indian" in the Indian race was to kill the tribe, by planting "treason to the tribe and loyalty to the nation at large."

*** Policymakers went even further, explicitly supporting intermarriage with Indians as an assimilation tool. In 1888, Congress enacted a law providing that Indian women who married white men would thereby become American citizens, so that their husbands could not gain rights to Indian allotments. The law was intended both to "prevent the marriage or miscegenation of ... degenerate whites with the Indian squaws," and to "encourage Indians to marry white men and become [assimilated] citizens of the United States." The debate on the law provides a neat summary of the role of Indians in American society. As "squaws," still tied to their tribes and land, Indians were reviled, and any whites that chose to join with them were "degenerate." By assimilating through marriage, however, female Indians would become both "women" and "citizens." As a matter of policy, moreover, so long as white preeminence was preserved, absorption of the original, now conquered, race was a fitting tribute. Echoing Thomas Jefferson, one policymaker observed, "while ten grains of Indian to one hundred of white man might be injurious to the quality of the white race, half a grain to one hundred might supply exactly the element needed to improve it ... What happy result can there be to the lamb, but in absorption, digestion, assimilation in the substance of the lion."

***

Throughout this period, citizenship was extended on an ad hoc basis as a reward for civilization, given to tribal members disavowing allegiance to their tribes or accepting their allotments, and awarded to Indian women marrying white men. In 1924, the same year Congress finalized the exclusion of Asians from citizenship, it extended citizenship to all Native Americans. Although the law provided a legal tool for Indians struggling for legal rights in non-Indian communities, it also symbolized the prevailing notion of American dominance over the Indian tribe.

Despite the advocacy of assimilation, Indians leaving reservations to join the broader community often found themselves shut out of public and social institutions. At times this was part of the general exclusion of people of color under Jim Crow. Ariela Gross documents the ways that officials struggled to categorize Mexicans as either Spanish, and therefore white, or Indian, and therefore colored, to fit them into an established racial taxonomy. But de jure discrimination was often on distinctly Indian grounds, focusing on the individual's connection with a tribe. Thus in *Elk v. Wilkins* in 1884, the Supreme Court upheld a Nebraska decision to deny the vote to an Indian man on the grounds that he was not a citizen. Although John Elk had left the reservation where he was born and severed his ties with the tribe over a year earlier, Indians born in tribal relations were not citizens of the United States, and did not acquire such citizenship automatically upon leaving their tribes. Citizenship, moreover, had a peculiarly descent-based spin, as seen when the Minnesota Supreme Court upheld the disenfranchisement of an entire community of mixed-blood men on the Red Lake reservation, finding that although they had "reached a degree of civilization superior to that manifested by many white men," and were likely the children of citizen fathers, they were also (the court assumed) illegitimate, and therefore took the status of their noncitizen Indian mothers.

We see exclusion on the basis of both color and tribal status in *Piper v. Big Pine School District of Inyo County*, a 1924 California Supreme Court decision. The school district had refused to admit California Indian Alice Piper, relying on a state statute providing that in areas within three miles of a federal Indian school Indian children could not be admitted to the general public schools. The court rejected the school district's argument, holding that because the child and her parents "are citizens of the United States and of this state" and had never "lived in tribal relations with any tribe of Indians or has ever owed or acknowledged allegiance or fealty of any kind to any tribe or 'nation' of Indians," it violated the Fourteenth Amendment to deny "admittance to the common schools solely because of color or racial differences without having made provision for their education equal in all respects to that afforded persons of any other race or color." In a testament to the flexibility of grounds for exclusion, however, the court took pains to affirm the constitutionality of the preceding section of the statute, which provided school districts with the power to "exclude children of filthy or vicious habits, or children suffering from contagious or infectious diseases, and also to establish separate schools for Indian children and for children of Chinese, Japanese or Mongolian parentage."

Despite the color prejudice many Indians experienced, individual Indian integration was publicly celebrated as another symbol of the triumph of European-American civilization over savagery. Boarding schools took before-and-after pictures of Indian children, first arriving in tribal dress and then arrayed in the trappings of whiteness, and circulated them for eager consumption by organizations in the east declaring themselves Friends of the Indian. Celebration of Indian assimilation also resulted in access to fora wholly barred to African Americans. Graduates of Indian boarding schools won academic and athletic scholarships to East Coast colleges, facilitating an Indian presence in professional sports that has not been matched since. The football star Jim Thorpe, the only professional Indian athlete most people can name, was a product of this phenomenon. Thirty-seven years before Jackie Robinson broke the black–white color barrier in major league baseball, Indians played on both sides in the 1911 World Series. Native actor-writer-director James Young Deer became the head of a major West Coast studio, while native opera singers were stars of the New York Metropolitan Opera, translating the fascination with the "disappearing" Indian culture into personal success and artistic influence.

*** Indians at the turn of the century were caught in a double bind. The denigration and near destruction of the Indian tribe was enshrined as part of the "grandeur of their race's imperial destiny." Tribes were not envisioned as governments, but rather as racial groupings fixed at an earlier moment of social evolution.

Assimilating those under the thrall of this innate "call of the wild" was a vindication of the white race, and the assimilated Indian was celebrated on the national stage. Individuals who chose to follow the white man's road, however, were blocked by color prejudice and stereotypes of the innately wild Indian. While the national ideology meant that the racial barriers to individual Indians were not as absolute as those faced by other groups, their options were circumscribed both as tribal savages and colored individuals.

III TWENTIETH CENTURY INNOVATIONS

The twentieth century saw two innovations in the racial understanding of Indian tribes. First, there was a short respite from policies that treated tribes as permanently inferior and Indians that chose to remain with them as racially misguided. During the Indian New Deal of the 1930s and 1940s, Indian policy and law recognized that securing wellbeing for native people required respecting their choices to remain with their tribes and culture, and accordingly sought to strengthen tribal governments. At the same time, native people seeking tribal rights self-consciously made claims to a distinct Indian ethnic identity. But in the following Termination Era of Indian policy, old assimilationist arguments were not only renewed, they were fortified by the emerging rhetoric of civil rights for individuals. By ignoring the different bases for Indian oppression and resistance, opponents of tribal equality were able to make the same old arguments in the name of equality itself. The Self-Determination policy that has replaced Termination is characterized by both elements, as support for tribal governments clashes with efforts to reimpose racial limitations when tribal rights undermine non-Indian expectations.

A *A Brief New Deal – A New Twist on the Old One: 1928–1968*

The assimilationist policy helped sow the seeds of its brief demise in the 1930s. A new generation of native people, educated at federal schools and liberal arts universities, used this education to publicize oppression of the Indian and organize against it. At the same time, the emphasis on the supposedly disappearing Indian and the attempts to gather information on this vanishing culture generated new interest in, and respect for, tribal traditions. Scholarly trends, including emergence of cultural relativism in anthropology, as well as social scientific documentation of the impact of forcible allotment and assimilation, also contributed to a new direction in Indian policy.

In 1934, under the direction of Commissioner of Indian Affairs John Collier, the federal government implemented a policy that for the first time sought to strengthen tribes and permit Indians to choose to maintain their tribal ties with dignity. The Indian Reorganization Act (IRA), the cornerstone Indian New Deal legislation, ended allotment, sought to restore and consolidate tribal territories, provided tribal economic development loans, enhanced Indian preference in the Bureau of Indian Affairs, and sought to facilitate tribal governmental organization. Felix Cohen, the legal architect of the Indian New Deal, recovered the elements of Indian law that had always, at least formally, recognized the status of tribes as governmental entities rather than racial groups and demanded some measure of respect for those governmental entities.

The policy's architects saw the Indian New Deal as fully consistent with equal rights for individual Indians. The IRA was accompanied by the Johnson–O'Malley Act which sought to counter state discrimination against Indians in the provision of governmental services. An administration lawyer issued an opinion declaring the unconstitutionality of voting restrictions on Indians who maintained tribal relations. But these policymakers also recognized that equality for American Indians required governmental rights for Indian tribes. As D'Arcy McNickle, one of the key players in the Indian New Deal, later declared of Collier, "He was saying that Indians are people, as good as any other people. They love their own values, and they should be allowed to work out their own destinies without being beaten down by superior power. That really is what the argument was all about."

The Indian New Deal did not survive the 1940s. World War II brought the rhetoric of individual Indian equality to the nationalism that had always existed in cries for Indian assimilation. Congressional reports protested against the policy of strengthening Indian tribes. In language reminiscent of Richard Pratt and Carlisle, a 1944 House Report declared:

> The goal of Indian education should be to make the Indian child a better American rather than to equip him simply to be a better Indian ... The present Indian education program tends to operate too much in the direction of perpetuating the Indian as a special-status individual rather than preparing him for independent citizenship.

Threatened with denial of funding for Indian programs if he remained in office, John Collier, the Commissioner of Indian Affairs who had been the principal champion of the policy, was forced out of office in 1945. His departure was followed by those of the other architects of the policy over the next few years. The way was clear for what became known as the Termination Era.

Under Termination, the federal government pursued a policy of ending its special relationship with Indian tribes and transferring tribal territories to the members individually or as shareholders in state chartered corporations. Despite the huge symbolic impact of termination, only about 3 percent of tribes were terminated, and many of those have now been restored to recognition. *** Most relevant for our purposes is the rhetoric of the termination policy. The clarion cry for termination was the need for individual Indian equality. Senator Arthur V. Watkins of Utah, the Chair of the Senate Committee on Indian Affairs and the most important legislative advocate of the termination policy, argued:

In view of the historic policy of Congress favoring freedom for the Indians, ... we should end the status of Indians as wards of the government and grant them all of the rights and prerogatives pertaining to American citizenship. With the aim of "equality before the law" in mind our course should rightly be no other ... Following in the footsteps of the Emancipation Proclamation of ninety-four years ago, I see the following words emblazoned in letters of fire above the heads of the Indians – THESE PEOPLE SHALL BE FREE!

*** Although the Termination Era reversed the congressional New Deal policy, the record in the Supreme Court was more mixed. Nineteen fifty-five saw a new low for judicial protection of tribal rights, as the Court held that the Takings Clause did not apply to federal acquisitions of tribal lands unless Congress had formally ratified the tribal property right. Nineteen fifty-nine, however, saw an even more important success. In *Williams v. Lee*, the Court held that state courts had no jurisdiction over a claim brought by a non-Indian against a Navajo couple to enforce a contract entered into on the Navajo Reservation. From an individual racial rights perspective, the decision might be seen as affirming a separate status of a people that are in part racially defined. But the Court emphasized the ways that the decision was necessary to ensure tribal equality, which rested on governmental rights that did not depend on the racial status of the parties:

> There can be no doubt that to allow the exercise of state jurisdiction here would undermine the authority of the tribal courts over Reservation affairs and hence would infringe on the right of the Indians to govern themselves. It is immaterial that respondent is not an Indian. He was on the Reservation and the transaction with an Indian took place there.

At least some of the justices understood the links between *Williams* and their civil rights decisions. Justice Frankfurter sent Justice Black a note on *Williams v. Lee* stating that he was "pleased to concur in this indirect affirmation of *Brown v. Board of Education*." Just as *Brown* was a landmark decision in the effort to undermine racial limitations on African American individuals, so *Williams* was a landmark in the effort to reverse the racially inferior position of Indian governments.

It is no coincidence that both decisions came in the same decade. Both African Americans and American Indians had served in large numbers in World War II and experienced the novelty of competition in a white arena. Both groups came back impatient with the limitations placed upon them by the country for which they had risked their lives. For American Indians, this generated new efforts to resist the restrictions placed on tribes. *Williams v. Lee* was a product of this movement, in particular of efforts by the Navajo Nation to develop and to assert the independence of its tribal courts. Nationally, Indian tribes began joining together to pursue their quest for tribal equality. The National Congress of American Indians, the first national supratribal organization focused on tribal survival, was created in 1954.

At the same time, Indian people fought the persistent political limitations placed on Indians who maintained their connection with their tribes. Long after Indians were declared citizens in 1924, several of the states with the largest Indian populations continued to deny Indians the right to vote. In 1928, the Arizona Supreme Court held that two Pima Indians residing on the Gila River reservation as "wards of the federal government" were "persons under guardianship" ineligible to vote. This decision was finally overturned in 1948, when two Mohave-Apache Indians, one of them a World War II veteran, again challenged the restriction. In 1927, New Mexico had responded to the 1924 Indian Citizenship Act by declaring that all "Indians not taxed" were ineligible to vote, a term that apparently excluded even reservation residents who paid some federal and state taxes. The legislature finally repealed this provision in 1951, after a 1948 federal court decision declared the law invalid. In 1956, the Utah Supreme Court held native people residing on reservations still could not vote because they were not "residents" of the state, rejecting arguments based on Indian citizenship, eligibility for the draft, and payment of taxes. The legislature finally repealed the restriction in 1957 after the US Supreme Court granted certiorari in the case. Idaho repealed its constitutional prohibition on voting by "Indians not taxed, who have not severed their tribal relations and adopted the habits of civilization" in 1950. In 1951, South Dakota repealed the statutory provision that Indians "maintaining tribal relations ... cannot vote or hold office." In 1960, Minnesota also finally removed the constitutional provision limiting the Indian vote to "persons of mixed white and Indian blood who have adopted the customs and habits of civilization" and "persons of Indian blood ... who have adopted the language, customs and habits of civilization, after an examination before any district court of the State," although it had apparently not enforced the restriction after 1934.

Just as native people were fighting to break the limitations placed on tribes as governments, they were defeating the limitations placed on them as individuals for their decisions to remain with their tribes. In the name of racial equality, the Termination policy had reversed the New Deal support for tribal self-government, and resurrected old habits of treating tribes as racial minority groups to be assimilated into the white mainstream. At the same time, however, native people were building the foundation for a resurgence of tribal rights that is continuing today.

B *Equality and Backlash: 1968 to the Present*

By the late 1960s, the Termination policy was moribund. All of the 1968 presidential election candidates opposed termination, and in 1970, President Nixon denounced termination as morally and legally unacceptable, initiating the Self-Determination Policy that has remained the official legislative and executive objective to this day. Under this policy, over half of governmental services for Indians have been turned over to tribal control, while other legislation has enabled tribes to protect their cultural and natural resources and has furthered tribal economic development. These measures have gone some way in restoring tribes to the position of governments rather than doomed minority groups. By undermining the power expectations built around the helpless ward status of Indian tribes, however, these changes catalyzed a backlash that uses the rhetoric of race equality in the service of the old racial order.

***

Although the romanticized noble savage remains a treasured part of popular culture, modern-day manifestations of Indian rights are met with less approbation. As tribes assert governmental rights that impinge on the privileges of whiteness, protesters attempt to re-race tribes and their members to undermine those rights.

One of the earlier manifestations of this phenomenon was in the treaty fishing battles beginning in the 1960s. Like many tribes, when the tribes of the Northwest and of the Midwest Great Lakes states ceded land by treaty in the nineteenth century, they preserved their right to hunt and fish in the ceded lands. In the twentieth century, however, non-Indian commercial overfishing and depletion due to pollution, dam projects, and introduction of invasive species led to increased restrictions on fishing practices. When this regulation resulted in crackdowns on tribal fishing, the tribes fought back, asserting their ancient treaty rights. For the tribes involved, these battles catalyzed the resurgence of tribal government and cultural identity.

The struggle generated a renaissance of racial attacks on the Indian tribe. Indeed, the district court hearing the Washington cases made the parallels between the tribal struggles and the demand for individual racial equality clear, noting that "except for some desegregation cases," in seeking to protect these treaty rights, "the district court has faced the most concerted official and private efforts to frustrate a decree of a federal court witnessed in this century." In the Great Lakes, for example, Indians had been incorporated into the tourism industry as guides, providing wealthy fishermen with indigenous access to the natural world. Now, however, they were asserting rights to fish free of state regulation that were superior to and, it was asserted, interfered with the rights of sport fisherman. The affront to the accepted racial–economic hierarchy brought hundreds of protesters to Anishinaabe fishing sites. As conflict with Indians had throughout history, the dispute resulted in the cheapening of Indian bodies and life. The Northwestern bumper sticker "Can an Indian, Save a Salmon" in the Midwest became signs saying "Spear an Indian: save a walleye" or even "Spear a pregnant squaw, save two walleyes."

In *Lac du Flambeau Band of Lake Superior Chippewa Indians v. Stop Treaty Abuse Wisconsin* the federal district court documented the Northern Wisconsin protests. Protesters used a barrage of racial epithets – "Tonto," "Redskin," and "timber nigger" – but also employed insults that recalled tropes of the racialized Indian tribe. They renewed the nineteenth century characterization of tribal members as lazy and dependent on government handouts, referring to the fishermen as "all you Indians that are on welfare" and "welfare warriors," and stating: "Look at those fat Indians. Eating all the commodities up at Flambeau there." Reasserting the history of Indian–white conflict, protesters yelled, "You're a defeated people; you are a conquered people," "the only good Indian is a dead Indian," and "Custer had the right idea." The protesters also challenged the spearers as lacking Indian authenticity, singing "[a] half breed here; a half breed there," mocking the cultural and religious significance of spearing, and circulating pamphlets stating that Chippewa spearers use spears "mass produced in China and Korea," and outboard motors "manufactured in Japan." The district court found that the protests sought to deny the Indians property rights because of their race in violation of 42 U.S.C. § 1982. Discarding the evidence of the leader of the protests that he had previously treated Indians well, Judge Barbara Crabb opined, "It is one thing to treat a group well when its members present no economic or personal inconvenience; it is quite another to continue to treat them that way when they have asserted interests in competition with one's own."

More recent examples of this truism come from the debates over Indian mascots and casino gaming. In further testament to the strange racial position of American Indians in the United States, Indians were until recently one of the most popular sports team names. The use of another racial group – African Americans, Mexicans, or Asians – in this fashion would generate horror in modern America. But Indian team names and the accompanying stereotypical depictions of native people are justified as honoring native peoples. This honor is reminiscent of the role of Pocahontas in the racist south. Absorbed within a white American nation, Indian mascots symbolize a pleasurable connection with the romanticized noble savage; when modern day Indians challenge non-Indian use of Indian images, however, they are quickly reduced to racist stereotypes. Efforts to replace Fighting Sioux as the University of North Dakota team name, for example, generated a poster representing Indians as an alcoholic, lazy, and defeated people dependent on government handouts: "If you get rid of the fighting Sioux we get rid of your free schooling," "Drink'em lots o' fire water," "Pay taxes," "Find something better for time [sic] 'like a job,'" and "You lost the war, sorry."

Protests against tribal casino gaming are particularly interesting, because they draw directly on a racially fixed image of the tribe. The accepted and honored tribe is poor, traditional, and close to the earth. By engaging in profitable commercial enterprises, tribes act as modern governments and violate this accepted Indian image. Others challenge the right to game on the grounds that tribal members are not racially Indian enough. As an Indian Law professor in Connecticut, the site of two vastly profitable tribal casinos, I have more than once been asked, "But are they really Indian?" Although the Indian, or more appropriately tribal, status required for eligibility to enter into a gaming compact does not depend on biological race but rather political status as a recognized tribe, the thrust of these questions is whether the asker would recognize the tribe's members as racially Indian. As one townsperson complained, "more than half [of the Mashantucket Pequots] are predominantly African American and the rest are mostly white." Renee Cramer notes the ways that cultural and racial traits blend in these critiques as the Pequots are also accused of being too successful, and therefore "too White," to be Indian. The rights of Indian tribes are thus fixed by their race, but efforts to assert those privileges in ways that interfere with white expectations result in challenges to racial authenticity.

Most recently, questions of race and Indian tribes have reached the national stage in a different posture, through the exclusion of descendants of African American slaves by the Cherokee Nation of Oklahoma. As discussed above, members of the Cherokee Nation held African slaves and enacted oppressive slave laws in the period before the Civil War. After the war, the Cherokee Nation agreed by treaty that former slaves would henceforth become tribal citizens. During the Allotment Period, the United States created rolls of tribal members; these rolls placed whites who claimed citizenship by marriage on "Intermarried White" rolls, those of Indian appearance or those who could prove Indian ancestry on "Cherokee by blood" rolls, and those of African appearance, frequently even if they possessed Indian ancestry, on "Freedmen" rolls. The Cherokee Nation has recently amended its Constitution to exclude from citizenship all those who cannot prove descent from the by-blood rolls, thus effectively excluding the few remaining descendants from the Intermarried White rolls as well as many more descendants from the Freedmen rolls. Although these measures do not exclude those with both African American and Cherokee descent, and many phenotypically black individuals are enrolled tribal citizens, the measures raises the specter of de facto racial discrimination in a powerful way.

A recent comprehensive doctoral dissertation shows that in enacting new restrictions limiting membership to those of tribal descent, these tribes are following the trend of most other tribes who have amended their membership requirements since the 1960s. Although federally influenced requirements of the 1930s were more likely to depend on residence and Indian blood quantum, more recently a number of tribes, seeking to establish historical continuity with their tribal ancestors in the face of geographic dispersion and intermarriage of their members, have shifted to a tribal blood standard. This trend should be seen as an effort to assert and to maintain sovereignty rather than racism, a turn from the racially Indian to the politically tribal. ***

We are in a time of shifting racial roles, with tribes no longer fully limited by their inferior Indian status and, for the first time since they were powerful trading partners with the colonists, possessing important negotiating power as governments. Both in law and popular culture, however, there is a resurgence of racialized limitations on the Indian tribe in an attempt to cabin this shift. The Supreme Court attempts to fix tribal jurisdiction by race, limiting it to tribal members only, while popular protest both uses old stereotypes of Indian tribes and attacks the racial authenticity of tribes that challenge established hierarchies of privilege. The history described in this Article suggests that, despite the new responsibilities sovereignty creates for tribes themselves, non-Indians concerned with racial equality should seek to protect meaningful tribal sovereignty rather than undermine it.

CONCLUSION

*** Native nations are in the midst of a cultural and political renaissance. Fueled by the refusal to give up the Indian identities that have sustained them, and supported both by intertribal action and overdue governmental encouragement, modern tribes have reemerged as formidable sovereigns. Development of tribal governments and economies has finally begun to shorten the gap between Indian and white health, education, and standards of living. By interfering with long-established hierarchies of power and non-Indian expectations, however, this renaissance has engendered protests that tribes are not governments but rather racial entities whose rights are fixed by their historic roles. Ironically, this effort to fix tribes in past-subordinate positions has been strengthened by the rhetoric of racial equality.

***

Shifting our understanding of the role of racism in Indian policy has important implications for equal protection law and its apparently anomalous treatment of American Indians. While classic equal protection jurisprudence can counter discrimination against Indians as individuals, it may pose obstacles to equality for Indians as members of tribes, because tribal membership often is, and will likely continue to be, dependent in part on tribal ancestry. Although the governing precedent upholds special treatment of Indians so long as those measures are "tied rationally to the fulfillment of Congress' unique obligation toward the Indians," thus permitting measures that are "reasonable and rationally designed to further Indian self-government," this precedent is under attack both as a matter of law and of policy. Understanding that the most devastating manifestations of racism for American Indians were denial of the governmental status of the Indian tribe and limitation of tribal status to that of a racially inferior group provides a new lens to understand why protection of tribal governments is in fact a necessary means to undermine racism toward American Indians. ***

NOTES & QUESTIONS

1. *Reading Indian Law*:
   - Berger directly contradicts the prevailing narrative that Indians were always oppressed or disadvantaged on the basis of race. Throughout American history, in what ways were Indians treated notably

differently than other racial groups? Building upon these collected examples, what might explain this different treatment?

- What is the role of the tribe in the creation of the racial Indian? What does Berger mean when she argues in the Introduction that the "basic racist move at work in Indian law and policy is to racialize the tribe, defining tribes as racial groups in order to deny tribes the rights of governments." How does it benefit the White majority to treat Indian tribes as racial groups instead of governments? Reflect on the examples Berger gives throughout her chronology. Can you reinterpret some of these examples in light of this framework?

- Think about the modern stereotypes of Indian people, both from your own knowledge and experience and from the latter part of Berger's piece. At a time when tribal governments are affirmatively reasserting themselves, how do racial images and tired tropes, like Indian mascots, seek to "cabin this shift" and threaten tribal sovereignty? Berger's piece identifies the use of this racial strategy in an attempt to limit the influence of tribal governments but proposes few concrete ways to combat it beyond urging a shift in our understanding. How might tribal governments act to ensure they are not defenestrated by these racial arguments?

2. *The Cherokee Freedmen*: Several times throughout *Red: Racism and the American Indian* Professor Berger raises the role membership battles have played in constructing tribal governments as racial collectives. Since *Red*'s publication, the interaction of race and membership has continued to play out throughout Indian country, raising questions of both the racial status of Indians and the sovereignty of tribal governments.

   The right to membership in an Indian tribe cannot be entirely controlled by the tribe when a treaty with the United States establishes some criteria for membership. In *Cherokee Nation v. Nash*, 267 F.Supp. 3d 87 (D.D.C. 2017) the US District Court for the District of Columbia addressed the disenrollment by the Cherokee Nation of the "Freedmen" – members who had traced their ancestry back to slaves owned by Cherokee citizens and then were freed by treaty. In 2007, the Cherokee voted to limit citizenship to only those persons who were Cherokee, Shawnee, or Delaware by blood. The Cherokee Nation argued that it was only the Cherokee Nation Constitution that had guaranteed citizenship to the Freedmen and that the Constitution could be changed in accordance with its amendment provisions. The Cherokee Freedmen brought suit alleging that their attempted disenrollment violated the Treaty with the Cherokee in 1866 and that their Cherokee citizenship is instead conferred by the Treaty which has never been abrogated.

The 1866 Treaty with the Cherokee contained a provision that discussed the enrollment of the Cherokees' freed slaves as members of the Cherokee Nation. The Court was called upon to resolve whether the 1866 Treaty guarantees a continuing right to Cherokee Nation citizenship for descendants of Freedmen listed on the Final Roll of Cherokee Freedmen as compiled by the Dawes Commission.

The Court reasoned that the 1866 Treaty's guarantee of "all the rights of Native Cherokee" included the right of citizenship. It also concluded that the language "and are now residents therein, or who may return within six months, and their descendants" included the current class of Freedmen petitioning the Court. The Court held that the 2007 amendment to the Cherokee Constitution violated the Treaty and was therefore unlawful.

The Court explicitly rejected the Cherokee Nation's argument that citizenship in the Nation is conferred solely by the Cherokee Constitution and is therefore subject to amendment. Instead, it held that the Cherokee have the right to determine their own membership and to change their membership criteria, but any changes must accord the rights conferred to the Freedmen by the 1866 Treaty.

Should tribes be able to decide for themselves who their members are? Should there be a required blood quantum or racial element to tribal membership, or could the tribe adopt anyone as a member and make them an Indian? Should a tribe be able to change its membership provision such that it is able to disenroll some of its members? Do individual Indians have a claim to tribal membership that should supersede the ability of tribal governments to decide membership criteria? These are difficult questions.

Disenrollment continues to be a pressing issue for Indian tribes. See if you can find some recent examples of disputes over the disenrollment of members. What is motivating this movement in Indian country? For an excellent and comprehensive discussion of the role of race, tribal sovereignty, and membership *see* Gabriel Galanda and Ryan Dreveskracht, *Curing the Tribal Disenrollment Epidemic: In Search of a Remedy*, 57 Ariz. L. Rev. 383 (2015).

3. *Birthright Citizenship*: In her discussion of racial policy and American Indians Professor Berger provides some discussion of Indian citizenship, noting that some states did not repeal their laws prohibiting Indians from voting until the mid-twentieth century. However the Fifteenth Amendment, enacted in 1870, says that "The right of citizens of the United States to vote shall not be denied or abridged by the United States or by any State on account of race, color, or previous condition of servitude." Despite the Fifteenth Amendment, Indians were denied the right to vote because they were not deemed "citizens" of the United States.

The Fourteenth Amendment says in part that "All persons born or naturalized in the United States and subject to the jurisdiction thereof, are citizens of the United States and of the State wherein they reside." But in *Elk v. Wilkins* (1884) the Supreme Court declared that Indians were not subject to the jurisdiction of the United States when they were born, and therefore are not entitled to birthright citizenship: "Indians ... although in a geographical sense born in the United States, are no more 'born in the United States and subject to the jurisdiction thereof,' within the meaning of the first section of the Fourteenth Amendment, than the children of subjects of any foreign government born within the domain of that government, or the children born within the United States, of ambassadors or other public ministers of foreign nations." Uniquely, under *Elk v. Wilkins* Indians are not entitled to birthright citizenship.

Elk v. Wilkins has never been overturned. Instead, as Professor Berger documents, all Indians were made citizens by an Act of Congress – the Indian Citizenship Act of 1924. While it is doubtful that the case would be upheld today, do you think it is meaningful that technically American citizenship is conferred upon American Indians by congressional statute while for most other Americans citizenship is conferred by birth under the Fourteenth Amendment? Is this different treatment on the basis of race?

4. *Morton v. Mancari*: Interestingly, the Supreme Court has rejected the "racial" status of Indians in the context of at least some governmental preferences. In *Morton v. Mancari* the Court was asked whether a policy at the Bureau of Indian Affairs which gave preference to American Indians for hiring and promotion constituted unlawful racial discrimination against non-Indian employees. The Supreme Court said it did not, because the preference was directed at those who were enrolled members of federally recognized tribes, a political rather than racial status:

> Contrary to the characterization made by appellees, this preference does not constitute "racial discrimination." Indeed, it is not even a "racial" preference. Rather, it is an employment criterion reasonably designed to further the cause of Indian self-government and to make the BIA more responsive to the needs of its constituent groups. It is directed to participation by the governed in the governing agency. *** The preference, as applied, is granted to Indians not as a discrete racial group, but, rather, as members of quasi-sovereign tribal entities whose lives and activities are governed by the BIA in a unique fashion.

Would Professor Berger approve of the outcome of *Mancari* whereby the Court recognizes all Indians together in a single racial group, yet also each a part of their own respective Indian tribe? From a more normative perspective, should the Court have treated membership in an Indian tribe as a 'political' instead of racial category in order to avoid the application of tougher constitutional standards which make it exceedingly difficult to treat people differently on the basis of their race?

5. *Historical Construction of Race*: Berger talks in several places about the different racial histories of African Americans and American Indians. The "One Drop Rule" suggested that an individual with any ancestor descended from sub-Saharan Africa should be considered racially Black. The treatment for American Indians was often more nuanced. For example, Virginia enacted the Racial Integrity Act of 1924 which adopted what became known as the "Pocahontas Exception" permitting some with small amounts of American Indian ancestry to still be considered white:

> It shall thereafter be unlawful for any white person in this State to marry any save a white person, or a person with no other admixture of blood than white and American Indian. For the purpose of this act, *** persons who have one-sixteenth or less of the blood of the American Indian and have no other non-Caucasic blood shall be deemed to be white persons.

Why might Virginia have treated American Indians differently than other racial groups when creating laws based on race? For additional discussion of the "Pocahontas Exception" *see* Kevin Noble Maillard, *The Pocahontas Exception: The Exemption of American Indian Ancestry from Racial Purity Law*, 12 Mich. J. Race and Law, 351 (2007).

6. *Beyond the Law*: There is no shortage of applications to the questions of race and racism found outside the law. For example, Carolyn Liebler from the University of Minnesota writes about American Indian self-identification during the US Census. *American Indian Ethnic Identity: Tribal Nonresponse in the 1990 Census*, 85 Social Science Quarterly 310 (2004). Dr. Liebler concludes that as many as 11 percent of American Indians do not identify themselves as racially Indian on the census, and determined that Indians were less likely to identify as such if they lived in states with smaller Indian populations, did not speak a native language or live with someone who could, and if they themselves had only a weak understanding of what it meant to be Indian.

Taking a more theoretical approach, Philip Deloria suggests in *Playing Indian* (Yale University Press 1999) that Indian identity goes far beyond race. There is something that has always attracted non-Indian Americans to the "Indian." Deloria traces Indian identity back to the Boston Tea Party, where revolutionary colonists dressed as Indians to throw tea into the bay; "In the early years of the new nation [colonists]

used Indianness to wed themselves to an essential American nationalism." Deloria contends that "[p]laying Indian encouraged people to
reject the stories and language that helped structure the common sense
of everyday life." Do you think that being "Indian" must have a racial
component, or is there something cultural or even countercultural
about Indian identity that permits it to transcend race?

FURTHER READING

- Gregory Ablasky, *Making Indians "White": The Judicial Abolition of Native Slavery in
Revolutionary Virginia and Its Racial Legacy*, 159 U. Pa. L. Rev. 1457 (2011).
- Bethany Berger, *"Power over This Unfortunate Race": Race, Politics and Indian Law in
United States v. Rogers*, 45 Wm. & Mary L. Rev. 1957 (2004).
- Matthew L. M. Fletcher, *Race and American Indian Tribal Nationhood*, 11 Wyo. L. Rev.
295 (2011).
- Carole Goldberg, *Not "Strictly" Racial: A Response to Indians as Peoples*, 39 UCLA L. Rev.
169 (1991).
- Sarah Krakoff, *Inextricably Political: Race, Membership, and Tribal Sovereignty*, 87
Wash. L. Rev. 1041 (2012).
- Carla Pratt, *Tribal Kulturkampf: The Role of Race Ideology in Constructing Native Ameri-
can Identity*, 36 Seton Hall L. Rev. 1241 (2006).
- Addie Rolnick, *The Promise of Mancari: Indian Political Rights As Racial Remedy*, 86 NYU
L. Rev. 958 (2011).
- Natsu Taylor Saito, *Race and Decolonization: Whiteness As Property in the American Settler
Colonial Project*, 31 Harv. J. Racial & Ethnic Just. 31 (2015).
- Paul Spruhan, *Indian As Race/Indian As Political Status: Implementation of the Half-Blood
Requirement under the Indian Reorganization Act, 1934–1945*, 8 Rutgers Race & L. Rev.
27 (2006).
- Gloria Valencia-Weber, *Racial Equality: Old and New Strains and American Indians*, 80
Notre Dame L. Rev. 333 (2005).
- Rose Cuison Villazor, *Blood Quantum Land Laws and the Race versus Political Identity
Dilemma*, 96 Cal. L. Rev. 801 (2004).
- Robert A. Williams, Jr., *Columbus' Legacy: Law as an Instrument of Racial Discrimination
against Indigenous Peoples' Rights of Self-Determination*, 8 Ariz. J. Int'l & Comp. L. 51
(1991).

4

(Tribal) Sovereignty and Illiberalism

Angela R. Riley

95 Cal. L. Rev. 799 (2007)

The US Constitution is not binding upon Indian tribal governments. Chief Justice Roberts put it bluntly: "Tribal sovereignty, it should be remembered, is 'a sovereignty outside the basic structure of the Constitution.' The Bill of Rights does not apply to Indian tribes." Plains Commerce Bank v. Long Family Land & Cattle Co. *Congress has long been concerned about this omission. In 1968 it enacted the Indian Civil Rights Act to require tribal governments to extend to tribal members some, but not all, of the rights guaranteed to individuals by the Constitution. Since then Indians and tribes have often disagreed in federal courts about the appropriate amount of judicial oversight or deference the federal system ought to bestow upon tribal activity. Recently federal courts have been less deferential, questioning whether they ought to sit as tribal appellate courts and commenting with increasing levels of disapproval upon tribal actions which limit the rights of individuals in order to maintain or promote culturally based tribal law.*

In this piece Angela Riley directly confronts the conflict between tribal sovereignty and illiberalism. She suggests that if federal courts are to remain faithful to the principles of tribal sovereignty, then they must defer to the decisions of tribal courts even when those decisions create tensions with existing legal norms. Riley endeavors to show how tribal governments occasionally need to act illiberally (or at least in a manner which is perceived as illiberal) in order to create systems and structures which are culturally responsive to the needs of tribal communities. She recognizes that illiberal tribal governance may implicate traditional justice systems, conceptions of gender, and even produce theocratic government – but that ultimately these seemingly illiberal institutions make tribal communities stronger. In the end, Riley places her faith in tribes to govern themselves without the imposition of normative values imposed by nonmembers who dangerously claim the right to review the actions of tribal actors.

As you read the following piece pay careful attention in the Introduction and throughout the first section as Riley defines the tension that exists between sovereignty and illiberalism. Try to articulate for yourself what she means when she says that some tribal actions are illiberal. Why is tolerance for illiberal action perceived as beneficial for tribal sovereignty? What is the conflict between the rights of individuals and tribal self-government? Do you have any concerns that a tribe's cultural, commercial, and governmental functions may be adversely impacted by an illiberal tribal government? Ultimately, are you persuaded by the benefits of illiberalism for Indian tribes, or do you believe that tribes should follow the same cultural and legal norms that exist in the states?

INTRODUCTION

Liberalism has a problem. Individual autonomy is its critical core, but pluralism remains a prominent tenet. This means that liberalism must navigate the sometimes treacherous course between upholding individual rights and accommodating a diverse array of cultures and organizations. Liberalism is challenged by this endeavor, particularly when individual rights are exercised in communities that espouse illiberal conceptions of the good.

This philosophical tension has manifested in very concrete intrusions on American Indians' tribal sovereignty. On the one hand, tribal sovereignty guards Indian nations' inherent right to live and govern beyond the reach of the dominant society. This "measured separatism" embodies liberalism's commitment to accommodating pluralism. On the other hand, critics charge that imposing liberalism onto Indian nations is necessary to prevent intrusions on individual rights by tribal governments. For these scholars, individual liberty must always take precedence over Indian nations' sovereignty and autonomy.

American Indian tribes have long been a subject of concern for the dominant society, particularly because Indian tribes are the only governmental bodies within the United States not bound by the US Bill of Rights. Unease over tribes' extra-constitutional status motivated Congress to enact the Indian Civil Rights Act (ICRA) in 1968, which extends provisions similar to those contained in the US Bill of Rights to Indian tribes. But ICRA has not alleviated concerns over potential violations of civil liberties by tribal governments. In fact, these concerns intensified after the Supreme Court's ruling in *Santa Clara Pueblo v. Martinez*, which limited federal court review of ICRA claims to habeas corpus petitions and left the interpretation and enforcement of the other ICRA protections to tribal courts. As a result, the Court upheld the Pueblo's authority to maintain its own membership rules, even though those rules discriminated against the children of women – but not of men – who married outside the Pueblo.

Today, scholars who critique the (sometimes merely perceived) illiberal actions of tribal governments point to *Santa Clara Pueblo* as evidence of the need for increased federal control over tribes and diminished tribal autonomy. And now it appears that the judiciary may be taking heed. Though *Santa Clara Pueblo* has never been overruled, there is evidence that federal courts are growing increasingly concerned over alleged civil rights violations by tribal governments and are seeking ways to intervene under ICRA even though the issue of federal court review of non–habeas corpus ICRA claims has long been settled.

Scholars have extensively debated to what extent liberal societies ought to accommodate illiberal groups, if at all. But in this Article I seek to address and fully examine another question concerning illiberalism, one related specifically to American Indian tribes: that is, to what extent are Indian tribes free to govern illiberally? As a descriptive matter, what is US law and policy concerning illiberal actions undertaken by the "domestic dependent nations"? And normatively, how should Indian tribal sovereignty inform US judicial and political reactions to the illiberal practices of these extra-constitutional governments? Answers to the questions raised here are critical, not only to Indian nations' sovereignty, but also to American democracy. And they must be confronted. With over 500 federally recognized Indian tribes in the United States, conflicts between individual tribal members and their tribal governments will continue to arise. Accordingly, it is imperative to examine – both descriptively and normatively – the scope and extent of federal power to intervene in purely intra-tribal disputes. ***

I ILLIBERALISM AND US LAW

A *Defining "Illiberalism"*

*** Though definitional concerns persist, illiberalism has taken on a generally accepted meaning. Illiberal groups are those that "simply assign particular roles and duties to people, and prevent people from questioning or revising them." Such immutable status is often placed on certain sub-groups – such as women, low-ranking social castes, and racial and ethnic minorities – where individuals are treated as "members of more and less respect-worthy natural kinds." As a result, many illiberal groups "are structured along patriarchal, theological, racist, classist or homophobic lines." For example, because of its gender-based rule excluding women from the priesthood, the Roman Catholic Church constitutes an example of an illiberal organization. ***

Even where a particular culture is characterized as illiberal – remembering that all cultures contain both liberal and illiberal strains – many scholars contend it may nevertheless be tolerated as long as the members enjoy the freedoms of exit (opt-out rights) and dissent (voice). If these rights are available, even groups advocating values at odds with liberal societies should retain wide latitude to maintain illiberal structures and practices. This is because allowing illiberal groups to exist within the liberal state advances liberalism's commitment to pluralism and personal liberty by providing individuals "with a diversity of options among communities." Thus, if a member is displeased with a particular group, she may simply opt out if she so chooses. Within this theoretical structure, a group such as the Boy Scouts of America, which discriminates against gays, but allows members to voice dissent and exit at will, is tolerable. But those that silence dissenting voices, or prevent members from opting out entirely, are beyond the bounds of liberalism's accommodation. The Taliban, which has been called "the most extreme instance of the self-conscious, intentional repression of women's rights anywhere in the modern world," serves as one such example.

Despite the widely-accepted views of classical liberalism, recent world events like the global rise in religious fundamentalism and an increased focus on the plight of women living under oppressive, patriarchal regimes have fueled arguments against accommodating illiberal groups, even those that freely allow members to voice dissent and exit at will. This is due, in part, to liberal scholars' skepticism regarding opt-out rights. They often contend that even where exit is not legally proscribed, its costs may be prohibitively high, or the right to opt out may be altogether illusory.

***

As they advance their claims, critics oftentimes neglect to acknowledge the important legal differences that distinguish the vast array of illiberal groups situated within the United States. Thus, the following section provides a brief overview of US law regarding illiberal groups, and then explains in greater detail how federal law relates, specifically, to the inner workings of sovereign Indian nations.

B *Indian Tribes and US Law*

The US Bill of Rights applies directly against the federal government and indirectly against the states via the Due Process Clause of the Fourteenth Amendment. Thus, federal, state, and local governments are all constitutionally prohibited from acting illiberally. In contrast, the freedom of (illiberal) association is constitutionally protected as a fundamental right under the First Amendment. As a result, most examples of illiberal practices within the United States – such as the Boy Scouts' decision to exclude gays – occur within the private sector, where organizations retain some leeway to act in ways that contradict principles of formal equality. In regard to illiberalism within the private sphere, the Supreme Court has delineated a "gradient of protectable expression with two diametrically opposed poles represented by political or intimate associations on the one hand (high levels of protection) and economic associations on the other (little or no protection)." Organizations situated somewhere between these two extremes – such as the Jaycees, a private social club with a quasi-commercial purpose – receive an intermediate level of protection.

Indian tribes are anomalous within this system. Unlike states, tribes are not bound by the US Bill of Rights. At the same time, tribes possess rights and responsibilities unique to their sovereign status, which also means they cannot be directly analogized to private clubs. Because the US Bill of Rights neither applies to nor limits domestic tribal nations, tribes cannot be encompassed in the "usual constitutional dialogue" of individual rights. Tribal sovereignty necessarily situates Indian nations beyond the federal-state paradigm that dominates individual civil liberties discourse within the US. In fact, the constitutional position of tribes – and their corresponding freedom to act beyond the scope of the US Bill of Rights in matters pertaining to individual civil liberties – prompted Congress to pass ICRA in 1968.

1 The Indian Civil Rights Act

The American civil rights movement of the 1960s inspired reformers to transform tribal governments. Senator Sam Ervin of North Carolina led this endeavor, introducing bills in Congress designed to extend constitutional protections to individual Indians via an Indian Bill of Rights. Ervin's aide, a Lumbee Indian, was partially responsible for inspiring Ervin's work on the bill. Ervin viewed the Lumbee tribe – an Indian nation that lacked a communal land base and had significantly assimilated into mainstream society – as a positive model for other tribes. When Ervin learned that the US Bill of Rights did not apply to individual Indians subject to the control of tribal governments, he commented that such a notion was "alien to popular concepts of American jurisprudence." Ervin thus sought to ensure that tribal governments offered protections to individual Indians similar to those enjoyed by citizens living under federal, state, and local governments.

Though much debate surrounded the initial bills, Congress succeeded in enacting ICRA as a rider to the Civil Rights Act of 1964. In language closely tracking the US Bill of Rights, the Act sets forth rights guaranteed to individual Indians vis-à-vis tribal governments, including the free exercise of religion and many of the protections guaranteed in the criminal process. Notably, ICRA also extends to individual Indians the right to equal protection and due process, as well as the writ of habeas corpus. Even though the Act closely mimics the US Bill of Rights in many respects, Congress nevertheless declined to apply the full complement of constitutional restraints to Indian tribes to further its two "distinct and competing purposes" in enacting ICRA: (1) to strengthen the position of individual tribal members within tribal governments and (2) to promote the well-established federal policy of furthering Indian self-government. Accordingly, Congress declined to extend to tribes the requirement of grand jury indictment, jury trials in civil cases, and the right to counsel for indigent defendants. Perhaps most importantly, Congress acceded to the desires of tribal elders and removed restrictions regarding tribal establishment of religion.

Whether Congress intended to authorize federal court review of ICRA claims was critical to questions surrounding the Act's enforcement. More than ten years after ICRA's passage, the Supreme Court resolved this issue in *Santa Clara Pueblo v. Martinez*, ruling that Congress intended to limit federal court review of ICRA claims to habeas corpus petitions, leaving all other ICRA claims within the jurisdictional purview of tribal forums.

2 *Santa Clara Pueblo v. Martinez*

Though Indian tribes have long been culturally and legally distinct from mainstream Americans, their status as (potentially) illiberal groups gained popular attention about thirty years ago, when the US Supreme Court decided the now infamous case of *Santa Clara Pueblo v. Martinez*. *Santa Clara Pueblo* involved a dispute over the membership status of the children of Julia Martinez, a member of the Pueblo, and her husband, Myles Martinez, a Navajo Nation citizen. A 1939 Santa Clara Pueblo membership ordinance states that children of men who marry outside the

Pueblo are eligible for tribal membership, but children of women who marry outside the Pueblo are not. Martinez attempted to persuade the tribe to change its membership rule in hopes of enrolling her children in the Pueblo. When unsuccessful, Martinez and her daughter filed an ICRA lawsuit against the tribe and its governor in federal district court. In her suit, Martinez sought to invalidate the 1939 membership ordinance and require the Pueblo to include her children as members.

Justice Thurgood Marshall wrote for the majority, ultimately concluding that federal courts lack authority to hear any ICRA claims other than habeas corpus petitions. Focusing on the purposes behind ICRA and the Pueblo's right to self-determination and continued traditional existence, the Court noted that ICRA's provisions were "similar, but not identical, to those contained in the Bill of Rights." It reasoned that, as compared with federal courts, the tribal courts were better situated to give effect to ICRA provisions consistent with traditional tribal norms and governance structures. In regards to membership decisions, the Court acknowledged that such determinations lay at the core of tribal self-government and that the Pueblo people are in the best position to determine what it means to be Santa Claran. Additionally, as Marshall pointed out, ICRA claims should be heard in tribal forums which "have repeatedly been recognized as appropriate forums for the exclusive adjudication of disputes affecting important personal and property interests of both Indians and non-Indians." The Court made no exception for tribes vesting judicial authority in a nonjudicial entity – such as a tribal council like in the Santa Clara Pueblo – calling such fora "competent law-applying bodies." As such, the Supreme Court affirmed what Congress recognized in passing ICRA: intra-tribal disputes are best left within the purview of the tribal courts.

Much of the Court's rationale rested on its faith in tribal dispute forums and its corresponding concern over the competency of the federal courts to decide issues critical to tribal governance. Marshall revealed great unease at the prospect of authorizing the federal courts to adjudicate disputes within Indian tribes, maintaining that to do so would threaten the survival of the tribal community as a distinct group. The Court stated: "Resolution of statutory issues under [ICRA] ... will frequently depend on questions of tribal tradition and custom which tribal forums may be in a better position to evaluate than federal courts." Furthermore, "efforts by the federal judiciary to apply [ICRA] ... may substantially interfere with a tribe's ability to maintain itself as a culturally and politically distinct entity." Accordingly, the Court construed ICRA narrowly. It held federal court review appropriate for habeas corpus violations alone as expressly provided for in the statute, reasoning that a contrary holding would undermine Congress's purpose of protecting tribal sovereignty and tribal self-government.

Santa Clara Pueblo caused a furor. By deferring to tribal sovereignty and denying federal court review, the Supreme Court allowed the Santa Clara Pueblo to continue determining membership pursuant to sexually discriminatory rules.

Mainstream feminists strongly criticized the result, while Indian scholars retorted with passionate pro-sovereignty arguments. With few compromises put forth, reconciliation between the camps has never been fully realized. *Santa Clara Pueblo* was certainly not the beginning of the schism between liberal theorists advocating for the primacy of individual rights and Indian scholars arguing for adherence to tribal sovereignty's "measured separatism." But in many instances this case drew liberal theorists' attention to Indian country for the first time, prompting a critique of tribal governments based on – oftentimes largely and singularly – one very public case.

C *Dissatisfaction with ICRA and* Santa Clara Pueblo

In 1996, nearly two decades after *Santa Clara Pueblo*, the Second Circuit Court of Appeals opened the door to broader federal court review of ICRA claims in *Poodry v. Tonawanda Band of Seneca Indians*. Plaintiffs were members of the Council of Chiefs for the Tonawanda Band of Seneca Indians who broke away from the tribe's legislative body in protest over alleged tribal law violations by other Council members. After Plaintiffs formed a competing government, the Council stripped them of their tribal citizenship and banished them from the tribe's territory. Plaintiffs brought suit in federal district court and made the unique argument that exclusion from the reservation provided a basis for a writ of habeas corpus under ICRA.

Though the district court dismissed the claim on the grounds that banishment did not trigger ICRA's habeas corpus provision, on appeal the Second Circuit considered whether the banishment constituted a "detention by order of an Indian tribe." The court emphasized that the plaintiffs had no access to review within the tribal community, so that "if the reasoning of *Santa Clara Pueblo* foreclosed federal habeas jurisdiction, the petitioners had no remedy whatsoever." Viewing the case through this lens, the Second Circuit decided the banishment constituted a criminal rather than civil sanction, meeting the first requirement for habeas review. Then, turning to the statute, the court acknowledged that "detention" for purposes of ICRA could be met by either physical imprisonment or "severe ... actual or potential 'restraints on liberty.'" Concluding that the banishment constituted a severe restraint on liberty, the Second Circuit held that federal court jurisdiction of Plaintiffs' ICRA claim was proper.

Poodry was monumental. It marked a change in the landscape of external review over intra-tribal matters, and its effects have been felt all across Indian country. Post-*Poodry*, federal courts are again grappling with the once-settled question of federal judicial review of ICRA claims. In *Quair v. Sisco*, for example, a federal district court in California relied on *Poodry* to allow federal court jurisdiction over plaintiffs' banishment and disenrollment claims against the Santa Rosa Rancheria Tachi Indian Tribe. Calling *Poodry* "authoritative" on the issue, the court held that the disenrollment and banishment of tribal members constituted "detention" under ICRA's habeas provision, authorizing federal court review of their claims.

Since *Poodry*, some federal courts have swiftly dismissed detention-based ICRA claims, even after applying its broad reasoning. But in another class of ICRA cases, decisions to decline federal court review of ICRA claims appear more complicated and potentially problematic. In these cases, courts have declined to authorize federal court review of tribal courts' ICRA decisions, but nevertheless express serious concern about tribal courts' exclusive jurisdiction over civil rights claims. In some instances these opinions convey judges' angst over evidence of potential abuses by tribal governments and urge Congress or the Supreme Court to intervene.

Poodry and its progeny manifest the concerns raised by the Supreme Court's pro-sovereignty decision in *Santa Clara Pueblo*; that is, that rogue tribal governments are engaging in unchecked violations of individual civil liberties. In this sense, these cases embody fears brewing since first contact between Europeans and Natives; namely, that Indian tribal governance is simply too far afield from Western liberalism to be tolerated. While the *Poodry* line of cases represents the real-world application of that belief, the illiberalism literature, discussed below, embodies its theoretical component. ***

II UNDERSTANDING TRIBAL SOVEREIGNTY

As the illiberalism literature reflects, *Santa Clara Pueblo* – and the corresponding perception of tribes as illiberal – retains a great deal of influence and continues to stir controversy. With stakes in tribal membership increasing due to a few tribes' rapidly changing economic circumstances, tribal governments are subject to greater scrutiny now than they have been for decades. Thus, it is critical for Indian nations' continued sovereign existence that outsiders understand both the historical foundations and contemporary expressions of tribal sovereignty.

***

1 Recognizing Tribal Sovereignty

Before the United States was even formed, and for many years since, treaties have governed the relationship between the Indian nations and colonial powers. And the authority to make treaties lies exclusively with nation-states. Thus, treatment of Indian nations as sovereigns, both in a historical and legal sense, is virtually indisputable, "given the long track record of diplomatic interaction between the European colonial governments and the Indian nations." Through treaty formation, tribal nations became participants in a sovereign-to-sovereign relationship with the colonial powers, which took on the role of protector of Indian tribes. Treaties with Indian nations spanned a wide variety of topics, including resolving boundary disputes, delineating hunting and fishing rights, and establishing peace between sovereigns. In the peace treaties in particular, tribes often ceded land and certain political rights to the dominant government, but reserved all rights not expressly ceded. The "reserved rights" rule of Indian treaty interpretation makes clear that the colonial powers did not grant rights to the Indians via treaty, but accepted cessions of rights from the Indians, who retained those rights not granted. This doctrine reveals much about Indian sovereignty: "Because tribal sovereignty is understood as being retained from a tribe's inherent, preconstitutional sovereignty rather than consisting of delegated power, the exercise of this sovereignty does not entail any federal or state action that would trigger the Constitution." Even though Congress ended treaty-making in the late 1800s, the reserved rights rule of treaty interpretation was substantiated by an early Supreme Court case and is still employed today.

In addition to treaty-making, the US Constitution also confirms the sovereign status of Indian tribes. At the time of the Constitution's creation, Indian nations were already established in the US and exercised inherent sovereignty over their people and territories. Thus, the US Constitution, which has never been amended to formally incorporate tribal governments into the federal-state system, does not regulate the conduct of Indian tribal governments. Even so, the Constitution expressly mentions Indian tribes three times. Specifically, it empowers Congress to regulate commerce with the Indian nations and authorizes both the President and the Senate to make treaties with them. ***

Finally, Congress also has reinforced and reinvigorated conceptions of Indian self-government. The 1934 Indian Reorganization Act is particularly significant, as it renewed congressional support for tribal self-governance and ended a policy period specifically geared toward assimilation of tribal peoples into US culture and government. Congress has passed other important legislation on behalf of Indian tribes as well. For example, the Indian Child Welfare Act of 1978 gave tribal communities control over the adoption of Indian children, and the Native American Graves Protection and Repatriation Act safeguards the human remains, sacred objects, and cultural patrimony of indigenous peoples. These laws, and others, reaffirm the federal government's commitment to act in furtherance of tribal rights and reinforce federal policy supporting Indian self-determination and self-government. ***

B *Tribal Sovereignty in Practice*

Tribal sovereignty touches virtually every component of tribal life within Indian country. Each day, hundreds of Indian tribes affirm the existence of tribal sovereignty through real and tangible everyday actions that span every facet of life, from the most basic and fundamental – birth, death, marriage, divorce, and prayer – to the most sophisticated and specialized – policing members, resolving disputes, and incarcerating law-breakers. While it is not my intention to lay out every facet of tribal governance or undertake a comprehensive empirical analysis, I do seek to show how tribal sovereignty manifests in three core components of Indian tribes' sovereign existence: tribal cultural, commercial, and governmental functions.

1 Cultural Functions

Indian tribes embody the most basic cultural unit in the human experience: they are, in many respects, families. Tribes are bound by bloodlines, clan affiliations, and kinship, with ancestry or descent often constituting the dominant factor in determining tribal membership. Family structure is a defining characteristic of tribal life. Even the political loyalties of individual Indians are often shaped around these identifiers.

Within tribal nations, the family structure also facilitates the formation of intricate social networks. Since many families trace their tribal roots back dozens of generations, tribal nations tend to be composed of groups of people – usually organized by family or clan – that have interacted with each other consistently for centuries. This long-standing social structure is deeply embedded within tribal nations and serves as the framework within which tribal people socialize, marry, worship, and feud. Given the closely knit nature of tribal communities, some scholars suggest that tribal cultures and Indian governance systems would suffer severely if civil rights protections are interpreted to apply to tribal governments just as they apply to the federal and state governments. ***

Indian tribes also serve as repositories for unique, ancient, and valuable indigenous knowledge that is kept alive by the continued existence of these threatened cultures. With vast differences between them, indigenous peoples possess working knowledge of tribally-specific pre-contact religions, medicinal remedies, burial traditions, and sacred practices. Hundreds of ancient languages and ceremonies are kept alive in flourishing, functioning tribal communities. These aspects of cultural identity are inextricably linked with tribal sovereignty. For example, in tribes that have consistently maintained separateness and sovereign authority within their aboriginal homelands – thus avoiding some of the losses that occurred through programs of assimilation and removal – tribal members are more likely to speak their native language and practice pre-contact religion. These tribal governments are also in a better position to develop and expand governance systems that are dependent on tribal custom and tradition. Thus, for tribes, political, territorial, and cultural sovereignty are intimately linked and mutually reinforcing.

2 Commercial Functions

For decades, Indian tribes have owned and operated tribal businesses as sovereigns. Though the popular perception of Indian commerce centers on the casino, in reality tribes have long engaged in a plethora of commercial enterprises. Tribes own auto-parts plants, timber management services, printing businesses, mills, grocery stores, golf courses, banks, and ski resorts, to name a few. Tribes are also actively engaged in media outreach to their members and surrounding communities, investing in newspapers, radio stations, and commercial telecommunications ventures.

Undoubtedly, the gaming industry has helped to further expand tribal holdings. Today, tribes cater to their visiting guests – both Indian and non-Indian – by developing hotels, resorts, restaurants, and other tourist attractions. In fact, gaming tribes alone contributed $32 billion in revenue, $12.4 billion in wages, and 490,000 jobs to the US economy in 2001. And those numbers are clearly growing. Some tribes have expanded commercial enterprises to the point that they are now among the largest employers in the regions or states in which they're situated.

Tribal sovereignty and tribal economic development are intertwined in a myriad of ways. The power to tax and regulate commerce on the reservation – powers reserved to sovereigns – generates income necessary for tribes to fulfill basic governmental functions, thus keeping tribal members engaged in tribal life. Such development also has allowed tribes to recover aboriginal territory lost after contact with Europeans. These lands are used to rebuild tribal communities, some of which included only a handful of members and a tiny or non-existent land base in the post-contact period. Finally, economic development has also enabled tribes to revitalize their traditional cultures, as generated income has been used to build tribal museums, restore indigenous languages, and repurchase once lost sacred lands.

3 Governmental Functions

Like all sovereigns, Indian tribes are governments. As such, tribes provide members a panoply of goods and services. Although these benefits vary by tribe, an Indian living with her tribe may have available to her housing and housing assistance (both on and off the reservation), health care benefits, education (from pre-school to the graduate level), and day care facilities owned and operated by the tribal government. With tribally owned gas stations, banks, grocery stores, fitness centers, gift shops, printing presses, newspapers and radio stations, tribal members oftentimes access all their daily necessities through tribal government or tribal enterprises. For an Indian who lives, works, socializes, exercises, and worships on a reservation, there is no other government that has a larger role in her day to day life than her tribe.

Tribal sovereignty and self-governance translates into tribes' legal authority. Most tribes enact, enforce, and live by their own tribal laws (either oral or codified), which apply to all tribal members. Criminal laws are usually enforced by tribal police, who may be cross-deputized with state or local law enforcement officials. Some tribes employ prosecutors who try crimes committed by Indians on the reservation. Disputes are resolved through indigenous justice systems that, in some cases, deviate significantly from Anglo-style courts. In some, tribal councils fill this role, while others rely on elders or clan leaders to settle disputes. There are a growing number of tribal courts in place to hear disputes – between both members and non-members – that arise on the reservation. Tribal courts vary widely in their structure: trial courts, appellate courts, Peacemaker courts, talking circles, drug courts, and specialized courts for domestic violence or child custody matters can all be found in Indian country. Among the tribal nations' many lawmaking functions are those reserved specifically for sovereigns: namely, the power to arrest, prosecute, and incarcerate those who break their laws. Along with the authority to exile and exclude, these are perhaps the most important powers of the tribal nations as sovereign entities.

III ASSESSING THE COSTS OF ICRA'S EXPANSION

Tribes are not only anomalous as compared to the federal and state governments; there is a vast range of governance systems within tribal communities as well. There are over 500 federally recognized Indian tribes in the United States, including Alaska, which contains over 200 tribal villages. Indian nations create, maintain, and are bound by their own tribal laws, which vary greatly from one community to another. Like the states and the federal government, many tribes follow a written constitution that serves as the paramount governing document and source for many tribal rights. Others govern without a written constitution, sometimes relying on codified law or legal custom passed down orally. Tribal leadership may be concentrated in a lone individual, or distributed among clans, families, or tribal councils. Some have laws and structures intentionally kept secret from the dominant society as required by tradition and religion or as part of a concerted effort to insulate some facets of tribal life from outside interference.

Critics of tribal sovereignty tend to overlook the vast spectrum of legal systems and practices found within Indian communities, and consequently fail to consider the consequences of homogenizing tribal governance. Some theorists endorse third-party intervention in tribal communities without acknowledging that such proposals will essentially require tribal cultures to become mirror images of the dominant society. Short of the wholesale application of federal law, federal courts have no clear rubric to decide which tribal rules constitute "illiberal" violations that "buttress the hegemony of cultural elites" and which ones are palatable. ***

Illiberalism within tribal communities is complicated and nuanced. Some nations are structured along matrilineal lines while others are patrilineal. Some tribes historically accepted transvestite, or berdache, members, while others have adopted the majority society's viewpoint and are now banning gay marriage. Some tribes retain traditional, pre-Columbian, theocratic structures, while others allow the entanglement of religion and government in the interest of furthering fundamentalist Christianity.

The continued recognition of tribal sovereignty and tribes' right of self-determination currently protects tribal laws and structures against a full-scale attack by the dominant society. There are two safeguards at work, functioning together to guard against ICRA becoming an entirely assimilative force. First, not all provisions of the US Bill of Rights were included in ICRA. Thus, certain provisions – like the

Establishment Clause – do not apply to tribal governments. Expanding ICRA to include all the US Bill of Rights provisions would eliminate the existing structure of selective application, ultimately subverting core tribal values. Second, tribal courts retain interpretive authority over ICRA provisions and need not interpret them "jot for jot" with federal courts. In other words, Indian tribes are authorized and encouraged to apply ICRA's provisions consistent with tribal values and traditions. In the absence of these safeguards, core facets of indigenous peoples' cultural and political existence – such as indigenous justice systems, gender-based systems of governance, and tribal theocracies – are at risk.

A *Indigenous Justice Systems*

Indigenous justice systems constitute the facet of tribal governance most vulnerable to destruction from an expansion of ICRA. In fact, even at the time that the initial civil rights bill was first introduced, testimony and debate surrounding the proposed Act revealed tribal leaders' fear that further federal encroachment into intra-tribal matters would wipe out Indian justice systems. During discussions on the proposed bill, tribal leaders' testimony focused on the importance of protecting traditional tribal dispute resolution methods. They emphasized the inconsistencies between the Anglo and Indian worldviews in regards to law and justice. For example, the Ute and Hopi Tribes noted:

> The defendants' standard of integrity in many Indian courts is much higher than in the State and Federal Courts of the United States. When requested to enter a plea to a charge the Indian defendant, standing before respected tribal judicial leaders, with complete candor usually discloses the facts. With mutual honesty and through the dictates of experience, the Indian judge often takes a statement of innocence at face value, discharging the defendant who has indeed, according to tribal custom, been placed in jeopardy. The same Indian defendants in off-reservation courts soon learn to play the game of "white man's justice," guilty persons entering pleas of not guilty merely to throw the burden of proof upon the prosecution. From their viewpoint it is not an elevating experience. We are indeed fearful that the decisions of Federal and State Courts, in the light of non-Indian experience, interpreting "testifying against oneself" would stultify an honorable Indian practice . . .

This testimony conveys concerns still relevant today. That is, if federal courts are authorized to review the practices and procedures of traditional tribal justice systems, they will have to reconcile these systems with mainstream constitutional principles. Such determinations are necessarily made within the context of the "non-Indian experience," compelling the courts to dismantle indigenous justice systems or practices inconsistent with mainstream constitutional law.

Other aspects of ICRA also raised concerns. Tribal leaders opposed the imposition of jury trials onto tribes, explaining that jury trials were seldom invoked by

Indian defendants, and tribal governments often viewed the jury process as inconsistent with tribal mores. The Pueblos explained:

> It [is] no more logical to use a jury system for the settlement of internal matters within the extended "family" that makes up a pueblo than it would be to use a similar system within the framework of an Anglo-American family as a means for enforcing internal rules or resolving internal disputes.

Other tribes, such as the Hopi and Ute felt similarly, and testified that "many accused Indian people feel they do not need a jury of peers to determine the facts already within the knowledge of the accused. The defendant enlightens a credulous court."

Statements by tribal leaders also emphasized the differences between the Anglo adversarial system and conceptions of justice within tribal nations. One Navajo leader explained that "it was difficult for Navajos to participate in a system where fairness required the judge to have no prior knowledge of the case, and where who can speak and what they can say are closely regulated." This is because Navajo conceptions of fairness and social harmony require full community involvement in each dispute and, in particular, the participation of elders and those knowledgeable about the matter. In the Navajo system, everyone is allowed to speak, and if private discussions with elders or decision-makers helps bring peace to the community, this is acceptable.

Perceptions of justice systems during the ICRA debates and now share a central theme: that the Anglo justice system is superior to indigenous ones. Indian leaders questioned this assumption at the time of the ICRA hearings, inquiring as to Congress's motivations in passing the Act. One tribal leader pressed this point, asking why tribes are not afforded "inalienable rights to be protected as our customs and traditions require" and why Congress saw fit to force Indians to "relinquish our right to self-government and submit to an alien code of reasoning that someone else knows better than we the safeguards of our sacred rights?" Another leader spoke about the majority society's failure to recognize the sophisticated and well-functioning Navajo legal system, emphasizing that Indian justice has long been viewed as "having nothing to contribute." He pointed out the ironic reality, that the Anglo judicial system had recently begun to emulate the indigenous methods of dispute resolution it had historically treated as inferior.

This testimony reflects Indian leaders' frustration with a majority legal system that historically devalued, misunderstood and trivialized indigenous justice systems. Furthermore, it highlights the inherent inconsistencies underlying further expansion of federal control over Indian tribes through ICRA; that is, the perception that some tribal practices deserve special protection, while others do not, and the framework pursuant to which such determinations are to be made is shifting. Tribal leaders feared broader federal power over tribal justice systems then, just as they do now. As Professor Alexander Tallchief Skibine argues, expanding ICRA to allow federal court review of tribal court decisions on purely intra-tribal matters will place every aspect of tribal governance – including membership decisions, election disputes, and freedoms of speech and religion – under the outside scrutiny of judges unfamiliar with tribal ways. Such a result will thwart the intentionally limited review authorized by ICRA, and will, as some scholars have warned, make tribal courts mere instrumentalities of the federal government.

This expansion may also jeopardize the existence of other indigenous justice systems that deviate from Anglo norms, such as talking circles, restorative justice processes, and consensus-building practices. Depending on the tribal court's utilization of particular procedures and/or interpretation of substantive law, these fora might impermissibly depart from federal constitutional law in a variety of ways. Informal resolution systems in which "everyone [is] allowed to speak," for example, may run afoul of procedural due process requirements. Similar problems may be raised by a system in which the decision-maker has prior knowledge of the dispute or is authorized to hold private conversations with the parties. Consider, for example, the Navajo Nation's Peacemaker court, which deviates in some significant respects from Anglo norms. The Peacemaker courts incorporate Navajo religion and ceremony in the dispute resolution process. Selected Peacemakers commence and conclude the proceedings with prayer, and participants call upon the supernatural to direct them in the reconciliation process. Peacemaking is effective for the Navajo precisely because it incorporates the Navajo worldview about the interconnectedness of the extraordinary (the sacred) and the ordinary (the secular) within its processes. However, despite its success – and its popularity – Peacemaking may be unable to withstand constitutional scrutiny. Even though Peacemaking is a "time-honoured procedure ensuring consensual decision-making" that promotes harmony, balance, and cultural continuity for the Navajo, it potentially could likely constitute an impermissible entanglement of religion and law by constitutional standards.

B *Traditional Gender-Based Systems of Governance*

Gender-based systems of governance – which may appear at first glance wholly incompatible with liberal conceptions of equality – are also vulnerable to destruction via ICRA's expansion. This is because some tribes maintain roles for men and women that are complementary and equal, but nevertheless fixed and immutable. For example, the Tonawanda Band of Seneca Indians – one of the six tribes comprising the Iroquois Confederacy – structures its government around eight clans. The clan system is matrilineally based and defines the cultural, social, and political aspects of tribal life, including how the tribe selects leaders. In this system, each clan selects a female Clan Mother by consensus. Together, the eight Clan Mothers appoint a man to serve as the tribe's chief. The Clan Mothers are vested with the authority to guide some of the Chief's actions, and may remove him if he fails to fulfill his duties. Because the clan system is fundamental to the selection of the Chief, women are held in high regard and wield significant political power within the tribe. One scholar notes this "system of gendered checks and balances sought to ensure, at least in theory, that women's voices could always be heard and respected on all issues of tribal policy." This gender-based model of governance is common to all of the Haudenosaunee Nations. At Onondaga, for example, Clan Mothers select men as Faith Keepers to serve on the tribe's governing council, and the Faith Keepers can be removed by the Clan Mothers for failing to act in the tribe's best interest.

The Navajo Nation and several of the Hopi tribes also define many legal rights through a matrilineal clan structure. At Hopi Pueblo, each Hopi village maintains its own lands, which are assigned to each village's matrilineal clans. Women are in charge of the lands, which are passed down according to matrilineal inheritance laws. The clans at Hopi-Tewa also hold the land, but women are the actual owners of the land and houses. Here too, ownership rights descend through the mother's line.

Not all gender-based practices or systems of governance are matrilineal, however. Some, like the Santa Clara Pueblo membership ordinance, preference the rights of men over those of women. But critics of gendered tribal systems often ignore evidence of matrilineal systems that reflect Indian women's authority in tribal communities. Historically, many Indian women possessed significant property interests, managed and controlled agricultural endeavors, and had the authority to initiate and end battles between nations long before similar rights were extended to Anglo women. And today, Indian women wield significant power in tribal communities. In fact, Indian women are more highly represented in prestigious tribal leadership positions than are non-Indian women in comparable American political institutions. As tribal cultures have evolved, some tribes have abandoned gendered systems of governance. But for other tribes such governmental structures have survived, as they are seen as providing an appropriate framework to distribute power and ensure cultural balance within the community.

From an American constitutional perspective, however, these gender-based systems are fundamentally flawed. Because federal law requires formal equality between the sexes, gender-specific laws in tribal communities could not withstand equal protection scrutiny. Thus, authorization for federal courts to review tribal court decisions on gender-based matters would mean the end of such systems, destroying the cultural foundation upon which tribal members seek to achieve balance in the community and in the world.

C *Theocratic Tribal Governments*

Finally, theocratic tribal governments are also vulnerable to destruction if ICRA is expanded. Liberal theory requires a strict separation between the state and religion and expressly disavows religion's infiltration into law. While many tribal govern-ments maintain the church–state distinction, such is not always the case, particularly among tribes that adhere to pre-contact religions. Nations such as the Pueblos, the Hopi, the Onondaga and the Meskwaki, for example, organize tribal government theologically. In these tribes, religion plays a dominant role in the selection of leaders. Often, religious figures select the tribe's leadership, or become leaders themselves due to their esteemed position within the tribe's religious hierarchy. As a result, the political and religious leadership is often one in the same. In such societies all aspects of tribal life – including governance, social structures, justice systems, and culture – are infused with religious meaning. Accordingly, if these tribes were prohibited from mixing religion and government, virtually every aspect of tribal society would be at risk of destruction.

The ICRA debates prominently reflected tribal leaders' fears regarding the exten-sion of the Establishment Clause to Indian tribes. Tribal leaders insisted at the time that applying the Clause to tribes would likely destroy tribal theocracies in existence much longer than the Constitution itself. Frank Barry, Solicitor of the Department of Interior, agreed. In explaining why the Department recommended no prohibition on the establishment of religion, he stated: "because religion is so deeply rooted in their system … it might be destructive of their government." Ultimately, Congress acknowledged that imposing the Establishment Clause onto all tribes could destroy their social and political foundations and imperil their governance systems. Con-gress avoided these disastrous consequences by declining to extend the Establish-ment Clause to Indian tribes, while maintaining protection of individual Indians' rights of free exercise. The result is that Indian tribes are the only constitutionally permitted theocracies within the United States. This exceptional status allows tribes to continue to self-govern according to their tribal customs and traditional religions, rather than suffer the alternative: destruction of tribal theocracies that could possibly undermine every aspect of traditional tribal cultures, resulting in absolute assimila-tion of theocratic tribal governments. ***

I do not mean to ignore the possibility that the critics of purportedly illiberal Indian tribes do, in fact, seek to culturally and legally assimilate Indian peoples in accordance with Western liberal ideals. The destruction of Indian culture has long been a goal of activists situated across the theoretical and political spectrum. Consider the now-infamous Dawes Act of 1887, which broke up communally held tribal lands into lots for individual ownership, decimating the tribal land base. This Act was, in significant part, the result of advocacy on the part of so-called Friends of the Indian. Convinced that the civilizing forces of individual, private property ownership and Christianity would improve the Indians' situation, these "friends" pushed the allotment policy into law, culturally devastating many Indian tribes. Still today, allotment is recognized as one of the most destructive pieces of legislation ever enacted in regards to tribal peoples. And it does not stand alone. Outsiders' desire to save Indians by way of destroying them is not new to indigenous peoples.

CONCLUSION

Political theorists have recently noted an increased desire on the part of contemporary liberals to impose liberalism on indigenous groups. This is a mistake. Despite heavy criticism fueled largely by *Santa Clara Pueblo*, evidence indicates that violations of civil liberties by tribal governments are, in fact, rare. And because Indian tribes vary dramatically in their governmental structures, cultures, and contemporary lives, Congress and the Supreme Court have recognized that the federal courts are ill-equipped to differentiate between them. Thus, forcing a one-size-fits-all approach to civil liberties onto Indian tribes is not only unjustified, it would seriously endanger Indian differentness.

Undoubtedly, Indian tribal governments owe duties to the tribal polity. And these duties should not be taken lightly. But these issues are better addressed by tribes themselves, who are in the best position to shape change in ways consistent with tribal values and traditions. This enables Indian nations to continue their own internal processes of cultural evolution and growth. Thus, as indigeneity as a way of life is increasingly threatened by an encroaching dominant culture, it is critical that the federal government take no further steps to force the assimilation and potential destruction of America's indigenous peoples.

NOTES & QUESTIONS

1. *Reading Indian Law:*
   - After reading *(Tribal) Sovereignty and Illiberalism* try to articulate for yourself what the tension is between individual liberties and tribal sovereignty. Can you define illiberalism as it is used in the article? Why does Professor Riley suggest that permitting tribes to organize themselves and to govern illiberally promotes tribal sovereignty? Do you agree that tribes ought to be free to govern themselves illiberally?
   - Toward the end of the piece Professor Riley highlights some of the ways tribes act illiberally: (1) through indigenous justice systems, (2) conceptions of gender, and (3) theocratic government. Would you be willing to give up your own individual protections to a tribal government in order to allow it to operate in a culturally sensitive, albeit illiberal, manner? Are any of the three differences articulated above more problematic than the others? If so, why?
   - Professor Riley uses the Boy Scouts as an example of a tolerant but illiberal organization, which was true when the article was written in 2007. Since 2007 the Boy Scouts have lifted the ban on both openly gay members and troop leaders. What effect does public opinion and/ or public pressure have on illiberal organizations? Might Indian tribes face this same pressure to alter illiberal rules based upon changing

community values? What is the relationship between community values, traditional culture, and illiberal governance?

2. *Acting Illiberally*: Professor Riley notes that one of the changes that was made to the Indian Civil Rights Act before it was enacted was the removal of any requirement that tribes refrain from establishing religion. This has led to some interesting examples of tribes acting illiberally in ways which perhaps show how some tribal governments attempt to police the religious practices of their members. Consider the following two examples:

(A) *Native American Church v. Navajo Tribal Council*, 272 F.2d 131 (10th Cir. 1959): The Navajo Nation outlawed the use, sale, or possession of peyote on the reservation. The Native American Church, to whom the use of peyote is an integral part of their religious practice, challenged the Navajo Nation's prohibition as a violation of their First Amendment rights. The Tenth Circuit denied the petitioner's claim, reasoning that tribes "have a status higher than that of states. They are subordinate and dependent nations possessed of all powers as such only to the extent that they have expressly been required to surrender them by the superior sovereign ... No provision of the Constitution makes the First Amendment applicable to Indian nations nor is there any law of Congress doing so."

(B) *Toledo v. Pueblo de Jemez*, 119 F. Supp. 429 (D.N.M. 1954): A group of six Protestant tribal members sued the Pueblo de Jemez for discriminating against them because they refused to adopt the Catholic faith: "the plaintiffs complain that the Pueblo has refused them the right to bury their dead in the community cemetery; denied them the right to build a church of their own on Pueblo land; prohibited them from using their homes for church purposes; refused to permit Protestant missionaries freely to enter the Pueblo at reasonable times; deprived some of them of the right to use a communal threshing machine which threatened the loss of their wheat crop. They also allege that the officials of the Pueblo threatened them with loss of their birthrights, homes and personal property unless they accept the Catholic religion."

The federal court held that it had no jurisdiction to hear the complaint because the Pueblo was not bound by the laws of New Mexico or the US Constitution. "There is, therefore, presented a serious charge of invasion of religious liberty by a Pueblo Indian tribal government. The question for decision is not whether the tribal government has the right to interfere with the religious beliefs and practices of its members but whether or not the objectionable

actions of the Pueblo come within the scope of the Civil Rights Act
*** There are some general allegations in the complaint that the
actions of the defendants amounted to a violation of the First
Amendment to the Constitution *** In these circumstances the
Court must conclude that since the defendants did not act under
color of state law, statute, ordinance, regulation, custom or usage
[Indian tribes are self-governing] no violation of the Civil Rights Act
has been alleged and the Court, therefore, has no jurisdiction."

Why does Professor Riley suggest that federal courts today may have
trouble reaffirming these admittedly illiberal opinions? (She speaks
specifically to *Santa Clara Pueblo* but generally includes an entire
canon of decisions permitting tribes to act illiberally.) Should tribal
governments play a role in policing the religious practices of their
members? Should they be able to?

3. *Membership & Illiberalism*: Professor Riley uses the Second Circuit's
decision in *Poodry* as an example of federal courts interfering with tribal
self-government. After *Santa Clara* the Supreme Court clearly limited
the ability of federal courts to review violations of the Indian Civil Rights
Act only through a writ of habeas corpus. *Poodry* expanded the scope of
habeas petitions in ICRA cases to permit federal review of punishments
where tribal members were banished from the reservation but not
otherwise incarcerated.

In 2017 the Ninth Circuit pushed back against *Poodry*'s expansion of
federal review of tribal actions. In *Tavares v. Whitehouse*, 851 F.3d 863
(9th Cir. 2017) the United Auburn Indian Community's Tribal Council
confirmed the banishment of several tribal members after they publicly
aired their concerns regarding the finances and management of the
Tribe. The Ninth Circuit limited the reasoning of *Poodry* and reaffirmed
the deference federal courts give to tribal punishments; "tribes have the
authority to exclude non-members from tribal land. If tribal exclusion
orders were sufficient to invoke habeas jurisdiction for tribal members,
there would be a significant risk of undercutting the tribes' power
because 'any person,' members and non-members alike, would be able
to challenge exclusion orders through § 1303. *** A temporary exclusion
is not tantamount to a detention. And recognizing the temporary exclusion orders at issue here as beyond the scope of 'detention' under the
ICRA bolsters tribes' sovereign authority to determine the makeup of
their communities and best preserves the rule that federal courts should
not entangle themselves in such disputes."

Do you think it is the role of federal courts to police the behavior of
tribal courts and/or tribal governments? Both Mr. Poodry and Ms.
Tavares are US Citizens in addition to tribal members, but the US

Constitution does not apply to tribal governments. What tension does that create? Do you think the US Constitution should protect the rights of individual tribal members when they are being punished by their tribal governments? If so, why isn't the Indian Civil Rights Act sufficient?

4. *Gay Marriage*: One of the more interesting developments of tribal illiberalism has occurred with the Supreme Court's recognition of same-sex marriage in *Obergefell v. Hodges*, 576 U.S. ___, 135 S. Ct. 2584 (2015). Because the Bill of Rights does not apply to tribal governments, when *Obergefell* required all states to allow same-sex marriage and to recognize those performed in other states, Indian reservations (and American Samoa) became the only places in the United States where the institution of marriage could legally continue to be reserved to a union of one man and one woman.

This has presented some difficult cultural questions for tribes and no consensus has yet emerged. Some tribes were among the earliest American jurisdictions to codify gay marriage into their laws. For example, the Coquille Indian Tribe legalized gay marriage in 2008 when only one US state (Massachusetts) had implemented a gender-neutral marriage law. Indigenous conceptions of gender, at least among some tribes, were historically more accepting, with many LGBTQI+ Indians identifying as "two-spirited" and tracing their identity back to cultural beliefs which celebrate their diversity.

Other tribes continue to oppose gay marriage. The Navajo Nation for example enacted an amendment to the tribal code in 2005 which banned same-sex marriage. While the amendment was vetoed by the Navajo president, the veto was overridden by the Navajo Nation Council.

When federal courts are asked to uphold a tribe's denial of marriage licenses to gay couples, they face the difficult conflict Professor Riley identifies. Should tribes be able to define marriage in ways which are unconstitutional? How would you decide between the promotion of tribal sovereignty and the protection of individual rights?

For an excellent discussion of exactly this problem *see* Marcia Zug, *Traditional Problems: How Tribal Same-Sex Marriage Bans Threaten Tribal Sovereignty*, 43 Wm. Mitchell L. Rev. 761 (2017).

5. *An Intersection of Ideas*: Professor Riley's piece is a perfect way to end this first part on foundational principles because it raises issues that are touched on throughout the modern Indian law canon. She writes about the importance of the role culture can play in creating a justice system, a point Chief Justice Yazzie makes directly in Chapter 5. In Chapter 6 Dean Newton builds upon this point, examining how tribal justice systems approach the law and finding both similarities and differences

in how law is interpreted by tribal courts. Dean Washburn in Chapter 15 continues the discussion about a disconnect between the Western legal system and traditional conceptions of justice when he critiques the role of the prosecutor and the lack of Indians on federal juries in Indian law cases. Finally in Chapter 13 Professor Resnik asks what we might learn about American justice and the construction of our judicial system through the tolerance of illiberalism.

As you read the other selections in this text, consider the observations Professor Riley has made in this piece. Would you place any limits upon the illiberal actions tribes might take?

6. *Beyond the Law*: At the core of tribal illiberalism is really a conversation about tribal culture and values. The law is a reflection of the values of the society it is supposed to govern. As new voices compete to define what is culturally relevant, new laws will emerge which may or may not be at odds with individual rights.

Scholars in sociology, anthropology, and gender studies have long been engaging in these questions about the ownership of tribal culture. For example, Robert Alexander Innes and Kim Anderson have edited an exceptional work on Indigenous conceptions of gender and identity, *Indigenous Men and Masculinities* (University of Manitoba Press 2015). Joanne Barker has similarly edited an impressive collection, *Critically Sovereign: Indigenous Gender, Sexuality, and Feminist Studies* (Duke University Press 2017). Together these works explore the role of gender, sexuality, and identity in indigenous communities and provide insight on the changing cultures which inform the attitudes of tribal policy-makers and, through them, tribal law.

FURTHER READING

- Gregory Ablavsky, *The Savage Constitution*, 63 Duke L.J. 999 (2014).
- Bethany Berger, *Liberalism and Republicanism in Federal Indian Law*, 38 U. Conn. L. Rev. 813 (2006).
- Jennifer Byrum, *Civil Rights on Reservations: The Indian Civil Rights Act and Tribal Sovereignty*, 25 Okla. Cty. U. L. Rev. 491 (2000).
- Carla Christofferson, *Tribal Courts' Failure to Protect Native American Women: A Reevaluation of the Indian Civil Rights Act*, 101 Yale L.J. 169 (1991).
- Matthew L. M. Fletcher, *Same Sex Marriage, Indian Tribes, and the Constitution*, 61 U. Miami L. Rev. 53 (2006).
- Matthew L. M. Fletcher, *American Indian Tribal Law* (Aspen Publishers 2011).
- Kevin Gover & Robert Laurence, *Avoiding Santa Clara Pueblo v Martinez: The Litigation in Federal Court of Civil Actions under the Indian Civil Rights Act*, 8 Hamline L. Rev. 497 (1985).
- Robert Laurence, *Martinez, Oliphant, and Federal Court Review of Tribal Activity under the Indian Civil Rights Act*, 10 Campbell L. Rev. 411 (1988).

- Stephen L. Pevar, *The Rights of Indians and Tribes* (Oxford University Press 4th ed. 2012).
- Angela Riley, *Good (Native) Governance*, 107 Colum. L. Rev. 1049 (2006).
- Katherine Robillard, *Uncounseled Tribal Court Convictions: The Sixth Amendment, Tribal Sovereignty, and the Indian Civil Rights Act*, 2013 U. Ill. L. Rev. 2047 (2013).
- Gloria Valencia-Weber, Santa Clara Pueblo v. Martinez: *Twenty-Five Years of Disparate Cultural Values: An Essay Introducing the Case for Reargument before the American Indian Nations Supreme Court*, 14 Kan. J.L. & Pub. Pol'y 49 (2004).

PART II

Voices

Most of the early federal Indian law scholarship was essentially a dialog between the academy and the bench or at least consisted of the academy attempting to educate the bench about the unique nature and doctrines of federal Indian law. As the number and diversity of professors increased, so did the voices of federal Indian law. The academy was not the only voice that multiplied during this period. As tribal governments and tribal courts became more robust, and began exercising their authority throughout Indian country, they began to make themselves heard. The voices of the tribal bench and bar added to the multiplicity of voices that emerged in the field.

The first article in this part, *"Life Comes from It": Navajo Justice Concepts* (rank 70/100), was written by The Honorable Robert Yazzie, former Chief Justice of the Navajo Nation. In his article, Justice Yazzie provides a Navajo perspective on law's origins and its place in governance, contrasting it with Anglo-American legal philosophy, and challenging the notion that the Anglo-American model has a monopoly on delivering justice. As Yazzie explains, Indian conceptions of law are not necessarily bound by a hierarchical premise and by technical principles like *stare decisis* but instead emerge from the mutual obligations and expectations of the community with a focus on healing. This forward-looking focus grows out of the traditional teachings of Navajo society, which take a collective view of society rather than a view centered on the "rights" of an individual. For the Navajo, the health and well-being of an individual rests on having a harmonious relationship with other members of the group.

Yazzie contrasts this with Anglo-American law's focus on individual rights which are designed to protect the individual against the rest of society and carve out a sphere of autonomy around each individual into which the government cannot intrude. Anglo-American law, asserts Yazzie, is thus concerned with social control and with establishing the dominance of one individual over another in a dispute – with determining who was in the "right" and who was in the "wrong." Yazzie's article discusses the development of Navajo common law – principles of law growing out of Navajo norms and expectations – and raises questions about the appropriateness of imposing on the Navajo Nation a system of law based in a different legal tradition.

The second article, *Tribal Court Praxis: One Year in the Life of Twenty Indian Tribal Courts* (rank 26/100), was written by Dean Nell Jessup Newton. Whereas Justice Yazzie's article provided insight into Navajo legal philosophy and a glimpse into the workings of the Navajo Nation's court system, Newton's article casts a broader net and examines in some detail the work of numerous tribal courts. *Tribal Court Praxis* was among the first scholarly explorations of tribal courts. The piece reacts to a common prejudice that tribal courts are biased in favor of Indian parties and are insufficiently rigorous to be proper guarantors of justice.

Newton surveys all tribal court opinions published in the 1996 edition of the *Indian Law Reporter* and ultimately shows that tribal courts are neutral, justice-administering institutions which, although varied in structure and composition, are actively engaged in a dialog about justice and legitimacy. Her review does reveal that many tribal courts have adopted doctrines and procedures from Anglo-American courts and examines spaces where tribal courts can, and have, carved out room for the development and use of tribal justice principles. Newton also calls for increased awareness and education regarding the work of tribal courts as a way to promote understanding and respect for their work.

The third article, Dean David Getches' *Beyond Indian Law: The Rehnquist Court's Pursuit of States' Rights, Color-Blind Justice and Mainstream Values* (rank 2/100), returns to the federal courts and documents the Rehnquist Court's shift away from a jurisprudence that permitted a sovereign people to control their own territory, and toward a "subjectivist approach" that allowed the Supreme Court to determine what Indian law *ought* to be. Getches documents this shift with statistics showing the comparative win/loss rate for tribes in cases before the Burger and Rehnquist courts. He uses these statistics to launch an inquiry into what caused the disparity.

That inquiry led Getches to the conclusion that the Court was motivated not by any particular aspect of Indian law but rather by motivations that cut across a broader swath of the Rehnquist Court's jurisprudence. Getches located these motivations by searching through empirical studies conducted by constitutional law scholars. These studies revealed that the Court appeared to be pursuing an agenda of its own: one that protected state interests and mainstream values. Getches' article traces the Court's agenda through its Indian law cases and demonstrates that the motivations identified by the constitutional law scholars also explain the results in Indian law cases. The article also reveals that the Court speaks with a voice motivated by principles other than serving as a neutral and objective seeker of truth, unmasking the larger motivations and narratives that exist within the Court's jurisprudential writing.

The fourth and final article, Professor Sarah Krakoff's *A Narrative of Sovereignty: Illuminating the Paradox of the Domestic Dependent Nation* (rank 20/100), takes us back to the reservation and looks at the tangible ramifications that Supreme Court decisions have had, and continue to have, on the ability of tribal governments to do their jobs. The piece focuses on the Navajo Nation and tracks how its tribal laws and policies have evolved with changing Supreme Court decisions from 1970 to 2003 to try to meet the needs of its people while living with the limits placed upon its authority by the courts. Krakoff concludes that courts need to be more cognizant of the effects of their decisions on reservation communities to ensure the cultural survival of American Indians. She calls upon tribal communities, and those who work with them, to create a narrative of sovereignty directed at educating federal and state courts about the work of tribal governments.

Together, these four articles illustrate the depth and breadth of the new voices that make up the field of federal Indian law. The field is no longer a narrow, constrained dialog focused on doctrinal issues, but rather is now a rich chorus of voices discussing and exploring the work of governments and courts and how best to serve the needs of all people within the boundaries of the United States. As you read the articles, try to identify the various voices that echo through each piece. This includes the voice of both the author of the article and the voice(s) of its subjects. What do these voices tell us about who is making decisions about the power and authority of tribal governments? What do they tell us about the foundations for those decisions? What do the voices tell us about who *should* be making those decisions and on what basis? Most importantly, what do they tell us about the destiny and direction of the field of federal Indian law?

5

"Life Comes from It": Navajo Justice Concepts

The Honorable Robert Yazzie

24 N.M. L. Rev. 175 (1994)

Numerous US Supreme Court cases speak of the right of Indians to make their own laws and be governed by them or make reference to the fact that tribal legal systems differ from the Anglo-American legal system. But what are these laws and how are they different?

The Navajo Nation Supreme Court has been very clear about its reliance upon Navajo custom and tradition in developing Navajo common law and in using Navajo common law as the basis for its decisions. "Common law" refers to law developed by judges and expressed in court decisions; "common law" is generally drawn from a society's shared customs and traditions regarding acceptable behavior. "Common law" is usually contrasted with "statutory" or "civil" law, which are the formal written laws enacted by a legislature.

The Navajo Nation Supreme Court not only publishes its court decisions, thereby making its opinions publicly available, the justices of the Court have also made concerted efforts to educate lawyers and law students about Navajo law and Navajo principles of justice. These efforts include holding oral arguments at law schools, lecturing at conferences and workshops, and writing articles.

In this article, former Chief Justice Robert Yazzie discusses the Navajo approach to conflict resolution and contrasts it with the Anglo-American approach. As you read the article, ask yourself how these differences would appear to a non-Navajo appearing in tribal court, as well as to a Navajo appearing in state or federal court.

INTRODUCTION

Navajo justice is unique, because it is the product of the experience of the Navajo People. Prior to contact with European cultures, Navajos developed their ways of approaching life through many centuries of dealing with obstacles to their survival. Likewise, Navajo concepts of justice are a product of the experience we have gained from dealing with problems. To fully understand these concepts, the essential character of Anglo-European law must be compared to that of Navajo law.

Law, in Anglo definitions and practice, is written rules which are enforced by authority figures. It is man-made. Its essence is power and force. The legislatures, courts, or administrative agencies who make the rules are made up of strangers to the actual problems or conflicts which prompted their development. When the rules are applied to people in conflict, other strangers stand in judgment and police and prisons serve to enforce those judgments. America is a secular society, where law is characterized as rules laid down by human elites for the good of society.

The Navajo word for "law" is *beehaz'aanii*. It means something fundamental, and something that is absolute and exists from the beginning of time. Navajos believe that the Holy People "put it there for us from the time of beginning" for better thinking, planning, and guidance. It is the source of a healthy, meaningful life, and thus "life comes from it." Navajos say that "life comes from *beehaz'aanii*," because it is the essence of life. The precepts of *beehaz'aanii* are stated in prayers and ceremonies which tell us of *hozho* – "the perfect state." Through these prayers and ceremonies we are taught what ought to be and what ought not to be.

Our religious leaders and elders say that man-made law is not true "law." Law comes from the Holy People who gave the Navajo people the ceremonies, songs, prayers, and teachings to know it. If we lose our prayers and ceremonies, we will lose the foundations of life. Our religious leaders also say that if we lose those teachings, we will have broken the law.

These contrasts show that while Anglo law is concerned with social control by humans, Navajo law comes from creation. It concerns life itself, and the means to live successfully. The way to a meaningful life can be learned in teachings which are fundamental and absolute.

Navajo justice is also pragmatic, and to explain how that is so, I will describe the problems Navajos address, contrast Navajo thinking with the major concepts of Anglo-European law, outline Navajo dispute resolution processes, and discuss the practical, problem-solving emphasis of Navajo law.

THE SOCIAL PROBLEMS NAVAJOS FACE

The core of Navajo justice is problem-solving. Navajo legal thinking requires a careful examination of each aspect of a given problem to reach conclusions about how best to address it. Navajos have faced different problems as they learned the ways of survival in a sometimes hostile environment. In the times of legend, Navajos slew monsters. Today, Navajos face new monsters, including:

- Domestic violence, involving abuse to spouses, elders, and children.
- Gang violence, where Navajo youths refuse to listen and do what they please.
- Alcohol-related crime such as driving while intoxicated, with resulting loss of productive lives; and disorderly conduct and fighting among neighbors and families in communities.

- Child abuse and neglect.
- The breakup of families in divorce and separation, with lasting effects upon children.

These problems are today's monsters; they are problems which get in the way of a successful life. The element which is common to all of the stated problems, including widespread alcohol abuse, is a loss of hope. There is a disease of the spirit which infects too many Navajos and leads to rising court caseloads. What do modern systems of justice offer to deal with these problems? Have the courts been effective in addressing them? Perhaps the very nature of these problems, grounded in a loss of self-respect and hope, gives us clues as to how they can effectively be addressed.

THE ADVERSARIAL SYSTEM: "VERTICAL" JUSTICE

The first modern courts were introduced to the Navajo Nation in 1892. Today's Navajo Nation courts were created in 1959 and reconstituted in 1985. The Courts of the Navajo Nation use the state model of adjudication, i.e. the adversarial system. There are obvious conflicts between Anglo-European justice methods and those of Navajo tradition. In trying to resolve these conflicts, Navajo Nation justice planners sometimes use models to help analyze the differences between the Anglo-European and Navajo legal systems. One useful model describes the Anglo-European legal system as "vertical" and the Navajo legal system as "horizontal."

A "vertical" system of justice is one which relies upon hierarchies and power. That is, judges sit above the parties, lawyers, jurors and other participants in court proceedings. The Anglo-European justice system uses rank, and the coercive power which goes with rank, to address conflicts. Power is the active element in the process. Judges have the power to directly affect the lives of the disputants for better or worse. Parties to a dispute have limited power and control over the process. A decision is dictated from on high by the judge, and that decision is an order or judgment which parties must obey or else face a penalty. The goal of the vertical system or adversarial law is to punish wrongdoers and teach them a lesson. For example, defendants in criminal cases are punished by jail and fines. In civil cases, one party wins and the other party is punished with a loss. Adversarial law offers only a win–lose solution; it is a zero-sum game. The Navajo justice system, on the other hand, prefers a win–win solution.

A fundamental aspect of the vertical justice system is the adjudicatory process. Adjudication makes one party the "bad guy" and the other "the good guy"; one of them is "wrong" and the other is "right." The vertical justice system is so concerned with winning and losing that when parties come to the end of a case, little or nothing is done to solve the underlying problems which caused the dispute in the first place.

For centuries, the focus of English and American criminal law has been punishment by the "state." The needs and feelings of the victims are ignored, and as a result no real justice is done. There are many victims of any crime. They include the direct recipients of the harm and those who depend on them, family members, relatives and the community. These are people who are affected by both the dispute and the legal decision. Often, the perpetrator is a victim as well, caught in a climate of lost hope, alcohol dependency and other means of escape.

The victims, or subjects of the adjudication, have little or no opportunity to participate in the outcome of a case. Their needs and feelings are generally not considered, and thus not addressed. They leave the courtroom feeling ignored and empty-handed. The adversarial system is "all or nothing," where strangers with power decide the future of people who have become objects rather than participants.

Money is a driving force in modern American society. Lawyers operate the adversarial system, and money buys lawyers. The best lawyers cost the most. Legal procedures are costly, and only the most wealthy litigants can afford them. Money for justice turns it into a commodity to be bought and sold. Many people in our wage and money-driven industrial society cannot afford redress so they sometimes turn to extralegal methods for a remedy. For instance, the verdict in the Rodney King case sparked angry outbursts in Los Angeles because the adversarial trial of police ignored systemic violence and racism.

What do consumers of law get from the adversarial adjudication process of the vertical system? This is a difficult question to answer since its methods do not repair damaged relationships, families, communities and society; instead this process promotes further conflict and disharmony.

Another element of the vertical system is a preoccupation with "the truth." The adversarial system dictates that there must be a winner and a loser. The side that represents the truth as it is perceived by the court wins, while the other side loses. "Truth" becomes a game where people attempt to manipulate the process, or undermine it where it does not suit their advantage. Each person has a version of "the truth," which represents that individual's understanding or perception of what happened.

People have strong feelings about truth, yet the vertical system does not allow the individual an opportunity to express his or her version of the truth in court. This role is taken from the individual and given to a power figure who is a stranger, both to the participants and the situation in question. Individual perceptions of the truth are based upon one's perspective; the "rules" of the vertical system prevent the parties from presenting their perspective. As a result, the parties feel disappointed and cheated because each of them knows what they think happened and the conclusions which should be drawn from that perspective.

When there must be a winner and a loser, truth is important. However, not all situations are best resolved through the adversarial determination of winner and loser. Sometimes solving the problem presented by a situation is more important than determining right and wrong and imposing penalties. Truth is irrelevant to a method of law that emphasizes problem solving.

For example, in a divorce, husbands and wives fight over property, child custody and hurt feelings. Each party views the situation from his or her perspective of the truth. Based on that "truth," each feels that he or she should win and that the other party should lose. The adversarial system calls upon a husband and wife to make important decisions about their future – and those of their children – at a time when they are not emotionally prepared to wisely look to the future. The couple is not allowed a means to express their hurt and anger, and because there is no opportunity to deal with emotions, lawyers and judges make unpalatable decisions for the couple. In the process, children are wounded, and the separated couple often fight more after the divorce than before. This process is alien to Navajo thought. In the Navajo tradition, there is a greater concern with the well-being of children and the ability of people to go on with life without hurt feelings.

Vertical justice looks back in time, to find out what happened and assess punishment for it. We may never know what really happened. Vertical justice does not look to the future. It does not try to find out what went wrong in order to restore the mind, physical well-being, the spirit, and emotional stability. I insist that any definition of "law" must contain an emotional element: one of spirit and feelings. Where the feelings of parties are separated from the process and the decision does not address them, dissatisfaction follows. Where the legal system ignores the emotions of the parties, there can be no restoration of relationships.

Vertical adversarial adjudication relies upon power, force and coercion. Where powerful figures abuse their authority, there is authoritarianism and tyranny. Navajo thought recognizes the danger of hierarchical or vertical systems. There is a Navajo maxim that one must "beware of powerful beings." Likewise, coercion is so feared in Navajo ethics that the invocation of powerful beings (e.g. calling upon them to use their force against another) – a form of coercion – is considered to be witchcraft. The inappropriateness of the vertical system, as imposed upon Indian nations in modern systems of law and courts, becomes more obvious when it is compared to the "horizontal" Navajo approach.

THE NAVAJO SYSTEM: "HORIZONTAL" JUSTICE

The "horizontal" model of justice is in clear contrast to the "vertical" system of justice. The horizontal justice model uses a horizontal line to portray equality: no person is above another. A better description of the horizontal model, and one often used by Indians to portray their thought, is a circle. In a circle, there is no right or left, nor is there a beginning or an end; every point (or person) on the line of a circle looks to the same center as the focus. The circle is the symbol of Navajo justice because it is perfect, unbroken, and a simile of unity and oneness. It conveys the image of people gathering together for discussion.

Imagine a system of law which permits anyone to say anything during the course of a dispute. A system in which no authority figure has to determine what is "true." Think of a system with an end goal of restorative justice which uses equality and the full participation of disputants in a final decision. If we say of law that "life comes from it," then where there is hurt, there must be healing.

Navajo concepts of justice are related to healing because many of the principles are the same. When a Navajo becomes ill, he or she will consult a medicine man. Patients consult Navajo healers to summon outside healing forces and to marshal what they have inside them for healing. A Navajo healer examines the patient to determine the illness, its cause and what ceremony matches the illness to cure it. The cure must be related to the exact cause of the illness because Navajo healing works through two processes: first, it drives away or removes the cause of illness; and second, it restores the person to good relations in solidarity with his or her surroundings and self.

The term "solidarity" is essential to an understanding of both Navajo healing and justice. Language is a key to law, and those who share common understandings of the values and emotions which are conveyed in words are bonded through them. Words are signs which also convey feelings. The Navajo understanding of "solidarity" is difficult to translate into English, but it carries connotations which help the individual to reconcile self with family, community, nature, and the cosmos-all reality. The sense of oneness with one's surroundings, and the reconciliation of the individual with everyone and everything, makes an alternative to vertical justice work. Navajo justice rejects simply convicting a person and putting them in prison; instead it favors methods which use solidarity to restore good relations among people. Most importantly, it restores good relations with self.

Navajo justice is a sophisticated system of egalitarian relationships where group solidarity takes the place of force and coercion. In it, humans are not in ranks or status classifications from top to bottom. Instead, all humans are equals and make decisions as a group. The process – which we call "peacemaking" in English – is a system of relationships where there is no need for force, coercion or control. There are no plaintiffs or defendants; no "good guy" or "bad guy." These labels are irrelevant. "Equal justice" and "equality before the law" mean precisely what they say. As Navajos, we do not think of equality as treating people equal before the law; they are equal in it. Again, our Navajo language points this out in practical terms.

Under the vertical justice system, when a Navajo is charged with a crime, the judge asks (in English): "Are you guilty or not guilty?" A Navajo cannot respond because there is no precise term for "guilty" in the Navajo language. The word "guilt" implies a moral fault which commands retribution. It is a nonsense word in Navajo law due to the focus on healing, integration with the group, and the end goal of nourishing ongoing relationships with the immediate and extended family, relatives, neighbors and community.

Clanship – *dooneeike'* – is a part of the Navajo legal system. There are approximately 210 Navajo clans. The clan institution establishes relationships among individual Navajos by tracing them to a common mother; some clans are related to each other the same way. The clan is a method of establishing relationships, expressed by the individual calling other clan members "my relative." Within a clan, every person is equal because rank, status, and power have no place among relatives.

The clan system fosters deep, learned emotional feelings which we call "*k'e.*" The term means a wide range of deeply-felt emotions which create solidarity of the individual with his or her clan. When Navajos meet, they introduce themselves to each other by clan: "I am of the (name) clan, born for the (name) clan, and my grandparents' clans are (name)." The Navajo encounter ritual is in fact a legal ceremony, where those who meet can establish their relationships and obligations to each other. The Navajo language reinforces those bonds by maxims which require duties and mutual (or reciprocal) relationships. Obviously, one must treat his or her relatives well, and we say: "Always treat people as if they were your relative." That is also *k'e.*

Navajo justice uses *k'e* to achieve restorative justice. When there is a dispute the procedure, which we call "talking things out," works like this: Every person concerned with or affected by the dispute or problem receives notice of a gathering to talk things out. At the gathering everyone has the opportunity to be heard. In the vertical legal system the "zone of dispute" is defined as being only between the people who are directly involved in the problem. On the other hand, as a Navajo, if my relative is hurt, that concerns me; if my relative hurts another, I am responsible to the injured person. In addition, if something happens in my community, I am also affected. I am entitled to know what happened, and I have the right to participate in discussions of what to do about it. I am within the zone of a dispute involving a relative. In the horizontal system the zone is wider because problems between people also affect their relatives.

The parties and their relatives come together in a relaxed atmosphere to resolve the dispute. There are no fixed rules of procedure or evidence to limit or control the process. Formal rules are unnecessary. Free communication without rules encourages people to talk with each other to reach a consensus. Truth is largely irrelevant because the focus of the gathering is to discuss a problem. Anyone present at the gathering may speak freely about his or her feelings or offer solutions to the problem. Because of the relationship and obligation that clan members have with each other, relatives of the parties are involved in the process. They can speak for, or speak in support of, relatives who are more directly involved in the dispute.

The involvement of relatives assures that the weak will not be abused and that silent or passive participants will be protected. An abused victim may be afraid to speak; his or her relatives will assert and protect that person's interests. The process also deals with the phenomenon of denial where people refuse to face their own behavior. For instance, a perpetrator may feel shame for an act done, and therefore hesitant to speak.

Relatives may speak to show mitigation for the act and to try to make the situation right. For example, Judge Irene Toledo of the Navajo Nation Ramah Judicial District has recounted a story in which the family helped a man confront the results of his actions.

The actions of this particular man commenced as an adversarial paternity proceeding familiar to today's child support enforcement efforts. The alleged father denied paternity while the mother asserted it. Judge Toledo sent the case to the district's Navajo Peacemaker Court for resolution. The parents of the couple were present for talking things out in peacemaking. It is difficult for a man and a woman to have a relationship in a small community without people knowing what is going on. The couple's family and everyone else who was present at the peacemaking were well aware of the activities of the couple. In light of the presence of family, the man admitted that he was the father of the child, and the parties negotiated paternity and child support as a group. The participation of a wider circle of relations is an effective means to address denial and get directly to a resolution of a problem rather than get sidetracked in a search for "the truth."

The absence of coercion or punishment is an important Navajo justice concept because there are differences in the way people are treated when force is a consideration. If, as in the vertical system, a decision will lead to coercion or punishment, there are procedural controls to prevent unfair decisions and state power. These safeguards include burdens of proof on the state, a high degree of certainty (e.g. "proof beyond a reasonable doubt"), the right of the accused to remain silent, and many other procedural limitations. If, however, the focus of a decision is problem-solving and not punishment, then parties are free to discuss problems.

Thus, another dynamic which we may see in Judge Toledo's example is that if we choose to deal with a dispute as a problem to be solved through discussion, rather than an act which deserves punishment, the parties are more likely to openly address their dispute.

Traditional Navajo civil procedure uses language and ceremony to promote the process of talking things out. Navajo values are expressed in prayers and teachings – using the powerful connotative force of our language – to bring people back to community in solidarity. Navajo values convey the positive forces of *hozhooji*, which aims toward a perfect state. The focus is on doing things in a "good way," and to avoid *hashkeeji naat'aah*, "the bad or evil way of speaking."

The process has been described as a ceremony. Outside the Navajo perspective, a "ceremony" is seen as a gathering of people to use ritual to promote human activity. To Navajos, a ceremony is a means of invoking supernatural assistance in the larger community of reality. People gather in a circle to resolve problems but include supernatural forces within the circle's membership. Ceremonies use knowledge which is fundamental and which none of us can deny. Traditional Navajo procedure invokes that which Navajos respect (i.e. the teachings of the Holy People or tradition) and touches their souls. Put in a more secular way, it reaches out to their basic feelings.

For example, traditional Navajo tort law is based on *nalyeeh*, which is a demand by a victim to be made whole for an injury. In the law of *nalyeeh*, one who is hurt is not concerned with intent, causation, fault, or negligence. If I am hurt, all I know is that I hurt; that makes me feel bad and makes those around me feel bad too. I want the hurt to stop, and I want others to acknowledge that I am in pain. The maxim for *nalyeeh* is that there must be compensation so there will be no hard feelings. This is restorative justice. Returning people to good relations with each other in a community is an important focus. Before good relations can be restored, the community must arrive at a consensus about the problem.

Consensus makes the process work. It helps people heal and abandon hurt in favor of plans of action to restore relationships. The dispute process brings people together to talk out a problem, then plan ways to deal with it. The nature of the dispute becomes secondary (as does "truth") when the process leads to a plan framed by consensus. Consensus requires participants to deal with feelings, and the ceremonial aspects of the justice gathering directly addresses those feelings. If, for any reason, consensus is not reached (due to the human weaknesses of trickery, withholding information or coercion), it will prevent a final decision from being reached or void one which stronger speakers may force on others.

There is another Navajo justice concept which we must understand for a better comprehension of Navajo justice, and that is distributive justice. Navajo case outcomes are often a kind of absolute liability where helping a victim is more important than determining fault. Distributive justice is concerned with the well-being of everyone in a community. For instance, if I see a hungry person, it does not matter whether I am responsible for the hunger. If someone is injured, it is irrelevant that I did not hurt that person. I have a responsibility, as a Navajo, to treat everyone as if he or she were my relative and therefore to help that hungry person. I am responsible for all my relatives. This value which translates itself into law under the Navajo system of justice is that everyone is part of a community, and the resources of the community must be shared with all. Distributive justice abandons fault and adequate compensation (a fetish of personal injury lawyers) in favor of assuring well-being for everyone. This affects the legal norms surrounding wrongdoing and elevates restoration over punishment.

Another aspect of distributive justice is that in determining compensation, the victim's feelings and the perpetrator's ability to pay are more important than damages determined using a precise measure of actual losses. In addition, relatives of the party causing the injury are responsible for compensating the injured party, and relatives of the injured party are entitled to the benefit of the compensation.

These are the factors that Navajo justice planners have used in the development of a modern Navajo legal institution – the Navajo Peacemaker Court. Before the development of the Peacemaker Court, Navajos experienced the vertical system of justice in the Navajo Court of Indian Offenses (1892–1959) and the Courts of the Navajo Nation (1959–present). Over that one hundred–year period, Navajos either adapted the vertical system to their own ways or expressed their dissatisfaction with a system that made no sense. In 1982, however, the Judicial Conference of the Navajo Nation created the Navajo Peacemaker Court. This court is a modern legal institution which ties traditional community dispute resolution to a court based on the vertical justice model. It is a means of reconciling horizontal (or circle) justice to vertical justice by using traditional Navajo legal values, such as those described above.

The Navajo Peacemaker Court makes it possible for judges to avoid adjudication and avoid the discontent adjudication causes by referring cases to local communities to be resolved by talking things out. Once a decision is reached, it may (if necessary) be capped with a formal court judgment for future use.

The Navajo Peacemaker Court takes advantage of the talents of a *naat'aanii* (or "peacemaker"). A *naat'aanii* is a traditional Navajo civil leader whose authority comes from his or her selection by the community. The *naat'aanii* is chosen due to his or her demonstrated abilities, wisdom, integrity, good character, and respect by the community. The civil authority of a *naat'aanii* is not coercive or commanding; he or she is a leader in the truest sense of the word. A peacemaker is a person who thinks well, who speaks well, who shows a strong reverence for the basic teachings of life and who has respect for himself or herself and others in personal conduct.

A *naat'aanii* acts as a guide, and in a peacemaker's eyes everyone – rich or poor, high or low, educated or not – is treated as an equal. The vertical system also attempts to treat everyone as an equal before the law, but judges in that system must single out someone for punishment. The act of judgment denies equality, and in that sense, "equality" means something different than the Navajo concept. The Navajo justice system does not impose a judgment, thereby allowing everyone the chance to participate in the final judgment, which everyone agrees to and which benefits all.

Finally, *naat'aanii* is chosen for knowledge, and knowledge is power which creates the ability to persuade others. There is a form of distributive justice in the sharing of knowledge by a *naat'aanii*. He or she offers it to the disputants so they can use it to achieve consensus.

Today's consumers of justice in the Navajo system have a choice of using the peacemaking process or the Navajo Nation version of the adversarial system. The Navajo justice system, similar to contemporary trends in American law, seeks alternatives to adjudication in adversarial litigation. The Navajo Nation alternative is to go "back to the future" by using traditional law.

NAVAJO JUSTICE THINKING

The contrast between vertical and horizontal (or circle) justice is only one approach or model to see how Navajos have been developing law and justice. We, as Navajo judges, have only recently begun to articulate what we think and do on paper and in English. Navajo concepts of justice are simple, but our traditional teachings which we use to make peace may sound complicated. Peacemaking – Navajo justice – incorporates traditional Navajo concepts, or Navajo common law, into modern legal institutions. Navajo common law is not about rules which are enforced by authority; it deals with correcting self to restore life to solidarity. Navajo justice is a product of the Navajo way of thinking. Peacemakers use the Navajo thought and traditional teachings. They apply the values of spiritual teachings to bond disputants together and restore them to good relations.

This paper uses English ways of saying things and English language concepts. It uses "paper knowledge" to try to teach you some of the things that go on in a Navajo judge's mind. To give a flavor of Navajo language thinking consider the following:

Never let the sun catch you sleeping. Rise before the sun comes up. Why? You must not be dependent. You must do things with energy and do things for yourself. You must be diligent or poverty will destroy you.

Watch your words. Watch what you say. Remember, words are very powerful. The Holy People gave them to us, and they created you to communicate. That is why you must think and speak in a positive way. Be gentle with your words. Do not gossip. Gossip has a name. It has a mind, eyes and a voice. It can cause as much trouble as you make by calling it, so do not call it to you. It causes disharmony and creates conflict among people. It is a living monster because it gets in the way of a successful life. So, as we and our young Anglo friends say, "What goes around comes around." Remember that there are consequences to everything you say and do.

Know your clan. Do not commit incest. You cannot court or marry within your own clan. If you do, you will destroy yourself; you will jump in the fire. Incest is something so evil that it will make you crazy and destroy you.

You have duties and responsibilities to your spouse and children. If you are capable and perform them, you will keep your spouse and children in a good way. If not, you will leave them scattered behind. You will not be a worthy man or woman. If you act as if you have no relatives, that may come to you.

The Holy People created human beings. Due to that fact, each must respect others. One cannot harm another. If so, harm will come back on you. There are always consequences from wrongful acts, just as good comes from good. Like begets like, so harm must be repaired through restitution (*nalyeeh*), so there will be no hard feelings and victims will be whole again.

These teachings, and many others, are spoken from the beginning of childhood. Navajo judges are beginning to look at familiar childhood experiences as legal events. For example, when a baby first becomes aware of surroundings and shows that in a laugh, there is a ceremony – the "Baby's First Laugh Ceremony." Family and relatives gather around the baby, sharing food and kinship, to celebrate with it.

What better way can we use to initiate babies into a world of good relationships and teach them the legal institution that is the clan?

These learned values serve as a guide in later years. As a child grows, he or she will act according to the teachings. Elderly Navajos tell us that we must always talk to our children so they can learn these Navajo values and beliefs. If we do not there will be disorder in the family and among relatives. The children will not listen, and they will have no responsibility to live by. We have youth violence because parents failed to talk to their children.

CONCLUSION

Traditional peacemaking is being revived in the Navajo Nation with the goal of nourishing local justice in local communities. The reason is obvious: life comes from it. Communities can resolve their own legal problems using the resources they have. Local decisions are the traditional Navajo way, in place of central control. Everyone must have access to justice that is inexpensive, readily available and does not require expensive legal representation. Peacemaking does not need police, prosecutors, judges, defenders, social workers or the other agents of adversarial adjudication. Peacemaking is people making their own decisions, not others forcing decisions upon them. There are 110 chapters or local governmental units in the Navajo nation. As of this writing, there are 210 peacemakers in 89 chapters, and we will extend the Navajo Peacemaker court to every community.

This revival assures that Navajo justice will remain *Navajo* justice, and not be an imported or imposed system. Navajo peacemaking is not a method of alternative dispute resolution; it is a traditional justice method Navajos have used from time immemorial.

AUTHOR'S NOTE

I adapted this article from an instructional outline I developed for presentations to non-Navajo lawyers and judges. It evolved in my thinking since January 20, 1992, when I assumed responsibilities as the Chief Justice of the Navajo Nation, and chose Navajo common law and the Navajo Peacemaker Court as personal priorities. These ideas will continue to grow as I discover more about my culture, language and traditions.

I draw upon two sources as I attempt to reconcile Navajo justice thinking with Anglo-European thought. I am a product of a Bureau of Indian Affairs (BIA) boarding school education which was so destructive of the Navajo culture. When I got out of boarding school, I was given a ticket to California to learn a manual skill in an electronics school. They told me I could not go to college, so I went to college. I was fascinated with the power, authority and (as I thought then) the money that went with being a lawyer so I went to law school. When I got my law degree, I put it to use as a trial judge in the Courts of the Navajo Nation. That returned me to another school – the school of Navajo life. Now, I seek to reconcile my paper knowledge with the vast knowledge that is held by my Elders – "the keepers of the tribal encyclopedia."

Sometimes I get impatient when I consider how traditional wisdom has so much value that has been forgotten. Sometimes I get angry about how Anglo law has overcome Navajo law, to the harm of Navajos. I read an evaluation of my talk on Navajo common law after a conference with state judges and lawyers which said, "Yazzie is bashing Anglo justice systems again." That is not my intent.

Emotions are important to me. The stereotype of the stoic, passive, or unemotional Indian is false, and emotions are an important part of Indian life. Navajos have a lot of pride, and when used in a good way, it is a very positive emotion. How else could I have thrown away a ticket to an electronics school and insisted that I was capable of getting a college degree? It took a lot of drive, and a little angry pride to tough it through law school in a time when non-Indians assumed that Indians were not capable of understanding the mysteries of "the law."

To me, and to many other Navajos, law is something that "just is." To explain it in my own mind and to you, I need a basis for comparison. That basis is the shortcoming of modern American adjudication, and I am not alone in decrying its destructive elements. I share a fondness for centuries of English-American common law traditions, but changing circumstances now require us to take a new look at that undefinable quality we call justice. As we of the Navajo Nation discuss the traditional knowledge that gives us power to survive in modern times, I find a property that is immensely valuable. I want to share it with you out of respect and to honor Navajo distributive justice. You, who have taken an interest to read this, are like a relative. This relationship will help us grow together in a good way because life comes from it.

NOTES & QUESTIONS

1. *Reading Indian Law*:
   - Justice Yazzie refers to the Anglo-American system of justice as "vertical" and the Navajo system of justice as "horizontal." What does he mean by these terms? How are they different from each other? How do these approaches impact what happens in the courtroom?
   - What does Justice Yazzie mean when he says the vertical system is overly preoccupied with "the truth"? How is the horizontal system different? How does that impact what happens in the courtroom? Which system do you prefer?
   - How is the *naat'aanii* selected? How does the role of a *naat'aanii* differ from that of a judge? What is the relationship of each to the parties? How does this impact the proceedings?

2. *Tribal Courts and Tribal Common Law*: The changes in federal Indian policy had a tremendous impact on tribal courts. As part of the late nineteenth-century policy of breaking up tribal governments and assimilating Indians into the general populace, the US government promulgated a Code of Indian Offenses and established Courts of Indian Offenses to enforce the new codes of conduct. The Code of Indian Offenses was published in the Code of Federal Regulations, resulting in the courts becoming known as "CFR Courts." These courts were empowered to "hear and pass judgment upon all such questions as may be presented to it for consideration by the agent, or by his approval, and shall have original jurisdiction over all 'Indian offenses' designated as such in *** these rules."

One of the rules, for example, declared that:

> The usual practices of so-called "medicine-men" shall be considered "Indian offenses" cognizable by the Court of Indian Offenses, and whenever it shall be proven to the satisfaction of the court that the influence or practice of a so-called "medicine-man" operates as a hinderance to the civilization of a tribe, or that said "medicine-man" resorts to any artifice or device to keep the Indians under his influence, or shall adopt any means to prevent the attendance of children at the agency schools, or shall use any of the arts of a conjurer to prevent the Indians from abandoning their heathenish rites and customs, he shall be adjudged guilty of an Indian offense, and upon conviction of any one or more of these specified practices, or, any other, in the opinion of the court, of an equally anti-progressive nature, shall be confined in the agency prison for a term not less than ten days, or until such time as he shall produce evidence satisfactory to the court, and approved by the agent, that he will forever abandon all practices styled Indian offenses under this rule.

What impact do you think CFR courts had on tribal traditions? In what way(s) do you think CFR courts differed from state and federal courts? How would this impact tribal legal systems?

During the Reorganization Era, many tribes established (or reestablished) tribal courts to replace the federally operated CFR courts. This practice continued during the Self-Determination Era. Although the courts of the Navajo Nation are perhaps the best known for their use and development of tribal common law, other tribal courts have also engaged in the process, and several articles have been published exploring these endeavors. *See, e.g.*, Sarah Deer & Cecilia Knapp, *Muscogee Constitutional Jurisprudence: Vhakv Em Pvtakv (The Carpet under the Law)*, 49 Tulsa L. Rev. 125 (2013); Pat Sekaquaptewa, *Evolving the Hopi Common Law*, 9 Kansas Journal of Law & Public Policy 761 (2000);

Justin B. Richland, *Arguing with Tradition: The Language of Law in Hopi Tribal Court* (University of Chicago Press 2008). *See also* Raymond D. Austin, *American Indian Customary Law in the Modern Courts of American Indian Nations*, 11 Wyo. L. Rev. 351 (2011).

In his article, Justice Yazzie discusses the concept of *nályééh*. The Navajo Nation Supreme Court has used this concept in defining the contours of tort liability:

> *Nályééh* is a unique Navajo principle that is used to redress civil wrongs. It is akin to but not quite the same as the Anglo-European concepts of restitution and reparation. The similarity is that *nályééh* requires payment or compensation to people who are injured, but it is quite different in its procedures. *Nályééh* does not simply require restitution or reparation, but calls upon the person who has caused or is responsible for an injury to talk out both compensation and relationships.

Benally v. Broken Hill, 8 Nav. R. 172 (S. Ct. 2001). How is this different from what would be required in a state or federal court? How does this concept fit with the "vertical" and "horizontal" concepts of justice?

Under state law, forcible entry and detainer statutes provide a way for landlords to remove tenants who refuse to comply with an eviction notice. In interpreting the Navajo Nation's forcible entry and detainer statute, the Navajo Nation Supreme Court declared that:

> The Navajo Nation Council appears to have adopted the five day rule from the Arizona forcible entry and detainer statute. *** The primary Navajo value that informs our due process analysis is *k'e*. In the context of Navajo due process, *k'e* ensures that individuals living in disharmony are brought back into right relationships and into the community to reestablish order. *** Under Navajo due process this Court cannot take the separation of a Navajo person from his or her home lightly, nor can we simply adopt a strict non-Navajo statutory interpretation of the law. Navajo due process includes the concept of fundamental fairness. *** It is fundamentally unfair to impose harsh and difficult timelines and to penalize a person by taking away their home without some strict requirements to assure due process. *** We take judicial notice of the fact that distances within the Navajo Nation are great, and transportation sometimes difficult. We do not do justice by expecting tenants to understand the unique eviction appellate requirement, to come into the court to see the judge, get the judge to set bond conditions, and then to comply with such conditions, all within five days of the order. We therefore hold that in order to assure due process, a district court's eviction order must give tenants notice of the appeal bond requirement, the timing

requirements, and the specific conditions for the bond set by the court. We also interpret the five days in the statute to be five working days from receipt of the order, to give tenants additional time to comply with the judge's conditions.

Fort Defiance Housing Corp. v. Lowe, 8 Nav. R. 463, 474–475 (S. Ct. 2004). How does the ruling compare to what is likely to happen in state court? How does the ruling of the Navajo Nation Supreme Court fit with the "vertical" and "horizontal" concepts of justice?

What are the advantages and disadvantages of using tribal common law to decide cases? How might that make tribal courts more "legitimate" in the eyes of tribal citizens? Do you think federal courts would view such decisions favorably or unfavorably? *See* Melissa L. Tatum, *Tribal Courts: Tensions between Efforts to Develop Tribal Common Law and Pressures to Harmonize with State and Federal Courts*, in *Harmonizing Law in an Era of Globalization: Convergence, Divergence and Resistance* (ed. Larry Backer, Carolina Academic Press 2007).

3. *Language*: The Navajo Nation requires that its judges speak the Navajo language. How important is that to developing tribal common law? Justice Yazzie used several Navajo words as part of his explanation of Navajo principles of justice. What is the connection between language and culture? In her article *Waging War with Words: Native Americans' Continuing Struggle against the Suppression of Their Languages*, 60 Ohio St. L.J. 901 (1999), Professor Allison Dussias documents US policy toward tribal languages at various points in history. In discussing the importance of tribal languages, she writes, "Native Americans and others also have expressed the interconnection between language and culture in terms of the link between a language and the worldview of those who speak it." *Id.* at 978.

4. *Peacemaking and Alternative Dispute Resolution*: As part of Justice Yazzie's comparison of the American and Navajo legal systems, he also discusses the Navajo Peacemaking process as an alternative to the formal court system. The American court system also has alternatives to formal court procedures, including mediation and so-called alternative dispute resolution. How do these American alternatives compare with Navajo Peacemaking? What, if any, role is played by the underlying principles of the two legal systems? See Carole Goldberg, *Overextended Borrowing: Tribal Peacemaking Applied in Non-Indian Disputes*, 72 Wash. L. Rev. 1003 (1997).

5. *Other Dispute Resolution Processes*: Traditional tribal dispute resolutions processes impact not only the work of tribal courts, they may also provide vehicles for solving other controversies. When the Zuni Pueblo

discovered that many of its *Ahayu:da* had wrongfully been removed from their shrines, the Zuni government began searching for the statues. Also known as War Gods, the *Ahayu:da* are carved sculptures whose purpose is to protect the Pueblo. The statues' powers are released as they are physically eroded by wind and weather. The Zuni discovered that many of the statues had been stolen and sold to museums or art collectors. Zuni tradition requires that a person with a grievance make four attempts to resolve the problem before taking stronger action. The Zuni followed this procedure in seeking return of the *Ahayu:da*, using the process to educate those in possession of the statues regarding the purpose of the statues and the need to return them. Using this process, the Zuni successfully repatriated every statue they located without having to initiate litigation. What objections would you expect museums and collectors to raise in response to efforts by the Pueblo to seek return of the *Ahayu:da*? How might the approach chosen by the Zuni resolve or avoid those objections? See T.J. Ferguson, Roger Anyon, and Edmund J. Ladd, *Repatriation at the Pueblo of Zuni: Diverse Solutions to Complex Problems*, 20 American Indian Quarterly 251 (1996).

6. *Beyond the Law*: The importance of Justice Yazzie's article reaches beyond its explanation of Navajo concepts of justice and its comparison of those concepts to the Anglo-American legal system. Justice Yazzie's article also helps break down stereotypes about tribal courts, how they function, and the processes through which they resolve controversies. Do you think those stereotypes have had an influence on the US Supreme Court's Indian law decisions? To what extent are those stereotypes perpetuated by the popular media? Professor Rebecca Tsosie has asserted the importance of the ability of Native people to control how they are depicted and how their stories are told. Rebecca Tsosie, *Reclaiming Native Stories: An Essay on Cultural Appropriation and Cultural Rights*, 34 Ariz. St. L.J. 299 (2002). Scholars of American Indian Studies have likewise challenged the stereotypes of Native peoples held by the dominant culture. *See, e.g.*, Vine Deloria, Jr., *Custer Died for Your Sins: An Indian Manifesto* (University of Oklahoma Press 1969); Elizabeth Cook-Lynn, *Who Stole Native American Studies?*, 12 Wicazo Sa Review 9 (1997).

A related problem concerns legitimacy. The multiplicity of voices contributing to federal Indian law scholarship increasingly raised questions about the legitimacy of federal authority over Indian affairs, and in particular the authority of the federal judiciary to define the contours of tribal jurisdiction. Inevitably, questions began to arise regarding the legitimacy of those contributing to federal Indian law scholarship.

Sometimes these questions focused on the substance and accuracy of the scholarship itself, and sometimes these questions arose regarding the author's authority to speak for a particular group of people. The controversy regarding Ward Churchill, a professor of Native Studies at the University of Colorado, contained elements of both. In his 1996 essay, John LaVelle questioned both Churchill's ability to speak with a Native voice and the quality of his research:

> *** Churchill gradually has emerged as a spokesman of sorts for those persons derisively referred to as Indian "wannabees" – individuals with no American Indian ancestry or tribal affiliation who nonetheless hold themselves out to the public as "Indians" by aggressively inserting themselves into the political affairs of real Indian people. Churchill's appeal among the "wannabees" lies both in the boldness with which he expresses contempt for Indian tribes, and in the scholarly facade he gives his anti-tribal propositions; indeed, many Churchill fans appear to have been won over by the mere fact that Churchill's books contain an abundance of endnotes. By researching those copious endnotes, however, the discerning reader will discover that, notwithstanding all the provocative sound and fury rumbling through his essays, Churchill's analysis overall is sorely lacking in historical/factual veracity and scholarly integrity.

John LaVelle, *Review Essay*, 20 American Indian Quarterly 109 (1996). After Churchill published a controversial article regarding those killed in the 2001 terrorist attack on the World Trade Center, the University of Colorado launched an investigation into Churchill, eventually terminating his employment based on irregularities identified in his scholarship. Controversy has also surrounded Professor Andrea Smith's claims to be Cherokee and to speak as a Native woman. Scott Jaschik, *Fake Cherokee?*, Inside HigherEd July 6, 2015. How should such claims be evaluated? What criteria should be applied to determine whether someone is Native and/or whether that person has the authority to speak on behalf of Native people? Is tribal citizenship necessary? Should it be sufficient in and of itself? What role (if any) should the federal government's concerted efforts at various points in history to break up tribal governments play in answering these questions?

FURTHER READING

- Raymond D. Austin, *Navajo Courts and Navajo Common Law* (University of Minnesota Press 2009).
- John Borrows, *Drawing Out Law: A Spirit's Guide* (University of Toronto Press 2010).

- Sarah Deer & Justin B. Richland, *Introduction to Tribal Legal Studies* (Rowman & Littlefield 3rd ed. 2015).
- Robert Cooter & Wolfgang Fikentscher, *Indian Common Law: The Role of Custom in American Indian Tribal Courts*, 46 Am. J. Comp. L. 287 (1998).
- Matthew L. M. Fletcher, *Rethinking Customary Law in Tribal Court Jurisprudence*, 13 Mich. J. Race & L 57 (2007).
- Jennifer Hendry & Melissa L. Tatum, *Justice for Native Nations: Insights from Legal Pluralism*, 60 Ariz. L. Rev. 91 (2018).
- B.J. Jones, *Tribal Courts: Protectors of the Native Paradigm of Justice*, 10 St. Thomas L. Rev. 87 (1997).
- Robert Porter, *Strengthening Tribal Sovereignty through Peacemaking: How the Anglo-American Legal Tradition Destroys Indigenous Societies*, 28 Columbia Human Rights L. Rev. 235 (1997).
- Gloria Valencia-Weber, *Tribal Courts: Custom and Innovative Law*, 24 N.M. L. Rev. 225 (1994).

6

Tribal Court Praxis: One Year in the Life of Twenty Indian Tribal Courts

Nell Jessup Newton

22 Amer. Ind. L. Rev. 285 (1998)

Many of the Indian law cases decided by the US Supreme Court involve tribal courts, often taking the form of challenges regarding the scope of tribal court authority. While some of the Court's decisions have been protective of tribal court authority, such as Williams v. Lee, *358 U.S. 217 (1959),* National Farmers Union v. Crow Tribe, *471 U.S. 845 (1985), and* Iowa Mutual v. LaPlante, *480 U.S. 9 (1987), more recent decisions have sharply limited the authority of tribal courts, particularly over parties who are not tribal members. See, e.g.,* Oliphant v. Suquamish Indian Tribe, *435 U.S. 191 (1978),* Duro v. Reina, *495 U.S. 676 (1990),* Strate v. A-1 Contractors, *520 U.S. 438 (1997), and* Nevada v. Hicks, *533 U.S. 353 (2001).*

These decisions necessarily rest on conclusions about tribal courts and the work they perform. For example, in his concurring opinion in Nevada v. Hicks, *Justice Souter (joined by Justices Kennedy and Thomas) wrote that the "ability of nonmembers to know where tribal jurisdiction begins and ends *** is a matter of real, practical consequence given the special nature of Indian tribunals, which differ from traditional American courts in a number of significant respects." 533 U.S. 353, 383 (2001) (internal quotations omitted).*

In this article, Nell Jessup Newton confronts some of the assumptions often made regarding tribal courts. She does so by discussing and analyzing the tribal court opinions published in the Indian Law Reporter *over the course of one calendar year. She concludes that tribal courts are more robust than many common stereotypes suggest, and that their opinions seek to engage their varied stakeholders and constituents in important dialog about the law itself. Dean Newton ultimately concludes that tribal courts are more complex than most assume, and that they are truly impartial arbiters of justice, deciding cases both for and against non-Indian parties, resolving difficult questions on jurisdiction and choice of law, and are trusted as the final mediators of political disputes. Her scholarship has helped to highlight the important role of tribal courts and calls for their opinions to be made more accessible and studied more broadly. As you read the article, ask yourself how the cases decided by tribal courts compare to cases decided by state and federal courts. How do the types of cases compare? How do the laws applied by the courts compare? How does the analysis compare? How do the outcomes of the cases compare? What do these comparisons say about the ability of tribal courts to dispense justice?*

I INTRODUCTION: ASSUMING THE WORST

In July 1997, Sen. Slade Gorton (R.-Wash.) appended a rider to the Interior Appropriations Act requiring all tribes receiving federal funds to waive sovereign immunity in federal court for cases brought by non-Indians. Although ultimately defeated, the rider was an attack on the entire tribal court system, because it was premised on the assumption that tribal courts are not neutral, justice-administering institutions. A recent letter to the editor of the *Washington Post*, written by a man whose son was killed in an automobile accident with a Yakima tribal police officer, makes this assumption painfully clear. Mr. Bernard Gamache's letter implied that he had no remedy because he could not sue the tribe in state or federal court. He apparently did not even attempt to file suit in tribal court, asserting that the tribe has a "makeshift court system that operates without a constitution." Mr. Gamache broadened this denunciation of the Yakima Tribal Court system to include all tribes: "Indian tribal courts have routinely shown their inability to administer justice fairly." Senator Gorton, in an op-ed piece published the same day, made the point only slightly more subtly: "[N]on-Indians and state governments may not seek justice in an *impartial* court when they have a dispute with tribal governments." Senator Gorton apparently is not disturbed by the fact that after *Seminole Tribe*, Indian governments may not seek justice against state governments in the federal courts, but rather are forced to take their disputes with the states into state courts. He also glosses over the numerous barriers presented by the common law and constitutionalized doctrines of sovereign immunity to suits against federal, state, and local governments.

Moreover, Mr. Gamache's letter is misleading because federal law has provided for a forum for such accidents *** under the Federal Tort Claims Act (FTCA). *** Mr. Gamache knew about this federal remedy when he wrote his letter because he had filed suit in federal court under the FTCA for $2 million. The case was scheduled to go to trial in December 1997, but was settled and dismissed by court order on November 26, 1997. Unfortunately, the public's ideas about tribal courts are so ill-informed that assertions like Mr. Gamache's are presumed to be the truth. Such assumptions require the application of a corollary presumption: that tribal courts are not justice-administering institutions.

When tribal courts have been subjected to intense scrutiny, as they have been in the last fifteen years, they have survived the test. Even investigations which began with apparent hostile intent have ended by stressing the strengths of tribal courts and noting that their weaknesses stem from lack of funding and not pervasive bias. The Reagan–Bush Civil Rights Commission held five hearings across the country targeted at a hot button issue: enforcement of civil rights on reservations. In 1991, the Commission issued its Final Report recommending no changes in federal law and rejecting proposals to bring the tribal judiciary under the control of the federal courts. Rather, the Commission pointed its finger at Congress by concluding that greater financial support should exist for the tribal court systems. In other words, those who examine what is actually occurring in tribal courts cannot help but be impressed with how well the courts function with the few resources at their disposal. Unfortunately, most people, including elites such as journalists and attorneys, know nothing about the existence, much less the day-to-day operation, of tribal courts.

***

*** [P]erhaps the best answer to Senator Gorton is to reveal that his proposal is premised on a false assumption that tribal courts are biased. This failure to address the actual and potential role of tribal courts as justice-administering institutions indicates that even those working on Indian political and legal issues are ignorant of the day-to-day work performed by tribal judges. This lack of knowledge is understandable. First, most tribal court opinions are not widely distributed. In 1996, for example, only twenty tribes submitted opinions to the *Indian Law Reporter*, a looseleaf service. Few law libraries subscribe to the *Indian Law Reporter*, probably because libraries respond to the needs of their faculty and student constituencies and most law professors and student researchers are not aware of the reporter's existence. Consequently, only those who routinely use tribal court opinions have access to them. A second factor contributing to the law community's ignorance of tribal courts is that tribal court jurisdiction is not generally publicized or acknowledged. Casebooks – the primary method of educating law students – do not include property, tort, or contract cases from tribal courts. Law review articles have begun to address the jurisprudence of tribal courts, but those articles might escape notice as seemingly addressed to a narrow area, holding little interest for those not concerned with Indian law.

If tribal court opinions were more widely available, the work of tribal judges would become visible to the legal as well as the general public. This education will in turn benefit the tribal courts and help to counteract and dispel accusations like those of Mr. Gamache which are now too readily published despite the lack of facts supporting them.

For a presentation to the Federal Bar Association Indian Law Conference in April 1997, I read the eighty-five cases published in the *Indian Law Reporter* during 1996. Although I have read many tribal court opinions in the past, I have never read so many unrelated cases in a sustained manner. I was struck by the diversity of the issues, the difficulty, complexity and subtlety of the choice of law, and other procedural and substantive issues addressed. I was most impressed by the richness of the dialogue in tribal court opinions – a dialogue between the court and the tribal councils, tribal people, and members of the bar. One may also read the opinions as initiating a conversation with the general public. A conversation requires listening, however, and until tribal court opinions are more widely available, accusations such as those of Mr. Gamache will remain unchallenged.

In this article, I will bring to light the work of tribal courts as reflected in the eighty-five opinions. ***

II OVERVIEW OF TRIBAL COURTS

A *Diversity and Legitimacy*

Tribal courts are a study in syncretism. Modern tribal courts had their genesis in the Courts of Indian Offenses, tools of colonialism imposed at the end of the nineteenth century to keep order on Indian reservations while educating tribal people in the dominant culture's norms. The Indian Reorganization Act of 1934 was designed to put an end to coercion, but continued the policy of assimilation by requiring tribes seeking the benefits of the IRA to organize Western-style governments. While the IRA constitutions did not provide for a separate judicial branch, tribal legislatures began creating court systems. This process has accelerated greatly since the enactment of the Indian Self Determination and Education Assistance Act in 1975. Today, most tribes have taken over the Courts of Indian Offenses. At the same time, the courts' jurisdiction has broadened from primarily criminal to include civil suits of increasing complexity. As a result, modern tribal courts vary in structure, jurisdiction, and substantive norms. Traditional non-judicial dispute resolution mechanisms continue to function in some tribes along with Peacemaker courts, courts of specialized jurisdiction, such as administrative commissions, gaming, small claims courts, and courts of general jurisdiction. These differences are a sign of creativity as tribal councils and courts balance variances among the tribes' traditions and present needs against the traditions and requirements of the dominant society's law.

Differences among tribal courts are to be expected given that law is one of the methods by which a community constitutes its own identity. Like all communities, tribal cultures are in a process of continual change, responding to pressures from various interest groups within tribes as well as pressures from the outside world. Tribal court systems create law and justice for a changing world as they apply tribal codes, constitutions, customary, and common law, as well as federal and state law. Nevertheless, because of their colonial origin, tribal courts must continually build legitimacy within the tribe, both among tribal members and with the Tribal Councils. To be sure, the opinions of courts on every level of federal, state, and local government serve to legitimate the work of these courts. The difference is that the legitimacy of state and federal courts is, for the most part, taken for granted, while tribal courts have only begun to thrive in the last fifty years. As a result, tribal courts do not yet have the same degree of respect among tribal people as do state and federal courts which have had hundreds of years of independent operation.

In addition to the ongoing project of establishing legitimacy among the people they serve, tribal courts must also counter attacks on their legitimacy by outside sources, to an extent not encountered by their state and federal counterparts. In other words, tribal courts work under a constant threat that the dominant legal society, acting through Congress or the federal courts, may react to one out of hundreds of tribal disputes in any given year by diminishing the judicial jurisdiction of *all* tribes. * * *

In conscious or unconscious anticipation to the possibility of federal interference with tribal authority, some tribal courts operate as nearly exact replicas of state courts. Although this strategy has been criticized by some, the reason for this strategy is understandable. The courts of gaming tribes, for example, frequently hear cases brought by non-Indians, especially those brought by non-Indian employees and customers injured on the premises. Given the large number of such suits, it is not surprising that at least two of the gaming tribes, Oneida and Mashantucket Pequot, have created courts very much modeled on the courts of the states within which they are located, both as to judicial personnel and the law applied. As the near success of Senator Gorton's rider indicates, whatever the background of the judge, whatever law is applied in tribal court, at least when non-Indian parties are involved, tribal judges adjudicate with a kind of Sword of Damocles over their heads.

B *Bringing the Work of Tribal Courts to Public Attention*

Unfortunately, the work of tribal courts is little known outside the circle of attorneys practicing before tribal courts on a regular basis and scholars of Indian law. Yet many others could benefit from exposure to tribal court opinions. On the most pragmatic level, attorneys and judges unfamiliar with Indian law called upon to struggle with an Indian law question would find such a source of legal norms invaluable. Unfortunately, since tribal court opinions are not widely available, busy practitioners often consult regional reporters or *Restatements* for insight into a wide variety of substantive issues in cases in which no tribal code provision or case precedent points the way toward a just resolution of a particular issue. More important, ready access to tribal court opinions could dispel some of the stereotypes regarding the ability of tribal courts to administer justice fairly. Attorneys representing clients sued in tribal court would then be able to research that particular court's treatment of certain kinds of cases. With greater knowledge of and access to the work of tribal courts, attorneys might well choose to bring some cases in tribal courts for the same reasons. Access to tribal court opinions may also aid federal courts called upon to review tribal court exercises of jurisdiction over non-Indians. Judges (and their clerks) may then be better able to put the occasionally ill-considered opinion in context, instead of assuming such an opinion represents the norm. Finally, legal scholars and the press may also benefit from a more nuanced understanding of the work of tribal courts, and thus be less apt to assume the worst when informed that tribal courts exist and even have jurisdiction over non-Indians in some cases.

As noted above, the *Indian Law Reporter* is the major source of tribal court opinions. Although those practicing frequently in tribal courts do subscribe to this excellent publication, many law libraries do not. It would be enormously helpful to have a reporter devoted solely to tribal court opinions which could then make an effort to contact all the tribal courts urging them to submit their opinions for publication. ***

***

A second method to bring the work of tribal courts to a larger audience is to encourage more articles on their work. Scholarly attention has begun to focus on tribal court opinions, with some excellent work on tribal law beginning to appear in law reviews. Greater availability of tribal opinions should cause this work to increase. An extremely beneficial undertaking for a law review would be to publish an annual review of tribal court decisions. The issues are fascinating and the opinions are often well-crafted. ***

*** [A]s criticisms of federal and state opinions must be informed by an understanding both of the law and the context of the case, so too must criticism of tribal courts be similarly grounded. While someone ignorant of tribal courts might chastise a court for not following the United States Constitution, someone with knowledge of tribal courts would understand the role of the tribe's own civil rights' ordinances or constitutional bills of rights as well as the Indian Civil Rights Act in developing a critical analysis of a tribal civil rights case.

In other words, students and scholars approaching tribal court opinions with respect for the tribal context would not automatically criticize deviations from state or federal law, but would understand that difference does not always mean inferiority. Moreover, just as tribal courts need not speak with one voice, those writing about tribal courts need not agree about whether a particular opinion is wise and just in context. One scholar may decry what she sees as overreliance on federal law in an opinion; another might think such reliance well placed, especially in a sensitive case; a third may argue a particular opinion is simply wrong on the law or bad policy. Although, some opinions may generate much more criticism than praise, such opinions might then be placed in better perspective. In short, it is the hope that articles like this reviewing the work of tribal courts each year may advance the understanding and legitimacy of tribal courts.

III ANALYSIS OF CASES PUBLISHED IN 1996

A *Methodology*

This report is based on the cases published in the *Indian Law Reporter* during the calendar year 1996. Although many of the opinions were dated in 1995 or 1996, some were dated as early as 1992. It must be stressed, therefore, that the sample of eighty-five tribal cases is much smaller than the actual number of cases heard by tribal courts. Tribes do not send all published opinions to the *Indian Law Reporter* and the reporter does not publish all trial court decisions submitted. Therefore, one should not regard this sample as complete even for those twenty tribes which submitted opinions published by the *Indian Law Reporter* in 1996.

It is difficult to give an accurate snapshot of the issues before tribal courts, because many cases involved multiple issues. For example, the opinion in *Estate of Tasunke Witko v. G. Heileman Brewing Co.* by the Rosebud Sioux Supreme Court dealt primarily with personal and subject matter jurisdiction, yet the underlying conflict raises important issues of tort, property, and customary law. Most of the opinions considered issues of civil or criminal procedure; only a relatively small number of criminal law cases reached the merits. Twenty cases addressed purely procedural issues, including statutes of limitations cases; some considered more thorny procedural issues, such as personal and subject matter jurisdiction and immunity from suit, which require an analysis of issues of tribal constitutional law and Indian Civil Rights Act questions. There were fifteen employment cases, representing a significant number in the sample, and a few property, tort, or family law opinions on the merits.

B *Sources of Law Applied in Tribal Courts*

1 Choice of Law and a Note of Caution

Tribal codes often contain choice of law provisions, which vary widely. All tribal courts must apply federal and tribal law on point. In ranking outside sources of law, tribal codes vary in some interesting ways. Some codes rank state law immediately after tribal law. The Colville Tribal Law and Order Code, for example, provides that: "In all cases the Court shall apply, in the following order of priority unless superseded by a specific section of the Law and Order Code, any applicable laws of the Colville Confederated Tribes, tribal case law, state common law, federal statutes, federal common law and international law." In the past many, if not most, tribal courts were directed to apply the law of the state within which the reservation was located. The Confederated Salish and Kootenai Tribes of the Flathead Reservation continue such a practice. Their tribal code directs courts to apply Montana law to decide issues not specifically addressed by tribal or federal law. Nevertheless, the tribal code provides an escape clause, noting that Montana law should be applied only where it is "just and appropriate." Since the Mashantucket Pequot Tribal Court has only been in existence since 1992, its code directs the tribal court to apply Connecticut law: "Until such time as a sufficient body of tribal court law has developed, the Gaming Enterprise Division, unless otherwise specified, shall apply the principles of law applicable to similar cases in Connecticut." Nevertheless, where tribal law differs, the court can and does develop common law.

For many tribes, the application of state law to fill gaps may be regarded as appropriate in light of the tribe's assessment of the basic fairness of state common law doctrines and of the tribal interest in making tribal courts accessible for non-Indian parties. For example, the Mashantucket Pequot courts entertain many personal injury and employment cases involving non-Indians. The Flathead reservation is heavily allotted, which may account for the acceptance of Montana state law in cases not governed by tribal law. As some tribes have repatriated their tribal courts, however, they have afforded those courts the opportunity to consult more sources of law, including the law of other tribes, and other states.

***

2 Tribal Law in Tribal Courts

On the one hand, all of the cases reviewed involved application of tribal law, whether tribal constitutions, codes, statutes, traditional, customary, or common law, including opinions which turn to federal or state law for norms applicable to the tribal context. Moreover, many tribal court opinions discuss the entire range of available norms. An excellent example is *Baylor v. Confederated Salish & Kootenai Tribes*, a case arising out of an on-the-job accident in which an employee of a tribal saw mill lost his right hand. The lower court denied the tribe's motion to dismiss, which was based on an argument that Montana's workers compensation law provided the exclusive remedy according to tribal law. When the tribe appealed the denial of the motion to dismiss, the injured worker argued that the tribe's final judgment rule barred the tribe's appeal. The Confederated Salish & Kootenai Tribal Court of Appeals agreed with the worker, and dismissed the tribe's appeal. In so doing, however, the Court had to interpret the scope of the tribe's final judgment rule, and in particular whether it should read tribal law, which permits the application of federal procedures in some situations, as adopting 28 U.S.C. 1292(b), which provides for narrow exceptions to the rule of finality. The court of appeals rejected this argument. Before arriving at this conclusion on the narrow issue of finality, the trial court and the court of appeals were required to engage in analyses of Montana workers compensation law, state judicial opinions, the opinion of a sister tribe, federal statutory and common law regarding the relations of states and tribes, tribal statutory law and the general policies regarding the relation of trial and appellate courts undergirded by the rule of finality.

With opinions covering such a wide scope of legal materials, it might not seem worthwhile to pigeonhole cases by whether tribal statutory or customary law or state or federal law was applied, but instead to analyze each substantive issue on its own terms. On the other hand, a major argument in favor of the tribal court system is that tribal judges are both familiar with tribal law and sensitive to the tribal context. In addition, tribal people and policymakers have increasingly invoked tribal traditions in a wide variety of contexts apart from judicial dispute resolution. In the wake of what some are hailing as a re-traditionalization movement, it is useful to examine the published cases, even though they are an imperfect sample of the reality of tribal court decision making, to determine the extent to which traditional or customary law is invoked in these tribal courts.

A) CUSTOMARY LAW Most tribes are directed to apply customary or traditional law where applicable. Tribal codes also frequently provide formal mechanisms for tribal courts to consult elders for help in determining appropriate customs and usages. The Winnebago Tribe of Nebraska provides, for example: "Where any doubt arises as to the customs and usages of the tribe, the court either on its own motion or the motion of any party, may subpoena and request the advice of elders and counselors familiar with those customs and usages." This practice is in sharp contrast to that followed in state and federal courts.

***

Perhaps because so many of the opinions printed in the *Indian Law Reporter* involve procedural issues and questions of first impression, only a few of the decisions in my sample were based solely on tribal customary or common law. ***

Although rarely the ratio decidendi of the published tribal cases, tribal traditions are often invoked when a tribal court examines a state or federal norm to determine whether the norm should be adopted in tribal court as tribal common law. Although tribal judges, many of whom are not tribal members, may lack familiarity with tribal law, invocations of tribal traditions can be a very powerful method of grounding the legitimacy of tribal decisions in tribal cultures, as well as tribal statutes and constitutions. Counsel, too, must make these links to traditional or customary law. In *Walker River Paiute Tribe v. Jake,* the criminal defense attorney may have missed an opportunity to use Northern Paiute or Walker River custom or tradition to persuade the tribal court to adopt a twenty-four-hour, rather than forty-eight-hour, time period for holding a criminal defendant without a probable cause hearing. Chief Judge Johnny adopted the forty-eight-hour rule enunciated by the Supreme Court in *County of Riverside v. McLaughlin,* in part because neither party had drawn the court's attention to any customs that might persuade it to adopt the shorter period. In the absence of any such persuasive authority, the court was much influenced by the realities of reservation life, in particular that "while this is the second largest Indian reservation in the state of Nevada ... there are presently only two tribal policemen ..."

***

Several of the opinions referred either to specific or general indigenous traditions in interpreting applicable law, or as an alternative ground of decision in a case in which tribal statutory law provided the ratio decidendi. Tribal cultural differences are most obviously marked in property and family law cases. Thus it is not surprising that an opinion deciding title to real property *** and several family law cases referred to tribal traditions. ***

B) TRIBAL STATUTES AND RULES OF PROCEDURE Most tribal court opinions resolved questions of tribal statutory law or procedural law. As Robert Porter has argued in a recent article, tribal procedures have been modeled on state and federal procedures, a practice he decries as a fatal step down the long road to assimilation because procedural rules are designed to promote the goals of an adversary system of justice, which is antithetical to traditional tribal dispute resolution. While he argues that such procedures may play a role in tribal court cases involving commercial issues, or resolving disputes between members of different tribes or non-Indians and tribal members, he is especially concerned about using an adversary model for intra-Indian disputes. The reported decisions, whether intra-tribal or involving disputes with non-members, do support his observation that tribal procedures are heavily influenced by state and federal law. When applying federal or state procedures as persuasive authority, several of the opinions adapt the procedure to the tribal setting or otherwise note that the procedural rules should not be applied with rigidity. Many times the courts merely applied the procedural norm without comment.

In addition to purely procedural issues, tribal courts also resolved questions in the grey area between substance and procedure, such as statutes of limitations, survival of tort actions, and interpretation of statutory waivers of sovereign immunity. For example, many of the Mashantucket Pequot cases interpreted the tribe's Tribal Sovereign Immunity Waiver Ordinance.

Other statutory issues of importance included cases concerning the interpretation of tribal regulatory laws. Fifteen of the opinions addressed employment law issues, usually cases challenging the termination of employees, but also cases based on tribal employment codes requiring accommodation of disabilities or protection of classes of employees from discrimination. While most of these involved casino employees, other cases, several of them significant, arose in other tribal employment contexts. Frequently tribal courts turned to common law to fill in the interstices of the statutory scheme. For example, several cases from the Mashantucket Pequot Tribal Court involved the extent to which an employee who resigned voluntarily can appeal his termination from employment in the tribe's Gaming Enterprise by arguing that his resignation was coerced or otherwise proffered under duress. In each case the tribal court turned to common law as expressed in federal and state opinions setting standards for what conduct constitutes coercion.

Although tribes require exhaustion of administrative remedies before seeking review in tribal court, the Ho-Chunk Tribe held that exhaustion was not necessary in a sensitive case involving a tribal agency reorganization plan, because on the facts of the case, exhaustion would be futile. Although tribal courts frequently upheld the tribal termination of employees, employees won some significant victories. * * *

Cases requiring interpretation of tribal statutes also raised difficult questions regarding the jurisdiction of tribal courts, waiver of sovereign immunity, the scope of the Indian Civil Rights Act, and the role of the tribal court in interpreting the tribe's constitution. These cases typically mix issues of tribal and federal law and

require great judicial sensitivity both to the role of the court in the tribe's political
system and public acceptance of tribal courts as justice-administering institutions.
* * *

3 The Law of Other Tribes

Tribal court opinions increasingly refer to the decisions of other tribal courts when
seeking persuasive authority in a case of first impression. As noted above, some tribal
codes direct tribal courts to consider the law of other tribes before considering state
law. But even without such direction, many judges have begun to refer to the law of
other tribes in a wide variety of cases. In *Lovermi v. Miccosukee Tribe*, holding that
the tribe had not waived its sovereign immunity to permit review of the tribal
Personnel Board's decision upholding a termination of employment, the court
first cited an earlier Miccosukee tribal court case but then turned to consider:
"[A]dditional legal precedent from sister tribal courts to support [defendants'] argument. A review of [these cases] may shed some light and show how other tribal
judicial systems have dealt with this issue." These references seem particularly apt in
cases, such as *Lovermi*, touching upon issues of great importance to all tribes, such as
sovereign immunity or the meaning of due process of law in the tribal context.
In *Colville Confederated Tribes v. Wiley*, the court considered a Ponca Tribal Court
case discussing the meaning of due process, cautioning: "parties to this action
should be cautious in evaluating due process in Anglo terms." In a difficult political
case, *Colville Confederated Tribes v. Meusy*, the court looked solely to other tribal
court opinions in deciding whether the separation of powers doctrine should apply
in the tribal context. Tribal courts also consider the opinions of sister tribal courts,
considering whether to endorse or distinguish them on more mundane matters.
Almost every tribal appellate court opinion I read referred to other tribal court
opinions. As more tribal court opinions are available, one may expect this reliance
on other tribal court opinions to displace reliance on state decisions.

4 State Law in Tribal Courts: The Influence of State Law
in Developing Tribal Law

Although many of the decided opinions refer to state or federal norms as persuasive
authority, the courts often do not discuss the extent to which these norms are
consistent with tribal customary law. Given that tribal courts continue to operate
as institutions of assimilation as well as to reflect the assimilation of tribal people into
the dominant culture, tribal courts looking for a solution to a knotty problem may
automatically consider Western common law as expressing commonsense solutions
to the problems of everyday life. In such opinions it is difficult to determine whether
the court made a separate assessment of whether those norms are consistent with the
tribe's past traditions and present needs.

As noted earlier, some tribal codes still point the court toward state law. Nevertheless, even these code provisions may contain discretionary language. For example, the Salish & Kootenai statute provides for application of tribal law, federal law where necessary, and then notes that the tribal court "may" decide the case according to the laws of Montana. In several cases the court referred to Montana precedents but did not adopt them blindly. For example, *** [i]n *Bick v. Pierce*, the court of appeals upheld a tribal jury damage award of $199,834.30 for injuries suffered by a tribal journalist in an automobile accident. The plaintiff's injuries were so substantial that even the defendant's own expert witness testified that the plaintiff suffered permanent injury. In fact, the defendant's medical evidence was stronger for the plaintiff than the plaintiff's own doctor's testimony. In upholding the award of $150,000 for pain and suffering, Chief Justice Peregoy cited Montana precedents regarding measurement of damages for pain and suffering and went into considerable detail in justifying the award as fair. The court noted that the plaintiff had forty-seven years of life expectancy and had been a healthy productive worker, earning $18 an hour as a journalist, but would now live in constant pain for the rest of his life. Applying a per diem analysis to demonstrate the reasonableness of the award, an analysis also used in Montana law, the court concluded that the compensation, though considerable, amounted to approximately $9 a day. It is this kind of careful explanation of damage awards that will do much to win legitimacy for tribal courts.

The Colville tribal courts also look to state law. Section 1.5.0.5 of the Colville Tribal Code permits a great deal of discretion in adopting procedures, stating "any suitable process or mode of proceeding may be adopted" if it is "conformable with the spirit of tribal law." The tribal court has rejected application of state law in some cases after considering both Colville law and the law of other tribes. ***

In sum, even when tribal codes direct the decision-maker to state law as an appropriate source of legal norms, it does not appear that any of the tribes studied required the courts to apply state law. For example, the Mashantucket Pequot Tribal Code directing the courts to apply state law refers to state common law and procedure until appropriate tribal rules are developed. Thus, tribal advocates should take care to argue that the particular norm urged on the court is not only the law of the particular state, but a good law that fits the tribal context as well.

5 Federal Law in Tribal Courts

As with the law of other jurisdictions, federal law may be applied because a tribal statute may point toward federal law. As noted above, the Winnebago Tribal Code requires application of tribal law, when federal law does not prohibit its application, then directs the courts to apply federal law, including federal common law, and the law of states or other jurisdictions which the tribal court finds compatible. Such tribal choice of law ordinances leave ample room for tribal court discretion and equal room for counsel to make arguments appealing to the context of the case and traditions of the tribe. Federal law can influence a tribal court opinion because it is a necessary part of a multilayered analysis, as when a difficult issue of tribal court jurisdiction over non-Indian parties or over particular subjects may begin with an examination of tribal law and end with an examination of federal law. Or, federal law can be a ready source of norms – especially procedural norms, but also norms concerning justiciability such as standing. In short, federal procedure, common law, constitutional law, or even statutory law may be applied as persuasive or mandatory authority in a case of first impression.

* * *

IV THE HARD CASES: SOVEREIGN IMMUNITY, CIVIL AND POLITICAL RIGHTS, AND NON-INDIAN PARTIES

A *Sovereign Immunity*

Sovereign immunity is a mixed constitutional, statutory and common law rule in federal courts. The doctrine is premised on the need to protect government coffers from what could be ruinous damage suits. In the pithy words of Judge Quinn of the Ho-Chunk Tribal Court, "It is the legislative and executive branches that deal with the nation's finances on a daily basis. It is not long ago that the only thing standing between the nation and bankruptcy was sovereign immunity." Tribal courts' analysis of sovereign immunity, while a matter of tribal law, is infused by an appreciation for the federal common law regarding this doctrine. Nevertheless, tribes differ in the extent to which they adopt various federal common law doctrines. To oversimplify the analysis, I will describe this process as involving three steps. First, it is necessary to determine to what extent the tribe both claims sovereign immunity and waives it by the tribe's constitution, by tribal ordinance, or as a matter of tribal common law. It is important to understand that some tribes extend sovereign immunity further than the federal government. For example, the Cheyenne River Sioux Tribe Law & Order Code 1-8-4 extends the tribe's sovereign immunity to officers and employees, while the federal doctrine is understood as limited to the government or agencies of the government. As a result, parties can sue federal officers acting in their individual capacities for money damages in certain circumstances. Recent federal court cases have held that tribes have the authority on their own to waive sovereign immunity, although in *Jones v. Chitimacha Tribe,* Chief Judge Dela Houssaye opined that tribes may not waive sovereign immunity without congressional authorization, but found that authorization in the Indian Gaming Regulatory Act. Although supported by 1940 opinion of the Supreme Court, this conclusion is not inevitable. Rather, most tribal courts assume that the tribe's inherent sovereignty includes the authority to waive sovereign immunity and certainly, permitting suits in tribal court would seem consistent with tribal policies of strengthening tribal courts and promoting self-determination in general.

Next, to determine what actions come within the waiver, one must study the tribal statutes carefully to determine to what extent the tribe has waived its sovereign immunity from suit in tribal court. Some tribal requirements are stricter than federal requirements. For example, the Cheyenne River Sioux Tribe Law and Order Code requires "a resolution or ordinance specifically referring" to sovereign immunity. These statutory waivers are typically construed strictly and are often regarded as jurisdictional. Some tribes like the Fort Berthold Tribe, specifically waive sovereign immunity for Indian Civil Rights Act cases, but limit that waiver to injunctive or declaratory relief. If a tribe has adopted a tort claims act, for example, it may have also adopted the many exceptions contained in federal or state tort claims acts. Like many states, tribal sovereign immunity ordinances may also limit damages. A frequent limitation is to the limits of the tribe's insurance policy. The Mashantucket Pequot Tribe has adopted a provision limiting damages to the actual damages suffered plus one-half of the actual damages for pain and suffering.

Second, if the tribal council has not waived sovereign immunity, it is necessary to determine whether the tribal court has adopted any of the federal common law ameliorating doctrines, such as the *Ex parte Young* doctrine permitting suits against federal officers seeking purely injunctive or declaratory relief and not affecting title to land, or *Bivens* actions for constitutional torts applied in Indian Civil Rights Actions. The Ho-Chunk Tribal Court has held that while the tribal constitution provides that officers and employees are immune for actions taken in the scope of their duties, equitable relief is available for actions taken beyond the scope of their duties. Many, but not all, of the tribal courts studied follow the *Ex parte Young* doctrine, including the Winnebago Supreme Court in *Rave v. Reynolds*. The *Rave* opinion contains an extensive review of tribal court cases and argues that tribes should distinguish between sovereign immunity, which does not normally attach to tribal officers, and official immunity, which provides a defense for officers to limit or avoid money damages in certain circumstances. One suspects Chief Justice Clinton's background as a Federal Courts professor impelled him to attempt to straighten out a thorny and confusing area of Indian law. In addition, the court has gone beyond the federal doctrine, by permitting declaratory and injunctive relief against tribal agencies as well as officers, criticizing the United States Supreme Court's refusal to extend the doctrine to agencies as unduly formalistic.

The third inquiry is whether Congress has abrogated the tribe's sovereign immunity from lawsuit. Some courts, like the Intertribal Court of Appeals of Nevada sitting in a case arising from the Walker River Paiute Tribe, have asserted that the ICRA by its own force becomes a part of the tribe's constitution and abrogates tribal sovereign immunity, at least for declaratory and injunctive relief in tribal court. Many tribes have waived sovereign immunity for injunctive or declaratory relief in civil rights cases.

B *Political Cases: Civil and Political Rights*

1 Civil Rights

Of the eighty-five cases submitted to the *Indian Law Reporter*, twenty-two raised civil rights questions. In eleven cases the tribal courts agreed with the party raising a civil rights claim. Many tribes have incorporated the ICRA into the tribal constitution or the law and order code; others have not, especially tribes that have not amended their constitutions since 1968, when Congress enacted ICRA. Thus, the issue can be discussed as a matter of tribal constitutional or statutory law, of the ICRA alone, or both. Tribal courts need not give the same definition to the "majestic generalities" of the ICRA's equal protection or due process clauses or the more specific provisions such as the rights of free speech and association. Some tribal courts continue to resolve these issues by reference solely to Supreme Court precedents without a discussion of the applicability of these precedents to the tribe's particular context, but there is a definite trend by tribal courts to assert that the tribe has leeway in interpreting these provisions.

Hall v. Tribal Business Council is illustrative. In *Hall*, the Fort Berthold District Court noted that in the context of Indian land, tribal member applicants for grazing unit leases have a due process right "to be treated culturally and legally with dignity and appropriate fairness," traditions that "are central to the history of the Three Affiliated Tribes." Because these traditions create a legitimate expectation for all tribal members that they will be eligible for grazing leases, the *Hall* court held that this tradition created a property interest triggering the fair procedures required by the due process clause.

Even in cases in which the tribal court ultimately decides to adopt the Supreme Court's precedents, it generally will note that it is not bound to follow this precedent but chooses to do so because the case before it fits the precedent. In *Clown v. Coast to Coast*, the Cheyenne River Sioux Tribe held that the proceedings in the trial court, when taken as a whole, violated plaintiff's due process rights in violation of the ICRA. The court noted that although the procedures in tribal civil cases where parties represent themselves may be less formal than otherwise and may be based on an inquisitorial, rather than adversarial format, parties must still be treated fairly and equally and be given a full, fair and meaningful opportunity to be heard. The defendant debtor, a member of the tribal council, had represented himself *pro se*, as had the plaintiff. The court of appeals noted that the trial court had become too embroiled in questioning the defendant and concluded that the number of errors effectively deprived the plaintiff of due process rights. In dicta, the *Clown* Court established a laundry list of guidelines applicable to subsequent cases to protect *pro se* litigants.

Finally, in some opinions, tribal courts put the burden on counsel to object to the Supreme Court precedents. Generally, these courts will apply the Supreme Court precedents if counsel does not argue that the court should interpret a tribal civil rights clause differently from the Supreme Court's interpretation of the federal constitution. Such was the approach of the Winnebago Court of Appeals in *Rave*.

Civil rights cases most often involved due process issues, with a few cases raising equal protection issues and one a free speech and assembly issue. *Simplot v. Ho-Chunk Nation Department of Health* is particularly noteworthy, because the Nation's Department of Health dismissed the plaintiffs, non-Indians, based upon an oral reorganization plan that had apparently issued from the Tribal President's office. The non-Indian employees argued that abolishing their positions while leaving the positions of Indian colleagues intact violated procedural due process and equal protection. Chief Trial Judge Butterfield granted summary judgment for the plaintiffs, holding that the Department denied the plaintiff employees due process when it did not follow any of its own policies with regard to reorganizations, did not inform the plaintiffs about bumping rights, and barred the employees from pursuing an administrative process. The court ordered the plaintiffs to be reinstated, their sick leave and seniority restored, and awarded each of them the damages permitted ($2000) under the limited waiver of sovereign immunity in the tribe's employment ordinance. Significantly, Judge Butterfield ordered the payment of these damages out of the President's budget. Judge Butterfield also pointedly noted that if the employees were successful in proving racial discrimination, other monetary relief may be available.

2 Political Cases

I use the term "political cases" broadly, to include cases adjudicating the rights of tribal members as citizens, such as voting rights, and those involving the structure of government, or clashes between branches of government, but not to sweep in all cases that may be political in the sense that the court's ruling may be controversial.

The opinions studied contained many political cases, with the main opinions discussing: (1) the authority of the judiciary to review legislative acts; (2) the separation of powers between the legislature and the courts; and (3) election disputes. These opinions indicate that to the extent tribes have incorporated separation of powers into their constitutions or judicial ordinances, tribal courts are addressing questions about the appropriate role of the tribal councils and the courts and asserting the power of judicial review.

Judicial review is a relatively new phenomenon in tribal courts. Most tribal constitutions did not contain provisions separating and dividing powers, but created a council system of government modeled more on municipal governments than state or federal governments. Under this system, the Council may have executive, judicial and legislative powers. The Tribal Chair is an elective position, but is also the chair of the council, taking part in enacting legislation. Tribal judges are usually appointed by the councils, although they are elected in some tribes. Critics of tribal courts often point to the fact that tribal courts may lack the authority to invalidate

tribal legislative or executive action. The trend in tribal court development, clearly
favored by the Congress and the Bureau of Indian Affairs, is to insulate tribal judges
from reprisals through contracts for a term, terminable only for cause, and providing
for judicial review of legislative acts.

Several of the reported cases addressed the duty of the court to interpret the law.
In *Thompson v. Cheyenne River Sioux Tribe Bd. of Police Commissioners*, the trial
court had remanded to the Police Commission to obtain Tribal Council interpretation of an ambiguous ordinance. The question was whether the ordinance's barring
employment of police officers with arrest records applied to detention officers. The
court of appeals reversed, holding the remand violated separation of powers principles of the Tribal Constitution. The Court noted that the tribal courts should not
avoid their obligation to decide the law because statutory interpretation is the very
"essence of the judicial function." Even without such a statute, however, tribes have
taken a leaf from Justice Marshall's opinion in *Marbury v. Madison* to interpret the
tribal constitution, tribal statutes, or tribal traditions as providing for judicial review.

Although tribal courts in some opinions merely flexed their muscles, so to speak,
by noting that the judiciary possessed the power to invalidate tribal ordinances, two
of the cases, *Colville Confederated Tribes v. Meusy*, and *Rave v. Reynolds*, invalidated tribal ordinances, although the later case was overturned on appeal, and one
imposed procedures for distributing grazing unit leases on the Tribal Council. In
Meusy, the tribal court invalidated a legislative response to an earlier tribal court
opinion, *Colville Confederated Tribes v. Tatshama*, refusing to grant deferred prosecution to criminal defendants on the grounds that the court could not create
deferred prosecution, a creature of statute, without violating the Colville Constitution's separation of powers provisions. After the tribal council responded by
providing for deferred prosecution, the court held that the council had gone too
far in the other direction by requiring the court to grant deferred prosecution when
requested by the tribal prosecutor because the resolution did not permit the court
any discretion in an inherently judicial arena and thus authorizes the tribal council
to determine the outcome of a case. The court thus invalidated the tribal resolution
as impermissibly intruding on the authority of the judiciary under the Colville
Constitution.

Opinions of tribes with separation of powers provisions in their constitutions
addressed other separation of powers principles. Several opinions referred to the
political question doctrine, a doctrine requiring federal courts to abstain from
deciding issues committed by the text of the constitution to a coordinate branch
of government for final decision. This argument was raised in two election cases,
Rave v. Reynolds, and *Coalition for Fair Government II v. Lowe*, and a case
challenging the removal of a tribal officer, *Frost v. Southern Ute Tribal Council*.
Like their federal counterparts, tribal courts considering this doctrine have rejected
its application to prevent the court from adjudicating cases with political issues.
Furthermore, the issue of whether a particular issue in fact raises a political question

doctrine issue requires an interpretation of the tribal constitution peculiarly within the court's province.

The most interesting political cases, however, are those arising in the context of election disputes or allegations of impropriety against tribal officers.

Rave v. Reynolds has been mentioned several times in this survey. These cases involved a challenge to a tribal council election in which a tribal council member, who was also a candidate for an upcoming election, made a motion for and voted in favor of disqualifying other candidates for the same election. In the first case, a special (pro tem) court invalidated a section of a tribal ordinance which stated that "[n]o one person shall attend or vote at more than one Caucus," as violative of the Winnebago Constitution's guarantee of free speech and assembly. The court also established a conflict of interest standard for tribal council members who are candidates in upcoming elections. Most significantly, the Court declared invalid the election result for having involved a possible conflict of interest and ordered a new election. The day after the Court issued its order, the courthouse was destroyed by fire.

The Winnebago Supreme Court reversed. The Supreme Court's discussion of tribal sovereign immunity has been noted above. On the merits, the Court applied an intermediate standard of review to assess the argument that the "one vote–one caucus" rule violated the freedom of association clause of the Indian Civil Rights Act. Under this analysis, the court concluded that the rule, although open to abuse and unwise, fell short of violating the Winnebago constitution and further held that the Council Member's participation in the vote to disqualify the candidates from the tainted caucus did not violate the procedural rights of the removed candidates under the due process clause. An innovation employed by the Supreme Court was to provide a syllabus of this complicated opinion, thus making the points in the opinion more accessible to the tribal community.

Coalition for a Fair Government II v. Lowe involved an attempt to remove several council members during a very short-held quorum of the Ho-Chunk Tribe. The Tribe's General Council is comprised of all eligible voters, of whom 20% must be present in order to constitute a quorum. Apparently it has always been difficult for the Council to maintain a quorum and since the percentage was raised from 10 to 20% in the 1994 Constitution, a quorum has rarely been achieved. According to the court, no General Council has held a quorum for more than one hour, until the meeting at which a vote was taken to remove three members of the Council. The Ho-Chunk Supreme court granted a preliminary injunction to postpone the special election called to fill the council members' seats, finding that the ousted council members had a likelihood of success on the merits that their removal violated due process.

In *Frost v. Southern Ute Tribal Council*, the tribal court denied a council member's application for a motion for a temporary restraining order to prevent the tribal council from beginning removal proceedings against him. The council member argued that he could only be removed for commission of a felony after taking office, which had not occurred and that the council's enacting regulations governing notice and procedures to be applied in removal cases after he was served with notice of removal violated the ex post facto provision of the ICRA and his right to due process. The Southern Ute tribal court rejected these arguments, relying first, on language in article V of the Southern Ute Constitution providing for discretionary removal of a council member upon the affirmative vote of four tribal council members, and, second, that enacting procedures for removal after he was given notice did not violate the guarantee against ex post facto laws in the ICRA or otherwise deny him due process.

3 The Rights of Non-Indian Parties

As noted above, critics of tribal courts make the basic assumption that non-Indians, in particular white people, will not get a fair trial in tribal courts. One method by which Indian tribes seek to establish their legitimacy in the eyes of non-Indians is by adopting Western structures and processes and by treating outsiders fairly in whatever process is applied.

As this paper demonstrates, most tribal courts are largely indistinguishable in structure and process from state and federal courts. Some tribes have adopted courts that are in almost every respect identical to state courts for cases primarily involving non-Indians. The gaming tribes in the sample have chosen this path not only because of the great number of non-Indian participants and the envy and distrust of some neighboring communities, but also as a way to gain trust and confidence from surrounding jurisdictions. While adopting many of the state court system rules and structures, however, these tribes have created court systems that serve tribal interests by limiting damages (common in many state courts) and by refusing to adopt Anglo court procedures that are not deemed helpful, such as the jury system for civil trials.

Tribes operating Westernized courts may also operate alternate systems of justice. Robert Porter urges tribes to focus more energy on recreating traditional court systems but to retain Westernized court systems for cases involving non-Indians. Some tribes have begun creating or recreating traditional court systems, such as the Navajo Peacemaker court. The Mohegan Tribe is in the process of setting up a Council of Elders, for example. In addition many informal nonjudicial dispute mechanisms exist in tribes and operate without burdening or invoking the formal tribal court system.

The second way to gain legitimacy is to treat outsiders fairly. My survey of these eighty-five cases indicates that tribal court judges work hard to make the tribal judicial system fair for all parties appearing before them. There have been and will be cases in which non-Indian parties are mistreated by the process; tribal judges are not immune from the rule that all judges are human. In this admittedly limited sample, however, the tribe does not always win against the individual, and the tribal member does not always defeat the non-Indian.

It would probably surprise Mr. Gamache and Senator Gorton that non-Indians are plaintiffs or defendants in eighteen of the cases studied and probably parties in nineteen others. Yet these non-Indian parties were treated fairly. In *Simplot v. Ho-Chunk Nation*, the court ordered non-Indian employees reinstated because their termination violated the Indian Civil Rights Act. In *Bartell v. Navajo Nation*, the court's ruling favored the insurance company defendant by limiting the damages that could be assessed. Non-Indians collect debts owed by Indian debtors in tribal courts, even when those debtors are members of the tribal council, *Clown v. Coast to Coast*. Tribal people also win, such as a journalist who was awarded $200,000 in damages for permanent injuries suffered in an automobile accident, *Bick v. Pierce*.

CONCLUSION

As with many other issues in Indian Law, the public opinion of tribal courts can be distorted by ignorance. Although federal and state courts often err in decision making, these errors are often overlooked and explained away by the old adage, hard cases make bad law. While the verdict in the O.J. Simpson trial was decried by many as an extreme injustice, no one argued that the California judicial system should be abolished.

Condemnation before adjudication, however, comes easy for critics of tribal courts as exemplified by Senator Gorton's and Mr. Gamache's biased and unsubstantiated reactions to tribal courts and their decisions. As demonstrated through this relatively small sample of tribal court cases, the tribal courts, although forced to engraft Western legal principles onto their consensual form of decision making, have been highly successful in doing so. In part, this is because they are sensitive to the potential loss of their independent adjudicatory systems if they were to overstep the boundaries placed upon them by the Congress and the courts, and in part because they have had to become adept at melding the traditions and customs of their cultures with those legal principles guiding the majority culture. Unlike their critics, tribal courts do not dismiss the well-reasoned opinions of the majority culture's courts but choose, instead, to use these Western principles with their own customary and traditional norms.

This ability to combine the principles of the majority and minority cultures is one that the dominant society should respect and honor. Unfortunately, this respect is not possible without these opinions being available to scholars, legislators, courts, and majority and minority communities. Not only will a wider distribution and coverage of tribal court opinions serve to eradicate misconceptions, it may also serve to allow for a critical dialogue with these opinions without eradication of the courts themselves.

NOTES & QUESTIONS

1. *Reading Indian Law*:
   - In the introduction to this article, Newton discusses allegations that tribal courts cannot be relied upon to reach fair results. Who was making those allegations? What were they based upon? Did Newton's review of tribal court opinions support or refute those allegations?
   - Where did Newton find the tribal court opinions she read and discussed? If she wanted to discuss the decisions of state courts or federal courts, where would she find those opinions? What is the importance of the difference in where the opinions are published?
   - What are some of the reasons Newton thinks people should read tribal court opinions? Who does she think should be reading them? What does she think they would learn?
   - Why is it important to know the sources of law relied upon by tribal courts in making their decisions? How does that help evaluate the work of tribal courts? Why do so many of the opinions discussed in the article concern issues of procedure, sovereign immunity, and civil rights? Could that be related to why they were selected for publication?

2. *Indian Law in Law Schools*: Despite the fact that tribal courts decide cases involving contracts, products liability, divorce, and child custody – the same types of cases heard by state courts – very few law school graduates learn anything about the work of tribal courts while in school. Indeed, many students graduate from law school without knowing that tribal courts even exist. This is because tribal court decisions are generally not included in law school textbooks and discussions of tribal courts are usually found only in specialized courses on Indian law. The majority of law schools do not offer such courses. Professors who teach Indian law have urged other faculty to include Indian law in their courses. *See, e.g.*, Aliza Organick, *Tribal Law and Best Practices in Legal Education: Creating a New Path for the Study of Tribal Law*, 19 Kan. J.L. & Pub. Policy 63 (2009); James Grijalva, *Compared When? Teaching Indian Law in the Standard Curriculum*, 82 N.D. L. Rev. 697 (2006); *Symposium: Integrating Indian Law into the Law School Curricula*, 37 Tulsa L. Rev. 481 (2001). A few other faculty have joined in this call. *See, e.g.*, Professor Resnik's article in Chapter 13 of this book; Wendy Collins Perdue, *Conflicts and Dependent Sovereigns: Incorporating Indian Tribes into a Conflicts Course*, 27 U. Tol. L. Rev. 675 (1996). Why do you think these calls for greater inclusion of Indian law and tribal court decisions have met with so little success? Is it a lack of understanding? Is there something unique about tribal courts that makes it inappropriate to

include their decisions in the general law school curriculum? Is Indian law sufficiently unique that it should be taught only as a specialized course?

Professor Robert Porter has argued that the standard law school curriculum actively harms tribal justice systems. Robert Porter, *Strengthening Tribal Sovereignty through Peacemaking: How the Anglo-American Legal Tradition Destroys Indigenous Societies*, 28 Columbia Human Rights L. Rev. 235 (1997). Why might this be the case? Does Justice Yazzie's article in Chapter 5 help provide an answer? Are Professor Porter's objections likely to be resolved in light of an increased number of Native law professors? *See, e.g.,* Rennard Strickland & Gloria Valencia-Weber, *Observations on the Evolution of Indian Law in the Law Schools*, 26 N.M. L. Rev. 153 (1996); G. William Rice, *There and Back Again – An Indian Hobbit's Holiday: Indians Teaching Indian Law*, 26 N.M. L. Rev. 169 (1996); Angelique EagleWoman, *Balancing between Two Worlds: A Dakota Woman's Reflections on Being a Law Professor*, 29 Berkeley J. Gender L & Just. 250 (2014).

3. *Access to Opinions*: Newton's article was published in 1998, and as she notes in the article, at the time, very few sources published tribal court opinions. While tribal court opinions are somewhat more readily accessible today, it is questionable whether this access has increased the number of people who make any systematic effort to read tribal court opinions. A few tribal courts publish reporters (printed and bound volumes) containing their opinions, some tribal courts make their opinions available via the internet (either on a website maintained by the tribal court or via a research service), and some tribes make printed copies available at various locations such as the tribal courthouse or a tribal government office. Many of these court decisions are not indexed or digested, meaning there is no easy way to research and locate court opinions relevant to any one particular topic. Instead, those wishing to find opinions on a certain topic must read through all the opinions issued by the court. The Navajo Supreme Court, for example, has published its opinions since 1969, but only a few of the bound volumes contain any index or digest to facilitate research, and those indexes that do exist are only for one particular volume. Newton's call for an annual survey of tribal court decisions, and for a single source in which to publish and research tribal court opinions, has not yet come to fruition. Why do you think this is the case? What would it take to cause these to come into being? What incentives would need to exist?

4. *Indian Civil Rights Act.* As is discussed more fully in Chapter 4, the individual rights provisions in the US Constitution do not restrict tribal governments. Through the 1968 Indian Civil Rights Act, however,

Congress has imposed many of the requirements on tribes. Despite ICRA's applicability, concern still exists that tribal courts do not provide sufficient protection for civil rights. To what extent does Newton's article support or refute these concerns? Does it matter whether the tribe provides its own set of civil rights? Does it matter whether the parties are members or nonmembers of the tribe? *See* Mark Rosen, *Multiple Authoritative Interpreters of Quasi-Constitutional Federal Law: Of Tribal Courts and the Indian Civil Rights Act,* 69 Fordham L. Rev. 479 (2000); Robert McCarthy, *Civil Rights in Tribal Courts: The Indian Bill of Rights at Thirty Years,* 34 Idaho L. Rev. 465 (1998); Elmer Rusco, *Civil Liberties Guarantees under Tribal Law: A Survey of Civil Rights Provisions in Tribal Constitutions,* 14 Am. Indian L. Rev. 269 (1989); James Zion, *Civil Rights in Navajo Common Law,* 50 Univ. Kan. L. Rev. 523 (2002).

5. *Beyond the Law:* In discussing what drew him to Indian law, Professor Frickey stated, "I think one of the reasons I am interested in federal Indian law is my upbringing in a small community, my sense of how such a place can work." Philip P. Frickey, *Tribal Law, Tribal Context, and the Federal Courts,* 18 Kan. J.L. & Pub. Policy 24 (2008). In their article *Law Stretched Thin: Access to Justice in Rural America,* Professors Lisa R. Pruitt and Bradley E. Showman, document that

> Rural areas in the United States face particular obstacles to achieving access to justice. These include socio-spatial obstacles associated with poor transportation infrastructure, lack of anonymity, population loss, shifting demographics, and social problems.

59 S.D. L. Rev. 466 (2014). These problems sound remarkably similar to those confronting tribal legal systems. Do you think that is the case? Is the US Supreme Court wrongfully attributing concerns to the tribal court context that are actually issues of geography? For a more nuanced discussion of how Indigenous people and rural communities often share the same legal aims *see* Zoltan Grossman & Winona LaDuke, *Unlikely Alliances: Native Nations and White Communities Join to Defend Rural Lands* (University of Washington Press 2017).

FURTHER READING

- Dennis Arrow, *Oklahoma's Tribal Courts: A Prologue, the First Fifteen Years of the Modern Era, and a Glimpse at the Road Ahead,* 19 Okla. City Univ. L. Rev. 5 (1994).
- Russel Lawrence Barsh, *Putting the Tribe in Tribal Court: Possible? Desirable?* 8 Kan. J.L. & Pub. Policy 74 (1998).
- Margery H. Brown & Brenda C. Desmond, *Montana Tribal Courts: Influencing the Development of Contemporary Indian Law,* 52 Mont. L. Rev. 211 (1991).

- Robert Clinton, *Tribal Courts and the Federal Union*, 26 Willamette L. Rev. 841 (1990).
- Sarah Deer & John Jacobson, *Dakota Tribal Courts in Minnesota: Benchmarks of Self-Determination*, 39 Wm. Mitchell L. Rev. 611 (2013).
- Vine Deloria, Jr. & Clifford M. Lytle, *American Indians, American Justice* (University of Texas Press 1983).
- Mary Jo B. Hunter, *Tribal Court Opinions: Justice and Legitimacy*, 8 Kan. J.L. & Pub. Policy 142 (1998).
- Melissa L. Koehn, *Civil Jurisdiction: The Boundaries between Federal and Tribal Courts*, 32 Ariz. St. L.J. 49 (1998).
- Sandra Day O'Connor, *Lessons from the Third Sovereign: Indian Tribal Courts*, 33 Tulsa L.J. 1 (1997).
- Frank Pommersheim, *Braid of Feathers: American Indian Law and Contemporary Tribal Life* (University of California Press 1997).
- Frank Pommersheim, *Tribal Court Jurisprudence: A Snapshot from the Field*, 21 Vt. L. Rev. 7 (1996).
- William P. Zuger, *A Baedeker to the Tribal Court*, 83 N.D. L. Rev. 55 (2007).
- Christine Zuni, *The Southwest Intertribal Court of Appeals*, 24 N.M. L. Rev. 309 (1994).

7

Beyond Indian Law: The Rehnquist Court's Pursuit of States' Rights, Color-Blind Justice, and Mainstream Values

David H. Getches

86 Minn. L. Rev. 267 (2001)

In the early 1970s, the federal government announced a shift in federal Indian policy. The new policy would encourage tribal self-determination, and the United States would work with tribal governments on a government-to-government basis. As part of this changed policy, Congress passed the Indian Self-Determination and Education Assistance Act, and federal agencies began making changes in their policies and regulations to implement this new understanding of the federal–tribal relationship.

Within a few years, however, the US Supreme Court began issuing a series of opinions that would ultimately restrict the power and authority of tribal governments and tribal courts, particularly their ability to exercise authority over non-Indians. A wave of law review articles ensued critiquing the Court's new approach and raising questions about whether the Court was usurping powers more properly exercised by the legislative and executive branches.

This article by David Getches was part of that wave, but in this article Getches goes a step further, adding some statistical information and using that data to launch an inquiry into what might be motivating the Court to change its course. As a result of that inquiry, Getches concludes that the Rehnquist Court is motivated by factors separate and apart from Indian law considerations.

As you read, think about the motivations identified by Getches and how those motivations connect to both the cases the Court agreed to hear and the Court's decision in each of those cases. In what ways have these motivations reshaped Indian law? Do these motivations explain the virtual abandonment of the principles laid out in the Marshall Trilogy? What, if any, insights do the motivations provide us in predicting how the Court will decide future cases? Does knowing these motivations provide any guidance as to what arguments are likely to influence the Court?

* * *

In a spate of cases beginning about the time Rehnquist became Chief Justice in 1986, the Court veered away from the foundations of Indian law. The Court began to alter the constitutionally anchored status of tribes to fit the fact situations of cases. It has not directly overruled precedent, but it has virtually ignored the Marshall trilogy, which had been the touch-stone of nearly all Indian law cases since the first Supreme Court. Since the 1992 Term, only two majority opinions of the Supreme Court in Indian law have cited any of the Marshall trilogy cases for support. Indeed, the Court has forsaken not only those foundational cases, but it has ignored most of the intervening 150 years of decisions, including nearly all of its approximately eighty modern era decisions. Three cases that had created apparently aberrant special rules concerning non-Indians – *Oliphant, Colville,* and *Montana v. United States* have now emerged from the modern era decisions as the most influential precedents for this Court.***

Beyond the departures from settled law, the cases show a stunning record of losses for Indians. Tribal interests have lost about 77% of all the Indian cases decided by the Rehnquist Court in its fifteen terms, and 82% of the cases decided by the Supreme Court in the last ten terms. This dismal track record stands in contrast to the record tribal interests chalked up in the Burger years, when they won 58% of their Supreme Court cases. It would be difficult to find a field of law or a type of litigant that fares worse than Indians do in the Rehnquist Court. Convicted criminals achieved reversals in 36% of all cases that reached the Supreme Court in the same period, compared to the tribes' 23% success rate.***

If the Court today were dealing with a disproportionate number of cases that implicate non-Indian interests and values, this might explain the different results. It is true that the Supreme Court has had some novel and difficult issues before it in recent years, especially cases involving unsettled questions of jurisdiction over non-Indians within reservations. The Court's departures from established principles of Indian law have been especially abrupt when control of non-Indian interests – property within a reservation, subjection to tribal regulation or judgments, the applicability of state law, or even non-Indian social values – was at stake. Its decisions creating exceptions and special rules in cases where tribes attempted to control non-Indians have been strongly criticized.

The Rehnquist Court's decisions have prevented tribes from trying and punishing non-Indian criminal defendants, from regulating nonmembers' fishing and hunting on non-Indian land, from zoning nonmember land in white communities on the reservation, from taxing non-Indian hotel guests on the reservation when the hotel is on non-Indian land, from hearing personal injury lawsuits between non-Indians for accidents on non-Indian land within the reservation, and from hearing suits brought by tribal members for torts committed against them on tribal land by non-Indian state officials. Moreover, even in cases where non-Indian interests were more attenuated, the Court has retreated from the deeply-rooted judicial approaches of respecting tribal sovereignty and deferring to congressional power in the field. The venerable principles that had guided the field since the nation's founding have been invoked only when a treaty or statute left little doubt about Congress's intent, and the result would only indirectly affect non-Indian expectations, or when the Court would have had to overrule a well-established decision to decide otherwise.

By contrast, perhaps the work of the Burger Court was dominated by more clear-cut cases involving unjustified extensions of state jurisdiction over Indians, to which it could more conveniently adapt the old precedents of the Marshall trilogy to define limits on state power in Indian country. If the Rehnquist Court has had to mediate thorny tribal assertions of jurisdiction over non-Indians while its predecessor dealt primarily with simpler cases in which Indians on reservations sought to be shielded from extensions of state law, the difference in subject matter might explain the different records of the two eras. The facts, however, do not justify this conclusion.

The non-Indian jurisdiction cases are not a recent phenomenon. Indeed, the Burger and Rehnquist Courts have dealt with about the same number of jurisdiction cases involving non-Indians, but the results were quite different. In cases where seemingly disenfranchised non-Indians within a reservation sought to escape tribal control, the Rehnquist Court's protection of non-Indian interests has been far greater. Of the ten cases in which tribal control over nonmembers' conduct or property was at issue, it rejected the tribe's claimed jurisdiction in all but two cases. It did not disturb tribal jurisdiction over non-Indians in *Iowa Mutual Insurance Co. v. LaPlante*, which simply extended a ruling made two years before in a nearly identical situation. In addition, one part of the deeply fragmented decision in *Brendale* allowed the tribe to extend its zoning authority over a nonmember's land in an isolated part of the Yakima reservation but subjected land in another part of the reservation to county zoning. By contrast, the Burger Court ruled in favor of subjecting non-Indians to tribal jurisdiction in six out of eight cases.

It remains true, however, that in fifteen terms the Rehnquist Court has decided fewer of the arguably easier cases in which Indian or tribal interests within a reservation claimed immunity from state law than the Burger Court did in its seventeen terms. The reason for this could be that review was sought in fewer such cases, but the difference in outcomes of the state jurisdiction cases that were decided by the two Courts is still notable: State jurisdiction over Indians in Indian country has prevailed in 54% of the cases in the Rehnquist Court compared to 38% of the cases in the preceding period. When the statistics for all the jurisdiction cases are combined, the record shows that tribal interests lost 70% of the time in the Rehnquist Court, while they won 63% of the time in the Burger Court.

There are several theoretical explanations for the radically different statistical results of the Rehnquist Court in Indian law. Although the subject matter of Indian litigation in the earlier period was not entirely different, the particular cases were somewhat simpler, perhaps today tribes are pressing claims at the margins of the law. It is doubtful that the trend in outcomes can be explained entirely by the heightened difficulty of the cases, however. The major cases of the preceding period were considered significant in their time too. In any event, the statistics are extreme enough to motivate a deeper search for explanations of the decisional trend. ***

VI ATTITUDES AND VALUES: DECISIONS IN OTHER FIELDS AS A GUIDE TO UNDERSTANDING THE REHNQUIST COURT'S INDIAN LAW

If the Court's approach to interpretation in Indian law is highly contextualized, and if the Court has no clear Indian law agenda, it may be necessary to look to the directions the Court is taking in other fields to find the values and attitudes that influence the Court's decisions. Identifying those directions and the underlying values may help predict the course of Indian law. Thus, I have searched the available scholarship on the Court's work in all fields of law to discern attitudes that explain the Court's work.

***

*** Constitutional experts have reviewed the Supreme Court's decisions in diverse fields with varying degrees of supporting data. I reviewed their analyses of outcomes and the language of several opinions, together with statistics compiled either as a part of those analyses or as separate tabulations. This method led to three surprisingly robust and discrete conclusions about the collective attitudes of the Rehnquist Court as indicated by its decisions in all fields: The Court tends to disfavor claims of racial minorities, to protect the interests of states, and to promote mainstream values. To the extent that these attitudes are implicated in Indian cases, they are likely to determine the outcome, change Indian law, and reshape Indian policy, even if the Court is indifferent about Indian law as a distinct field. One or more of these three clearly identifiable attitudes of the Rehnquist Court is at the core of virtually every Indian case, given the facts and parties typically found in such cases, so they offer valuable insights into the directions Indian law will take if the Court stays its present course.

A *The Court Disfavors Claims of Racial Minorities*

One scholar has summarized the Rehnquist Court's record in cases involving claims of equal protection as follows: "[T]he Court has tightened the restrictions on civil rights suits, limited affirmative action remedies, made it easier to challenge affirmative action and set aside programs for women and blacks, reversed earlier desegregation decisions, and avoided expanding the net of equal protection ... scrutiny traditionally granted racial and gender discrimination cases."

Almost every race-conscious remedial program has been rejected. This approach "functions to restrict the reach of legal measures designed to actively intervene in racism" because it is based on "the theory that the appropriate response to ongoing racism is for the government and the law to refuse to recognize race as a relevant category." The "color-blind" approach, according to one observer, marks "a major shift away from the Court's traditional concern for fairness and justice for racial minorities." The resulting rejection of programs that attempt to reverse past patterns of racially disparate allocation of government-provided opportunities has been criticized as "an enormous setback to minority efforts to achieve equal opportunity." This theory of equality is especially destructive when misapplied to laws relating to Indians.

* * *

B *The Court Protects the Interests of the States*

According to Professor Laurence Tribe, "'The most consistent commitment of the current [C]ourt is probably to a vision of federalism that gives states considerably more autonomy and protection from the national legislature than any [C]ourt in decades has done.'" This is borne out by an empirical study of cases involving state interests such as Eleventh Amendment immunity, state taxing authority, and treatment of Congress's Commerce Clause power relative to state power. The study concludes that "whether the state interest wins or loses on the merits ... is a function of the degree to which the 'legitimate activities of the states' ... drive the controversy, encumbered by neither the Supremacy Clause nor the national government's enumerated powers." Moreover, the Court has elevated the states' right to "set their own rules" over an ideal of "a nation in which its citizens had the same rights and liberties wherever they resided."

The conclusion that the Rehnquist Court prefers the interests of states has overwhelming statistical support. When a state loses in a lower court and the Supreme Court accepts the case, it reverses in favor of the state 93% of the time. By contrast, when the state wins below the Court reverses only 47% of the time. * * *

C *The Court Favors Mainstream Values*

Decisions in several fields of law indicate that the Court is strongly inclined to follow what the Justices believe to be the mainstream values of American society. A dedication to the status quo, often exemplified by "traditional values," is a common theme that can be synthesized from the work of writers who have proposed several different explanations for the Court's decisions. For instance, some scholars argue that recent cases show that the Court is enforcing moral imperatives of a social majority. Others discuss the increasing tendency of the Court to cite "tradition" as a means of aligning norms of constitutional interpretation with mainstream values. Studies show that the Court's First Amendment decisions are better explained by their protection of mainstream values related to their content and context than by simply a desire to advance the inherent values of freedom of expression and religion. Where economic issues are concerned, the Court favors the status quo, opting for stability and protection of expectations.

* * *

The synthesizing thread in the racial discrimination, free expression, and criminal justice decision making trends identified in several hundred cases studied is that the Rehnquist Court tends to disfavor interests of minorities when they conflict with interests of the majority in society. The Rehnquist Court's approach, then, may be seen as intervening to correct choices that do not embrace "traditional," majoritarian, democratic principles.

***

Other commentators have noted the tendency of the Court to extend constitutional protections to economic rights as well as to personal freedoms, departing from the Court's practice of leaving economic matters largely to the political process. Mark Tushnet has observed that "[t]he best description of the modern Court is that it acts in ways that satisfy a rather well-to-do constituency." The best example of this phenomenon has been the expansion of constitutional protection for rights of property owners against legislative changes that are inconsistent with their reasonable expectations and therefore could amount to a "taking" of property without due process. These status quo-oriented decisions tend to favor economically powerful interests (haves) against less advantaged interests (have-nots) such as those seeking regulatory controls of pollution, land use, labor practices, and so on. In this sense they favor mainstream, not marginal, interests.

***

*** Thus, with few exceptions, *** the Court allows majoritarian institutions to decide issues when they protect mainstream values, but steps in to protect individual rights when the political branches go too far in protecting peculiar, non-mainstream religious views.

VIII INDIAN LAW AS CRUCIBLE

Identifying the dominant attitudes of the Rehnquist Court sheds light on its approach to decision making, and the three trends successfully explain the outcomes of most of its cases. The judicial attitudes evident from the Court's decisions have considerable predictive value for similar cases in the future. The question, however, is whether one gains much predictive value for Indian cases from the three attitudinally driven trends or whether Indian law cases are exceptional.

***

Although the question of whether a tribe or a state has jurisdiction over a reservation dispute might be perceived as a minority group's claim for undemocratic, special protection under the law, an Indian law expert would view it differently. A jurisdiction case defines tribal sovereignty and tests federal preemption; it is not simply a states' rights matter. These cases concern primarily political rights, not racial justice or civil rights. The larger issue at stake in nearly all Indian law cases is the relationship of tribes to the United States – a matter rooted in centuries-old policy created as part of the nation's constitutional framework.

The Justices, however, do not appear to comprehend Indian law cases as implicating a set of ancient policies that define the nation's relationship with tribes. Although these policies were vividly important to the Framers, they may have become obscure and insignificant to the present Court. Today, Indian cases appear to interest the Court primarily for their intersections with issues that provoke judicial concerns with federalism, minority rights, and mainstream values, not because they raise distinct questions of Indian law that need to be resolved in order to clarify and perpetuate a historically unique political arrangement.

Indeed, Indian law has become a crucible for forging a larger agenda important to majorities of the Court. This explains why a number of Indian cases are on the Court's docket, as well as the obvious lack of attention to established Indian law principles in the opinions in virtually all of them. Certainly at least some of the Supreme Court's Indian cases are no more than auspicious factual settings for the Court's majorities to use in announcing views on momentous issues completely apart from their impact on Indians or Indian law. This section examines several Indian law decisions to illustrate the ways in which the three Supreme Court trends are being developed in an Indian law crucible.

The Rehnquist Court's 2001 decision in *Nevada v. Hicks* is a stunning example of how it pursues the Justices' larger agendas in Indian cases while ignoring and misapplying Indian law principles. The Court catapulted fragments of dicta from a few cases into sweeping rules that limit tribes' sovereignty over their reservations. The mission for a majority of the Court was apparently to vindicate the authority of the state. To do so it had to relieve non-Indian state officials of the risks and burdens of being subjected to tribal court jurisdiction when they violated personal and property rights of Indians on a reservation. While the decision strengthened state prerogatives, it also curtailed the capacity of separate tribal court systems to apply standards of justice that might not comport with mainstream values.

In *Hicks*, state game wardens suspected a member of the Fallon Paiute-Shoshone Tribes in Nevada of illegal hunting. They obtained a warrant from a state judge to search the tribal member's home located on tribal land and had it validated by the tribal court. The search resulted in the seizure of two mounted sheep heads that turned out not to be evidence of any crime. After the search, the tribal member brought a trespass and civil rights suit in tribal court against the wardens individually, alleging that they had exceeded the scope of the search warrant and had damaged the sheep heads. The Supreme Court held that the tribal court lacked jurisdiction to hear the case.

The cases leading up to *Hicks* had made narrow departures from the usual presumption favoring tribal civil jurisdiction on reservations for special cases on lands not controlled by tribes. The departures were based on congressional policies that the Court found to have the effect of limiting tribal authority over non-Indians. The *Hicks* opinion conflates these special rules into general principles.

The majority opinion in *Nevada v. Hicks* epitomizes the use of states' rights as the lodestar for deciding an Indian case while disregarding or dismissing traditional Indian law principles. An overview of the applicable principles shows that Justice O'Connor was not overstating matters when she said that the main portion of the majority's decision "is unmoored from our precedents."

Writing for the court, Justice Scalia stressed that "the State's interest in execution of process is considerable enough to outweigh the tribal interest in self-government even when it relates to Indian-fee lands." As Justice O'Connor observed, "The majority's sweeping opinion, without cause, undermines the authority of tribes to make their own laws and be ruled by them." From the perspective of one knowledgeable in Indian law, "The majority's analysis … is exactly backwards." As surprising as *Hicks* may be, it essentially accelerates a trend in the Court's approach to Indian law that began about the time William Rehnquist became Chief Justice.

Established Indian country jurisdiction rules are relatively clear. Generally, Indians on a reservation are immune from the application of state law and subject to tribal law. At the core of the applicable rules is an inquiry into the impact on tribal sovereignty of the proposed assertion or denial of jurisdiction. When a *state* seeks to extend its jurisdiction over *non-Indians* in Indian country the Court has said that "absent governing Acts of Congress, the question has always been whether the state action infringed on the right of reservation Indians to make their own laws and be ruled by them."

Different rules apply to non-Indian (or nonmember) conduct when the tribe is asserting jurisdiction. In *Oliphant v. Suquamish Indian Tribe* the Supreme Court announced that when tribes were incorporated into the United States they lost the power to try and punish non-Indians for crimes committed in their territory. The Court presumed that the tribes' inherent sovereignty must be limited because the ability to deprive non-Indians of personal liberties would be "inconsistent with their status."

Oliphant's rule did not extend to tribal civil jurisdiction and the Court later recited that "[c]ivil jurisdiction over [nonmember] activit[y] presumptively lies in the tribal courts unless affirmatively limited by a specific treaty provision or federal statute." Then in *Montana v. United States* the Court announced a new presumption against tribal civil jurisdiction when nonmember conduct occurs on non-Indian land. The Crow Tribe was trying to regulate hunting and fishing by a non-Indian on non-Indian-owned fee land within its reservation. The Court denied the tribe's jurisdiction but still declined to extend *Oliphant*'s blanket rule denying tribal criminal jurisdiction over non-Indians to civil jurisdiction matters. While the Court decided that tribes presumptively do not have jurisdiction over non-Indians on non-Indian land, it said that "([t]o be sure, Indian tribes retain inherent sovereign power to exercise some forms of civil jurisdiction over non-Indians on their reservations, even on non-Indian fee lands." Thus, the presumption against tribal jurisdiction over non-Indians on fee land could be rebutted if the non-Indian had entered into consensual relations with the tribe or its members or if the non-member's conduct would threaten or affect the political integrity, economic security, or health and welfare of the tribe.

The Court in *Hicks* treated *Oliphant* as if its flat denial of tribal jurisdiction had been applied in *Montana v. United States*, calling it "the 'general proposition' derived from *Oliphant*." *Oliphant*, however, was based on the Court's view that the restriction on personal liberty in a criminal case was "central to the sovereign interests of the United States," like the tribes' power to dispose of their lands without the national government's consent and their power to engage in foreign relations, both of which were lost upon the discovery of the continent by Europeans.

When the Court addressed civil jurisdiction over non-Indians in *Montana v. United States*, it did not follow the *Oliphant* rationale. It looked at treaty and statutory language and found that it was the congressional policy of allotment, opening the reservation up to settlement and occupation by nonmembers, that had qualified the tribe's jurisdiction. Thus, the "land alienation occasioned by that policy [had an effect] on Indian treaty rights tied to use and occupation of reservation land." Accordingly, in a case decided the next term, the Court allowed a tribe to exercise the jurisdiction over non-Indian hunting and fishing that it had denied in *Montana v. United States*, noting that the essential distinction between the cases was that the activity took place on tribal land, not on non-Indian fee land as in *Montana v. United States*.

By the time the Court decided *Hicks*, however, it would acknowledge only that "tribal ownership is a factor in the *Montana* analysis." Moreover, the *Montana v. United States* analysis went from a rebuttable presumption against tribal jurisdiction to a nearly absolute rule when the Court refused to apply the broadly worded exceptions that would allow tribal jurisdiction in many cases.

The exception for consensual relations was dismissed in a footnote as not intended to apply to arrangements like the cooperative effort of the tribe and the state in jointly approving a search warrant. The tribal interests exception was not even analyzed to determine whether a state official abusing his authority by invading the rights of a tribal member on tribal land could "threaten or ha[ve] some direct effect on the political integrity, the economic security, or the health or welfare of the tribe." Justice Scalia said that addressing these concerns was unnecessary because tribes are "guaranteed" that "the actions of these state officers cannot threaten or affect th[eir] interests . . . by the limitations of federal constitutional and statutory law to which the officers are fully subject." This seems to say that when state officials violate state or federal laws while on tribal property, their conduct could not possibly affect self-government or other tribal interests, because theoretically, there are legal remedies in other fora.

Justice Scalia applied the purported "'general proposition,'" derived from dicta in *Oliphant*, saying that "'the inherent sovereign powers of an Indian tribe do not extend to the activities of nonmembers of the tribe'" except to the extent "'necessary to protect tribal self-government or to control internal relations.'" He concluded that tribal regulatory jurisdiction over the game wardens in the particular case was unnecessary. This approach resembles a long-discredited version of the infringement test. Not only has the Supreme Court never applied the test of whether state action infringes on the right of reservation Indians to be governed by their own rules to *tribal* jurisdiction cases but, when it has used the test, the Court has clearly rejected arguments that state jurisdiction should presumptively apply whenever no infringement can be proved. Justice Scalia's opinion includes several other dicta that are troubling from the standpoint of maintaining the integrity of Indian law but which seem to be motivated by an agenda that goes beyond Indian law.

In *Hicks*, the Court changed Indian law in its vindication of states' rights. In other cases, the Court has used Indian cases to make rules of law that are much broader than Indian law. For instance, the Court's decision in *Seminole Tribe v. Florida* is perceived by scholars, and I believe was intended by the Court, primarily to announce a new rule on the sovereign immunity of states and to limit Congress's power under the Commerce Clause. These reforms in constitutional law are motivated by a Court majority's attitude toward states' rights. Choosing an Indian case to announce them actually might have made the changes more palatable to swing voters on the Court, not to mention to a public insensitive to the Indian law implications.

* * *

In *Idaho v. Coeur d'Alene Tribe*, the Court again used an Indian case to address its interest in states' rights. The decision bolstered state sovereign immunity by preventing a tribe from suing the state to vindicate its property rights to submerged lands. The Court curtailed the reach of the so-called *Ex parte Young* doctrine, which had been widely used to circumvent state immunity by bringing suit against a state official instead of naming the state. In some earlier cases concerning state ownership of submerged lands, the Supreme Court recognized that the political relationship and historical situation leading to the establishment of an Indian reservation could justify a reversal of the usual presumption that all submerged lands pass to new states on statehood. By denying a forum to determine whether Congress intended to extinguish or preserve the tribe's rights in the submerged lands in *Coeur d'Alene*, the Supreme Court rendered largely theoretical the tribe's ability to claim sovereign and proprietary rights that preceded the state's existence. Thus, tribes were lumped with private claimants rather than with sovereigns in applying Eleventh Amendment jurisprudence, an area where the Court has gone beyond the text of the Amendment to perpetuate the immunity of states from suit by relying on various implications and understandings divined from its reading of history.

In another Indian case, the Supreme Court scrapped the well-established "compelling interest" test for judging whether state laws infringe the right of free exercise of religion under the First Amendment. The case the Court used as a crucible for formulating this pronouncement was *Employment Division, Department of Human Resources v. Smith*. It may have seen in *Smith* an appealing factual situation for ruling that states should not be burdened with proving a compelling interest to enforce its laws every time someone claims to have violated the law in the name of religion. A drug counselor took drugs and was fired for cause, then asked the state to pay unemployment benefits. Apparently moved by the prospect that a state might be liable to compensate a discharged drug-taking employee unless it can prove a compelling interest, Justice Scalia said that "such a system would be courting anarchy, . . .[and] that danger increases in direct proportion to the society's diversity of religious beliefs, and its determination to coerce or suppress none of them." When Alfred Smith, an elderly Indian man, braved a rainy night to attend a meeting with a few fellow members of the Native American Church, he must not have realized as he took the sacrament, placing a bitter peyote cactus button in his mouth, that so much was at stake.

Because of its unusual facts, unlikely to be replicated in mainstream religion cases, *Smith* may have been the "best case" for the Court to choose as a vehicle for changing First Amendment law and giving governments more latitude to regulate religious practices that are contrary to mainstream norms. Nevertheless, scholars broadly criticized the ruling, as did representatives of organized religion who feared that it could be extended over practices of more popular religious faiths. So they persuaded Congress to pass legislation restoring strict scrutiny of government actions inhibiting religious practice. The Court then asserted its power by striking down the remedial legislation. By being at the center of a First Amendment debate, *Smith* has gotten far more attention than most Indian decisions. Although its impact on the fundamentals of Indian law is not pervasive (because it did not deal with tribal sovereignty or reservation rights), it illustrates the Court's marginalization of Indian values as it selects cases to further a larger agenda.

Two years before *Smith*, the Court had declined to protect Indian sacred sites on federal land from destruction without applying the compelling interest test. *Lyng v. Northwest Indian Cemetery Protective Ass'n* was little noticed outside Indian law, however, because it did not purport to strike down the well-established general rule but instead found the test inapplicable to a conflict between public land laws and Indian religious practices on federal lands, a situation that evoked little empathy, even from erstwhile free exercise advocates. Yet *Lyng* is even more emblematic of the depreciation of values to be maintained by the "measured separatism" of Indian tribes because it involved the place-based religion of Indians, making it even less like mainstream religions than the communion-like (albeit hallucinogen-ingesting) sacrament involved in *Smith*. Ultimately, land and nature provide the nexus for all Indian social, political, and religious values. Without a basic acceptance, if not understanding, of this reality, the Court is less likely to consider Indian law very "important."

In *Lyng*, the Court assumed that allowing the government to build a highway into the sacred lands of the tribal claimants within a national forest "could have devastating effects on traditional Indian religious practices." In fact, the lower court had found that the land use decision in question would "virtually destroy the ...Indians' ability to practice their religion." As the Court candidly acknowledged in *Smith*, "[L]eaving accommodation to the political process will place at a relative disadvantage those religious practices that are not widely engaged in; but that [is an] unavoidable consequence of democratic government ..."

Other Rehnquist Court decisions have manifested the discomfort the Justices feel for upholding "special treatment" of Native Americans under the law. The case of *Rice v. Cayetano* could have been selected and decided as a crucible for advancing the Court's "color-blind" approach to racial justice. The Court reversed a decision allowing the state of Hawaii to conduct a Natives-only election of trustees to administer a trust to benefit Native Hawaiians. It found that the Fifteenth Amendment, adopted after the Civil War to prevent states from denying the elective franchise to former slaves, prevented Hawaii's attempt to address a perceived history of injustice toward its Native peoples.

The Court struck down a state constitutional amendment that had been adopted by a vote of the citizens (including the non-Native majority). The Court disregarded the circumstances, motives, and historical backdrop that led to a majority-sanctioned special election of trustees for the benefit of a disadvantaged Native minority. These facts would take the case out of the purpose of the Fifteenth Amendment, which was to prevent the white majority from excluding racial minorities from the basic civil right of participating in democratic government. A wooden application of the law, of course, is essential to the Court's negative approach to affirmative action programs and other government measures that take race into account. In *Rice*, however, it was not necessary for the Court to confront that issue because the precedents support the constitutional authority of Congress to legislate on behalf of Native peoples. Thus, regardless of the Court's views on the construction of the Fifteenth Amendment, it might have distinguished the case as being within the power of Congress in Indian affairs. Instead of deciding the case on Indian law principles, it seized the moment to press the color-blind approach to which several members adhere.

Several Indian cases decided by the Court, like those reviewed here, surely were crucibles for developing legal principles that, in the minds of the Justices, have nothing to do with Indian law. However, this still does not explain the preponderance of other Supreme Court Indian decisions that raise issues peculiar to Indian reservations and that result in decisions concerning only questions of governance of Indian country. Even cases not selected as crucibles for developing specific legal rules important to the Court may attract the Court's interest by implicating the Justices' strongly held attitudes. The typical reservation governance case involves some or all of the Court's concerns with states' rights, apparent special treatment of minorities, or conflicts with mainstream values. The Court's concern with these issues may draw the Justices to Indian law cases and, when deciding them, provide a forum for expressing their attitudinal preferences without focusing on Indian law principles or the consequences for the political position of tribes in our system.

The results in Indian cases support the Court's strong preference for the position of states as reflected in the entirety of its record. This is significant because 68% of all Indian cases decided by the Rehnquist Court have involved a state as a party or a question of state jurisdiction. The Court does not always rule in favor of states in such cases. Indeed, in the last ten years, tribes have prevailed over state interests in four cases. In *Rice v. Cayetano*, for example, the state had taken a position supporting Native American interests. The Court rejected the state's position. The Court's attitude favoring states and states' rights, however, is well-illustrated in the Eleventh Amendment cases like *Seminole Tribe*, as well as by the statistical record.

Similarly, the confluence of the Justices' distaste for racially defined institutions and their preference for mainstream values with states' rights is seen in the opinions denying tribal jurisdiction. Consider, for instance, *Strate v. A-1 Contractors*. A plaintiff who had lived her adult life on the reservation and whose children were all tribal members sued the defendant in tribal court for injuries she sustained in an accident on a reservation road. The Supreme Court said that the plaintiff could not sue in her own community on the reservation but would have to take the case to a "state forum [that is] open to all who sustain injuries on North Dakota's highway." The Court found that "requiring [the non-Indian defendants] to defend against this commonplace state highway accident claim in an unfamiliar court is not crucial to" the tribe's interests. In joining a later decision relieving a state official from having to defend himself in a suit for trespass to an Indian home on tribal land, Justice Souter wrote in *Nevada v. Hicks*,

> Tribal courts also differ from other American courts (and often from one another) in their structure, in the substantive law they apply, and in the independence of their judges. Although some modern tribal courts "mirror American courts" and "are guided by written codes, rules, procedures, and guidelines," tribal law is still frequently unwritten, being based instead "on the values, mores, and norms of a tribe and expressed in its customs, traditions, practices," and is often "handed down orally or by example from one generation to another." The resulting law applicable in tribal courts is a complex "mix of tribal codes and federal, state, and traditional law," which would be unusually difficult for an outsider to sort out.

In the tribal court jurisdiction cases, the issue was not the specific denial of any fundamental right, but a general concern with difference – the kind of difference that might be expressed with the laws of any other country or, indeed, among states which, in our federal system, may apply their own mix of laws ranging from the common law of England to unique local ordinances. In these cases, however, the

Court has treated the matter as if the most powerful factors were the unfamiliarity of the tribal court to the defendant. The Court acknowledged the impact on the tribe's interests in maintaining reservation health and safety through the exercise of sovereignty over reservation activities but, unlike a traditional conflict of law analysis, gave no weight to the preference for the local law of the place of injury. If the Court's role in these cases had been to make a conflict of law balancing decision, even without applying Indian law principles, it arguably did not do so with a full appreciation of the tribal interests that were at stake.

The Court in *Strate* had to indulge incredible legal contortions to deny jurisdiction to the tribal court. To circumvent usual Indian law rules, Justice Ginsburg first explained away the Court's own recent statement that civil jurisdiction over non-Indians "presumptively lies in the tribal courts" as meaning that if a tribe had established its regulatory jurisdiction then it also would have judicial jurisdiction. Besides converting that statement of law from the 1987 *Iowa Mutual* case into a tautology, her explanation was implausible given the context of that case, which had nothing to do with regulatory jurisdiction.

Next, Ginsburg recast an element of basic property law by saying that the tribe's conveyance of a road right-of-way passed the equivalent of fee title to the state. This was necessary to revise the facts of *Strate* so they would look more like *Montana v. United States*, where the Court held that, subject to certain exceptions, tribes lack jurisdiction over the activities of non-Indians on their own fee land. Then she had to overcome an exception to the *Montana* rule for non-Indians who were in a consensual relationship with the tribe. The defendant in *Strate* was working on a tribal contract to landscape the tribal headquarters when he was driving his truck along a road in front of the plaintiff's reservation home and collided with her car. Justice Ginsburg refused, however, to apply the exception to the defendant because the *plaintiff* was not also a party to the tribal contract.

The other exception to the *Montana* rule recognized the inherent power of tribes over non-Indians, even on non-Indian land, whenever the conduct "threatens or has some direct effect on the political integrity, the economic security, or the health or welfare of the tribe." Ginsburg had to admit that this exception, on its face, "undoubtedly" applied. Yet she said that to apply it in circumstances where tribal self-government was not more seriously threatened "would severely shrink the [*Montana*] rule."

Consistent with its preference for mainstream values, the Court also has used Indian cases to advance the view that statutory interpretation should not result in major shifts in wealth. In two recent cases, enormous economic benefits from natural resources development were at stake for tribes. To uphold the tribal position required, in one case, disgorging millions of dollars from a state treasury, and in the other, denying millions of dollars in royalties to private non-Indian entities. The Court upheld the status quo and expectations of the state and the private landowners in the two cases, although these parties had relied on assumptions that proved legally incorrect in the first case and factually incorrect in the other. In *Montana v. Crow Tribe*, both the state and the tribe imposed taxes on coal produced from lands where the tribe owned the mineral estate. The tribe secured a court of appeals decision that the state tax was illegal and the tribal tax was lawful. In the meantime, the state had collected millions of dollars in taxes. The Court reversed a lower court order that the funds collected by the state pursuant to its unlawful tax should be disgorged and paid over to the tribe, finding that it would be "inequitable" to the state to alter the status quo under the circumstances.

In *Amoco v. Southern Ute Indian Tribe*, the Court revived a popular misconception about the nature of coal-bed methane gas to avoid altering an arrangement where royalties were paid to overlying non-Indian landowners rather than to the tribe that owned the coal estate. The United States had conveyed rights to minerals to surface owners along with title to the surface, but reserved coal rights, which it later conveyed to the tribe. As between the surface owners and the tribe that owned the coal estate, the surface owners prevailed. The Court recognized that the methane gas in coal seams was a dangerous waste produced along with coal and that it had not been understood to be a valuable, extractable mineral at the time of the conveyance of mineral rights to the surface owners. Nevertheless, the Court held that when the conveyance was made, coal was thought of only as a solid substance, and since methane is a gas and not solid (a "fact" that is not entirely true until the coal seam is opened and the gas is liberated from the coal), rights to the methane were not reserved along with the coal. The Court seemed concerned that the landowners and methane producers had been influenced by and relied on an opinion of a government attorney in 1981 that the methane had passed apart from the coal as part of the mineral estate.

The non-Indian reliance concerns in these cases are similar to those in two earlier Indian water rights decisions. In *Nevada v. United States*, the Court refused to reopen a water rights decree where a tribe had been represented by government attorneys who had a conflict of interest and had claimed little water for the benefit of the tribe. The Court held that the tribe was bound by the earlier decree under *res judicata* principles, noting that both parties and non-parties "have relied ... on the *Orr Ditch* decree in participating in the development of western Nevada... "Likewise, in *Arizona v. California*, federal attorneys representing the tribes had not claimed all of the irrigable acreage to which the tribes were entitled, resulting in the Court awarding them rights to less water. The tribes tried to reopen the case to claim a greater share of the water but were turned back by the Court. The opinion did not question the fact that the tribes had suffered from inadequate legal representation at the hands of the government, but cautioned that "[c]ertainty of rights is particularly important with respect to water rights in the Western United States." So the Court held that the tribes must be content with a lower quantity of water based on the "compelling need for certainty in the holding and use of water rights."

In rare cases, the Rehnquist Court has resurrected foundational Indian law principles to uphold Indian rights. It seems to have done so primarily in order to add gravity to outcomes that largely comported with reliance interests of non-Indians. This was true in three of the five cases in which tribal interests have prevailed in the last ten terms of the Supreme Court. In *Minnesota v. Mille Lacs Band of Chippewa Indians*, the Court recited in detail the history of the Chippewa treaties and the principles of reserved rights to uphold off-reservation fishing rights in Minnesota. The interpretation and application of treaty rights in that case emulated the factually similar 1979 US Supreme Court decision in *Washington v. Washington State Commercial Passenger Fishing Vessel Ass'n*. Moreover, the Minnesota decision was nearly identical to lower court decisions that were being implemented successfully after contentious tribal–state litigation by other bands of the Chippewa Tribe in neighboring Wisconsin, and followed decisions regarding Indian treaties in Michigan litigation. A reversal by the Supreme Court would have created an anomaly and disregarded the agonized history of Indian–white relations in the region that had finally produced a working relationship through a negotiated arrangement that assumed the correctness of judicial interpretations reached during eighteen years of litigation.

As all these cases illustrate, Indian rights can be misunderstood as outside the mainstream by judges unschooled in Indian law. If the Supreme Court sees tribes as a racial group pressing for special rights, rather than as sovereign entities vindicating a political relationship grounded in the Constitution, they will be at a severe disadvantage. Indeed, the potential coincidence of the three dominant attitudes in the Rehnquist Court's decisions almost invariably produces results that disfavor legal protection for tribal sovereignty and cultural integrity and that eschew limits on state power in Indian country. Justices who, in other settings, might adhere to stare decisis, but who find the precedent in this area to be odd, are tempted to disregard authority and break new ground. The concept of legally separating Indian people from the rest of society is difficult in the abstract and may be more so in a fact situation notorious enough to bring the dispute all the way to the Supreme Court. Justices, who otherwise would rely on coordinate branches to solve the problem, are inclined to wade in and set things right. Even Justices who see the Court as playing an important counter-majoritarian role – and who attribute importance to the Court's role in protecting minority rights in a system where majorities rule – may resist the idea of tribal autonomy. They may not appreciate that the cultural and political survival of tribes is at the mercy of a homogenizing majority. Only if Indian law is kept in the context of an American legal tradition, supported by the Constitution and reflected in solemn bargains secured by treaties, can it transcend the categories typical of mainstream adjudication.

IX THE NEED TO REDISCOVER INDIAN LAW

The Supreme Court's failure to appreciate that Indian law is *sui generis* denies deep traditions that preceded the nation's founding, were memorialized in the

Constitution, and have been perpetuated by the judiciary until recently.
The cornerstones of Indian law – that tribes have sovereignty over their territory,
that state powers are severely limited in Indian country, and that these principles
may be changed only by Congress – are essential to our political structure. Earlier
Supreme Courts have characterized the relationship of tribes to the United States as
unique. Departing from basic approaches and rules may seem compelling under the
facts of a particular case, but in Indian law, pulling on a single thread can unravel
the entire fabric. Indian law is not, as some might see it, a collage of incoherent
rules; the incoherence in the field today is largely the product of the decisions of the
Rehnquist Court. The field has always been complex and curious in many respects
and has not produced results that entirely pleased any one set of interests. Furthermore it carried the stigma of its colonial roots, but it has served to referee with
predictability, if not perfect justice, the intense jurisdictional battles among federal,
state, and tribal interests.

Leaving Indian legal rights and the powers of Indian tribes to the mercies of the
American political system has its risks. Felix Cohen poignantly addressed the
potentially dramatic impact of imposing law and policy on Indians:

> [T]he Indian plays much the same role in our American society that the Jews played
> in Germany. Like the miner's canary, the Indian marks the shifts from fresh air to
> poison gas in our political atmosphere; and our treatment of Indians, even more
> than our treatment of other minorities, reflects the rise and fall in our
> democratic faith.

The tragedy of the Indian as miner's canary has been rehearsed several times in
our history. Indian policies made by the political branches were sometimes extensions of national policies that were deemed "right" for the dominant society. This
tested the practical limits of otherwise acceptable policy and often caused tragic
consequences for Indians. Time and again, when policies that captured the nation's
collective imagination were pressed beyond the mainstream of society, they have
had disastrous effects on Indians.

One example was Congress's extrapolation of the country's 1880s public land
policy to Indian affairs. The Jeffersonian ideal of the yeoman farmer that inspired
experiments in home-steading was forced on tribes in the well-intentioned but ill-
fated "allotment" policy. It was designed to carve up reservations and give individual
Indians allotments in tribal lands, with the "surplus" lands going to non-Indian
farmers. Reservations were broken up into family farms with horrific consequences:
poverty, loss of land, and destruction of tribal governments. Congress recognized its
mistake and repudiated the allotment policy, but not before Indians had sacrificed
ninety million acres, tribal governments had failed, and reservations had been
wracked by poverty and dismal social conditions.

"Termination" was another policy that foisted on Indian country ideals that
seemed desirable for the dominant society. In the 1950s, some supporters of the

policy thought they were promoting racial equality. Others wanted to eliminate communally governed groups. The post-war zeal for unifying the nation combined with otherwise divergent political strains to find consensus in the idea of terminating the special status of Indian tribes and bringing them into the mainstream of society.

Congress perfunctorily embraced the policy with little reflection and virtually no Indian participation. The termination policy destroyed several tribes and drove their members into severe social and economic distress before it was rejected. Congress then spent years trying to put the pieces back together by "restoring" terminated tribes.

In eras when Congress was imposing versions of grand national policies on Indians, the Supreme Court's role was to ensure, for better or worse, that neither states nor courts interfered with the essentially political decisions involved in the field of Indian affairs. Sweepingly destructive policies like allotment and termination were enacted with little or no involvement or communication with tribes. Perhaps this is unsurprising, given the awesome prerogatives that the Court historically conceded to the political branches of government notwithstanding a relative lack of transparency that allowed untoward results to be hidden from public view. Moreover, these policies were adopted when tribes lacked the level of political and economic influence that they have gained in recent years.

Since the days of John Marshall, the Supreme Court has eschewed a judicial role that adjusted the nation's anomalous political relationship with Indian tribes, thus leaving the task to the political branches. In the past, lower courts have occasionally indulged their sympathies for states or settlers, or for individual Indians or tribes. To the extent that these rulings departed from the nation's political relationship with tribes, the Supreme Court has been the super-ego in the system. It has made decisions that seemed courageous or cowardly, depending on one's perspective, but which were consistent with foundational principles. The Court started with the premise that tribes would maintain their autonomy and control over historical territory, but Congress would be in charge of the relationship. This meant that the Court tolerated explicit, sometimes drastic, exercises of congressional power invading tribal sovereignty and Indian rights or curbing state governmental incursions or infringements of Indian rights. It tolerated unequal bargains in which the tribal land base was decimated. It also meant that, unless and until Congress acted deliberately, or the executive exercised authority delegated by Congress, states, local governments, private companies, land speculators, resource developers, and others could not interfere with Indian rights or self-governing powers. In its historical context, this tradition of deference would seem appealing to all but the most imperious judge.

Congress appears to have internalized the lesson of history that toxic limits on broad national policies are often discovered when they are insinuated into Indian policy. The last two generations of American Indians, under the prevailing self-determination policies, have had to cope only with the pockets of poisonous gas that linger from old federal policies. Since the termination era ended, congressional activity has been less headstrong, with anti-Indian politicians indulging in only occasional forays that would curtail tribal authority or rights.

Indian legislative activity has never before been as mindful of tribal interests as it has during the last thirty-five years. Indeed, no sooner had the brief termination era ended than Congress began reversing its actions by restoring terminated tribes. It has also implemented the prevailing self-determination policy with an impressive body of laws and programs strongly supporting the sovereignty of tribes.

These laws provide for Indian control of education and health care, tribal regulation of environmental quality on reservations, and the restoration and consolidation of the tribal land and resource base. Congress has even tried to roll back some of the Supreme Court's ventures into policymaking that were in conflict with tribal political and cultural autonomy.

Although there may be serious challenges to Indian interests by members of Congress, tribes today are part of every legislative debate that affects them and they have a growing influence in national and state politics. They are represented by experienced and educated leaders and often retain skilled professional lobbyists, consultants, and lawyers. In no small way, they have been aided by the wealth some tribes have gained from gambling businesses. The threat of Congress's abuse of its plenary power in Indian affairs remains, but the prospect of its being used to destroy tribal rights and powers is more limited than ever because tribes are better equipped to participate in the political process.

Now it is the Supreme Court that appears intent on fitting Indians into norms of the dominant society's legal system rather than waiting for Congress to fill gaps and address issues. Moreover, the judicial gap-filling seems especially intrusive on congressional prerogatives in an era when the winds of policy from the political branches favor the tribal sovereignty while the Court rolls back self-governing powers. The Rehnquist Court's decisions, meanderings from the settled principles and approaches embraced by all its predecessors, have created a judicial atmosphere that threatens economic development efforts as well as the political and cultural survival of Indian tribes. It is ironic that, in an era when tribes have gained sufficient respect and competence to deal effectively in the political arena, the Court should, for the first time in the nation's history, claim the prerogative of designing Indian policy instead of deferring to Congress.

The Rehnquist Court has used Indian cases to promote values important to a majority of the Justices. Some cases may have been selected because they presented an opportunity to tackle an issue like state sovereign immunity or limits on the free exercise of religion and the case just happened to involve Indians. In others, Justices' values have informed their view of the merits of cases that, in another era, would be seen as uniquely Indian law matters.

Putting Indian decisions back on a more predictable course, one consistent with judicial traditions in the field, might be somewhat easier than if the Court were dedicated to pursuing a specific "Indian agenda." By renewing its appreciation of the distinctness of Indian law, the Court could return the field to a foundational approach. That approach requires the Court, in the absence of clear legislation limiting the historic status of tribes, to defer to Congress rather than conjure up its own policy. If the Court appreciated the place of tribes in the constitutional structure it would force more issues into the political arena. This would certainly not ensure that tribes will always "win"; not all the decisions of the Rehnquist Court that are adverse to tribes are "wrong" in their outcome, though few employ traditional analysis. Under the plenary power doctrine, tribal rights and powers can be whittled and even eliminated, but only by clear legislative statements and after appropriate debate that weighs the policy change in light of a variety of potential contexts. In this age of greater sophistication of tribal leaders, there will surely be Indian participation in the debate.

The rediscovery of Indian law requires an understanding of the basic principles and traditions of Indian law apparently lacking on the present Court. Short of taking a course in Indian law, the Justices need only appreciate why this is a special field, like international relations, where the judicial role is appropriately more limited than in others. It is not a field where the Court should plunge in and decide, on balance, what the relations of tribes and their neighbors "ought to be" by applying the values it brings to bear on other cases where such balancing and interpretive license may be more fitting. In addition, rediscovery demands that the Court not yield to the temptation to use Indian cases as crucibles for forging and testing principles favored by the Court's majorities but that are unspecific as to Indian law. Returning the Court to thoughtful consideration of the foundational principles of Indian law would end the current trend that grossly disserves tribes by lumping Indian law cases with cases involving racial preferences, attacks on state rights, and aberrations from the mainstream.

The Justices must also understand that their recent decisions have begun to dismantle Indian policy, and that this inevitably will cause confusion among state, local, and tribal governments, heighten tensions among Indians and their non-Indian neighbors, undermine reservation economic development efforts, and frustrate lower federal and state courts. *** Indian rights should be seen for what they are, and historically have been: the fulfillment of a political relationship between the United States and self-governing tribes.

***

NOTES & QUESTIONS

1. *Reading Indian Law*:
   • What is the significance of the statistics Getches discusses in the first part of his article? What do they tell us? What do they *not* tell us?
   • Why does Getches look to the work of constitutional law scholars as a way to determine what might be motivating the Court in deciding

Indian law cases? What changes occurred between the Burger Court and the Rehnquist Court? How do those changes impact Indian law?

- In his article, Getches uses a very famous quotation from Felix Cohen. Who was Felix Cohen? How did he contribute to Indian law? What did Felix Cohen mean when he compared Indians to the miner's canary? Why did Getches use this quotation in his article?

2. *Tribal Governments and the Political Structure of the United States*: The US Constitution establishes the structure of the federal government and sets forth the guidelines for the relationship between the federal and state governments. The primary legislative authority of the federal government rests in Congress, which has a bicameral structure. Each state is given two seats in the US Senate, and the seats in the House of Representatives are apportioned among the states based on population. Unlike states, tribal governments have no formal place in the federal structure. Congress does, however, possess the power to enact laws relating to federal Indian policy. What influence do tribal governments have on Congress? What mechanism exists for tribes to have a voice in federal Indian policy? In what ways are tribes different from states? What is the significance of that difference?

3. *Separation of Powers and the Role of the Judicial Branch*: The US Constitution creates a federal government with three branches – legislative, executive, and judicial – and establishes checks and balances to ensure that no one branch gains a disproportionate amount of power. In looking at the relationship between the judicial and legislative branches, the legislative branch is supposed to express the "will of the people" and the judicial branch is supposed to ensure that in doing so, the legislative branch does not trample on the rights of those individuals who might not share the beliefs of the majority. In his article, Getches argues that one of the motivating factors for the Rehnquist Court is "protection of mainstream values." How does this comport with the view that the judicial branch is supposed to protect those in the minority from the "tyranny of the majority"? How does that play out in Indian law cases?

The federal courts have developed several doctrines to ensure that the judicial branch does not intrude too deeply into the work of the legislative and executive branches. Several of these doctrines call for the courts to defer to the judgment of Congress and of administrative agencies in cases requiring a weighing and balancing of political and budgetary factors. Can these calls for deference be reconciled with the Rehnquist Court's decisions disfavoring racial minorities, ensuring states' rights, and protecting mainstream values? Is the US Supreme Court fulfilling the duties of the judicial branch as envisioned in the US Constitution? Has the Court redefined its role?

As you consider these questions, reflect on the relationship between the Constitution and Indian tribes discussed by Professor Riley in Chapter 4. In a case involving whether the Navajo Tribe could prohibit the use of peyote by members of the Native American Church, the Tenth Circuit has placed Indian tribes beyond the reach of the Constitution and given them a sovereign status higher than that of states:

> The First Amendment applies only to Congress. It limits the powers of Congress to interfere with religious freedom or religious worship. It is made applicable to the States only by the Fourteenth Amendment. Thus construed, the First Amendment places limitations upon the action of Congress and of the States. But *** Indian tribes are not states. They have a status higher than that of states. They are subordinate and dependent nations possessed of all powers as such only to the extent that they have expressly been required to surrender them by the superior sovereign, the United States. The Constitution is, of course, the supreme law of the land, but it is nonetheless a part of the laws of the United States. Under the philosophy of the decisions, it, as any other law, is binding upon Indian nations only where it expressly binds them, or is made binding by treaty or some act of Congress.

Native American Church v. Navajo Tribal Council, 272 F.2d 131, 134–135 (10th Cir. 1959). After reading the Getches piece, do you think the Supreme Court today would afford tribes such a powerful position? What has changed since 1959?

4. *The Tribal Supreme Court Project*: In 2001, the same year Getches' article was published, a group of tribal leaders formed what became known as the Tribal Supreme Court Project. The purpose of the Project is to coordinate in a concentrated and strategic manner the briefing and arguments in Indian law cases presented to the US Supreme Court. The Tribal Supreme Court gets involved both when the Supreme Court is considering accepting a case and after the case is placed on the Court's docket. Why do you think such strategic coordination is necessary? Does the article by Getches help answer that question? An article in the Native American Rights Fund newsletter (NARF plays a major role in the Project) cites the statistics set forth in Getches' article when discussing the reasons the Project was created. *The Tribal Supreme Court Project*, 30 NARF Legal Review 1 (2005). What kinds of cases would the Project want to keep out of the Court? How could the Project make it more likely that certain cases would be accepted by the Court? In answering these questions, be sure to read Professor Matthew Fletcher's article excerpted in Chapter 16.

5. *Critical Legal Studies*: The Critical Legal Studies movement and Critical Race Theory, an offshoot of CLS, are schools of thought that developed in the 1970s and 1980s. Both schools of thought argue that the legal system, and in particular the courts, are not institutions committed to justice. These movements argue instead that the legal system is a creature of the existing power structure and exists to reinforce the authority of those in power. Would Critical Legal theorists or Critical Race scholars agree or disagree with Getches' arguments? Do the motivations of the Rehnquist Court, as identified by Getches, support or refute these theories? Consider Professor Williams' discussion in Chapter 2 regarding the philosophical underpinnings of the Marshall Trilogy and his critique of modern Indian law.

6. *Beyond the Law*: Although tribal governments lack an official voice or representation in the US government, individual tribal members are US citizens (at least since 1924) and thus have the same right to vote under the law as any other US citizen. Translating this legal right into political reality, however, has not been an easy task. States have erected a number of obstacles to prevent or dilute the Native vote. The *Harvard Law Review* has documented some of the most recent stories:

> Naomi White resides outside Window Rock, Arizona, an area within the Navajo Nation so rural that the Postal Service does not provide home delivery. Because White's voter-registration application bore a physical address that was "too obscure," the Apache County Recorder, the agency charged with election administration for the county, could not assign her to a voting precinct, considered her to be an inactive voter, and did not allow her to vote by absentee ballot. As a result, White, who is Navajo, was kept from voting in at least two elections in 2012.
>
> Agnes Laughter, another member of the Navajo Tribe, resides in Chilchinbeto, a community in the Navajo Nation 170 miles northeast of Flagstaff, Arizona. Laughter speaks only Navajo, does not read or write, and does not have an original birth certificate. When the state of Arizona passed a law requiring that voters provide certain forms of identification, Laughter was forced to travel to Flagstaff, and was able, but only after substantial effort, to obtain a form of identification that would be accepted at the polls – but not before she was kept from voting in the 2006 elections.
>
> Thomas Poor Bear is a member of the Oglala Sioux Tribe and resides in Wanblee, Jackson County, South Dakota, on the Pine Ridge Reservation. In order to register to vote or to vote absentee in person, Poor Bear and other members of the Oglala Sioux Tribe must travel almost sixty miles round-trip to Kadoka, the county

seat – even though an estimated 22% of Indian households in Jackson County do not have access to a car. Poor Bear had asked the County to establish a satellite elections office in Wanblee, the population center of the Jackson County portion of the Pine Ridge Reservation, but the County initially refused. Only after Poor Bear and other members of his tribe filed suit did the County open the satellite office.

Securing Indian Voting Rights, 129 Harv. L. Rev. 1731, 1731 (2016). *See also* David E. Wilkins & Heidi Kiiwetinepinesiik Stark, *American Indian Politics and the American Political System* 206–210 (Rowman & Littlefield 4th ed. 2018). For an exploration of the cases brought under the Voting Rights Act, *see* Daniel McCool, Susan M. Olson, & Jennifer L. Robinson, *Native Vote: American Indians, the Voting Rights Act, and the Right to Vote* (Cambridge University Press 2007). If Native Americans, as a practical matter, do not possess the same ability to vote as other US citizens, how does that impact the representation they receive in Congress? What incentives does that give Representatives and Senators to listen to the Native vote?

FURTHER READING

- Grant Christensen, *Judging Indian Law: What Factors Influence Individual Justice's Votes on Indian Law in the Modern Era*, 43 U. Tol. L. Rev. 267 (2012).
- Matthew L. M. Fletcher, *Indian Courts and Fundamental Fairness: 'Indian Courts and the Future' Revisited*, 84 U. Colo. L. Rev. 59 (2013).
- David Getches, *Conquering the Cultural Frontier: The New Subjectivism of The Supreme Court in Indian Law*, 84 Cal. L. Rev. 1573 (1996).
- L. Scott Gould, *The Consent Paradigm: Tribal Sovereignty at the Millennium*, 96 Colum. L. Rev. 809 (1996).
- Ralph W. Johnson & Berry Martinis, *Chief Justice Rehnquist and the Indian Law Cases*, 16 Pub. Land L. Rev. 1 (1997).
- Melissa L. Koehn, *The New American Caste System: The Supreme Court and Discrimination among Civil Rights Plaintiffs*, 32 Mich. J.L. Ref. 49 (1998).
- John LaVelle, *Sanctioning a Tyranny: The Diminishment of Ex Parte Young, Expansion of Hans Immunity, and Denial of Indian Rights in Coeur d'Alene Tribe*, 31 Ariz. St. L.J. 787 (1999).
- Alexander Tallchief Skibine, *The Supreme Court's Last 30 Years of Federal Indian Law: Looking for Equilibrium or Supremacy?*, 8 Colum. J. Race & L. 22 (2018).
- Robert A. Williams, Jr., *Like a Loaded Weapon: The Rehnquist Court, Indian Rights, and the Legal History of Racism in America* (University of Minnesota Press 2005).

8

A Narrative of Sovereignty: Illuminating the Paradox of the Domestic Dependent Nation

Sarah Krakoff

83 Or. L. Rev. 1109 (2004)

The federal Indian law decisions of the US Supreme Court reflect a wide spectrum of opinions about the power and authority of tribal governments. Some decisions, such as Worcester v. Georgia, *are very protective of a tribal government's ability to regulate what happens within its borders. Other decisions, such as* Montana v. United States, *are quite restrictive in limiting the tribal government's jurisdiction.*

In this article, Sarah Krakoff argues that many of these Supreme Court opinions are made on the basis of little to no understanding of just what it is that tribal governments do and how they function. She calls upon those working in tribal government and in federal Indian law to develop a more robust narrative of sovereignty.

Professor Krakoff uses the Navajo Nation as an example of how to build such a narrative. Rather than focusing on the work of tribal courts, she has studied the actions of the Navajo Nation's legislative and executive branches and uses the resulting information to paint a picture of the problems confronting the Navajo Nation and the solutions it has implemented. Into this narrative, she weaves the decisions of the US Supreme Court, examining the ways in which the Court's decisions have impacted the efforts of the Navajo Nation.

As you read the article, ask yourself how the information provided by Professor Krakoff impacts your understanding of tribal governments and the challenges they face. Before reading the article, what did you know about the work of tribal governments? Where did that information come from? Where do you think the US Supreme Court gets its information about tribal governments? After reading the article, do you think the Supreme Court has an accurate view of tribal governments?

Does American Indian tribal sovereignty exist? In some sense it is a strange question to ask. More than 540 federally recognized American Indian tribes function as sovereign nations in many significant respects. To the members of these tribes and to many non-members who spend time in Indian country, the answer is a resounding "yes." Yet the doctrine of American Indian tribal sovereignty is a legal and conceptual conundrum. "Domestic dependent nations," as Justice John Marshall famously labeled Indian tribes, are unique and paradoxical constructions. Sovereignty ordinarily entails powers of self-protection for which a nation-state requires no positive legal authority, as well as the right of a state to exercise power freely within its territory. American case law, however, has limited tribal governmental authority to domestic and internal matters, and has declared that even these powers are subject to defeasance by Congress. Because of these limitations and the often inscrutable way in which the Supreme Court arrives at them, the legal construct of Indian tribal sovereignty has been subject to much criticism, including most recently by members of the Court itself. In *United States v. Lara*, a case affirming Congress's power to recognize inherent tribal criminal jurisdiction over non-member Indians, Justice Thomas concurred in the result but wrote separately to decry what he sees as the contradictory premises that lie at the heart of the doctrine of tribal sovereignty. Justice Thomas suggested that one solution is for the Supreme Court to declare that tribal sovereignty does not exist.

Such a declaration would be met with shock and outrage by many members of tribal nations for whom "sovereignty" is as common and heartfelt a term as "rights" is to most other Americans. Many tribal members perceive that their cultural survival is inextricably linked to their existence as separate, self-governing nations, and that dealing a final blow to the legal doctrine of sovereignty would be akin to terminating tribal people themselves. Former Chief Justice of the Navajo Nation Robert Yazzie, in testimony before the US Senate Committee on Indian Affairs, put it this way: "In short, the Navajo Nation is faced with nothing less than a threat of cultural, economic, and political genocide." These are strong words, particularly when aimed at the least dangerous branch of government, one that sits at quiet remove from the daily struggles for survival in Indian country.

How can we account for the gap between Justice Thomas and Justice Yazzie? A critique of the legal doctrine is not enough. What is required is a narrative of sovereignty that informs courts, legislators, and the public about what tribal sovereignty actually looks like on the ground and why it matters. This Article provides that narrative by examining the interplay between US Supreme Court decisions defining the contours of tribal sovereignty and actions by and within the Navajo Nation regarding its sovereignty from 1970 to 2003. In studying the legal and political developments within the Navajo Nation, this Article addresses the following questions: What impacts have US Supreme Court decisions had on the development of the Navajo Nation's political and legal systems? How, in turn, have the functions of Navajo sovereignty been affected? Those functions include concerns of practical governance, such as providing economic opportunities and peace and security, as well as the more elusive expressive aspects associated with preserving a distinct and endemic culture.

Providing a narrative of sovereignty is particularly salient now due to the active role that the Supreme Court is taking in defining tribal governmental powers. The

Supreme Court has granted certiorari on a surprisingly disproportionate number of Indian law cases during the last several decades. The Court's recent decisions in these cases have left scholars with ample questions concerning the constitutional and common law underpinnings of the Court's reasoning, and much scholarly attention has been devoted to addressing these questions. The cases have also left scholars and tribal advocates with the more practical problem of how to respond to the Court's narrowing of tribal powers. The Court's activity and the legal and practical questions it raises highlight the need for an engaged discussion about what tribal sovereignty is in practice, how it is affected by Supreme Court decisions, and why it matters.***

I THE NAVAJO NATION: A CASE STUDY IN ENACTING SOVEREIGNTY

The Navajo Nation is one of the most studied tribes. Academics, journalists, and others are drawn to the Diné homeland, located in the four corners area of the Southwest, for a variety of compelling reasons. It is the Indian nation with the largest land base; Navajo Indian country comprises twenty-seven thousand square miles, or roughly seventeen million acres, which is slightly larger than West Virginia and comparable in size to Ireland. It is also the second-most populous Indian nation, with 298,197 tribal members, 168,000 of whom reside in Navajo Indian country. For legal scholars, the Navajo Nation's highly active and developed tribal court system and substantial body of decisional law, including Navajo customary law, constitute a significant draw. For historians and anthropologists, the Navajo's resilience and consequent ability to maintain an intact yet ever evolving culture provide ample fodder for study. And for all of these reasons and more, the Navajo Nation is an interesting and unique place to spend time. In addition, with respect to this study in particular, access to research materials such as council resolutions and minutes, interviews with key participants in the Navajo legal system, and other intangibles making research possible were facilitated by my familiarity with the place and at least some of its players.

First, a brief word on methodology is called for. The primary sources reviewed for this study included legal documents (comprising tribal council resolutions and minutes as well as tribal case law), periodicals, tax department documents, and other material relevant to how the Navajo Nation has reacted to Supreme Court decisions defining the contours of tribal sovereignty from the period between 1970 and 2003. In addition, I interviewed key participants in the Navajo legal and political systems. During many of the interviews, it was clear that there is an aspect of tribal sovereignty that is expressive for tribal members. They feel deeply that sovereignty matters, and that any unilateral incursions by the Supreme Court are an affront to justice, or even survival, for Indian people. While it is hard to quantify these expressions of sovereignty, they are an integral part of my conclusions concerning the centrality of tribal political sovereignty to the continued existence of Indian tribes as separate cultures. The study thus includes quantitative as well as qualitative elements in its attempt to assess the impacts of federal law on some of the core values that sovereignty, by almost any definition, is intended to protect.***

A Legal Sovereignty: Introduction to the Framework of Federal Decisional Law

American Indian tribes have a unique legal status. They are sovereign nations whose existence pre-dates the Constitution, and yet they have been folded into the United States and its domestic legal framework through a series of court decisions and other legislative and political acts. ***

*** It has been largely from the early 1970s on that the Court has refined the contours of tribal sovereignty. On one end of the spectrum, the Court has affirmed and strengthened the inherent sovereign authority of tribes. These cases *** include ones in which the Court recognizes inherent tribal powers to govern tribal members or non-members as well as those in which the Court has held that states lack power to regulate the activities of tribal members or non-members within Indian country. *** On the other end of the spectrum, the Court has limited tribal governmental authority in two ways. *** [First,] the Court has allowed greater and more intrusive forms of state regulation within Indian country. *** [Second,] the Court has limited tribal authority over non-members in Indian country. Almost all of the Supreme Court decisions that might have some direct effect on tribal governance fit within these three categories.***

B Historical Background of the Navajo Nation

***

Recognizing the Navajo as a people who self-define through attachment to place rather than solely through lineal descent is one key to understanding the political nature of Navajo identity, which has been forged by adaptation and change. The indispensable constant in historical times has been connection to the beautiful, sparse, dry, and wind-swept landscape between the Navajo's four sacred mountains. With identity firmly rooted in place, the Navajo have been otherwise free to incorporate other people, their traditions, their economic practices, and still remain Navajo. The political nature of Navajo identity reinforces the significance of the tribe's sovereignty; without the status of a sovereign, the Navajo Nation would not be able to protect the distinct evolving nature of Navajo culture. The constancy of place leaves room for the changing nature of what is still distinctly Navajo.

***

C Strands of Sovereignty in the Modern Era

***

The Supreme Court has affirmed the general notion that Indian tribes retain inherent authority to govern, through civil regulation or adjudication, the activities of tribal members and non-Indians within the boundaries of tribal territory.

The cases recognizing inherent tribal powers to regulate and adjudicate and restricting the reach of state authority in Indian country appear to endorse a vision of tribal evolution to govern a range of civil matters, including matters involving non-Indians. The cases, when considered together, also appear particularly solicitous of tribal courts and the extent to which federal intermeddling could undermine tribal judicial authority. Subsequent cases are not so solicitous, and have placed significant limitations on tribal authority over non-members. But the vision and institutional sensitivity of the *** cases nonetheless resulted in significant opportunities for tribes to develop their regulatory and judicial systems.

The Navajo Nation has taken advantage of these Supreme Court decisions in a range of ways, and today has a robust government that has taken on many of the same functions as state governments. First, the Navajo have developed, and re-tribalized, one of the most respected and busy American Indian tribal court systems in the country. The development of the Navajo Nation judicial system has been studied by many legal scholars. In addition, Navajo Nation Supreme Court justices have been prolific themselves, and have shared many insights concerning the history and development of Navajo law. That work will therefore not be repeated here, but it is important to note that the common refrain is the unique melding of Anglo-American-style judicial systems and traditional Navajo customary law. In the context of its court system, the Navajo Nation story of mutual infusion persists. On one hand, principles from federal law, such as the interpretation of due process in the context of personal jurisdiction, have been adopted by the tribal courts. On the other, the Navajo Nation has incorporated Navajo customary law and traditional dispute resolution into its legal system so successfully that the concepts have been studied for application elsewhere. The Navajo Nation has enacted inherent sovereignty in the judicial realm by developing a judicial system that successfully straddles two worlds, providing a fair and familiar forum for non-Navajo persons and a culturally coherent body of laws and procedures for tribal members.

Less has been written about substantive Navajo law, and in particular Navajo legislation. The Navajo Nation has enacted laws that protect individual rights and liberties, some of which exceed the protections in the US Constitution. In 1967, the Navajo Nation enacted a Bill of Rights, including due process and equal protection provisions. In 1980, the Navajo Nation took a step that the United States has yet to take: the Navajo Tribal Council voted by an overwhelming majority to adopt an Equal Rights Provision, explicitly providing for legal equality between the sexes.

*** [T]he era of self-determination also gave the Navajo Nation the breathing room to develop consumer protection, employment, and other statutory laws that relate to core aspects of practical sovereignty, such as provision of jobs and protection from unfair economic practices. ***

The Navajo Nation has also exercised its governmental powers to attempt to provide educational opportunities that simultaneously prepare Navajo children to compete in a non-Indian world and reinforce Navajo language and culture. ***

During the allotment period and for a long time afterwards, education was primarily a tool to kill off any vestiges of tribal language and culture. ***

The Navajo Nation thus faces a significant challenge to turn education from a threatening, negative influence into one that can provide positive opportunities. To meet this challenge, the Navajo Tribal Council passed a law requiring all schools on the Navajo Nation to teach Navajo language and culture in all grades. The Diné Division of Education oversees the implementation of the law, assisting the many state public schools on the Navajo Nation to meet the requirement through its Office of Diné Language, Culture & Community. The Navajo literature repeatedly expresses the link between inherent sovereign powers and the ability to take steps to preserve Navajo language and culture. The preamble to the Diné Office of Language, Culture & Community's programs states: "The Navajo Tribe, as a sovereign nation, has a responsibility to its people to oversee the education in whatever schools or school systems they are being educated."

***

With its inherent power to regulate and adjudicate, the Navajo Nation has taken many significant steps toward: providing for peace and security, through its respected and fair court system; economic opportunities, both by protecting consumers and employees; and furthering Navajo cultural practices, by incorporating Navajo law into judicial decision making, by taking steps to encourage tribal members to stay within the Navajo Nation, and by incorporating Navajo language and culture into education. The Supreme Court's decisions recognizing inherent tribal powers and limiting the reach of state jurisdiction appear, from these examples, to have provided room for a distinctly Navajo political and cultural life to continue.

b Responding to Concurrent State Authority to Regulate

In *Cotton Petroleum Corp. v. New Mexico*, the Court hinged its decision to allow states to tax non-Indian activity in Indian country in part on the services provided by the state to the tribe and tribal members. The obligation of states to provide certain services is constitutionally based. At the end of the allotment era, Congress passed a statute that declared that all American Indian tribal members would henceforth be US citizens. Pursuant to the Fourteenth Amendment of the United States Constitution, American Indian tribal members are also therefore citizens of the states where they reside. A string of cases in which tribal members have pressed for their rights to equal state services confirm that the Fourteenth Amendment's equal protection guarantees apply to them, notwithstanding the complication of their political membership in an Indian tribe. Navajo tribal members and the Navajo Nation itself have relied on this line of authority in order to obtain benefits for tribal members that allow them to continue living on the Navajo Nation.

***

*** While it might seem anomalous to assert the sovereign right to be free from state authority in some circumstances, and yet to sue the state to provide services in others, the complicated hand that "domestic dependent nations" have been dealt requires flexibility in terms of strategies. State public schools are a staple of American Indian reservation life. The federal government has chosen to meet its obligation to educate American Indian children in part by providing funding to state school districts, both through the ability to tax non-Indian activity in Indian country and more directly through a variety of federal funds that compensate for lost tax revenue and/or provide additional funds for the special needs of American Indian children. States are paid, in other words, to assist them in meeting their constitutional obligations. Thus, while the best long-term solution might be to replace state public schools with tribal schools, for the foreseeable future Navajo children will attend schools run by the states. Requiring states to provide adequate, local, culturally appropriate educational programs is one way of assuring a Navajo future for tribal children.

The Navajo Nation has also recruited the state as an initially unwilling partner in the problem of child support enforcement for tribal members. The federal statute requiring states to provide child support enforcement services for recipients of welfare omitted any reference to Indian tribes. Tribes therefore had no direct access to the federal funds that accompanied the mandate. The Navajo Nation, spurred on by indigent tribal members who had been denied state enforcement services, negotiated with New Mexico and Arizona and ultimately achieved a solution that brought some child support enforcement services to the reservation.

As the examples of public education and child support demonstrate, the Navajo Nation and Navajo tribal members have responded flexibly to the issue of concurrent state authority in Indian country. While many Navajo officials likely believe that the best long-term solutions are clear territorial boundaries and increased funding and autonomy for the Nation to provide its own services, that day is not at hand. In the meantime, *Cotton's* legal framework of overlapping authority and responsibility for services has resulted in context-specific tactics that attempt to ensure that the needs of Navajo Nation residents can be met.

***

c Effects of Categorical Limitations on Tribal Inherent Power to Regulate
and Adjudicate

***

The Supreme Court's decisions *** limiting tribal civil jurisdiction over non-Indians have had a range of impacts on the Navajo Nation. First, in the expressive category, Navajo tribal officials and other tribal members have reacted strongly to what they perceive to be an attack on their separate existence. Second, litigants seeking relief in tribal court must often wade through several layers of jurisdictional proceedings in tribal and federal court before obtaining a final answer to the question of whether the tribal court can hear their claims. Third, the transactional environment for the Navajo Nation has been negatively affected by the apparent flip in presumptions concerning tribal jurisdiction over non-Indian activity. And related to these impacts, non-Indian resistance to tribal substantive law affects the Navajo Nation's ability to safeguard, through employment and tort law, the economic and physical security of Navajo tribal members.

Navajo tribal officials, in both formal and informal statements, have condemned the Supreme Court's decisions limiting tribal inherent powers. In various ways, these officials express the link that they see between sovereignty and survival of the Navajo people. As noted in this Article's introduction, former Chief Justice of the Navajo Nation Robert Yazzie describes the Court's decisions as creating the "threat of cultural, economic, and political genocide." These are strong words, and yet they are not the isolated perceptions of one Navajo Justice. Navajo Nation Legislative Counsel Raymond Etcitty concludes that the federal courts "are trying to do what the federal, executive, [and legislative] branch[es] have learned they cannot do—eliminate tribes." Mr. Etcitty also describes what he sees as hypocrisy in the Supreme Court's decisions on at least two fronts. First, the Court's solicitude for federalism illogically stops at respect for the separate political approaches of Indian nations. "What about the concept of laboratories for democracy?" Etcitty wonders, paraphrasing the famous quote by Justice Brandeis. Second, Etcitty asks with evident frustration and anger, "How does the US government have the audacity to tell other governments what to do with their indigenous people when it doesn't deal appropriately with its own?"

***

Another recurring theme in the responses of Navajo Nation officials is that the Court's decisions are based, at least in part, on ignorance. Etcitty does not mince words: "Ignorance drives the Court's decisions." In particular, Etcitty cites to the Court's lack of knowledge about Navajo concepts of due process, which he believes contributes to the Court's reluctance to submit non-Indians to tribal jurisdiction. "Our concept of 'Nalyeeh,' is more generous than due process," Etcitty asserts, referring to a Navajo common-law concept that embodies principles of fair treatment and restitution. Navajo Nation Supreme Court Justice Lorene Ferguson comments that there was a time when the federal government understood Indian issues. She believes that time has passed, and that today the Court and Executive Branch appear alternately ignorant and hostile. ***

The comments of these Navajo Nation officials, in both tenor and substance, indicate the extent to which Navajo tribal members perceive their distinctness as a people to be bound up with their political existence as a sovereign. ***

In terms of impacts on practical governance, there is evidence to suggest that the concerns of Navajo officials are warranted. Navajo consumer protection and employment laws, in which the Navajo Nation has exercised its sovereign powers to serve the functions of providing economic security as discussed above *** face uncertainty as a result of the Supreme Court's cases. Tort cases filed in Navajo courts are also vulnerable. Non-Indian litigants are more prone to challenge the tribe's jurisdiction over them in these cases, which creates prolonged uncertainty regarding the application of Navajo law. Such challenges may ultimately result in federal decisions that non-Indians, even when they engage in substantial activity in Indian country that depends upon Navajo labor and services of various kinds, are not subject to Navajo law at all.

***

Finally, the Supreme Court's cases that divest Indian tribes of categories of civil jurisdiction have compromised the transactional environment for tribes. As a result of *Strate* and *Hicks*, the Navajo Nation has adopted a policy of requiring consent to tribal jurisdiction in every lease, contract, or other consensual agreement. But every negotiation with a non-Indian business is now conducted in a context in which non-Indian perceptions of the uncertainty and strangeness of tribal law are bolstered by their sense that these laws need not apply to them. Obtaining consent to tribal law and jurisdiction in these circumstances is awkward if not impossible. *** The Court's jurisprudence has altered jurisdictional expectations in a way that creates barriers to transactions, and therefore potentially interferes with tribal economic development.

*** Providing economic security through employment is a key function of sovereignty. Researchers at the Udall Center for Studies in Public Policy and the Harvard Project on American Indian Economic Development have determined that "tribal control over tribal affairs is the only policy that works for economic development." If providing services and a secure business environment to non-Indian businesses on the Navajo Nation does not result in the potential to increase Navajo employment, a significant benefit of economic development is lost, and that functional aspect of sovereignty is impaired. Likewise, the sovereign interest in protecting citizens from unscrupulous and/or harmful behavior through consumer protection and tort law is at risk due to the instability of tribal legal jurisdiction.

***

2 Taxation

A ACTING ON THE INHERENT POWER TO TAX "The right to tax is an inherent right of the Navajo Nation and one aspect of its sovereignty." This quotation does not come from a federal case. These are the words of the Navajo Nation Tribal Council in its 1974 resolution establishing the Navajo Tax Commission. Emboldened by the new era of self-determination and committed to creating a homeland that could nurture its people in ways the federal government had repeatedly failed to do, the

Navajo Nation set out to collect revenue to fund programs. As the Council resolution also stated, "Various studies and surveys made by and on behalf of the Navajo Tribe have shown that taxation within a comprehensive taxation program would be in the best interests of the Navajo people."

In the four years following the establishment of the Navajo Tax Commission, the Commission continued to study the question of whether and how much to tax. In 1978, the first Navajo taxes – a possessory interest tax (hereafter PIT, which is a type of ad valorem tax) and a business activity tax (hereafter BAT, which is a type of gross receipts tax) – were enacted by the Tribal Council. In enacting both of these taxes, the Tribal Council again declared that "[t]he right to tax is part of the inherent sovereignty of any Nation." In addition, the economic need for the taxes was articulated: "Navajo population and Navajo needs are increasing, with the increase in the need for services partly a result of increased employment and development within the Navajo Nation." In these pronouncements, the Council makes clear the direct link between sovereign authority and revival and protection of the Navajo people.

Almost as soon as the Navajo Nation BAT and PIT were passed, non-Indian businesses extracting coal within the Navajo Nation filed suit, objecting to the taxes on jurisdictional and other grounds. While these cases were winding their way through the federal courts, the Supreme Court heard two other challenges to tribal taxes, and in both affirmed the inherent tribal power to tax. ***

Given the green light to pass taxes in order to raise revenue and fund essential governmental programs, many tribes passed a variety of tax provisions. Some of these taxes raised issues that would later result in de facto and de jure limitations on the tribal power to tax, as discussed *** below. But the Court's unambiguous recognition of the tribal power to tax affirmed the notion of modern tribal sovereignty, in the context of one of the most important powers possessed by any government. The Navajo Nation has seized on this power, in both expressive and practical ways.

*** Subsequent taxes enacted by the Navajo Nation include the Oil and Gas Severance Tax, passed in 1985, the Hotel Occupancy Tax, passed in 1992, the Tobacco Products Tax, the Fuel Excise Tax, and the Sales Tax. The revenue from these taxes constitutes an increasingly significant percentage of the Navajo Nation budget. A certain percentage of the revenue is earmarked for distribution to particular funds. These include five percent to the Tax Administration Suspense Fund, two percent to the Land Acquisition Fund, two percent to the Chapter Development Fund, and twelve percent to the Permanent Trust Fund. In addition, portions of particular taxes are earmarked for specific uses. For example, the net revenue from fuel taxes goes to road maintenance and construction, and the net revenue from the hotel tax goes to a tourism fund. Each of these funds, in particular the Land Acquisition Fund and the Permanent Trust Fund, plays a significant role in furthering the core aspects of sovereignty. The Land Acquisition Fund enables the

Navajo Nation to purchase non-Indian fee lands, and thereby restore the land base as well as address some of the jurisdictional problems raised by checkerboard patterns of ownership. The Permanent Trust Fund, which was established by former Navajo Nation President Peterson Zah in 1985, is intended to provide a replacement revenue stream for oil and gas royalties. Revenue from the Fund is not available until 2005. The Navajo Nation needs long-term financial security for the day when income from fossil fuels ceases, or at least diminishes greatly, due to depletion of the resource. Using tax revenues in this way is a creative solution to the serious gaps in economic development opportunities in Indian country.

After the earmarked funds are subtracted from the tax revenue, the remainder goes in the Navajo Nation General Fund. This Fund includes revenue from all sources, including other tribally generated revenue, such as royalties from mineral production, as well as federal and state grants. From 1990 to 2002, tribal taxes accounted for a low of seven percent of the fund to a high of fifteen percent of the fund.

Tax revenue thus supports a variety of programs that ensure the health, security, and long-term viability of the Navajo Nation and its people. The money goes to basic infrastructure, which is essential to further other forms of economic development, as well as long-term investment in the Permanent Trust Fund. Moreover, taxes are becoming an increasingly significant aspect of the Navajo governmental budget. The Court's affirmation of the inherent power to tax has enabled the Navajo Nation to fund essential governmental programs today as well as plan for a more secure economic future.

B RESPONDING TO CONCURRENT STATE JURISDICTION TO TAX At the same time that the Supreme Court was affirming tribal inherent power to tax non-Indians, it was expanding concurrent state taxation of non-Indians in Indian country. Non-Indians in Indian country as a general matter now have three potential layers of taxes to pay—tribal, state, and federal. Other than the federal income tax, taxation is typically a local matter, and so the paradigmatic contest created by the Court's cases is between states and tribes for tax revenue.

***

The cases *** in which the Supreme Court has affirmed concurrent state taxation of non-Indians in Indian country, have impacted the Navajo Nation in two ways. On one hand, it is clear that tribal revenue is less than it could be in the absence of multiple taxation. Unlike states, tribes cannot market tax exemptions in order to lure customers into their jurisdictions. The tax rate in Indian country for non-Indians will therefore always be set at a floor of the state tax rate. On the other hand, the Navajo Nation has approached state governments in order to address the problem of multiple taxation on a government-to-government level. Through tribal and state legislation as well as intergovernmental agreements, the Navajo Nation has been able to mitigate some of the harsher effects of the Supreme Court's multiple taxation cases.

The revenue impacts of the *Cotton* rule are apparent in the context of the Navajo Nation Sales Tax. The sales tax is currently set at three percent of the gross receipts of any sale. The range set by the statute is between two percent and six percent, but in an environment of dual taxation for non-Indian visitors to the reservation, it is not practical to set the tax any higher than three percent. In 2003, the revenue from the sales tax exceeded $4 million. If that revenue doubled, there would obviously be more money and more flexibility. According to Amy Alderman, legal counsel for the Navajo Nation Tax Commission, one option would be to earmark some of a larger pool of sales tax revenues for sorely needed social programs. And with respect to all tribal taxes, *Colville* stands for the proposition that it is unacceptable for tribes to generate revenue by attracting non-Indian customers into Indian country by competitively pricing goods and services through the mechanism of tribal taxes that are lower than state taxes. The potential revenue from this type of competitive taxation is therefore completely lost to tribes.

Within this framework of constraints, the Navajo Nation has found room to maneuver. Neither the surrounding states nor the Navajo Nation want the multiple tax burden to inhibit non-Indian business altogether. In such circumstances, both governments lose out on the potential revenue stream because there is no business to tax at all. As a result, the Navajo Nation has approached New Mexico, Arizona, and Utah and achieved agreements that, for the most part, mitigate the harshest effects of multiple taxation on non-Indians.

New Mexico in particular has proved to be an important partner in addressing multiple taxation. In 2001, the Office of the Navajo Tax Commission worked with members of the New Mexico legislature to reduce the dual taxation effects on coal extracted from the New Mexico portion of the Navajo Nation. The negotiations resulted in mutual legislation to address the problem. New Mexico passed laws providing for severance and gross receipts tax credits to offset the Navajo taxes, and also authorized entry into cooperative agreements with the Navajo Nation. The Navajo Nation likewise approved amendments to the BAT. The result is that businesses extracting coal from the New Mexico portion of the reservation pay a comparable tax rate to businesses extracting coal from non-Indian country lands in New Mexico.

Similar legislation and intergovernmental agreements have been reached regarding other taxes. There is an intergovernmental agreement with Arizona related to tobacco tax revenue sharing and enforcement, and Arizona has passed legislation that essentially caps the cumulative tobacco tax on the reservation at the state tax rate. Arizona and the Navajo Nation have also entered into intergovern- mental agreements with respect to enforcement of the Navajo Nation BAT and the Hotel Occupancy tax. In Utah, the Tax Commission worked with state legislators to reduce the effects of concurrent state and tribal taxes in the context of hotel occupancy and fuel excise taxes. Utah passed laws mitigating the dual taxation effects, and an intergovernmental agreement was finalized. Also regarding fuel excise taxes, intergovernmental agreements exist with Arizona, New Mexico, Texas, and California

This complex of Navajo and state legislation and intergovernmental agreements has, in many significant respects, eliminated concurrent taxation. The Navajo Nation has thus been able to counteract the effects of the Supreme Court's concurrent taxation jurisprudence, to the advantage of taxpayers as well as tribal and state governments. By approaching other governments to achieve a taxing environment that does not discourage economic investment and development, the Navajo Nation exercises its sovereignty against the backdrop of federal decisional law in a positive, and mutually beneficial, way. The Navajo Nation's response can only go so far, however. The Court's concurrent taxation cases have virtually eliminated the possibility that tribes could use competitive tax policies to attract non-Indian businesses onto the reservation. And new tribal taxes, such as the Navajo Nation Sales Tax, are lower than they could be in the absence of dual taxation. Yet within these very real constraints imposed by the Court's legal definition of sovereignty, the Navajo Nation nonetheless is enacting sovereignty on the ground in creative and powerful ways.

c Effects of Categorical Limitations on the Inherent Power to Tax

In *Atkinson Trading Co. v. Shirley*, the Supreme Court in 2001 addressed the question of whether the Navajo Nation could collect a hotel occupancy tax from the non-Indian owner of a hotel located on non-Indian fee land within the Navajo Nation's boundaries. Until *Atkinson*, the Court's treatment of tribal inherent powers to tax appeared to differ from that of other tribal governmental powers. In 1982, two years after the *Montana* decision, the Supreme Court declined to follow *Montana's* framework in *Merrion v. Jicarilla Apache Tribe*. In *Merrion*, the Court affirmed the tribe's power to tax non-Indians, and found that the tribal power to tax was not merely an extension of the tribal power to exclude non-Indians from the reservation. As noted in *Merrion*, it had long been the understanding of the executive branch that tribes retained the power to tax activities on lands in which they had a significant interest, irrespective of land title. That understanding was bolstered by an early circuit court opinion affirming tribal taxes on non-Indian businesses located on non-Indian lands within a reservation.

The argument that the taxing power is different, and should not be measured by land title, is also supported by the justification for the power to tax. Governments provide services to areas within their geographical region, irrespective of land title. The power to raise revenue to fund those services is a necessary and indispensable attribute of government. In *Atkinson*, however, the Court concluded that neither

Merrion nor the governmental services argument were sufficient to distinguish the taxing power from other forms of jurisdiction over non-Indians. *Atkinson* arose on the Navajo Nation, and a brief examination of its facts shed light on some of the dignitary and economic consequences of the case.

The Atkinson Trading Company ("Atkinson"), the plaintiff in the case, owned a very small island of fee land in Cameron, an area that is within the Navajo Nation's boundaries and is otherwise predominantly composed of tribal trust land. Atkinson owns and operates the Cameron Trading Post, located on Atkinson's patch of fee land. As the Navajo Nation noted in its briefs before the Supreme Court, the Navajo Nation provides fire and police protection, emergency medical services, and health inspection services to the Cameron area. The Navajo Nation is thus the primary governmental authority ensuring health, safety, and security for Atkinson and its customers. In addition, Atkinson draws customers to its business by advertising itself as a gateway to Indian culture. The website shows photographs of Navajo waitresses, walls adorned with Navajo rugs, and includes the following marketing blurb:

> Time was when it would take days, sometimes months, to travel across the reservation and trade for the fine Native American Indian arts and curios at Cameron Trading Post. *** The Cameron Trading Post today is a center for local trade as well as a source for Native American Indina [sic] art representing many Native American Indian cultures throughout the American Southwest. In traditional patterns passed down through generations, this selection of hand crafted Navajo rugs and textiles, baskets, pueblo pottery, Native American Indian jewelry, carvings, & Southwestern art are mementos to be treasured, found in a variety to suit any vacation budget.

Atkinson thus benefits from being located on the Navajo Nation both because of the governmental services provided and the cultural milieu, which Atkinson deliberately markets. Nonetheless, the Court declined to follow *Merrion* and instead applied "*Montana* straight up," and found that neither the consensual relationship exception nor the "direct effects" exception applied. As to the former, the Court interpreted the exception narrowly, requiring nothing short of an express agreement with the tribe or its members, whereas the lower court had found a consensual relationship by virtue of the hotel customers' knowing entry into Navajo territory. Regarding the direct effects exception, the Navajo Nation argued that the Cameron Trading Post had direct effects upon the Navajo Nation in that it employs up to one hundred tribal members, derives business from tourists attracted to the Navajo Nation, and is located in an area that has overwhelming Navajo character. The Court again was not persuaded, finding that the inability to tax customers at the Trading Post would not "imperil" the political integrity of the tribe. *Atkinson* thus stands for the proposition that non-Indians on non-Indian fee lands within tribal nation boundaries exist in tribal tax-free zones. The Navajo Nation's authority to tax non-Indians is, as a practical matter, limited to circumstances in which the Navajo

Nation can require consent to tribal taxation. In instances of tribal taxes imposed for non-Indian activities on tribal trust lands, *Atkinson* itself does not impose a significant barrier. But when non-Indian business occurs on non-Indian fee land, or its equivalent, within Navajo Nation boundaries, it may be difficult for the tribe to induce the non-Indian to consent to tribal taxation.

Atkinson has clear, if not deep, revenue effects on the Navajo Nation. The Navajo Nation Hotel Occupancy Tax ("HOT") was passed by the Navajo Nation Tribal Council in 1992. Prior to the *Atkinson* decision, the tax was imposed on non-Indian guests at fourteen hotels located within Navajo Nation boundaries, as well as a small number of "bed and breakfast" establishments. Since *Atkinson*, the Navajo Nation has ceased collecting the tax from two hotels on non-Indian fee land. The Navajo Nation has also stopped collecting the Navajo Nation Sales Tax for any transactions between non-Indians on non-Indian fee land.

The revenue impacts of *Atkinson* are evident in the context of the Hotel Occupancy Tax. In the three years preceding the *Atkinson* decision, when the two hotels located on non-Indian fee land were collecting the HOT from non-Indian customers, revenue from the HOT ranged from $1,167,353 to $1,169,686. In 2001, the year *Atkinson* was decided, the revenue from the HOT dipped to $881,533. In 2002, HOT revenue totaled $948,291, and HOT revenue for 2003 was $624,000. The amount of revenue lost is not enormous. Although both of the hotels on non-Indian fee land are significant tourist establishments on the Navajo Nation, they still only constitute two out of fourteen hotels within reservation boundaries. But the lost revenue is also not likely to be recouped. Some Navajo Nation officials have suggested creative ways to induce a consensual agreement with the non-Indian owners of the hotels. For example, Navajo Nation District Court Judge Allen Sloan speculates whether the Navajo Nation's withdrawal of the provision of police and other emergency services from the Cameron area would cause Atkinson to consent to pass on the tax in exchange for these services' being restored. But whether the Navajo Nation would adopt this somewhat confrontational strategy is at best uncertain. Furthermore, whether Atkinson would consent even under such circumstances is highly speculative. It seems likely that Atkinson's resistance to the Navajo HOT was largely ideological, given that the tax was passed on to transient, non-repeating customers, and therefore not a factor in hotel profits. The tax revenue that is lost due to the direct effects of the *Atkinson* decision is therefore likely lost for good. The Navajo HOT funds tourism-related services provided by the Navajo Nation government. The loss of this income therefore hurts the Navajo Nation's ability to engage further in this relatively non-exploitative form of economic development. Extrapolating from the Navajo experience, it is likely that this fairly non-negotiable outcome has more significant revenue impacts on other tribes, almost all of which have far more non-Indian fee land within their boundaries than the Navajo Nation.

Another effect from *Atkinson* in the taxing context is the negotiation posture that the Navajo Nation now takes with respect to consent to rights of way and other limited interests in land across Navajo Indian country. *Strate* held that for the purposes of tribal civil jurisdiction, non-Indian rights of way across tribal trust land are the equivalent of non-Indian fee land. Therefore, to preserve the authority to tax the use of such rights of way and similar interests in land, the Navajo Nation Department of Justice now includes consent-to-taxation clauses in all of its right-of-way agreements. While this appears to be a responsive solution, there is some question as to whether it creates barriers to negotiating with non-Indian businesses that did not exist prior to *Strate* and *Atkinson*. As discussed above ***, non-Indian businesses are more likely to object to these clauses because they may believe that non-Indians can successfully resist tribal jurisdiction.

For the Navajo Nation, Supreme Court decisions imposing categorical limitations on the authority to tax non-Indians have small, but nonetheless significant, revenue effects. Moreover, the Navajo Nation is challenged more than in the concurrent taxation context to exercise its sovereignty in responsive and creative ways. *Atkinson* is thus a significant legal setback for the Navajo Nation. The case presents a virtually non-negotiable barrier to the ability to collect income from non-Indians doing business on non-Indian fee land within reservation boundaries. This is so regardless of whether the Navajo Nation provides the benefits of governmental services to the area, and regardless of whether the cultural and aesthetic benefits of the Navajo Nation are the primary reasons for the non-Indian presence. The lost revenue, although limited in amount, is also highly unlikely to be recovered. Moreover, *Atkinson* and the related cases limiting tribal civil jurisdiction of all kinds create a climate of awkward business negotiations with non-Indians.

In *Merrion* and *Kerr-McGee*, the Supreme Court recognized that the power to tax is foremost among the powers of any government. Without the power to raise revenue, there is no ability to fund infrastructure or services; in short, without money there is no ability to govern. The Navajo Nation has taken full advantage of this power, and has also responded in creative and flexible ways to the Supreme Court's decisions permitting concurrent state taxation of non-Indians. Yet the story of Navajo Nation taxation also reveals the ways in which the Court has limited economic growth and development on the Navajo Nation. Notwithstanding compacts and agreements with states, concurrent state taxation places outer limits on the level at which the Navajo Nation can impose taxes. Even more significantly, in its decisions categorically limiting tribal jurisdiction to tax, the Court has created common-law barriers to transactions with non-Indians.

II TOWARD AN EXPERIENTIAL THEORY OF AMERICAN INDIAN TRIBAL SOVEREIGNTY

The framework of federal law is inescapable, yet federal law renders tribal sovereignty a fragile concept, resting vulnerably in the hands of potentially unconstrained federal courts that articulate a nebulous common law and legislators who exercise an insufficiently constrained plenary power. The commentary on this unsatisfactory state of doctrinal affairs is extensive. There is not much left to say about the doctrine of tribal sovereignty, at least from the perspective of federal law. Yet, as the foregoing study shows, the lived experience of tribal sovereignty is something else again. Sovereignty, as witnessed on the Navajo Nation, is resilient, not fragile. The Navajo Nation has enacted sovereignty in the shadow of federal law, sometimes in response to it and sometimes not. The relationship between legal sovereignty and sovereignty on the ground is not precisely linear, yet neither is there no relationship. This study points toward the need for a theory of tribal sovereignty that does not depend upon legal definitions, but nonetheless acknowledges them.

Consistent with this study's attempt to shift the gaze away from exclusive focus on the federal courts, some legal scholars have begun to consider how tribes enact their sovereignty from within. For the most part, commentators have focused on tribal judicial systems, analyzing how they can be vehicles for reviving and sustaining uniquely tribal forms of law and dispute resolution. These articles complement the growing body of literature by scholars from other disciplines who theorize about tribal life and identity. Emerging from some of these writings, directly and indirectly, is a conception of tribal sovereignty that is vital, evolving, and intertwined with the maintenance of American Indian identity.

* * *

Group identity, at present an embattled and waning concept in some quarters, also lies at the core of these alternative theories of tribal sovereignty. Sovereignty protects the ability of the group, as a distinct cultural and political unit, to continue to exist. Indeed, the other strands – culture, wisdom, and land – both depend on and foster the continuation of group identity. Thus, for example, there is an indelible sense of what it means to be "Navajo," notwithstanding that a part of being Navajo is and has always been to incorporate successfully the traditions and practices of others. Tribal sovereignty serves to perpetuate that sense of being Navajo as distinct from just being an American Indian by ethnicity. This perceived link between sovereignty and culture is evident in the comments in the foregoing sections by various Navajo tribal members. And, to relate this to the strands of wisdom, culture, and land, group identity exists because of the relationship of the group to particular places, and the wisdom and cultural practices that grow from those places.

The theory of tribal sovereignty that emerges is that tribes should continue to exist as sovereigns because tribal political institutions foster and protect a unique group identity that stems from place-based wisdom and culture. The emphasis on a process-based understanding of this group identity avoids the tendency to fix American Indian tribes in a particular time period, and also allows for history's impact on tribes to be considered. * * *

CONCLUSION

In the shadow of federal decisional law, the Navajo Nation is doing what it has always done: adapting and resisting in order to remain a distinct Navajo people. The Navajo are not, and have never been, frozen in one particular historical period, like an Edward Curtis photograph of an exotic time past. Inherent tribal powers that the Supreme Court has affirmed have been essential and well-used to ensure that the process of adaptation continues. The power to adjudicate has been crucial to the development of a home-grown Navajo court system. The power to regulate has allowed for Navajo employment and consumer protections. The power to tax has enabled the Navajo to plot an economic future that does not depend solely on limited natural resource extraction.

With respect to Supreme Court decisions that allow concurrent state authority, the Navajo Nation has responded creatively to the challenge. At times the Navajo Nation has used these decisions to force states to live up to obligations to provide equal services. And regarding dual taxation, the Navajo Nation has reached out to the surrounding states and negotiated with them as a sovereign to achieve a mutually beneficial economic solution. The cases that deprive Indian tribes of categories of authority provide fewer avenues of response. In some instances, there is nothing the Navajo Nation can do but seek redress in Congress, which it is attempting to do along with other tribes. For Navajo, the immediate economic effects of these decisions may not be great, but the long-term effects on the Nation's ability to negotiate on equal terms with non-Indian businesses will suffer. The ability to impose standards of behavior in contexts that pose serious health or economic threats to Navajo people is also badly compromised.

Navajo perceptions about the link between sovereignty and survival are grounded in these practical realities, as well as a larger intangible sense that their culture has greater significance than the transient presence of a recent, though overwhelmingly powerful, colonizing government. The Navajo have found ways to live with, and even within, that government. But it is clear in many of their reactions that they worry that the Court's creeping challenge to their separate political existence will be the final step in the uneven march toward Indian conquest.

It seems probable, though not certain, that the Supreme Court will continue in this vein of unilateral common-law divestment of tribal powers. If so, it will remain to be seen how well tribes can continue to adapt and enact sovereignty in the shadow of federal law. The working conclusion from this research is that tribes need enough legal sovereignty to ensure their continued existence as separate nations, capable of fostering growth and development of their endemic cultures. Part of that growth and development, as it turns out, has been to grapple with the federal legal doctrines restricting sovereignty. But too much intermeddling by the Supreme Court, a body that is unaccountable and extremely difficult to override in Congress, might well be more than even the Navajo Nation, a Nation formed by adaptation, can absorb. For the Navajo Nation, and for the rest of us who benefit from the living culture and link to history that our American Indian nations provide, let us hope that the experience of tribal sovereignty can ride out this historical moment, just as it has so many other apparently greater challenges. It seems probable that it will. Raymond Etcitty certainly believes so: "Let's let it run its course ... In the greater scheme of things, it doesn't matter as long as there are tribal members, [tribes] will still be here ... Tribes are full-bore ... they're not going away." Implicit in Raymond Etcitty's comment is the notion that tribal sovereignty originates from tribal people. "We the People." It has a familiar ring. For the Navajo, "we" historically has been a flexible and inclusive term. And for the Navajo, "we" also includes ancestors who pre-date European arrival. As we, the United States, proceed to temper tribal sovereignty through the rule of law's quiet colonialism, perhaps we can keep in mind the moral force behind the notion that unaccountable attacks on self-governance violate, if not a higher law, then at least our highest conceptions of ourselves.

NOTES & QUESTIONS

1. *Reading Indian Law*:
   - Krakoff focuses primarily on the work of the Navajo legislative and executive branches as opposed to the work of the Navajo courts. Why did she choose this focus? What does the work of the tribal council tell us that the work of tribal courts does not?
   - What are some of the topics of Navajo laws discussed in Krakoff's article? Were you surprised by any of the laws? How do you think they compare to the work of state governments?
   - Krakoff documents the challenges faced by the Navajo Nation in the wake of the US Supreme Court's decision in *Strate v. A-1 Contractors* and *Atkinson Trading Co. v. Shirley*. What were some of those challenges? How did the Court's decisions in *Strate* and *Atkinson* change the way the Navajo Nation conducted the business of government?
   - Did reading this article give you a better understanding of what tribal governments do and how the decisions of the US Supreme Court impact that work? Why or why not? Do you think the experiences of the Navajo Nation are typical of the experiences of other tribal governments? What impact, if any, do you think geography has on your answer? Does your answer depend on the size of the reservation? The percentage of allotment? The tribal population?
2. *Laboratories of Democracy*: Responding to US Supreme Court opinions limiting the authority of tribal governments, one Navajo official quoted in Krakoff's article queried, "what happened to laboratories of

democracy?" He was referring to Justice Brandeis's dissenting opinion in *New State Ice Co. v. Liebmann*, 285 U.S. 262 (1932), which declared:

> Denial of the right to experiment may be fraught with serious consequences to the nation. It is one of the happy incidents of the federal system that a single courageous State may, if its citizens choose, serve as a laboratory; and try novel social and economic experiments without risk to the rest of the country.

Is the US Supreme Court less willing to allow tribal governments room to experiment? Why or why not? Is the Court less willing only when non-Indians are involved? On what do you base your opinion?

3. *Cultural Match*: As discussed in Krakoff's article and Justice Yazzie's article (see Chapter 5), the Navajo Nation makes an effort to ensure that its laws are rooted in Navajo tradition and culture. Several scholars have discussed this concept of cultural match. *See, e.g.*, Gloria Valencia-Weber, *Tribal Courts: Custom and Innovative Law*, 24 N.M. L. Rev. 225 (1994); Stephen Cornell & Joseph P. Kalt, *Where's the Glue? Institutional and Cultural Foundations of American Indian Economic Development*, 29 Journal of Socio-Economics 443 (2000). Cultural match is important because "where there is cultural match, citizens are able to trust in government and actually work with it to achieve desired community ends." Melissa L. Tatum, Miriam Jorgensen, Mary E. Guss, & Sarah Deer, *Structuring Sovereignty: Constitutions of Native Nations* 16 (UCLA American Indian Studies Center 2014). Federal Indian policy, with its vacillations between assimilation and self-determination, has had a tremendous impact on many tribal governments. How might these policies impact the ability of a tribal government to achieve a cultural match? What changes in tribal government have occurred as a result of the different eras of federal Indian policy?

Many tribes have sought creative ways to work within the confines of federal, state, and local laws to serve the needs of those within their borders. Some tribes have opened businesses, some have developed innovative ways to package and deliver governmental services, and some have sought to merge the two. Specifically, reflecting on Krakoff's article, how has the Navajo Nation reacted? The Honoring Native Nations Awards, organized by the Harvard Project on American Indian Economic Development, single out for recognition the best of these tribal government approaches. More information on Honoring Native Nations Awards, including profiles of nominees can be found at https://hpaied.org/honoring-nations.

4. *Beyond the Navajo*: The Navajo Nation is not an IRA tribe and, like Great Britain, does not have a written constitution. The Navajo Nation

also differs from many other tribes in that it has a very large land base (larger than ten states), less than 10 percent of the reservation's inhabitants are non-Indian, and the Navajo are still on their traditional homelands. Very few tribes can make similar claims. How important do you think these factors are to the preservation of Navajo traditional culture? What role do they play in enabling the Navajo Nation to govern effectively?

Although the Indian Reorganization Act of 1934 encouraged (but did not require) tribes to re-form their government and adopt a constitution, many of these constitutions were based on a model or "boilerplate" prepared by the Bureau of Indian Affairs. As a result, many of the constitutions bear a marked resemblance to each other and very little resemblance to traditional tribal government structures. *See* David E. Wilkins & Sheryl Lightfoot, *Oaths of Office in Tribal Constitutions: Swearing Allegiance, but to Whom?* 32 Amer. Indian Quarterly 389 (2008). Constitutions provide a "blueprint" for a government, laying the foundation for who will exercise legislative, executive, and judicial powers and how those entities will relate to each other. What are some of the ways these boilerplate constitutions may differ from traditional tribal governments? Do you think there might be any similarities? What impact might these boilerplate constitutions have on the ability of the tribe to govern effectively? To respond to Supreme Court decisions in a culturally appropriate manner?

5. *Beyond the Law*: Disputes over who possesses authority to regulate activities in Indian country have long been the source of friction between tribal and state governments. These disputes can be increasingly polarized when they involve issues of authority to levy and collect taxes. Think back over the US Supreme Court's Indian law decisions discussed in the articles you have read so far. How many of those cases involved disputes over regulating and/or taxing certain activities? Litigation can be a time-consuming and expensive way to resolve these disputes, and regardless of who prevails in court, the inevitable hardening of positions means that tension will continue between the parties. In an effort to resolve some of these tensions, tribal governments in several states have commissioned studies regarding the contributions to state economies made by tribal undertakings. These studies usually demonstrate that tribal economic ventures do not take money out of state coffers, but rather have a net positive impact on state economies. *See, e.g.*, Jonathan B. Taylor, *The Impact of Tribal Government Gaming in Arizona* (2012), concluding that:

> In fiscal year 2012, these contributions amounted to $97.3 million. By the terms of the compacts, tribes contributed $12.4 million of that

directly to cities, counties, and towns for government services that benefit the general public including public safety, gaming impact mitigation, and economic development. The remaining amount, $84.9 million in fiscal 2012, went to the Arizona Benefits Fund, which the Arizona Department of Gaming distributed to its own budget ($8 million), problem gambling ($1.7 million), school district instructional improvement ($42.1 million), trauma & emergency services ($21.1 million), wildlife conservation and tourism ($6.0 million each).

See also *The Statewide Impact of Oklahoma Tribes* (2012) (concluding that tribes in Oklahoma produce an estimated $10.8 billion impact on the state's production of goods and services). For an examination of methods of tribal economic development, *see* Robert Miller, *Reservation "Capitalism": Economic Development in Indian Country (Native America: Yesterday and Today)* (Praeger 2012).

FURTHER READING

- Robert Cooter & Wolfgang Fikentscher, *American Indian Law Codes: Pragmatic Law and Tribal Identity*, 56 Am. J. Comp. L. 29 (2008).
- Harvard Project on American Indian Economic Development, *The State of Native Nations* (Oxford University Press 2007).
- Miriam Jorgensen (ed.), *Rebuilding Native Nations* (University of Arizona Press 2007).
- Patrice Kunesh, *Constant Governments: Tribal Resilience and Regeneration in Changing Times*, 19 Kan. J.L. & Pub. Policy 8 (2009).
- Frank Pommersheim, *A Path Near the Clearing: An Essay on Constitutional Adjudication in Tribal Courts*, 27 Gonzaga L. Rev. 393 (1992).
- Robert Porter, *Strengthening Tribal Sovereignty through Peacemaking: How the Anglo-American Legal Tradition Destroys Indigenous Societies*, 28 Colum. Hum. Rts. L. Rev. 235 (1997).
- Keith Richotte, *Legal Pluralism and Tribal Constitutions*, 36 Wm. Mitchell L. Rev. 447 (2010).

PART III

Property

In a sense, the entire history of federal Indian law and policy can be told as a struggle for control over land and property. Since they first arrived on the continent now known as North America, Europeans have staked a claim to land in the name of their religion, their political leaders, and their civilization. Tribes have just as fervently fought to keep their homelands. Kristen Carpenter, one of the authors in this section, has observed that "For many indigenous people, every facet of culture, identity, and existence – including tribal religions, Native languages, ceremonies, songs, stories, art, and food – is tied up with the land from which they came."[1]

Questions of property ownership underlie the entirety of Indian law. The first Indian law cases decided by the Supreme Court, *Fletcher v. Peck* and *Johnson v. M'Intosh*, were at their core disputes about property ownership. The articles in this part each explore the role property has played in the development of federal Indian law. Collectively these pieces illustrate how changes in thinking about Indian property drove changes in federal administrative policy, from attempts to cordon Indian tribes onto reservations and then force the admission of non-Indian neighbors to using access to land as a bartering tool to force concessions from Indian people.

This part also explores the different attitudes toward property. Unlike the Anglo-American legal system which is focused upon individual landownership and considers that land is used best when it maximizes its economic utility, Indigenous conceptions of property may be as focused on preservation as utilization. Indigenous land use planning encourages decision makers to consider the state of the land future generations will inherit and questions whether economically remunerative "development" should proceed if it risks disturbing burial grounds or tribal sacred sites.

First up is Professor Joseph Singer's article *Sovereignty and Property* (rank 15/100). Singer uses the US Supreme Court's 1989 decision in the case of *Brendale v.*

---

[1] Kristen Carpenter, A *Property Rights Approach to Sacred Sites Cases: Asserting a Place for Indians as Nonowners*, 52 UCLA L. Rev. 1061, 1063 (2005).

Confederated Tribes as a vehicle for exploring the ways in which the United States government, and the United States Supreme Court in particular, has treated Indian property differently than it treats property owned by non-Indians. Ostensibly a dispute over whether the county or the tribe possessed the power to impose zoning regulations within reservation boundaries, *Brendale* was actually a much deeper struggle whose roots originate with promises made to Indians at statehood and in treaties.

Singer's article explores these roots, taking the reader on a tour through treaties, legal battles, and federal legislation, using each stop on the tour as an opportunity for examining the role played by property. He uses these examples to demonstrate that the Court's inconsistent treatment of tribal governments – sometimes treating tribal governments like sovereign governments and sometimes like private property owners – is driven by a particularly Western European philosophical conception of property. Singer's article also illustrates that although the federal government defines property and landownership according to Western European norms, those definitions are not in and of themselves sufficient to achieve the federal government's goals of displacing tribes in the quest for dominion and control over land. Rather, only by constantly changing the rules was the federal government able to achieve its objectives.

The second article, Professor Judith Royster's *The Legacy of Allotment* (rank 3/100), focuses on the breakup of the reservation. In a sense, the General Allotment or Dawes Act of 1887 was the ultimate example of the federal government changing the rules to ensure it could continue to control tribal property. Professor Royster explores the factual and political history of allotment, tracing the statutory changes and BIA implementation through which tribes lost approximately two-thirds of their remaining lands. By opening up so-called surplus lands to non-Indians, allotment resulted not just in a mixed system of land tenure in Indian country, but also a very mixed demographic of inhabitants. Not all reservations were allotted, and not all allotted reservations experienced a significant shift in population, but the changes were sufficiently widespread to bring about a permanent change in Indian law.

As Royster demonstrates in her article, however, the change need not have been as far-reaching as it became. The continuing consequences of allotment are primarily the result of actions by the US Supreme Court, and not the actions of the political branches. She explores how the Court played a particularly egregious role in the loss of tribal land by eliminating the requirement that tribes must consent to the allotment process. Royster extends her analysis by looking at the Court's treatment of tribal land even after the Indian Reorganization Act of 1934 formally renounced the policy of allotment. She observes that the Supreme Court could undo much of the harm caused by allotment not by giving effect to Congress's intent in enacting the Dawes Act, but by emphasizing that Congress has expressly repudiated the ill effects of allotment, preferring instead the promotion of tribal sovereignty and tribal self-government.

Royster's article explores the ways in which the federal courts have used the consequences of the federal allotment policy to make permanent and far-reaching changes in the foundations of Indian law. The US Supreme Court in particular has relied on various aspects of the allotment policy in its decisions diminishing Indian country and reducing the sovereign authority of tribal governments. Ultimately, Royster's article demonstrates that the Supreme Court's actions have been contrary to the Court's own precedents and have usurped congressional authority over Indian affairs.

The third article, Professor Philip Frickey's *A Common Law for Our Age of Colonialism: The Judicial Divestiture of Indian Tribal Authority over Nonmembers* (rank 1/100), picks up this theme and documents instances in which modern US Supreme Court decisions depart from historic first principles. The most consistently cited Indian law article from 1985 to 2015, it demonstrates that many of these changes have come in cases involving individuals who are not tribal members. Frickey shows how the Supreme Court has used the changes in landownership patterns resulting from allotment to break down not just the physical barriers of Indian country, but also the legal barriers establishing tribal governments as true sovereigns with authority to regulate activity occurring within their borders.

As Frickey demonstrates, the Supreme Court's changing jurisprudence has resulted in the virtual evaporation of the canons of construction – the critical foundation establishing Indian law as a unique field of law rooted in a shared history between sovereigns, as opposed to a field of law built around a disadvantaged minority. Once these foundational elements disappeared, the door was opened for the Court to begin homogenizing Indian law by importing principles from other areas of law. The result, as the article makes clear, is profoundly troubling for the future of Indian law.

The fourth and final piece, *In Defense of Property* (rank 6/100), was written by Professors Kristen Carpenter, Sonia Katyal, and Angela Riley. While the first three articles in this part focus almost exclusively on land – that is, on real property – *In Defense of Property* begins by cataloging the various types of property and the ways in which Indigenous and European conceptions of property differ. It then proceeds to illustrate ways in which those conceptions have been stereotyped, thus leading to mistaken assumptions about the incompatibility of the two approaches.

To illustrate these commonalities, Carpenter, Katyal, and Riley begin with Radin's theories of property and personhood and build from there, using concepts of fiduciary duty and stewardship as substantial pillars in constructing a bridge between Indigenous and Anglo-American conceptions of property. These commonalities create areas for mutual understanding and room in which negotiations can proceed regarding ownership and control over various types of property. Through the lens of stewardship, the authors explore how Indigenous interests in cultural property, intangible property, and real property may be protected even if Indigenous communities cannot "own" the property itself.

Collectively, the four articles in this part explore the role property has played in the foundations of federal Indian law and policy. As you read each article, ask yourself: What form of property is being discussed? Who defines what that property consists of and what it means to own that type of property? What is the role played by property in each dispute and in each era of federal Indian policy? What standards are being used to define property and property rights? What is the relationship between the various types of property? Are disputes concerning intellectual and cultural property meaningfully different from disputes over real property? After reading all four articles, you should be able to tell the story of federal Indian law through a narrative of property.

9

Sovereignty and Property

Joseph William Singer

86 Nw. U. L. Rev. 1 (1991–1992)

The acquisition, ownership, and protection of private property hold a fundamental place in Anglo-American law. The Declaration of Independence famously asserts that "We hold these truths to be self-evident, that all men are created equal, that they are endowed by their Creator with certain unalienable rights, that among these are life, liberty and the pursuit of happiness." The Declaration goes on to state that protecting these rights is the primary purpose of government. These assertions draw heavily on the work of John Locke, whose most famous work, Two Treatises on Government, *declares that government exists to protect an individual's rights to life, liberty, and property. The centrality of property in the Anglo-American system, and in particular the centrality of land, is illustrated by the fact that it is known as "real property" or "real estate."*

In this article, Joseph Singer raises questions about the philosophical foundations of property, in particular real property. He asks those questions in the context of exploring the United States Supreme Court's 1989 decision in the case of Brendale v. Confederated Tribes and Bands of the Yakima Indian Nation, 492 U.S. 408 (1989). Brendale *was ostensibly a zoning case. Most zoning cases involve a dispute between the owner of a piece of property and the city or county government. The disputes typically arise when a landowner is told she cannot do something on property she owns because it violates the local zoning regulations. The courts must then balance the ability of the government to make and enforce comprehensive land use planning decisions with the rights of the individual property owner.*

In Brendale, *however, the dispute concerned which government – the county or tribe – possessed authority to make comprehensive land use decisions and impose those decisions on the private property owner. As part of his examination of the Supreme Court's badly fractured decision, Professor Singer explores both arguments that could have been presented to the Court and arguments that actually were presented to the Court. Professor Singer's analysis demonstrates how the Court's inconsistent treatment of tribal governments – sometimes treating tribal governments like sovereign governments and sometimes like private property owners – is driven by the Court's Anglo-American conceptions of property.*

As you read each argument, ask yourself whether the Supreme Court is treating the tribe like a government or an individual. Then ask yourself what the consequences of that approach will be in the context of this case. How does Professor Singer interpret those consequences? Do you agree or disagree with his interpretation?

I SHINING PINE NEEDLES AND JUST FORMS OF GOVERNMENT

In his first annual message to Congress in 1817, President James Monroe proposed that American Indian nations be forced to open their lands to settlement by non-Indians. "No tribe or people," he explained, "have a right to withhold from the wants of others more than is necessary for their own support and comfort." The proposed method for accomplishing this goal was to force land cessions from Indian nations through treaties. In return, the United States would promise in those same treaties either to recognize the land reserved by the tribes as their sovereign territory or to grant the tribes a new land base for that purpose. This policy was diligently pursued for over fifty years. But the demand for Indian lands did not subside. The treaties – once the vehicle for obtaining land cessions – became seen as obstacles to further expansion by the United States.

If the United States had viewed its treaty commitments with American Indian nations seriously, it would have attempted to renegotiate the treaties with its treaty partners. Sometimes the federal government adopted this path. When it did, the result was almost always to force further land cessions from the tribes. More often, however, the United States simply abrogated the treaties. The federal government has a long and appalling history of breaking treaties with Indian nations whenever it was convenient for the United States to do so.

If the treaty commitments had been viewed in the same light as other contractual agreements of the federal government, such as promises made to holders of United States bonds or those made to government contractors, the federal government would have had to make good on its commitments or pay just compensation for its failure to do so. Yet the United States has repeatedly cast aside its solemn promises to Indian nations and arranged for the seizure and dispersal of tribal property without paying just compensation. Sometimes, the United States has made efforts to compensate Indian nations for lost property and treaty rights. Much of the time, however, the United States has paid less than would be required for non-Indian property. Moreover, many rights based on treaties are not classified as "property" rights by the Supreme Court, thus allowing the federal government to ignore those interests with impunity.

The federal government has often justified its coercive interference with the property and sovereignty of American Indian nations by claiming to be acting in good faith exercise of its trust responsibilities toward American Indians. When the United States breaks a treaty, it almost always claims to be doing so for the good of tribal members. Yet the result has been nothing short of catastrophic for American Indians.

It is not too surprising to find that the Congress and the President have often failed to honor treaty commitments by seizing American Indian property without just compensation. After all, as the elected branches of government, they are vulnerable to the vocal demands of powerful political majorities for access to Indian lands. What is surprising is the role the Supreme Court has played in this area. At crucial moments in American history, the Supreme Court has abdicated its responsibility to protect tribal property rights. In a nation dedicated to the protection of property, with a Supreme Court that has not generally proved to be insensitive to the interests of property owners, it is notable that the Supreme Court has failed to protect the property rights of American Indian nations.

***

The issues in these *** cases are complicated, as is the history of relations between the United States and American Indian nations. Yet they teach us a great deal about both the social meaning of property rights and about the just and unjust exercise of governmental power. Indeed, a close analysis of the reasoning in these cases reveals alarming insights. It also places in doubt some of the most cherished truisms about the meaning of private property in America.

***

These *** themes emerge with special clarity in the *** case of *Brendale v. Confederated Tribes and Bands of the Yakima Indian Nation*. This recent outrage in the tragic history of federal Indian law presented the question of whether the Yakima Nation, located in the state of Washington, had the power to zone fee property owned by non-members of the tribe located within the borders of the Yakima Reservation. Four members of the Court would have held that Indian nations have no power whatsoever to regulate directly the use of fee lands within Indian country owned by nonmembers of the tribe. Two members of the Court passed the deciding votes holding that Indian nations only have the power to zone fee lands located in areas within Indian country that have no significant non-Indian presence. Three dissenters would have held that Indian nations have the power to zone all lands located within Indian country, unless a federal statute or treaty limits that power.

A close analysis of the three opinions in *Brendale* illustrates the *** themes outlined above. These are hard lessons to learn. But if they are correct, then federal Indian law is not simply a peripheral subject of interest to a small minority. Rather, it is an entryway to understanding the complex relations between property and sovereign power in United States law. Exploration of this relation will reveal how law allocates both property rights and political power along lines of racial caste. Federal Indian law therefore raises serious questions about the meaning of democracy, property, equality and the rule of law in the United States.

Yet these insights may also signal the beginnings of a way out. If property is a form of political power, and political power is a source of property, then responsibility for poverty and inequality rests, to a large extent, with the legal system itself. Such responsibility imposes obligations on those with the power to implement the rule of law. "[T]he recognition of private property as a form of sovereignty is not itself an argument against it. Some form of government we must always have," explained Morris Cohen. "At any rate it is necessary to apply to the law of property all those considerations of social ethics and public policy which ought to be brought to the discussion of any just form of government."

* * *

II TRIBAL PROPERTY AND SOVEREIGNTY

B *The Yakima Nation and the United States*

By a treaty signed on June 9, 1855, the fourteen tribes that make up the Confederated Tribes and Bands of the Yakima Indian Nation involuntarily ceded to the United States most of their ancestral lands, reserving for themselves an area to be known as the Yakima Indian Reservation. The Treaty provided that the reservation was for the "exclusive use and benefit" of the Yakima Nation. Pursuant to later legislation, including the Dawes Act and a special allotment statute passed in 1904, a substantial portion of the lands inside the Yakima Reservation was opened to settlement by non-Indians. The Yakima Reservation, however, was never disestablished. The result of this series of events is that a significant portion of the land inside the Yakima Reservation is now owned by non-Indians or by American Indians who are not members of the Yakima Nation. Like many other Indian nations, the Yakima Nation has three kinds of property. Twenty percent of the property is owned in fee simple, mostly by non-Indians or by nonmembers of the tribe. The other 80% of the land is held either by the tribe as a whole under a form of ownership known as "recognized Indian title" or by individual tribal members in the form of restricted trust allotments. Tribal property in the form of recognized Indian title is held by the Yakima Nation as a whole under a "right of occupancy" subject to ultimate fee title held by the United States in trust for the benefit of the Yakima Nation or individual members of the Yakima Nation. Individual allotments are held by individual tribal members, subject to restrictions and control by the Bureau of Indian Affairs.

Throughout its history, the Yakima Nation has divided the Yakima Indian Reservation into two parts. The closed area has historically been closed to all outsiders, except those who own property there, who travel on public roads, or who obtain permits from the tribe. Very little – roughly three percent (3%) – of the land in the closed area is fee land. The open area of the Reservation is open to outsiders, and it includes three towns incorporated under state law; almost half of the land in the open area is fee land, and the bulk of that land is located in these towns.

* * *

Brendale involved two cases in which the zoning ordinance of Yakima County allowed proposed developments on the Reservation while the Yakima Nation zoning ordinance prohibited them. * * *

III PROPERTY

*** The Constitution grants the federal government the power to enter treaties with Indian tribes, so the question is whether this power, or the power to regulate commerce with the Indian tribes, gives the federal government absolute power over Indian nations. The plenary power doctrine of *Lone Wolf v. Hitchcock* is often invoked to defend the proposition that the United States has absolute power over Indian nations. However, Milner Ball has convincingly demonstrated that the reference to plenary power in the early Marshall Court opinions cited in *Lone Wolf* simply meant that the power to deal with Indian nations was reserved to the federal government; the states had no power in this area. In this sense, federal power was plenary; it pre-empted the field. Marshall did not conclude, however, that the United States had absolute power to abolish tribal sovereignty and take tribal property. Rather, Marshall concluded exactly the reverse. According to Chief Justice Marshall, the original understanding of the sovereignty and property rights of Indian nations was that Indian tribes would retain both an absolute right of occupancy of their lands and a sovereign power to exercise governmental authority within their territory, until voluntarily ceded to the United States.

If this is correct, then an involuntary cession of land and sovereignty by an Indian nation is unconstitutional. As Justice Marshall explained in *Cherokee Nation v. Georgia*, "the Indians are acknowledged to have an unquestionable, and, heretofore, unquestioned right to the lands they occupy, until that right shall be extinguished by a voluntary cession to our government . . ." An involuntary cession may be unconstitutional because the Constitution simply does not grant any branch of the federal government the power to take over Indian lands by force. Or a forced cession of Indian lands may be unconstitutional because it constitutes a taking of property without just compensation prohibited by the fifth amendment. Robert Clinton has suggested that "[i]n Lockean social compact terms, Indian tribes never entered into or consented to any constitutional social contract by which they agreed to be governed by federal or state authority, rather than by tribal sovereignty."

***

A second reason the validity of the Treaty was not raised in favor of the Yakima Nation, however, is a case called *Tee-Hit-Ton Indians v. United States*. Unknown to most lawyers, including those who specialize in property law, this case holds that seizure by the federal government of Indian property held under original Indian title does not constitute a taking of property under the fifth amendment. Only if Indian property is recognized by treaty or statute does it constitute "property" protected from seizure by the government. The holding in *Tee-Hit-Ton* means that, under current constitutional law, it does not, and did not, constitute a taking of property for the United States to force the Yakima Nation to cede most of its territory for less than its fair market value. Property held under original Indian title is not "property" protected by the Constitution. The *Tee-Hit-Ton* Court explained this remarkable and outrageous principle by contending first, that the property rights of native peoples of America were not of the type envisioned by the fifth amendment because they were owned, if at all, communally by the tribe, rather than individually. Second, the Court argued that Alaskan native peoples had not exercised possessory rights in the lands claimed by them. They had merely used the lands for hunting and fishing purposes, roaming over them rather than enclosing them and establishing individual parcels.

Neither of these arguments makes sense. The fact that Indian lands are owned communally rather than individually does not exclude them from consideration as property. After all, the American legal system recognizes many forms of common ownership, including joint tenancy, tenancy in common, partnership and corporate ownership, community property, and non-profit organization or trust ownership. Corporations, as well as individuals, are capable of obtaining ownership of property by adverse possession or purchase. An Indian tribe is simply an alternate form for the exercise of common ownership. Nor do hunting, fishing, and dwelling seasonally on land constitute non-possessory uses; in fact, the activities engaged in by the Tee-Hit-Tons were as much or more than those activities routinely recognized as sufficient to create actual, open and notorious possession for purposes of adverse possession doctrine. This means that the tribal property rights in *Tee-Hit-Ton* were accorded less protection than that routinely granted to other comparable forms of property in the United States. We can conclude from this that the formal arguments given in the *Tee-Hit-Ton* opinion do not account for the real reasons for the result.

The real reason for the *Tee-Hit-Ton* holding can be found in Professor Robert Williams's recent argument that a major point of John Locke's philosophical writings was to justify the seizure of land in America from Indian nations. Scholars ordinarily understand Locke as presenting an argument for property rights based on possession and labor in the state of nature; the state of nature, in this conception, represents a philosophical, rather than an historical concept. Williams argues, in contrast, that the state of nature was, in fact, an historical concept. In the beginning, Locke explained, "all the world was America." Locke's *Second Treatise of Government* provides a philosophical foundation for European conquest and possession of the New World. It did so by distinguishing between Indian relations with the land and European conceptions of property in land. American Indians, according to Locke, had not established property rights in land both because they had wasted it by not developing it and because they did not recognize the same kinds of possessory rights associated with fee ownership. ***

B *Did the Treaty Reserve the Yakima Nation's Sovereignty Over All Lands on the Reservation?*

Assuming that the Treaty lawfully divested the Yakima Nation of some of its sovereign powers, the next question is whether the powers reserved by the Yakima

Nation in the Treaty include the power to regulate the use of all lands on the Yakima Reservation. To answer this question we must interpret the meaning of the Treaty. The Treaty provided that the land retained by the Yakima Nation "shall be set apart ... for the exclusive use and benefit of said confederated tribes and bands of Indians, as an Indian reservation." One clear implication of this provision is that the Yakima Nation would be able to exercise sovereign power within the borders of the Yakima Reservation. The right to continue the tribal government is explicitly preserved. The Treaty further provided that "[no] white man, excepting those in the employment of the Indian Department, [shall] be permitted to reside upon the said reservation without permission of the tribe and the superintendent and agent." Do either of these provisions limit the sovereign power of the Yakima Nation to trust lands owned by the tribe?

* * *

Justice White made it look as if he was applying the language in the Treaty to the facts in the case before him. He noted that the conditions contemplated in the Treaty no longer obtain and that it can therefore no longer be a source of sovereign power over alienated lands. "The Yakima Nation no longer retains the 'exclusive use and benefit' of all the land within the Reservation boundaries ..." This made it seem as if it were an historical accident that this occurred, or a result of the choice of the Yakima Nation. White nowhere honestly admitted that the reason the Yakima Nation no longer retains exclusive use of the Reservation is because the United States broke its word and failed to abide by the Treaty. The conditions contemplated under the Treaty no longer obtain because the United States violated the Treaty when it provided for the allotment of Yakima lands.

* * *

Like Justice White, Justice Stevens made it appear as if the Yakima Nation had made a decision to allow nonmembers to purchase property on the Reservation. He argued, for example, that the question is whether the "Tribe ... exercised its power to exclude nonmembers from trust land." But, it is quite clear that the Yakima Nation never made a decision to allow nonmembers to buy property on the Reservation. The Treaty, although allowing for allotment, required allotments to be made to tribal members who would use the property as a "permanent home." The Treaty did not authorize the transfer of these future allotments to non-Indians. On the contrary, it provided that the Reservation was to be retained "for the exclusive use and benefit" of the Yakima Nation and that "[no] white man ... be permitted to reside upon the said reservation without permission of the tribe and the superintendent and agent."

Justice Stevens pointed to no evidence that the Yakima Nation made a decision to open the Reservation to settlement by nonmembers. In fact, the information on the record pointed to the opposite conclusion. The Yakimas objected vigorously to the 1904 federal statute which allotted the lands of the Yakima Nation and opened it to settlement by non-members in violation of the promises of the United States in the Treaty. Like Justice White, Justice Stevens failed to focus on the fact that settlement of the Reservation by non-Indians was not a policy decision of the Yakima Nation; it was the result of the violation of the Treaty by the United States.

C. Was the Treaty Lawfully Superseded by Later Legislation?

In addition to suggesting that the Treaty never reserved the right to exercise sovereign power over non-Indians inside the Reservation, Justice White's position was that whatever the meaning of the Treaty, it was superseded by the Dawes Act. The Treaty reserved sovereign power over the Reservation to the Yakima Nation and provided that the Reservation should be for the "exclusive use and benefit" of the Yakimas. White considered this language inapposite to this case because subsequent events – namely, the Dawes Act and the eventual conveyance of tribal lands to non-Indians – changed the situation such that the "Yakima Nation no longer retains the 'exclusive use and benefit' of all the land within the Reservation ..." Justice White argued that because the Reservation was opened for settlement by non-Indians by operation of the Dawes Act, "the Yakima Nation no longer has the power to exclude fee owners from their land within the boundaries of the Reservation." The Reservation no longer was for the exclusive use of the Yakima Nation; Justice White concluded that the Treaty had therefore been superseded and "any regulatory power the Tribe might have under the treaty 'cannot apply to lands held in fee by non-Indians.'" "[I]t defies common sense," White stated, "to suppose that Congress would intend that non-Indians purchasing allotted lands would become subject to tribal jurisdiction when an avowed purpose of the allotment policy was the ultimate destruction of tribal government."

One objection to its argument is that while it is true that the ultimate goal of the Dawes Act was to abolish tribal governments, it is quite clear that the Dawes Act did not itself abolish tribal governments or sovereignty. To the contrary, the Court has held numerous times that allotment of lands did not, by itself, result in disestablishment of a reservation. Final termination of a tribal government required specific legislation to that effect.

A second objection is that it is simply not the case that the Court has consistently held that tribal governments have no sovereign powers over the activities of non-Indians located inside the Reservation. In fact, the Court has upheld the power of Indian nations to tax business activities located inside the Reservation.

In the allotment legislation, Congress provided for the entry of non-Indians into permanent occupation of land inside the Yakima Reservation without the consent of the tribe as required by the Treaty. Was Congress constitutionally free to abrogate the Treaty in this way? Justice White assumed that Congress was perfectly free to abrogate the Treaty. If a treaty is equivalent to a federal statute, then a later statute takes the place of an earlier statute whose terms are inconsistent with it. If this is true, then the fact that the Treaty was abrogated by the unilateral act of the Congress is of no consequence – it is an irrelevant, but mildly interesting fact. This is because the Supreme Court has held, with one exception discussed below, that Congress has plenary power under constitutional law to abrogate treaties entered into with Indian nations.

I argued earlier that the Treaty unconstitutionally took the property of the Yakima Nation without just compensation. The Supreme Court has held that this argument is unavailable because property held under original Indian title is simply not protected from government seizure by the Constitution. But the Supreme Court has held that Indian property that is recognized by treaty or statute is protected by the fifth amendment. Why then wasn't the allotment and sale of property inside the Yakima Nation subject to the constitutional requirement of paying just compensation? After all, the Dawes Act and subsequent legislation resulted in the taking of two separate property interests of the Yakima Nation: the right of the Yakima Nation to exclude non-Indians from the Reservation and the right of the Yakima Nation to hold property as a tribe.

The answer lies in the Court's failure to extend to Indian nations the same constitutional protections afforded to non-Indians. In *United States v. Sioux Nation*, the Court held that the fifth amendment protection against uncompensated takings does not apply when Congress acts in its role as trustee over Indian tribes and property. If Congress authorized the seizure of recognized title [to] tribal land without paying any consideration, its actions would certainly be deemed a taking of property and not a good faith exercise of the federal government trust powers. However, if Congress provides "equivalent value" for the land taken in a good faith effort to exercise its trust responsibility to manage tribal land for the benefit of the tribe, then Congress has merely "transmute[d] the property from land to money, [and] there is no taking" in violation of the fifth amendment.

The requirement of "equivalent value" does not constitute a requirement that the government pay the "fair market value" as would be required for a physical seizure of non-Indian property. This test more closely resembles the test for determining when a government regulation has gone "too far" and constitutes a taking. Nell Jessup Newton explains that this means that unless the courts are vigilant, Congress may take recognized title property "under the guise of management and sell it at less than fair market value without liability, as long as the tribe receives some proceeds."

It is important to note that proceeds of sales of Indian land are ordinarily deposited in accounts held by the federal government and managed by the Bureau of Indian Affairs, not the tribes. The BIA has often spent this money in ways that were not supported by the tribal governments they were intended to benefit. When tribes notified Congress of their objections to the expenditure of tribal funds without the tribes' consent, the response was simple: "*Lone Wolf*." Nor is this response limited to the distant past. In 1985, the Supreme Court held, in *United States v. Dann*, that even when the federal government has taken Indian property and paid just compensation, it has no obligation actually to distribute money to the tribe whose property was seized; payment had occurred when the government appropriated funds and deposited them in a trust account with the government as trustee for the Shoshones.

Where non-Indian property is physically seized, the fifth amendment is not satisfied if the government makes a "good faith effort" to provide "equivalent value" for the property interest taken. Rather, the Constitution affirmatively requires the government, if it insists on taking the property, to pay the full amount that would be required by "just compensation." When the federal government attempted to force a landowner to open a privately developed marina to the public, on land which had not previously been connected to public, navigable waters, the Supreme Court in *Kaiser Aetna v. United States* found a taking of property which could not be accomplished without paying just compensation, or the fair market value for the highest and best use of the land. On the other hand, the forcible and involuntary divestment of the Yakima Nation's treaty right to exclude non-Indians from the Reservation does not entitle the Yakima Nation to just compensation. The available historical evidence indicates, moreover, that the allotment process allowed non-Indians to purchase "surplus" lands for unconscionably low prices, not for the "just compensation" otherwise required by the constitution.

The Yakima Nation did not agree to give up the right to exclude non-Indians from the Reservation. In fact, the Yakimas refused, after repeated attempts, to consent to the sale of Yakima lands to nonmembers. The Yakima Nation explained these facts to the Supreme Court in its brief. As stated in the Report of the Committee on Indian Affairs to the United States Senate in support of the legislation providing for the sale of surplus or unallotted lands on the Yakima Reservation:

> No agreement has been made with these Indians, and their consent has not been secured for the opening of the reservation and the disposal of the unallotted lands. The failure to secure such consent or agreement, however, does not rest with the Government. Repeated attempts have been made to reach an agreement with these Indians and very liberal terms have been offered, but the Indians have declined to enter into such an agreement.

The legislation forcing the Yakima Nation to sell unallotted lands to nonmembers was passed in 1904, one year after the Supreme Court decision in *Lone Wolf v. Hitchcock*. The *Lone Wolf* Court held that Congress had absolute power to abrogate Indian treaties. It also upheld forced allotment without the need for obtaining the consent of the tribes, which previously had been thought to be constitutionally required. Congress wasted no time in opening up the Yakima Reservation to settlement by non-Indians.

In addition to the loss of the right to exclude non-Indians from the Reservation, the Yakima Nation was forced to allot its tribal property among individual members of the tribe. This was accomplished without the consent, and over the strenuous objections, of the Yakima Nation. The Supreme Court has held that seizure of tribal property and its allotment to individual tribal members is not a taking of property requiring just compensation even if that tribal property is recognized by treaty or statute and allotment violates the treaty. Rather, the Court has characterized allotment as merely a change in the form of investment; the property – although taken from the tribe – is partitioned among tribal members. For this reason, no compensation is required.

The failure to identify a forced allotment of tribal property as a taking requiring just compensation distinguishes tribal property from other forms of commonly owned property in the United States. Imagine how the Supreme Court would react if Congress passed a statute authorizing the President to seize the factories, offices and other property of General Motors, divide it up into thousands of physically divided units and give specific squares of real property to individual shareholders. Rather than owning a share of stock in General Motors, a shareholder would own in fee simple a room in GM's corporate headquarters, or perhaps a 25 foot square area inside a GM factory. This scheme would obviously deprive the corporation of all its real property while giving individual owners pieces of the corporation's property that are likely to have far less value than they would as assets of General Motors as a going concern. This mere "change in the form of the investment" would cut deeply into the property rights both of the corporation itself and of its shareholders. It would be quite surprising if such an uncompensated re-distribution of property rights were upheld in the absence of just compensation.

D Why Wasn't Tribal Sovereignty Restored by the Indian Reorganization Act of 1934?

In their analyses of the legal effects of the Treaty, Justices White and Stevens focused on the policies underlying, first, the Treaty itself and second, the allotment legislation which, contrary to the terms of the Treaty, opened the Reservation to settlement by nonmembers. But after the allotment policy was found to be an abysmal failure, Congress repudiated the policies underlying the allotment legislation which had favored eventual disestablishment of tribal governments. In 1934, Congress passed the Indian Reorganization Act of 1934. That statute repealed the Dawes Act, stopped the allotment policy and provided for the reorganization and revitalization of tribal governments. The Act had far reaching effects. It helped to revitalize the tribes and tribal governments, and gave an impetus to the development of tribal courts.

If the Dawes Act was repealed by the Indian Reorganization Act, why did Justices White and Stevens focus on the policies underlying the Dawes Act? As a matter of ordinary statutory interpretation, it is distinctly odd for the Court to focus on the intent of the legislature that passed the Dawes Act, rather than the intent of the legislature that passed the later Indian Reorganization Act. After all, the Indian Reorganization Act expressly repudiated the policies underlying the earlier statute and was intended to reinvigorate tribal government. In the usual case, when two statutes conflict, the later statute applies, unless it is unconstitutional.

* * *

Both Justices explicitly assumed that a rational Congress would never have subjected non-Indians to political control by Indian tribes, and refused to come to that result in the absence of clear language in the legislation requiring it. For example, Justice White argued that "it defies common sense to suppose that Congress would intend that non-Indians purchasing allotted lands would become subject to tribal jurisdiction when an avowed purpose of the allotment policy was the ultimate destruction of tribal government." This statement might mean that White believed that the Congress that passed the Dawes Act intended to limit the tribe's sovereign power. But I believe White meant more than that. He appears to have meant that he could not imagine that any Congress – including the Congress that sought to reinvigorate tribal government by passing the Indian Reorganization Act – could rationally subject non-Indians to political control by Indians.

The Supreme Court may also have assumed that the establishment of Indian sovereignty over fee lands would infringe on the property interests of the fee owners who purchased property inside the Reservation based on the belief that the tribe would eventually be disbanded. Suppose the non-Indian purchasers relied on the government's promise in the Dawes Act that tribal government would eventually – although not immediately – be abolished. Those purchasers may have bought in reliance on this expectation. To infringe on those reasonable, investment-backed expectations might interfere with vested rights protected by the takings clause.

Moreover, property owners may claim a right to participate in the government that has regulatory power over their land use. Property rights may constitute a source of sovereignty; ownership of property may seem to entail the right to use and develop that property unless those use rights are limited by regulations promulgated by a democratic government with which the owner has a social contract. If one is a citizen of the regulatory government, it might be argued that one has impliedly consented to regulations imposed by that government since one has had the chance to participate in the political process that generated the regulation. On the other hand, if one is not a citizen of a government, one has not implicitly consented to regulation of one's property by that government. Nonmembers, by definition, do not participate in the tribal government on the same terms as members. Under this line of reasoning, non-Indians have a right to be zoned by the County, rather than by the Yakima Nation, because they are citizens of the County government but not the tribal government. As between the sovereignty of the County and the Yakima Nation, the County should prevail because only the sovereign powers of the County are compatible with the property rights of nonmembers of the tribe. This result is not unfair to the Yakimas since they too are citizens of Yakima County with the right to vote in the elections which establish the County government.

Justice Stevens made a related argument. He suggested that the extent of non-Indian ownership determines the extent of tribal sovereignty. Fee ownership does not automatically entitle one to participate in the government that zones one's land, but does so only if a significant number of persons who own fee land are non-members of the governing political authority. This means that fee property is partly individual and partly communal in nature. White seems to have assumed that all individual fee owners have, as a mixed property/citizenship interest, the right to participate in the government that regulates their real property. This premise allowed White to choose between competing sovereigns: the County versus the Yakima Nation. Stevens argued, in contrast, that fee interests generate a claim on sovereignty only if an owner is joined by others like her such that they form a distinct minority (or majority) within the area. When non-Indian fee ownership becomes substantial, then this group has a right to be governed by the County, rather than the tribe of which it is not a part.

This line of argument may explain why both Justices White and Stevens assumed, without any explanation, that the Indian Reorganization Act could not have been intended to establish tribal sovereignty over lands owned by non-tribal members. The ownership of land in fee simple creates a presumption which is conclusive for White and merely presumptive for Stevens that the owner's land use should be regulated by a government of which the owner could become a member.

The assumptions implicit in the analysis of Justices White and Stevens are unwarranted. It is simply not true that property owners have inherent rights to vote in the government entity empowered to zone their property. If I buy property in several states, I am subject to the zoning laws of the places where the property is located, even though I am entitled to vote in only one state. If I, as a citizen of the United States, buy property in France, I am obligated to comply with French land use regulations, even though I have no right to participate in the French political process by voting in French elections. Many landowners in the United States are not citizens; they are bound by United States zoning laws even though they have no right to vote in any elections at all. This is standard conflicts law.

One might argue in response that under United States law, one is almost certainly entitled under the Constitution to register to vote in the area where one has one's home, and that there is some kind of right to participate in the government that regulates one's property. However, the *Brendale* case did not raise this issue. Both Brendale and Wilkinson were asking for the right to subdivide and develop property for profit; they were not claiming rights to use their home in ways prohibited by the Yakima zoning law.

The racially contingent nature of the Court's analysis can be understood by considering a counter-example. A Japanese corporation recently purchased Radio City Music Hall in New York City. Japanese companies now own a substantial chunk of Manhattan real estate. If we assume that many of the shareholders of Japanese companies are Japanese citizens, we have the circumstance of non-citizens buying property in New York, yet having no right to participate in New York City elections. By Justice White's reasoning, it should be illegitimate to subject these Japanese owners to New York zoning law; rather, the property should be zoned by the legislature in Tokyo. This result is absurd, as Justices White and Stevens themselves would certainly agree. Yet it is structurally equivalent to the assumptions underlying their arguments in *Brendale*.

In *Brendale*, Justice Blackmun noted that, at the time of the Dawes Act, non-Indian purchasers should have been on notice that they were buying property in Indian country which might be subject to regulation by the Indian nation. The Dawes Act did not abolish tribal governments, although Congress contemplated that they eventually would be abolished. Non-Indian purchasers were therefore arguably in the same position as United States citizens buying property in another state or country where they are clearly subject to local zoning law even though they have no right to vote in local elections. Even if these non-Indian purchasers were unaware that they were buying property in Indian country, traditional principles of constructive notice in property law would dictate that their land would be subject to whatever servitudes or encumbrances they would have discovered if they had made a reasonable investigation.

The majority of the Justices on the Court in *Brendale* ignored this traditional rule of property law. In so doing, they granted non-Indian purchasers greater rights than they would have had if their property had been located off the Reservation. Once more we face the bedrock assumption that American Indian property and sovereignty interests are subject to defeasance to protect the interests of non-Indians.

IV SOVEREIGNTY

If the Treaty cannot form a legitimate basis for zoning power by the Yakima Nation, a second possible basis for tribal sovereignty is the doctrine of inherent tribal sovereignty. This sovereign power is not granted by the United States. Rather, it pre-existed the United States, and persists unless divested by federal law.

Justice White argued that the general rule of law is that tribes may regulate their own members in Indian country, but that Indian nations may not regulate the use of fee lands on reservations, unless the non-Indian owners of those fee lands have entered into consensual relations with the tribe or if their land use "threatens or has some direct effect on the political integrity, the economic security, or the health or welfare of the tribe." ***

*** Justice White would adopt an incredibly narrow substantive standard to determine whether the County's zoning decision harms tribal interests. According to White, the standard is whether the proposed zoning would "do serious injury to and clearly imperil the protectable tribal interests identified in this opinion." Those interests include the "political integrity, economic security, or the health or welfare" of the tribe. To overcome the presumption that Indian nations cannot regulate the use of fee lands, the Yakima Nation must demonstrate that the impact of the state zoning regulation on those tribal interests is "demonstrably serious."

* * *

White argued that it is imperative not to interpret the legitimate interests of the tribe broadly. To do so, he argued, would equate Indian Nations with states by interpreting tribal health and welfare to encompass all the interests included in the police power available to the states. This would be inconsistent with the status of Indian tribes as dependent domestic sovereigns. This argument, however, fails to account for the complex nature of tribal sovereignty. White was trying to fit Indian nations into a dual sovereign structure of federal and state government. Land use regulation by zoning is generally allocated to municipal governments that derive their power from the state; here the relevant municipal government is the County. But Indian nations are not subordinate to the states; they are subordinate to the federal government, and in many areas, are coordinate with the states. For example, Indian nations, in general, have plenary power to regulate their own members on the reservation. They may also regulate the conduct of non-Indians they permit to come on the reservation, and this regulatory interest is not limited to vital tribal interests. The only difference in the *Brendale* case is that the nonmembers own property on the reservation. While the ownership of property complicates the issue further, it does not justify retreating to a dual model of federal–state sovereignty.

The one nod White gave to tribal sovereignty was to limit state zoning authority when the tribe's interests are seriously threatened by the County's land use decision. How serious was the threat here? White argued, amazingly, that the proposed development of land in the open area of the Reservation does "not imperil any interest of the Yakima Nation."

How could the Court conclude that the County's land use decision will not affect the interests of the Yakima Nation in any way, when the County is allowing a development ... that is expressly prohibited by Yakima law? Assuming that the Yakima Nation prohibited the development for a reason, we can only conclude that the interests of American Indians are simply not recognized as real. White's argument that the County's decision does not impinge on any interest of the Yakima Nation is reminiscent of *Lyng v. Northwest Indian Cemetery Protection Association*, in which the Court held that building a highway through sacred tribal lands imposed no burden on religion, even though it would have the effect of destroying the ability of the Yurok, Karok and Tolowa Indians to practice their religion. *Brendale*, like *Lyng*, stands for the proposition that American Indian perspectives are irrelevant in federal courts. American Indian religious and sovereignty interests will be recognized only to the extent they are seen to fit within non-Indian paradigms.

What about the rights of non-Indians? * * *

Private land sales cannot ordinarily divest a government of jurisdiction. If a citizen of Arizona sells his estate to a citizen of New York, the territory of Arizona is not diminished, nor is the territory of New York enlarged. We have never, however, overcome the convenient pretense that sales of Indian land imply cessions of sovereignty.

The usual means of protecting the interests of nonresident property owners is the takings clause, not divestiture of sovereignty. The takings clause does not apply to tribal governments. However, the Indian Civil Rights Act of 1968 has extended takings protection to non-Indian property located inside reservations. Moreover, that statute is enforceable in tribal courts rather than in state or federal courts. What would be wrong with that?

Non-Indians fear that tribal courts will be biased against them. They also fear that the tribal court will not adhere to the basic rights contained in the Bill of Rights, even though most of the elements of the Bill of Rights have been officially imposed on Indian nations by the Indian Civil Rights Act of 1968.

These are real fears. Tribal courts are not perfect. Tribal courts may develop different conceptions of the meaning and extent of property rights than those promulgated by non-Indian courts. But how does transferring jurisdiction to the state administrative system and the federal courts solve the problem?

***

V POWER, SOCIAL RELATIONS, AND THE LAW OF PROPERTY

*** If "property is a set of social relations among human beings," the legal definition of those relationships confers – or withholds – power over others. ***

Suppose we started our analysis of property by taking seriously the history of the legal treatment of American Indian nations. What would our constitutional and private property system look like if *Worcester v. Georgia* were as central to American jurisprudence as *Marbury v. Madison* and *Brown v. Board of Education*? If we took American Indian law seriously, it becomes clear ... that the legal system currently confers less protection on American Indian property than it does on non-Indian property. The rules about just compensation for takings of property either do not apply to Indian property (original Indian title may be taken without just compensation) or impose lesser constraints on the government than in the non-Indian context (recognized title may be taken without just compensation if the government, in good faith, is exercising its fiduciary power to manage Indian affairs for the good of the Indians under its trust relationship with Indian nations). Further, non-Indian property rights appear to be granted super-protection when they are located on Indian reservations (non-Indians appear to have a right to vote in the government which zones their property only if that property is located on an Indian reservation). This super-protection of non-Indian property inside reservations limits the sovereign power of Indian nations in a way that does not apply to non-Indian municipal governments, and infringes on the property rights of the Indians who are neighbors to the non-Indians.

Recent controversies about off-reservation fishing and hunting rights in Wisconsin and Washington states are affected by this double standard. The treaties imposed on the Indian nations in those states reserved to the tribes the rights to hunt and fish on public lands ceded to the federal government. In recent years, many non-Indians have reacted with anger to the exercise of these rights. They feel that those treaties create special benefits for Indians; the treaties appear to grant unequal rights of access to public lands based on race. However, those rights are explicitly protected by treaty. If we thought of treaties as deeds or fee patents, rather than agreements with Indian tribes, the situation might appear quite different. Those hunting and fishing rights are easements reserved by the grantor – the various Indian nations which ceded the land to the United States. If Nelson Rockefeller had granted land to the United States, but reserved the right for himself and his heirs to have access to the land for specific purposes, it would be clear that that reservation constituted a property right which others would be bound to respect. Yet somehow the reserved rights of Indian nations are not accorded the same respect.

Property in the United States is associated with a racial caste system. Nor is this a phenomenon of the past; the law continues to confer – and withhold – property rights in a way that provides less protection for property rights of American Indian nations in crucial instances than is provided for non-Indian individuals and entities. This means that if we want to help a client determine the extent of its property rights, the first thing we need to know is whether the client is an American Indian nation or, say, a business corporation. The law provides a certain level of protection for the interests of General Motors and a quite different level of protection for the interests of the Yakima Nation. Imagine having to explain this to a client, and being asked why. This divergent treatment is not simply a minor fact of injustice that could be corrected by strategic changes in contemporary constitutional law doctrines. Rather, it means that the distribution of property rights in land in the United States has less than auspicious origins. Unless it is rectified – unless it can be rectified – the distribution of real property is inherently suspect. The history of United States law, from the beginning of the nation to the present, is premised on the use of sovereign power to allocate property rights in ways that discriminated – and continue to discriminate – against the original inhabitants of the land. Changing a few doctrines of law would not erase this history of injustice, nor undo its effects on the current situation of Indian nations. If the injustice cannot be easily rectified, then it places continuing obligations on the present and future generations to attend to the meaning of the past. If those who benefit from this history of injustice claim a vested right to its benefits, they should be aware that what they claim is a right to the benefits of a system of racial hierarchy.

Nor is this lesson confined to American Indian nations. Black Americans, torn from Africa, placed in slavery, and then "freed," were never given the land, education, and other resources that had been available to many other Americans. Unless we join the Supreme Court in calling a halt to history, we need to understand the current distribution of property in the United States as growing out of this history of injustice. We must see the ways in which the rules in force are implicated in the social construction of race. We need to understand the racial context in which property law developed and in which the distribution of wealth has been established and continues to be established. This context gives us no reason to feel confident that the distribution of wealth in the United States is just.

* * *

4. Property Rights are Defined and Allocated by the State – There is an image many Americans have of settlers going out to the frontier, staking their claims, and possessing property in the wilderness. They mixed their labor with the land, as John Locke would say, and therefore made it their own. This image of the origin of property in first possession focuses attention on the free activities of private citizens operating in a state of nature. Government is not present; nor are these settlers stealing or appropriating property from anyone else. First possession is the root of their title, and that title was acquired justly. Government followed these settlers, protecting their pre-existing claims based on first possession.

This image is a fantasy. What really happened is that the United States was inhabited by hundreds of Indian nations. The settlers did not walk into vacant land; they invaded Indian territory. The United States government, at periodic intervals, promised to respect the right of occupancy of the various tribes. Every so often it would send out the cavalry to oust the non-Indian invaders from Indian country. But when enough settlers came to an area, the cavalry was assigned a different task – backing up the United States when it sent representatives to force the tribes to sign treaties of cession, either reserving limited lands for themselves or "agreeing" to be removed to lands far away.

What happened after these treaties were signed? Who owned the land? Under the holding of *Johnson v. M'Intosh*, the land was owned by the United States government, which then decided how to distribute the land. It did so in a variety of ways by defining the course of action individuals could take to stake claims to the land. The government then issued titles to the persons who followed those procedures.

Why was the land taken? It was taken because the Indians were thought not to need it and because they were misusing it by engaging in a hunting, rather than an agricultural economy. It was taken because it was needed by the non-Indians.

Focusing on American Indian property thus gives us a rather different picture of the origin of property rights than that to which most of us are perhaps accustomed. The historical basis of original acquisition of property in the United States is not individual possession in the state of nature, with government stepping in only to protect property rights justly acquired. Rather, it is redistribution by the government from those who were thought not to need the property or to be misusing it to those who were thought to need it – a different picture, indeed.

VI. THE CONTINUING CONQUEST

*** The Supreme Court's failure over the last fifteen years to identify American Indian claims as protectable property rights has resulted in greater and greater intrusions into the interests of Indian nations. By often failing to recognize treaties either as creating vested property rights or as describing reserved powers of sovereignty, the Court has perpetuated a system that grants less protection to the property rights of American Indian nations than to the property rights of non-Indians and non-Indian corporate entities. The Supreme Court has defined as exercises of sovereignty by Indian nations actions that would be recognized as exercises of property rights by business corporations; then, by holding that there can be no rival sovereigns to the states and the federal government, the Court has cut back on both tribal sovereignty and property. In this way, the Court has deprived Indian nations of protection for interests that are routinely recognized in the non-Indian context.

Conquest is not something that happened in the distant past which cannot be corrected. Rather, the Court is attempting to conquer Indian nations now by its failure to protect tribal property rights and inherent sovereignty.

When tribes would benefit from being classified as property holders, the courts often classify them as sovereigns. Thus, when the courts cut back on the property rights of American Indian nations, they claim they are simply limiting the sovereign power of those nations. Given the history of the plenary power doctrine, the Supreme Court has come more and more to assume that tribal sovereignty concerns personal power over tribal members rather than geographic power over land bases on the reservations. By classifying the tribes as public entities, rather than as private property owners, the Court can cut back on tribal control over tribal land without appearing to violate the takings clause. According to the Supreme Court, when Congress took from the Yakima Nation the right to exclude nonmembers from its territory, it was not taking a property right but simply cutting back on tribal sovereignty. The Yakima Nation was not a property owner for the purpose of obtaining protection from loss of its property to the state.

On the other hand, when tribes would benefit from being classified as sovereigns, the courts often treat them as private associations. Thus, when the Court analyzes the extent of the sovereign power of Indian nations, it assumes that it is inappropriate for those nations to exercise sovereignty over nonmembers. The Court does this despite the fact that all states in the nation have the power to exercise sovereign authority over outsiders that come into those states. For example, the state of Washington has the power to arrest New Yorkers who come into Washington and violate Washington law even though those outsiders had nothing to do with forming that law. Their presence in the state is taken as implied consent to jurisdiction. Similarly, the state of Washington has the power to enact zoning laws to restrict the use of land owned in Washington by New Yorkers who have no right to vote in Washington. Yet, according to the Supreme Court, nonmembers who own property inside the Yakima Reservation have the right not to be regulated in most instances by the tribal government of the Yakima Nation. The Yakima Nation is not treated as a sovereign for the purpose of exercising power in a way that affects nonmembers.

The Supreme Court has therefore given Indian nations the worst of both worlds. They are often not treated as property owners for the purpose of protection from confiscation of their property by the state, and they are often not treated as sovereigns for the purpose of governing the conduct of nonmembers inside their territory. * * *

NOTES & QUESTIONS

1. *Reading Indian Law*:
   - One of Singer's primary arguments is that the US Supreme Court treats the property interests of Indians differently than the property interests of non-Indians. What examples does he provide to support his position? Do you agree or disagree?
   - What does Singer mean when he asserts that non-Indian property located in Indian country receives "super-protection"? How is this protection different from what the property would receive outside Indian country?
   - Many of the US Supreme Court decisions discussed in Singer's article addressed the nature of Indian land title. Why was the seizure of Indian land not considered a "taking" under the Fifth Amendment? What would be the consequences if the seizure of Indian land *had* been considered a "taking"?
2. *Western European Conceptions of Property*: The "State of Nature," where life is "nasty, brutish, and short" (Hobbes, *Leviathan*), is a common conceptual tool in Western European political philosophy. It is used to analyze the legitimacy and purpose of government by exploring what happened in a theoretical time before the existence of government and why individuals would band together and create a government. The term "social contract" refers to the agreement whereby individuals would surrender some of their freedoms to the newly created government in return for the government protecting the remaining individual rights. The Declaration of Independence borrowed heavily from this philosophy in asserting the American Revolution was justified because the British Government had failed to fulfill its obligations toward the Colonies. The US Constitution also relied heavily on this political theory; the Preamble makes it clear that the Constitution is the embodiment of the Social Contract. Since the Constitution was an agreement between the former colonies and the citizens of those former colonies, and tribes were not part of that agreement, what justifies the federal government's authority over Indians and tribal governments?

Treaties? What happens to that authority when the treaty is broken? Does the answer lie with the Doctrine of Discovery?

3. *Individual v. Collective Rights*: In justifying the role of government, Social Contract theory assumes that the basic rights holder – that is, what existed prior to government in the State of Nature – are individuals. This approach asserts that protection of individual autonomy and individual rights is not only the most efficient form of government, it is the only legitimate form of government. This belief is not shared by many Indigenous cultures. Many Indigenous cultures believe that the purpose of government is to protect the peace and harmony of the community from individuals who would disrupt that harmony. Can a system based on individual rights be reconciled with a system based on group rights? How could the two systems work together? *See* N. Bruce Duthu, *Shadow Nations: Tribal Sovereignty and the Limits of Legal Pluralism* (Oxford University Press 2013); *see also* Jennifer Hendry & Melissa L. Tatum, *Human Rights, Indigenous Peoples, and the Pursuit of Justice*, 34 Yale Law & Policy Review 351 (2016).

4. *Tribal Property Law*: As Professor Singer details in his article, the US Supreme Court relied on the Doctrine of Discovery and Locke's theory of property to justify the appropriation of Indian lands. Locke and others argued that property interests are acquired when a person "mingles their labor with the soil." The United States Supreme Court's decisions in *Johnson v. M'Intosh* and *Tee-Hit-Ton Indians v. United States* declared that Indians did not possess the type of property interest recognizable under US law. The US thus did not owe tribes compensation under the Fifth Amendment's Takings Clause.

This argument rests on a depiction of tribes as nomadic hunter-gatherer societies, moving seasonally around a geographic territory and taking the berries and animals that they might happen to find. It ignores the reality that many tribes, particularly in the northeastern and south-western parts of what would become the United States, had very sophisticated agricultural economies. It also ignores the fact that many tribes had their own systems of property ownership and property law. *See, e.g.,* Kenneth H. Bobroff, *Retelling Allotment: Indian Property Rights and the Myth of Common Ownership*, 54 Vanderbilt L. Rev. 1559 (2001).

Congress did eventually provide a mechanism for tribes to seek compensation for land taken by the United States. At first this was done on an ad hoc basis, with Congress enacting a series of special jurisdictional statutes allowing specific tribes to file suit in the United States Court of Claims. In 1946, however, Congress created the Indian Claims Commission which heard cases for three decades before being dissolved in 1978. *Final Report of the United States Indian Claims Commission:*

August 13, 1946 to September 30, 1978. The cases still pending before the Commission when it was dissolved were transferred to the United States Court of Claims. The last of those cases, filed by the Pueblo de San Ildefonso, was finally resolved in 2006 with the passage of Public Law 100-286.

The Indian Claims Commission and the US Court of Claims were authorized to award only monetary compensation. This limitation frustrated some tribes, who sought return of the land itself. Why would Congress provide only monetary compensation? What else could it have done? *See, e.g.*, Edward Lazarus, *Black Hills, White Justice: The Sioux Nation versus the United States 1777 to the Present* (University of Nebraska Press 1999). For more information, see H.D. Rosenthal, *Their Day in Court: A History of the Indian Claims Commission* (Garland Publications 1990); Imre Sutton (ed.), *Irredeemable America: The Indians' Estate and Land Claims* (University of New Mexico Press 1985).

5. *Native Title in Canada*: Canada has taken a different approach to the property rights of its First Nations. Although Canada borrowed from *Johnson v. M'Intosh* and adopted the Doctrine of Discovery, it did not hold that Aboriginal title was not a compensable property right. Instead, in a series of cases, the Canadian Supreme Court held that Aboriginal title is a unique form of title, as it is both communal and inalienable. This line of cases also declares that the Canadian government can infringe upon Aboriginal title, but the government must pay compensation for any infringement. *See, e.g.*, *Delgamuukw v. British Columbia*, 3 SCR 1010 (1997). What does this mean for First Nations in Canada? How might it put Canadian First Nations in a different position than tribes in the United States? *See* Renee Racette, *Tsilhqot'in Nation: Aboriginal Title in the Modern Era*, in *Indigenous Justice: New Tools, Spaces, and Approaches* 90 (Palgrave Macmillan 2018).

6. *Zoning*: Philosophical differences about the nature of property rights are not the only problematic aspect of *Brendale*. The US Supreme Court's 1926 decision in *Village of Euclid v. Ambler Realty Co.*, 272 U.S. 365, recognized the power of a local government to enact and enforce zoning laws. The purpose of zoning laws is to create and implement comprehensive land use planning decisions. How can this be reconciled with the result in *Brendale*, which allowed the tribal government to apply its comprehensive zoning laws to only one section of the reservation? Can any system of zoning work on a reservation under the restrictions imposed by the Supreme Court? What happens if the demographics change?

7. *Beyond the Law*: The differing nature and treatment of property have far-reaching economic consequences for tribal government. As Professor

Angelique EagleWoman has written, "Land as the basis of capital asset creation is of primary importance to the foundation of economic property in the nineteenth and twentieth century. Trust land is inalienable and cannot be sold, taxed, mortgaged, or used for collateral." Angelique EagleWoman, *Tribal Nations and Tribalist Economies: The Historical and Contemporary Impacts of Intergenerational Material Property and Cultural Wealth within the United States*, 49 Washburn L.J. 805, 819 (2010). If trust land cannot be used for collateral, how would that impact tribal economic development? What alternatives are available to tribal governments? Is there any way tribal governments can avoid or lessen the impact of these limitations? *See* Jenny Small, *Financing Native Nations: Access to Capital Markets*, 32 Rev. Banking & Fin. L. 463 (2012–2013); W.G. Guedel, *Capital, Inequality, and Self-Determination: Creating a Sovereign Financial System for Native American Nations*, 41 Am. Indian L. Rev. 1 (2016).

FURTHER READING

- Milner S. Ball, *Constitution, Court, Indian Tribes*, 1987 Am. Bar. Foundation. Res. J. 1 (1987).
- Raymond Cross, *Sovereign Bargains, Indian Takings, and the Preservation of Indian Country in the Twenty-First Century*, 40 Ariz. L. Rev. 425 (1998).
- Melissa L. Koehn, *The New American Caste System: The Supreme Court and Discrimination between Civil Rights Plaintiffs*, 32 Mich. J.L. Reform 49 (1998).
- Nell Newton, *Compensation, Reparations, & Restitution: Indian Property Claims in the United States*, 28 Ga. L. Rev. 453 (1994).
- Jo Pascualucci, *International Indigenous Land Rights: A Critique of the Jurisprudence of the Inter-American Court of Human Rights in Light of the United Nations Declaration on the Rights of Indigenous Peoples*, 27 Wis. Int'l L.J. 51 (2009).
- Frank Pommersheim, *Broken Landscape: Indians, Indian Tribes, and the Constitution* (Oxford University Press 2009).
- Lindsay G. Robertson, *Conquest by Law: How the Discovery of America Dispossessed Indigenous Peoples of Their Lands* (Oxford University Press 2007).
- Wenona Singel & Matthew Fletcher, *Power, Authority, and Tribal Property*, 41 Tulsa L. Rev. 21 (2005).
- Rebecca Tsosie, *Land, Culture, and Community: Reflections on Native Sovereignty and Property in America*, 34 Ind. L. Rev. 1291 (2001).
- David E. Wilkins, *Hollow Justice: A History of Indigenous Claims in the United States* (Yale University Press 2013).
- Mary Wood, *Indian Land and the Promise of Native Sovereignty: The Trust Doctrine Revisited*, 1994 Utah L. Rev. 1471 (1994).

10

The Legacy of Allotment

Judith V. Royster

27 Ariz. St. L.J. 1 (1995)

When Congress passed the General Allotment Act in 1887 its goal was to eradicate tribal governments, transform individual Indians into farmers, and absorb them into the general populace, thus putting an end to "the Indian problem." The General Allotment Act failed to achieve these goals, but it did forever change the face of federal Indian law.

Congress repudiated the allotment policy in 1934 and dramatically reversed the course of federal Indian policy with the passage of the Indian Reorganization Act. That was not, however, the end of the allotment policy, as the consequences of that policy continue to influence the decisions of the US Supreme Court up through the present day.

In this article, Judith Royster traces the factual, political, and legal history of the General Allotment Act. The article takes the reader on a tour not just of the broad strokes of the workings of the Allotment Act, but through the on-the-ground practical realities of the ways in which the actions of administrative officials actually resulted in undercutting Congress's goals. Royster observes that while the elected branches of government subsequently embraced the government-to-government relationship enjoyed between tribes and the United States, the Supreme Court has at times forsaken that renewal and focused instead on how allotment altered tribal communities. She argues that if the Court would consider the full context of allotment, it might reconsider how it approaches questions of tribal sovereignty and congressional plenary power.

As you read the article, ask yourself how the allotment policy continues to make itself felt through the Supreme Court's decisions. Why are the residual impacts still influencing the course of federal Indian law? Are these continued effects an inescapable fact of life for those in Indian country? Could the Court have reached a different conclusion? How?

I INTRODUCTION: TERRITORIAL SOVEREIGNTY

The first principle of federal Indian law is the sovereign status of the Indian tribes. ***

Sovereignty is inextricably tied to territory. Governments may exist in exile during times of political upheaval and cultures may survive for centuries dispersed across nations, but sovereignty demands a territory over which the governmental authority of the sovereign extends. Control over territory is the most essential element of sovereignty. ***

Indian tribes have territories. For most tribes, the major territory is the reservation, but tribal territories are more accurately determined as the Indian country, encompassing not only the entirety of the reservations, but certain lands outside reservation boundaries. *** Without that territory, without territorial sovereignty, tribes are too easily reduced to little more than "private, voluntary organizations."

Nonetheless, tribal territorial sovereignty has come under increasing and increasingly virulent attack. In the early nineteenth century, Chief Justice John Marshall proffered a vision of great "conceptual clarity." In *Worcester v. Georgia*, he held that the State of Georgia had no authority to extend its laws into Cherokee country, even though Cherokee territory was encompassed within the boundaries of the state and even though Georgia was attempting to apply its laws to non-Indians entering the Cherokee country. For Marshall, Cherokee country was under the sovereign control of the Cherokee Nation, subject only to the exercise of federal power. The territorial sovereignty of the tribes was complete, and inviolate against attempted incursions by the states.

By the late twentieth century, however, the Supreme Court was dismissively referring to "platonic notions" of tribal sovereignty that ought not bind the Court to Marshall's vision. By 1980, the Court was comfortable in positing that: "Long ago the Court departed from Mr. Chief Justice Marshall's view that 'the laws of [a State] can have no force' within reservation boundaries." Nonetheless, *Worcester* has never been overruled and the Court consistently notes that tribes possess sovereign rights over their territories. Thus, even as it retreats from the plain meaning of *Worcester* and Marshall's declaration of tribal territorial sovereignty, the Court continues to recognize, at least to some extent, the strong territorial component of tribal governmental authority.

The importance of territory to tribal sovereignty is demonstrated by the fluctuations of federal Indian policy over the last century. When the government's attention has turned to the assimilation of Indians into the majoritarian society and the dissolution of the tribes, tribal territory is the focus of the attack. During the allotment era of the late nineteenth and early twentieth centuries, the assimilationist goal rested on the allotment of reservations in severalty and the sale of the remaining lands. During the termination era of the 1950s, the approach was even cruder: wholesale withdrawal of federal protection from tribal territories, forced sale of lands, and distribution of the proceeds.

The opposite is also true. When federal Indian policy has turned to the protection and promotion of tribal autonomy, territory is again a central feature. At the repudiation of the allotment era, Congress ended all further depredations on the tribal land base and provided mechanisms for the return of unsold lands and the acquisition of "new" additional lands. With the reversal of the termination policy came the restoration acts, generally providing the restored tribes with some land base. Today, the recognition of groups as federally recognized tribes also carries with it the demand for territory.

The greatest and most concerted attack on the territorial sovereignty of the tribes was the allotment policy of the 1880s to the 1930s. The allotment policy was overtly directed to the dissolution of the tribes and the extinguishment of tribal territories. But the allotment policy was also a failure: it did not transform the Indians into yeoman farmers, but it did wreak destruction within tribal communities. Recognizing the atrocity of allotment, Congress formally ended the practice in 1934 and repudiated its policy underpinnings.

That should have been the end of allotment. But its legacy lingers on, and in recent years has been revived by the Court in a series of cases that give present effect to the discredited policy of allotment and assimilation. In the process, the Court has chosen to diminish tribal territories and to restrict tribal sovereign control over the territory that remains. By deciding cases in accord with the assimilation policy, the Court has undercut the sovereignty and territorial integrity of the Indian nations.

This article traces the legacy of allotment in the Court's recent opinions and argues that the decisions giving effect to the allotment policy are contrary to interpretive rules, precedent, and federal policy *** Unfortunately, the *** Supreme Court *** not only persists in giving effect to a policy that has failed, but does so in ways that disrespect the branch of government charged with authority over Indian affairs and mock the Court's own precedents in the field.

II DISMANTLING THE LAND BASE, 1885–1934

***

A *Allotment and Assimilation*

Prior to the late nineteenth century, federal Indian policy was primarily oriented toward the separation of tribes and citizens. In the early decades of the century, removal of the tribes to "unsettled" territory west of the Mississippi was the preferred federal approach. The removed tribes were accorded lands in the new country in exchange for their cession of aboriginal territories in the southeast. By the end of the Civil War, however, the focus of the separatist idea had shifted. As non-Indian settlement of the trans-Mississippi West burgeoned, federal policy shifted from the removal of tribes to the Indian Territory to the isolation of tribes in pockets of lands carved out of aboriginal territories.

The purposes of the reservation policy were diverse. In part, like the removal policy, the reservation policy was intended to ease hostilities and tensions between tribes and settlers by segregating the two groups from one another. Moreover, reservations were designed to preserve the tribes from destruction and, at the same time, to provide a laboratory for teaching Indians the virtues of agriculture and civilization. Indian lands set aside as reservations were eventually recognized as being "in trust" for the tribes; under that trust status the United States holds the fee while the tribes retain beneficial ownership.

Contained within the reservation policy of the mid-to-late nineteenth century were the origins of the allotment policy to come. Treaties concluded in the 1850s to make way for white settlement of Kansas and Nebraska included provisions for allotment of lands, as did treaties in the Pacific Northwest. Throughout the reservation era, various Commissioners of Indian Affairs advocated the allotment of the reservations as the next logical step toward the civilization and improvement of the Indians. Nonetheless, widespread dissatisfaction with the reservation policy was slow to build. Not until the late 1880s did Congress begin actively pursuing a new approach.

The 1880s witnessed the fundamental shift in federal policy from separatism within reservations to assimilation. And yet the goals of the allotment and assimilation era were in many respects continuations of the reservation goals: agriculture, Christianity, and citizenship were to be the ultimate outcome. Federal policy, however, was no longer content with separating the tribes, protecting their autonomy, and providing Indian agents as teachers of change. Instead, federal policy turned toward the assimilation of Indians into the general body of citizens.

The primary agent of civilization and citizenship was to be private land ownership. Despite the "flat, miserable failure" of previous experiments in allotment, advocates of the policy believed that individual ownership of property would turn the Indians from a savage, primitive, tribal way of life to a settled, agrarian, and civilized one. Assimilation was viewed as both humanitarian and inevitable. The cornerstone of this social engineering, this "legal cultural genocide," was the replacement of tribal communal ownership of land with private property. In the General Allotment, or Dawes, Act of 1887, Congress authorized the break up of the reservations. Indians were to receive allotments of land in severalty, and the remaining surplus lands were to be opened to settlement.

1 Allotments and Fee Patents

The central feature of the General Allotment Act was the allotment of the reservations in severalty. Under the Act, individual Indians received a certain number of acres of reservation land. In recognition of prior failed attempts to allot Indian lands in fee, however, Congress provided that allotted lands would be held in trust for the individual allottee for a period of twenty-five years. During that time, the allottee was expected to assimilate to agriculture, to Christianity, and to citizenship. At the end of the twenty-five year transition period, the individual would receive a patent in fee, free of encumbrance and fully alienable. With the acquisition of a fee patent, the allottee would also be subject to the civil and criminal laws of the state.

The twenty-five year trust period came under attack, however, by those who viewed the continued federal guardianship as an obstacle to the goal of assimilation. As a result, Congress amended the General Allotment Act in 1906 to authorize the early issuance of fee patents. The Burke Act authorized the Secretary of the Interior to issue a fee patent to an allottee at any time, upon a determination that the individual was "competent and capable of managing his or her affairs." Upon the issuance of one of these premature patents, the land was expressly subject to alienation, encumbrance, and taxation.

The effect of the Burke Act was immediate and substantial. In the three years following the passage of the 1906 act, patents were issued upon the recommendation of the Indian superintendent. Of the 2744 applications made during those years, all but 68 were granted. Surveys in 1908 showed that more than 60 percent of the premature patentees lost their lands. In 1909, an alarmed Commissioner of Indian Affairs began requiring a more detailed showing that the allottee was competent, and the approval rate dropped to approximately 70 percent of all applicants.

That relief was short-lived. In 1913, a new Commissioner of Indian Affairs not only reinstated the liberalized policy, but expanded upon it. Initially, the Indian superintendents were ordered to submit the names of competent Indians, but that procedure was soon replaced by "competency commissions," charged with roaming the reservations in search of allottees who could be issued premature patents. Under pressure to liberate the Indians from federal guardianship, the Indian Office issued patents to unqualified allottees and, in many cases, to allottees who neither applied for nor wanted to accept them. Despite reports showing that in many cases 90 percent or more of premature and forced-fee allottees lost their lands, the liberalized policy was formalized and further expanded in 1917.

In that year, Indian Commissioner Sells announced that fee patents would simply be issued to all allottees of less than one-half Indian ancestry, while competency determinations would still be required for those of one-half or more Indian blood. The effects were again devastating. In the eighteen months following Sells' policy announcement, the Indian Office issued premature patents for approximately one million acres, more than had been patented in the previous ten years. Similarly, between 1917 and 1920, more than 17,000 patents were issued, twice as many as were issued in the previous ten years. The havoc caused by Sells' policy resulted in a loss of support for liberalized patenting, and in 1920 a new Commissioner abolished the competency commissions and declared that no fee patents would issue without a determination of competency regardless of blood quantum.

Between the two methods – expiration of the trust period and premature patents – thousands of patents in fee were issued, often amounting to several thousand in a single year. Once a patent in fee was issued, the land could be alienated, encumbered, and at least as to Burke Act patents, taxed. Thousands of Indian owners disposed of their lands by voluntary or fraudulent sales; many others lost their lands at sheriffs' sales for nonpayment of taxes or other liens. By the end of the allotment era, two-thirds of all the land allotted – approximately 27 million acres – had passed into non-Indian ownership.

2 Surplus Lands

Despite the devastating effect of fee patents, the 27 million patented acres lost to non-Indians represented only about one-third of the tribal losses during the allotment era. More than twice as much land – some 60 million acres – was lost under the surplus lands program. The General Allotment Act provided that, once reservation lands were allotted in severalty, the remaining "surplus" lands could, at the discretion of the President, be opened to non-Indian settlement. Non-Indian settlement interspersed with Indian allotments, assimilation advocates believed, would promote interaction between citizens and Indians and encourage the allottees to adopt white ways. Allotment would remove the "dead weight" of communal tribal lands that kept the Indians from full participatory citizenship.

As enacted, the General Allotment Act called for tribal consent to cession of the surplus lands. Although multiple cession agreements were negotiated with tribes, many of the early efforts were thwarted by the tribes' refusal to sell or their demand of a high price. In 1903, however, the Supreme Court held in *Lone Wolf v. Hitchcock* that tribal consent to the loss of surplus lands was not required, notwithstanding either the General Allotment Act or a specific treaty provision requiring written consent to any cession agreement. Thereafter, Congress unilaterally enacted surplus lands acts, contending that rapid disposal of the surplus lands would increase the value of Indian allotments, give the Indian allottees role models to emulate, and generally "be a great improvement upon their present condition." The Commissioner of Indian Affairs concurred, noting that if Congress waited for tribal consent, "it will be fifty years before you can do away with the reservations." Within two years of the *Lone Wolf* decision, Congress enacted six surplus lands acts without tribal consent or negotiation, and in 1905 four of the affected reservations were opened to white settlement.

The post-*Lone Wolf* surplus lands acts followed a pattern. "They were proposed by western politicians, approved by a voice vote in Congress, and greeted with cheers from local settlers and businessmen." Tribal advocates were reduced to campaigning for adequate compensation for the homesteaded lands. Once tribal consent was no longer at issue, the focus of the surplus lands program had shifted from assimilation of the Indians to the development and white settlement of the western states.

B Repudiation of Allotment

The 1920s represented a decade of transition from the devastation of the allotment years to a formal change in federal policy in the early 1930s. In 1921, the liberal policy of granting forced-fee and other premature patents was officially abandoned, and the number of premature patents steadily declined throughout the 1920s. By the early 1930s, the Indian Office rejected more than 50 percent of patent applications, and issued fewer than 300 patents in a two-year period. Nonetheless, patentees continued to lose their lands in "staggering" numbers. As a result, the Indian Office began to urge legislation that would permit the cancellation of forced-fee patents, a proposal that received considerable impetus from a Ninth Circuit decision holding that fee title did not pass to the allottee under a forced-fee patent. Congress responded in 1927, authorizing the Secretary of the Interior to cancel forced-fee patents. The effect of the legislation was limited, however; patents could be canceled only if the patent was issued without the application or consent of the allottee and if the owner had not sold or mortgaged the land. Because of those limitations, the Interior Department ultimately canceled only some 470 forced-fee patents out of approximately 10,000 that were issued.

The decade culminated with the issuance of the Meriam Report in 1928. The report, a nongovernmental study undertaken at the request of the Secretary of the Interior, investigated Indian policy and administration and their impacts on Indian life. The destructive effects of the allotment policy documented in the Meriam Report – effects on the economic, social, cultural, and physical well-being of the tribes – generated sympathy and popular support for a change in the federal approach. The report also called for greater respect for Indian culture, an attitude that reflects what historian Frederick Hoxie has termed the early twentieth-century "redefinition of Indian assimilation" to accommodate cultural diversity. Publication of the Meriam Report was closely followed by appointment of a new Commissioner of Indian Affairs, who had some success in implementing the recommendations of the report.

The appointment of John Collier as Commissioner in 1933, however, set the stage for wide-ranging reform of federal Indian policy and programs. Within four months of taking office, Collier effectively put an end to allotment and the practice of issuing fee patents by directing the superintendents not to submit either certificates of competency or fee patents. The following year, Collier's goal of legislation to reverse allotment was realized when Congress enacted the Indian Reorganization Act of 1934.

With the Indian Reorganization Act ("IRA"), Congress put an official end to the allotment program and formally repudiated the assimilation policy. The first sections of the IRA contained what Collier called the "repair work" regarding tribal lands. Section 1 of the IRA prohibited any further allotment of tribal land. Section 2 provided that any allotments then held in trust status would continue in trust until Congress provided otherwise. Section 3 authorized the Secretary of the Interior to restore any remaining surplus lands to tribal ownership, and the Secretary subsequently halted any disposition of surplus lands on thirty reservations pending the implementation of § 3. Finally, § 5 authorized the Secretary to take new lands into trust and to add those lands to reservations.

In effect, Congress halted the allotment program where it stood in 1934, and provided that certain ravages of the policy could be in part ameliorated. What Congress did not do, however, was restore fee patented or homesteaded lands to tribal ownership. Although the Secretary was authorized to acquire fee lands and return them to trust status and tribal ownership, these provisions affected only a fraction of the millions of acres lost to fee ownership. The vast majority of lands that had passed into fee during the allotment years remains in fee today: the legacy of allotment that gives rise to the modern Court decisions divesting tribes of both territory and sovereignty.

C The Modern Policy Era

The reorganization era was short-lived. Criticism of the IRA began immediately and, coupled with pro-assimilationist social forces revived after World War II, led to the termination era of the 1940s and 1950s. Termination was assimilation with a vengeance. Congress withdrew federal recognition, liquidated tribal assets, including the land base, and transferred jurisdiction over Indians to the states. The loss of tribal territory and sovereignty was immediate and complete. In that sense, termination was if anything more brutal than allotment, but it affected, by comparison, few people and little land.

Like the reorganization era that it replaced, the termination era also was short-lived. Even as the final termination plans were developed and implemented in the late 1950s and early 1960s, federal policy turned against the forced termination of tribes. The swing in federal policy back to the protection and promotion of tribal autonomy was ushered in by President Johnson, who called in 1968 for a policy of "self-help, self-development, and self-determination" for Indians. Two years later, President Nixon inaugurated the modern federal Indian policy of self-determination, proposing federal promotion of tribal self-determination, sovereignty, and control over Indian country. In line with the executive branch, Congress shortly embarked on a legislative agenda designed to carry the self-determination policy into effect.

Subsequent administrations have continued and expanded the basic self-determination policy announced by Nixon. In 1983, President Reagan proclaimed a "government-to-government" relationship between the tribes and the United States. The government-to-government policy was reaffirmed by President Bush and most recently by President Clinton, who promised as well "to honor and respect tribal sovereignty." Congress also has continued to legislate for tribal control over Indian country.

The cornerstones of modern federal Indian policy – tribal control over the Indian country and the government-to-government relationship – are diametrically opposed to the tenets of the assimilation policy. Instead of the assimilation-era goal of breaking up tribal territories into allotments and fee lands, modern policy promotes

and protects tribal control over Indian country. Far from contemplating the dissolution of the tribes, modern policy rests on an intergovernmental relationship
between the federal government and the Indian nations. Respect for tribal sovereignty is the stated aim of the current administration.

Federal Indian policy is set by Congress and the President; those branches of
government determine the tenor of federal relations with the tribes during any given
policy era. But full implementation of federal policy requires the cooperation of the
judicial branch. Despite disingenuous statements that the Court does not make
policy, the Court certainly furthers or impedes policy in the course of its decisions.
And the difficulty in federal Indian law today, in cases implicating the allotment
policy or its lingering effects, is the Court's insistence upon rendering decisions
consistent not with the modern policy of self-determination, but rather with the
allotment policy of the assimilation years. The Court has determined upon a path of
effectuating the allotment policy, to the detriment of the tribes and the schizophrenia of federal interactions with the Indian nations.

* * *

III THE DAWES ACT RIDES AGAIN: *COUNTY OF YAKIMA V. YAKIMA INDIAN NATION*

The allotment policy is reminiscent of a horror movie villain, defeated in the final
scenes and officially dead. But as the closing credits roll, the faint continuing throb
of a heartbeat can be detected, and soon sequel after sequel resurrects the villain to
continue its course of destruction. Like the villain, allotment was pronounced dead
in 1934 with the passage of the Indian Reorganization Act. But like the villain, the
allotment policy lurked on below the surface, waiting to break free. Over the last two
decades, under the activating hand of the Supreme Court, the policy has sprung
back to life. If the Court continues on its present course of giving effect where
possible to statutes and policies of the allotment era, tribal sovereignty – tribal
territorial sovereignty – is at risk.

The Court's recent interpretation of the General Allotment Act itself is in many
ways the paradigm illustration of the problem. In *County of Yakima v. Yakima
Indian Nation*, the Court was asked to determine whether the General Allotment
Act permitted state property taxation of former allotments now held in fee by Indian
owners. Despite conflicting plausible interpretations of the statute, and despite being
squarely presented with the inconsistency between the policy of allotment and the
present policy of self-determination, the Court chose to read the General Allotment
Act in light of its assimilationist underpinnings. In holding that the Act permitted
state real property taxes, the Court construed the Act to further the goals of the
allotment policy, notwithstanding the congressional repudiation of both the policy
and its underlying doctrine of assimilation.

* * *

In so holding, the Court discarded two principles of interpretation of Indian statutes that are crucial to the protection of tribal autonomy. The first of these is the long-standing rule that state taxation of Indian lands is barred unless Congress has made its intent to authorize that taxation "unmistakably clear." Since at least the mid-nineteenth century, the Court has consistently refused to permit state taxation of Indians, Indian interests, and particularly Indian lands within Indian country absent congressional consent.

***

The second interpretive principle neglected by the Court is the canons of construction designed to interpret legislation enacted for the benefit of the tribes. Originally developed for the interpretation of treaties, the canons provide that statutes are to be construed, and that ambiguities are to be resolved, in favor of the tribes. In essence, the canons call for courts to construe statutes broadly when Indian rights are recognized or established, and narrowly when those rights are limited or abrogated. The canons thus act as "the tribes' tenth amendment," ensuring that powers and authority remain with the tribes unless ceded by treaty or agreement with the tribes' clear consent and understanding, or plainly and deliberately appropriated by Congress.

Application of the canons of construction to § 5 of the General Allotment Act would require the narrow interpretation of that section, construed liberally in favor of the tribes.

***

In addition to this wholesale rejection of long-standing principles of statutory interpretation in federal Indian law, the Court declined to consider Congress's express repudiation of allotment and its supporting policy of assimilation. The Yakima Nation argued that the termination of the allotment program in 1934, Congress's express rejection of the assimilation policy in the Indian Reorganization Act, and the present federal policies of tribal self-government and self-determination blocked state jurisdiction over land in Indian country. The Court dismissed that argument as "a great exaggeration," stating that "the mere power to assess and collect a tax on certain real estate" would not significantly disrupt tribal self-government. That statement has potentially nasty implications for tribal sovereignty.

***

The Court's decision in *County of Yakima* is thus a paradigm of the legacy of allotment in Indian law. Faced with conflicting plausible interpretations of the General Allotment Act regarding state taxation of fee lands, the Court chose to manipulate its rule concerning congressional authorization of state taxes, to ignore the canons of construction, and to construe the Act to carry forward the policies of allotment and assimilation.

*** Attempts to draw easy, bright-line rules require a court to forego the difficult and detailed analysis that the issues deserve. One of the most destructive legacies left by the Court in *County of Yakima* may be this apparent permission for the lower courts to further the assimilationist policies of the past with casual indifference to history, policy, and precedent.

IV ALLOTMENT AND TERRITORY: THE RESERVATION DISESTABLISHMENT CASES

While *County of Yakima* represents the Court's interpretation of the General Allotment Act itself, most of the Court's legacy of allotment derives from the present effects of the allotment program. In particular, the Court has focused on non-Indian fee ownership within Indian country, a direct outgrowth of the allotment years, as a justification for divesting tribes of territorial sovereignty. The cases terminating territorial sovereignty have fallen into two general categories: first, the reservation disestablishment cases, which concern the loss of territory itself with the concomitant loss of sovereignty; and second, the decisions, generally in regulatory jurisdiction cases, that abrogate full tribal sovereign authority over the territory that remains. *** The reservation disestablishment cases, those that look at the loss of tribal territory, arise out of the surplus lands acts of the allotment years. ***

A generation after the tribes lost ownership of the surplus lands to non-Indian homesteaders, the Supreme Court took up the issue of whether the tribes had also lost territorial sovereignty. Over the next two decades, the Court developed an obscure and essentially ad hoc approach to determining whether individual surplus lands acts terminated the reservation status of the surplus lands.

The early reservation disestablishment cases appeared to establish a relatively workable test based largely on the language and intent of the particular surplus lands act. ***

Where the language of the surplus lands act did not *** expressly provide for termination of the reservation status, the Court turned to the intent of both Congress and the tribes as indicated by tribal "consent" to the loss of the lands. In *DeCoteau v. District County Court*, the Court found that the language of the Sisseton and Wahpeton surplus lands act was ambiguous. Unlike surplus lands acts which unambiguously "abolished" or "discontinued" the reservation status of the lands or expressly "vacated and restored [the lands] to the public domain," the Sisseton–Wahpeton act ratified an agreement by which the tribes agreed to "cede, sell, relinquish, and convey to the United States all their claim, right, title, and interest in and to all the unallotted lands" of the reservation. While the act clearly divested the tribes of title to the unallotted lands, the language did not expressly "abolish" or "discontinue" or "vacate" the reservation itself. Nonetheless, the Court found that congressional intent to disestablish the reservation could be found "unmistakably" both on the face of the surplus lands act and from the surrounding circumstances and legislative history. Untroubled by the lack of plain language terminating the reservation, the Court discovered disestablishment in the factors constituting the "surrounding circumstances and legislative history." First, the Court found it significant that the tribe had consented, in negotiations leading to an agreement that was then ratified by Congress, to convey "all" its interest to the government for a sum certain: in other words, that the tribe ceded the land in exchange for payment in full from the government. Second, the Court noted that the language of the Sisseton–Wahpeton act paralleled that of other contemporaneous acts which all parties agreed terminated portions of the affected reservations. Third, the sponsors of the ratifying legislation had "stated repeatedly" that the Sisseton–Wahpeton lands would be returned to the public domain. Hitching the language of the act to the statements of the congressional sponsors, the Court held that the act disestablished the entire Sisseton–Wahpeton Reservation.

The decision in *DeCoteau* represented a significant and troubling departure from the Court's previous disestablishment analysis. Most disturbing was the retreat from the express language of the act. In both of its prior disestablishment cases, the Court had based its ultimate holding squarely on the language of the act. In neither case did the act expressly authorize termination of the surplus lands from the reservation, and the Court consequently refused to infer any congressional intent to do what the act did not provide. In *DeCoteau*, by contrast, the Court said it found an unmistakable intent to terminate on the face of the act, but its analysis relied solely on the circumstances surrounding the act's passage. The language of the Sisseton–Wahpeton act was relevant only in passing. Moreover, to the extent that the language of the act at issue in *DeCoteau* was ambiguous, the canons of construction would call for the language to be interpreted to the benefit of the tribe. Given that the act did not expressly terminate the reservation, that Congress is capable of making its intent to terminate plain when it wishes to do so, and that disestablishment is detrimental to the tribe, application of the canons should have led the Court to determine that the act did not terminate the Sisseton–Wahpeton Reservation.

As troubling as the analysis in *Decoteau* was, however, the subsequent cases ultimately proved even more troubling for tribes subject to the surplus lands program. Within two years of its decision in *DeCoteau*, the Court declared that many of the factors it found relevant to diminishment in that case – a sum-certain payment for the ceded lands and tribal consent to the cession as shown through a negotiated agreement preceding the surplus lands act – were in fact not dispositive. In *Rosebud Sioux Tribe v. Kneip*, the Court stated that the only truly relevant factor in its prior cases had been congressional intent. Circumstances such as tribal consent and provision for a sum-certain payment were mere aids to the determination of congressional intent, but were not in themselves dispositive one way or the other.

* * *

Throughout its disestablishment cases, the Court has concentrated on congressional intent to terminate reservation status. Arguably, this standard would have been a reasonable approach to the surplus lands acts if the Court had stuck with its original analysis in *Seymour*, focusing on the language of the act itself. Thus, reservation disestablishment would perhaps be a reasonable determination if the language of the act expressly or plainly showed that Congress intended to terminate the reservation status of the land and return the land to the public domain, and Congress carried out that intent by paying the tribe a sum certain for the territory terminated as reservation lands, and the act ratified a negotiated agreement between the tribe and the federal government. But the Court faltered in its application of congressional intent. First it moved away from the requirement that Congress make its intent to disestablish plain on the face of the act, and then it introduced the legal niceties of the "surrounding circumstances" standard and the offensive racism of whether the surplus lands retained their Indian character by not becoming too white.

In implementing that approach to the disestablishment question, the Court has given effect not to Congress's intent in the surplus lands acts, but to the general intent of the repudiated allotment policy. Only where the surplus lands act contains *no* language that could arguably be construed as language of either cession or termination has the Court, in recent years, been willing to find an absence of congressional intent to disestablish. Moreover, the Court is adamant about clinging to that approach even when it concedes that it has "no way of knowing for sure" what Congress intended in any given act. Not only is that approach fundamentally flawed under the canons of construction, but more destructively it is designed to further the policies of the allotment era even if the particular surplus lands act did not contemplate an end to the reservation status of the opened lands. The lack of clear congressional intent, the repudiation of the allotment policy, and the modern policy of encouraging tribal governmental status all appear irrelevant to the Court's disestablishment analysis.

As in its interpretation of the General Allotment Act in *County of Yakima*, the Court in the disestablishment cases could have chosen a reasonable interpretation of the surplus lands acts that would have taken account of those factors. Had it focused solely on congressional intent as expressed through the plain language of the particular surplus lands act, it could have given effect both to the express intent of Congress and to tribal territorial sovereignty. Instead, the Court chose to further the legacy of allotment by straining to find whenever remotely possible that the surplus lands acts terminated the reservation status of those lands, and therefore terminated tribal sovereignty over the disestablished lands.

V ALLOTMENT AND SOVEREIGNTY: THE REGULATORY JURISDICTION CASES

The reservation disestablishment cases discussed in the previous part address the legacy of the allotment policy with regard to the territory encompassed today by reservation borders. But even within existing and recognized reservation boundaries, the modern legacy of allotment has divested tribes of sovereign control over the territory. In particular, the Court has used the effects of allotment to wrest from tribes sovereign authority over non-Indian-owned fee lands within tribal territories.

One of the primary tenets of sovereignty is the concept that within its territorial limits, the sovereign's power is exclusive. Since the foundations of federal Indian law and the denomination of tribes as "domestic dependent nations," however, tribal sovereign powers have been subject to federal control. Until the 1880s, federal authority in Indian affairs was largely confined to the exercise of authority over relations between the tribes as sovereigns and the American people. Aside from those powers of external sovereignty, powers the Court had declared inconsistent with the dependent status of the tribes, tribal sovereign authority within tribal territory remained exclusive. In the 1880s, however, Congress and the Supreme Court made significant inroads into this exclusivity.

Those nineteenth century incursions primarily focused on the application of criminal laws in the Indian country. In 1885, Congress asserted its first direct control over the internal affairs of the tribes. With passage of the Major Crimes Act, the federal government for the first time exercised authority to determine the relations among tribal members within tribal territory. In addition to that intrusion into tribal sovereignty, the Supreme Court held in the 1881 case of *United States v. McBratney* that federal courts were without jurisdiction to prosecute crimes between non-Indians occurring in Indian country. While *McBratney* itself determined only that the federal courts had no jurisdiction, it has come to stand for the proposition that states, by virtue of their admission into the union, acquired criminal jurisdiction over crimes involving only non-Indians. Crimes not involving Indians, the Court determined, implicated no tribal sovereign interests requiring federal or tribal jurisdiction.

Despite these early inroads on tribal authority to govern all conduct within tribal territory, arguably the most serious and far-reaching curtailment of tribal power occurred in 1978 with the decision in *Oliphant v. Suquamish Indian Tribe*. In *Oliphant*, the Court resurrected the notion that tribes were, upon their incorporation within the United States, impliedly divested of all powers "inconsistent with their status." Those powers inconsistent with tribal status, the Court determined, were not limited to the powers of external sovereignty, but encompassed all powers other than the right to govern relations internal to the tribe. Accordingly, the Court held, Indian tribes were divested of any sovereign power to criminally prosecute non-Indians.

While *Oliphant* did not directly implicate the allotment program, the Court made a point of noting the effects of allotment on the Suquamish Indian Reservation. Nearly two-thirds of the reservation land was held in fee by non-Indians, and most of the trust land was "unimproved acreage upon which no persons reside." Out of a total population of nearly 3000, only about fifty persons were members of the

Suquamish Tribe. While these facts were technically irrelevant to the holding, their influence on the Court's decision is suspect. Underlying the Court's decision is a clear sense of unease in permitting tribes to exercise criminal jurisdiction over non-Indians, particularly in situations where the tribe is vastly outnumbered in land ownership and population.

What may have been merely an influence in *Oliphant*, however, became the dominant factor in *Montana v. United States*, where the Court divested the tribe of sovereign powers on the basis of the effects of allotment. Like most tribes, the Crow Tribe of Montana had been subject to the allotment program: tribal lands had been allotted; surplus lands had been sold; and considerable land had passed into non-Indian ownership, leading inevitably to a significant non-Indian presence within the Crow Reservation. As a result of the allotment years, by 1981 more than one-quarter of the Crow Reservation was held in fee by non-Indians. While more than two-thirds of the Crow territory continued in trust, most of the remaining trust lands were held as trust allotments.

In 1974, the Crow Tribal Council adopted a resolution prohibiting all hunting and fishing within the reservation by anyone not a member of the Crow Tribe. The prohibition extended throughout the territorial boundaries of the reservation, and consequently barred non-Indians from hunting and fishing even on fee-owned lands. In *Montana*, the Supreme Court struck down the resolution as beyond the sovereign powers of the Tribe to regulate that legacy of allotment: non-Indians on non-Indian fee land. The Court held that the effects of allotment in Crow country divested the tribe of both its treaty-recognized and its inherent rights to territorial sovereignty.

The 1868 Treaty of Fort Laramie established the Crow Reservation as land "set apart for the absolute and undisturbed use and occupation" of the tribe, and obligated the United States to prevent non-Indians from passing through or residing in the Crow territory. While these treaty provisions arguably recognized a right of the Crow Tribe to control hunting and fishing, the Court said, they did so *only* as to those lands over which the Tribe retained its "absolute and undisturbed use and occupation." Lands now held in fee by non-Indians as a result of the allotment policy, the Court then held, are not lands over which the Tribe now exercises exclusive use and occupation. Allotment, in other words, divested the tribes of territorial sovereignty over allotted lands subsequently lost to non-Indian owners.

Moreover, the Court found that it would be inconsistent with the purposes of the allotment policy to interpret the treaty as recognizing tribal authority over non-Indian lands. "It defies common sense," the Court asserted, "to believe that Congress intended to subject non-Indian fee owners to tribal jurisdiction when the ultimate purpose of the allotment policy was the "destruction of tribal government." The Court expressly rejected any notion that it should interpret the Treaty of Fort Laramie in light of Congress's repudiation of the allotment policy in 1934. On the contrary, the Court insisted, the only "relevant" inquiry was the effect of allotment on land ownership within the Crow Reservation.

Having eliminated the treaty as a source of tribal rights over non-Indian fee owners, the Court then turned to the inherent sovereign authority of the Tribe. Those inherent rights, the Court held, were insufficient to support the authority of the Crow Tribe to regulate activities on non-Indian fee land. For support, the Court turned to its decision three years earlier in *Oliphant*. The Court reiterated the doctrine underlying *Oliphant*: that Indian tribes, by virtue of their dependent status, have been implicitly divested of all sovereign rights inconsistent with that status. In particular, the dependent status of tribes is inconsistent with tribal control over non-Indians; the retained sovereign powers of the tribes extend only to the relations among the tribe and its people. Based on this broad sweep of the idea of implied divestiture, the Court stated that *Oliphant* stands for "the general proposition that the inherent sovereign powers of an Indian tribe do not extend to the activities of nonmembers of the tribe."

The Court immediately, however, recognized exceptions: instances in which tribal sovereign authority extended to non-Indian conduct within tribal territory. First, the Court held, tribes retain inherent authority to regulate the activities of non-Indians who enter into consensual relationships with the tribe or its members. Second, even as to non-Indian activities on fee land, tribes retain inherent authority to regulate conduct which "threatens or has some direct effect on the political integrity, the economic security, or the health or welfare of the tribe." Despite the apparently broad sweep of these exceptions, however, the Court held that neither was relevant to the exercise of Crow jurisdiction over non-Indian hunting and fishing. Non-Indians hunting and fishing on fee lands do not enter into any consensual dealings with the Crow Tribe. Nor do their activities have any direct effect on tribal sovereignty. In particular, the Court noted that because the State of Montana had historically regulated hunting and fishing on fee lands and because the Crow Tribe had asserted no authority over non-Indian hunting and fishing on the reservation at the time of the Crow Allotment Act, tribal control of hunting and fishing on fee lands "bears no clear relationship to tribal self-government or internal relations." Accordingly, it is a power inconsistent with the dependent status of the Crow Tribe and therefore divested.

Montana thus directly tied tribal sovereign regulatory powers to the fee lands legacy of the allotment years. Whatever general regulatory powers inhered in the tribe as a sovereign or were guaranteed to the tribe by treaty, the Court held, those powers were abrogated by operation of the General Allotment Act. Because of the change in title and the loss of tribal ownership, the tribe also lost the sovereign authority to regulate certain conduct within its territory. Despite the fact that fee lands within reservations are part of Indian country and that Indian country generally represents the territorial boundaries of tribal sovereignty, the Court bifurcated tribal powers along land tenure lines. As to regulation of conduct on trust lands, including the conduct of non-Indians, tribal power remains plenary. But as to regulation of that same conduct on fee lands by non-Indians, tribal power is divested absent some direct effect on tribal sovereignty.

The "direct effects" test that the Court constructed to provide exceptions for conduct on fee lands begged the question. Territorial integrity – the right of the sovereign to control persons and activities within its territory – is a central tenet of sovereignty. Any loss of territorial integrity necessarily has a direct effect on tribal sovereignty: it trenches upon a basic sovereign right. To argue, as the Court did, that the loss of the power to regulate activities within the sovereign's territorial borders "bears no close relationship" to self-government is oxymoronic.

Despite its lack of logic, the direct effects test proved highly useful to tribes in the years following the *Montana* decision. Tribes were, virtually without exception, able to convince lower federal courts and tribal courts that a range of non-Indian conduct on fee lands would have sufficient direct effects on tribal sovereignty to justify tribal regulation. For all practical purposes, the direct effects exception swallowed the "general proposition" that tribes were divested of sovereign authority over non-Indian fee lands.

* * *

VI "SHALL WE PERSIST IN A POLICY THAT HAS FAILED?"

In 1885, at the dawn of the allotment era, former Commissioner of Indian Affairs George Manypenny wrote of his disillusionment with the allotment program. As Commissioner, Manypenny had negotiated a number of treaties with western tribes to make way for the organization of the Kansas and Nebraska territories. For the most part, those treaties called for the Indian lands to be allotted in severalty, provisions which Manypenny believed at the time to be "wise and judicious." By 1885, Manypenny's reaction to allotment was quite different:

> When I made those treaties I was confident that good results would follow. Had I not so believed I would not have been a party to the transactions. Events following the execution of these treaties proved that I had committed a grave error. I had provided for the abrogation of the reservations, the dissolution of the tribal relation, and for lands in severalty and citizenship; thus making the road clear for the rapacity of the white man. I had broken down every barrier. I had committed a grevious [sic] mistake, and entailed on the Indians a legacy of cruel wrong and injury. Had I known then, as I now know, what would result from those treaties, I would be compelled to admit that I had committed a high crime.

Manypenny's wisdom was, unfortunately, lost on Congress. Within two years of Manypenny's article of contrition, Congress enacted the General Allotment Act, clearing the way for widespread application of the program that Manypenny decried. For nearly fifty years thereafter, tribes were subjected to the "cruel wrong and injury" of the allotment policy. Although allotment ceased in 1934 with official congressional repudiation of the policy and program, its legacy lingers on in the Supreme

Court. With decisions in such diverse areas as taxation, reservation disestablishment, and regulation of fee lands, the Court continues to give effect to the purposes of a long-dead policy.

The political tenor of our times is no longer much amenable to arguments that the present effects of past policies must be corrected by the legal system. And yet that is the only approach that will work for the Indian tribes. Unless the Court is willing to act affirmatively to halt the devastating present effects of allotment, or Congress is willing to step in, tribal territorial sovereignty is in danger of becoming a curio in the history of the Republic.

If the Court were willing to repudiate the policy of allotment, it has the tools to do so. In none of the cases critiqued in this article was the outcome foreclosed by treaty, by federal statute, or by precedent. Instead, in each of the cases, the Court had one or more avenues available to reach conclusions protective of tribal territorial sovereignty: the canons of construction, the repudiation of allotment in the Indian Reorganization Act, and the current federal Indian policy of tribal self-determination.

A careful application of the Indian law canons of construction would go far toward mitigating the persistent effects of the allotment policy. First, the General Allotment Act itself should be interpreted according to the canons. Either the Act should be viewed in its historical context as legislation enacted for the benefit of Indians and therefore interpreted liberally in favor of the tribes, or the Act should be viewed in its post-1934 context as legislation abrogating Indian rights and therefore interpreted narrowly to limit those rights only where Congress was unmistakably clear. The results should be identical either way. The Act would not, for example, authorize state property taxes on fee-patented lands owned by Indians unless Congress said so, and Congress did not. Similarly, the Act would not strip tribes of sovereign rights over fee-patented lands sold to non-Indians unless Congress clearly mandated that result in the Act, and it did not. Finally, legislation implementing the Act would not divest reservations of homesteaded land unless Congress and the tribes had intended an outright cession of reservation lands, and few of the surplus lands acts evidence that plain intent. Had the Court chosen to interpret the Dawes Act and its implementing legislation liberally in favor of the tribes and to resolve all ambiguities in favor of the tribes, the Court could have reached results consistent with both the statutes and the preservation of tribal territorial sovereignty. However naive it may be to expect the present Court to engage in conscientious application of the canons of construction, that interpretative approach is clearly available to the Court.

In addition to the canons, the Court could also employ an interpretation of the General Allotment Act and its implementing legislation that takes into account the repudiation of the allotment policy in the 1934 Indian Reorganization Act ("IRA"). In the IRA, Congress recognized the devastation wrought by allotment, halted further allotments and surplus lands acts, extended trust periods on existing trust allotments, authorized the addition of lands to reservations, and promoted the "reorganization" of tribal governments. Congress, in simple terms, terminated the allotment policy. Given the express terms of the IRA, the modern Court could choose to interpret the present effects of the allotment policy not in light of the intent of the 1887 Congress, but in light of the intent of the IRA.

If the purposes of the IRA become the context, then the important factors are the preservation of the land base and the perpetuation of tribal self-government. When the General Allotment Act, its implementing legislation, and its present effects are viewed against those purposes, the outcomes of the allotment-based cases should be radically different. State taxation of Indian-owned former allotments interferes with the tribe's ability to govern its members within its territory, and therefore obstructs the IRA purpose of promoting tribal government. The surplus lands acts are in direct opposition to the purposes of the IRA regarding the preservation, consolidation, and expansion of tribal territory, and therefore should be interpreted to diminish reservations only when they clearly implement an agreement ceding a tract outright to the federal government. Finally, divesting tribes of regulatory jurisdiction over nonmember fee lands contravenes both the IRA goal of tribal self-government and the principle of territorial integrity.

Time after time, however, the Court has flatly refused to consider the IRA and its purposes in deciding allotment-based cases. Justice Scalia has dismissed the importance of the IRA in this context, stating that "Congress made no attempt to undo the dramatic effects of the allotment years on the ownership of former Indian lands." While it is true that Congress did not, in the IRA, restore to tribal ownership lands then owned in fee by non-Indians, the purposes and intent of the IRA clearly support tribal territorial sovereignty. But the Court is using that one aspect of the IRA to find that it need not consider any other aspect of the Act – in particular, the intent of the Congress that enacted it – in looking at the present effects of allotment-era legislation.

Moreover, the Court takes the same approach to a consideration of modern federal Indian policy. For 25 years, presidents have pledged to protect and promote tribal self-determination, and for the past decade that pledge has included a specific recognition of the "government-to-government" relationship between the federal government and the Indian tribes. Congress has concurred, consistently enacting legislation over the past two decades that recognizes tribal self-government and control over tribal territory. But as with the policies of the IRA, the modern policies of Congress and the Executive are apparently irrelevant in the Court's eyes. Nowhere in its allotment-derived cases does the Court recognize the "ongoing relationship" between Congress and the tribes or the importance of that relationship. Indeed, the Court seems to have no compunction about interfering with that relationship by implementing the allotment policy rather than the current policy of tribal self-determination. If Congress is indeed the branch responsible for federal Indian policy, as the Court repeatedly states, then the Court should be supporting rather than undermining congressional attempts to ameliorate the effects of the allotment era. ***

NOTES & QUESTIONS

1. *Reading Indian Law*:

- At the beginning of the article, Royster mentions that property has played a role in every major era of federal Indian law, and indeed, an examination of the role of property can tell us much about each era. What was the role of property in the Treatymaking Era, including the removal and reservation sections of that era? What was the role of property in the Allotment Era? Reorganization? Termination? Self-Determination?

- Under allotment, the lands reserved to a particular tribe were divided into 40- to 160-acre parcels and assigned to individual members of the tribe. The title to these parcels was held in trust by the federal government, typically for twenty-five years. Why was the title held in trust? What were the conditions for releasing the title from its trust status? Why were some of these titles released early? What is a forced fee patent and what role did it play in the Allotment Era?

- In what ways did the allotment policy influence US Supreme Court decisions after Congress repudiated that policy? What, if anything, do you think the Supreme Court should have done differently? Was there a way the Court could have avoided the influence of the allotment policy?

2. *Lone Wolf and Challenging Allotment*: *Lone Wolf v. Hitchcock*, 187 U.S. 553 (1903) was a case challenging the constitutionality of the allotment policy, with tribal stakeholders arguing that the policy violated the 1867 Medicine Lodge Treaty. In rejecting the challenge, the US Supreme Court declared that

> In effect, the action of Congress now complained of was but *** a mere change in the form of investment of Indian tribal property, the property of those who, as we have held, were in substantial effect the wards of the government. We must presume that Congress acted in perfect good faith in the dealings with the Indians of which complaint is made, and that the legislative branch of the government exercised its best judgment in the premises. In any event, as Congress possessed full power in the matter, the judiciary cannot question or inquire into the motives which prompted the enactment of this legislation.

187 U.S. at 568. What did the Court mean when it described the allotment policy as a "mere change in the form of the investment"? Do you agree or disagree with that description?

In the words of Professor Phillip Frickey:

> *Lone Wolf v. Hitchcock* has been called "the Indians' *Dred Scott* decision." *Dred Scott* is notorious because of its racism – its

inhuman conceptualization of the African-Americans – and because of its troubling aftermath – it greased the slide into the Civil War. *Lone Wolf* is similarly shocking. ***

Philip P. Frickey, *Doctrine, Context, Institutional Relationships, and Commentary: The Malaise of Federal Indian Law through the Lens of* Lone Wolf, 38 Tulsa L. Rev. 5 (2013). How would you compare *Dred Scott* and *Lone Wolf*? Do you think it is fair to call *Lone Wolf* the Indian's *Dred Scott*?

3. *The* Cobell *Litigation*: When Congress enacted the IRA in 1934 all of the parcels of land allotted out to individual Indians, but still held in trust by the federal government, were to remain in trust indefinitely. While these parcels are in trust status, officials at the Bureau of Indian Affairs (BIA) are responsible for managing the land on behalf of the legal owners. This meant that the federal government negotiates leases for grazing, timber harvesting, mineral exploration, and collects the royalties or other payments for these activities. The payments were deposited into Individual Indian Money (IIM) accounts managed by the BIA. The proceeds were then periodically disbursed to the legal owners of the property, or that is how the system was supposed to work. Over 100 years of poor record keeping resulted in the federal government being unable to account for billions of dollars of money that flowed through the IIM accounts.

In 1996, a class action lawsuit was filed against the government demanding an accounting for these monies. (An accounting merely means that the government was asked to show what monies were deposited and withdrawn from each IIM account.) The plaintiffs alleged that the government had committed an egregious breach of trust and as evidence of this breach asserted that among other errors: over 15,000 duplicate accounts existed, more than 54,000 accounts had no address for the individual, and more than 21,000 accounts existed for deceased individuals and had not been distributed to their heirs. As part of the litigation, several auditors were hired to reconstruct the accounting books but none were able to do so. After a decade of litigation, including multiple findings that various government officials were in contempt for failing to comply with court orders, the federal government settled with the parties. What do you think would have happened if these funds had been private trust funds managed by a bank? Should the government be held to a different standard? Millions of acres of land are still held in trust. What should be done with them?

For a critique of how the settlement will not resolve the underlying problem *see* Jered Davidson, *Comment: This Land Is Your Land, This Land Is My Land? Why the Cobell Settlement Will Not Resolve Indian Land Fractionation*, 35 Am. Indian L. Rev. 575 (2011).

4. *The Problem of Fractionation*: The *Cobell* litigation addressed the accounting issues regarding allotted land held in trust, but it did not address the problem of fractionation. When the original allottee passed away, that person's heirs inherited undivided portions of the land. If the original allottee had four children, each child inherited one-fourth of the property. With each successive generation, allotted lands became increasingly fractionated. The now (in)famous Tract 1305 is an example of the problems that result:

> Tract 1305 is 40 acres, and produces $1,080 in income annually. It is valued at $8,000. It has 439 owners, one-third of whom receive less than $.05 in annual rent and two-thirds of whom receive less than $1. The largest interest holder receives $82.85 annually. The common denominator used to compute fractional interests in the property is 3,394,923,840,000. The smallest heir receives $.01 every 177 years. If the tract were sold (assuming the 439 owners could agree) for its estimated $8,000 value, he would be entitled to $.000418. The administrative costs of handling this tract are estimated by the Bureau of Indian Affairs at $17,560 annually.

Hodel v. Irving, 481 U.S. 704, 713 (1987). Congress attempted to resolve these problems with the Indian Lands Consolidation Act, which provided a means by which some of these increasingly small fractions of land would revert to the ownership of the tribal government. Owners of these small fractions of land filed suit, challenging the statute as violating the Fifth Amendment. The Fifth Amendment declares that the government must pay "fair compensation" if private land is taken for public purposes. The US Supreme Court upheld these challenges, sending Congress back to the drawing board. Congress eventually responded with the American Indian Probate Reform Act of 2004, which created new procedures for handling estates containing trust land. What problems do you foresee with this type of approach? What complications might occur? Is there a way to avoid those problems? *See, e.g.*, Douglas R. Nash & Cecelia E. Burke (2006) *The Changing Landscape of Indian Estate Planning and Probate: The American Indian Probate Reform Act (AIPRA)*, 5 Seattle J. for Social Justice 121 (2006).

5. *Beyond the Law*: The Meriam Report, more formally known by its official title, *The Problem of Indian Administration*, was a report commissioned by the Secretary of the Interior and prepared by what would later become known as the Brookings Institution. After visiting ninety-five jurisdictions (reservations, collections of urban Indians, Indian schools and hospitals, and communities where Indians had migrated), Lewis Meriam issued a scathing report on the failure of the government's

Indian policies. The report was rich in detail, with sections on health, education, the status of the family and Indian women, economic development, the work of missionaries, etc. The report attributed the problems of poverty, joblessness, lack of education, low life expectancy, and poor living conditions directly to the current manner in which the Department of Interior and Bureau of Indians Affairs were working with Indians and demanded changes be made immediately.

The report declared that the health of the Indians "is bad" and that with few exceptions the medical facilities "must be generally characterized as lacking in personnel, equipment, management, and design." The report also declared that the "income of the typical Indian family is low." As a result, "with comparatively few exceptions, the diet of the Indians is bad. It is generally insufficient in quantity, lacking in variety, and poorly prepared," and "the prevailing living conditions among the great majority of the Indians are conducive to the development and spread of disease." The report attributed primary blame for these conditions largely to the failings of the federal government generally and to the allotment and assimilation policy specifically. The report was a significant factor contributing to Congress's decision to end the allotment policy and enact the 1934 Indian Reorganization Act.

Eighty years later, conditions on reservations were still poor. In 2003, a report of the US Commission on Civil Rights asserted that "Native Americans still suffer higher rates of poverty, poor educational achievement, substandard housing, and higher rates of disease and illness. Native Americans continue to rank at or near the bottom of nearly every social, health, and economic indicator." US Commission on Civil Rights, A *Quiet Crisis: Federal Funding and Unmet Needs in Indian Country* 4 (2003).

> Native Americans have a lower life expectancy than any other ethnic group in the United States, and they suffer higher rates of illness for many diseases. *** Elderly Native Americans are 48.7% more likely to suffer from heart failure, 173% more likely to suffer from diabetes, and 44.3% to suffer from asthma than the general population.

Armen H. Merjin, *An Unbroken Chain of Injustice: The Dawes Act, Native American Trusts, and* Cobell v. Salazar, 46 Gonz. L. Rev. 609, 612 (2010). What, if any, conclusions can be drawn from these statistics? Why so little improvement? What message do they send to tribes? To the federal government? What should the response be? *See* Jennie R. Joe and Francine C. Gachupin (eds.), *Health and Social Issues of Native American Women* (Praeger 2012).

FURTHER READING

- Kenneth H. Bobroff, *Retelling Allotment: Indian Property Rights and the Myth of Common Ownership*, 54 Vanderbilt L. Rev. 1559 (2001).
- Kathleen R. Guzman, *Give or Take an Acre: Property Norms and the Indian Land Consolidation Act*, 85 Iowa L. Rev. 595 (2000).
- Christine A. Klein, *Treaties of Conquest: Property Rights, Indian Treaties, and the Treaty of Guadalupe Hidalgo*, 26 N.M. L. Rev. 201 (1996).
- Robert Laurence, *The Dominant Society's Judicial Reluctance to Allow Tribal Civil Law to Apply to Non-Indians: Reservation Diminishment, Modern Demography, and the Indian Civil Rights Act*, 30 U. Rich. L. Rev. 781 (1996).
- Richard A. Monette, *Governing Private Property in Indian Country: The Double-Edged Sword of the Trust Relationship and Trust Responsibility Arising out of Early Supreme Court Opinions and the General Allotment Act*, 25 N.M. L. Rev. 35 (1995).
- Jessica Shoemaker, *Like Snow in the Spring Time: Allotment, Fractionation, and the Indian Land Tenure Problem*, 2003 Wis. L. Rev. 729 (2003).
- Rebecca Tsosie, *Land, Culture, and Community: Reflections on Native Sovereignty and Property in America*, 34 Ind. L. Rev. 1291 (2001).
- Mary Christina Wood, *Indian Land and the Promise of Native Sovereignty: The Trust Doctrine Revisited*, 1994 Utah L. Rev. 1471 (1994).

11

A Common Law for Our Age of Colonialism: The Judicial Divestiture of Indian Tribal Authority over Nonmembers

Philip P. Frickey

109 Yale L.J. 1 (1999)

The final stages of the Treatymaking Era focused on separating settlers and Indians, first by removing Indians west of the Mississippi River and later by confining Indians to reservations. The Allotment Era ended this separation, most particularly by lifting reservation barriers and creating an influx of non-Indians.

Ending this separation inevitably gave rise to friction between tribes and non-Indians who were now living and working in Indian country. This friction did not create much impact initially, largely because federal Indian policy cycled fairly quickly once the Allotment Era ended, with the Reorganization and Termination eras each lasting approximately twenty years. As the United States settled into the Self-Determination Era, and tribal governments had time to become reestablished and start exercising more authority, the friction between tribal governments and the non-Indians living within their borders increasingly gave rise to litigation.

This article by Philip Frickey explores the impact of these lawsuits on the development of federal Indian law, and the ways in which the changing land tenure patterns in Indian country reshaped the way the US Supreme Court approached Indian law cases. Because many of the principles articulating the boundaries of power between tribes, states, and the United States are constructed by courts instead of by Congress, the Supreme Court has been particularly influential on the development of Indian/non-Indian relations. The breakdown in the borders between Indian country and the rest of the United States has manifested itself in a breakdown of tribal sovereignty.

As you read Professor Frickey's article, think about the ways in which ownership of land by non-Indians reduced the sovereignty and authority of both tribal courts and tribal governments. Why do you think this is the case? Why did the US Supreme Court view non-Indian landownership as a game changer? When individuals purchase land within a different state, that purchase of land does not carry with it the potential ability to change the scope of state governmental authority. Why should it be different in Indian country?

I INTRODUCTION

Surely Oliver Wendell Holmes, Jr. gave federal Indian law no thought when he wrote that "experience" – including "[t]he felt necessities of the time" and "even the prejudices which judges share with their fellow-men" – contributes more "than the syllogism" to the development of judge-made law. Nor was federal Indian law on his mind when he contrasted an "ideal system of law" based on "science" with the one he inhabited, in which "tradition, or vague sentiment" produced doctrines that were "accidental relics of early notions." Yet his aphoristic analysis strikingly reson-ates with both sides in a key dispute of federal Indian law – whether a tribe may regulate all persons within the historical boundary of its reservation – that has produced both incoherent Supreme Court precedents and incandescent controver-sies in the lives of the people subject to them. Consider an example.

Located in rural South Dakota, the Cheyenne River Sioux Reservation may seem far removed from the great legal controversies of our day. Yet, in less than a decade, it was the setting for two important cases concerning contemporary tribal authority. In the first, *Solem v. Bartlett*, the Supreme Court held that reservation borders specified in a nineteenth-century treaty survived the later enactment of a federal statute that opened the reservation for non-Indian homesteading and that has resulted in a significant non-Indian population there. The Court concluded:

> When both [the statute] and its legislative history fail to provide substantial and compelling evidence of a congressional intention to diminish Indian lands, we are bound by our traditional solicitude for the Indian tribes to rule that diminishment did not take place and that the old reservation boundaries survived the opening.

As a result, the tribe has potentially significant authority over non-Indian reserva-tion landowners. At least some of these non-Indians feel betrayed. In their view, *Solem* ignored their reasonable expectations and those of their predecessors that non-Indian lands were outside the reservation. They complain of being subject to a sovereign in which they have no say, a sort of "taxation without representation" foreign to America. They could invoke Holmes to contend that "tradition, or vague sentiment" – what the Court in *Solem* called its "traditional solicitude for the Indian tribes" – has produced an "accidental relic" of tribal sovereignty inconsistent both with longstanding congressional and private expectations and with fundamental fairness.

In the second case, *South Dakota v. Bourland*, the Court held that the tribe could not regulate non-Indian hunting and fishing in an area where Congress had taken reservation land to build a dam, reservoir, and public recreation area. Even though the land remained within reservation boundaries, the Court concluded that, "when Congress has broadly opened up such land to non-Indians, the effect of the transfer is the destruction of preexisting Indian rights to regulatory control."

Bourland and *Solem* fit together awkwardly in both law and life. Doctrinally, the focus in *Bourland* on the *effect* of the congressional alienation of Indian land seems inconsistent with *Solem*, where the reservation remained intact despite the congressional alienation of Indian land because no clear congressional *intent* to diminish tribal authority had been shown. As a practical matter, *Bourland* probably antagonizes tribal members as much as *Solem* angers non-Indian reservation residents. Because of *Bourland*, the tribe lacks integrated regulatory authority over its territory. Tribal leaders, too, could invoke Holmes in contending that tribal sovereignty, long recognized by the Supreme Court, was displaced by a one-sided perception of non-Indian "felt necessities" to be free from tribal authority that are rooted in the "prejudices which judges share with their fellow-men [and women]."

The controversy at Cheyenne River is contemporary federal Indian law in microcosm. What the Supreme Court said long ago remains true today: The relation of Indian tribes to the broader American system "has always been an anomalous one and of a complex character." The Constitution does not clearly delineate the relationship among tribes, the federal government, and the states. It is unsurprising, then, that the task of rationalizing the field has largely fallen to the Supreme Court. Given the lack of guidance in positive law, the complexity of the issues, and the tangled normative questions surrounding the colonial displacement of indigenous peoples to construct a constitutional democracy, it is also not surprising that the resulting decisional law is as incoherent as it is complicated.

As the Cheyenne River cases indicate, one of the most vexing clusters of questions involves the geographical extent of reservations containing many non-Indians and the authority of tribes to regulate nonmembers found in "Indian country." Over the past four decades, the Supreme Court has decided six cases concerning reservation boundaries in addition to *Solem*. Although the cases purport to follow *Solem's* injunction that only clear congressional intent may work a reduction in reservation size, *** their results cannot be squared with that standard. *** [O]ver the same period the Court has decided the remarkable number of fourteen cases involving tribal criminal, civil, and judicial authority over nonmembers found on reservations. Tribes prevailed in two seemingly easy cases – considering whether Congress could authorize tribal civil regulation of nonmembers and whether a tribe could tax the sale of a product to a nonmember – as well as in three more controversial settings.

Three other cases reached peculiar compromises. The other six decisions diminished the tribal capacity to deal with nonmembers who fail to comply with reservation law. Are these opinions defeats for legitimate tribal authority, a kind of ongoing judicial colonization in Indian country? Or do they reflect a proper respect for the civil rights of American citizens who, because they cannot participate in tribal government or serve on tribal juries and are not members of the ethnic group exercising sovereign authority, lack the actual and virtual representation that provides the customary nonjudicial protection from governmental abuse in the United States? Moreover, whatever might be the appropriate normative conclusions about these decisions, do they fit together into a conceptual whole or disaggregate into incoherence?

This Article examines the concept of tribal sovereignty that was originally developed by the Supreme Court and that has evolved as the result of clashes with the interests of nonmembers. *** [T]he traditional model of tribal authority, *** at least implicitly assumed that tribes have geographical sovereignty over their reservations and all persons found there. In recent years, the Supreme Court has undercut this understanding in two fundamental ways. *** [T]he Court has sometimes reduced tribal geographical sovereignty by diminishing reservation boundaries to free largely non-Indian areas from tribal control. *** [T]he Court has also substantially undermined tribal authority even within acknowledged reservation borders by concluding that tribes have no criminal, and only limited civil, jurisdiction over nonmembers found there.

On the surface, the analysis *** seems to reveal an incoherence between the outcomes of these decisions and their purported doctrinal underpinnings. [This article] suggests, however, that an unstated assumption underlies all of them: Tribal sovereignty over non-Indian areas and tribal authority to regulate significant nonmember interests are inconsistent with what the Supreme Court presumes to be the wishes of Congress. Because in these cases the congressional intent is unstated, however, the outcomes turn on judicial presumptions, rather than legislative resolutions, concerning the question whether tribes are sovereigns or merely membership organizations. Thus, it is the Court, not Congress, that has exercised front-line responsibility for the vast erosion of tribal sovereignty. The coherence that underlies the doctrinal confusion in the cases is a strong, albeit largely unarticulated and undefended, judicial aversion to basic claims of tribal authority over nonmembers that is implicitly projected upon Congress as well.

That the Court has exercised this extraordinary authority in an area in which Congress has long operated with plenary power supports the disturbing conclusion that the Court has assumed a legislative function – that of implementing the ongoing colonial process. *** [T]he Court has done so by flattening federal Indian law into the broader American public law by importing general constitutional and subconstitutional values into the field. The Court has undertaken this task without congressional guidance. A half-millennium after the colonial process began, in our time of great skepticism concerning colonization, our least democratic branch has become our most enthusiastic colonial agent.

* * *

II THE BASIC MODEL OF TRIBAL SOVEREIGNTY

A *Foundational Premises*

Questions concerning tribal power are, of course, not new. In his monumental attempt to systematize federal Indian law, Felix Cohen addressed the place of tribal power within the American scheme of governance. Cohen concluded that "[t]he whole course of judicial decision" adhered to three basic principles. First, prior to European contact, a tribe possessed "all the powers of any sovereign state." Second, the European colonial process, which Cohen labeled "[c]onquest,"

> renders the tribe subject to the legislative power of the United States and, in substance, terminates the external powers of sovereignty of the tribe, e.g., its power to enter into treaties with foreign nations, but does not by itself affect the internal sovereignty of the tribe, i.e., its powers of local self-government.

Third, tribes therefore retain internal sovereignty "subject to qualification by treaties and by express legislation of Congress." Thus, tribal powers generally are not "delegated powers granted by express acts of Congress," but instead are "inherent powers of a limited sovereignty which has never been extinguished." Consistently with established canons of interpretation, ambiguities in federal statutes that might be read as invading tribal authority are construed narrowly to protect tribal interests. Similarly, provisions of Indian treaties that might undercut tribal authority are also read narrowly, based on two key assumptions: The treaty transaction was a cession of rights by the tribe rather than a granting of rights by the United States, and these cessions, along with all other treaty provisions, are to be interpreted as the Indians would have understood them.

* * *

In addition to being rooted in precedent, Cohen's three principles represented a normative accommodation of our colonial heritage and a judicial respect for tribal survival as a self-governing authority. The principles accept the inevitable: The United States resulted from a colonial process that cannot be undone at this late date, no matter the normative concerns that might be raised about it. Thus, in light of "the actual state of things," courts viewed themselves as impotent to consider basic challenges to historical colonization, such as the involuntary loss of tribal authority to engage in government relations and land transactions with any entity other than the United States and the presumed supremacy of Congress over Indian affairs. Moreover, tribes themselves had ceded away other important interests on a treaty-by-treaty basis. Despite these factors, however, and in the face of the historical justifications for colonization, the Supreme Court had assumed that the relationship between the colonizers and the tribes was benign, one of trust and cooperation rather than of annihilation. Thus, treaties were viewed as solemn agreements between cooperative sovereigns under which the tribe, not the federal government, granted rights, which as in derogation of their own sovereignty should be narrowly construed. So, too, although Congress had the authority to destroy Indian rights, the assumption was that Congress would not do so lightly, and thus canons of interpretation protecting tribal interests were applied to statutory as well as treaty interpretation.

These principles combine to form an institutionally sensitive approach to the ongoing American colonial process – the centuries-old but continuing series of conflicts between indigenous peoples and those elements of the dominant society seeking to displace their institutions and prerogatives. Under the canons of interpretation, positive law on the books (treaties, statutes, and so on) is construed narrowly to preserve tribal sovereignty against all but crystal-clear losses. This technique forces opponents of tribal power to bear the heavier burden in litigation – they must marshal the complexities of the case persuasively – and leaves the reviewing court a simple way to cut through the confusions of federal Indian law. If, as should often occur, tribal authority survives this challenge, its opponents then must bear the burden of legislative inertia. Although Congress may change the outcome, it may do so only openly, by clear statutory language that should flag the issue for legislators and lobbyists who favor Indian interests and that should ensure a fairer legislative fight. Because it is much easier to kill legislation than to enact it, tribal interests have significant advantages in the legislative struggle. Thus, the courts place significant side constraints on the imposition of new colonial intrusions while leaving the ongoing issues of the relationship of tribes and the larger society in the hands of Congress.

B The Fragility of These Principles in the Context of Non-Indians in Indian Country

Under these principles, tribes possess all authority not lost as a result of original European contact, explicit treaty cessions, or unambiguous unilateral congressional action. Accordingly, absent treaty or statutory language to the contrary, non-Indians found on an Indian reservation would seem to be subject to tribal authority. Moreover, all three of these categories have significant limiting principles that further undercut any non-Indian immunity to tribal regulation.

As defined by the Marshall Court, the first category concerns the loss of authority to have government relations and land transactions with any entity other than the "discovering" European sovereign or its successor, the United States. It reflects the essential premises necessary to rationalize colonization from its outset and to promote the efficient displacement of indigenous interests on an ongoing basis. Under these assumptions, the colonial process is bilateral, involving subordinated tribes locked into an exclusive relationship with the dominant United States. The non-Indian side of the process is centralized in Congress, which is empowered to carry out the colonization of the continent. Thus, when a diminished tribal authority is traceable to this category, the reason is that the tribal power in question is inconsistent with the capacity of Congress to engage in efficient colonization. The rights of private individuals – such as non-Indians found in Indian country – are, accordingly, irrelevant.

* * *

*** [I]t would seem inescapable that tribes retain territorial sovereignty over their reservations unless some federal treaty or statute has plainly abrogated it. Absent clear immunity in such positive law, non-Indians who find themselves on an Indian reservation would seem to be subject to the authority of the tribe, just as they would be subject to the authority of New York when strolling across Central Park. That is not how the law has turned out, however. *** [T]he canons have lost much of their bite in the context of tribal regulation of nonmembers. *** [T]the Court has also undermined tribal sovereignty by reopening the category of tribal powers that are inconsistent with domestic dependent status and then evaluating nonmember complaints about assertions of tribal authority on a case-by-case basis.

At least two factors explain the fragility of the principles that seemingly mandate tribal geographical sovereignty. First, they were developed in cases contesting the authority of tribes vis-à-vis the federal or state governments or the tribe's own members, not vis-à-vis non-Indians. The conclusion that tribes have authority to regulate non-Indians found on reservations follows logically from these cases, but was not at issue in any of them. The second, related factor is that these understandings were developed against the backdrop of a simple context, in which Indian reservations were perceived to be enclaves for Indians only. Congress shattered that understanding when it adopted the General Allotment Act of 1887, a policy directive that reservations be divided up into allotments for tribal members, with the land left over opened to non-Indian homesteading. Implemented on a tribe-by-tribe basis, the allotment process was designed to assimilate Indians into the larger society. The allotments were to be held in trust for a period of time, rendering them inalienable and free from state taxation and providing an opportunity for the allottees to learn western agricultural ways. The theory was that, when the trust period ended and the land was transformed into fee simple status, the Indian owners would be assimilated into the agricultural economy. Reservations would disappear over time, and the "Indian problem" would be solved.

It never turned out that way. Allotment was a disastrous policy. When the allotments became alienable, sometimes much more quickly than originally planned, huge amounts of Indian land were lost through sales and tax foreclosures. By the 1920s, it had become clear that allotment was a failure. In the Indian Reorganization Act of 1934, Congress embraced this reality, extending the trust period for all remaining allotments in perpetuity and providing that no further allotments be made. Congress did not attempt to undo the effects of allotment, however.

Federal Indian law has not been the same since the allotment era. Because of allotment, many reservations today have a significant non-Indian population and a checkerboard land pattern with non-Indian fee property mixed in with Indian allotments and collective tribal property. Indeed, the demographic diversity in Indian country today is remarkable. At one extreme, over ninety-six percent of the residents of the Navajo reservation are Indian. At the other extreme, the Port Madison Reservation of the Suquamish Indian Tribe in Washington contained over 2900 non-Indians and only fifty members at the time the tribe engaged in major litigation concerning its authority to regulate nonmembers.

During the allotment era, another factor also undermined the simple "we/they" context of federal Indian policy. In 1924, Congress unilaterally conferred citizenship upon Indians who had not yet attained that status. Like it or not, Indians were now citizens of both the United States and their state of residence as well as members of their tribes.

These developments substantially complicate any analysis of contemporary federal Indian law. Where it was once plausible to imagine that the only important relationship in the field was a bilateral one between Congress and the tribes, the interests of individuals – Indian and non-Indian alike – are now salient by virtue of the congressional policies of allotment and Indian citizenship. Nonetheless, the federal policy of promoting tribal sovereignty was restored in 1934 and remains in place today. How might one rationalize this more complex context? To return to Holmes's aphoristic analysis: Which is today's "accidental relic," the presence of nonmembers on reservations long after the abandonment of allotment, or the continuation of tribal sovereignty itself? Can federal judges adjudicate disputes in this controversial environment by following the "felt necessities of the time" without falling victim to "shared prejudices"?

It is probably not surprising that, in this more muddled context, courts have sometimes limited tribal authority over nonmembers. Two basic strategies have emerged. As *Solem* indicates, one method is to reexamine the location of reservation boundaries in order to free largely non-Indian areas from tribal control. Because neither Congress's embrace of the allotment policy nor its subsequent abandonment of it explicitly dealt with the question of reservation boundaries, Congress created a conundrum of treaty and statutory interpretation concerning the limits of reservations. ***[D]espite the canons of interpretation, the contemporary Supreme Court has sometimes interpreted century-old allotment statutes as diminishing reservation size. A second avenue for truncating tribal authority is to conclude, as *Bourland* did, that nonmembers are immune from tribal power even if found on a reservation. *** [T]he disruptive impact of allotment has led to a contemporary reevaluation of which tribal powers are inconsistent with current domestic dependent status.

V DOING WHAT COMES NATURALLY: METHODOLOGICAL
RECONCEPTUALIZATIONS OF THE COURT'S OPINIONS
CONCERNING TRIBAL AUTHORITY OVER NONMEMBERS

A *Judicial Lawmaking in the Guise of Routine Statutory Interpretation*

The most obvious methodological point about contemporary federal Indian law is that, in the absence of targeted congressional guidance, the Supreme Court stands ready to protect arguably significant nonmember interests rather than to wait for Congress to address the problem. It does not seem to make much difference whether, as in *Oliphant*, the Court acknowledges that no authoritative text controls and that the Court is engaged in federal common-lawmaking that divests tribes of inherent sovereignty or whether, as in *Yankton*, the Court purports to rely upon statutory or treaty text to diminish tribal interests. In both scenarios, the Court reaches whatever result seems most practical in the current context. The Court has, in effect, embraced a common law for our age of colonialism.

A striking evolution in judicial methodology has occurred in order to free the Court to pursue this mission. The canons of interpretation that once seemed to influence strongly, if not control, outcomes in federal Indian law cases have lost their force in the context of significant nonmember interests. ***

***

The apparent merger of statutory interpretation and common-lawmaking in these cases is highlighted by the role played by developments subsequent to the allotment of the reservation. In the reservation-diminishment cases, the Court has admitted that, in "interpreting" the allotment agreement or statute in question, it takes into account postenactment factors such as contemporary demographics and jurisdictional patterns that have arisen over time. This approach makes no sense if the interpretive touchstone of the agreement or statute in question is plain textual meaning (there is none), specific congressional intent about reservation boundaries (there is none), or original general congressional purposes (which are always assimilative, such that adhering to them would require that the tribes always lose, which they have not). This approach does become understandable, however, if we conceptualize the judicial role in these cases to be achieving a common-law-like resolution of a current dispute based on current context.

***

B *Harmonizing Federal Indian Law with the Anglo-American*
Legal Landscape

The basic thrust of the Court's statutory interpretation and quasi-constitutional decisions in federal Indian law has been to domesticate tribal power by harmonizing federal Indian law with basic Anglo-American legal values and assumptions.

The Court has produced a profound "flattening" of federal Indian law into the broader public law. The precedents and the canons of interpretation that have rendered the field of Indian law a unique exception to many general public-law principles have now been diluted in the name of legal uniformity and the protection of the perceived reasonable reliance of nonmembers upon their assumptions about the rule of law and the roles of lawmaking institutions within the United States.

This judicial missionary work of bringing the general law into Indian country may explain at least some of the Indian law precedents that are not simply rooted in statutory interpretation or quasi-constitutional elaboration. The clearest example is *Strate*. Recall that the case involved a suit brought in tribal court by a nonmember surviving spouse of a member decedent and by his member children against a nonmember concerning an auto accident on a state highway. These facts might seem analogous to the common situation in which a citizen brings suit in her home state's court against a citizen of another state. One of the most basic elements of civil procedure is that this scenario raises fears that the defendant will be unfamiliar with local processes or will be "hometowned" by the local judge or jury. Accordingly, in its wisdom, Congress enacted legislation allowing the out-of-state defendant to remove the case to federal court. But, it would seem, the Court in *Strate* concluded that Congress lacked infinite wisdom, for it has never enacted legislation allowing nonmember defendants to remove cases from *tribal* court to federal or state court. Overtly analogizing to removal from state courts, the Court simply filled the gap in federal law by adopting a federal common-law approach precluding tribal-court authority on the facts of *Strate*, thereby compelling similarly situated plaintiffs, in the absence of diversity of citizenship and an amount in controversy authorizing federal jurisdiction, to bring the case in state court.

On the surface, *Strate* may seem defensible as similar to other decisions that borrow statutorily rooted policies to inform federal common-law evolution. Perhaps the most famous of these is *Moragne v. States Marine Lines* in which the Supreme Court abandoned the common-law rule barring recovery for wrongful death in light of the repudiation of that approach in numerous federal and state wrongful death statutes. Few would quarrel with the general logic of *Moragne* that "legislative establishment of policy carries significance beyond the particular scope of each of the statutes involved. The policy thus established has become itself a part of our law, to be given its appropriate weight not only in matters of statutory construction but also in those of decisional law." Now that federal Indian law is being folded into the general public law at an unprecedented rate, we might expect to see more *Moragne*-like reasoning importing principles from the "general law" in an effort to make the field less arcane – to domesticate it as a branch of general federal public law rather than to allow it to retain its complicated conglomeration of unique doctrines.

The potential consequences of this technique for federal Indian law would be hard to overstate. They easily transcend those of the Court's more established approaches – loose statutory interpretation and quasi-constitutional lawmaking – to accommodating nonmember interests. For, if broadly implemented, the *Moragne* technique could well mean the end of the field of federal Indian law as we have known it. This is so because, unlike loose statutory interpretation and quasi-constitutional lawmaking, which are at least both tied to presumptions about congressional purposes, moving *Moragne* into Indian law would suggest that the many aspects of federal Indian law that are in tension with general public-law principles should be judicially waved aside in the name of harmonization. Judges could then look to any source of general American legal principles – statutes, administrative regulations, state as well as federal common law – and when, as will often be the case, an inconsistency appears, displace the established unique aspect of Indian law in the name of legal uniformity, all without any specific congressional guidance.

The *Moragne* method has influenced doctrinal evolution in such basic domains as torts and landlord–tenant relations, where certain aspects of the ubiquitous backdrop of the common law have been statutorily modified so consistently that it is clear that a more appropriate policy has been legislatively identified. Despite these important inroads, however, the method is probably generally unfamiliar to American-trained lawyers, who may assume that a statute can intrude into a common-law domain only when its terms govern the case. In my judgment, this traditional assumption does take a crabbed view of the capacity of legislatures to articulate reasoned principles counseling legal evolution. That the *Moragne* move is a legitimate tool for the reassessment of hoary doctrines in basic common-law fields in no way counsels the automatic use of the technique to flatten all unique legal regimes into more general patterns, however. Indeed, "[a] possible danger . . . is that the very unfamiliarity of the doctrine will give it an immediate superficial attractiveness. Initially grasped, the methodology seems capable of giving almost any solution desired for a particular problem."

In particular, where the courts have adopted special approaches to construct fine-tuned "interpretive regimes," there has been a judicial understanding that the legal domain in question has unique qualities legitimately distinguishing it from the "general law." An obvious example is criminal regulation: Statutory codes have displaced the common law of crimes, and those criminal statutes are construed narrowly so that the citizenry has fair notice of what conduct triggers sanctions. In such areas of law, special considerations counsel that doctrinal evolution generally requires direct legislative intervention, not common-law evolution.

Federal Indian law is best understood as one of these domains. It represents a structural, sovereign-to-sovereign arrangement that seeks to meld historical practices of colonization with a current commitment to tribal survival. Federal Indian law came first. It legitimated for non-Indian purposes the colonial processes used in the acquisition of Indian lands and the displacement and involuntary partial

incorporation of indigenous peoples. It thereby made room – both literally and
figuratively – for the construction of the general American legal system, which
continues to sit awkwardly on top of internal tribal law and the federal–tribal
relationship. Given this background and its contemporary consequences, an interpretive regime requiring clear congressional action to displace tribal prerogatives
further draws force from precedent and principle alike. It follows that using the
Moragne move to harmonize federal Indian law with the general American law
would be judicial colonization of the first order.

If increasing the clarity and predictability of federal Indian law is a prime impetus
for this technique, it is also likely to be unavailing. For example, in *Brendale*, Justice
White, writing for a four-Justice bloc, argued that the tribe had no sovereign
authority to zone nonmember reservation property, but did have a property interest
in being free from usage of nonmember property that imperiled the tribal interest in
using its own land as it reasonably saw fit. According to White, this federal property
interest might be enforceable only through the county zoning process and whatever
appeals or litigation might lie beyond it under state law. Then again, White seemed
to indicate that the tribe might have a way to invoke federal-court jurisdiction at
some point to protect its property interest. In the final analysis, the opinion stands as
an example of analogical reasoning in an endless loop, a descent into the maelstrom
of judicial freewheeling that leads everywhere in general but nowhere in particular.
The confusion and unpredictability are compounded by the fact that five Justices
did not join the White opinion, with two of them opting for an outcome based on
the Indian character of the area in question and three others arguing for the
traditional notion that tribal sovereignty to zone should be territorial in scope.
Brendale demonstrates that any judicial effort to undertake first-line responsibility
for bringing coherence to federal Indian law by harmonizing it with the broader law
may produce more, not less, of a conceptual mess. There are too many choices and
not enough judicial consensus, even leaving aside the nagging question whether
there is sufficient justification to overrule the many longstanding precedents recognizing unique tribal interests where Congress also has authority to displace such
settled law.

As a final example, recall *Duro*. The *Moragne* technique suggests that a well-
established statutory pattern of policy counsels reconsideration of an inconsistent
common-law rule. Yet in *Duro*, the Court adopted a new constitutionally inspired
common-law rule – that tribes had no criminal jurisdiction over nonmember
Indians – in the face of a pattern of federal statutes suggesting that Congress had
long assumed tribes had such jurisdiction and that, far from promoting a coherent
harmonization of criminal jurisdiction in Indian country, produced a serious gap in
it. The outcome in *Duro* starkly demonstrates that the three judicial techniques that
have emerged in federal Indian law during the past two decades are not always
compatible. Taken together, these techniques may well promise more, not less,
incoherence in federal Indian law.

D *The Consequences of Doing What Comes Naturally: Anglocentric Analogical Reasoning*

Analogical reasoning is a key judicial tool. In an area as murky as federal Indian law, analogizing to more mainstream areas of law may be almost irresistible, especially for judges who have not developed any appreciation for why federal Indian law has grown up to be as unusual as it is. The Court's jurisprudence on tribal authority over nonmembers is saturated with analogical reasoning. Unfortunately, the Court's analogical exercises seem more ad hoc than adept, more Anglocentric than analytical.

In the diminishment cases, the Court seems to have jettisoned the canonical approach to the interpretation of statutes and treaties in favor of a fact-based analogical process. The basic inquiry is whether the reservation area in question is, in the Justices' minds, analogous to off-reservation areas. To put it bluntly, the Court seems to be asking, "is this area like the rest of South Dakota, or is it truly Indian in nature?" One might question the objectivity of this analysis from a group of jurists who may know little about South Dakota, much less about Indian reservations found there. Whatever vision is conjured up of a truly "Indian reservation" may have little to do with contemporary reality and imposes an essentialist, static conception upon the inherently dynamic institutions of tribal governance and contexts of tribal life.

In *Oliphant* and its progeny, the Court has embarked upon a process of bringing the values of the broader legal system to Indian country. The Constitution does not apply to tribal governmental action, and Congress has imposed only a qualified set of analogous limitations upon tribes in the Indian Civil Rights Act. Nonetheless, the Court has "improved" upon the congressional solution by diminishing tribal power when it threatens the judicial conception of fundamental rights untouched by ICRA, such as the threat that all-member juries might treat nonmembers unfairly. In these situations, the Court seems to view tribal processes as analogous to those of state and local governments, rather than as a different sort of sovereignty – one that predates the Constitution, possesses inherent, retained indigenous authority rather than constitutionally rooted reserved or delegated power, and is subject to "Anglo-cization" (colonial assimilative impositions) through the congressional rather than the judicial process. Even more remarkably, *Strate* suggests that seemingly foundational subconstitutional values, such as the availability of removal from potentially biased local courts, are also fair game for analogical implementation despite the fact that Congress has never seen fit to impose them upon the tribes.

It should be obvious that bringing the Constitution to Indian country and promoting evolution of the federal common law of Indian affairs to harmonize it with our general law are radical steps that could disintegrate the established doctrines of federal Indian law. It is ironic, indeed, in a field in which the Court says that Congress has plenary power, that this destructive drive toward uniformity has taken place without *any* supporting congressional action. Indeed, the only recent congressional lawmaking directly involving the concerns of this Article – the legislation overturning *Duro* by acknowledging tribal authority to prosecute non-member Indians – was motivated solely by a desire to undo a Supreme Court decision designed to make federal Indian law more uniform. It is ironic, as well, that this judicial shift has occurred in a time in which the express congressional and executive policy has been to promote, not undercut, tribal sovereignty.

Nor has the Court openly acknowledged that it has gone a long way toward abandoning its prior practices of using canons of interpretation to prevent all but congressionally mandated losses of tribal interests. In the reservation-diminishment cases and the implicit-divestiture cases like *Bourland,* where the Court purported to rely upon statutory or treaty text, it is hard to avoid the conclusion that the Court paid the canons lip service, but ended up embracing its sense of general congressional assimilative purposes where the context under litigation was seen as heavily non-Indian in nature. But note that the general congressional purposes in these cases relate to statutes adopted long ago, during a different era in federal–tribal relations, and represent obsolete congressional purposes as against current congressional and executive policies. Why should the Court prefer old purposes to new ones, especially where, as in all these cases, the statutory text does not compel any particular outcome and the canons favoring the protection of Indian interests have both a longstanding pedigree and a substantial basis in policy?

In the implicit-divestiture cases like *Oliphant* and *Duro,* where the Court has fallen victim to a "dormant plenary power impulse" to bring constitutional values to Indian country, the canons have played an even less significant role. The Court in these circumstances imposed such federal common-law rules where Congress has been essentially silent (*Oliphant*) and even where Congress has sent strong signals contrary to the judicial outcome (*Duro*). To the extent that the Court has considered nonconstitutional values as informing its authority to alter federal common law in this domain, as occurred in *Strate,* it has arrogated to itself even more power than was involved in *Oliphant* or *Duro,* for the Court seems to believe that all values found in general law, not just well-established constitutional values, are relevant to the new harmonization of federal Indian law. To put it bluntly, this approach suggests that, to the extent that federal Indian law is inconsistent with what law students learn in their required courses and foundational electives, federal Indian law is out of step and in need of reform. The current congressional and executive policies promoting tribal self-government are, apparently, irrelevant to this inquiry, except to the extent that they suggest to the Court that tribes have allies available who might be willing to overturn the Court once in a while and restore to tribes some authority that was judicially removed, as with the legislation effectively overruling *Duro.*

This technique turns federal Indian law on its head. The field is best understood as reflecting a stark compromise between colonialism (overriding power) and limited government (the rule of law): Congress has virtually untethered authority over Indian affairs, but the courts stand ready, through the canons of interpretation, to force Congress to do its ongoing colonial work expressly. The vagaries of existing law are interpreted to preserve tribal sovereignty, and those seeking to diminish tribal power must bear the burden of overcoming legislative inertia to obtain express congressional authorization. This approach provides the courts with a course to chart through the immense complexities of the field, preserves the status quo from the Indian perspective, and gives tribes and their allies fair notice and a meaningful chance to defeat proposals to implement colonization more broadly. The new harmonization threatens to jettison this well-established mediating method rooted in congressional responsibility and judicial checks in favor of a one-sided imposition of colonial values where courts, not Congress, assume front-line colonial responsibility.

If the judges borrow concepts from the general law, not simply from constitutional values and general congressional purposes associated with particular statutes, the uniqueness of federal Indian law may evaporate. In a decade or two, law schools may have no reason to offer a course in "Federal Indian Law"; instead, it might be enough to teach a chapter called "Indian Lands" in a casebook on public lands and natural resources. Tribes will have lost all sovereignty and, from the outside, might appear to be little more than ethnocentric Elks Clubs. To be sure, tribes and their members will endure as best they can. But even if the doctrinal drift alone is unlikely to revive the nineteenth-century non-Indian notion of the "vanishing Indian," it is the harbinger of the vanishing Indian law.

Of course, nothing like a complete collapse of federal Indian law into the broader public law has yet occurred. What I have described is merely a trend that the Court itself has embarked upon without evident reflection. Particularly in a field as slippery and complicated as federal Indian law, a host of choices remains viable. In the next Part, this Article concludes by briefly examining some of them.

VI CONCLUSION: SOME ALTERNATIVES TO THE NEW HARMONIZATION OF FEDERAL INDIAN LAW

The end of a lengthy article is hardly the place to examine with requisite care the choices available to Congress and the Supreme Court in this second quincentennial of the colonization of this continent. Instead, what I hope to do is merely suggest some of the plausible avenues open to these institutions in addressing what seems to be the root problem in the cases involving judicial diminishment of tribal authority: the presence of nonmembers in Indian country.

In many respects, the simplest option for the Court would be to freeze the law as it now stands, embrace what it can retrieve of the traditional concepts, and force Congress to undertake any further relief for nonmembers in Indian country. This approach would leave the doctrines incoherent – it would maintain precedents favoring tribal sovereignty like *Williams* and *Merrion*, while likewise entrenching nonmember-protecting precedents like *Oliphant* and *Montana*. Any real freezing of the doctrinal status quo would have to avoid more decisions like *Bourland* and *Strate*, which refused to find rather evident distinctions between their facts and prior precedents. Such a judicial change of direction might seem unfair to nonmembers, who have been able to convince courts of the injustice of tribal regulation on a case-by-case basis. But a fundamental problem with the Court's new common law of colonization is that it relieves Congress of its responsibility to visit these issues. A further problem is that the disputes come up in a concrete litigative situation in which an abstract and poorly understood concept with little cross-cultural currency – tribal sovereignty – is weighed against perceived real hardship to an identified individual with whom the judges share more cultural affinity. It is no surprise how that balance has been struck in recent cases – that, to borrow from Holmes again, it is tribal sovereignty, not the presence of nonmembers in Indian country, that strikes judges as an "accidental relic of an early notion." But the fundamental question is which institution should be attempting to strike the balance in the first place. Under our longstanding assumptions in the field, that institution should be Congress, not the Court. The only way that Congress is likely to take on these matters is if the Court retrocedes to it front-line responsibility for them.

To divert the Court from its doctrinal drift, such considerations of comparative institutional competence are probably paramount, but other factors are also relevant. Most fundamentally, the Court is unlikely to take a more favorable view of tribal sovereignty in the contemporary context without being presented with a salient argument for following the traditional constructs of the Marshall Court that transcends a mere exhortation to adhere to the formalisms of hoary precedent. At bottom, the Court needs a contemporary comfort level with the proposition that tribes are governments, not voluntary membership associations; it is surely discomfort with this conclusion that has led the Court to impose a creeping constitutionalism in federal Indian law. There is no escaping the normative character of any defense of tribal sovereignty along these lines, although practical factors, such as scholarship indicating that economic development in Indian country works best when tribes are capable of autonomous sovereignty, make the case as well.

What might Congress do in response to the agonizing problems faced both by tribes and nonmembers, as well as by states that have potentially overlapping jurisdiction with tribes? No doubt tribal leaders would do their best to prevent Congress from further diluting tribal sovereignty, and no one should begrudge them that effort. If Congress is bestirred to attempt to achieve a principled compromise, however, it should encourage a wide scope to the imagination of good-faith advocates for all sides. Consider a few possibilities, which I offer merely as illustrations of places where such a conversation might begin.

If Congress deemed tribal courts to be inferior institutions to adjudicate claims against nonmembers, it might consider increasing federal funding and other supportive measures for these courts. Perhaps the quid pro quo could be a limited federal appellate review, akin to certiorari, from the highest tribal court to the Supreme Court, to the federal court of appeals for that circuit, or to a special Court of Appeals for Indian Affairs.

Another possibility would be the enactment of an "Unallotment Act." Bruce Duthu once imagined such a federal statute that would provide that, after the passage of a certain amount of time, perhaps a decade, all nonmembers who remain in Indian country would be subject to full tribal territorial sovereignty. Duthu acknowledged the political implausibility of the proposal, but there may be more politically feasible revisions to the idea. For example, Congress might provide the tribe with a right of first refusal concerning any transfer of fee simple land within the reservation, so that the tribe would have the privilege of purchase. Of course, for most tribes, funds are not readily available for such an effort, and thus Congress would have to provide financial assistance. A more aggressive program would recognize a tribal power of eminent domain concerning fee simple reservation land. As a matter of compromise, Congress could limit such programs to reservations, or portions of reservations, where land consolidation seems most feasible. Interestingly, such efforts may have a significant chance of success on some Indian reservations today, which because of depopulation trends by non-Indians have an increasingly "Indian character."

At bottom, the issues seem to be more about political economy than law. Indeed, the Court itself has engaged in its own brand of amateur political economy in recent years, evaluating demographics and land ownership patterns in deciding whether reservation boundaries should be diminished and whether tribal authority should remain over nonmembers concededly found within the reservation. In light of the doctrinal confusion and practical chaos that these lines of cases have produced, however, it strikes me as fruitful to shift the intellectual debate in federal Indian law in order to spark the imagination of professional political economists and to dampen the influence of litigation. The only institution capable of encouraging such innovation designed to find local solutions to local problems is Congress – and to do so it would itself need to avoid one-size-fits-all statutory solutions and instead provide incentives for the play of imagination and bargaining.

Of course, many other legislative possibilities exist, including some that would seriously intrude upon or even terminate tribal sovereignty.

Colonialism is a dangerous political game, and congressional considerations of these problems could go in a variety of directions, some of them devastating to tribes. In anticipation of such possibilities, there are those of us in the academy who would provide some judicially enforceable side constraints upon unilateral congressional colonial action. For present purposes, however, it seems sufficient to note what the examination of Supreme Court decisions in this Article has demonstrated: that any effort to mediate the tension between tribes and nonmembers in Indian country is inherently political and not easily subject to judicial balancing and resolution.

Dialogue and compromise among sovereigns – Congress, tribes, and states, which have incentives to provide an effective voice to nonmembers – are likely to be superior methods of achieving anything remotely approaching a lasting solution in this context of multi-sided and sharply contrasting visions of "accidental relics of early notions" and "felt necessities of the time." What makes sense is a constructive conversation, not a common law, for our age of colonialism.

NOTES & QUESTIONS

1. *Reading Indian Law*:
   - Frickey discusses ways in which legal doctrines from outside Indian law are being imported into Indian law. What are some of those doctrines? How did they influence the outcome of the cases? How might the cases have been decided differently if those doctrines had not been introduced?
   - The US Supreme Court has elevated the significance of landowner-ship by non-Indians in Indian country, especially in establishing the boundaries of tribal government and tribal court authority. Why does the Supreme Court think this landownership is so important? What is significant about it? How has the ownership of land in Indian country changed since the beginning of the Allotment Era? How has the intrusion of non-Indians into Indian reservations changed tribal governments? Federal Indian law?
   - Frickey discusses alternatives to "harmonizing" federal Indian law. What alternatives does he propose? Do you think those suggestions are workable? Can you think of other suggestions? What would be different if Indian tribes did regain sovereignty over all non-Indians and fee lands on the reservation? Frickey claims such an arrangement is politically unfeasible. Why? Who would object to this arrangement?
2. *The Canons as the Tribes' Tenth Amendment*: Frickey's article discusses the ways in which the Supreme Court's decisions are no longer treating Indian law as a distinct field and are instead harmonizing Indian law with other legal doctrines. Professor Royster suggested in her article (see Chapter 10) that the Canons of Construction served as the tribes' Tenth Amendment. The first ten amendments to the US Constitution, collectively known as the "Bill of Rights," were adopted simultaneously with the ratification of the Constitution. The first eight of these amendments focus specifically on rights held by individuals against the government. The Ninth and Tenth Amendments are more structural, with the Tenth Amendment declaring that "The powers not delegated to the United States by the Constitution, nor prohibited by it to the States, are reserved to the States respectively, or to the people." Although there has been a

great deal of debate about the exact meaning and contours of the Tenth
Amendment, it is generally accepted that one of the main purposes of
this amendment was to establish boundaries on the political relationship
between the states and the United States. *See* Kathryn Abrams, *On
Reading and Using the Tenth Amendment,* 93 Yale L.J. 723 (1984). Do
you agree with Professor Royster that the Indian Canons of Construction
served much the same purpose for tribes? Where did those canons come
from? Who has the authority to change or modify them? Does that make
a difference in deciding whether the Indian canons are equivalent to the
Tenth Amendment?

3. *Nonmembers and Criminal Jurisdiction*: Frickey is highly critical of the
common law adopted by the Supreme Court regarding the ability of
tribes to assert their criminal jurisdiction over non-Indians. Non-Indians
own land in fee on reservations only because Congress engaged in
allotment, a project so universally recognized as foolhardy that Congress
expressly repealed it in 1934. While it is not the fault of Indian tribes that
non-Indians now own property in Indian country, the Supreme Court
has reasoned that tribal courts lack inherent criminal jurisdiction over
non-Indians and may exercise such authority only with congressional
permission. *See Oliphant v. Suquamish Indian Tribe.* In reaching this
conclusion, the Supreme Court quoted from its opinion in *Ex Parte
Crow Dog,* which held that the federal government lacked the authority
to prosecute an Indian who killed another Indian in Indian country. In
reaching that conclusion, the *Crow Dog* Court expressed concern about
subjecting Indians to the unfamiliar laws of a different culture:

> It tries them, not by their peers, nor by the customs of their people,
> nor the law of their land, but by superiors of a different race,
> according to the law of a social state of which they have an imperfect
> conception, and which is opposed to the traditions of their history, to
> the habits of their lives, to the strongest prejudices of their savage
> nature; one which measures the red man's revenge by the maxims of
> the white man's morality.

Ex Parte Crow Dog, 109 U.S. 556 (1883). Why is the Court so concerned
in *Oliphant* about subjecting non-Indians to the criminal laws of tribal
governments? The non-Indians in that case lived on the reservation. If
someone moves from one state to another, or even from a foreign
country into the United States, they are not excused from following
the laws of the state where they reside. Why is it different for non-Indians
who move into Indian country?

4. *Nonmembers and Civil Jurisdiction*: Frickey is likewise highly critical of
the common law adopted by the Supreme Court regarding the ability of

tribes to assert their civil or regulatory authority over non-Indians. The rules developed for civil jurisdiction are even more complex than those developed for criminal jurisdiction. Tribal governments are deemed to have authority to regulate the conduct of their citizens everywhere within the tribe's Indian country. The ability of tribes to regulate the conduct of non-Indians in Indian country is dependent on who owns the land on which the conduct occurs. If that land is Indian land, then the tribe can regulate the conduct. If that land is fee land owned by a non-Indian, then the tribe is presumed to lack jurisdiction over the conduct of non-Indians. The tribe can rebut the presumption by demonstrating either that the non-Indian engaged in consensual relations with the tribe or one of its members and that the conduct arose out of that relationship *or* that the non-Indian's conduct directly impacts the tribe's ability to govern itself. Again, this is a very different standard than the one used to evaluate state authority. Why do you think the Supreme Court treats tribal and state governmental authority differently? Should it do so?

One of the concurring opinions in *Nevada v. Hicks* thought the test for tribal civil jurisdiction was unduly complex and advocated simplifying the rule:

> A rule generally prohibiting tribal courts from exercising civil juris-diction over nonmembers, without looking first to the status of the land on which individual claims arise, also makes sense from a practical standpoint, for tying tribes' authority to land status in the first instance would produce an unstable jurisdictional crazy quilt. Because land on Indian reservations constantly changes hands (from tribes to nonmembers, from nonmembers to tribal members, and so on), a jurisdictional rule under which land status was dispositive would prove extraordinarily difficult to administer and would pro-vide little notice to nonmembers, whose susceptibility to tribal-court jurisdiction would turn on the most recent property conveyances.

533 U.S. 353, 383 (2001). What do you think of this proposal? Why not simplify it by using the same test as for state civil jurisdiction?

5. *Indian Character:* Professor Frickey notes that the Supreme Court placed a great deal of emphasis on whether a reservation had lost its Indian character in cases like *Brendale* and *Solem* (i.e. whether the demographics of the reservation continue to make the reservation "look" Indian by virtue of having a substantial proportion of the reservation enrolled). The Supreme Court has recently walked this standard back, finding that even though less than 2 percent of tribal members live in the open part of the Omaha reservation, the tribe still had regulatory author-ity over non-Indian owned businesses located there because Congress had not diminished the reservation.

This subsequent demographic history cannot overcome our conclusion that Congress did not intend to diminish the reservation in 1882. And it is not our role to "rewrite" the 1882 Act in light of this subsequent demographic history. After all, evidence of the changing demographics of disputed land is "the least compelling" evidence in our diminishment analysis, for "[e]very surplus land Act necessarily resulted in a surge of non-Indian settlement and degraded the 'Indian character' of the reservation, yet we have repeatedly stated that not every surplus land Act diminished the affected reservation."

***

Petitioners' concerns about upsetting the "justifiable expectations" of the almost exclusively non-Indian settlers who live on the land are compelling, but these expectations alone, resulting from the Tribe's failure to assert jurisdiction, cannot diminish reservation boundaries. Only Congress has the power to diminish a reservation. And though petitioners wish that Congress would have "spoken differently" in 1882, "we cannot remake history."

Nebraska v. Parker, 136 S. Ct. 1072, 577 U.S. ___ (2016). How does *Parker* challenge the direction of Supreme Court jurisprudence that is part of Frickey's narrative? Would tribes benefit if the Court deferred to Congress like this more often? Do you think the Court is really willing to intrude regularly on the "justifiable expectations" of non-Indians living in Indian country?

6. *Beyond the Law*: In his article, Professor Frickey accuses the Supreme Court of "flattening" Indian law, that is, removing the part of federal Indian law that makes it unique and, once that barrier has been removed, freely importing other legal principles with no thought to whether they are an appropriate fit. In other words, Professor Frickey asserts that the Supreme Court has homogenized the field. In essence, this is what Congress sought to do with the policies of allotment and assimilation. While the allotment policy sought to change patterns of property ownership on reservations, the boarding school process sought to eradicate tribal culture from the lives of Indian children.

One of the proponents of the boarding school system was Richard Henry Pratt, to whom the phrase "Kill the Indian and Save the Man" is attributed. Pratt described his education philosophy:

It is a great mistake to think that the Indian is born an inevitable savage. He is born a blank, like all the rest of us. *** Transfer the infant white to the savage surroundings, he will grow to possess a savage language, superstition, and habit. Transfer the savage-born infant to the surroundings of civilization, and he will grow to possess a civilized language and habit. These results have been established

over and over again beyond all question; and it is also well established that those advanced in life, even to maturity, of either class,
lose already acquired qualities belonging to the side of their birth,
and gradually take on those of the side to which they have been
transferred. *** The school at Carlisle is an attempt on the part of
the government to do this. ***

When we cease to teach the Indian that he is less than a man; when
we recognize fully that he is capable in all respects as we are, and
that he only needs the opportunities and privileges which we possess
to enable him to assert his humanity and manhood; when we act
consistently toward him in accordance with that recognition; when
we cease to fetter him to conditions which keep him in bondage,
surrounded by retrogressive influences; when we allow him the
freedom of association and the developing influences of social
contact – then the Indian will quickly demonstrate that he can be
truly civilized, and he himself will solve the question of what to do
with the Indian.

Richard H. Pratt, *The Advantages of Mingling Indians with Whites*, in
*Americanizing the American Indians: Writings by the "Friends of the
Indian" 1880–1900* (Harvard University Press 1973).

Indian children at boarding schools were given Anglo names,
required to speak English, dress in Anglo clothing, and attend Christian
church services. Children were punished for speaking their Native
language, wearing their traditional clothing, and for any other manifest-
ation of tribal culture. Children often spent their entire formative years
living in dormitories, with no knowledge or experience of life in a typical
nuclear family. What problems would you expect children raised in
these circumstances to suffer? How are they likely to handle being
parents? How do you think they would fit back on the reservation after
graduation? Would it be different in a city? For more information about
US Indian boarding schools, see Brenda J. Child, *Boarding School
Seasons: American Indian Families, 1900–1940* (University of Nebraska
Press 1998); K. Tsianina Lomawaima, Brenda J. Child, & Margaret
L. Archuleta (eds.), *Away from Home: American Indian Boarding School
Experiences, 1879–2000* (Heard Museum 2nd ed. 2000).

FURTHER READING

- Bethany Berger, *Justice and the Outsider: Jurisdiction over Nonmembers in Tribal Legal
Systems*, 37 Ariz. St. L.J. 1047 (2005).
- Kirsten Matoy Carlson, *Congress and Indians*, 86 Univ. Colo. L. Rev. 77 (2015).
- Grant Christensen, *Creating Bright-Line Rules for Tribal Court Jurisdiction over Non-
Indians: The Case of Trespass to Real Property*, 35 Am. Indian L. Rev. 527 (2010).

- Allison Dussias, *Geographically-Based and Membership-Based Views of Indian Tribal Sovereignty: The Supreme Court's Changing Vision*, 55 Univ. Pitt. L. Rev. 1 (1993).
- Angelique EagleWoman & G. William Rice, *American Indian Children and U.S. Indian Policy*, 16 Tribal Law Journal 1 (2016).
- Matthew L. M. Fletcher, *The Supreme Court and Federal Indian Policy*, 85 Neb. L. Rev. 121 (2006).
- Stacy L. Leeds, *The Burning of Blackacre – A Step toward Reclaiming Tribal Property Law*, 10 Kan. J.L. & Pub. Pol'y 491 (2000).
- Peter Maxfield, Oliphant v. Suquamish Tribe: *The Whole Is Greater Than the Sum of Its Parts*, 19 J. Contemp. L. 391 (1993).
- Nell Jessup Newton, *Indian Claims in the Courts of the Conqueror*, 41 Amer. U. L. Rev. 753 (1992).
- Joseph Singer, *Canons of Conquest: The Supreme Court's Attack on Tribal Sovereignty*, 37 New Eng. L. Rev. 641 (2003).
- Alexander Tallchief Skibine, *Duro v. Reina and the Legislation That Overturned It: A Power Play of Constitutional Dimensions*, 66 S. Cal. L. Rev. 767 (1992–1993).

12

In Defense of Property

Kristen A. Carpenter, Sonia K. Katyal, and Angela R. Riley

118 Yale L.J. 1022 (2009)

Struggles over land – that is, "real property" – are not the only property disputes causing friction between tribes and the United States. Disputes exist with respect to every category of property: real property, personal property, intellectual property, and cultural property.

These disputes are generally analyzed as arising either out of a different perspective or approach to the concept of property or out of a different way of valuing the property in question. For example, a tribe may value a particular sculpture for cultural and religious reasons, while museums and private collectors may value the same sculpture for artistic reasons. These different ways of valuing property make it difficult to find common ground.

This article by Professors Carpenter, Katyal, and Riley argues that the Anglo-American and tribal approaches to property are perhaps not as different as they might appear on first glance. The authors draw on two strands of thought to support their position. The first strand relies heavily on Margaret Jane Radin's work demonstrating that Anglo-American property law recognizes that not all types of property are fungible or easily reduced to monetary value. The second strand looks at legal concepts of agency and uses these concepts to develop a theory of stewardship.

As you read the article, think about both of these strands and the role played by each. Examine each step in the argument carefully. How do the authors use Radin's concepts of property and personhood? How do these relate to tribes and "peoplehood"? How do the authors define "stewardship" and how is this definition related to cultural property?

* * *

Cultural property has been referred to as property's "fourth estate" – the other three arenas being real property, intellectual property, and personal property. Traditionally, cultural property referred to tangible resources bearing a distinct relationship to a particular cultural heritage or identity. Because of their cultural significance, these tangible resources – including documents, works of art, tools, artifacts, buildings, and other entities that have artistic, ethnographic, or historical value – were thought to transcend ordinary property conceptions and to merit special protection.

Consider a paradigmatic example. Sometime between the years 1801 and 1812, Thomas Bruce, the Earl of Elgin, physically removed about half of the surviving sculptures from the Greek Parthenon and sold them to the British Museum for a substantial sum. Almost two hundred years later, after numerous requests, the British Museum continues to refuse calls from the Greek government to repatriate the sculptures. In response to the museum's refusal, one prominent Greek minister, Melina Mercouri, explained,

> [T]hey are the symbol and the blood and the soul of the Greek people ... [W]e have fought and died for the Parthenon and the Acropolis. [W]hen we are born, they talk to us about all this great history that makes Greekness ... [T]his is the most beautiful, the most impressive, the most monumental building in all Europe and one of the seven miracles of the world.

To this day the Elgin Marbles remain in the British Museum, where they are kept on display despite repeated requests for repatriation.

The case of the Elgin Marbles demonstrates that, notwithstanding the myriad statutes and international declarations that honor the right to culture, cultural property remains a politically complicated fixture. Unlike real, intellectual, and personal property, each of which has substantial prominence in the classic annals of property theory, cultural property falls into the grey area between these other realms. As Patty Gerstenblith has observed, cultural property is "composed of two potentially conflicting elements": "culture," which embodies group-oriented notions of value, and "property," which traditionally has focused on individual notions of ownership. Partly as a result, cultural property is often considered anathema to traditional property constructs and accordingly is afforded scant treatment in property theory. Today, because cultural property is partially intended to repair the ruptures associated with a history of colonization and capture, it also raises questions about the utility and appropriateness of property law as a remedy for harms suffered by indigenous peoples.

In the past several years, revolutionary changes in the cultural property field have contributed both to the salience of indigenous peoples' claims and to the arguments of theorists in opposition. The first major shift in the field involves a tremendous expansion of subject matter, loosening the requirements of materiality outward from "cultural property" and into the domain of "cultural heritage." As a result, cultural property has expanded from the domain of the tangible into the domain of the intangible. Contemporary legal instruments now include both long-recognized tangible resources (for example, land, water, and timber) as well as intangible ones (for example, medicinal knowledge, folklore, and Native religion). Furthermore, by some definitions, the concept also now encompasses collections of fauna, flora, minerals, or other goods that may be of interest to paleontologists, anthropologists, and researchers in other specialized fields of knowledge, in addition to property that relates to history and events of national importance. A second shift involves the increased visibility of indigenous peoples generally and a burgeoning movement to protect indigenous cultural existence. While the body of law known as cultural property affects all peoples (and likewise all nations), it carries a particular potency when situated alongside the interests of indigenous peoples. Though the term "indigenous" continues to be contested, every prevailing definition considers a people's deep, historical, ancestral roots to traditional lands as integral to indigeneity. Numerous instruments and principles of international law have long provided potential protection for indigenous interests in cultural property. Such international law instruments, including the American Convention on Human Rights and the American Declaration on the Rights and Duties of Man, recognize indigenous rights to property, religion, culture, association, and resources.

* * *

Somewhat different cultural property protections have emerged in the United States, not through the language of human rights, but through the vehicle of property law. Some of these protections preserve American cultural property generally (which can include indigenous cultural property but is not specific to it) and some, such as NAGPRA [the Native American Graves Protection and Repatriation Act] and the Indian Arts and Crafts Act (IACA), are specifically directed at Indian cultural property. The breadth of the regulation and of the property interests in question has paved the way for a wide divergence of cases. Consider the following.

Sometime in the nineteenth century, the New York State Museum acquired from the Onondaga Nation twenty-six belts of "wampum" (colored clam and conch shells), which are used for trade and for recording significant community events. When the tribe sought repatriation, the museum refused to return the belts. Although the tribe initially lost the case, public outcry against the decision was so strong that the New York legislature passed an act requiring repatriation so long as the tribe preserved the belts at museum-grade standards.

In 1998, while visiting a storeroom at the American Museum of Natural History in New York, a Tlingit clan elder heard an "inner voice" calling him to a particular shelf. When he reached the shelf, he was astonished to see a central part of Tlingit culture – an intricately carved wooden beaver – staring back at him. The carving had been sold by a clan member and had been missing since 1881. Under NAGPRA, the carving was returned to the Tlingits at their request.

In 2004, seventy-two members of the Havasupai tribe, a geographically isolated tribe based at the foot of the Grand Canyon, filed suit against Arizona State University for performing allegedly unauthorized genetic studies on four hundred blood samples that researchers had gathered, allegedly for the purpose of testing for diabetes. The researchers regarded the blood samples as a virtual "gold mine," given the tribe's geographic isolation, and used them to conduct research on schizophrenia and inbreeding and to explore the Bering Strait migration theory. After discovering the deception, the tribe decided to place a moratorium on biomedical research on their reservation.

In 2005, the National Collegiate Athletic Association (NCAA) instituted a policy against the use of Native American mascots on uniforms, clothing, and logos by sports teams during postseason tournaments, calling the use of such mascots "hostile" and "abusive" forms of speech. A representative for the organization explained, "[A]s a national association, we believe that mascots, nicknames or images deemed hostile or abusive in terms of race, ethnicity or national origin should not be visible at the championship events that we control."

As these examples illustrate, indigenous groups have, at times, successfully raised cultural property claims. Yet these claims have generated a number of powerful critiques in legal scholarship and anthropology, with some focusing on the role of culture and cosmopolitanism, while others question the ability of property law to address the incommensurable concerns raised by indigenous peoples. Cultural property's uncertain place in the property literature flows partly from the inadequacy of traditional property theory to embrace the unique vision it offers. Because its definition is partly grounded in theories of incommensurability, cultural property introduces a significant rupture in classic economic theories of property that are premised on a presumption of fungibility. Cultural properties therefore reflect several layers of incompatibility from within: at the same time that they reflect group identities and values that are incommensurable, some cultural artifacts and goods command high prices on the private market. Thus, some kinds of cultural properties are often caught between their attractiveness as high-value objects and their integral role in the formation of indigenous group identity and community.

* * *

II PEOPLEHOOD AND CULTURAL STEWARDSHIP

Previously we suggested that indigenous groups require a robust conception of property to help them secure rights to land and related cultural products and expressions. Yet it is precisely on that ground, the use of property law, that cultural property critics mount their most vociferous challenges. As these critiques indirectly suggest, putting cultural property alongside other forms of property raises an important question of whether cultural property is really property at all. At the same time, there is something disconcerting about placing the wide breadth of entitlements sought by indigenous peoples in the singular box of "cultural property."

We believe that cultural property is, at heart, a form of property, but that the existing theoretical framework for cultural property is insufficient to capture its normative and doctrinal possibilities. In that spirit, we draw upon our recent work regarding property and peoplehood to establish a framework for reconceptualizing and justifying indigenous cultural property claims. Section II.A argues that certain property deserves legal protection because it is integral to the collective survival and identity of indigenous groups. After establishing this background on the concept of peoples and its role in international and domestic law, we turn our focus in Section II.B to the connection between peoplehood and property claims, showing how some cultural property considerations are motivated not by ownership but rather by stewardship concerns.

A *From Personhood to Peoplehood*

Margaret Jane Radin's theory linking property and personhood altered the way many think about property. Put simply, Radin argued that some property deserves a higher level of legal protection because it expresses individual personhood and should be nonfungible. Nearly three decades after the publication of *Property and Personhood*, Radin's widely applied proposition hardly seems radical, yet it has been instrumental in challenging the ubiquitous assumption that property loss can, in every instance, be remedied in monetary terms. Radin rejected the then-prevailing view in our legal system that property is universally "commensurable," "commodifiable," or "alienable." Instead, she postulated that property that is constitutive of personhood should be regulated to protect against private market incursions and governmental interference. In such varied contexts as family heirlooms, the donation and sale of human organs, adoption, reproductive freedoms, takings, criminal justice, and the regulation of cyberspace, Radin has persuasively argued that the personal nature of some property requires specialized consideration. The ultimate aim of legal protections should be to further Radin's concept of "human flourishing," which she offers as an alternative, or complement, to wealth-maximization rhetoric.

***

1 Conceptualizing Peoplehood from Personhood

*** Radin's model is potentially transformative for indigenous property rights. But in the indigenous context, her work is somewhat limited by its explicit foundation in a philosophical tradition of individual personhood. *** Thus, we propose considering the extensive literature (political, legal, sociological, and indigenous) on peoples and peoplehood to identify group interests that have a role to play in contemporary law and policy, especially with respect to property.

Descriptively, the term "people" connotes a collective association of individuals based on political affiliation, religion, culture, language, race, ethnicity, history, and other factors, while "peoplehood" is the state of being a people or the sense of belonging to a people. ***

Turning to the United States, we argue that American Indian nations satisfy both narrow and broad definitions of peoples, and that their peoplehood claims can be consistent with important national ideals of equality and democracy. Moreover, in the cultural property context, we believe that the claims of a particular people need not obviate those of the larger world community nor violate widely accepted legal norms. Like many other domestic minority groups, American Indians within tribes share a "common descent – a shared genealogy or geography" as well as "contemporary commonality, such as language, religion, culture, or consciousness." American Indians often identify, on a tribal-specific basis, as peoples, and carry on many of the distinctive traditions that give their communities cohesion and endurance against assimilation into the majority society. Yet, unlike other American minority groups, American Indian tribes enjoy formal legal status as peoples or sovereigns under domestic and international law. The US Supreme Court has held that Indian tribes are "a separate people" within the larger American polity. As both a formal and practical matter, American Indian peoples enjoy a form of sovereignty that includes governing authority over tribal members and territory, and a government-to-government relationship with the United States.

Thus, American Indian tribes and their experiences satisfy most definitions of peoples and peoplehood. We argue, moreover, that they also deserve treatment as peoples, and legal protection for their expression of peoplehood, as a matter of reasonable pluralism and its specific expression in tribal sovereignty. ***

To a unique extent, US law recognizes the importance of preserving the "differentness" of American Indian peoples, and does so through the model of "tribal sovereignty." A significant body of federal statutory and common law is devoted to the enhancement of tribal self-determination and reflects, to some extent, tribal interests in maintaining a "measured separatism" within the national polity. ***

American Indian peoplehood is a critical component of our nation's legal, social, and moral fabric, and is essential to democratic ideals and reasonable pluralism. As we describe in further detail below, American Indians can only survive as distinct peoples if they enjoy legal protection of, and autonomy over, their cultural resources.

2 Indigenous Peoplehood and Cultural Property

Patty Gerstenblith reminds us that once items are designated as cultural property, they assume a powerful role in linking group identity and property ownership, for a few reasons. First, because the identity of a people is inextricably linked to an object, Gerstenblith argues that a group might acquire ownership rights over the object. Second, to the extent that this property is intimately tied to the identity of a group, it is viewed as inalienable not only because of the group's contemporary norms but also because future generations are unable to consent to transactions that may affect their own identity and culture. In this Subsection, we examine these dynamics in the context of indigenous experiences, focusing on the land-based quality of many indigenous cultures and the challenges of cultural survival in the wake of colonization and territorial dispossession.

In the United States, American Indians have experienced a unique legacy of dispossession. Millions of acres of traditional tribal lands are now owned and controlled by non-Indians as a result of European and American colonization. In our view, the loss of real property is inextricably linked to the formation of cultural property claims, a point that has largely escaped scholars. This problem is illustrated most poignantly by the 1988 decision in *Lyng v. Northwest Indian Cemetery Protective Ass'n*, in which the Supreme Court denied several Indian tribes' Free Exercise Clause challenges to a Forest Service plan to build a road through traditional Indian sacred sites. The Court held that even if the government would "virtually destroy" the Indians' religion, it did not violate the First Amendment, in part because "[w]hatever rights the Indians may have to the use of the area ... those rights do not divest the Government of its right to use what is, after all, *its* land." Even with respect to lands that the tribes retained, jurisdictional limitations have at times affected the tribes' powers to protect cultural resources within reservation boundaries.

Of course, the close relationship between indigenous peoples and land is so well known and oft-repeated by scholars, advocates, and indigenous peoples themselves that it may begin to sound cliché. Indeed, the contention that a relationship with the land is a definitional element of what it means to be indigenous invites charges of essentialism and romanticism. We too recognize the diversity of indigenous groups and do not assert that each indigenous person, on an individual basis, necessarily maintains special attachment to the land. We do contend, however, and illustrate through several examples below, that a connection between land and identity is a defining element of indigenous peoplehood. In light of these ongoing collective attachments to land, it is impossible to protect indigenous peoplehood without also protecting indigenous relationships with tribal lands and the culture that grows out of those lands.

Consider NAGPRA, for example. The repatriation statute was necessary not to secure Indians' *special* rights, but to counteract federal and state laws that facilitated the excavation, examination, and destruction of Indian burial grounds, which were situated predominantly on lands taken from tribes by non-Indians. Other cultural property directives, such as the National Park Service's cooperation agreement concerning Indians and recreationalists at Devils Tower National Monument, similarly sought to protect the religious rights of Native peoples that had been undermined by the dispossession of Indian lands. The Lakota reserved the Black Hills – including Devils Tower – in the Treaty of Fort Laramie of 1868 because of the site's central importance in Lakota religion. Shortly thereafter, the US government repudiated the Treaty and invaded Lakota territory, placing *Mato Tipila* (Lakota for "Bear Lodge") squarely on what is now federal land where Indian religious practitioners must compete with rock climbers for time and space to conduct their ceremonies.

***

A *From Ownership to Stewardship*

As we suggested in Subsection II.A.2, a vision of peoplehood underlies conceptions of cultural property, both in a descriptive and normative sense. Contemplating cultural property through the lens of peoplehood redefines our understanding of cultural property claims and forces us to grapple with an emerging, alternative model of property that challenges ownership as the fundamental nexus of property interests.

The notion that property concerns the absolute rights of owners to do whatever they wish with their possessions has long influenced the development of property law, and it seems to continue to influence cultural property critics. Anglo-American property law springs from a vision of property as "that dominion which one man claims and exercises over the external things of the world, in exclusion of every other individual." In more contemporary terms, Richard Pipes has surmised that "[*p*]*roperty* refers to the right of the owner or owners, formally acknowledged by public authority, both to exploit assets to the exclusion of everyone else and to dispose of them by sale or otherwise." These rights add to the perception that an owner enjoys a wide degree of autonomy over her property, enabling her to "us[e] it all up," or even to destroy her property, depending on the context.

Viewed through the classic prism of owners' rights, cultural property would understandably appear like a threatening legal device to scholars who appreciate culture as a collaborative enterprise developed and shared among multiple members of society. Fortunately, the absolute ownership model of property is neither the only nor the leading approach to property theory today. Rather, we would argue that cultural property protection reflects, in part, the now pervasive view that property is a bundle of relative, rather than absolute, entitlements, including limited rights to use, alienate, and exclude. In its disaggregation of these rights among individuals and groups, property law functions as a system of "[s]ocial [r]elations," structuring relationships among persons with respect to things.

As we discuss further below, contrary to the presumptions of its critics, cultural property approaches do attempt to reconcile the interests of owners and nonowners in drawing on a particular resource. Indigenous peoples, rather than holding property rights delineated by notions of title and ownership, often hold rights, interests, and obligations to preserve cultural property irrespective of title. That is why the language used within these approaches draws upon the themes of custody, care, and trusteeship, rather than comparably more fungible conceptions of property. As Rebecca Tsosie has explained in the context of real property,

> Although Native peoples, like all people, share the need to use the land for their physical sustenance, they hold different notions about the appropriate relationship and obligations people hold with respect to the land. The mere fact that the land is not held in Native title does not mean that the people do not hold these obligations, nor ... that they no longer maintain the rights to these lands.

This principle – the exercise of rights and obligations independent of title – lies at the heart of cultural stewardship.

1 Introducing Cultural Stewardship: Views from Indigenous, Corporate, and Environmental Theory

While specific traditions vary widely, many indigenous communities in the United States exhibit a strong duty of care toward the land and related resources as a spiritual obligation. For example, the Navajo Nation Code provides that the Navajo "have the sacred obligation and duty to respect, preserve and protect all that was provided for we were designated as the steward for these relatives." The belief that humans maintain duties to – rather than dominion over – the earth and its Creator is common among indigenous peoples. Such concepts are often expressed in culturally specific terms that convey the interdependence between the tribe and its environment and that underscore the fiduciary obligation felt by many tribes toward their natural resources. The Hopi, for example, explained in *Navajo Nation v. U.S. Forest Service* that their tribal interest in protecting the San Francisco Peaks stems from a spiritual covenant with *Ma'saw*, a holy presence that directed them to care for the land at the time when the Hopi first emerged into this world. In other communities, tribes express specific duties to the subsistence landscapes, water sources, or ancestral remains that perpetuate tribal lifeways and peoplehood.

Stewardship concerns – involving the fiduciary duty of care or the duty of loyalty to something that one does not *own* – are not unique to the indigenous context. There is a fascinating, overlooked parallel in corporate management with respect to the notion of stewardship. In the corporate context, stewardship is conceived of as "the willingness to be accountable for the well-being of the larger organization by operating in service, rather than in control, of those around us." In the context of organizational management, the concept of stewardship has been an underlying factor in providing a substantive theoretical alternative to classical agency theory, which focused on a variety of ways to incentivize employees to behave productively in the absence of ownership of the company. Traditional agency theory, like much of property law, postulates a model of the rational actor – whether an agent or a principal – who seeks to maximize his utility within the modern corporation, which is based on a clear separation between ownership of the firm and control. Given that employees do not own the corporations that they manage, agency theory directs that firms must balance their interests in maximizing profits with a studied attention to structuring employee compensation and benefits in such a way that channels the employee's self-serving behavior toward the benefit of the owners.

Predictably, the agency model often receives substantial critique from other theorists, who point out that its baseline presumption of opportunism depicts subordinates as "individualistic, opportunistic, and self-serving" and fails to take into account the complexities of human motivation. As such, some organizational theorists have grown to emphasize the development of stewardship theory as an alternative. Stewardship theory, in contrast to agency theory, postulates a model that "pro-organizational, collectivistic behaviors have higher utility than individualistic, self-serving behaviors." The behavior of a steward is motivated out of concern for the collective, as opposed to the individual, and is "constrained by the perception that the utility gained from pro-organizational behavior is higher than the utility that can be gained through individualistic, self-serving behavior." In short, stewardship behavior is more akin to a fiduciary model, requiring "constant and unqualified fidelity" to the corporation, rather than a self-interested model. Often, these fiduciary duties require directors and officers to exercise the degree of care, skill, and diligence that each normally would employ in the service of his or her own affairs.

The emergence of stewardship theory in the corporate context, as an alternative to classical agency theory, provides us with much more than a purely facial parallel in the indigenous cultural property context. In conceptualizing property management, a vision of corporate stewardship differs from that of a traditional agency model in three major ways. First, like the pluralistic conception of peoplehood, which diverges from a single-minded focus on individual self-actualization, stewardship prioritizes service to the organization or group over self-interest, and is concerned with treating employees more like owners and partners than like specific agents. Whereas agency theory presupposes a clear separation between the principal and the agent, the stewardship model views both principal and agent as part of the collective enterprise, thus merging the governance of authority. Here, the index of identity, like the notion of peoplehood itself, is collective; it is organizational and pluralistic in nature, rather than individualistic.

Second, this bond of collective enterprise radically alters notions of duty and obligation, rupturing the classic distinctions at play in common agency models of responsibility and bringing to the forefront the concept of fiduciary obligation. In the classic agency-contractual relationship, "each party acts to benefit himself or herself in carrying out the common enterprise," whereas a fiduciary relationship is premised on acting only in the beneficiary's interests, and thus often precludes such opportunistic behavior. Lawrence Mitchell has argued that the fiduciary construct implicates a key assumption: "that persons can and will subordinate self-interest to the interests of others," and that the fiduciary serves largely as a surrogate to ensure that the dependent beneficiary's best interests are addressed in all relevant contexts. In the corporate law context, these duties are legally imposed in the categories of a duty of loyalty and a duty of care.

In the cultural property context, while the fiduciary ethic is asserted, the neat delineations between fiduciary and beneficiary often overlap. Instead of a hierarchical separation between these parties, there are multiple levels of interactivity in the cultural property regime, as well as overlapping and sometimes opposing obligations, rights, and duties regarding fiduciaries and beneficiaries at different points along the cultural property spectrum. For example, regarding the repatriation of human remains and funerary objects, NAGPRA is primarily concerned with enabling a tribe (itself a beneficiary of the "trust" relationship with the federal government) to exercise its own fiduciary responsibilities to a variety of constituencies – its current members, future generations, and past members now deceased – in reacquiring cultural property.

In the multiple contexts where cultural property interests emerge, the tribe holds a duty of loyalty and of reasonable diligence in acting on behalf of these interests. In these instances, the tribe accepts responsibility even in the absence of title, and does so sometimes at odds with the divergent interests of the individual title-holder. Inherent in these tribal obligations is the concept of stewardship and its corollary of fiduciary responsibility – a duty of loyalty to act in the beneficiary's interest, along with a duty of care to undertake reasonable actions on the beneficiary's behalf. In contrast to ownership, which locates the majority of these rights and obligations within the owner's sphere of responsibility, stewardship distributes these rights, duties, and responsibilities along a spectrum of collective or group obligations, focusing on notions of "custody" and "trusteeship" rather than on title.

The concept of trusteeship in cultural property is often overlooked, but it is especially important to capture through the lens of stewardship, because it indirectly suggests that while a tribe may act as a fiduciary on behalf of its own tribal members, a much wider framework of beneficiaries stand to benefit from the protection of the tribe's cultural property. ***

Beyond the corporate context, stewardship is perhaps even more clearly evident in the foundational ethos of the environmental movement. Here, the notion of stewardship is closely tied to conservation and the requirement that humans engage in use and management of resources in such a way that protects and preserves their environmental quality. Modern environmentalism is undoubtedly inspired in part by American Indian approaches to land, as it unswervingly attempts to identify a fiduciary – indeed, familial – relationship between humans and the environment. In contrast to the Christian tradition, which emphasizes human dominion over land, non-Western and indigenous approaches to property imbue the land itself with a particular spiritual significance. Instead of casting humans as rightfully dominant over nature, the stewardship view considers first what is best for the planet, emphasizing the principle that "[n]on-human life has intrinsic value unconnected to its human usefulness, and humans have no right to reduce non-human richness."

Thus far, we have examined the concept of stewardship in varied contexts, ranging from corporate organizational management to native environmental sovereignty, suggesting that long-term fiduciary obligations can be exercised by those outside the letter of ownership. Although there are competing visions even among environmentalists as to the proper relationship between humans and the environment, adherents to the movement universally believe that the earth's resources should not be exploited to the point of depletion. Stewardship, as opposed to ownership, plays a critical role in the environmentalists' conception of human–nature interactions, and it also offers a different conception of the role and concept of utility in economic theory. Consider this observation, from *Stewardship-Based Economics*:

> As inhabitants of Earth, we cannot claim ownership of the Earth or any part of it; we are its stewards. The Earth in its entirety has been bestowed on us for our care. More importantly, it is also meant for future inhabitants, human and otherwise. While ownership is only a legal device used to facilitate transactions among people, the purpose of stewardship is to increase the utility function for ourselves and all other living beings on the planet.

While we might disagree with the author's narrow conception of ownership, his proposition that a purely market-based system of property fails to consider the value of sustainability comports with indigenous perspectives. Consider, for example, the mission statement of the Natural Resources Defense Council, which seeks to "establish sustainability and good stewardship of the Earth as central ethical imperatives of human society" and "strive[s] to protect nature in ways that advance the long-term welfare of present and future generations."

This statement echoes a conviction common to many indigenous belief systems that living tribal members owe duties both to their ancestors and to the coming generations. The interests of the so-called Seventh Generation must be carefully safeguarded. As an Iroquois leader stated:

> In our way of life ... we always keep in mind the Seventh Generation to come. It's our job to see that the people coming ahead, the generations still unborn, have a world no worse than ours – and hopefully, better. When we walk upon Mother Earth we always plant our feet carefully because we know the faces of our future generations are looking up at us from beneath the ground. We never forget them.

Through religion, law, and culture, many indigenous communities express the duty to preserve natural resources, maintain tribal culture and lifeways, keep language alive, and ensure the continuance of ceremonies for the generations yet to come.

At times, these shared obligations have enabled indigenous and environmental activists to make common cause with each other and to work in concert to achieve stewardship goals. For instance, a number of conservation land trusts have been created in response to the Native environmental sovereignty movement and the desire to correct deficiencies in environmental law. The intersection of these two interests has led to the formation of conservation trusts that demonstrate adherence to an emerging stewardship model of fiduciary duty. These conservation trusts are held by Native parties, private parties, or by the government, but each embodies some fiduciary obligation to the land. In each of these formulations, a variety of non-owning parties hold fiduciary obligations to each other and to the resource in question and, in the case of conservation easements, may independently coexist along with the individual property owner's interests.

Stewardship theory – whether rooted in indigenous, corporate, or environmental sources – facilitates an understanding of resource protection that extends beyond the traditional ownership model. The stewardship concept also embodies a notion of mutual trusteeship – enriched by a view of the interdependence between present and future generations and between different peoples – that acknowledges the fact of global cohabitation and mandates a sense of shared responsibility. Stewardship requires contemplation of natural resources as deserving of respect independent of their utility to human interests, and posits that their survival should be facilitated and that their worth exceeds their market-based monetary value. ***

Through the lens of stewardship, claims for cultural property protection are neither special nor exceptional, but rather part of a spectrum of property, liability, and inalienability rules that – like so many other areas of property – can embrace and theorize the rights of indigenous nonowners alongside the claims of owners. This is not to say that greater acknowledgment or increased implementation of a stewardship framework of property necessarily means that stewardship trumps ownership, or that the interests of nonowners always should prevail over those of owners. There may be cases – such as disputes over the proper use of sacred sites now located on federal public lands – where Indians believe that stewardship concerns require the absolute exclusion of non-Indians. Nevertheless, in such cases, absolute rights of exclusion as against the public or the title-holder might either be unfeasible or legally impermissible. We therefore do not assert that stewardship mandates predetermined outcomes that always favor indigenous groups. Rather, by integrating stewardship concerns alongside the common expectations that ownership often dictates, we can resituate cultural property claims within this broader spectrum of property law's relationship with property, liability, and inalienability rules. In some cases of tribal cultural resources, integrating stewardship concerns mandates that the interests of indigenous peoples – who may lack title (and therefore the ownership-based right to exclude) largely as a result of a history of land dispossession, removal, or illegal transfer – be contemplated as raising legal claims that are equal to, and in some unique cases superior to, those of title-holders.

***

III INDIGENIZING CULTURAL PROPERTY

Classic property theory, which rests on a monopolistic conception of the owner, focuses primarily on the liberal, autonomous individual. We believe that many critics of cultural property rely in part on this narrow understanding of property law – as fundamentally defined by ownership, with its rights of alienability and exclusion and its norms of commodification and commensurability. This conception leads to a potential overdetermination of the rights of the owner over all other actors, overlooking the emergent nature of other interests along the dual trajectories of static and dynamic rights. As a result, some critics discount the possibility that cultural property is a dynamic expression of human relationships – or that in some settings, property law can be both essential to, and as flexible as, culture itself.

Fluid conceptions of property underlie indigenous peoples' group claims to those items most closely and intimately tied to peoplehood and group identity: indigenous cultural property. Once indigenous peoples' cultural property claims are examined within the framework of stewardship, as opposed to ownership alone, a more nuanced conception of property emerges that captures the unique ways in which indigenous groups may exercise cultural property entitlements as nonowners. Consider, for example, the complexities that arise when dealing with certain objects that may not be owned at all, those that are inalienable by definition, or those for which possession is subject to shifting custodial arrangements rather than absolute rights of title. In many such cases, the custody of such items may in fact be situated in the fiduciary obligations of a collective "people," rather than rooted in claims of individual ownership. ***

A Tangible Cultural Property

*** The historical record about the treatment of Indian remains and funerary objects in the United States that led to Congress's passage of NAGPRA is now well documented. Early grave protection laws were designed according to European conceptions of private property, which conceived of graves as clearly identified, fenced off from society, and located in private cemeteries. But many Indian graves, in contrast, were unmarked and fell outside of tribal territory due in large part to federal Indian policy. During the infamous removal period, which spanned the years 1830 to 1861, thousands of Native people were removed from their aboriginal homelands and driven across the United States to lands unwanted (at least at the time) by whites. Thousands of Native people died and were buried along the way during the infamous death marches. Consequently, Indian graves and their contents were treated as abandoned and therefore available for appropriation under American law.

Colonizers' morbid curiosity, combined with official federal policy, resulted in a perfect storm of mass appropriation of Indian remains and ceremonial items buried with the dead. Federal laws like the Antiquities Act of 1906 – which was intended to protect American archaeological resources discovered on federal lands and which classified Indian remains as federal property – allowed the US government to secure its own collection of Indian bodies and artifacts. At times, US policy effectively endorsed the mass excavation and looting of Indian gravesites by encouraging grave robbers to turn their contents over to federally funded museums so that studies could be done to confirm the assumed racial inferiority of Indian people.

American museums served as repositories for the exhumed evidence of Europeans' love affair with "Indians" and the romanticized West. All of these forces converged to create a unique property phenomenon: unlike most individuals in the United States, who possessed the right to bury deceased members of their families, Native Americans found that Indian remains and the objects buried with the dead were propertized and turned into fungible goods. In the end, hundreds of thousands of Indian remains were exhumed and sent off to federally funded museums. By 1986, the Smithsonian Institute alone held the remains of almost 18,500 Indians in its collections. Today, it is estimated that the remains of hundreds of thousands of indigenous people ultimately will be accounted for through museum inventories.

NAGPRA sought to reverse this history, specifically by empowering tribes, as peoples, to regain access to and custody of Indian remains and artifacts in a manner consistent with their own lifeways and beliefs. *** But NAGPRA's salience, we contend, is most clearly embodied in stewardship conceptions of property. Consider the property consequences of repatriation under the Act. NAGPRA is primarily concerned with reconfiguring custody and possession, not title and ownership. Human remains and funerary objects, for example, cannot actually be "owned" by anyone. ***

Thus, we posit that both the policy considerations driving NAGPRA and the Act's statutory language embody a stewardship approach to the treatment of human remains and funerary items that most nonindigenous people already possess.

***

B *Intangible Cultural Property*

Although cultural property law and theory initially encompassed only tangible property – focusing on "objects of artistic, archaeological, ethnological, or historical interest" – contemporary definitions are far more expansive. Today, it is well accepted that cultural property includes the intangible effects of a culture and encompasses "traditions or histories that are connected to the group's cultural life," as well as "songs, rituals, ceremonies, dance, traditional knowledge, art, customs, and spiritual beliefs." ***

It would be impossible to discuss here all the ways in which a stewardship property model relates to indigenous peoples' relationships with their intangible cultural property. Certainly, claims involving the misuse of genetic human material – such as that of the Havasupai against Arizona State University researchers for nonconsensual use of blood samples – will raise very different legal issues than, for example, a tribe's efforts to keep a popular music group from using its sacred ceremonial song as part of a performance that parodies Indians. Because the laws governing intellectual property are multilayered (international, national, local, and tribal) and quite complex, indigenous peoples' approaches to using law in various intangible property-related disputes undoubtedly will reflect these variances. ***

It is its unique flexibility and capacity for giving voice to claims of both owners and nonowners that make stewardship a uniquely powerful normative framework for considering indigenous peoples' intangible property claims. Moreover, as a model, stewardship aptly captures the language with which many indigenous groups already articulate their desire for intangible property protection. In pursuing claims to traditional medicinal knowledge, for instance, indigenous groups do not commonly seek the power to prevent access by the rest of the world, but rather a role in the dynamic process of developing, disseminating, and seeking compensation for the good. Commonly, this stewardship role manifests itself in indigenous peoples' desires to participate in the disclosure of sacred or confidential information that may be tied up with the medicinal knowledge. Or the group may simply seek to have access to the decision-making process that will define where and how the information will be obtained, particularly when it might affect their aboriginal territories.

***

C Real Cultural Property

For many indigenous people, every facet of culture, identity, and existence – including tribal religions, Native languages, ceremonies, songs, stories, art, and food – is tied up with the land from which they came. While many people have deep ties to particular geographic locations, for indigenous groups, land is sacred. This relationship between land and culture is captured in a statement by a chief of the Gwich'in: "We hurt because we see the land being destroyed. We believe in the wild earth because it's the religion we're born with." His assertion reflects a common understanding shared by many of the world's indigenous peoples: as a people, they literally came from the land, are defined by the land, and have a responsibility to the earth that is integral to their identity as peoples. ***

Because all aspects of indigenous cultural survival relate back to the land, it is perhaps the most important – and most threatened – of all cultural properties. Although in some cases indigenous peoples still seek the return of tribal lands wrongfully taken, many contemporary Native Americans' claims primarily reflect stewardship concerns. Without ownership rights, Indians have had to fight fiercely to retain access to sites that are necessary for their worship and cultural survival. Many sacred sites are currently owned by the US government, which secured title to those lands either through purchase or conquest. In contemporary times, the way in which the government chooses to manage that land – for example, whether to allow rock-climbing on Devils Tower, tour groups and alcohol consumption at Rainbow Bridge, flooding of the Tennessee River Valley, or construction of a road through the "High Country" – can have devastating effects for indigenous peoples who hold these lands to be sacred. ***

Our argument for reliance on stewardship concepts to protect the real cultural property interests of indigenous peoples is both tactical and normative. ***

Although Indians have had limited success in cases framed largely by the ownership model of property, they have secured greater protections through negotiated agreements reflecting stewardship conceptions of property. The agency consultation process has led to the development of an accommodation model of land management. Many of the recent land management plans acknowledge the limited access interests of multiple parties – recognizing, for example, rock climbers' interests in climbing Devils Tower National Monument, but asking them to refrain from doing so while the annual Lakota Sun Dance takes place there. Another management plan prevents logging on Forest Service lands around a sacred site, and still another requests that all visitors refrain from touching or walking under a sacred site managed by the Park Service. Notably, none of these programs mandates a shift of title or widespread exclusion of others from the resource. They do, however, expressly recognize the interests of American Indians in the preservation and maintenance of, and continued access to, sacred indigenous places.

* * *

CONCLUSION

In this Article, we have suggested that operating beneath the subtext of cultural property governance is another form of regulation that involves the evolving notion of stewardship. In many respects, we believe that the stewardship approach to property offers theoretical coherence and practical utility for cultural property law. Contrary to the suggestions of critics, cultural property considerations do not always mandate a shift in title, but rather illuminate the myriad ways in which property law can reconcile the interests of owners and nonowners. The stewardship model captures, for example, the fiduciary or custodial duties exercised by tribes in the absence of title and ownership. It also explains why a number of key "sticks" in the proverbial bundle of property rights – rights of use, representation, access, and production – can be exercised by nonowners in the context of tangible and intangible properties. Our model is deeply grounded in lived indigenous experiences, including the collective relationships that indigenous peoples often enjoy with the land and the unique cultures growing out of those relationships. In the absence of title, stewardship becomes necessary to enable the continued cultural survival of indigenous peoples. * * *

NOTES & QUESTIONS

1. *Reading Indian Law*:
    - The authors rely heavily on Radin's concept of property and personhood. What is that concept? How does Radin's theory challenge traditional Anglo-American concepts of property? The authors generalize from the concept of "personhood" to the concept of "peoplehood." How do the authors draw this connection? What constitutes the connection? How does that connection relate to cultural property?

- The authors also look to parts of Anglo-American property law to develop their concept of stewardship. Where in property law do they look? What kind of stewardship is this? How do the authors translate this concept into cultural property?
- The piece argues in favor of the stewardship model for cultural property, intangible property, and real property. How does the concept of stewardship manifest itself in these three areas? Is stewardship better suited to some kinds of property than others? Explain.

2. *What Is Cultural Property?*: Professor Patty Gerstenblith has written extensively about cultural property and has defined cultural property as property which reflects and defines a given culture. *See* Patty Gerstenblith, *Identity and Cultural Property: The Protection of Cultural Property in the United States*, 75 Boston Univ. L. Rev. 559, 570 (1995). Defining an object as cultural property carries with it, according to Gerstenblith, three interrelated concepts: the culture becomes the owner of the item, that ownership is communal, and the ownership is based on the Lockean notion that the group is the creator of the object.

This third element of cultural property – that ownership is based on the group's status as the creator of the object – poses potential obstacles for some claims by Indigenous cultures. As Professors Carpenter, Katyal, and Riley discuss in their article, many Indigenous groups have a special connection to land. The article suggests that this connection and its accompanying stewardship obligations fit within the concept of cultural property. What obstacles might be presented by the third element described by Professor Gerstenblith? What gives rise to those obstacles? Is there a way to avoid them?

Professor John Henry Merryman, another leading scholar of cultural property, has written that "[t]here are obvious affinities between concerns for cultural objects and for the natural environment." John Henry Merryman, *The Public Interest in Cultural Property*, 77 Calif. L. Rev. 339, 342 (1989). Despite these affinities, Merryman asserts that the differences are substantial and critical, "the cultural object is an approach to the study of humanity, of ourselves; the environment is a separate part of reality, something outside of ourselves." *Id.* Do you agree or disagree with Professor Merryman? Would Indigenous communities agree or disagree with Professor Merryman? Does his argument rest on any particular view of the connection between land and human beings?

The National Historic Preservation Act (NHPA) provides a mechanism for protecting specific sites important to the national heritage of the United States. 54 U.S.C. § 300101 et seq. Congress amended the NHPA in 1992 to include protection for "Traditional Cultural Properties," including geographic sites. These provisions have been used to protect sites sacred to tribes. *See* Patricia L. Parker & Thomas F. King, *Guidelines for Evaluating and Documenting Traditional Cultural Properties*, National Register Bulletin No. 38, US Dept. Interior (1998); Jill Kappus Shaw & Melissa L. Tatum, *Law, Culture & Environment* (Carolina Academic Press 2014).

3. *Crazy Horse Malt Liquor*: That protecting intangible property has proven difficult for Native people is illustrated by the case of Crazy Horse Malt Liquor. Crazy Horse Malt Liquor was a brand of alcohol conceived of, and produced by, companies in the northeastern United States. Crazy Horse was, however, a real person who was on record as objecting to alcohol. When word of the manufacture and distribution of the malt liquor reached the descendants of Crazy Horse they objected and attempted to put a stop to the product. Congressional efforts to ban the use of the name Crazy Horse were struck down by the federal courts as violating the companies' commercial free speech rights. Once these efforts failed, the descendants of Crazy Horse filed a civil suit in tribal court. The suit, brought in the name of Crazy Horse's estate, was based on several grounds including the right of the Estate to control the use of the name Crazy Horse. These are the same grounds used, for example, by the Estate of Elvis Presley to control the use of Elvis's name and image. The companies filed a lawsuit in federal court challenging the ability of the tribal court to hear the case. The federal court agreed that the tribal court lacked jurisdiction. *Hornell Brewing Co. v. Rosebud Sioux Tribal Court*, 133 F.3d 1087 (8th Cir. 1998). The federal court's decision rested primarily on the fact that the companies had not marketed or sold the product on the reservation. For more details regarding the case, see Nell Jessup Newton, *Memory and Misrepresentation: Representing Crazy Horse*, 27 Conn. L. Rev. 1003 (1994–1995), and Frank Pommersheim, *The Crazy Horse Malt Liquor Case: From Tradition to Modernity and Halfway Back*, 57 S.D. L. Rev. 42 (2012). Why do you think the court focused on the marketing and sale of the product rather than on the harm suffered by the Estate? What harms were suffered by the Estate? Should those harms have been deemed to be located on the reservation?

4. *Using Intellectual Property Law*: Tribes have attempted to use various aspects of intellectual property law, including copyright, patent, and trademark, to protect Native stories, art, plant knowledge, dances, traditional designs, songs, and even their names. For example, the sun symbol used as its official emblem by the State of New Mexico was appropriated without permission from the Zia Pueblo. Many efforts to stop these wrongful appropriations fail, either because too much time has passed and/or because the identity of the person who originally

created the song, story, or dance is unknown. Most fundamentally, the intellectual property system in the United States is designed to provide economic incentives to create knowledge. These economic incentives last for a fixed period of time, after which they expire, and the knowledge moves into the public domain. *See* Jane Anderson, *Indigenous/Traditional Knowledge & Intellectual Property*, Duke University Center for the Study of the Public Domain (2010). Why would a system based on economic incentives be incompatible with the goals of Native people? Why do tribes want to protect their traditional knowledge? Who do they want to protect it from? How long do they want it protected?

Even when they can overcome these hurdles, Native people still face other difficulties. When the Navajo Nation filed suit to stop Urban Outfitters from selling a line of products including "Navajo panties," a court dismissed part of the suit, ruling that even though the Navajo Nation had trademarked the word Navajo it was not sufficiently well known as to cause consumer confusion. The Navajo Nation and Urban Outfitters ultimately reached a settlement in which they agreed to collaborate on an authentic line of products. For an excellent discussion of this controversy *see* Angela R. Riley and Kristen A. Carpenter, *Owning Red: A Theory of Indian (Cultural) Appropriation*, 94 Texas L. Rev. 859, 903–904 (2016).

5. *International Law and Traditional Knowledge*: Issues regarding the exploitation and protection of traditional knowledge also arise in the international arena, particularly with respect to the cosmetic and pharmaceutical industries. Both of these industries spend billions of dollars researching and developing products. They often seek to reduce these costs by working with Indigenous communities to learn about traditional uses of local plants. The companies often patent this knowledge to protect their investment and prevent competitors from using this information. Profits from these patents are rarely shared with the Indigenous people who provided the knowledge on which they are based. After years of studying the issue, the World Intellectual Property Organization (WIPO) has begun advocating for the development of *sui generis* ways of handling these disputes. In other words, WIPO has determined that standard intellectual property approaches are inadequate to handle issues of fair compensation, and that more customized procedures should be developed. *See Intellectual Property and Traditional Knowledge Bulletin No. 2*, World Intellectual Property Organization, WIPO Bulletin 920(E) (2009). What should these systems look like? How should fair compensation be determined? How do you decide who is entitled to compensation?

Consider as a starting point Article 31 in the United Nations Declaration on the Rights of Indigenous People (UNDRIP):

> Indigenous peoples have the right to maintain, control, protect and develop their cultural heritage, traditional knowledge and traditional cultural expressions, as well as the manifestations of their sciences, technologies and cultures, including human and genetic resources, seeds, medicines, knowledge of the properties of fauna and flora, oral traditions, literatures, designs, sports and traditional games and visual and performing arts. They also have the right to maintain, control, protect and develop their intellectual property over such cultural heritage, traditional knowledge, and traditional cultural expressions. ***

Does UNDRIP protect all the classes of cultural property discussed by the authors? How should nation-states go about implementing UNDRIP's protections?

6. *Beyond the Law*: Issues regarding control of Native stories go beyond the legal arena and involve debates over who has the ability and/or the authority to use Native stories in their writing. These issues are fairly easy to resolve with respect to nonfiction. Authors who obtain information from Indigenous people should disclose the purposes for which they seek the information and should abide by any restrictions placed on the sharing of the information. The issues are even clearer if it is determined that the information was falsified and the work of "nonfiction" is actually a work of fiction. Such was the case with Carlos Castaneda, who wrote a series of popular books allegedly based on time spent with a traditional Yaqui medicine man. The books were later revealed to be fabricated.

   The issues are much more difficult with respect to writing fiction. Fiction is, by definition, the creation of a writer's imagination even if it is rooted to some degree in truth. To what degree is it appropriate or inappropriate for a non-Native writer to use Native characters and Native settings in their fiction? Tony Hillerman for example is not Native, but he wrote a very popular series of mystery novels set on the Navajo reservation. Was it improper of him to do so?

   Does it make a difference if the writer is Native? If the writer is or is not a member of the group whose story she is using? Rebecca Roanhorse has gained national attention for her book *Trails of Lightning*, which uses Navajo stories in a futuristic setting. Roanhorse, however, is not Navajo; she is of Ohkay Owingeh and African American descent. In a guest column in the *Navajo Times*, Professor Jennifer Rose Denetdale declared that

If "Trail of Lighting" is meant to create Indigenous/Diné protagonists and storylines to empower readers and remind everyone to resist colonialism, it shouldn't come at the expense of harming the very culture that it supposedly honors.

Jennifer Rose Denetdale, *New Novel Twists Diné Teachings, Spirituality*, Navajo Times, Nov. 21, 2018. Do you agree or disagree with Professor Denetdale? What, if any, restrictions do you think there should be on the use of Native stories in fiction? *See, e.g.*, Rebecca Tsosie, *Reclaiming Native Stories: An Essay on Cultural Appropriation and Cultural Rights*, 34 Ariz. St. L.J. 299 (2002).

FURTHER READINGS

- Christopher S. Byrne, Chilkat Indian Tribe v. Johnson *and NAGPRA: Have We Finally Recognized Communal Rights in Cultural Objects?*, 8 J. Envtl. L. & Litig. 109 (1993).
- Kristen A. Carpenter, *A Property Rights Approach to Sacred Sites Cases: Asserting a Place for Indians as Nonowners*, 52 UCLA L. Rev. 1061 (2005).
- Kristen A. Carpenter, *Real Property and Peoplehood*, 27 Stan. Envtl. L.J. 313 (2008).
- Graham Dutfield, *TRIPS-Related Aspects of Traditional Knowledge*, 33 Case W. Res. J. Int'l L. 233 (2001).
- Richard A. Guest, *Intellectual Property Rights and Native American Tribes*, 20 Am. Indian L. Rev. 111 (1995).
- Nancy Kremers, *Speaking with a Forked Tongue in the Global Debate on Traditional Knowledge and Genetic Resources: Is US Intellectual Property Law and Policy Really Aimed at Meaningful Protection for Native American Cultures?*, 15 Fordham Intell. Prop. Media & Ent. L.J. 1 (2004).
- Angela R. Riley, *Recovering Collectivity: Group Rights to Intellectual Property in Indigenous Communities*, 18 Cardozo Arts & Ent. L.J. 175 (2000).
- Angela R. Riley, *Straight Stealing: Towards an Indigenous System of Cultural Property Protection*, 80 Wash. L. Rev. 69 (2005).
- Naomi Roht-Arriaza, *Of Seeds and Shamans: The Appropriation of the Scientific and Technical Knowledge of Indigenous and Local Communities*, 17 Mich. J. Int'l L. 919 (1996).
- Jack Trope & Walter EchoHawk, *The Native American Graves Protection and Repatriation Act: Background and Legislative History*, 24 Ariz. St. L.J. 35 (1992).

(Mis)Understandings

Tribes, states, and the United States comprise three distinct sovereigns that must coexist within the American system. The tension between these sovereigns forms the basis for most disputes underlying federal Indian law. Many federal Indian law cases emerge due to misunderstandings or fundamental disagreements between the very nature of competing sovereigns. Tribes want to be respected as independent entities, the federal government wants to assert plenary power over Indian affairs, and states want to control what happens within their territory irrespective of whether that land is also held as an Indian reservation.

Part IV concludes this volume by looking at the structure of law itself, and inquires whether the rules of the system justly allocate power between competing sovereigns. This part focuses on the misunderstandings that underlie these conflicts. In some ways the pieces in this part are the most distinct from each other, but at the same time each focuses on the dynamic relationship between tribes and the United States. Each piece tackles the concept of plenary power in its own way, critiquing a federal government that claims it knows how to treat Indian tribes without really listening to them. Together these pieces argue that constitutional interpretation, criminal procedure, and even appellate rules have been structurally constructed to the disadvantage of Indian tribes. The authors do not claim that these are necessarily conscious decisions, but each piece suggests that if the Court spent more time considering the perspective of tribes and their sovereign position, it might treat them differently. The authors all normatively agree that tribes are disadvantaged by the current rules.

Judith Resnik's *Dependent Sovereigns* (rank 9/100) examines the tension between tribal and federal sovereigns. Unlike states, Indian tribes have never ceded their sovereignty to the federal government but appear to have lost much of it anyway, slowly eroded by the decisions of the federal judiciary. Resnik utilizes a federal courts perspective to argue that there is space in American jurisprudence to accommodate tribes as part of the interdependence of sovereigns in the American system, and that a review of Indian law cases by students and scholars outside of federal Indian law would provide valuable insight into the federal judiciary.

Resnik uses the Supreme Court's opinion in *Santa Clara Pueblo v. Martinez* to review the interrogative space between tribal and federal courts. In concluding that federal courts lacked the authority to hear Ms. Martinez's claim that the tribal courts denied her due process and equal protection of the law, the Supreme Court established precedent that it was willing to tolerate judicial decisions and procedures which differed, in some ways markedly, from its own. Resnik suggests that by looking at cases like *Santa Clara* it is possible to determine the scope of pluralism permitted in the American judiciary and learn about the tolerance federal courts are likely to show "other" judicial bodies. In this way, studying challenges to tribal court authority in federal courts says as much about what the federal courts are as it does about the power of tribal courts.

Robert Clinton's *There Is No Federal Supremacy Clause* (rank 4/100) illustrates how the Supreme Court's federalism jurisprudence has recognized the rights of states and placed new limits on the powers of the federal government, even while the courts have steadfastly deferred to the "plenary power" of Congress in the area of Indian affairs. Clinton suggests that the plenary power doctrine has never been consistent with a textualist reading of the Constitution and urges instead an interpretation where there is no federal power over Indian tribes at all without their consent manifested through treaty or agreement.

Clinton designs his argument to speak directly to a Supreme Court which has reinvigorated the principles of federalism. If the federal government may exercise only those powers specifically articulated in the Constitution, Clinton reasons, then no constitutional basis exists for federal control over Indians. While Indian tribes are mentioned specifically in the Commerce Clause, the authorization is limited to legislating the interaction of non-Indians with Indian tribes and not the internal workings of tribal government. Instead Clinton returns to the Treaty Clause and argues that because tribes never ratified the Constitution, the proper way to bring tribes into conformity with federal law is by securing their consent through treaty or agreement. Absent consent, there is no federal power over Indians.

Kevin Washburn's *American Indians, Crime, and the Law* (rank 12/100) looks at criminal justice in Indian country not from the perspective of Indian law and policy but through the lens of criminal procedure. It recognizes that criminal jurisdiction in Indian country places disproportionate weight on the federal prosecution of on-reservation crime because tribes and states have limited and disparate criminal powers. Washburn questions whether prosecutorial discretion can be appropriately exercised when outsiders prosecute local crimes in Indian country and when juries often fail to include tribal members.

Washburn recognizes that the admirable goals of criminal justice – including permitting the accused to be tried by a jury of his/her peers and allowing the community to participate in the criminal justice process – are often impossible in federal criminal cases which originate in Indian country. He pays particular attention to the role of the community. Federal prosecutors often lack the support and cooperation of the community in helping to prosecute crime because they are foreign to the tribe. Moreover, when federal criminal trials are held in federal courthouses, sometimes hours from tribal communities, few tribal members are able to attend the proceedings. Without being able to participate in the system, tribal communities become inured to not knowing what happens to tribal members who are prosecuted. Washburn encourages tribal courts to play a more active role in criminal justice to solve the problem of community disengagement.

Matthew L. M. Fletcher's *Factbound and Splitless* (rank 81/100) recognizes the US Supreme Court's preeminent role in resolving disputes between tribes, states, and the federal government. However, because the Supreme Court hears only cases that can earn four votes for certiorari, the direction of federal Indian law is controlled as much by the choice to hear a case as by the ultimate decision that is issued. Fletcher examines the Supreme Court's behavior in Indian law cases at the certiorari stage in order to explain how modern Court behavior is changing the landscape of Indian law without even deciding some of the most important legal issues.

Fletcher's piece is innovative in that it uses both empirical methods and recently released Supreme Court memos to examine the behavior of the Supreme Court at the certiorari stage, a position ignored by many scholars because of the difficulty in contextualizing the material. He finds that a federalist bent at the Court has resulted in many more Indian law appeals being granted when the petitioning party is a state rather than a tribe – which has corresponding consequences on the development of Indian law because the Court reverses a majority of cases it decides. His analysis pays special attention to Rule 10, which nominally governs the review of appeals. Fletcher argues that the rules themselves are structurally designed to disadvantage Indian law cases because Indians are concentrated in just a few federal circuits and many Indian law issues are often tied up in the factual or historical nature of the subject matter.

As you read these last four pieces consider how each of them is directed toward the misunderstandings that tribal, state, and federal sovereigns manifest toward one another. Resnik suggests that we can tell a lot about federal courts by looking at their Indian law jurisprudence. What would Fletcher have to say after conducting his study of the Supreme Court's certiorari decisions? Are either of these pieces at tension with the Washburn piece, which suggests that tribal courts should hear more criminal cases at the expense of federal courts? Where does each piece stand on plenary power? Do any of the pieces agree with Clinton that the federal government has no constitutional power to govern Indian tribes? Where do states fit into this analysis? Would state criminal authority address the problems identified by Washburn? Would Resnik suggest that state cases can tell us as much about federal courts as tribal cases? When state supreme courts get the law wrong, does Fletcher suggest the US Supreme Court will step in to correct the error? Collectively these articles talk to each other as well as to the relationship between competing sovereigns.

13

Dependent Sovereigns: Indian Tribes, States, and the Federal Courts

Judith Resnik

56 U. Chi. L. Rev. 671 (1989)

Federal courts and state courts are distinct from one another. When a state supreme court issues an opinion interpreting state law, that decision cannot even be appealed to the US Supreme Court unless the state law violates the US Constitution or conflicts with another federal law. Federal and state judicial systems are in this way parallel, or horizontally oriented to each other; cases do not run first though a state court system and then begin in the federal courts. What about tribal courts? The Supreme Court has long ago clarified that states have limited powers in Indian country, but federal law does occasionally permit federal courts to review the decision of tribal courts. Yet tribes are still sovereign – capable of making, enforcing, and interpreting their own laws. What then is the proper relationship between federal and tribal courts?

In this piece, Judith Resnik uses the Santa Clara Pueblo v. Martinez *case to begin a conversation about the interaction between federal and tribal courts. In addition to her Indian law work, Professor Resnik is a noted scholar of federal courts. She argues that cases like* Santa Clara *should be taught more regularly outside of Indian law because how the Supreme Court treats tribal courts is indicative of how much pluralism the federal courts are willing to allow. Professor Resnik recognizes that there is an assimilative force to encourage courts to coalesce around an inevitably "federal" interpretation of the law, but that tribal courts are good examples of "other" courts which experiment with developing their own laws and rules. Tolerance and even support of these "other" courts provides a diversity of perspectives to the judicial resolution of conflict.*

The piece begins with a discussion of a single US Supreme Court case, Santa Clara Pueblo v. Martinez. *As you read Professor Resnik's description of the case, think about the difficult choices faced by the Court in resolving a conflict between the protection of cultural practices and fundamental principles like the equal protection of laws. How does the Supreme Court resolve this choice? How are tribal courts different than federal courts? Should federal courts be able to review the decisions of tribal courts? What does judicial deference to tribal courts mean for the wider schema of the judiciary? What can be learned from the interaction of federal and tribal courts?*

INTRODUCTION

In 1941, Julia Martinez, a member of the Santa Clara Pueblo, and Myles Martinez, a Navajo, were married. The couple resided on the Santa Clara Pueblo; they had several children. In 1939, the Santa Clara Pueblo promulgated an ordinance detailing its membership rules. The ordinance provided that children of female members who married outside the Pueblo would not be Santa Clarans, while children of male members who married outside the Pueblo would be members. In the early 1970s, Julia Martinez and her daughter Audrey filed a lawsuit under Title I of the Indian Civil Rights Act (ICRA) of 1968. Having been unsuccessful in their efforts to persuade the Pueblo to change its membership rules, Julia and Audrey Martinez asked the federal court for declaratory and injunctive relief – to invalidate the Santa Clara Pueblo's ordinance and to require that the Pueblo count the Martinez children as members.

In 1978, the United States Supreme Court decided the case of *Santa Clara Pueblo v. Martinez*. Justice Thurgood Marshall, writing for the majority, interpreted Title I of the ICRA to impose "certain restrictions upon tribal governments similar, but not identical, to those contained in the Bill of Rights and the Fourteenth Amendment." However, the only express jurisdictional and remedial provision of the statute was habeas corpus. *Santa Clara Pueblo* thus raised the question of whether the federal court should imply a right of action and federal court jurisdiction to hear the alleged violation of the Indian Civil Rights Act. According to the Court, implication of a right of action and federal court review for claims such as those raised by Julia and Audrey Martinez would undermine the Congressional purpose of preserving "tribal sovereignty" and "self-government." Therefore, no implied cause of action existed, and the federal courts could not hear the discrimination charge.

Santa Clara Pueblo is a major case in federal Indian law. *Santa Clara Pueblo* also offers a fascinating illustration of how the United States government conceives of its citizens as holding simultaneous membership in two political entities. According to the Indian Citizenship Act of 1924, all Indians are United States citizens, but that citizenship cannot "impair or otherwise affect" their rights to tribal property. The 1968 Indian Civil Rights Act provides that "[n]o Indian tribe in exercising powers of self-government shall ... deny to any person within its jurisdiction the equal protection of its laws." Julia and Audrey Martinez represented a group of Santa Claran women who had married non-Santa Clarans and the children of such marriages. The Martinez women came to federal court to obtain "equal protection." The obvious problem with this claim was the tension arising from being a member of two governments, the Santa Clara Pueblo and the United States.

That tension was addressed by the Court in *Santa Clara Pueblo* when it declined to imply a private right of action. *** In *Santa Clara Pueblo*, Justice Marshall described the extent of federal control over Indian tribes: All "aspect[s] of tribal sovereignty ... [are] subject to the superior and plenary control of Congress." But, Justice Marshall explained, Indian tribes retain a substantial measure of sovereignty; they "remain a 'separate people, with the power of regulating their internal and social relations.'" Thus, according to the Court, if federal courts were to imply a power to "intervene" in tribal decisions, the courts would undermine the authority of a group whose powers have already been limited. "A fortiori, a resolution in a foreign forum of intra-tribal disputes of a more public character, such as the one in this case, cannot help but unsettle a tribal government's ability to maintain authority." Congress intended to protect the tribes from "undue interference." Hence, the federal courts should not imply jurisdiction and remedies beyond the one (habeas corpus) specified in the legislation. Julia and Audrey Martinez were sent back to the tribal forum, which had already refused their requests for reconsideration of the tribal ordinance.

Two themes, power and sovereignty, were central to the *Santa Clara Pueblo* case. Those themes also dominate the scholarship of "federal courts" jurisprudence. The theme of power, of its allocation and constraint by separation of functions, is typically examined by discussion of the relationships between the federal courts and the Executive, the Congress, and the agencies within the federal government. The theme of sovereignty, often described as "federalism," addresses the relationships among the governmental entities in the United States, and specifically, between the federal courts and the states. A central problem is how two "sovereigns" can and should coexist in the United States. These questions of separation of powers and of federalism arise when considering the extent of Congressional control over the jurisdiction of the federal courts, the delineation of responsibilities among the branches of the federal government, the relationship between the state and federal court systems, and the distinctive treatment accorded states as litigants in the federal courts.

The bountiful literature of federal courts' jurisprudence does not, however, consider problems of the relationship between Indian tribes, the federal government, and the states. "We" who teach and write about the federal courts, we who list ourselves as the definers of the domain, speak and write relatively rarely about the federal courts and their relationship to Indian tribes. *Santa Clara Pueblo* and other "Indian tribe" cases are not often found in books about "the" federal courts or in discussions about the problems of multiple sovereigns coexisting in the United States. While there is a wealth of scholarship about Indian tribes, that scholarship is not integrated into federal courts' jurisprudence. ***

Recent articles have attempted to understand what Richard Fallon has called the "ideologies of federal courts law" – to explicate the underlying assumptions and aspirations of the discipline. This essay continues that enterprise: to consider why federal courts' jurisprudence has not spoken much about Indian tribes when telling the story of the federal courts, and to learn what that silence has to teach. I hope to show what Indian tribe cases have to bring to federal courts' jurisprudence, to what is meant by the concept of state sovereignty and allocation of power between the state and federal governments.

In contrast to many of the states, Indian tribes are arguably truly distinct sovereigns, which did not cede sovereignty with the adoption of the Constitution but which lost most of it anyway. Exploration of the responses of federal courts – when individuals ask for federal protection from the tribal government, as in *Santa Clara Pueblo*, and when tribes claim intrusion by the state and federal governments – can inform contemporary discussions of the domain of the federal courts. How the United States government has treated Indian tribes and those in conflict with the tribes teaches us about the enormous power of the federal government. The capacity of the United States government to try to obliterate smaller "sovereigns" illuminates reasons to respect and maintain semi-sovereigns and demonstrates the complexity of the interaction and interdependence of "sovereigns" in the United States. ***

I CREATING THE BOUNDARIES OF JURISPRUDENTIAL THOUGHT ABOUT THE FEDERAL COURTS

*** Several of the current federal courts casebooks begin with *Marbury v. Madison*, which is used to state basic principles: that the government of the United States is one of "powers limited"; that the Supreme Court holds the power to decide when other branches of the federal government have unconstitutionally "transcended" their powers; and that the Constitution is the repository of statements of the powers and limits of the federal government. Of course, the matters of "powers limited" is much more complex, as each account of the federal courts' "story" quickly develops. For example, when considering the power of the Congress over the jurisdiction of the federal courts, questions soon emerge about the breadth of authority granted in Article III to the Congress. Congress is often said to have "plenary power" over the federal courts' jurisdiction. But not quite. Most commentators assume that a law that provided jurisdiction in the federal courts for white citizens but not for blacks would be unconstitutional – not because it violated the text of Article III, but because another part of the Constitution, the Bill of Rights, constrains congressional action.

Constitutionality is at the heart of discussions of the federal courts. From the principle of limited governmental powers constrained by constitutional commitment (if not always by the text itself), a problem arises: how to explain and rationalize the growth of national powers in the context of a history of dual sovereignty, of a government founded on the idea that the states have consented to some form of simultaneous yet non-identical power-holding by state and federal governments. The recurring questions are: Who – the federal government or the states – gets to decide what issues? What kind of deference is owed by federal courts to the state courts? ***

The task for federal courts' jurisprudence is to understand what might be meant by a claim of allegiance to more than one sovereign and what meaning, if any, inheres in the idea of states as "sovereigns." In an array of circumstances, federal courts' jurisprudence must question whether shared and concurrent jurisdiction remains viable and must explore whether to embrace or resist the pressures toward nationalization and homogenization. Are the states really coherent descriptions of viable political entities, or are they a fiction left over from an earlier era? Will and should the federal government tolerate sustained deviation from its norms? Are the forces of centralization and assimilation so great that the only laws that matter, ultimately, are national laws? Should the country strive to have a central government (with some measure of decentralization or delegation) or try to preserve some form of distinction between governments and encourage multiple sovereignties, multiple court systems, and multiple norms? While some federal courts' scholars address some of these issues in the context of state and federal relations, the law about Indian tribes helps underscore the centrality of these questions for federal courts' jurisprudence and helps to suggest some of the kinds of responses available.

II THE INDIAN TRIBES' RELATIONSHIP TO THE UNITED STATES

I have had the opportunity to discuss the issues raised in this paper with many people. I have learned that, at least within the legal academy, a common perception is that federal Indian law is complex, foreign, very different, and thus an area set aside for "experts" alone. This essay is an effort to demonstrate that one need not know "everything" to speak a little, that just as those of "us" (within the legal academy) who are not economists, philosophers, political scientists, or feminist theorists integrate insights from economics, philosophy, political science and feminist theory, we can also integrate an area of law that challenges, admittedly and interestingly, some of the rules we take for granted.

* * *

Supreme Court case law repeatedly creates and then recognizes the enormity of the "plenary" federal power over the Indian tribes. Take, for example, a statement quoted in a recent Supreme Court case: "[A]ll aspects of Indian sovereignty are subject to defeasance by Congress." Ordinary constitutional exegesis would oblige the Court then to make reference to some provision in the Constitution, or other documents such as treaties, by which the Indian tribes ceded powers to the central government. Moreover, ordinary constitutional exegesis would also describe federal powers as having boundaries, albeit sometimes vague ones. Even when constitutional theorists believe in the plenary power of one branch of the federal government in particular instances, reference is made to constraints, to power that is checked – either by political recall, dependence upon other branches for implementation of the decisions made, or by other constitutional guarantees. Recall the example mentioned above, that Congress has "plenary power" over the federal courts' jurisdiction. While federal courts scholars are used to hearing that claim, they are similarly used to explaining that "plenary power" always comes with the caveat: but see the Bill of Rights.

Not so for Congress's power over the Indian tribes. There is no "but see the Bill of Rights" because the United States Supreme Court has held that the Bill of Rights has little application to Indian law. Members of Indian tribes cannot make Bill of Rights claims against their tribes, and Indian tribes are not protected by the Bill of Rights from federal decisions. For example, the Supreme Court has stated that "Indian occupancy, [on land] not specifically recognized by action authorized by Congress, may be extinguished by the [federal] Government without compensation." ***

The history of United States' dealings with the peoples who inhabited the continent before Western Europeans arrived is one of conquest, exploitation, and eradication. Phrases like "allotment," "discovery," and "relocation," capture events that are deeply embarrassing to those committed to a vision of a United States founded upon consent and dedicated to non-discriminatory treatment. Unlike the disturbing history of slavery, no arguably comfortable mileposts are available. No *Brown v. Board of Education* exists for Indian tribes. ***

Federal courts' jurisprudence must struggle with claims of "sovereignty." Inclusion of materials about Indian tribes does more than deconstruct some of the traditional wisdom about the limits of the federal government's power. Learning about the interaction between federal, state, and Indian governments is learning about how some form of group identity and governance can survive in the midst of domination – and learning that the survival of such identity and governance is a product of decisions by both the smaller and the larger groups, and of their interactions. The point is not that states and Indian tribes are equivalent. Profound differences – of history, sociology, and politics – exist between a state and an Indian tribe. But there is much to learn from thinking about both the differences and the similarities.

The claim of sovereignty arises when one group makes a claim to be or to sustain rules different from another. A central question for federal courts' jurisprudence is how much difference between state and national laws the federal government should encourage or tolerate. The relationship between the federal and state governments and the Indian tribes reminds "us" to take claims of difference seriously and to explore the meaning of claimed distinctions between "sovereigns." Perceiving "difference" between the Santa Clara Pueblo and the United States may be easier than perceiving difference between New Jersey and the United States. But the very ease of perceiving difference between Indian and non-Indian may also obscure interaction and influence. Exploration of the relationship between the Santa Clara Pueblo and the United States shows complex interweavings of two "sovereigns." Texts about federal Indian law enable insight into what deviations from its norms the federal government will tolerate and what it will attempt to preclude, and thus provide insight into what federal norms really are.

III REASONS TO GIVE VOICE

Analytically comparable problems, embarrassment, and a belated sense of obligation to speak about the history of treatment of Indian tribes are sufficient to give rise to a claim for inclusion of materials about Indian tribes in federal courts' jurisprudence. But Indian tribe cases offer more than a chance to display appropriate sensitivity to the experiences of many within this country. Indian cases provide vivid insight into three central themes for federal courts' jurisprudence to explore: (1) whether and when the United States will tolerate subgroups that seek to be different and distinct and to express such distinctions by self-governance; (2) whether such differences can be sustained, given the interdependencies of the subgroup and the federal government; and (3) whether distinct governance structures are to be desired and preserved or forbidden and eroded. ***

B *Separate but Assimilated*

*** Starting in the middle of the 1960s, an era during which civil rights consciousness was great, members of Congress began to express concern about the rights of Indians vis-à-vis their tribes. One result was the Indian Civil Rights Act of 1968 (ICRA). Billed both as insuring civil rights of Indian tribe members and as protecting the sovereignty of Indian tribes, the ICRA made some, but not all, of the Bill of Rights applicable to Indian tribe members. As noted above, ICRA specified only one remedy, habeas corpus, which reflected the particular concern that tribal decisions about incarceration be made subject to reconsideration by a federal court.

Before the Supreme Court heard *Santa Clara Pueblo v. Martinez*, many lower courts had implied remedies beyond habeas corpus for breaches of rights enumerated in the ICRA. However, by the time *Santa Clara Pueblo* was before the Court, federal policies about tribal sovereignty and about federal rights had shifted once again. In 1968, President Johnson had termed Indians "the forgotten American," and in 1970, President Nixon's executive proclamation steered federal policies again toward tribal sovereignty. Stating that "[s]elf-determination among the Indian people can and must be encouraged without the threat of eventual termination," Nixon announced a legislative package to permit Indian tribes to administer federal service programs. Soon thereafter, justices appointed by President Nixon to the Supreme Court turned that institution's attention away from articulation of individual rights, away from implication of remedies from federal statutory schemes, and towards an emphasis on state sovereign powers. In the 1978 *Santa Clara Pueblo* decision, the federal policy of tribal self-determination, ambivalence about women's rights, and the limited federal court willingness to imply remedies coalesced, and Julia and Audrey Martinez were told that the federal courts could not help them.

1 Sovereignty and Jurisdiction

[F]ederal court support for the principle of tribal sovereignty has limits as well. Just two months before deciding *Santa Clara Pueblo*, the Supreme Court held that Indian tribes lack authority to punish non-Indians who commit crimes on tribal reservations. *Oliphant v. Suquamish Indian Tribe* arose when two non-Indian residents of the Suquamish Tribe's reservation sought habeas corpus relief from criminal convictions in the tribal court. *** While the Court drew upon a number of sources, its underlying assumption is that tribal sovereignty is not unbounded but limited – because the tribes are not fully another government but a dependent group. Justice Rehnquist's opinion for the Court stated that tribal powers were not "limited only by specific restrictions in treaties or congressional enactments"; tribal powers could not "conflict with [the] ... overriding sovereignty" of the United States. Justice Rehnquist spoke of the United States' interest in protecting citizens (implicitly, non-Indian citizens) from "unwarranted intrusions on their personal liberty." While Justice Rehnquist stated that "some Indian tribal courts have become increasingly sophisticated and resemble in many respects their state counterparts," his concern was that tribal justice would not always comport with United States definitions of due process.

Since *Oliphant*, the Court has had several occasions to delineate the respective jurisdictions of the federal, state, and tribal courts regarding litigation to which Indians are parties. The issues are made complex by federal statutes, some of which assert jurisdiction over "major crimes" by Indians on Indian land, some of which cede federal jurisdiction to some states if they exercise the option, and some of which – including the Indian Civil Rights Act of 1968 – could be read to permit tribal jurisdiction to be at least a first, if not a final, forum.

The recent major jurisdictional cases have probed the relationships between non-Indians, who are either doing business with tribes or living on reservations, and Indians. From *National Farmers Union Insurance Company v. Crow Tribe* and *Iowa Mutual Insurance Company v. LaPlante*, the rule has emerged that federal courts should not exercise civil jurisdiction over activities arising on tribal lands at least until after tribal remedies have been exhausted, and possibly not thereafter. While many issues about the overlapping jurisdictions remain open, federal courts students and scholars will find the modes of analysis familiar. Federal court jurisdiction is understood to be intrusive to the decision making of another sovereign; rules of comity mandate deference to that other court system. Federal courts do not "lack" subject matter jurisdiction but, as a result of prudentially based comity doctrines, must defer to another court system.

The Indian tribe comity cases offer more than familiar analytic exercises, for the differences between sovereigns – federal and tribal – enable an understanding of why courts' exercise of jurisdiction can be described as "jurispathic." The term is Robert Cover's and its meaning is that courts can kill law created by communities. For many of us who think about the interaction between federal and state systems, it is often difficult to perceive federal courts as jurispathic vis-à-vis states. Given federal regulatory structures in place since the New Deal and federal civil rights rulings, the differences between "New Jersey," "California," or "Virginia" justice and "federal" justice seem small, and the "harm" to any state, if federal courts "intrude," seems more theoretical than real. Federal and state lines have blurred, at least for those who move from state to state and often have affiliations with more than one jurisdiction.

In contrast, as both the *Santa Clara Pueblo* and *Oliphant* opinions insist (albeit drawing different conclusions), Indian tribes are "other." Their culture and norms are not federal culture and norms; their rules are theirs. Given the possible divergences in culture between tribal modes of governance and federal norms, the use of jurisdiction as a means of control is more apparent than the claimed interference when federal courts preclude state court decision making. Jurispathic courts seem not an exaggeration but a real threat; federal court reluctance to exercise jurisdiction seems like an appropriate response to a claim that these people really do have a federally recognized place as "not federal."

But that place is unevenly respected. In some instances, federal court rules accord greater deference to tribal courts than to state courts, while in others, less solicitude for tribal authority is expressed. For example, some forms of comity, in which a federal court defers to a state court, are premised upon an assumption that the state court will apply federal law; the explicit vision is that a state court is equal to the federal court in fidelity to and enforcement of federal norms. Further, the state court decisions on federal law can, at least in theory, be reviewed by the United States Supreme Court. In contrast, when federal courts defer to tribal courts under both *Santa Clara Pueblo* and *Iowa Mutual Insurance v. LaPlante*, the tribal courts may not always follow federal law and, whether obliged to or not, their decisions in noncriminal cases are not reviewable by the federal courts. The *Oliphant* case, however, exemplifies the other version – when federal courts are less deferential to tribal courts than to state courts. Under *Oliphant*, tribes cannot enforce their criminal laws against non-Indians but must instead depend upon other sovereigns' law enforcement interests. Yet, when criminal defendants in state court come to federal court to assert protection from state prosecution, the federal court declines – because of the centrality of criminal law to the states as "sovereign."

2 Tribal Courts, Federal Courts, and State Courts

Doctrines of deference to other court systems assume that those court systems are "other." Just as the 1939 membership ordinance at issue in *Santa Clara Pueblo* must be seen not as a pure artifact of Santa Clara Pueblo culture but as a product of the interaction between Santa Clara Pueblo and the United States, so a closer look at the Indian tribal courts reveals many aspects of their operation to be a product of the interaction between tribal customs and the Bureau of Indian Affairs [BIA], the Department of Interior, and federal Indian policy.

Many commentators have described the tribal courts, and I will simply sketch the outlines. The 1883 case of *Ex Parte Crow Dog* is often credited with bringing attention to Indian tribal dispute resolution. The federal court for the Territory of

Dakota convicted an Indian for the murder of another Indian on Indian lands. The Supreme Court interpreted the governing statutes and treaties as not authorizing federal jurisdiction and therefore voided the conviction. In response, in 1884, the Secretary of Interior issued regulations establishing "courts of Indian offenses" and staffing those courts with Indian judges. The purpose of these courts was expressly jurispathic; to "civilize" tribes by banning tribal custom and imposing federal norms. In 1885, Congress passed the "Major Crimes Act," which conferred federal jurisdiction over Indians in Indian country for seven specified felonies. The Supreme Court upheld that grant of jurisdictional control as an appropriate exercise of federal guardianship powers over Indians.

Two mechanisms were used to infuse federal norms into Indian dispute resolution. The first was divesting tribes of jurisdiction over issues deemed outside their competence, either by making that jurisdiction federal or by turning jurisdiction over to the states. The second was to instruct and to influence tribes about how to exercise what jurisdiction remained theirs.

During the late nineteenth and early twentieth centuries, federal control over tribal courts was pervasive. By 1926, seventy Indian judges were paid by federal funds and worked in Indian courts run pursuant to Interior Department regulations. After the 1934 enactment of the Indian Reorganization Act, the Department of the Interior provided model regulations for tribes to structure justice systems. Although some tribes retained their traditional tribal courts, many tribes adopted court structures based upon the Interior Department regulations. These courts have become known as "CFR courts," after the sections of the Code of Federal Regulations that set forth the court procedures, the selection and removal of judges, and a compilation of "Indian Tribal Offenses." Indian justice rules "were copied verbatim or patterned to a considerable extent upon the [then] new Departmental rules." Indeed, some Indian tribes adopted Interior Department-inspired codes and constitutions that limited Indian court jurisdiction and made Indian tribal decisions dependent upon approval by the Secretary of the Interior. The enactment, in 1968, of the Indian Civil Rights Act exerted additional pressures to adopt the United States' modes of dispensing justice. As one group of commentators who surveyed tribal courts in the late 1970s describes: "[T]he 1968 Indian Civil Rights Act implies to many Indians that self-determination is acceptable only to the extent that tribes develop sophisticated, anglicized tribal court systems." Only a few tribes followed customary law, while the majority adopted justice mechanisms like those in the United States – albeit with extremely limited funding and resources.

Yet these tribal courts are not simply federal products, for they developed from an interaction between federal regulation and Indian tribal customs. As a consequence, many Indian tribal courts have aspects that are not so familiar to those schooled in United States' court practices. Most notably from the perspective of the United States, federal traditions of separation of powers are not commonplace. Some commentators report that tribal councils influence tribal court decision making in a variety of ways, including judicial selection, retention, and recall. Further, in some instances, tribal councils act as appellate bodies as well as executive decision makers. The sources of law, permissible styles of argument, and structure of the proceedings may vary substantially from what practitioners have come to expect in federal courts.

Thus, when the federal courts require litigants to submit to tribal courts in the name of tribal sovereignty, many of those court systems have been framed and regulated by the BIA but also maintain proceedings and procedures at some variance from federal and state courts. The question is whether the federal government will tolerate such deviations by respecting and deferring to tribal court jurisdiction, or whether federal rules of deference and comity depend upon the similarity between the two court systems.

3 Federal Oversight via Relitigation

One vehicle for federal review is the habeas corpus provision of the Indian Civil Rights Act; by that provision, Congress authorized federal courts to consider "the legality of ... detention by order of an Indian tribe." In August 1988, Senator Orrin Hatch, who is often identified with legislation aimed at stripping, rather than conferring, federal court jurisdiction, suggested that an additional route to the federal court be provided. He introduced S 2747, entitled "The Indian Civil Rights Act Amendments of 1988." The proposed amendments would overturn *Santa Clara Pueblo* to a large extent by authorizing jurisdiction in the federal courts over "civil rights actions alleging a failure to comply with rights secured" by the legislation. The Hatch proposal requires exhaustion of tribal court remedies and then permits return to the federal courts for "any aggrieved individual ... or the Attorney General on behalf of the United States." Such plaintiffs could obtain declaratory and equitable relief against tribes or their officials for a variety of failings of tribal court decision making, including the failure of a tribal court to be "fully independent from the tribal legislative or executive authority," the failure to "resolve the merits of the factual dispute," the failure to "adequately develop material facts," and the failure to afford "a full and fair hearing." In short, the proposed legislation would permit extensive federal court "oversight" of or "intrusion" into tribal courts. ***

Senator Hatch's introductory comments to the legislative proposal illustrate his concerns. He discussed in detail the case of *Little Horn State Bank v. Crow Tribal Court*, which involved a bank's effort to obtain a forklift from a defaulting debtor. There, despite United States Supreme Court mandates of deference to tribal court decision making, a federal trial judge declined to defer and instead enjoined enforcement of the tribal court order protecting the alleged debtor. Senator Hatch quoted at length from the federal court opinion, in which the judge characterized the tribal court as a "sort of 'kangaroo court' [that] has made no pretense of due process or judicial integrity ... It would appear that the Crow Tribal government changes judges at a whim, to the detriment of non-Indian litigants, and of the Tribe."

As a result, the Tribal Court lacks any continuity and uniform precedent which is the foundation of our judicial system . . . If the Crow Tribe wishes to earn the respect and cooperation of its non-Indian neighbors, it must do more to engender that respect and cooperation . . ."

I know nothing of the merit of the trial judge's description of the Crow Tribal Court's methods. Nor do I know whether the informality and the connection between tribal council and tribal judge that the federal court found offensive are so very different from small town state court proceedings, or how frequently such informality is found in tribal courts. What is plain is that the federal trial judge found the Crow tribal processes very different from those that he identified as essential to "judicial integrity" and that, given the absence of similarity between the two systems, the federal judge declined to permit the tribal ruling to stand. Further, the federal judge was remarkably unrestrained in his language; he did not employ the polite discourse common when federal judges speak of state court decision making. The Hatch proposal builds upon the assumptions of the *Little Horn Bank* case; the proposal would authorize the position taken by the federal judge in that case. Like federal habeas corpus review of state court decisions, the Hatch proposal is designed to insure that another sovereign's court system follows the norms of the federal sovereign. Both the habeas statute and the Hatch proposal are efforts to assimilate – to permit "independence" only upon condition that the "other" process mirrors the federal one. ***

IV THE LESSONS LEARNED

A *Familiar but Altered Themes*

Those familiar with federal courts' jurisprudence can easily feel at home with federal Indian law, despite its absence from the canon. Federal habeas corpus jurisdiction expanded when federal courts and Congress perceived state courts as inhospitable to enforcement of federal rights. Relitigation of state court civil rights decisions expanded, briefly, when federal courts questioned state courts' adherence to federal rights enforcement and receded in face of claims of state court "parity." Federal court relitigation of claims of discriminatory employment practices, decided adversely in state and federal administrative agencies, is still available. If *Little Horn Bank* is illustrative of federal courts' attitudes, or if the Hatch proposal is enacted, federal court relitigation of tribal court decisions may similarly expand, as federal judges and members of Congress perceive tribal courts to be inhospitable to United States forms of procedure and to the enforcement of federal rights.

Again and again, in the contexts of both state and tribal courts, we watch the interplay between multiple court systems, between expansion and contraction of jurisdiction, sometimes to affirm norms of diversity and, at other times, to encourage assimilation by the application of nationwide norms. The state/federal and Indian tribe/federal patterns are not identical, but at many points, doctrine and explanation overlap. ***

B *The Question of the Survival of "Other" Courts*

With fluctuations over time, the federal government and its courts have consistently permitted other (lesser) power centers to function and sometimes even to flourish. Federal courts have crafted doctrines of comity and deference, and have ceded jurisdiction and authority to other court systems – state and tribal – and to quasi-court systems, such as agencies and arbitration.

What animates this support for other decision centers? Answers vary over time and with different actors. For some, the hope is that community-based processes still thrive in smaller units of government. Others claim a commitment to an "ethic of promising," that the federal government entered into compacts even though it might try to exercise the power of rescission. Yet another explanation comes from the uses that the federal government can find for states and tribes. For example, the federal system does not want to decide all the disputes in the country, but wants to maintain its elite status by having only a subset of cases and, sometimes, final authority over cases otherwise distributed.

Responses to the question about the continuing vitality of tribal and state governments emerge not only from the perspective of the federal government, but also from the perspective of the tribes and states. The tenacity of tribal governance, despite sustained efforts by the federal government to extinguish it, is remarkable. Given that Indian tribes are politically dispersed, have limited resources, and must contend with oppressive majoritarian rules, explanations of the resilience are needed. Similar exploration of the persistence of state governments is also needed, but the issue is less obvious. Just as Indian "tribes" are "historic inventions, tendentious and changing," so are states. Once the instability of the construct "tribe" is used to demonstrate the instability of the construct "state," then one is free to ask why and when to support the construction of either of those entities. Again, the answers need not be parallel, nor is the question solely one for the dominant culture to answer.

C *The Assimilationist Pressures*

Inclusion of Indian tribal cases also clarifies the force of assimilationist pressures. Just as the federal government self-consciously cedes power, so it presses the "other" government to act as its surrogate. For better or worse, federal support for other court systems turns out, in many instances, to be contingent upon their performance as measured by federal court standards. This assimilationist pressure is desirable if one is enthusiastic about the standards imposed. Many of us celebrated the imposition of federal norms on communities that said that their culture, their custom, was to treat whites differently than blacks. Many of us are prepared to celebrate the imposition of federal norms, if they exist, that demand the non-subordination of women. Many of us worry about courts in which judges are dependent upon the executive or legislative branches, and many of us have a deep commitment to the values that go under the label "due process of law." State courts have, upon occasion, failed to insist upon racial and gender equality and on due process in decision making. Hence, one might look to the federal government in an effort to persuade it to exercise its power and insist upon such rules.

Watching the interaction of federal, state, and tribal courts is instructive because one sees that the decision of the federal system to trump an "other's" decision varies with the strength of the federal norm at issue. When racial equality came to be seen as a national norm, toleration of the states' interest in racial inequality waned. When racial oppression was tied to criminal justice systems, federal attention was turned to state conviction processes. When federal interest in both racial equality and its impact on the administration of criminal justice wane, state sovereignty emerges again as a theme.

When "federalization" is occurring, one has to ask whether the idea of "dual sovereigns," meaning state and federal courts, really has much meaning. Are these "other" court systems simply sub-systems of the federal courts? Once again, the context of Indian tribe law sharpens a question implicit in federal courts' jurisprudence but often not articulated: We say we have dual sovereigns, with dual court systems, dual norm generation, and dual citizenship, but are the forces of federalization so strong that the duality is more true on paper and in rhetoric than in reality? *Santa Clara Pueblo* and *Little Horn Bank* help make plain that policies described as "theirs," as those of a sub-community, are always the product of interaction between a larger and a smaller group. The wealth of interdependencies demonstrates the complexity of "we"/"they" distinctions and reminds us to be skeptical of the dominant group when it purports to be supporting the sovereignty of the "other."

D The Utility of the "Other"

Given these interdependencies and assimilationist pressures, the question emerges: What is the point of the "other"? A large part of the record of tolerance of the "other" is of tolerance of similarity, not dissimilarity. The effort is to make the "other" like "us" – in the case of United States interaction with the Indian tribes, explicitly to "civilize" them. Understanding the attempts to change the "other" is important for federal courts' jurisprudence, which assumes the actual existence of an "other" – the "other" branches of the federal government and the "other" sovereignty, the states.
***

One possible conclusion from acknowledging the assimilationist pressures is to perceive the states as not really "other," but as subdivisions of the federal government. If one believed that subdivisions were all that existed, then the argument for their continuation would rest upon a claim of efficiency – that the scale of the smaller units is better able to govern than the larger unit. Decision making in cases about federalism would then be governed by views about whether the smaller unit's claim enhances its capacity to serve as a subdivision of the federal government.

But there is a risk of overstatement. The state courts are not totally clones of the federal courts. At some points, state courts announce rules of law and of practice that are at some distance from the federal courts. And, despite enormous federal pressures, tribal courts are still "struggling to maintain their identity." There are assimilationist pressures but not complete assimilation. Something more than subdivisions of the federal government currently exist.

*** From the perspective of the dominant society, the question is how much "subversion" and "invention" should be tolerated and encouraged. At the core of federal courts' jurisprudence is a question that has often gone under the name of "sovereignty" but may more fruitfully be explored in the context of difference. If the word "sovereign" has any meaning in contemporary federal courts' jurisprudence, its meaning comes from a state's or a tribe's ability to maintain different modes from those of the federal government. The United States has often made claims about the richness of its pluralist society – made claims that the loss of state or tribal identity would not only be a loss to states and tribes, but would also harm all citizens because of the benefit of living in a country in which not all are required to follow the same norms. Some deep-seated emotional respect for group governance may be at work here, some sense that these self-contained communities are "jurisgenerative" (again, to borrow from Robert Cover) and that their traditions and customs must sometimes be respected and preserved. In the tribes, cities, states, and regions of the country, one can find not only individuals, but also the individual as part of a community – a community that has had continuity over time. In these communities there are social ties, there is a shared history, there is a network of relatedness. In contrast, the federal system appears to some as individualistic and atomistic. We are attracted by these smaller institutions, these subsets, these multiple sovereignties; we like the scale, the sense of history, the intimacy.

But we also know that some communities are communities of oppression. In Marilyn Friedman's words, "[b]esides excluding or suppressing outsiders, the practices and traditions of many communities are exploitative and oppressive toward many of their own members. This problem is of special relevance to women." Of course, interpretations of communities as "exploitative and oppressive" depend upon the perspective of the viewer. While one reading of Julia and Audrey Martinez's decision to go to federal court to obtain alteration of membership rules could be that they found the Santa Clara Pueblo to be oppressive to women, many interpretations are possible. In one sense, the very act of asking the federal court to dictate to the Pueblo could be understood as an act of self exclusion. By seeking federal court assistance, Ms. Martinez signaled that she stood outside the community in which she sought to have her children included and perceived the community as a source of oppression. In another sense, the decision to seek federal court help could be understood as demonstrating how deep Ms. Martinez's affiliation with the Pueblo was, for she was willing to risk a good deal of hostility to enable her children to continue to live on the Pueblo and to inherit land as members of the Pueblo. Ms. Martinez was not alone in seeking federal court relief from tribal decisions. Many other cases have been filed by Indians challenging the decisions of their communities, indicating that, at least for some, embeddedness in a jurisgenerative community may be problematic, that "communities of place" may not always be responsive to the needs of their members.

How are we to interpret the Supreme Court's instruction to Ms. Martinez? "You are a citizen of the United States, but go back to your community and make your claims there." We must acknowledge that the decision is an act of exclusion, that Ms. Martinez's claim of connection to the United States was rejected at the same time that the Court affirmed both her affiliation with the Santa Clara Pueblo and federal power to control the relationship between her and the Pueblo – had Congress chosen to exercise its power. *** These seem to be federal statements enforcing the continued importance of "communities of place" and ignoring claims that those communities are at least nonresponsive if not outright oppressive. ***

If notions of "checks and balances" are at work, if the "other" must have power so as to limit and diffuse the power of the federal government, then federal courts should sustain differences that enhance the ability of the other to hold power sufficient to check the federal government. One of the problems with the *Santa Clara Pueblo* decision is that the Court never confronted the claim that the Pueblo was being used for some purposes as a subdivision of the federal government – to distribute Indian benefits for the government. Yet another problem in *Santa Clara Pueblo* was the implicit public/private distinction endorsed by the Court. The arena in which tribes have most authority are "intratribal disputes," matters including issues such as membership, marriage, and family matters. To cut off that set of activities from federal rule making is to assume that the structures of families and communities are not decisions of national political importance. Hence, "letting" tribes have control over these issues is not recognizing them as serious power holders, but only as holding power over that which has little import.

But *Santa Clara Pueblo* did not send only Julia and Audrey Martinez's claim for non-discriminatory membership rules back to tribal governments for decision. The Supreme Court said that, absent Congressional direction, no federal court could entertain any private civil action for violation of the ICRA, whether those claims are of denial of equal protection, deprivations of free speech, illegal searches and seizures, wrongful takings, or denial of due process. One might then conclude that *Santa Clara Pueblo* is evidence of a serious commitment to the tribal courts as competing power centers for the enforcement of different cultural norms. However, the Court justified its refusal to permit federal court jurisdiction by stating that "[t]ribal forums are available to vindicate rights created by the ICRA [which had] . . .

the substantial and intended effect of changing the law which these forums are obliged to apply." Tribal courts have the power to decide, but their decisions must be in accordance with the federal law, albeit with no federal court supervision of compliance.

If tribal courts are simply vehicles for federal lawmaking, what is the definition of tribal "sovereign" interests that the Court claimed in *Santa Clara Pueblo* to respect? "Sovereignty" in this context seems to mean that a tribe need not explain itself to the federal courts, but must follow federal law. (Will tribes, like state courts, be presumed by federal judges to be equal to federal courts in their fidelity to federal law?) But perhaps a stronger definition of sovereignty can be pulled from the lines of the *Santa Clara Pueblo* opinion. If the tribal courts are the interpreters of the meaning of federal law, can use tribal law, and have the authority to interpret without federal court oversight, then divergent, idiosyncratic expressions can emerge. "The vast gulf" that Justice Marshall referred to "between tribal traditions and those with which the federal courts are more intimately familiar" can be preserved and even enlarged. But, as *Oliphant* and *Little Horn Bank* remind us, when non-Indians are involved and tribal criminal law is invoked, or when non-Indian creditors seek enforcement of their claims, federal court interest in "tribal sovereignty" wanes.

One way that the federal government can use "other" sovereigns is to learn something about itself. *Santa Clara Pueblo* and *Little Horn Bank* help to clarify that what the federal government is prepared to tolerate in "them" depends upon how it defines itself and what effect it perceives "their" decisions to have. When federal and "other" norms converge, toleration and claims of "sovereignty" are easy to make. *** The Supreme Court's tacit reliance upon dichotomies such as Indian and non-Indian, public and private, demonstrates the ways in which the *Santa Clara Pueblo* opinion avoided responding to the underlying problems: the coherence of the conception of Indian tribes as a "separate people" (in the sense of disconnected) and the assumption of a "domestic sphere" as apolitical. Interconnections weave together Indians and non-Indians, families and the "market." The clashes are not avoided, but only postponed.

While *Santa Clara Pueblo* illustrates deep underlying convergences between the tribal conception of its role and the federal conception, *Little Horn Bank* and the Hatch proposal exemplify moments when normative divergences are closer to the surface. At some point, from the perspective of the dominant group, the "vast gulf" becomes too vast – differences emerge that the federal government tries to obliterate. At such points, the federal government attempts to remind the dominated group of its dependence upon the larger collective and works to bring the smaller group into compliance with federal norms. Implicit in the *Little Horn Bank* decision is a view that courts with procedures different from the federal ones may cause harm to creditors' ability to collect debts and may undermine the fluidity of commercial transactions. Toleration of such differences in this "public" arena of debt collection were not to be countenanced by at least one federal district court. Further, the techniques for assimilation need not always be judicially or legislatively based. Economic pressures may also be exerted to try to bring tribal courts into compliance with federal norms; banks can refuse to do business if their debt collection efforts will be thwarted by tribal or state courts. As a descriptive matter, we must note these assimilationist pressures; as a normative matter, we must debate the desirability of them.

An "other" sovereign serves a valuable purpose for the federal government. The degree of toleration of the "other" sovereign's decisions enables the federal government to make plain what its own values are. *** The most difficult issues for federal courts' jurisprudence are to explain how to engender differences, how deep the respect should be for difference, when the federal government's right to assert a baseline exists, and then to ascertain where that federal floor should be. Constitutional and case law exegesis alone cannot accomplish these tasks. Rather, on-going relational struggles illuminate the changing shapes of the floors that are continually to be sought. ***

CONCLUSION

*** Thus far, the official canon of the federal courts has not included the relationship between the federal courts and Indian tribes. Little is said about the federal courts' role – sometimes destroying Indian tribal culture and occasionally respecting it. We have also not much spoken of the sources of federal power over Indian tribes: conquest, violence, force. In the context of states, basic aspects of the power relationship are similarly not much discussed; when the Supreme Court imposes federal rules, it refers to parts of the Constitution, not to the Civil War. Yet it was the Civil War and then again the use of federal force in the 1960s that established the federal power to insist that federal norms trumped "state sovereignty."

It is time, I think, to review the stories we have been telling about the federal courts, to acknowledge the role played by brute force, to make plain the limits of constitutionalism and of history in explicating constitutionalism. It is time to revise the canon, to include texts less noble than the ones we have preferred, and with their inclusion, learn more about the present and what future we want to craft.

NOTES & QUESTIONS

1. *Reading Indian Law*:
   • Explain how *Oliphant* and *Santa Clara* are two different examples of federal intrusion upon tribal sovereignty. Both cases are still good law. How can the two cases be reconciled together? What does each case have to say about the assumption of the power of federal courts over Indians?

- Resnik talks about the ability of courts to be "jurispathic" and "jurisgenerative." What does she mean by those terms? Can you give examples of each? What role do tribal courts play in the construction or application of these terms?
- Are tribal courts really extensions of federal courts? Resnik argues for the inclusion of tribal courts in the study of federal courts because federal tolerance of tribal courts tells us something about the federal court system. What can we learn about tolerance, diversity, inclusion, and/or plurality by observing the interaction between federal and tribal courts? How different is a tribal court permitted to be before federal courts exercise their oversight?

2. *Santa Clara Pueblo Membership Ordinance*: In *Santa Clara* the Supreme Court denied relief to Julia and Audrey Martinez, reasoning that the federal courts did not have jurisdiction to hear their case because they were not detained. (The Indian Civil Rights Act provides for federal court review only upon a writ of habeas corpus.) The result left the Martinez family with no federal recourse, and instructed them to again seek redress from the tribe.

   It took thirty years, but in 2012 the Santa Clara Pueblo voted by a 2:1 margin to change their membership ordinance to include the children of female members with men of other cultures. Is it better to have the Tribe change its own rules or to have federal courts require the Tribe to implement the change? What can be learned from the fact that the Santa Clara Pueblo decided on their own to rewrite their membership ordinance? Does this provide evidence that federal courts should continue to defer to tribal decision making?

3. *Federal Courts*: Professor Resnik is not the only Indian law scholar to see a role for a discussion of Indian law cases within the context of federal courts. Professor Frank Pommersheim from the University of South Dakota has at least twice commented on the importance of Indian law to an understanding of the construction and power of federal courts. *See* Frank Pommersheim, *Tribal Courts and Federal Courts: A Very Preliminary Set of Notes for Federal Court Teachers*, 36 Ariz. St. L.J. 63 (2005) and Frank Pommersheim, *"Our Federalism" in the Context of Federal Courts and Tribal Courts: An Open Letter to the Federal Courts Teaching and Scholarly Community*, 71 U. Colo. L. Rev. 123 (2000).

   For example Professor Pommersheim specifically encourages federal courts scholars to explore the doctrine of exhaustion (discussed by Professor Resnik in response to the *National Farmers* and *Iowa Mutual* cases) and relate the doctrine to the concept of abstention, where federal courts could exercise jurisdiction but choose not to.

Exhaustion and abstention appear similar because they both require federal courts in some circumstances to defer to the courts of another sovereign, whether state or tribal, and stay their hand. This similarity is governed by the shared policy concern of comity and respect. Yet there remains an important shade of difference. Comity in the exhaustion context moves beyond respect to include a specific commitment to support and advance tribal courts. This additional benevolence is at least implicitly required as a matter of federal policy in order to advance the tribal sovereign, which otherwise would not be as sufficiently or constitutionally protected as the state sovereign.

36 Ariz. St. L.J. at 70–71. What does the concept of exhaustion teach us about the federal courts' tolerance or indulgence of tribal courts? What is comity and what role does it play in the relationship between courts?

4. *Hatch Proposal*: Professor Resnik notes that in response to the perception that tribal courts offer an inferior form of justice, Senator Orrin Hatch (R-UT) introduced The Indian Civil Rights Act Amendments of 1988. 134 Cong Rec S 11652 (Aug. 11, 1988). Importantly the proposal did not become law. It was introduced in the Senate, referred to the Judiciary Committee's Subcommittee on the Constitution, and no further action was taken during the 100th Congress. It was introduced again by Senator Hatch during the 101st Congress, but the legislation gained only one co-sponsor (Senator Pressler R-SD) and no further action was taken. How would Indian law be different had it been enacted? What would the law have done to the balance between federal and tribal courts?

Professor Resnik is not the only noted Indian law scholar to write about Senator Hatch's proposal. Professor Williams (author of the article presented in Chapter 2) has also taken up a pointed criticism, noting that the rhetoric deployed to support the proposal uses a variety of strategies that attempt to treat all Indians as an identikit, constructing a problem from a small number of isolated examples to justify federal intervention.

While Senator Hatch's discourse suggests strong reliance on strategies of difference and assigning negative values to difference to support his proposal to constrain the exercise of tribal sovereignty by tribal courts, what is more alarming is the Senator's totalizing approach in advocating a remedy for "systemic" and "institutional" Indian Civil Rights Act problems. Senator Hatch acknowledged at several points in his introductory remarks that the "problems" with enforcement of the ICRA which motivated him to submit his bill were limited to only "some tribes," and were "not necessarily occurring in all or even a majority of the tribal governments." His bill, however, would extend federal court review of tribal court ICRA decisions to all tribes. Hatch claimed that the isolated "problems" and abuses of tribal enforcement of the ICRA were so "serious" in his opinion that generalized federal court review of all tribal court ICRA-related decisions was mandated.

Robert A. Williams, Jr., *Documents of Barbarism: The Contemporary Legacy of European Racism and Colonialism in the Narrative Traditions of Federal Indian Law*, 31 Ariz L Rev 237, 273 (1989). Do you find Professor Williams' observations compelling? What is the problem with making a law for all Indian tribes based upon the behavior of only a few? What insights do proposals like The Indian Civil Rights Act Amendments of 1988 provide to instruct how the federal government perceives tribal courts?

5. *Habeas Corpus and the ICRA*: While the Supreme Court has not taken another case interpreting the habeas corpus remedy in the Indian Civil Rights Act, the lower federal courts have been regularly asked to overturn tribal court judgments. The United Auburn Indian Community has an ordinance that prohibits any member from defaming the reputation of the tribe, its officials, or its employees. Jessica Tavares, and a small group of other tribal members, disagreed with the internal governance of the tribe and circulated press releases detailing their complaints to local media. In response to the press releases, the Tribal Council voted to terminate the members' per capita benefits and banish the members from the reservation for a term of years. A tribal Appeals Board upheld the sanction, and the tribal members applied to the federal court for relief – alleging violations of their right to free speech and due process. A divided panel of the Ninth Circuit concluded that federal courts did not have authority to hear the appeal:

> A temporary exclusion is not tantamount to a detention. And recognizing the temporary exclusion orders at issue here as beyond the scope of "detention" under the ICRA bolsters tribes' sovereign authority to determine the makeup of their communities and best preserves the rule that federal courts should not entangle themselves in such disputes. *** The petitioners raise free speech and due process claims that implicate the substantive protections Congress saw fit to grant Indians with respect to their tribes through the ICRA. *** But the petitioners' remedy is with the Tribe, not in the federal courts.

Tavares v. Whitehouse, 851 F.3d 863 (9th Cir. 2017). How does *Tavares* extend the Supreme Court's holding in *Santa Clara*? What does it say about federal courts that they are willing to refuse to read into ICRA an implied remedy to address alleged violations of free speech, equal protection, or due process? How do these opinions build tribal sovereignty?

6. *Federal Courts Are Not Tribal Appellate Courts*: In *Eagleman v. Rocky Boy Chippewa-Cree Tribal Bus. Comm. or Council*, 699 Fed. Appx. 599 (9th Cir. 2017) three tribal members originally filed common law claims in tribal court against the tribal housing authority. The tribal court dismissed the claims on the basis of sovereign immunity. The plaintiffs then filed suit in federal court seeking a declaratory judgment that the tribal court erred in dismissing their claims. The Ninth Circuit affirmed the dismissal of plaintiff's petition. The Ninth Circuit went on to discuss the relationship between courts in the United States:

> The Eaglemans essentially ask the district court to sit as a general appellate body to review the decision of the tribal court. This miscomprehends the relationship between the federal government and Indian tribes. Tribal courts are not vertically aligned under the federal judicial hierarchy. They are institutions within coordinate sovereign entities vested with the power to regulate internal tribal affairs. Asserting jurisdiction here would effectively expand this court's authority to superintend matters of tribal self-governance. And because we lack general appellate power over the tribal court, we would be unable to afford effective relief to the Eaglemans even if we determined that the tribal court erred.

The Ninth Circuit's summary is a concise description of the interaction between federal and tribal courts. Should federal courts be able to hear appeals from parties who claim that tribal courts have come to the wrong decision? What does the Ninth Circuit mean when it says that tribal courts are not vertically aligned under federal courts? What is the relationship between federal and tribal courts? For a discussion of other times federal courts have refused to sit as tribal appellate courts *see* Grant Christensen, *A View from American Courts: The Year in Indian Law 2017*, 41 Seattle U.L. Rev. 805 (2018).

7. *Beyond the Law*: The issues raised by *Santa Clara* have resounded well beyond the legal context. As Professor Resnik indicates in her discussion of the case, the "ambivalence about women's rights" may have played a role in the decision which ultimately protected tribal cultural practices over gender equality. Noted feminist scholar Catherine MacKinnon has dedicated a chapter in her book *Feminism Unmodified: Discourses on Life and Law* (Harvard University Press 1987) to a critique of the *Santa Clara* decision:

> I want to suggest that cultural survival is as contingent upon equality between women and men as it is upon equality among people. The sex division in this case undermined the ability of Native Americans to survive as autonomous cultures. *** the tribe was willing to

sacrifice *her tribal connection,* her full membership in the tribal community, in the face of a white male supremacist threat.

Ruth Swentzell, a Santa Clara woman married to a nonmember, defends the decision of the Supreme Court because it preserves tribal sovereignty. She writes powerfully about the origins of the tribe's membership ordinance and about the tribe's history.

> In summary, as our myths, stories, and songs tell us, there are tensions and struggles in life. Our traditional beliefs tell us that we are all relations, that we are all children of the community, which is part of the universe, which daily harmonizes opposites. It also tells us that it is an inclusive, not exclusive, world that we share and cooperation, not competition, is ideal behavior. That world also knows that "things come around" – that things will change.

Testimony of a Santa Clara Woman, 14 Kan. J.L. & Pub. Pol'y 97, 101 (2004). Are you persuaded by either side? If forced to pick between protection of culture or gender, which do you find more important?

FURTHER READING

- Bethany R. Berger, *Indian Policy and the Imagined Indian Woman,* 14 Kan. J.L. & Pub. Pol'y 103 (2004).
- Naomi Cahn, *Family Law, Federalism, and the Federal Courts,* 79 Iowa L. Rev. 1073 (1994).
- Matthew L. M. Fletcher, *Resisting Federal Courts on Tribal Jurisdiction,* 81 U. Colo. L. Rev. 973 (2010).
- Matthew L. M. Fletcher, *The Supreme Court's Indian Problem,* 59 Hastings L.J. 579 (2008).
- Kevin Gover & Robert Laurence, *Avoiding* Santa Clara Pueblo v. Martinez: *The Litigation in Federal Court of Civil Actions under the Indian Civil Rights Act,* 8 Hamline L. Rev. 497 (1985).
- B.J. Jones, *Welcoming Tribal Courts into the Judicial Fraternity: Emerging Issues in Tribal–State and Tribal–Federal Court Relations,* 24 Wm. Mitchell L. Rev. 457 (1998).
- Melissa L. Koehn, *Civil Jurisdiction: The Boundaries between Federal and Tribal Courts,* 29 Ariz. St. L.J. 705 (1997).
- Robert Laurence, *A Quincentennial Essay on* Martinez v. Santa Clara Pueblo, 28 Idaho L. Rev. 307 (1992).
- Sanford Levinson, *On Political Boundary Lines, Multiculturalism, and the Liberal State,* 72 Ind. L.J. 403 (1997).
- Gary Lawson, *Territorial Governments and the Limits of Formalism,* 78 Calif. L. Rev. 853 (1990).
- Judith V. Royster, *Stature and Scrutiny: Post-Exhaustion Review of Tribal Court Decisions,* 46 Kan. L. Rev. 241 (1998).
- Gloria Valencia-Weber, Santa Clara Pueblo v. Martinez: *Twenty-Five Years of Disparate Cultural Visions: An Essay Introducing the Case for Re-argument before the American Indian Nations Supreme Court,* 14 Kan. J.L. & Pub. Pol'y 49 (2004).

14

There Is No Federal Supremacy Clause for Indian Tribes

Robert N. Clinton

34 Ariz. St. L.J. 113 (2002)

The United States Constitution contemplates a federal government of limited powers, reserving to the states those powers not explicitly delegated to one branch of the federal government. By ratifying the Constitution the states explicitly agreed to cede those limited powers in order to solemnify a larger union. In this way the Constitution is a compact between sovereigns, apportioning power in a manner designed by the nation's forefathers and articulated in its founding document. Indian tribes are sovereign governments but they are not given a place in this didactic compact between the federal government and the states. At the same time, while tribes exist within a state and within the United States they are not perfectly a part of either. Since the nineteenth century Congress has assumed virtually unlimited (i.e. plenary) powers in the area of Indian affairs, and the courts have regularly recognized or affirmed that power even though the tribes themselves have never consented to be congressional subjects.

In this foundational contribution to Indian legal scholarship Robert Clinton argues that the long held assumption of plenary power ought to be exposed for the myth that it is. He observes that under the leadership of Chief Justice Rehnquist the Supreme Court developed a federalist bent, acting to regularly restrict the powers of what it saw as an overactive federal government. However, notably absent from this jurisprudential movement was any attempt by the Court to question the origins of congressional plenary power over Indian tribes. Instead the Court assumes that federal laws over Indians bind the practice of tribal governments through the Supremacy Clause. Professor Clinton contends that because Indian tribes are not truly a party to the Constitution, an understanding of the federal government as an agent with limited powers requires a reexamination of the origins of plenary power. He concludes that the Constitution nowhere delegates to Congress the ability to enact laws governing the internal affairs of Indian tribes, and that therefore tribes should not be bound by congressional attempts to limit their inherent powers.

As you read Professor Clinton's piece, observe how the Constitution notably omits delegating to Congress power over Indian tribes. How does a government legitimately claim and exercise power? What does it mean for Congress to assume the right to legislate for Indian people absent an express authorization or delegation of that power in the Constitution? What role does the Supremacy Clause play? Pay attention to how the Supreme Court has responded to the assumption of federal power over Indians. Where does the Court claim this power comes from, and is the assumption of this power consistent with the Court's behavior in other areas of the law? What implications might this have for Indian country?

INTRODUCTION

Indians often describe life and the universe as a circle. So it may also be for constitutional law. Once again, American constitutional law is concerned with finding and enforcing limitations on the authority of the federal government to protect another sovereign within the country, the states. After many years of federal judicial deference to Congressional initiatives in adjusting the balance of power between the federal government and the states, the United States Supreme Court has recently become more active in protecting the sovereign prerogatives of the states against federal legislative and judicial intrusion. The Supreme Court has wielded the Interstate Commerce Clause, the Tenth Amendment, the Eleventh Amendment and the general structural arrangements of the United States Constitution as constitutional weapons to support its heightened scrutiny of national initiatives that impinge on state authority.

This essay reflects on the failure of the federal judiciary to employ any similarly probing analysis with respect to the breadth of authority the federal government claims over another sovereign directly referenced in the Commerce Clause – Indian tribes. Specifically, this essay suggests that application of the Supreme Court's historically-based, originalist methodology to those portions of the Constitution dealing with federal power over Indian affairs compels the need to reexamine several basic Indian law doctrines, most notably the so-called federal Indian plenary power doctrine. It also suggests that such scrutiny is consistent with perhaps the most revered principle of the United States Constitution – namely, that all legitimate governmental authority derives from the consent of the people who have chosen to delegate only certain limited powers to the federal government (a theory often called "popular delegation" or "popular sovereignty").

*** This essay challenges the federal government and, most notably, the federal judiciary, to honor American legal traditions by abiding by the nation's own founding principles with respect to the nation's first people. Thus, the essay offers primarily a historically-derived immanent, rather than an external, critique of American constitutional law applied to Indian affairs. It challenges the American legal structure to rethink its colonialist past and to revisit its concern for democracy, local control, consent, and territorial sovereignty in application to the nation's Indian tribes, just as it has recently done in affording greater protections to state sovereignty.

The ultimate conclusion of this essay, nevertheless, is far more provocative in American constitutional terms. It is simply that there is no acceptable, historically-derived, textual constitutional explanation for the exercise of any federal authority over Indian tribes without their consent manifested through treaty. Reduced to its starkest statement, this thesis means that, unlike the legal primacy the federal government enjoys over states by virtue of the Supremacy Clause of the United States, the federal government has no legitimate claim to legal supremacy over

Indian tribes. Consequently, neither Congress nor the federal courts legitimately can unilaterally adopt binding legal principles for the tribes without their consent. This essay also suggests that this constitutional arrangement accurately reflects the founders' original understanding of the United States Constitution. Subsequent late-nineteenth century doctrinal departures from this original understanding resulted from racist, ill-reasoned, constitutionally illegitimate efforts to legally rationalize colonialism in Indian country. This essay suggests that those developments cannot be reconciled with the basic popular delegation principles of American constitutional theory, whatever their legality under international or tribal law.

* * *

I INTRODUCTION: THE ORIGINAL BASELINE UNDERSTANDING OF THE TRIBAL FEDERAL RELATIONSHIP

*** [I]n *Worcester v. Georgia* *** Chief Justice Marshall offered the following accurate description *** to explain the contemporary legal status of Indian tribes:

> Certain it is, that our history furnishes no example, from the first settlement of our country, of any attempt on the part of the crown to interfere with the internal affairs of the Indians, farther than to keep out the agents of foreign powers, who, as traders or otherwise, might seduce them into foreign alliances. The king purchased their lands when they were willing to sell, at a price they were willing to take; but never coerced a surrender of them. He also purchased their alliance and dependence by subsidies; but never intruded into the interior of their affairs, or interfered with their self-government, so far as respected themselves only.

Thus, the hallmark of the early conception of Indian sovereignty was the tribes had the complete right of self-governance over their lands. The tribes relied on federal authority and the federal government could legitimately assert power only with respect to external affairs, i.e., negotiations between the tribes and foreign nations and their protection from foreign invasion. The federal government had not claimed, and the tribes had not conceded, any power to regulate internal tribal affairs without tribal consent. *** [T]he Chief Justice reflected this relationship when he wrote:

> The Cherokee nation, then, is a distinct community occupying its own territory, with boundaries accurately described, in which the laws of Georgia can have no force, and which the citizens of Georgia have no right to enter, but with the assent of the Cherokees themselves, or in conformity with treaties, and with the acts of Congress.

The quoted language reflects not only the lack of power of the State of Georgia over Cherokee lands, but also that of the federal government. Thus, Georgia citizens could only enter Cherokee country either with the assent of the Cherokees themselves, i.e., in conformity with Cherokee law, or pursuant to an act of Congress and, then, only if "in conformity with treaties." Congress could act with reference to Cherokee lands only if confirmed by the consent of the Cherokee Nation through a treaty. Congress possessed no unilateral power under the Indian Commerce Clause or otherwise to legislate for the Indians themselves or for their territory. Exercises of congressional power that directly affected an Indian tribe had to be authorized and confirmed by treaty entered into with the affected tribe. Unilateral federal legislative power was limited to governing nonmembers subject to its authority in their dealings with Indian tribes. Significantly, because power over non-Indian missionaries constituted the basis for the jurisdictional contest in *Worcester*, the case must hold that the Cherokee Nation had complete sovereignty over its territory and that state power over the same territory was accordingly ousted. *Worcester*, therefore, suggests that tribal sovereignty, like federal and state sovereignty, was conceived at the time as territorial and not dependent on the political allegiance of the party involved. ***

II DELEGATION AND CONSENT OF THE GOVERNED: AMERICAN CONSTITUTIONAL FIRST PRINCIPLES ON THE LEGITIMACY OF GOVERNMENTAL POWER

*** The most basic tenet of American constitutional law has long sought to analyze the legitimacy of the exercise of federal governing power by grounding and confining such authority to the scope of the popular delegation contained in the Constitution. For example, in the most classic statement of the test for the constitutionality of legislation, Chief Justice Marshall wrote in the famous case of *McCulloch v. Maryland*, "Let the end be legitimate, let it be within the scope of the constitution, and all means which are appropriate, which are plainly adapted to that end, which are not prohibited, but consist with the letter and spirit of the constitution, are constitutional."

Thus, the touchstone of constitutional exercises of federal power involves confining the exercises of federal power to express and implied grants of authority delegated by the people in the document and not running afoul of any prohibition on the exercise of power contained in the Bill of Rights and elsewhere. American constitutional theory, therefore, is fundamentally grounded upon and enforces the idea of popular delegation of authority. ***

This reminder that the historical and contemporary theory of popular delegation provides the basis for determining the constitutional legitimacy of the exercise of governmental power fully explains the foundation in American constitutional law for the baseline understanding of the limited nature of federal power in Indian affairs. The Indian tribes and their members, unlike the states and their citizens, were not part of the "We the People of the United States" who drafted the United States Constitution. They constituted separate sovereign peoples which federal Indian law would later label domestic dependent nations. They were outside the federal union and owed no allegiance to it other than bi-national alliances created by treaty. The very exclusion of tribal Indians from the census by the "Indians not taxed" clause contained in Article I clearly recognizes that status in the text of the Constitution itself. As such, unlike the states, the citizens of the tribes never delegated any power to the federal government!

Thus, under basic American principles of constitutional authority, the federal government could not directly exercise any authority over the Indian tribes or their members in Indian country, except by their consent through treaty. Indeed, the treaty provisions, *** demonstrate contemporary understanding that federal legislation could not directly reach or act upon Indian tribes without their consent through treaty. Congress had no power to legislate for or upon them directly. Therefore, the grant of power to Congress in the Indian Commerce Clause to regulate commerce with Indian tribes merely constituted a delegation of authority to regulate those persons who were subject to United States authority who entered into Indian country to engage in such commerce. Properly understood in conformity with America's basic principles of governmental legitimacy, the constitutionally delegated power consisted of authority to regulate commerce "with the Indian tribes," not a power to regulate the commerce of the Indian tribes. It was a power to regulate non-Indians who dealt with the tribes and to manage the American side of the bilateral diplomatic, economic, political and social intercourse with tribes. That delegation did not include any power to directly regulate tribal Indians, who, of course, had not delegated authority to the federal government, other than perhaps a claimed power to protect American citizens from harm.

The basic theory of American constitutional law, therefore, not only explains the baseline understanding of power and authority in the tribal federal relationship, it also explains why virtually all federal laws enacted prior to 1885 only applied to non-Indians who dealt with Indians, rather than regulating the Indian tribes directly. Since the Indian tribes were not part of the federal union and their citizens (members) were not part of "We the People of the United States," they had delegated no authority to the federal government other than through treaty. Federal and state powers simply could not be asserted over them directly without the benefit of their agreement through treaty.

***

Since the very text of the Constitution conclusively demonstrates that the people of the United States did not include the Indian tribes or their citizens, the document had no power whatsoever to limit tribal authority or to assure federal supremacy over tribal authority. Based on the first principles of the American constitutional system, Congress, therefore, has no authority to legislate directly for the tribes. Furthermore, nothing in the Constitution or in any legislation can or should be thought to limit tribal authority to simply ignore federal law. The federal government has no greater claim to supremacy for its law over the Indian tribes than it has for the supremacy of its law over Great Britain, Canada, or Mexico! None of those sovereign powers were parties to the American original constitutional compact and none are legally bound by it. Of course, the subsequently-admitted states similarly had no seat at the table when the original constitutional compact was crafted. Unlike the Indian tribes and foreign nations, however, the voluntary requests by the later-admitted states for admission to the Union required them to abide by the United States Constitution, and thereby, to principles of popular delegation of authority and federal supremacy. In short, *** there not only is no legitimate basis for the exercise of direct federal legislative power over Indian tribes, but there also is no federal supremacy clause for Indian tribes!

III PLENARY POWER OVER INDIAN AFFAIRS AND THE RISE OF AMERICAN COLONIALISM

Colonialism can be conveniently defined as the assertion of political sovereignty or other authority over a separate people, often of a different race, without their consent. So defined, it is clear that colonialism is centrally at odds with America's first principles. If all legitimate governing authority derives from the consent of the governed through constitutional delegation, then the assertion of political hegemony over another people without their consent does not constitute a legitimate exercise of governing authority. Of course, such colonialism is also diametrically opposed to the now internationally-recognized right of the colonized people to self-determination. The decolonization movement of the post–World War II era, which finally has enforced for some peoples that right of self-determination, has had profound implications for redrawing of boundaries and spheres of legitimate governing power everywhere in the world except the Americas, where perhaps the first wave of mass European colonialism occurred. ***

B *The Emergence of an Activist Judicial Indian Plenary Power Doctrine from a Judicially Conservative Court*

*** The growth of judicial federal plenary power began with the United States Supreme Court decision in *Oliphant v. Suquamish Indian Tribe*, in which the Court held that Indian tribes lacked inherent criminal jurisdiction over non-Indians. The opinion of the Court, authored by then Justice Rehnquist, engaged in an inventive process of judicial historical revisionism to suggest that Indian tribes were never understood to exercise criminal jurisdiction over non-Indians. Since most tribal justice systems of the nineteenth century were informal and restorative, rather than punitive, the Court not surprisingly found few examples of Indian tribes actually punishing whites after trial during the period. Nevertheless, to solidify its historical point, the Court was forced to marginalize early treaties that expressly provided that Indian tribes could punish illegal white settlers. ***

More important than the revisionist nature of the history in the *Oliphant* opinion was its rationale. While the opinion contains references to the lack of non-Indians on the Suquamish juries and adverts to a claimed lack of civil liberties protections despite enactment of the Indian Civil Rights Act of 1968, at core the rationale of the opinion rests on the notion that tribal exercise of criminal jurisdiction over non-Indians is "inconsistent with their [dependent] status." Thus, the exercise of judicial plenary power picks up where legislative plenary power left off, with the Court applying a wardship theory to determine limits on tribal sovereignty, limits created by their supposed dependency. As part of the claimed limitations on tribal power, later cases explained *Oliphant* on the grounds that tribal powers of self-government were merely internal and did not include external powers, by which they meant that tribes could govern their members but not others. *** Suddenly Indian tribal sovereignty no longer meant what sovereignty means in other Euro-American contexts – governing authority over all persons and property within the exterior borders of the sovereign government. For Indians, and Indians alone, their right of self-government had come to mean their power to govern themselves, but no one else, within their territory. Instead of focusing on the sovereign governing portion of the term "self-government," the Court chose to focus on the idea of self. *** Thus, the Court suggested that the federal government, rather than the tribe, exercised criminal jurisdiction over non-Indians for crimes occurring in Indian country against the person or property of Indians.

The *Oliphant* reshaping of the baseline understanding of tribal authority was significantly assisted by the grant of jurisdiction contained in the Indian Civil Rights Act of 1968, authorizing the federal courts to hear habeas corpus petitions for those held in tribal detention in violation of federal law. While ostensibly designed to permit the enforcement of the criminal procedure guarantees contained in the Indian Civil Rights Act, it was employed in *Oliphant* and later cases to attack the existence of tribal jurisdiction, rather than the manner of its exercise, as originally contemplated. No similar grant of jurisdiction expressly authorizes federal courts to review the regulatory or taxing authority of tribal councils or the civil adjudicatory jurisdiction of tribal courts. Nevertheless, in the exercise of judicial Indian plenary power, the federal courts undertook to adjudicate the limitations on tribal power in these areas, employing general grants of federal question jurisdiction. In these cases, the tribes were often complicit with this effort since they frequently initiated litigation in federal courts, rather than tribal courts, to establish their jurisdiction or to limit state authority over Indian country.

***

Obviously, in a post-*Brown v. Board of Education* world, some non-racial explanation of this effort was necessary in order to mask the overt racism and colonialism involved in the Court's most recent foray into the world of Indian wardship, dependency and plenary power. *Duro v. Reina* supplied that rationale. In this case, the Court returned to the theme of the reach of a tribe's inherent criminal jurisdiction, this time in a case involving criminal prosecution of an Indian who was an enrolled member of a tribe other than the one where the crime occurred. Since *Oliphant* had held that Indian tribes lacked criminal jurisdiction over non-Indians, if the Court sustained tribal jurisdiction in *Duro*, it clearly would draw a racial line for criminal jurisdiction between Indian and non-Indian nonmembers of the Tribe. Yet, the *Oliphant* determination of whether the exercise of a tribal power was inconsistent with its dependent status theoretically had been based on a historical inquiry to determine whether Indian tribes traditionally exercised such jurisdiction. * * *

Justice Kennedy's opinion for the Court clearly jettisoned the historic constitutionally recognized roots of the tribal federal relationship, by suggesting "[w]hatever might be said of the historical record, we must view it in light of petitioner's status as a citizen of the United States." Thus, according to the *Duro* opinion, Indians, like other citizens, can look to the federal government to find protection against unwarranted intrusions on their personal liberty. Finding that criminal punishment involving the deprivation of personal liberty was so serious a punishment, the Court suggested, relying solely on *Oliphant* and without any historical support, that "its exercise over non-Indian citizens was a power necessarily surrendered by the tribes in their submission to the overriding sovereignty of the United States." Yet for the Salt River Maricopa Community involved in *Duro*, the Court did not and could not cite any treaty the tribe ever entered into by which it submitted to any overriding sovereignty of the United States. Thus, the theory of *Duro* totally ignored *Crow Dog* and *Worcester*, both of which specifically held that treaty guarantees of protection were not relinquishments of sovereignty or jurisdiction, but instead, federal guarantees of protection of that sovereignty. More important was the Court's finding of "a submission to the overriding sovereignty of the United States" even where there was no treaty whatsoever expressing any tribal intent to submit. The alleged submission was nothing more than a renewed statement of colonial dominance imposed without tribal consent. It was a judicially-constructed wardship theory not grounded in any historical facts surrounding the dealings between the Salt River Maricopa Community and the federal government.

The penultimate theoretical paragraph of *Duro* clearly states a new, radically different, and highly limited paradigm for tribal powers of self-government. Justice Kennedy wrote:

> As full citizens, Indians share in the territorial and political sovereignty of the United States. The retained sovereignty of the tribe is but a recognition of certain additional authority the tribes maintain over Indians who consent to be tribal members. Indians like all other citizens share allegiance to the overriding sovereign, the United States. A tribe's additional authority comes from the consent of its members, and so in the criminal sphere membership marks the bounds of tribal authority.

Indian tribal sovereignty, therefore, was no longer conceptualized by the Court as complete territorial sovereignty for which some tribes had carefully negotiated in prior treaties. Rather, the federal and state government shared the territorial sovereignty, and tribes simply had certain "additional authority" derived from consent of their members. Since non-Indians and nonmembers had not consented to tribal criminal jurisdiction, there was none. Ironically, as this essay notes, given the stress the *Duro* opinion placed on the fundamental constitutional principles of consent and delegation of power, it never stopped to analyze the central question posed by this issue – whether tribes ever consented to any exercise of paramount overriding federal power over themselves and their land. As this essay suggests, the consent rationale works both ways.

*** By common law development [the Supreme Court] has charted its own Indian policy and formulated its own conception of tribal sovereignty which is far narrower than anything the tribes negotiated for or were guaranteed in their treaties and narrower, even, than the Congressional policies reflected in modern statutes. Indeed, Congress reacted quickly to *Duro* by overturning its result by statute. Nevertheless, the consent paradigm adopted by *Duro* as the touchstone of tribal sovereignty remains and continues to pervade the federal cases in the area. Thus, today federal courts are actively invoking the notion that the federal common law conception of tribal sovereignty comes from the "overriding sovereign," as *Duro* put it, and have actively sought to limit the exercise of tribal power on numerous fronts.

***

In *Nevada v. Hicks* the United States Supreme Court brought the exercise of judicial plenary power to its ultimate conclusion, all but overruling the baseline understanding of the tribal federal relationship[.] *** The precise question involved in *Hicks* was whether the Fallon Paiute-Shoshone Tribal Court could entertain both a tort action and an action under 42 U.S.C. § 1983 brought against state conservation officials who had damaged the personal property of a tribal member on Indian-owned land within the Reservation while executing state search warrants for an alleged off-reservation crime pursuant to supplemental warrants issued by the tribal court. Consistent with the trend of its judicial plenary power decisions, the Supreme Court unanimously ruled that the tribal court lacked any jurisdiction to enforce either tribal or federal legal standards against the state conservations officials despite the fact that (1) the injured party was a tribal member, (2) the event took place on Indian-owned land within the reservation and (3) the state conservation officials' power over tribal members on-reservation initially had been thought by all parties involved in the case (other than the United States Supreme Court) to derive solely from warrants issued by the tribal court.

Despite the fact that *Montana* and every case that applied its tests until *Hicks* had involved tribal governance over non-Indian owned lands within Indian country, the Court in *Hicks*, *** announced by sheer judicial fiat that the *Montana* exceptions henceforth would constitute the test for determining tribal authority over nonmembers anywhere within Indian country, i.e., on Indian, as well as non-Indian, owned land. The nature of the land ownership within a reservation simply became, according to the *Hicks* opinion, a factor for a court to weigh in applying the *Montana* tests, rather, than a determinative question governing which test to apply, as it had operated in all prior cases under the judicial plenary power doctrine. ***

Justice Scalia's opinion for the Court in *Hicks* went to great lengths to explain why the Nevada conservation officials' invocation of tribal authority was simply unnecessary. In the process, the Court, over some objection from concurring justices, converted a case about tribal court jurisdiction into a case about state power and, in dicta, purported to greatly enlarge the scope of state authority over tribal Indians on-reservation at the expense of tribal authority. Specifically, Justice Scalia's opinion suggested that the state had inherent authority to enforce its search warrant against a tribal member on-reservation for an off-reservation crime over which it otherwise had subject matter jurisdiction. Contrary to the baseline understanding of the tribal federal relationship and the historical intent of the Indian Commerce Clause, Justice Scalia plainly assumed that states had jurisdiction everywhere within a state, including Indian reservations, except where expressly preempted by federal law. Totally ignoring the express requirements for tribal extradition which were contained in many Indian treaties that assumed complete tribal territorial control over their Reservations, even where off-reservation crimes are concerned, Justice Scalia wrote, "[T]he States' inherent jurisdiction on reservations can of course be stripped by Congress. But with regard to the jurisdiction at issue here that has not occurred."

The contrast between *Worcester* and *Hicks* could not be more stark. In *Worcester*, the criminal defendant charged by the state was non-Indian and the Court, nevertheless, sustained the exclusive territorial jurisdiction of the Cherokee Nation over the matter. Federal law therefore preempted all exercise of state power over Cherokee lands in order to protect the territorial sovereignty of the Cherokee Nation. By contrast, in *Hicks*, the Court assumed complete state jurisdiction over the reservation except where expressly preempted by federal law. In *Hicks*, the non-Indian state conservation officials, consistent with *Worcester*, had actually invoked the power the of the Fallon tribal court to support execution of their state search warrant. The Supreme Court, nevertheless, rejected the existence of any tribal jurisdiction over the matter. Far from the complete tribal territorial jurisdiction guaranteed by the original baseline understanding of the tribal federal relationship reflected in *Worcester*, Justice Scalia's opinion in *Hicks* suggested that tribal authority could only be sustained over nonmembers in Indian country where "'necessary to protect tribal self-government or to control internal relations,' [or where] such regulatory jurisdiction has been congressionally conferred." In short, state sovereignty and authority, even in Indian country, constituted an unquestioned norm, while tribal sovereignty and jurisdiction, previously guaranteed by treaty and the baseline understanding of the tribal federal relationship, now existed, according to Justice Scalia, at the sufferance and whim of the Supreme Court. Justice Scalia was not oblivious to the stark contrast between his ruling and that of Chief Justice Marshall, since he sought to limit the *Worcester* decision virtually to its facts, if not overrule it altogether. Thus, Justice Scalia wrote:

> Our cases make clear that the Indians' right to make their own laws and be governed by them does not exclude all state regulatory authority on the reservation. State sovereignty does not end at a reservation's border. Though tribes are often referred to as "sovereign" entities, it was "long ago" that "the Court departed from Chief Justice Marshall's view that 'the laws of [a State] can have no force' within reservation boundaries. *Worcester v. Georgia*, 6 Pet. 515 (1832) ... "Ordinarily," it is now clear, "an Indian reservation is considered part of the territory of the State."

*** *Hicks* therefore brought the exercise of federal judicial plenary power to its ultimate conclusion. In *Hicks*, the Supreme Court accepted, albeit in dicta, the precise argument that it rejected in *Worcester*, i.e., that states have some ill-defined inherent authority over matters affecting tribal Indians in Indian country. ***

IV FEDERAL SUPREMACY DOES NOT APPLY TO INDIAN TRIBES

Today, Indian tribes face a problem they have not previously confronted – whether to honor federally developed Indian law. At first glance, the problem may appear simple, but it involves a far more complex set of choices than may be apparent. Most tribes made no agreement expressly giving up their sovereignty and some even negotiated for and received express treaty promises of complete territorial jurisdiction over their reservations. While such guarantees were explicit in some treaties, implicit in all creation of Indian country, at least until recently, was the assumption created by the baseline understanding of the tribal federal relationship – that Indian reservations or other areas of Indian country were set aside for exclusive governance by the Indian tribes governing the areas. The Indian tribes still recognize those promises and the original understanding of the tribal federal relationship. Since there is no easy way for the tribes to seek rescission and get their ceded lands back as a result of federal breaches of treaty promises, the tribes insist that Congress and the federal courts honor the original bargain. Indeed, many tribal codes contain jurisdictional provisions that continue to assert such complete territorial jurisdiction over their reservation. ***

The growing gap between the Indian territorially-based conception of tribal sovereignty and federal courts' efforts to curtail the scope of tribal authority creates a clear legal dissonance for most Indian tribes. The problem which results both from federal statutes enacted under the Indian plenary power doctrine and from federal common law limitations on tribal sovereignty imposed by the federal judiciary is whether the tribe should adhere to its own conception of its authority, often guaranteed by treaty and certainly reinforced by the original understanding of the tribal federal relationship, or whether it should bend to and follow the allegedly paramount and overriding power of the federal government in Indian affairs. Not surprisingly, these questions often arise in tribal courts. Careful analysis of the themes in this paper and of the doctrines of stare decisis suggest that the tribes and the tribal courts should continue to adhere to their own conceptions of their sovereignty and should simply ignore contrary federal statutes and judicial decisions.

Tribal courts, like federal and state courts, can consider the constitutionality of legislation brought to the court for enforcement. That power of judicial review includes not only tribal laws, but also federal laws. Thus, the constitutionality of federal statutes enacted under the guise of the federal plenary power doctrine constitutes a question open for tribal court decision, although almost no tribal decisions have actually challenged the constitutionality of federal legislation. Given this fact, it is surprising that parties rarely challenge the constitutionality of federal statutes based upon the colonialist federal Indian plenary power doctrine in either tribal or federal court. At least when challenged in tribal court, such statutes can and should be subjected to searching scrutiny.

Such careful scrutiny reveals the intellectual bankruptcy of the federal Indian plenary power doctrine. *** Applying conventional constitutional analyses derived from notions of delegated power, the Indian plenary power doctrine *** has no basis whatsoever in American constitutional law. It was not grounded in any traditional conception of enumerated, delegated federal authority.

*** [T]ribal and federal courts can and should reconsider the scope of Indian affairs powers of Congress in light of the limited delegation of such authority contained in the Indian Commerce Clause. Given popular sovereignty notions, the delegated governing could only include federal power over those then subject to authority of the United States, i.e., the non-Indian side of Indian commerce. Explication of the historic baseline tribal federal relationship reflected in the federal treaties, the history of the Indian Commerce Clause, and the very limited Congressional understanding and implementation of federal authority in Indian affairs for the first century of the nation's existence, all explain why the Indian Commerce Clause does not grant Congress plenary power over Indian affairs. Indeed, the Indian Commerce Clause originally was not intended to grant Congress any power to regulate Indian tribes or their members who were not founding members of the American union and were not even citizens of the United States. The federal power delegated to Congress in the Indian Commerce Clause was the power to regulate non-Indians subject to the authority of the United States who dealt with tribes and the exclusive power of the United States, rather than the states, to manage diplomatic and economic relations with Indian nations. The Indian tribes were simply separate nations existing geographically within the United States[.] *** Indian tribal courts, therefore, can and should reject the federal Indian plenary power doctrine in favor of the original understanding of the baseline tribal federal relationship, often guaranteed in a treaty creating the tribal reservation.

The problem, of course, is that current federal judicial precedents claim a far broader power for Congress under the guise of the Indian plenary power doctrine. *** This essay certainly suggests that such a reexamination is long overdue and would lead to the conclusion that the claims of plenary federal power in Indian affairs are just as much relics of America's racial past as the contemporaneously developed doctrine of "separate but equal." Furthermore, the worldwide revulsion at western colonialism and the post–World War II decolonization movement also suggest that reconsideration of the plenary power doctrine derived from wardship is long overdue. Such a reconsideration should lead to the realization that Congress possesses only very limited power under the Indian Commerce Clause to regulate non-Indians who deal with Indian tribes and their members and to manage the United States' relations with Indian tribes. If the federal courts will not undertake such a reexamination, the tribal courts should!

Consistent with the original American constitutional tradition, the federal government can secure power to directly regulate Indian tribes or their members only through exercise of the treaty power. Because of doctrines of stare decisis, lower federal courts may not be at liberty to engage in such a reappraisal until the Supreme Court signals the non-controlling nature of the Indian wardship cases that produced the federal Indian plenary power doctrine. That observation, however, does not mean that tribal courts may not engage in such a reappraisal. But are tribal courts, or Indian tribes, bound by United States Supreme Court decisions on the scope of their jurisdiction (exercises of judicial Indian plenary power) or by the plenary nature of the power of Congress to curtail and limit their sovereignty?

Since Indian tribes are sovereign, they have the power to adopt any approach to precedent and stare decisis they desire. Nevertheless, since most tribes today, outside of Alaska and a few southwestern tribes, have some variant of a western style tribal court, almost all tribal courts of record more or less follow American legal traditions with respect to the binding effect and use of precedent. Under those traditions, a court is technically bound only by the holdings of the same court or a court with authority to review its decisions. Presently, no Act of Congress authorizes the United States Supreme Court or any federal court to review tribal decisions. Indeed, given the limited nature of Indian commerce power argued for in this essay, perhaps any federal statute extending such review should be subject to serious constitutional challenge. Whatever the constitutionality of extension of such federal review powers, at present, the simple fact is that none exists. As a consequence, the tribal appellate courts are truly courts of last resort, with no possibility of a direct appeal to the United States Supreme Court or any other federal or state court. As such, they technically are bound only by their own precedents and the Indian tribes are not technically bound as a matter of stare decisis by decisions of the Supreme Court or lower federal courts purporting to curtail their jurisdiction or sustaining the constitutionality of federal statutes that attempt to regulate Indian tribes or purport to curtail their sovereignty.

Certainly, under the doctrine of stare decisis, decisions of the Supreme Court and other lower federal courts may have persuasive effect if their reasoning withstands close analysis. The message of this essay, of course, is that the inconsistency of these cases with the basic norms of American constitutional thought, their inconsistency with the original understanding of the Indian Commerce Clause, their tendency to undermine and invert the original baseline understanding of the tribal federal relationship, and the tainted roots of the wardship notion based on notions of racial superiority of late-nineteenth century colonialism, all significantly undermine, and indeed, totally destroy, the persuasive force of these decisions. *** They have no basis whatsoever in the American constitutional tradition of consent or limited delegated federal powers. Thus, Indian tribal courts can, and perhaps should, decline to follow both the federal judicial plenary power cases and other federal cases purporting to limit tribal authority and sustaining the application of broad federal statutes to Indian tribes.

* * *

An important cautionary practical note, however, must be added to this conclusion.[458] This essay is intended to explore the important constitutional theory surrounding the tribal federal relationship. It is not offered as a prescription for future tribal governmental behavior. Even if American constitutional law cannot offer any satisfactory constitutional theory binding Indian tribes to unilaterally adopt federal law or judicial decisions limiting tribal authority, ignoring such decisions can have significant adverse costs for tribes. First, whatever the original constitutional theory, Indian tribes over time have in fact become enmeshed with and often financially dependent on the federal government, often in ways not unlike the states. Just as the states can resist perceived federal governmental overreaching, as they recently have done, but are in no financial or other position to simply ignore or flaunt the federal government, likewise Indian tribes, which often are substantially more dependent on the federal government for social service program funding or the protection of their lands, cannot now and never have been able to simply ignore the policy of the federal government in Indian affairs. Failure to recognize and often cooperate with federal policy objectives can easily lead to loss of important federal economic,

---

[458] After hearing a necessarily abbreviated oral presentation of portions of this article, Philip S. Deloria, the Director of the American Indian Law Center, Inc., rightly cautioned the author that if tribal leaders irresponsibly flaunt federal law in response to the author's legal theories, it could make life far worse for many Indian communities, whose socioeconomic data already places them at the bottom of most material and health measures of American society. These perceptive comments suggest that, whatever the original constitutional theory of federal power with respect to Indian tribes and irrespective of the nature of the relationship developed when treaties were negotiated, the model of the tribal federal relations in fact has been a historically evolutionary one in which Indian tribes increasingly have become enmeshed with, controlled by, and economically dependent upon the federal government. Whatever its theoretical constitutional legitimacy, that practical reality clearly suggests that tribal leaders and tribal judges must be extremely cautious in exercising the powers they legitimately can claim.***

logistical, and political support for tribal governments. Since federal law often constitutes the major bulwark against Indian country being overrun by aggrandizing efforts by the states to increase their political hegemony over Indian peoples, the loss of federal support very well could make tribal governance a practical impossibility, whatever its legal legitimacy.

Second, while not technically binding on tribal courts, the decisions of the Supreme Court in the area of Indian law certainly constitute precedents that must be considered for their persuasive analytical force. Tribal courts that simply ignore federal law or Supreme Court precedents clearly will be seen by other courts in the federal system as acting illegally. Since such courts often need to cooperate on the enforcement of judicial decrees, criminal extradition, the execution of search warrants, cross-deputization arrangements and the like, tribal courts and judges cannot afford the reputation of becoming judicial "loose canons." No sovereign is an island. All are interdependent. Tribal governments, leaders and judges must exercise tribal sovereignty responsibly in ways that both foster the social, economic, and political welfare of tribal members and facilitate the intergovernmental cooperation on which tribal well-being often depends.

***

VI POLISHING THE CHAIN OF FRIENDSHIP BY RECONSIDERING THE LEGAL LEGACY OF AMERICAN COLONIALISM

Just as America could not redress its racist legacy of slavery without directly addressing and overturning the late-nineteenth century doctrine of "separate but equal" announced in *Plessy v. Ferguson,* so the nation really cannot redress its racist history of colonialism in Indian country without confronting the Indian plenary power doctrine announced by the same court a decade before *Plessy* and defended on similarly racist grounds. *** Whatever the reason for the failure of the nation to address its racist legacy of colonialism in Indian country, the nation should no longer pretend to legitimate its exercise of authority over Indian tribes by asserting Indian plenary power, a doctrine that has no basis whatsoever in any textual delegation of constitutional power and whose roots are deeply stained with late-nineteenth century racism. Only by limiting the exercise of federal power to the original scope under the Indian Commerce Clause and by abandoning the racially-motivated colonial pretense of federal plenary power dominance of Indian tribes can the nation rebuild any respectability or legitimacy, with Indians and the rest of the world, for its practices in Indian country. That effort certainly would begin to brighten and renew the chain of friendship that long ago bound Indian tribes in alliance to the United States and, indeed, significantly contributed to the founding of the nation during the American Revolution.

More importantly, it is worth considering what abandonment of the Indian plenary power doctrine would mean. First, and foremost, it would mean that unilateral exercises of federal legislative power would be limited to textual sources of delegation – the Indian Commerce Clause and treaty powers. For purposes of the Indian Commerce Clause the nation must engage in the painful reexamination of the limited power implicit in that clause. *** Under the Interstate Commerce Clause, *** Congress can only enact statutes that directly regulate interstate commerce, protect and secure the channels and instrumentalities of interstate commerce, or regulate other economic transactions that have a substantial effect on commerce. The ostensible reason offered for rigorous judicial enforcement of such limitations is to protect state sovereignty otherwise recognized in the Constitution and to assure that exercises of federal authority do not unduly intrude on legitimate realms for state regulation. Applying a similar approach to the Indian Commerce Clause suggests that this clause grants Congress no power whatsoever to regulate Indian tribes or their members and that the exercise of congressional Indian commerce authority is limited to nonmembers subject to federal authority who deal with tribes and to the management of federal relations with the tribes. *** The power granted under the Indian Commerce Clause was a power to regulate the non-Indian side of the tribal federal relationship, not a power to regulate the Indians themselves. It was a power to regulate commerce with the tribes, not the commerce of the tribes. Congress could only regulate those who legitimately were subject to the authority of the United States, which did not include tribal Indians. ***

Second, abandonment of the Indian plenary power doctrine would require the federal government to abandon the pretense of having a dominant colonial authority in Indian country. Relinquishing the claim to the overriding supremacy of federal law over tribal authority in Indian country would follow as a necessary result. Absent such overriding federal colonial power, the federal government could claim no authority to unilaterally abrogate Indian treaties in a fashion that enlarges federal power over Indians. ***

Third, to the extent that the federal government desires to assure application of federal laws to Indians tribes, abandonment of the Indian plenary power doctrine would require the federal government to formally negotiate with the Indian tribes and obtain their consent, as it did by treaty when the Constitution was drafted and throughout the treaty period. Thus, for Indian tribes, the missing Constitutional component for the legitimate exercise of federal power is supplied through treaty or, if constitutional, treaty-substitutes, such as the agreements negotiated with Indian tribes after treaty-making ended. *** Thus, abandonment of the Indian plenary power doctrine requires a return to the mutual intergovernmental respect that was part of the original tribal federal relationship reflected in the treaty process, i.e., a model of treaty federalism. Consequently, if the 1871 statute ending Indian-treaty making is constitutional at all, it must be repealed if the United States actually desires to assure application of its laws to Indian tribes.

While some might regard the process of securing individual tribal consent for the application of federal law as onerous, inconvenient or impossible, a few observations about its feasibility are in order. Historically, the federal government long employed monetary incentives in the form of federal program services and annuities to secure tribal consent in treaties, just as it uses foreign assistance and offers trade incentives and benefits to encourage appropriate behavior from foreign nations. Given the heavy reliance of many tribes on federal program funds, such incentives would produce significant leverage to encourage cooperation with federal policies or goals, just as Congress today still can employ program-relevant conditions on federal spending measures to encourage appropriate cooperation from sovereign states, even in areas over which it may have no direct regulatory power. In this respect, federal negotiation of treaty-like agreements with tribes to implement federal programs might resemble the spending-power based deals increasingly imposed on states. In both cases, the sovereign impacted by federal policy initiatives could avoid application or enforcement of the federal rule within its jurisdiction by refusing participation in the federal program, albeit not without the cost of some lost federal program funds.

Additionally, during the treaty-making period, the federal government actually negotiated some treaties under which the contracting tribal party agreed to accept the supremacy of federal law. Such negotiations therefore are not impossible. For example, the guarantees of exclusive jurisdiction over their new land made to the Choctaw Nation contained in the Treaty of Dancing Rabbit Creek (1830) expressly provided that:

> The US shall forever secure said Choctaw Nation from, and against, all laws except such as from time to time may be enacted in their own National Councils, not inconsistent with the Constitution, Treaties, and Laws of the United States; and except such as may, and which have been enacted by Congress, to the extent that Congress under the Constitution are required to exercise a legislation over Indian Affairs.

*** Some have proposed that the historic lack of federal power over Indian tribes might be cured by a constitutional amendment that clearly spells out the place of Indian tribes in the federal union. While that process might, perhaps, be preferable to incremental and inconsistent adjudication of such questions in federal courts, it fails to supply the essential constitutional element currently lacking in all claims to federal Indian plenary power – tribal consent and delegation of authority to the federal government. Since amendments are proposed by Congress, where the Indian tribes have no structural protections and virtually no effective representation, and are ratified by the states, not the tribes, any such constitutional amendment might be thought to resolve technical legal defects about the purported scope of federal authority under the Indian Commerce Clause, but cannot supply the consent of the Indian tribes required to bring the exercise of power over the Indians into conformity with America's basic commitments to constitutional delegation of authority by those governed. Only a treaty-like process, i.e., a treaty federalism model, can accomplish that result. Thus, abandonment of the pretense of colonial federal plenary power necessarily requires the return of the United States to the bargaining table with Indian tribes, just as recent Indian negotiations in Canada have rejuvenated the treaty process. A return to treaty federalism, i.e., the bilateral negotiation of the tribal federal relationship, constitutes the only conceptual solution to the basic constitutional problem raised in this article. Such mutual respect and recognition would go far to redress the legacy of colonialism and polish the chain of friendship which once bound the Indians to the United States and helped secure the very existence of the United States during the American Revolution.

VII CONCLUSION

The short version of this lengthy exegesis on the illegitimacy of the federal Indian plenary power doctrine and the lack of federal supremacy over Indian tribes is simply that the emperor has no clothes! It is high time legal scholarship routinely speaks truth to power in the hope that constitutional scholars, lawyers, and judges will conclude finally that what Congress and the Supreme Court have long claimed as a legitimate federal plenary power over Indian tribes, in fact, simply has no constitutional textual or original historical basis. The federal Indian plenary power doctrine is nothing more than a raw assertion of naked colonial power ostensibly cloaked with an aura of constitutional legitimacy by mere judicial fiat. ***

The failure of the Supreme Court to protect Indian tribal sovereignty by applying the same constitutional delegation analyses it rigorously invokes to protect state sovereignty and its failure to explore and enforce the original conception of constitutional limitations on federal power over Indian tribes speaks volumes about the continued institutionalization of colonialism and racism with respect to Indians in the American legal system. The only effective way to clothe the emperor with constitutional legitimacy and redress America's legal colonialist legacy with respect to Indian tribes is to polish the chain of friendship that previously bound Indian tribes to the United States by restoring mutual respect through treaty negotiation and the fulfillment of treaty obligations. That process necessarily involves abandoning all colonialist pretenses of federal plenary power and supremacy over Indian tribes. ***

NOTES & QUESTIONS

1. *Reading Indian Law*:
   - Why does Clinton feel that the *Oliphant* decision was an inflection point in the direction of the Court's treatment of Indian tribes, and how did *Duro* further limit their inherent power? What does he mean when he says that the Court focused on the "self" part of self-government, and what power(s) did tribal sovereigns lose that other sovereigns retain? Why does Clinton feel this interpretation is

inconsistent with the original understanding of tribal powers embedded in Constitutional history?

- Why is it constitutionally important that Indian tribes never consented to the plenary power of the United States? What role does the Supremacy Clause play in the conversation regarding plenary power? If Congress lacks the delegated power to enact laws to govern Indian tribes directly, does the Constitution provide any limitation on the power of tribal governments?
- Why does Clinton argue that the exercise of plenary power over Indian tribes undermines Constitutional legitimacy? What challenges would need to be overcome in order to give tribes meaningful consent to federal law? What might Indian tribes require in exchange for this concession? How might the United States respond if Indian tribes refused to consent?

2. *Colonialism & Consent*: Professor Clinton analogizes plenary power to colonialism because it asserts congressional power over Indian tribes without their consent. In building his argument against plenary power he notes that colonialism is antithetical to American values. In many ways the problem of plenary power is directly confronted throughout this text; both explicitly by Professor Williams in Chapter 2 and Professor Riley in Chapter 4, but also implicitly by Dean Getches in Chapter 7 and Professor Krakoff in Chapter 8. Are you persuaded by Professor Clinton that the assumption of plenary power over Indian tribes without their consent is a form of colonialism? Think broadly about the ideas underlying plenary power. How would modern Indian law and policy be different if Congress were unable to legislate for Indian tribes? Consider the large number of federal statutes which would now have no immediate force in Indian country: Indian Gaming Regulatory Act, Indian Civil Rights Act, Indian Mineral Leasing Act, Tribal Law and Order Act, Indian Self-Determination and Educational Assistance Act, etc.

3. *United States v. Lara*: In *Duro* the Court held that tribal courts lacked the power to criminally prosecute Indians who were nonmembers of the tribe. It reasoned that tribes lost those inherent criminal powers when they submitted to the overriding sovereignty of the United States. Professor Clinton rejoins: "The alleged submission was nothing more than a renewed statement of colonial dominance imposed without tribal consent."

The *Duro* opinion was issued in May of 1990 and by November of 1990 Congress had acted to overturn the decision by amending the Indian Civil Rights Act. The revision amended Congress's understanding of the inherent powers of tribal government:

"powers of self-government" means and includes all governmental powers possessed by an Indian tribe, executive, legislative, and judicial, and all offices, bodies, and tribunals by and through which they are executed, including courts of Indian offenses; *and means the inherent power of Indian tribes, hereby recognized and affirmed, to exercise criminal jurisdiction over all Indians* [emphasis added].

25 U.S.C. § 1301(2). The constitutionality of this *Duro*-fix was affirmed by the Supreme Court two years after Professor Clinton published his article. In *United States v. Lara*, 541 U.S. 193 (2004) the Spirit Lake Tribe prosecuted a member of the Turtle Mountain Band of Chippewa in its tribal court pursuant to the *Duro*-fix. Lara then challenged Congress's ability to recognize the inherent powers of tribal courts to criminally prosecute nonmember Indians. The Supreme Court held that "the Constitution authorizes Congress to permit tribes, as an exercise of their inherent tribal authority, to prosecute nonmember Indians. We hold that Congress exercised that authority in writing this statute. That being so, the Spirit Lake Tribe's prosecution of Lara did not amount to an exercise of federal power, and the Tribe acted in its capacity of a separate sovereign." This reaffirmation of inherent tribal powers is an important hedge against the casual erosion of tribal sovereignty perpetuated by the Courts since *Oliphant*.

Justice Thomas wrote an important concurrence in *Lara* that speaks to many of the constitutional problems Professor Clinton has identified. For example, Justice Thomas questions whether Congress has the authority to take away the right to negotiate treaties with Indians (which Clinton notes occurred in 1871) and at the same time claim to legislate for any subject which could have been in a treaty (i.e. plenary power):

The treaty power does not, as the Court seems to believe, provide Congress with free-floating power to legislate as it sees fit on topics that could potentially implicate some unspecified treaty. Such an assertion is especially ironic in light of Congress' enacted prohibition on Indian treaties. *** The Federal Government cannot simultaneously claim power to regulate virtually every aspect of the tribes through ordinary domestic legislation and also maintain that the tribes possess anything resembling 'sovereignty.' In short, the history points in both directions.

541 U.S. at 225. Justice Thomas's concurrence in *Lara* goes even further suggesting, as Professor Clinton does, that there may be no constitutional justification for congressional regulation of Indian affairs:

The Court should admit that it has failed in its quest to find a source of congressional power to adjust tribal sovereignty. Such an

acknowledgement might allow the Court to ask the logically antece-
dent question whether Congress (as opposed to the President) has
this power. A cogent answer would serve as the foundation for the
analysis of the sovereignty issues posed by this case. We might find
that the Federal Government cannot regulate the tribes through
ordinary domestic legislation and simultaneously maintain that the
tribes are sovereigns in any meaningful sense.

Id. at 226. However, Justice Thomas and Professor Clinton come to
different conclusions about what a lack of a constitutional basis for
plenary power might mean. While Professor Clinton calls for negotiation with tribes in order to obtain their consent to federal power, Justice
Thomas suggests that tribes may not be sovereign at all.

the time has come to reexamine the premises and logic of our tribal
sovereignty cases. It seems to me that much of the confusion
reflected in our precedent arises from two largely incompatible
and doubtful assumptions. First, Congress (rather than some other
part of the Federal Government) can regulate virtually every aspect
of the tribes without rendering tribal sovereignty a nullity. Second,
the Indian tribes retain inherent sovereignty to enforce their criminal laws against their own members. *** In my view, the tribes
either are or are not separate sovereigns, and our federal Indian law
cases untenably hold both positions simultaneously.

Id. at 214–15. Where do Justice Thomas and Professor Clinton agree, and
where do they part ways? How might Professor Clinton respond to
Justice Thomas's concurrence in *Lara*?

4. *Effect of Ignoring Plenary Power:* If Professor Clinton is right and both
federal laws and Supreme Court decisions are not binding on Indian
tribes, then tribes are free to ignore the concerns of outsiders and
proceed to organize themselves or legislate with disregard for Constitutional principles. What is the problem with ignoring more than
200 years of federal law developed by federal entities?

The ramifications of condemnation from outside Indian country
would surely be severe. Professor Clinton therefore notes that his article
"is not offered as a prescription for future tribal governmental behavior.
Even if American constitutional law cannot offer any satisfactory constitutional theory binding Indian tribes to unilaterally adopt federal law or
judicial decisions limiting tribal authority, ignoring such decisions can
have significant adverse costs for tribes." What are these adverse effects?
How might tribes overcome them without fully consenting to an extension of federal power over them?

Professor Clinton focuses specifically on the judicial reaction if tribal
courts were to suddenly ignore judicial precedents; "Tribal courts that

simply ignore federal law or Supreme Court precedents clearly will be seen by other courts in the federal system as acting illegally." Do tribal courts need the assistance of other courts in order to function? Would tribal courts be injured if their actions were perceived to be unlawful by other courts? How so?

5. *Responding to Professor Clinton*: Professor Robert Laurence from the University of Arkansas responded directly to Professor Clinton's article. *Indian Law Scholarship and Tribal Survival: A Short Essay, Prompted by a Long Footnote*, 27 Am. Indian L. Rev. 503 (2003). The footnote referenced in the title of the article is note 458, which is also reproduced in relevant part in this chapter. Professor Laurence's critique echoes Sam Deloria's from the footnote: "oral presentations are necessarily abbreviated and, without great care, necessarily misleading. When the listeners are non-lawyer tribal decision makers, such misleadings can have real impacts on the ways tribes do business, and when the message is that the federal government is without power over tribes, the consequences may threaten in real ways the survival of the tribe." *Id.* at 509. What consequences are contemplated by Professor Laurence? Do you agree with the critique? What role does legal scholarship have in the practice of law? How might it be used by tribal leaders?

6. *Commerce Clause*: The Constitution does specifically mention Indian tribes in a couple of places. Most relevant, Article I, Section 8, Clause 3 gives Congress the power "To regulate Commerce with foreign Nations, and among the several States, and with the Indian Tribes." Why doesn't the Commerce Clause delegate the power to Congress to legislate on behalf of Indian tribes? What is the difference between regulating non-Indians who deal with Indians, and regulating the tribes themselves?

7. *Beyond the Law*: The doctrine of plenary power transcends the law, with roots in history and implications for policymaking. David Wilkins has examined the basis of plenary power from a historical perspective. *The US Supreme Court's Explication of 'Federal Plenary Power': An Analysis of Case Law Affecting Tribal Sovereignty 1886–1914*, 18-3 Am. Indian Quarterly 349 (1994). He explores contrasting views of tribal sovereignty, noting that for the Supreme Court sovereignty deals primarily with questions of self-governance while from an Indigenous perspective, as Vine Deloria Jr. has articulated, sovereignty "can be said to consist more of continued cultural integrity than of political powers and to the degree that a nation loses its sense of cultural identity, to that degree it suffers a loss of sovereignty." *See* Vine Deloria Jr., *Custer Died for Your Sins* (University of Oklahoma Press 1969). How might these different visions of sovereignty effect perceptions of plenary power?

Wilkins places plenary power in a historical context. He explains that even during the historical apex of plenary power there were still elements of tribal consent embodied in congressional policy toward Indian tribes. "Frequently, tribal leaders and their constituencies simply voted down pending bilateral agreements or law perceived as potentially injurious or unfair. These laws, treaties, or agreements would then be returned to Washington for revision or tabled indefinitely if Washington could not secure tribal consent." Why might Congress have deferred to the tribes instead of forcing through the laws vetoed by tribes? Does this perspective change your understanding of Clinton's thesis regarding tribal consent?

FURTHER READING

- Richard B. Collins, *Indian Consent to American Government*, 31 Ariz. L. Rev. 365 (1989).
- Seth Davis, *American Colonialism and Constitutional Redemption*, 105 Calif. L. Rev. 1751 (2017).
- Carla F. Fredericks & Jesse D. Heibel, *Standing Rock, the Sioux Treaties, and the Limits of the Supremacy Clause*, 89 U. Colo. L. Rev. 477 (2018).
- Philip Frickey, *Domesticating Federal Indian Law*, 81 Minn. L. Rev. 31 (1996).
- Nell Jessup Newton, *Federal Power over Indians: Its Sources, Scope, and Limitations*, 132 U. Penn. L. Rev. 195 (1984).
- Robert Odawi Porter, *The Inapplicability of American Law to the Indian Nations*, 89 Iowa L. Rev. 1595 (2004).
- Angela R. Riley, *Good (Native) Governance*, 107 Colum. L. Rev. 1049 (2007).
- Natsu Taylor Saito, *The Plenary Power Doctrine: Subverting Human Rights in the Name of Sovereignty*, 51 Cath. U.L. Rev. 1115 (2002).
- Wenona Singel, *The First Federalists*, 62 Drake L. Rev. 775 (2014).
- Alex Tallchief Skibine, *Formalism and Judicial Supremacy in Federal Indian Law*, 32 Am. Indian L. Rev. 391 (2008).
- Alex Tallchief Skibine, *Constitutionalism, Federal Common Law, and the Inherent Powers of Indian Tribes*, 39 Am. Indian L. Rev. 77 (2015).
- Robert A. Williams, Jr., *Like a Loaded Weapon: The Rehnquist Court, Indian Rights, and the Legal History of Racism in America* (University of Minnesota Press 2005).

15

American Indians, Crime, and the Law

Kevin K. Washburn

104 Mich. L. Rev. 709 (2006)

Criminal jurisdiction in Indian country is full of presumptive rules. Tribes have inherent criminal jurisdiction over all Indian persons who commit crimes on tribal lands, but no criminal jurisdiction over non-Indians unless authorized by Congress. Unlike state courts, tribal courts are severely limited by federal law in the criminal penalties they may impose. The United States can impose substantial penalties upon criminal defendants and has concurrent jurisdiction over Indians who commit crimes in Indian country under a series of federal statutes. However, these prosecutions occur not on the reservation but in federal courthouses which are often hours away from the tribal community. Given the restrictions on tribal court jurisdiction, many of the most serious crimes committed in reservation communities are prosecuted by the federal government. States generally lack criminal jurisdiction over crimes committed in Indian country, but retain the power to prosecute non-Indian on non-Indian crime. This patchwork of jurisdictional rules is confusing and has not served Indian communities particularly well. Rates of violent crime in Indian country, particularly rates of domestic violence and interracial violence, well exceed the national average.

In this piece Kevin Washburn argues that the current state of criminal justice in Indian country serves tribal communities particularly badly. Tribal courts lack the authority to impose the most serious penalties and so end up delegating law enforcement authority to the United States. Washburn notes that this arrangement serves no one especially well. Federal prosecutors are unfamiliar with tribal communities and therefore may use prosecutorial discretion especially poorly. Moreover, given the lack of trust many Indians have in the federal government, federal prosecutors have a difficult time cultivating the relationships necessary to find cooperative witnesses and achieve successful prosecutions. Prosecutions take place away from the reservation community, so tribal members do not see the justice system in action. Finally, Washburn argues that federal juries seldom include any Indians, let alone a jury of the defendant's peers, which is damaging to the rights of the defendant and the tribal community.

As you read the following piece on crime in Indian country try to make a list of all the problems Washburn identifies with the structure of the current criminal justice system. What role do prosecutors, juries, and tribal communities play in the promotion of criminal justice? Why is it problematic that most actors in the federal criminal justice system are not Indian? How can the problems Washburn identifies be corrected? Can tribal court systems play a role in solving the criminal justice deficit identified in the piece?

INTRODUCTION

When a Navajo tribal member commits a serious felony against another Navajo on the remote Navajo Indian Reservation, the crime sets in motion not a tribal criminal investigation and tribal court proceeding, but a federal investigation and federal court proceeding under the federal Major Crimes Act. For trial, the Navajo defendant, the Navajo victim, and the witnesses (all of whom are also likely to be Navajo) will be summoned to a federal district court far away from the reservation and the specific community where the crime occurred. Unlike a felony involving only non-Indians, which would be routinely adjudicated at the local county or district courthouse, the Navajo felony will be tried in a distant federal court in Phoenix, Salt Lake City, or Albuquerque.

The federal court operates in a language that is foreign to many Navajos; thus the Navajo defendants, victims, and witnesses may require interpreters to translate the proceedings. Neither the judge, the court reporter, the prosecutor, the court security officers, the deputy marshals, nor the defense attorney or investigator are likely to be Navajo or even understand or speak the Navajo language. Perhaps even more importantly, the federal jury that hears the evidence is unlikely to include a Navajo, or even an Indian, or any other member of the community where the crime occurred.

While the Navajo Nation provides a compelling example of such alienation because it ranges across three states and is inhabited by more than 180,000 people in hundreds of distinct Indian communities, this federal criminal justice regime spans more than one hundred Indian reservations across the United States and involves thousands of federal cases opened each year within "Indian country" as that term is defined by federal law. ***

As a result of a series of federal statutes, felony criminal justice is primarily a federal responsibility on hundreds of Indian reservations *** In the United States, criminal justice is an inherently local activity as a matter of constitutional design; American criminal justice systems are carefully designed to empower local communities to solve internal problems and to restore peace and harmony in the community. Viewed in this light, many of the practical problems outlined above, and more serious ones discussed below, may represent violations of fundamental constitutional norms. In short, federal justice in Indian country simply may not accord with many of the basic legal principles that guide American courts, prosecutors, and law enforcement officials.

Consider some of the most obvious questions raised by a federal Indian country prosecution: Does an Indian defendant receive a trial by a jury of his peers when he faces a federal jury in a distant city composed of non-Indians who are foreign to the Indian community, who may very well speak a different language and who are subject to a different set of laws and a different process for adjudicating them? Does an Indian community have a voice in issues of public safety when its local felonies are prosecuted, defended, and adjudicated in distant and foreign tribunals by federal officials who are not accountable to tribal leaders or the community? Are basic requirements of fairness and due process met when defendants, crime victims, and witnesses are summoned to court hundreds of miles away to testify about simple but serious local crimes that occurred in their own backyards? Can a community enjoy its right to a "public trial" when a local crime is adjudicated in a non-televised trial hundreds of miles away in a city that is difficult to reach from the reservation? As these questions suggest, the federal Indian country criminal justice scheme is subject to a host of criticisms derived from implicit constitutional values of federalism and localism and explicit constitutional requirements of criminal procedure. ***

For thirty-five years, federal policymakers have moved more and more decisively in the context of Indian law and policy toward an approach that fosters "tribal self-determination" and have sought to restore the powers of tribal governments. As a result of the advance of federal Indian policy, the federal criminal justice system in Indian country no longer rests comfortably within the mainstream of federal Indian policy. To some degree it seems to be a relic, perhaps, of colonialism. While the notion of community "self-determination" has been enthusiastically embraced only fairly recently in federal Indian policy, it is a long-standing and hallowed norm in American criminal justice. Indeed, many of the key institutions of the federal criminal justice system, such as juries, were designed to assure community control of criminal justice. Given that American criminal justice is designed in many respects to build in "self-determination" as its own guiding principle, it is perhaps ironic that criminal justice in Indian country has been resistant to such notions.

Thus, rather than challenging the existing system on the grounds that it is inconsistent with federal Indian policy, this Article instead asks a more fundamental question: is this federal criminal justice system consistent with its own prevailing norms? In other words, this Article evaluates the federal Indian country criminal justice regime, not against norms of Indian law and policy, but against those of criminal law and policy. Specifically, this Article evaluates the federal constitutional norms that lie at the heart of American criminal justice and that are designed to ensure the legitimacy of federal criminal trials. ***

I THE MODERN STRUCTURE AND PROCESS OF INDIAN COUNTRY CRIMINAL JUSTICE

A A Legal Description of the Indian Country Regime

The federal Indian country criminal justice regime consists primarily of a trio of federal laws that create a complex jurisdictional framework. The first of the three statutes is 18 U.S.C. 1151, which defines no offenses but merely sets forth the geographic scope of federal Indian country jurisdiction. ***

The other two key statutes are the Major Crimes Act, set forth at 18 U.S.C. 1153 and another statute known variously as the Indian Country Crimes Act or the General Crimes Act (the latter will be used here, in contradistinction to "Major Crimes Act"). The General Crimes Act provides that the general federal laws enacted to apply to locations within exclusive jurisdiction of the federal government, also known generally as the federal enclaves laws, apply in Indian country. One of the federal enclaves laws, the Assimilative Crimes Act, provides that any state criminal law of the state in which the lands are located can be assimilated if there is no federal criminal law on point. Because of this provision, the General Crimes Act allows a federal prosecution for virtually any conceivable offense, whether misdemeanor or felony. ***

Viewed together, the Indian country definition, the Major Crimes Act, and the General Crimes Act constitute the jurisdictional apparatus for bringing criminal cases in Indian country into federal court. None of these laws, however, provides the substantive offenses to which they refer. The substantive definitions must be found elsewhere in the criminal code and, if the Assimilative Crimes Act is used, in state law. This means, of course, that the serious crimes in Indian country are defined by federal and state officials, not by tribal officials.

Complementing this trio of federal statutes is the Indian Civil Rights Act. That Act strips tribes of jurisdiction over crimes punished by sentences greater than one year of imprisonment or a fine of more than $5000. As a result, tribes may define and prosecute any offense, but because of the sentencing limitation, tribal offenses would be labeled federally as misdemeanors. As a result, though many tribes have active criminal court dockets, only the federal government – and not tribes – can address serious crimes with felony sentences. The Indian Civil Rights Act thus has the effect of elevating the importance of the federal criminal justice regime in Indian country and giving it primacy.

B A Practical, Critical Description of the Process of an Indian Country Case

*** The first substantive prosecutorial step in a federal major crimes case is review of the evidence and the determination of whether or not to pursue a prosecution. Following the arrest, federal prosecutors work with the arresting officer to prepare a criminal complaint or else direct that the perpetrator be released. If the United States Attorney's Office ("USAO") decides to proceed, it will file a criminal complaint. The perpetrator will then be taken to the nearest federal court for an initial appearance. During that appearance, the federal prosecutor may file a motion for a detention hearing. If so, the defendant is "bound over" and remains in custody pending the hearing.

If the defendant is indigent, an attorney will be appointed to represent him in later proceedings. A substantial number of Indian country defendants are indigent and are represented by the Federal Public Defender or, if that office is unavailable or has a conflict, an attorney selected by the court from a panel of attorneys on a court-approved list of criminal defense attorneys who are willing to take cases under the court's modest fee structure. ***

In the federal system, no felony prosecution, including those for major crimes in Indian country, may proceed without an indictment issued by a grand jury. Thus, whether or not the defendant is held in detention, the United States Attorney must next present an indictment to the grand jury or risk having the case dismissed. A federal grand jury consists of up to twenty-three citizens selected randomly to serve for a lengthy term – often one year, though a longer time is authorized. Grand jurors screen and evaluate prosecutorial charging decisions by ensuring that the evidence presented by the prosecutor is sufficient to meet a legal standard of probable cause. Though the American criminal justice system uses a grand jury for this function primarily to ensure that the community has a role in the administration of criminal justice, few or none of the grand jurors in most Indian country cases actually reside in any Indian country community.

*** For reasons that will be addressed fully below, the venire from which the jury is selected is unlikely to have a single member of the Indian community in which the crime occurred. At trial, neither the prosecutor, the defense attorney, the marshals, nor the court security officers, the court reporter, the judge, or law clerks are likely to live within the community where the offense occurred. In many cases, the only other tribal member in the courtroom will be the interpreter, if one is needed, and the witnesses. In that sense, the tribunal may seem alien to the defendant, and he may not feel that he is being judged in any sense by his own community. ***

II FEDERAL PROSECUTORS IN INDIAN COUNTRY

*** An implicit justification for the modern federal Indian country criminal justice regime is that the United States has a responsibility to preserve public safety on Indian reservations. Indeed, the regime does not purport to be primarily responsible for public safety throughout the general community encompassing the entire federal judicial district or state but merely concerns those communities that lie within the jurisdictional confines of "Indian country," as that term is defined in the United States Code. In other words, the regime is designed to provide public safety and criminal justice in Indian country and the statutory scheme is geographically defined as applying only to that area. Given that background, the apparent responsibility of the prosecutor in an Indian country case is to represent – and protect – the Indian country community.

1 The Prosecutor as Representative of the Community

For a variety of reasons, one might be highly skeptical of the ability of a federal prosecutor to represent the Indian country community. Unlike the usual circumstances, in which the prosecutor internalizes and acts in accordance with the mores and values of the community (of which she theoretically is a part), a federal prosecutor in Indian country may live hundreds of miles from the reservation and may not even speak the language used in that community. She may not be able to understand and internalize the values of the community that she theoretically protects.

The federal prosecutor's lack of membership in the Indian country community is not the only obstacle she will face in intuiting community values. First, she is not present on a daily basis within the community to participate in ongoing communications about community values and mores. She will not know, firsthand, what the community is talking about or concerned about. Second, since many Indian communities are closed and suspicious of outsiders, it is unrealistic to believe that they will easily confide in a federal prosecutor about matters that are important to them. ***

The Indian country regime, in explicitly creating a scheme for prosecuting local offenses with no national nexus and applying only to Indian country, offers insight into our national psyche. While federal law may not consciously single out African American communities, its willingness to single out "Indian country" for special treatment in this way may be cause for broader concerns by other communities. In Indian country, the federal prosecutor is alien to the community and less able or unable to understand, internalize and protect, or even act in accordance with, the community's values. Perhaps such an official simply is not institutionally competent. This gives rise to a related problem.

2 The Accountability Problem

The alignment between the prosecutor and community values that serves as the normative foundation for broad prosecutorial discretion is supported, in most American jurisdictions, by prosecutorial accountability through the political process. *** The political power of Indian tribal communities over their (federal) prosecutors is strikingly different from the political power over the prosecutors who bring the same kind of cases in non-Indian communities. Because federal prosecutors are appointed, rather than elected, direct political accountability is absent in all Indian country cases, increasing the gulf between the interests of the prosecutors and the community. ***

Some federal Indian country prosecutors undertake extraordinary formal and informal efforts to get to know their Indian communities. Such knowledge is absolutely crucial to the task. One federal prosecutor has explained, for example, the Navajo cultural norm against looking a person in the eye, which can be considered "offensive, an affront, even a challenge to the other person." Knowledge of and respect for such a cultural norm might make a difference in whether the prosecutor will gain or lose the assistance of a key witness. A misstep here can make the difference between a righteous conviction and a colossal waste of federal resources.

But even for federal prosecutors who are sensitive to cultural differences and concerned enough to make extraordinary efforts, the sheer distance between United States Attorney's Offices and many of the federal Indian reservations they serve presents tremendous obstacles that the average violent crime prosecutor in the state system does not face. Perhaps as a result, United States Attorneys have been widely criticized for decades for failing to give proper attention to Indian country cases. The substance of such complaints almost always involves the failure to prosecute aggressively enough and almost never involves complaints of "over-prosecution."

Because of the non-reviewability of decisions to decline prosecution or to under-prosecute, the weak or nonexistent political accountability of federal prosecutors to tribal communities, and the lack of media interest in Indian country prosecutions, federal prosecutors feel little external pressure to treat Indian country cases seriously. Under such a scheme, well-intentioned federal prosecutors will work hard in Indian country, and many do. But even high levels of commitment and interest by federal prosecutors are no substitute for actual accountability. Those prosecutors who are not committed to Indian country cases will simply not pursue them. And in Indian country, it is often the decisions not to prosecute, called "declinations," that cause the most grief and consternation. As a result, it would appear that federal Indian country prosecutors are failing in precisely the area in which their discretion is subject to the least scrutiny and accountability. The extensive critical commentary in academic literature may be the most serious negative repercussion that these federal officials face. The result is that criminal justice in Indian country is occasionally pursued aggressively and is sometimes ignored, making criminal justice a haphazard event at best for Indian tribes. ***

3 Federal Prosecutors and the Cavalry Effect

*** In Indian country, the federal government is held in the esteem it has earned in more than two centuries of federal–tribal relations. Its reputation in Indian country has been forged, in part, by the nineteenth-century cavalry officers who committed atrocious actions, such as murder, and the Indian agents who committed atrocious omissions, such as the withholding of treaty-guaranteed food and supplies in winter. Its reputation was formed by the actions of government officials who used gifts of smallpox-infected blankets to destroy tribal communities and by federal officials who unilaterally violated treaties and encouraged private actors to do the same, and, in more recent years, the federal trustee that lost track of the records of millions and perhaps billions of dollars of Indian assets held by the Department of the Interior in tribal accounts and Individual Indian Money accounts.

Enter the well-intentioned federal prosecutor seeking to prosecute a violent crime in Indian country. While federal prosecutors may be talented and committed public servants who are trying to "do good" by helping to provide public safety or bringing justice to Indian country, each carries tremendous moral, emotional, and symbolic freight of which he may not even be aware. Indians and Indian tribes have long memories. Such is the power of oral traditions.

Though experiences vary from tribe to tribe, the federal prosecutor in Indian country is, in some respects, the direct lineal descendant of the blue-coated, sword-wielding cavalry officer; the prosecutor represents the very same federal government that committed cruel and violent acts against Indian tribes for more than a century. He represents the government that has made and then broken sacred promises. Yet he shows up on the tribal member's doorstep with the claim, "I am here to help you obtain justice." Given the history of federal–tribal relations, tribes have every reason to be suspicious of such an official and such a claim. In a real sense, for many reservation Indians, the federal government continues to represent the enemy.

In such a context, the federal prosecution creates a political dynamic in the tribe that must be addressed in virtually every case. Consider a typical case of sexual abuse of a child: after the child victim reluctantly reports an incident of abuse by another family member, it is surprisingly common for the victim's family members to align themselves with the defendant and against the victim. This is not unheard of outside Indian country, but it represents a particularly serious problem in Indian country cases. The dynamic, though extremely unfortunate, is explainable. When the federal government accuses a community member of a heinous offense and brings a criminal complaint or an indictment, the community may naturally become protective of the accused defendant in the face of this outside authority, even if the charges are based on a report by another tribal member. The family may not perceive its choice as one between the perpetrator and the victim, but between a tribal member and the United States government. As a result, when the family chooses sides, it may line up behind the perpetrator and against the child who has been victimized.

Given the long history of federal–tribal relations, the federal prosecutor simply may not be anyone whom the community has any reason to trust. The result is that the child victim is victimized anew by a political dynamic that aligns the victim with the United States and against the community and the defendant. This dynamic may well cause further psychological injuries to the child victim of sexual assault and lead to the victim's alienation and estrangement from family members. In that respect, a new harm is done to the child that might not have occurred in the absence of the federal prosecutor. According to experts in the field, this alienation of a child from the family often has psychological ramifications that are even more serious than the harm done by the perpetrator of the sex offense. In addition to harming victims, the dynamic may cause numerous lesser evils, such as practical problems in prosecutions. It sometimes, no doubt, causes victims to recant and frustrates effective prosecutions of sexual predators. As a result, sexual predators are not effectively removed from the community.

Use of a federal prosecutor likely creates a host of other less-serious problems as well. Even leaving out the emotional and historical baggage that creates the political dynamic that I will characterize as the "cavalry effect," child sex abuse cases are among the most difficult cases to prosecute successfully, even in the best of circumstances. As an alien to the community, the federal prosecutor is likely to find it difficult to communicate with the Indian child and even more difficult to convince the child victim to participate in a trial. As evidence that these problems are very real, federal prosecutors have taken to employing "victim-witness coordinators" who often work to bridge the cultural gap between the Indian victims and the federal prosecutors. Without the assistance of the victim-witness advocates, Indian country prosecutions would be far less successful. ***

The cavalry metaphor offers one other key insight: the cavalry chooses its battles carefully and then leaves when the battle is over. One telltale sign of the lack of trust of federal law enforcement and prosecutors is the fact that many crimes are never even reported. One key reason for the failure to report is that victims do not trust the federal authorities to protect them from retaliation. Like the cavalry, federal prosecutors and FBI agents swoop in occasionally to prosecute a perpetrator, but they do not maintain a constant presence and do not necessarily consider the broader impact of their work. They address only the serious offenses and they leave when each case is concluded. It is up to the tribal community to address other offenses and the aftermath of the felony and to attempt to restore the fabric of the community. Even assuming that the federal prosecutors who agree to handle such cases are generous, selfless, and committed to bettering the lives of the reservation community (as most of them no doubt are), even the best of intentions may not always be able to overcome the handicaps noted herein.

Consider one obvious alternative approach: a tribal prosecutor. As a member of the Indian country community, a tribal prosecutor might face few of the handicaps that the federal prosecutor faces. A tribal prosecutor would not be forced into the same dynamic – she could represent the community and the community would feel less of a need to attempt to protect the defendant against an external authority. In addition, unlike the federal prosecutor, a tribal prosecutor would presumably live within the community. This would convey a much stronger sense of interest and investment in the community and would allow the prosecutor to help the community address the collateral issues that arise from the prosecution. The presence of the prosecutor within the community might also give greater comfort to those victims of crime who are unwilling to come forward. Moreover, a tribal prosecutor might act – in a variety of ways – in a fashion more compatible with community norms.

4 Obstacles to Tribal Governance and Self-Determination

In addition to the problems noted above, the role of federal prosecutors creates a serious obstacle to tribal self-determination. Use of a federal prosecutor to address

major crimes between Indians sends a clear message of inferiority about tribal law
enforcement and tribal courts, that is, that tribes cannot handle felonies. And it robs
the tribal community of leadership in one of the most important areas of governance: maintenance of public safety and criminal justice. In some respects, the
system can create a vacuum of tribal leadership on public safety issues that can
exacerbate crime problems by sidelining the people who might be best able to
address these serious issues. * * *

Tribal officials are likely more knowledgeable than federal officials about remote
Indian reservations and are also likely to be much more responsive to the tribal
community. Yet a tribal leader running for election would be ill-advised to promise
his constituents that he could address serious public safety and criminal justice
problems on the reservation; he simply lacks control of the key resources. To make
such a promise, he would need to have assurances from federal officials. Given the
history of promises by federal officials, even in sacred treaties, a tribal official would
be foolish to count on any such assurance. As a result, even in circumstances in
which tribal governments do not actively seek to frustrate federal prosecutions, tribal
leaders are much less likely to be invested in felony criminal justice. One of the
telltale signs of the lack of official interest in these issues is the fact that crime
statistics are so difficult to obtain for Indian reservations. One would be hard-pressed
to find a mayor of a major American city who was unaware of the crime rate for that
city. Yet tribal leaders do not routinely collect such data and would be hard-pressed
to answer such a question, partially no doubt because they often do not have line
authority over the law enforcement officers involved. If tribal political leaders are
unwilling to use their limited resources or stake their reputations on improvement in
this key area of tribal public policy, then improvements may never occur. * * *

In short, the federal Indian country regime creates an unfortunate and indefens-
ible paradox. It wrests control of the key and inherently local issue of felony criminal
justice away from tribal leadership and places control over these issues in the hands
of federal officials who have little accountability to the tribal community and little
incentive to be responsive. The result is not only irrational from a criminal justice
standpoint; it is contrary to the stated federal policies of tribal self-determination and
self-governance.

C *Concluding Thoughts about Federal Prosecutors*

Locating the power to prosecute in a federal official from outside the reservation
poses numerous practical problems, such as difficulty in obtaining the cooperation
of witnesses at trial, and creates structural problems by often converting the tribal
government into an opponent of the prosecution, even when the prosecution would
otherwise have worked to produce a safer reservation environment. The cavalry
effect and other problems related to the Indian country criminal justice system
inflict serious costs on the community and serious damage to individual Indian

defendants and victims. This model of criminal justice, in which prosecutions are handled by an outside authority and not the tribal government, creates a system that smacks more of colonialism than of rational criminal justice policy. It simply is not consistent with modern principles of federal Indian policy and it is dysfunctional from the standpoint of federal criminal justice policy. It is for this reason that federal Indian country prosecutions should be "de-colonized."

III JURIES AND JURY COMPOSITION IN INDIAN COUNTRY

While the prosecutor is ideally supposed to "represent" the community, the greatest opportunity for the community to participate affirmatively in the administration of criminal justice is, of course, through juries. In the American criminal justice system, the jury trial is constituted not only as a key procedural safeguard to the defendant, but to give the community a central role in the administration of criminal justice. ***

B *Representative Juries and Anti-Discrimination in Jury Composition*

Because of the key role that the jury plays in representing the community, the Supreme Court began addressing racially discriminatory jury composition soon after the Civil War. In *Strauder v. West Virginia* in 1879, the Supreme Court overturned a black man's murder conviction because the state had explicitly excluded blacks from serving on the jury, holding that the Fourteenth Amendment's Equal Protection Clause prohibits exclusion of black jurors from juries in state courts. The Court discussed two different types of rights in its decision. First, it recognized that the black community has a "right to participate in the administration of the law" that may not be denied through racially discriminatory state laws. Second, the Court recognized the right of the black defendant to a trial by a jury selected without discrimination against others of his race.

The very next year, in *Neal v. Delaware*, the Supreme Court held that even de facto discrimination was actionable. In that case, even though Delaware's law was not explicit in excluding blacks, the Supreme Court overturned a black defendant's rape conviction on the basis of de facto discrimination in light of evidence establishing that a black person had never served on a jury in the entire state of Delaware. In other words, the jury's representative role was so important that the Court was willing to protect it against even possibly accidental and unintentional actions that diminished the jury's representativeness. ***

In 1968, during the civil rights movement, Congress enacted a law governing the selection of federal juries that codified much of the anti-discrimination jurisprudence enunciated by the Supreme Court in these cases and others. The Jury Selection and Service Act ("JSSA") now provides the basic legal rules that apply to jury selection in federal cases, including those arising in Indian country. The JSSA generally provides that all litigants in federal courts who are entitled to trial by jury "shall have the right to grand and petit juries selected at random from a fair cross section of the community." ***

C *Underrepresentation of Native Americans on Indian Country Juries*

Despite the normative principle of representativeness, Indians tend not to be well represented in federal juries in Indian country cases. Even in states with large Indian populations, Indians remain a very small fraction of the population. As a result, Indians would be expected to have minimal representation in the jury venire. However, the statistics indicate lower numbers than one would expect. Under-representation even of the existing small fraction of the population may occur for a variety of reasons. First, Indians are among the poorest Americans. Because juries in most federal districts are chosen from state voter rolls, "federal jury venires underrepresent the poor" who are less likely to register to vote and, even if they have registered, are more likely to have moved since they last registered. *** Since juries are routinely selected from voter registration lists of state political subdivisions, even relatively politically active and aware tribal members may nevertheless not be represented if they focus their activism solely within the tribal government. While the JSSA seems to allow use of tribal voting registration lists, it does not require such use.

Perhaps most important, however, is the geographic aspect of the problem. *** Consider, for example, the federal District of Arizona. In Arizona, the Navajo reservation sends more cases to the United States Attorney's Office than all other tribes in the state combined. Federal trials of these cases routinely occur in Prescott or Phoenix. *** Prescott is around one hundred miles, as the crow flies, from the closest point on the Navajo Reservation and more than two hundred miles from the heart of that reservation. By highway, these distances are much greater. ***

As a result of the geographic factors and the other phenomena mentioned previously, Native Americans are poorly represented on all federal jury panels. Because juries in Indian country cases are selected in the same manner as all other federal criminal juries, Indians are almost never well-represented as jurors in Indian country cases. In that sense, they share many of the traditional complaints of other minority communities related to the composition of juries.

D *Legal Challenges*

In an early Eighth Circuit case, *United States v. Clifford*, the defendant presented evidence that Indians living within the division from which the trial jury was selected constituted 15.6% of the total populace, but that only 8.4% of the jurors who served during a two-year period were Indian. This evidence demonstrated an "absolute disparity" (the difference between the figures) of 7.2% and a "comparative disparity" of 46%. In other words, each jury had, on average, 46% fewer Indians than it would have had if its composition matched the representation of Indians in the general population.

*** [T]he Eighth Circuit recognized that Indians are a "distinctive group" that should be represented in a fair cross-section of the community. However, the Eighth Circuit held *** that the disparity established by the evidence was not substantial enough as a matter of law to constitute a violation of the JSSA or the Sixth Amendment. Accordingly, the defendant was unable to establish a prima facie violation and was unable even to reach the third step of showing that the under-representation was due to "systematic exclusion." Since that time, other challenges in the Eighth Circuit have been equally unsuccessful.

The Tenth Circuit first addressed the issue at about the same time and reached a similar result. In *United States v. Yazzie*, an Indian defendant presented evidence that the proportion of Indians in the grand jury was 45% lower than the proportion of Indians over age eighteen in the general population of the state. The defendant also presented evidence that the proportion of jurors on the petit jury was 46% lower than the proportion of Indians in the general population over age eighteen in the division from which the jury was drawn. The Tenth Circuit in *Yazzie*, like the Eighth Circuit in *Clifford*, held that such disparities were not substantial enough to demonstrate that the venire was "not [a] fair and reasonable" representation of the community. Just as in the Eighth Circuit, no Indian country defendant in the Tenth Circuit has ever successfully challenged jury composition on such a basis.

*** The "fair cross-section" issue arose again [in] the Ninth Circuit in *United States v. Bushyhead*. The defendant, an Indian prosecuted for a murder on the Pyramid Lake Paiute Reservation in northern Nevada, argued that his conviction should be reversed because he was denied a panel constituting a "fair cross-section" of the community; the jury selection plan in the District of Nevada drew only from county voting lists and not from tribal voting lists. The Ninth Circuit rejected Bushyhead's argument. The JSSA generally authorizes the district court to select the political subdivisions from which it will obtain voting lists. It seems to allow, but does not require, the district court to select among other appropriate subdivisions of government from which it will draw lists. The Ninth Circuit noted that people living on reservations in Nevada also live within Nevada counties and thus are not purposefully excluded from the county voting lists; they may register for elections like any other citizens within those counties. Therefore, the court held that Bushyhead could not establish that the jury selection plan was not fair or reasonable *** or that it caused "systematic exclusion" of Native Americans[.] *** Thus, the Ninth Circuit joins the Eighth and Tenth Circuits in never having entertained a successful challenge by an Indian to an Indian country prosecution for lack of a jury constituting a "fair cross-section" of the community. Together these three circuits make up the vast majority of Indian country jurisdiction in the United States.

E A Critique of Jury Composition Cases in Indian Country

In each of the challenges discussed above, the parties argued that the jury pools failed to constitute representative cross-sections of the community because they excluded Native Americans. The parties and the courts have made three general types of analytical errors in these cases.

1 Representativeness and a Jury of One's Peers

*** In Indian country cases, obtaining jurors from the entire district results in using jurors from outside the Indian country jurisdiction of the court. Although neither the Constitution nor the Sixth Amendment use the term "peers," the Supreme Court has, from time to time indicated that the right to trial by jury means a right to a jury of one's peers. Since the term is not explicitly constitutional, it has never been effectively defined, at least for federal purposes. However, the Court has suggested that the term is implicit within the definition of jury and that the term means to include only those persons with the same legal status as the defendant, those who live within the reach of the same laws. Since no off-reservation person can be prosecuted for an Indian country offense unless he ventures into Indian country and commits a crime, the average juror in an Indian country case is simply not in any practical sense a "peer" to the defendant in the case. ***

2 Considering the Indian Law Context of These Cases

Litigants and the courts have also failed to give proper consideration to the Indian law context of these cases. As the Supreme Court recognized when it first upheld the Major Crimes Act, "[Indians] owe no allegiance to the States, and receive from them no protection. Because of the local ill feeling, the people of the States where they are found are often their deadliest enemies." Given that one of the justifications for the Indian country criminal justice regime is the federal government's duty of protection toward Indians and, often, as against state authority (and state authorities), how can state voter registration lists be the appropriate resources for creating a jury pool? In other words, why should federal courts look to the people whom the Supreme Court once described as the Indians' "deadliest enemies" to construct a jury pool that is impartial for purposes of the Sixth Amendment? ***

3 Focusing on "The Community"

While the routine approach to jury selection may be legitimate in the context of general federal criminal laws, the Indian country laws are not federal laws of general applicability with nationwide application. Indian country prosecutions are not brought to protect the national "community." They are brought to protect the Indian reservation community. Thus, a jury pool that represents a fair cross-section of the judicial district or a division thereof will not constitute a cross-section, fair or otherwise, of the Indian country community. And it is only the existence of the crime within the Indian country community that justifies federal jurisdiction. ***

To frame the overarching problem in a slightly different way, jury panels in federal Indian country cases are not underinclusive because they fail to include adequate numbers of Native Americans but rather overinclusive because they include persons who do not live in Indian country and are not routinely subject to federal Indian country jurisdiction. The composition of Indian country juries is thus akin in the non-Indian context to using a statewide jury pool to adjudicate a local crime. Not only is such an approach difficult to justify as [a] matter of criminal justice practice, it would violate state constitutions in many states. A proper analysis thus involves a more careful and explicit examination of the word "community."

The "fair cross-section of the community" rhetoric grows from the Sixth Amendment's interest in creating an "impartial jury." Federal courts have tended to construe "community" as the entire judicial district in which the offense occurred or as a division, which is a smaller subunit of the district. *** In future cases, defendants should make the straightforward argument that jurors in Indian country cases cannot be drawn from addresses outside Indian country because "Indian country" is the community that the law is designed to protect.

*** The crimes enumerated in the Major Crimes Act are serious but routine offenses of a local nature with significant local effects and few effects beyond the locality. Yet most federal juries are unlikely to include a single representative from the local Indian community where the offense occurred and likely will not even include a single person who lives within Indian country. If the Sixth Amendment's requirement of a jury that is fairly representative of the community arises from the theory that the jury exists to ensure that the affected community plays a role in the provision of criminal justice within that community, then these purposes fail miserably in Indian country prosecutions. Because a federal jury is not composed of members of Indian reservation communities, it cannot claim to represent the Indian communities where major crimes occur. Thus, such juries do not ensure the legitimacy of criminal verdicts.

4 Practical Effects of These Errors

While such convictions are thus illegitimate as a formal matter, serious pragmatic ramifications follow from the errors in composing federal juries.

First, actual substantive errors may well creep into verdicts. Substantive criminal law is replete with statutory language that calls for interpretations of language by the local community, through the jury, in adjudicating crime. For example, some crimes and defenses hinge on whether an action or perception was "reasonable."

The word "reasonable" is inherently subject to context and cultural norms. It is, to a large degree, an empty vessel that lawmakers and courts intentionally leave empty to be filled by jurors in any given case. In other words, the jury is the carrier of cultural norms of what is reasonable in any given community. A jury that is not representative of the community may well provide the wrong definition of the word "reasonable," and thereby reach an erroneous verdict. Given the open texture inherent in language and the peculiar role of juries in providing meaning in different contexts, it is possible for such errors to occur in a variety of contexts in criminal adjudications.

Second, consider a practical, but even more fundamental problem. The impact and the importance of any single criminal conviction lies in its broader meaning. Each conviction derives its normative force from what criminal law theorist Henry Hart called the "moral condemnation of the community." Indeed, expression of the moral condemnation of the community is one of the most profound purposes of the criminal justice system. Since, in Indian country cases, the defendant's community is absent, a convicted Indian country defendant is not likely to feel the weight of the condemnation of his own community. He is thus much less likely to feel the moral weight of the verdict. That weight, which causes the defendant to feel shame, is a powerful force driving the rehabilitative effects of criminal justice. Absent shame, one of the core purposes of punishment will not be met.

In summary, the regular federal jury selection process simply does not allow the jury to serve its fundamental purpose in Indian country cases. *** Because the jury's chief importance in American criminal justice is to give the community a role and because that role is crucial to the system's legitimacy, the verdicts produced through the existing jury process are not legitimate. The legacy of colonization is present in each of them.

IV PUBLIC ACCESS, VENUE, AND PUBLIC TRIALS

Closely related to the jury composition problems in Indian country cases is a related set of issues in the constitutional doctrines of publicity and venue. While jury composition principles address which community decides a case by focusing on which community comprises the jury, the venue provisions address which community hosts the trial.

A *Rights of Public Access to Criminal Trials*

Public access or publicity for criminal trials is guaranteed by two separate constitutional provisions. The Sixth Amendment protects the defendant's right to a public trial on the theory that the public will provide safeguards to corruption or oppression by government officials. The First Amendment creates a constitutional right of access to criminal trials for general members of the public who are not parties to the case. The Supreme Court has repeatedly emphasized the importance of public access in criminal trials. While the federal Indian country criminal justice regime may pose few formal barriers to public access, the regime creates substantial de facto barriers that prohibit meaningful public access to criminal trials and thus may violate the constitutional rights of both the defendant and the Indian country community.

1 The Source and Rationale for the Right to Public Trials and Public Access

The Sixth Amendment explicitly guarantees the defendant's right to a public trial: "In all criminal prosecutions, the accused shall enjoy the right to a speedy and public trial ..." *** The Supreme Court has held that "public access to criminal trials ... is essential to the proper functioning of the criminal justice system." ***

> When a shocking crime occurs, a community reaction of outrage and public protest often follows. Thereafter the open processes of justice serve an important prophylactic purpose, providing an outlet for community concern, hostility, and emotion ... The crucial prophylactic aspects of the administration of justice cannot function in the dark; no community catharsis can occur if justice is done in a corner or in a covert manner. [And] results alone will not satiate the natural community desire for "satisfaction." A result considered untoward may undermine public confidence, and where the trial has been concealed from public view an unexpected outcome can cause a reaction that the system at best has failed and at worst has been corrupted.

The Court has also explained that without access, the community will not understand the system in general or its particular workings in a specific case, and it is difficult for a community to accept what it cannot observe. *** Without access to the trial by the interested community, neither the defendant's interests nor the public's interests are served.

2 Public Access and Indian Country Defendants

As explained above, trials for local offenses in Indian country routinely occur more than a hundred miles away from the communities where the crimes occurred. In light of the tremendous distances, deep poverty, and other daily facts of life on Indian reservations, the defendants, their families, the victims, the witnesses, and other members of the community are often unable to attend criminal trials. While there may be no formal bar to access, the federal regime's removal of the trial from the community where the crime occurred to a distant city creates a routine, de facto denial of public access to trials. ***

Consider first the defendant's right to a public trial as a criminal procedural safeguard. One stated justification for public trials is to ensure the "integrity and quality" of the testimony offered at trial and to encourage witnesses to perform their duties more conscientiously. Given those concerns, access by members of the affected community – friends and neighbors, in other words, rather than strangers – is likely to be much more effective in insuring witness conscientiousness and honesty. Practical experience suggests that it is harder to lie in front of friends than strangers. Indeed, the absence of any members of the relevant community in the gallery or on the jury may embolden a witness who is prone to lie or may at least allow the witness to be more careless with the facts. In such circumstances, the witness is not directly accountable to his own community for the testimony he provides. *** The Supreme Court has also justified public access on the expectation that publicity may "induce unknown witnesses to come forward with relevant testimony." Certainly, this cannot be so unless the specific community in which the witnesses are located has easy access to the trial.

* * *

V A FRAMEWORK FOR ANALYSIS OF REFORM

*** A serious effort at reforming criminal justice in Indian country ought [ ] to look outside the federal system. Put another way, the reform analysis ought to begin one step prior to evaluation and reform of the federal system. Such an effort might begin by asking whether the federal government is the proper governmental institution to provide law enforcement and criminal justice on Indian reservations. After all, the federal government is only one of the possible providers of criminal justice and public safety on Indian reservations.

In the United States today, there are three different providers of criminal justice in Indian country. In addition to the federal system, many tribal systems are involved in criminal justice, though their jurisdiction is limited to misdemeanors. And in some states (those in which Public Law 280 or similar laws prevail), state and local governments have criminal jurisdiction on Indian reservations. A careful focus on reform of criminal justice in Indian country would evaluate each of these three government-types and determine which is best suited to the important responsibility of Indian country criminal justice. Each of the three government types has advantages and disadvantages compared to the others.

For example, while the existing federal system has all of the problems set forth above (and more), state authority in this realm also poses some problems. Although the fundamental geographic and accountability issues posed by prosecutions by distant federal prosecutors might be mitigated by use of local state prosecutors, new problems might arise. Given that the federal system was justified by the notion that local state citizens were the tribe's "deadliest enemies," we might see serious pushback and concern by tribes in response to a proposal to turn criminal authority over to the states. *** Yet, despite the problems related to federal and state prosecutors, real concerns might be raised in some quarters about giving tribes more power over criminal justice. To outsiders (and sometimes to insiders), tribal governments are sometimes viewed as being tugged in inappropriate directions by warring political factions and the reputations of tribal officials are sometimes tarnished by assertions of corruptibility. As a result, some might view the independence and lack of accountability of federal prosecutors as a distinct advantage that helps them, in most cases, to make charging decisions in a fairer and more objective fashion. As this analysis of the prosecutorial function illustrates, careful analysis for purposes of a reform agenda is a complex task. ***

CONCLUSION

The Constitution implicitly and explicitly recognizes that crime is a local problem and should be addressed by local institutions. Two of the key institutions of American criminal justice, prosecutor and juries, have been designed in such a way to execute this fundamental constitutional norm. Both prosecutors and juries, however, fail to meet their constitutionally envisioned responsibilities in federal Indian country cases, primarily because they do not embrace the Constitution's clear preference for local criminal justice solutions to local crime problems.

In most of the United States, addressing violent acts in criminal trials is an expressive community act. Indeed, most felony prosecutions in this country are conducted under the direct authority of prosecutors who are elected by the community they serve. Because the Indian country is dealt out of its criminal justice system, the process of criminal justice on Indian reservations is neither an affirmation of community mores nor a formalized expression of community outrage. To the local community, it is, at best, a hollow effort. At worst, it is simply another imposition of authority by a foreign government that does not even seriously intend to occupy the soil upon which it seeks to impose its will. It is a relic of the colonialist roots of the American criminal justice system. ***

If a fundamental principle of American governance and of criminal jurisprudence is that crime and criminal justice are local issues, then Indian communities deserve a far greater role in the criminal justice system that affects them. The United States Constitution may well demand it.

NOTES & QUESTIONS

1. *Reading Indian Law*:
   - Washburn suggests that self-determination has been a consistent goal of federal Indian policy, but rules limiting both the jurisdiction of tribal courts and the penalties they may impose interfere with that goal. What policy changes are needed to encourage tribes to play a larger role in criminal justice? How is the tribal community impacted when trials are held in federal courthouses? Why does the location of

a criminal trial matter? Explain why public trials are important to criminal justice.

- Articulate what role a prosecutor plays in a criminal proceeding. What is prosecutorial discretion and how does it affect federal prosecutions in Indian country when the prosecutor is not a member of the tribal community? Would it be enough to hire more Indian people as federal prosecutors or are more fundamental structural changes necessary to promote justice in tribal communities?

- Washburn argues that criminal defendants are entitled to a jury of their peers, but observes that federal prosecutions often include no Indian jurors. In fact Washburn notes that some jury systems are structurally designed in ways that discourage calling Indian jurors because they use only state, but not tribal, voter rolls. Why is it important that a jury hearing a criminal case arising out of Indian country contain members of the tribal community? Are there structural or even constitutional problems to using jury pools drawn from federal districts instead of tribal communities?

2. *Indian Status As an Element of the Crime*: Building on the discussion of race presented by Professor Berger in Chapter 3 and the critique presented by Professor Clinton in Chapter 14 suggesting Congress lacks the authority to legislate for tribal communities – the federal statutes relied upon for most Indian country prosecutions require the prosecutor to prove the Indian status of one of the parties. Non-Indian prosecutors sometimes forget this is a required element of the offense and neglect to offer sufficient evidence, resulting in an acquittal. Consider *United States v. Seymour*, 684 Fed. Appx. 662 (9th Cir. 2017):

> Here, the government did not produce any evidence that Seymour has "some quantum of Indian blood" as required for his convictions under the [Major Crimes Act]. To prove Seymour's Indian status, the government relies primarily on a "Tribal Affidavit." The Tribal Affidavit is signed by a Tribal Enrollment Officer of the White Mountain Apache Tribe and states merely that Seymour is "an enrolled member of the White Mountain Apache Tribe," but says nothing about Seymour's Indian blood. ***
>
> The government now contends that the Tribal Affidavit, along with other circumstantial evidence, proves Seymour's blood quantum when considered in light of the White Mountain Apache Tribe's constitution, which establishes criteria for tribal membership. But without any evidence regarding the basis for Seymour's enrollment in the tribe, or about Seymour's ancestry, even construing the facts in the light most favorable to the prosecution, we cannot say that any rational trier of fact could find that Seymour has "some quantum of Indian blood." *** We are compelled to hold on this thin record

that no rational jury could find beyond a reasonable doubt the blood-quantum element of Seymour's offenses, as required by our precedent.

Because the government failed to introduce sufficient evidence of Seymour's Indian blood quantum, the case is reversed and remanded to the district court with direction to enter judgment of acquittal.

Seymour illustrates some of the problems with federal criminal prosecutors that Dean Washburn illustrated in *American Indians, Crime, and the Law*. In a tribal court it would be sufficient for a tribal prosecutor to show that the accused is a member of the tribe, as tribes have authority over their members and their territory. A tribal prosecutor would also pay more attention to the Indian status of the defendant because the accused is a member of the tribal community.

What role does race play in this discussion of criminal justice? What are the negative effects of having the federal court attempt to define the contours of tribal court criminal jurisdiction and restrict the penalties tribes may impose? How would cases like *Seymour* work differently if they were heard in tribal court?

3. *Tribal Law and Order Act*: Dean Washburn attributes one of the problems with criminal justice in Indian country to the limited criminal power of tribal courts. He notes that Congress only permits tribes to assert misdemeanor criminal jurisdiction with a maximum penalty of one year in jail or $5,000. That changed in 2010 with the passage of the Tribal Law and Order Act (TLOA).

TLOA permits tribes to impose much harsher penalties; up to three years in jail per offense and a maximum nine years per event and a financial penalty of up to $15,000. But in order to take advantage of these enhanced criminal powers tribes must comply with some enhanced protections for criminal procedures.

(c) Rights of defendants. In a criminal proceeding in which an Indian tribe, in exercising powers of self-government, imposes a total term of imprisonment of more than 1 year on a defendant, the Indian tribe shall—

    (1) provide to the defendant the right to effective assistance of counsel at least equal to that guaranteed by the United States Constitution; and

    (2) at the expense of the tribal government, provide an indigent defendant the assistance of a defense attorney licensed to practice law by any jurisdiction in the United States that applies appropriate professional licensing standards and effectively ensures the competence and professional responsibility of its licensed attorneys;

(3) require that the judge presiding over the criminal proceeding–
    (A) has sufficient legal training to preside over criminal proceedings; and
    (B) is licensed to practice law by any jurisdiction in the United States;
(4) prior to charging the defendant, make publicly available the criminal laws (including regulations and interpretative documents), rules of evidence, and rules of criminal procedure (including rules governing the recusal of judges in appropriate circumstances) of the tribal government; and
(5) maintain a record of the criminal proceeding, including an audio or other recording of the trial proceeding.

How does the enhanced criminal sentencing given to tribes under TLOA address the problems Dean Washburn identified? Does TLOA promote tribal self-governance? Now that tribes have enhanced criminal powers, do you think tribal communities will play a more active role in criminal justice?

It is worth noting that some tribes have opposed TLOA's requirements because they force tribal courts to 'look' like state or federal courts. Tribes that are protective of their own autonomy, or those without the funds to comply with the enhanced procedures, continue to only assert misdemeanor criminal jurisdiction. For a discussion of the choice TLOA requires tribes to take see Angela Riley, *Crime and Governance in Indian Country*, 63 UCLA L. Rev. 1564 (2016).

4. *Criminal Jurisdiction and Culture*: Dean Washburn is the third author in this text to suggest that traditional or cultural attitudes toward criminal justice are different in Indian communities. Recall Professor Riley in Chapter 4:

> The defendants' standard of integrity in many Indian courts is much higher than in the State and Federal Courts of the United States. When requested to enter a plea to a charge the Indian defendant, standing before respected tribal judicial leaders, with complete candor usually discloses the facts. With mutual honesty and through the dictates of experience, the Indian judge often takes a statement of innocence at face value, discharging the defendant who has indeed, according to tribal custom, been placed in jeopardy.

And Chief Justice Yazzie in Chapter 5:

> Under the vertical justice system, when a Navajo is charged with a crime, the judge asks (in English): "Are you guilty or not guilty?" A Navajo cannot respond because there is no precise term for "guilty" in the Navajo language. The word "guilt" implies a moral

fault which commands retribution. It is a nonsense word in Navajo law due to the focus on healing, integration with the group, and the end goal of nourishing ongoing relationships with the immediate and extended family, relatives, neighbors and community.

Putting these chapters together, what role does culture play in the creation and promotion of a criminal justice system? In Chapter 2 Professor Williams calls for a return to autochthonous legal systems grounded in cultural traditions. How might tribal justice systems work differently if they were freed from federal restraints? Are you concerned that such a system might not respect the rights of the accused, and if so what checks might be placed upon a purely chthonic justice system? For a discussion of Indigenous approaches to criminal justice see David Milward, *Not Just the Peace Pipe but Also the Lance: Exploring Different Possibilities for Indigenous Control over Criminal Justice*, 43:1 Wicazo Sa Review 97 (2008); Chris Cunneen & Juan Tauri, *Indigenous Criminology* (Bristol University Press 2016).

5. *Beyond the Law*: From Criminal Justice, to American Indian / Indigenous Studies, to Women and Gender Studies the problems of violence against women in Native communities are particularly acute. Sarah Deer writes in *The Beginning and End of Rape: Confronting Sexual Violence in Native America* (University of Minnesota Press 2015) that "the legacy of relocation, chronic poverty, and historical trauma significantly reduces the opportunities available to Native women and makes them vulnerable to prostitution and sex trafficking." In a report funded by the US Department of Justice and authored by professors of sociology and criminal justice, the authors conclude that Native women in some communities in the United States are murdered at rates up to ten times the national average. They are more likely to be raped, sexually assaulted, and physically assaulted than women of any other racial group, while cultural factors make it less likely that Native women will report this abuse; "Cultural barriers also prevent some American Indian and Alaska Native women from seeking assistance from those outside the community, while issues of privacy may also prevent others from seeking help inside close-knit tribal communities where 'everyone knows everyone else's business.'" Ronet Bachman et al., *Violence against American Indian and Alaska Native Women and the Criminal Justice Response: What Is Known* (US Dept. Justice, August 2008; available at www.ncjrs.gov/pdffiles1/nij/grants/223691.pdf).

How can tribal communities address these issues of gender violence that are not unique to, but are particularly common within, Indian country? Why are Native women particularly vulnerable? The Violence Against Women Act (VAWA) of 2013 expanded tribal criminal jurisdiction to permit tribal courts to prosecute some non-Indians who commit acts of dating or domestic violence in Indian country. For a discussion of VAWA's expanded tribal authority see Maura Douglas, *Sufficiently Criminal Ties: Expanding VAWA Criminal Jurisdiction for Indian Tribes*, 166 U. Pa. L. Rev. 745 (2018).

FURTHER READING

- Barbara Creel, *The Right to Counsel for Indians Accused of a Crime: A Tribal and Congressional Imperative*, 18 Mich. J. Race & L. 317 (2013).
- Samuel Ennis, *Reaffirming Indian Tribal Court Criminal Jurisdiction over Non-Indians: An Argument for a Statutory Abrogation of Oliphant*, 57 UCLA L. Rev. 553 (2009).
- Elizabeth Kronk, *The Emerging Problem of Methamphetamine: A Threat Signaling the Need to Reform Criminal Jurisdiction in Indian Country*, 82 N.D. L. Rev. 1249 (2006).
- Brian L. Lewis, *Do You Know What You Are? You Are What You Is; You Is What You Am: Indian Status for the Purpose of Federal Criminal Jurisdiction and the Current Split in the Courts of Appeals*, 26 Harv. J. Racial & Ethnic Just. 241 (2010).
- Richard Monette, *Indian Country Jurisdiction and the Assimilative Crimes Act*, 69 Or. L. Rev. 269 (1990).
- Judith Resnik, *Tribes, Wars, and the Federal Courts: Applying the Myths and the Methods of* Marbury v. Madison *to Tribal Courts' Criminal Jurisdiction*, 36 Ariz. St. L.J. 77 (2005).
- Molly Schiffler, *Women of Color and Crime: A Critical Race Theory Perspective to Address Disparate Prosecution*, 56 Ariz. L. Rev. 1203 (2014).
- Kevin Washburn, *Federal Criminal Law and Tribal Self-Determination*, 84 N.C. L. Rev. 779 (2006).

16

Factbound and Splitless: The Certiorari Process As Barrier to Justice for Indian Tribes

Matthew L. M. Fletcher

51 Ariz. L. Rev. 933 (2009)

Thousands of cases are appealed to the Supreme Court every year, and yet the Court often decides fewer than one hundred. The cases it accepts become canonical, articulating interpretations of the law that are binding on courts across the country. Given the stakes, it is important to understand how the Court selects the cases which are ultimately decided. In 1925 Congress expanded the Court's discretionary jurisdiction which precipitated the creation of the modern 'Rule of Four'. Essentially, during their weekly conference the justices vote on which cases to decide. It takes four votes to grant 'certiorari' and schedule the case for briefing, argument, and decision. The Court has further established some guidelines to help it determine when a case is cert-worthy. These rules do not treat all cases equally, but instead attempt to highlight cases the Court feels are the most important to decide.

This groundbreaking piece by Matthew L. M. Fletcher argues that Indian law cases are uniquely disadvantaged by some of the rules the Supreme Court applies to the selection of cases, and that Indian tribes in particular struggle to get the Court's attention when they are the appellants. This scholarship marries quantitative methodology with narrative, and utilizes primary sources to provide insight on the Court's behavior. Fletcher argues that because so many Indian law cases involve litigating history, many cases which may be decided incorrectly by lower courts are deemed 'Factbound' and denied further consideration. He further argues that Indian law cases are often termed 'Splitless' because an improper interpretation of a treaty will seldom result in a split among federal circuits. Fletcher concludes that Indian law cases are thus at a structural disadvantage when it comes to consideration by the Court. While this excerpt focuses more on the narrative than the quantitative methodology, the entire piece is worthy of nuanced examination.

As you read Fletcher's work, consider the enormity of the implications of the patterns he uncovers. Pay special attention to his discussion of Rule 10. Does the rule systematically discriminate against tribal interests? What does it mean for Indian law advocates if the Court is more willing to hear cases appealed by states than by tribes? How can Indians trust a federal judicial system led by a Supreme Court which privately admits that it is sometimes asked to review a case which is wrongly decided or poorly reasoned, but decides not to correct the error because the issue is considered not of sufficient national importance? Are some communities more disadvantaged than others? Is there a solution? What can tribes do to better attract the attention of the Supreme Court?

INTRODUCTION

Professor Edward Hartnett once asserted that the certiorari process, which defines the Supreme Court's power to decide its own docket, "has had a profound role in shaping our substantive constitutional law." The power to choose a few select cases among several thousand petitions each year is an awesome power. Hartnett challenged future scholars to perform an empirical analysis of the impact of the certiorari process on substantive constitutional law. There are a growing number of empirical studies of the Supreme Court's agenda-setting through the certiorari process, but few scholars have examined the impact of the certiorari process on a substantive area of constitutional law. This Article takes up that challenge.

To meet Hartnett's challenge, this Article reviews 163 preliminary memoranda written by Supreme Court clerks in the certiorari decision-making process (the "cert pool memos") during the 1986 through the 1993 docket years, memoranda only recently made public in the Digital Archive of the Papers of Justice Harry A. Blackmun. The Article only studies memos from federal Indian law cases. A study of the cert pool memos in a single subject area offers unique possibilities. It is, after all, the Supreme Court clerks who serve as the first gatekeeper to the Supreme Court. Moreover, the influence of the cert pool memo in moving a case onto the Court's "discuss list" and then to certiorari is critical, yet understudied. In most instances, the cert pool memos are the only writing from the Court discussing the cases in which the Court denies certiorari. Studies show that when the author of a cert pool memo recommends denial, other Justices' clerks generally spend little or no time arguing to grant certiorari.

Federal Indian law was a natural choice of focus, not only because of this author's experience in the subject matter, but also because of the fortuitous timing of the memos' release. Something extraordinary has been happening in federal Indian law. From 1959, the generally recognized beginning of the modern era of federal Indian law, to 1987, when the Supreme Court decided the major Indian gaming case *California v. Cabazon Band of Mission Indians,* Indians and Indian tribes (to whom this Article will often call "tribal interests") won nearly 60% of federal Indian law cases decided by the Supreme Court. But since *Cabazon,* tribal interests have lost more than 75% of their cases. The sample under study – from 1986 to 1993 – covers the first years of this radical turnaround. Consistent with the overall pattern of the period, tribal interests lost about 75% of their cases during the period under study.

The research presented in this Article reveals powerful evidence that the Supreme Court's certiorari process harshly discriminates against the interests of Indian tribes and individual American Indians. During the period analyzed in this study – October Terms (OT) 1986 through 1993 – the Supreme Court granted certiorari once out of ninety-two Indian tribe and tribal interest petitions (excluding three unpaid *in forma pauperis* prisoner petitions involving indigent Indians in which the Court granted certiorari). During the same period of time, the Court granted cert fourteen times out of a mere thirty-seven petitions filed by states and local units of government against tribal interests – more than a third of the petitions. Other petitioners opposing tribal interests did not fare as well as state governments, but the Court still granted their petitions significantly more often than tribal parties (four grants out of twenty-eight petitions). This difference is statistically significant. Because so few tribal petitions are granted, and relatively so many petitions filed by opposing parties are granted, the number of cases where a tribal party is the respondent – and at a clear disadvantage statistically – is overwhelming.

*** The question remains – how does the Court's certiorari process discriminate so wildly against tribal interests? The Supreme Court's certiorari process, which includes the clerks that do much of the Court's work, discriminates against Indians and Indian tribes in two ways. First, the Court undervalues the merits and importance of petitions filed by tribal interests. Second, the Court overvalues the merits and importance of petitions filed by the traditional opponents of tribal interests – state governments and, to a lesser extent, the federal government and private entities. In shorthand, if a tribe or an Indian loses in the federal courts of appeal, the Court will almost never review the case, but if a state loses against a tribe or an Indian, the Court often grants certiorari. This imbalance skews the development of federal Indian law doctrine.

Emblematic of how the certiorari process undermines tribal interests is *Elliott v. Vermont. Elliott* is a case about aboriginal hunting and fishing rights of the Abenaki people. The cert pool memowriter recommended that the Court deny the petition because it was both factbound and splitless, as are nearly all Indian treaty claims. But the memowriter acknowledged that the petitioners had a valid claim. The Vermont Supreme Court applied the wrong standard – in fact, that court had created a new common-law standard out of whole cloth – and the court had refused to consider important evidence favoring the exercise of the aboriginal rights. Despite a strong showing that the lower court had committed reversible error, the Supreme Court denied the petition.

This Article argues that the certiorari decisions made by the Supreme Court tend to prejudice tribal interests because the entire certiorari process – especially the participation of the clerks – slants the Court's certiorari decisions against tribal interests in subtle but unmistakable ways. It would be tempting to argue that the Supreme Court's agenda has shifted from more of a balance of tribal and non-tribal interests since 1987 to an agenda that is opposed to tribal interests on most levels. This Article, backed with empirical support drawn from the cert pool memos, offers a theory different than mere agenda-setting: that the certiorari process itself creates conditions that lead the Supreme Court to accept cases that are likely to be decided against tribal interests.

Elliott is a good example of how the certiorari process and the cert pool create conditions that prejudice tribal interests. *Elliott* is typical of cases that arise between tribal interests and others; namely, that conflict arises out of attempted enforcement of Indian treaty rights and the subsequent exclusion of state law and regulation. Critically, memowriters recognize that tribal claims are usually based on a single treaty or statute grounded deep in American history. The treaty's terms and history are bound to a particular territory, so a law clerk would be hard-pressed to argue that the case has national implications. Because Indian law cases have limited territorial reach, splits in lower court authority are unlikely. Jurisdictional splits are the most important objective factor favoring a grant of certiorari. Moreover, these cases are complex and involve "factbound" applications of settled law. The petitioner is therefore praying the Court to correct a lower court error applying rules of law previously determined by the Supreme Court. This, according to the Court's own rules, it will rarely do. Finally, as memowriters demonstrate time and again, the cert pool members assume tribal interests are not important to their audience. ***

I THE CERTIORARI PROCESS

***

B *The Mechanics of Modern Certiorari Decision-Making*

The way the Supreme Court decides to accept a petition for certiorari has long been a virtual mystery, except perhaps to those involved in the process. What is known is that the Court grants cert in only a handful of cases – often less than 100 a year – out of over several thousand petitions filed each Term. When a litigant receives an adverse judgment from a federal court of appeal or the highest court of a state judiciary, the party may seek Supreme Court review. To do so, it must file a petition for certiorari with the Court – a "cert petition." *** Each of the Supreme Court Justices hires clerks – usually recent law school graduates with some experience in lower federal courts – who review all the cert petitions, cert oppositions, and amicus briefs. The clerks prepare a short memorandum, formally known as a "preliminary memorandum," in which they summarize the facts, the procedural history, and the claims of the parties. They include a short discussion with candid commentary on the relative merits of the petitions and recommend the Court either grant or deny the petition. In some instances, especially when the federal government has an interest or special expertise in an area of law addressed by a cert petition (federal Indian law being a prime example), they recommend that the Court seek input from the United States, represented by the Solicitor General – Call for the Views of the Solicitor General (CVSG).

Seven of the nine current Justices (Justices Alito and Stevens excluded) participate in what is known as the "cert pool," whereby the law clerks are assigned a docket number and asked to write a preliminary memorandum (colloquially known as a cert pool memo) about the petition. During the period addressed by this study – the 1986 through the 1993 Terms – fewer Justices participated in the pool. Justices

Brennan, Marshall, and, as noted above, Stevens, did not participate, although they each received copies of every cert pool memo.

The cert pool memos are the Court's first take on whether a case is "certworthy," an internal term of art that can be best defined by referring to Supreme Court Rule 10, which governs the exercise of judicial discretion the Court is allowed when making certiorari decisions. Rule 10 indicates that the Court will review petitions for numerous factors, including: (1) whether "a United States court of appeals has entered a decision in conflict with the decision of another United States court of appeals on the same important matter;" (2) whether "a United States court of appeals ... has decided an important federal question in a way that conflicts with a decision by a state court of last resort;" (3) whether "a United States court of appeals ... has so far departed from the accepted and usual course of judicial proceedings, or sanctioned such a departure by a lower court, as to call for an exercise of this Court's supervisory power;" (4) whether "a state court of last resort has decided an important federal question in a way that conflicts with the decision of another state court of last resort or of a United States court of appeals;" (5) whether "a state court or a United States court of appeals has decided an important question of federal law that has not been, but should be, settled by this Court;" or (6) whether "a state court or a United States court of appeals ... has decided an important federal question in a way that conflicts with relevant decisions of this Court." Running throughout the rule is the requirement that the question presented must be "important." Rule 10 also states that "[a] petition for writ of certiorari is rarely granted when the asserted error consists of erroneous factual findings or the misapplication of a properly stated rule of law."

*** The Court avoids petitions asking it to review a lower court's findings of fact or application of a settled legal standard to specific facts. In the parlance of the cert pool memo, cases in which there is no split in authority are "splitless." Cases in which a party is asking the Court to review a lower court's application of specific facts to a settled legal principle are "factbound." It is clear from reading the cert pool memos contained in Justice Blackmun's archives that the vast majority of Indian law-related cert petitions are "factbound" or "splitless" – and often both.

Cert pool memos feature the Supreme Court clerks' recommendations on whether to grant or deny a petition *** These recommendations often are hedged by a note that a case is a "close call." Not even the clerks can predict when the Court will find a case "important" enough to justify granting the petition. The Court might find some clear circuit splits too insignificant to resolve. In other instances, the clerks note that a split is weak or illusory, *** or that the kind of dispute creating the split is unlikely to recur. In short, most cases that are important enough are placed on the so-called discuss list. Once the "discuss list" is compiled, the Justices confer, reviewing the merits of granting cert to each case. Ultimately, if four Justices vote to consider a case, cert is granted. If the requisite four votes are not obtained, cert is denied.

II THE RISE AND FALL OF FEDERAL INDIAN LAW

F *Applying the Rule 10 Criteria to Indian Law Cert Petitions*

1 Circuit Splits and Splits in Authority

As Rule 10 suggests, the best way to convince the Court to grant cert in a particular case is to identify a circuit split or a conflict with Supreme Court precedent. In general, the study found few splits in authority regarding federal Indian law, perhaps because the vast majority of the cert petitions in the sample were from just three circuits – the Eighth, Ninth, and Tenth Circuits. Cert petitions labeled "split-less" are usually relegated to the dustbin. In some criminal law and Eleventh Amendment cases where a split did exist, however, the Court granted cert. Circuit splits tend not to arise in Indian law cases because often the only possible split is between a state court and a federal circuit. For example, a cert pool memo authored by a Kennedy clerk disposed of a petition arising out of Alaska by noting, "Because of the local nature of this dispute, no conflict will arise in the circuits." In *South Dakota v. Spotted Horse*, Justice Blackmun's clerk wrote a supplemental memo to the cert pool memo in which she noted, "As the poolwriter noted, there will never be a split on the question of South Dakota's jurisdiction over these tribal highways because both [Eighth Circuit] and the [South Dakota Supreme Court] agree that the State is without jurisdiction." In *Tarbell v. United States*, a criminal case involving the application of a federal statute that applied to New York Indians, the cert pool memowriter, an O'Connor clerk, noted, "Of course, [New York] state is probably the only other jurisdiction that would have an opportunity to rule on the issue."

Moreover, the lack of circuit splits also can be attributed to the subjective character of many federal Indian law doctrines, such as the federal Indian law preemption doctrine or the reservation diminishment cases, rendering "factbound" what might otherwise be an apparent split in authority. Because these doctrines are subjective, different outcomes between circuits may be attributable to different facts. If cases are considered "factbound," Rule 10 weighs against granting cert, even where a split in authority can be identified. As one Blackmun clerk noted in the cert pool memo in *White Mountain Apache Tribe v. Arizona State Transportation Board*: "A final factor which may be considered either as supporting a grant or denying a grant is that the case involves pre-emption in the context of Indian law. Cases involving pre-emption claims by Indian tribes may merit a different analysis."

One cert pool memo, involving a claim that federal Indian law preempted a state's taxation of attorney fees, demonstrated the difficulty in establishing a circuit split. The memowriter, a Blackmun clerk, identified three Supreme Court decisions that applied to the question, but the cases' disparate fact patterns created different applications of the federal Indian law preemption rule – "I think [appellant] has the better of the argument, though [appellant] overstates its case by suggesting a direct conflict with this Court's prior decisions. Rather, I think the question is open." ***

During the study period, the Court sometimes did not act on cases in which the petitioner alleged a viable split or conflict with prior precedents if the split was "weak" or "illusory." In *Osceola v. Florida Department of Revenue*, a case involving the application of the Tax Injunction Act to individual Indians seeking immunity from state taxes, the memowriter noted that the older case in the split probably would have been decided differently if it were reconsidered in accordance with later Supreme Court precedent.

Another cert pool memowriter described the apparent split in authority in *Washington v. Confederated Tribes of Colville Reservation*, a case where the State "wanted to enforce petty traffic laws against Indians on reservations," as "not clean." There, what seemed to be a circuit split turned out to be illusory because the character of the two state laws involved differed – one was explicitly criminal, the other was a civil traffic statute. Explaining away the apparent split in authority with a kind of logical leap, the memowriter concluded, "It remains possible that either [court], if someday faced with the facts of the other's case, would come out just as the other did."

The Court is also less likely to grant certiorari when a split of authority is based in state law. *Richardson v. Mt. Adams Furniture* involved tribal sovereign immunity in the context of off-reservation business activities. The cert pool memo recommended seeking the Solicitor General's input after the "[petitioner] identified an existing division of authority among state supreme courts regarding the extent of tribal immunity from suit with respect to commercial activities undertaken by tribal entities off the reservation." The memowriter explained:

> Tribal immunity is a creature of federal law and can be adjusted only by Congress. To the extent immunity reflects federal policies regarding tribal autonomy and relations with outsiders, the Government may have an interest in ensuring that the Court selects an appropriate vehicle for addressing the immunity question.

*** It is often the case that a fact pattern will be unique to a particular tribe or reservation, rendering the possibility of a split very unlikely. In cert petitions brought by the Oneida Nations of New York and Wisconsin in the New York land claims, the cert pool memowriter wrote:

> This is a case of some practical significance inasmuch as there is a great deal of land in the balance, but the questions are not of general legal significance meriting the plenary review of this Court.
>
> . . . .
>
> There is no indication that these issues have arisen before or that they will arise again.
>
> . . . .
>
> There is no split of authority on the relevant powers or limitations found in the Articles of Confederation or the Treaty of Fort Stanwix.

*** One certiorari denial, *Circle Native Community v. Alaska Dept. of Health and Social Services*, demonstrates the enormous complexity of federal Indian law questions. It was an Alaskan case involving tribal authority to decide internal child custody matters after federal statutes purported to divest Alaskan Native villages of their tribal character. The case also posed the question of whether Alaskan Native villages retained sovereign immunity. The cert pool memowriter found that the splits in authority (there were two in this instance) were "square," meaning that the case squarely presented the splits for resolution. The memowriter concluded, "Although the issues are not very interesting and seem to have little national significance, they are quite important to Native–State relations in Alaska, and only this Court can resolve the conflict. I therefore unenthusiastically recommend [a Call for Response with] a view to GRANT."

But the state of Alaska threw a monkey wrench into the proceedings – they questioned the legal status of the petitioner, often a confusing question in Alaskan Native disputes. Cert was subsequently denied. The supplemental memo drafted by the clerk notes the clerk's confusion:

> In short, there may be good answers to the problems [respondent] raises, but I do not know what they are, and in any event the Court need not address the [jurisdiction] question presented in a case that would require preliminary resolution of other thorny and legally insignificant issues.

As a result, the clerk recommended denial. After the petitioner replied to these questions with copies of tribal council resolutions and a trial court order recognizing the Community's right to intervene, Justice Blackmun's clerk noted, "I recommend that the Court [call for the views of the Solicitor General]. The split is real and conceded. The [Solicitor General] may help to sort out the preliminary problems." Regardless, only two Justices (Blackmun and Stevens) voted to seek the views of the Solicitor General, while the rest voted to deny certiorari.

The emphasis on locating a split in authority affects federal Indian law, perhaps, more than in most other areas of law. Consider *Sokaogon Chippewa Community v. Exxon Corp.* The case involved a highly contested land claim of immense importance to the tribal community and its neighbors, focusing on an 1854 treaty that was far from plain. The cert pool memowriter dismissed the cert petition's claims with a curt blurb:

> I think Judge Posner correctly interpreted the 1854 treaty as extinguishing the occupancy [rights] under the 1842 treaty in exchange for establishment of reservations and payments. [Petitioner], having lost on its interpretation argument in both the [district court and the Seventh Circuit], now seeks further appellate review. Absent a split, I see no reason for the [Court] to look further into this issue.

Of course, there likely would never be a split in authority on the 1854 treaty because that case might be the only case ever turning on the treaty. Of all the cert pool memos in the sample, only one memowriter – an O'Connor clerk – recognized that "splits are rarer in Indian cases .... ." And yet, he recommended denial of cert in *Lummi Indian Tribe v. Whatcom County* even though he was not "sure that [the Ninth Circuit] got this right – it's a close case – but there's no split, and the issue doesn't seem crucial enough to be independently certworthy."

2 Error Correction ("Factbound")

Many Indian law-related cert petitions are based in historical and treaty claims that arise in facts limited to a particular tribe or region. Rule 10 notes that "[a] petition for a writ of certiorari is rarely granted when the asserted error consists of erroneous factual findings or the misapplication of a properly stated rule of law." These claims are often labeled "factbound" and denied.

This issue is endemic to Indian treaty claims brought by tribal interests. The number of cases where Indian tribes lost below and a Supreme Court clerk noted that their petition was at least colorable, if not compelling, but where the clerk recommended the denial of cert anyway, is surprisingly high. The standard in these cases usually is described as: (1) Did the lower court correctly state (as opposed to apply) the applicable rule?; (2) If yes, deny. As such, because few courts commit the gross error of stating the wrong standard, the Court will hear few Indian treaty petitions brought by tribal interests who lost below. Even in instances where the lower court did state the wrong standard *** the Court may still deny cert.

The number of cases classified as "factbound" is the most significant subgroup of the sample. One example is *Little Earth of United Tribes, Inc. v. Kemp*. The petitioner brought a race discrimination claim (amongst other claims) because the United States foreclosed the mortgage of the only public housing project for transient urban Indians. On the cert petition, the pool memowriter noted that the case was based entirely on the factual findings of the district court and recommended denial. Justice Blackmun's clerk agreed with the recommendation but annotated the cert pool memo to state, "sad case." ***

Similarly, a cert pool memo in *Lummi Indian Tribe v. Washington* denigrated the Lummi Tribe's claims by noting:

> [Petitioner] is unhappy with [the Ninth Circuit]'s determination of the boundaries of the Lummi Reservation. Based on little more than the testimony of a 100-year-old man in the early 1900s, [petitioner] wants this Court to hold contrary to the plain language of the treaty, the facts found by the [district court], and the presumption against conveyance of land under navigable waters. The [petition] should be denied.

Ultimately, the cert pool memo recommended denial on the basis of unimportance.

Perhaps a more significant example of the fact-heavy character of Indian law cases was *Elliott v. Vermont*, a case addressing whether the Abenaki people retained their aboriginal rights after the State of Vermont was incorporated into the Union in 1791. The state prosecuted Missisquoi Indians attempting to exert their fishing rights on land they believed to be owned by the tribe in aboriginal title. Under Rule 10, the Court is unlikely to grant cert in a case where the lower court allegedly misapplied a properly stated rule of law. As the cert pool memowriter noted:

> At bottom, [petitioners] complain that the Vermont Supreme Court[] misapplied the rule of extinguishment [of aboriginal title], not that the Court misstated it. Indeed, the Vermont Court did an excellent and extensive summary of the law of extinguishment, which appears to be correct in all its particulars. Nonetheless, [petitioners] appear to have a substantial argument that the admission of Vermont into the Union, and Congress' concomitant de facto recognition of Vermonter's land claims under the Wentworth grants, are not sufficient to establish the clear intent required to extinguish aboriginal title. Although the Vermont Court's opinion is both exhaustive and scholarly, it does not take account of a fair bit of evidence introduced by [petitioners] that suggest that even after 1791, the Abenakis continued to exercise aboriginal fishing rights. The case is *sui generis* and probably does not warrant a grant of certiorari absent a more meaty legal issue . . . .

This somewhat internally inconsistent cert pool memo (calling the Vermont Supreme Court's opinion "excellent and extensive" while noting that the court ignored the critical evidence raised by the Indians) places the claim in the "factbound" category. The Court did not discuss this case in conference, according to Justice Blackmun's docket sheet.

The lesson from *Elliott* appears to be that, so long as the lower court states the proper test (a purely superficial exercise), the Supreme Court will not review the lower court's application of the test except in "rare" circumstances. Note that the cert pool memowriter must have had a short period of time to review the history of the State of Vermont (probably a well-documented history) and the history of the western Abenaki people; specifically, the Missisquoi people (probably not as well documented). It is unlikely that a cert pool clerk confronted with a case like *Elliott* could marshal the historical and legal knowledge in a short period of time to conclude that the Vermont Supreme Court was wrong.

Indian law scholars, however, have concluded that the Vermont Supreme Court in *Elliott* adopted a new test on aboriginal title extinguishment divorced from the Court's precedents – the "increasing weight of history" test. The petitioners' reply brief in support of its cert petition argued, in the words of Justice Blackmun's clerk, "Vermont [Supreme Court]'s 'weight of history' approach conflicts [with] this [Court]'s requirement that extinguishment be 'clear and unambiguous.'" To be fair to the memowriter, he did note that "an argument can be made that the Court has a special responsibility to ensure that Indian land claims are resolved properly, with due regard for the traditional federal policy of solicitude for Indian tribes." Even Justice Blackmun's clerk concluded that the petition was factbound and not certworthy.

Recent law graduates would have to have unusual knowledge about Indian history to conclude that a court was so wrong on most questions based in history and fact as to recommend that the Court grant cert. The chances of this happening, especially with Rule 10's admonition that it is "rare," in an Indian law context where a tribal interest is the petitioner, are all but zero. This structural problem likely affects tribal claims, most of which are based in history, more than any other constitutional subject area.

3 Importance

Rule 10 factors in the relative "importance" of a case in the certiorari process. "Importance" is the greatest subjective factor that affects whether or not the Court will grant cert in a particular case. The importance factor also provides the Court great leeway to set a federal Indian law agenda, should it choose to do so. The cert pool memos reflect clerks' predictions about what the Justices might find sufficiently important to grant cert. Many memos, too numerous to discuss in detail, evidence clerks hedging their bets by making recommendations to deny.

Many Indian law cases do not reach the discuss list because they are labeled too unimportant to consider. Yet in several cases, such as *Lyng v. Northwest Indian Cemetery Protective Association* and *Employment Division v. Smith (I and II)*, the Court granted certiorari despite a clerk's recommendation of a denial and noting the case to be factbound and splitless.

As the following examples demonstrate, when a case is brought by a state government, a local government, or the federal government against a tribal interest, the cert pool memos either trumpet the importance of the case because of the governmental interest involved or take it as a given that the case is important because a state or the federal government filed the petition. Even if the memowriter does neither and recommends denial, the Court might disregard the recommendation, as was the case in *Lyng*, *Smith I*, and *Smith II*. It may be that the Court reviews some cases recommended for denial because the Justices are concerned with leaving a lower court ruling in place that could apply to several states.

Brendale v. Confederated Tribes, a case involving the zoning authority of Indian tribes on reservation land, was sufficiently important to be granted cert. Amicus briefs filed by numerous states and counties noted that "the case is of national importance: of the 930,000 people who reside within Indian reservations nationwide, some 380,000 (41%) are non-Indians." The memowriter, a Rehnquist clerk, argued:

> To me, the [*Montana*] question appears certworthy, as it is not clear from *Montana* just exactly how much civil regulatory authority a tribe possesses over nonmembers within a reservation.
>
> . . . .
>
> And, as amici point out, the question of tribal zoning is potentially a very large issue, affecting many states and many private property owners, who would be divested of

some say in local zoning laws if it were held that tribal zoning preempted state regulation.

Justice Blackmun's clerk argued that the lower court decision favoring the tribes was "basically correct – zoning jurisdiction over non-Indian parcels is important to proper, consistent regulation of land uses. I would wait for further development." But five Justices voted to grant certiorari, perhaps on the basis that the number of non-Indians affected by the case was so large.

Some cases are important because of practical problems that would arise if a particular dispute is not resolved. *Mississippi Band of Choctaw Indians v. Holyfield*, the only Indian Child Welfare Act case granted certiorari by the Supreme Court to date, was splitless. Nonetheless, the memowriter argued that the Mississippi Supreme Court's decision "creates a jurisdictional 'black hole' because Indian Health Service had a practice of transporting expectant mothers off the reservation to give birth" in order to avoid the application of the Act. The Act required the adoption of all Indian children domiciled on the reservation to be adjudicated in tribal court. The Court had granted cert in a similar case years earlier, but that case had been settled and dismissed. After *Holyfield*, the Court has denied cert in every Indian Child Welfare Act-related case. ***

Often, the initial cert pool memo recommends that the Court seek the views of the Solicitor General to help in determining the importance of a case. Sometimes, a petition headed for denial for lack of importance is resurrected by a recommendation from the government to grant certiorari. *Negonsott v. Samuels*, one of the rare unpaid petitions in which the Court granted certiorari, is one such case. The cert pool memowriter noted a clear circuit split between the Eighth and Tenth Circuits, but argued against a grant because of the lack of importance of the case. After the cert pool memo recommended the Court call for a response from the State of Kansas, Kansas recommended that the Court grant certiorari. The memowriter remained uncertain because of the limited impact of the older Eighth Circuit decision and the complexities of Indian law. The Court then sought the views of the Solicitor General, which urged the Court to grant cert, which it did.

For whatever reason, Supreme Court clerks rarely find cert petitions filed by tribal interests to be important. For example, there are a good number of cert petitions brought by tribal interests the clerks found to be compelling, novel, or even interesting claims, but where the clerks also wrote that the underlying cases were unimportant for a variety of reasons, usually related to the narrow factual question. In short, claims brought by tribal interests are almost never important unless there is a non-Indian law-related question of importance attached to the petition. Often, the proxy for "importance" is whether a state government filed the cert petition.

One illustrative case is *Hoffman v. Native Village of Noatak*. There, the Ninth Circuit held that the Eleventh Amendment did not bar suit by Indian tribes against states. The cert pool memo begins, "Because these are complicated and far-reaching

matters of federal jurisdiction, and because there is a split with the 8th Circuit on the
11th Amendment issue, I recommend that the petition be granted." Justice Blackmun's clerk argued valiantly against a grant in a supplemental memo, noting:

> I agree with [the cert pool memowriter] that the 11th Amendment aspect of this case
> is certworthy. However, I think it would be appropriate for the Court to wait to see
> the actual consequences of [the Ninth Circuit]'s decision. [Petitioner's] contention
> that this decision will open the floodgates to litigation by Native Americans is
> empirically verifiable. Further, if [petitioner's] prediction is accurate, the Court
> will have ample opportunity to revisit the issue. The results of litigation from
> circuits other than [the Ninth Circuit] and [the Eighth Circuit] would also be
> helpful. Finally, while I believe the [Ninth Circuit] may have reached the correct
> result given the unique status of Native American tribal governments in the United
> States, the [Ninth Circuit] opinion in this case is less than careful in its analysis.
> The Court might well wait for a better reasoned opinion.

The argument did not dissuade the Court or even Justice Blackmun, who offered to
serve as the fourth vote for certiorari if necessary.

Another example is *South Dakota v. Bourland*, where the Court narrowly granted
cert despite a recommendation to deny. The cert pool memowriter noted that the
lower court decision favoring the Cheyenne River Sioux Tribe might have been
incorrect for failure to follow relevant Supreme Court precedent. But the memo
recommended denial because there was no split, nor could one be alleged. And yet,
despite the lack of a split and the recommendation of the cert pool memo, Chief
Justice Rehnquist and Justices White, Stevens, and Thomas voted to grant certiorari.
Is this a case of four Justices voting reflexively in favor of a cert petition from a state?

Consider the Oklahoma Tax Commission, the entity involved in more certiorari
petitions in this sample than any other except the United States – five as a petitioner
and four as a respondent. The Court granted certiorari in four of the five petitions
filed by the Oklahoma Tax Commission, but in none of the petitions brought by
tribes against the Commission. Ultimately, the Commission lost two of the three
cases it litigated to a final result in the Supreme Court – *Sac and Fox* and *Citizen
Band Potawatomi* – while winning in *Graham*, a relatively insignificant case with
only tangential Indian law issues. But in the cert pool memos, the clerks described
the interests of the Oklahoma Tax Commission as raising "important concerns of
federalism," while similar tribal petitions were "of no general significance."

Other petitions brought by state governments or agencies implicated the power of
states to enforce criminal laws against peyote, the power of states to enforce its taxes
on non-Indians in Indian Country, and the water rights of states and their constituents. The Court granted certiorari in all these cases.

Conversely, claims brought by tribal petitions often are labeled unimportant
without much discussion. One exemplary case is *Pueblo of Santo Domingo
v. Thompson*. The United States and the Pueblo had brought claims that the Pueblo

Lands Board had invalidly extinguished Pueblo title to certain lands in New Mexico. The cert pool memowriter noted, "It seems clear that the Board erred 60 years ago when it extinguished Pueblo title in this overlap land; section 14 of the 1924 Act prohibited such a result." But the poolwriter recommended denial because the outcome of the case would affect only a few tribes. Even Justice Blackmun's clerk wrote in the margin, "While I think [the Tenth Circuit] may have erred, I see no issue of general importance."

* * *

Similarly, the cert pool memowriter in *Makah Tribe v. Washington* noted that the lower court's decision may have been "a clearly unwarranted departure from precedent," but recommended denial of the petition because "review would be merely for error correction." The Ninth Circuit held that prevailing tribes in the *United States v. Washington* litigation could not recover attorney fees under federal civil rights statutes. Justice Blackmun's clerk's annotation, while sympathetic to the tribal petitioner, still doubted the importance of the question:

> This is a hard call. It seems to me that [petitioners] are right in every respect: [the Ninth Circuit]'s decision is wrong as a matter of law and has no obvious limiting principle. On the other hand, my instinct is that the memowriter may be correct in viewing this case as an isolated blunder. Since I'm also sympathetic to [petitioners] on the merits, [I'd] be inclined to keep their claim alive. I'm really not sure what the [Solicitor General] would have to say. I appeal to your judgment.

As with determinations that a case is "factbound," clerks often conclude that the limited geographic import of a particular claim renders the case less important – unless a state government brought the claim.

4 Gross Error

More rarely, the cert pool memos will assert that a lower court decision is clearly wrong, or in the Rule's language, "has so far departed from the accepted and usual course of judicial proceedings . . . ." As the language suggests, this happens less often than circuit splits. The complexity and ambiguity of federal Indian law, however, creates circumstances where lower courts do seem to deviate from Supreme Court precedents, perhaps more often than in other contexts. The classic example is *Department of Taxation and Finance of New York v. Milhelm Attea & Bros., Inc.* That case reached the Supreme Court twice: the first time, the Court GVR'd the case in light of *Oklahoma Tax Commission v. Citizen Band Potawatomi Indian Tribe of Oklahoma*; the second time, the Court reversed the New York Court of Appeals on the merits. The Court's opinion in *Milhelm Attea* noted that the outcome turned on "the narrow[] question of whether the New York scheme is inconsistent with the Indian Trader Statutes." The cert pool memos indicated another reason for the Court to decide the case. The memowriter indicated that a line of New York Court of Appeals' decisions were not aligned with Supreme Court precedent. Even prior to the *Milhelm Attea* remand, the Court had GVR'd an earlier New York Court of Appeals decision on similar grounds. The poolwriter noted:

> The [New York Court of Appeals] has not "moved' on this issue since the [Supreme Court] vacated and remanded *Herzog* in 1988, the decision below is at least suspect, and if [New York]'s regulatory approach is the only effective way petitioners can police the retail sale of taxable cigarettes on Indian reservations, the [courts] below have put [petitioners] in a tough spot.

After another decision from the New York Court of Appeals reaching the same outcome the cert pool memowriter wrote, "The [New York Court of Appeals] stubbornly refuses to alter its questionable preemption analysis, despite two GVR's from this [Court] (one in this case, and one in *Herzog*) . . . ." Moreover, according to the memo, "the issue, however, is important both legally and practically, and the [New York Court of Appeals] does not seem willing to heed anything but a reversal on the merits." Justice Blackmun's clerk objected, annotating the cert pool memo in the first *Milhem Attea* petition with this grumble: "Is this such an important case? What 20 [pages] of memos comes down to is this: the [New York Court of Appeals] misread one of this [Court]'s cases. What happened to the word 'split'[?]" ***

In other cases, the clerks focus on non-Indian law-related questions. One example is *Rhodes v. Vigil*. The Indian Health Service had lost at the lower court level on the question of its discretion to eliminate a program for handicapped Indian children. The cert pool memowriter noted, "There is no clear split in authority, but the decision below is certainly in tension with the Court's decisions, and the D.C. Circuit's approach . . . ." But the cert pool memowriter acknowledged that the split was not clean. The memowriter recommended granting cert on the basis of "the egregiousness of the [Tenth Circuit]'s errors . . . ." Justice Blackmun's clerk wrote a supplemental memo arguing against granting certiorari on the basis that the Indian law character of the claim made the split illusory. The argument won over Justice Blackmun, but the Court still granted certiorari.

G The Structure and Mechanics of the Certiorari Process Discriminates against Tribal Interests

1 The Mechanics of the Certiorari Process

There is a great deal of circumstantial evidence that the factors articulated in Rule 10 create a structural barrier to the fair disposition of cases brought by tribal interests. In short, the subjective and objective factors the Supreme Court's clerks look for in the certiorari process encourage the dismissal of tribal arguments.

Professor David Stras has broken down the import of the clerks in the Supreme Court's cert pool, first noting that the creation of the cert pool has "led to a homogenization of the [certiorari] process ... ," largely because the clerk in the cert pool now writes for "anywhere from five to eight Justices." Also, Stras points out, political science scholar H.W. Perry's interviews with former clerks "suggest that, because recommendations to deny a case are the norm, law clerks pay far less attention to those recommendations than to recommendations to grant during the annotation process, increasing the likelihood that an issue of importance will be overlooked." *** Stras argues that three factors push cert pool clerks to recommend a denial in tough cases: (1) it is less risky because a recommendation to deny will receive less scrutiny from clerks in other chambers; (2) it avoids cases in which the Court might be forced to dismiss a grant of certiorari as improvidently granted (apparently a result that clerks "dread"); and (3) general signals from the Court that the fewer cases the better.

Finally, the inexperience of the clerks hurts tribal petitions: "Incoming law clerks, often fresh off of a clerkship with a judge on the United States Courts of Appeals, have little training and even less experience screening petitions for certiorari." [T]here are several cert pool memos that evidence a clerk's lack of understanding of multiple aspects of federal Indian law. For example, some clerks seem surprised that Indian tribes have immunity from suit. Other clerks complain about the vagueness of federal common law tests. In many circumstances, the data indicates that a Supreme Court clerk will always recommend the denial of a petition filed by a tribal interest for the reasons Professor Stras suggests.

The cert pool Justices in the study period, except Justice Blackmun, constituted the core of the Court that would bring federalism jurisprudence to the forefront of American constitutional law in the 1990s – mainly Chief Justice Rehnquist and Justices White, O'Connor, Scalia, Kennedy, and Thomas. Cert pool clerks knew that they were writing for an audience that consisted of Justices often interested in states' rights. There must be different tugs on a memowriter. The audience cannot be ignored, but the memowriter wants to be fair and candid about the petitions. Early in a law clerk's one-year stint, before a memowriter becomes confident and experienced in this unusual job, he or she is perhaps more likely to write to this audience of "federalism" Justices that constitute the core of this audience. And so the cert pool memos, whether the clerks intend to or not, are less likely to trumpet the merits of a legal position put forward by a tribal interest than a state interest. A cert pool memo candidly noting that a state's position is weak in comparison to a tribe's position likely will not win points with the conservative Justices in the cert pool, while a memo understating the possible strength of a tribal position might undermine the cert pool memowriter's reputation. This suggests the possible creation of a cert pool culture, as suggested by David Stras, himself a former clerk. However, the import of the cert pool can be overstated. It bears mention that the Court several times rejected the recommendation of the poolwriters.

In the cases decided since the end of this study, from 1994 to the present, the ratio of wins and losses remains the same. Now, seven of the nine Justices participate in the cert pool, including three Democratic appointees. The "audience" for the cert pool clerks includes four "federalism" Justices (Roberts, Scalia, Thomas, and Kennedy), and three others (Breyer, Ginsburg, and Sotomayor). One would expect the cert pool memos in the last fifteen years or so to reflect the presence of the non-federalism Justices, but one could also expect that the focus of the cert pool memos would not reflect the minority. The cert pool memos appear to function as a means to crystallize the thinking of the Court on a particular case before any individual Justice reviews the materials. Anyone who negotiates contracts knows that the key to controlling the final product is to prepare the first draft, which then forms the basis for the entire negotiation. A Justice who supports a pro-tribal interest outcome in a matter might have to work from the first cert pool memo, which was written for an audience of a majority of Justices who disfavor tribal interests as opposed to state interests. Given that Indian law tends to not excite the "judicial libido," in Justice Scalia's pithy words, a Justice who starts out in the minority might be less inclined to use his or her institutional capital to persuade the rest of the Court to change a presumptive vote against tribal interests, interests that do not appear to have any special supporters in the Roberts Court, a role that Justice Blackmun most recently played.

CONCLUSION

The stated purpose of the Supreme Court's discretionary docket is to remove "patently uncertworthy" cases from consideration. In general, the certiorari process as currently constituted in Rule 10 appears to meet this goal. The Court will agree to decide few "splitless" or "factbound" cases unless there are extraordinary circumstances, such as unusual importance to the question or an atypical lower court error.

In the field of federal Indian law, with questions often far removed from the mainstream of constitutional jurisprudence, the certiorari process appears to prejudice the interests of Indians and Indian tribes, who are often engaged in a multitude of complicated legal disputes with states and state agencies.

The modern certiorari process, with its dependence on law clerks applying the Court's Rule 10, virtually guarantees that the cert pool will denigrate petitions filed by tribal interests. Tribal petitions, often involving the interpretation of Indian treaties or complicated and narrow common law questions of federal Indian law, are readily deemed "factbound" and "splitless." Conversely, the cert pool values and perhaps better understands the interests of state and state agency petitions. The pool's audience (a majority of the Roberts Court, including Justice Alito) also highly understands and values the states' interests. Thus, the pool's recommendations favor states and state agencies. The result, frankly, is that tribal petitions on a question will almost never be favored, whereas state petitions on the same question will often be favored.

The solutions to this discrepancy are not simple to effectuate. The Court's commitment to the certiorari process and the cert pool is powerful and not subject to outside interference. This commitment likely is linked to the Court's interest in placing all cert petitions – with the notable exception of original jurisdiction petitions – into one category.

As the occasional clerk and the occasional Justice recognize, however, federal Indian law resists categorization into the mainstream. The certiorari process simply does not work for federal Indian law. The cert pool, and its reflection of the political makeup of the Court, cements the prejudice that tribal interests face in the certiorari process.

Finally, while the admonition that tribal interests should do their very best to avoid the Supreme Court is not new, the findings of this study also demonstrate with increased force and clarity that Supreme Court adjudication is an extraordinarily hazardous process for tribal interests. The only cases the Court is likely to accept are cases in which the party opposing tribal interests lost at the lower court level. In short, a tribal victory below appears to be viewed as an aberration that the Court is more willing to correct than not.

One very important tactical benefit to this study for both tribal interests and those that oppose them is the perspective it gives to the certiorari process. It is one thing to read and understand Rule 10, but it is another to see it in action as interpreted and applied by the cert pool clerk. There is no doubt that the people writing these memoranda are some of the finest legal minds in American law and their assessment – colored as it is by Rule 10 – of the strengths and weaknesses of a particular petition is an invaluable tool for future litigators. If nothing else, the list of Indian law-related certiorari petitions filed during the study period will allow Indian law litigators to better assess their chances in the certiorari process.

NOTES & QUESTIONS

1. *Reading Indian Law*:
   - Articulate in your own words what it means for a case to be "factbound" or "splitless." Is it possible for a case to be both? Why are Indian law cases more likely to fall into these categories? Which of the cases Fletcher discussed caught your attention? Do you agree that these cases are "factbound" and/or "splitless"? How might Indian law be different had the Court granted certiorari in one or more of them?
   - Fletcher's piece encompasses not just the difficulty for Indian law cases to attract the attention of the Court, but also how different appellants are treated differently. Why is it problematic for tribal interests if the Court is more likely to hear cases when the state is the appellant? What might be motivating this behavior? The United States, through its trust responsibility, sometimes litigates cases on

behalf of the tribe. Does federal support cure the problems you have identified above?

- The certiorari process is not as simple as the Rule of Four might at first imply. How do the factors laid out in Rule 10 alter the cases the Court selects? What role do judicial clerks and the cert pool play in the selection of cases? How might these rules and processes be altered in order to give Indian law cases more favorable consideration or what could advocates do to improve the chances of getting an Indian law case accepted by the Court?

2. *An Indian Law Champion*: Professor Fletcher observes that it is helpful to Indian interests to have an advocate on the Court; "a Justice who starts out in the minority might be less inclined to use his or her institutional capital to persuade the rest of the Court to change a presumptive vote against tribal interests, interests that do not appear to have any special supporters in the Roberts Court, a role that Justice Blackmun most recently played." Throughout the modern era of Indian law there have been several justices willing to play this role. Perhaps contrary to popular assumptions, advocates for tribal interests are not always democratic appointees. Justice Brennan (an Eisenhower appointee) was largely seen as a friend to tribal interests, and, as *Factbound and Splitless* notes, Justice Blackmun (a Nixon appointee) played a pivotal role in trying to protect Indians and Indian tribes at the Court.

Justice Blackmun is not the only justice to have performed this role. Justice William O. Douglas has historically been the strongest advocate. Measured on the merits, he voted in favor of the tribal interest in a staggering 33 of 37 Indian law cases (89.2 percent) that reached the merits stage between 1959 and his retirement in 1975. Similarly Justice Thurgood Marshall voted in favor of the tribal interest in 64 of 87 cases (73.6 percent) during his tenure on the Court.

Since Professor Fletcher's article was published, a new champion for Indian law may be emerging. Justice Sonia Sotomayor was confirmed to the Court just as *Factbound and Splitless* was being published in 2009. Through the end of the October 2017 term she had voted with the tribal interests in 9 of 12 cases that reached the merits stage (75 percent). Further cementing her Indian law credentials, Justice Sotomayor's first lone dissent was in *United States v. Jicarilla Apache* where she wrote:

> Federal Indian policy, as established by a network of federal statutes, requires the United States to act strictly in a fiduciary capacity when managing Indian trust fund accounts. The interests of the Federal Government as trustee and the Jicarilla Apache Nation (Nation) as beneficiary are thus entirely aligned in the context of Indian trust fund management. *** The Court's decision to the contrary rests on

false factual and legal premises and deprives the Nation and other
Indian tribes of highly relevant evidence in scores of pending cases
seeking relief for the Government's alleged mismanagement of their
trust funds. But perhaps more troubling is the majority's disregard of
our settled precedent that looks to common-law trust principles to
define the scope of the Government's fiduciary obligations to Indian
tribes. Indeed, aspects of the majority's opinion suggest that
common-law principles have little or no relevance in the Indian
trust context, a position this Court rejected long ago.

564 U.S. 162, 188 (2011). Lone dissents are important because they signal
a justice's willingness to disagree with her eight colleagues and stand
alone for their interpretation of law. How important is it for the Court to
have a strong advocate for an understanding of Indian law that is
sympathetic to tribal interests? How might that advocate help change
the Court's jurisprudence during both the certiorari and merits stages of
Supreme Court litigation?

3. *Federalism and Indian Law*: Professor Fletcher argues that by the end of
the 1980s the Supreme Court had accumulated a collection of "federalist" judges (i.e. Chief Justice Rehnquist and Justices White, O'Connor,
Scalia, Kennedy, and Thomas). In this context, federalism implies
justices who are interested in tipping the balance between state and
federal power back toward the states – implying a more limited role for
federal governance. Why might these justices be less inclined to vote in
favor of hearing cases appealed to the Court by Indian tribes? (Reflect on
your understanding of Indian law, either from earlier chapters in this text
or your outside knowledge.)

Five of the six named federalist justices who participated in cert
decisions during the period of Professor Fletcher's study no longer sit
on the Supreme Court. How might changes in the composition of the
justices, as well as changes in the justices who participate in the cert
pool, alter the outcome of cert decisions? For a valuable discussion of
how Indian tribes embrace and engage with federalism *see* Wenona
T. Singel, *The First Federalists*, 62 Drake L. Rev. 775 (2014).

4. *The Role of the Clerk*: One of the things Professor Fletcher's piece
highlights is just how important Supreme Court clerks are as gatekeepers
of the Court's docket. As more justices opt into the cert pool, a single
clerk has the ability to contextualize a case for a majority of the Court. As
Fletcher contends, "Anyone who negotiates contracts knows that the key
to controlling the final product is to prepare the first draft, which then
forms the basis for the entire negotiation." Can you describe the role the
clerk plays in helping the Court to determine whether to hear a case?
Are you comfortable with clerks having this much control over the

Court's docket? Are you surprised by how candidly some clerks declare cases "unimportant" or even "uninteresting"?

For an in-depth look at the role of the clerk consider Artemus Ward & David L. Weiden, *Sorcerers' Apprentices: 100 Years of Law Clerks at the United States Supreme Court* (New York University Press 2006). The authors provide a history of the changing role of the Supreme Court clerk and suggest that clerks can sometimes change the mind of their justices. They note that clerks often work together, even across chambers, on the development of strategies to bring certain cases or arguments to the attention of the justices. However, as Fletcher notes, justices also do not always follow the recommendation of the clerks.

5. *Beyond the Law*: Legal scholarship is only just beginning to explore the possibilities offered by quantitative analysis. Political scientists have been working with these methods for much longer. John R. Hermann has done the most quantitative work with Indian law. In his *American Indians in Court: The Burger and Rehnquist Years*, 37 Soc. Sci. J. 245 (2000) he argues that being the appellant and having the support of the Solicitor General are important indicators of tribal success. Surveying the pool of Indian law cases actually decided by the Court from 1969 to 1992 (a period which overlaps with Fletcher's analysis of cert petitions), he concludes that tribal interests won 70 percent of the cases in which they were the appellant but only 32 percent of the cases when the Solicitor General appeared in person or on brief in opposition.

A focus on quantitative analysis is no longer only the purview of the hard sciences. Dr. Michael Yellow Bird has suggested that "we (in American Indian/Indigenous studies) are more than a bit light in teaching our students to be voracious consumers, advocates, and experts in using empirical methods as a form of critical thinking." *The Future of American Indian Studies in the Time of Global Warming*, 23:2 Wicazo Sa Review 91, 92–93 (2008). Dr. Yellow Bird points out that increasingly grant applications (of use to professors, students, and tribal leaders) ask for a research plan with the capability of producing statistically significant results. New scholarship must be "evidence based."

How do you think Indian legal advocates might be influenced by quantitative work in law or other disciplines? Are the insights provided by this analysis helpful? How does Fletcher's work encourage empirical thinking about problems? Do you find his case analysis and use of new primary materials to be sufficiently "evidence based" and persuasive such that you would be comfortable advocating for real and practical changes to the way Indian interests advocate at the Court on the basis of his article? Why is statistically significant or evidence based scholarship so valuable? Professor Fletcher has also grounded his empirical scholarship in part as a response to a call to change the goals and methodologies of traditional Indian law scholarship. *See* Matthew L. M. Fletcher, *American Indian Legal Scholarship and the Courts: Heeding Frickey's Call*, 4 Calif. L. Rev. Circuit 1 (2013).

FURTHER READING

- Grant Christensen, *Judging Indian Law: What Factors Influence Individual Justice's Votes on Indian Law in the Modern Era*, 43 U. Tol. L. Rev. 267 (2012).
- Daniel Epps & William Ortman, *The Lottery Docket*, 116 Mich. L. Rev. 705 (2018).
- Adam Feldman & Alexander Kappner, *Finding Certainty in Cert: An Empirical Analysis of the Factors Involved in Supreme Court Certiorari Decisions from 2001–2005*, 61 Vill. L. Rev. 795 (2016).
- Matthew L. M. Fletcher, *The Supreme Court's Indian Problem*, 59 Hastings L.J. 579 (2008).
- Emily Grant, Scott A. Hendrickson, and Michael S. Lynch, *The Ideological Divide: Conflict and the Supreme Court's Certiorari Decision*, 60 Cle. St. L. Rev. 559 (2012).
- John R. Hermann, *American Indian Interests and Supreme Court Agenda Setting: 1969–1992 October Terms*, 25 Am. Pol. Q. 241 (1997).
- John R. Hermann & Karen O'Connor, *American Indians and the Burger Court*, 77 Soc. Sci. Q. 127 (1996).
- Karl J. Kramer, Comment, *The Most Dangerous Branch: An Institutional Approach to Understanding the Role of the Judiciary in American Indian Jurisdictional Determinations*, 1986 Wis. L. Rev. 989 (1986).
- David M. O'Brien, *Join-3 Votes, the Rule of Four, the Cert. Pool, and the Supreme Court's Shrinking Plenary Docket*, 13 J.L. & Politics 779 (1997).
- Barbara Palmer, *The "Bermuda Triangle?" The Cert Pool and Its Influence over the Supreme Court's Agenda*, 18 Const. Commentary 105 (2006).
- Angela Riley, *The History of Native American Lands and the Supreme Court*, 38 J. Sup. Ct. Hist. 369 (2013).
- Alexander Tallchief Skibine, *The Supreme Court's Last 30 Years of Federal Indian Law: Looking for Equilibrium or Supremacy?*, 8 Colum. J. Race & L. 22 (2018).

Glossary

amici	A party that submits an amicus brief to the court.
amicus brief	An amicus brief is submitted by a person or entity who are not themselves a party to the lawsuit but who have specialized knowledge of the subject matter or are uniquely affected by the potential outcome of the litigation. Often these are legal scholars, states, nonprofits, or other policy-focused organizations.
autochthonous	Indigenous, aboriginal. Something is autochthonous if it comes from, originates from, or is native to a certain place.
canon / canonist	A canon is a general rule or legal principle often used to help judges resolve a legal dispute. A canonist is someone who believes the law should be resolved using the relevant legal canons.
certiorari	An agreement by an appellate court to review a decision of a lower court. At the United States Supreme Court four justices can agree to grant a writ of certiorari, at which point a case is scheduled for formal consideration.
comity	Judicial respect. Comity is the principle by which one court recognizes another court's judgment or reasoning even though they are not required to.
dicta	Language or reasoning used in a judicial opinion which is not strictly necessary to resolve the legal question asked and therefore does not carry binding authority on other courts.

diminishment	The legal principle that by virtue of congressional action some portion of a reservation has been returned to the state. A diminished reservation typically leaves Indian tribal governments with control over only those lands owned by the tribe, its members, or held in trust by the United States.
disestablishment	The legal principle that by virtue of congressional action some Indian reservations no longer exist; Congress has by statute removed the protected status of tribal lands, placing the old reservation community entirely under the control of the state.
Doctrine of Discovery	A legal principle applied in the Marshall Trilogy which justified the European appropriation of land. The Doctrine of Discovery suggests that in exchange for Christianity and "civilization" the Indians lost the right to alienate their lands to anyone but the first Christian nation to "discover" them.
Eleventh Amendment	The Eleventh Amendment to the US Constitution prevents the federal government from waiving a state's immunity to suit in any court proceeding.
ex post facto	A Latin phrase meaning "from a thing done afterward," it is the legal principle that a law may not be applied retroactively, but may have legal force governing only disputes which occur after the law has been enacted.
fee patent	Land previously held by the United States but now titled over to an individual. As part of allotment, fee patents issued to Indians were held in trust status. Those lands did not become subject to state jurisdiction until the trust restrictions were released.
fee simple	All permanent and absolute rights in a piece of real property (land).
grand jury	A group of typically twenty-three persons selected to examine the evidence and determine whether the government has a sufficiently strong case that it may bring felony charges against an accused citizen.
GVR	A grant, vacate, and remand order typically issued by the Supreme Court. A GVR does three things at the same time without requiring the parties to submit additional briefs or scheduling the case for an oral argument. The order grants consideration by the court, vacates the lower court judgment for

reasons given in the order, and remands the case back to a lower court for additional consideration.

habeas corpus
Literally "show me the body" or "produce the body," a petition for a writ of habeas corpus is the document filed with a court to challenge the physical detention of an individual.

in forma pauperis
A Latin term for "in the manner of a pauper," this is a request asking a court to hear a claim without paying a filing fee because the accused cannot afford to pay the fees.

inalienable rights
Natural rights. Rights which may not be revoked by government.

Indian country
A legal term of art which generally describes the lands over which tribes may have authority. It includes all reservation lands, dependent Indian communities, and allotments.

Indian fee lands
Lands now owned by individual Indians or Indian tribes but not held in trust by the United States. These lands may be taxed or subject to regulation by the state in which they are located.

indictment
A formal written criminal charge brought by a prosecutor and approved by a jury, typically a grand jury.

judicial review
The act of a court reviewing the legality of a law or action.

jurisprudence
A catchall term for the philosophy of law.

just compensation
Typically the fair market value of land that a property owner is entitled to when the government confiscates their property for a public purpose using its power of eminent domain.

legislative history
Documents produced by Congress in the consideration of a piece of legislation. These may be statements from members, transcripts of debates on the floor, committee hearings and reports, or other material entered into the record relating to the legislation. Courts sometimes look to the legislative history to interpret what Congress meant when it wrote a law.

Manifest Destiny
A nineteenth-century belief that the United States was fated to stretch from the Atlantic to the Pacific ocean.

Marshall Trilogy	A series of three US Supreme Court cases decided by Chief Justice Marshall in the early nineteenth century which established the foundation of many principles of Indian law. The three cases are *Johnson v. M'Intosh* (1823), *Cherokee Nation v. Georgia* (1831), and *Worcester v. Georgia* (1832).
nonjusticiable	A case or subject matter over which a court may not exercise power. For example, a plaintiff must have standing to bring a case and the issue before the court must be an actual controversy that is ripe for review but not yet moot.
original jurisdiction	A court has original jurisdiction over cases which may be brought before it in the first instance. The Supreme Court has original jurisdiction over disputes between states, but appellate jurisdiction over disputes that arise in lower courts.
originalism / originalist	Originalism is the theory that the Constitution should be interpreted as the founders understood it. An originalist is a person who believes in originalism.
personal jurisdiction	The power of a court to compel a defendant to defend a claim in front of it. The doctrine developed out of concern for fairness to the defendant, reasoning that the defendant must have some connection to the place where they are being sued.
petit jury	A jury, typically constituted by twelve persons, which sits at a trial and issues final verdicts on criminal or civil matters.
plenary power	In the context of Indian law, an assumption that Congress has virtually unchecked authority to make laws respecting Indian tribes.
political question doctrine	Asks whether the judiciary is the proper branch of government to resolve a dispute. It is premised on the idea that some conflicts are inherently political rather than legal in nature and so should be resolved by the elected branches of government.
practically irrigable acreage	A method of calculating a tribe's water rights, it implies that a tribe has the right to the water necessary to cultivate the land on the reservation which can reasonably be used for agriculture or food production.

preemption	In the context of Indian law, preemption asks whether the interests of the United States in furthering tribal self-government and self-sufficiency, combined with the interests of the tribe to regulate on reservation conduct, are sufficiently strong so as to overcome any interest of the state in asserting its power over the reservation.
prima facie	A Latin term meaning "at first face," generally referring to minimum elements the government must establish to prove its case.
pro se litigant	A Latin phrase meaning "for oneself," a pro se litigant is a party that appears in litigation without the assistance of a lawyer or advocate.
probable cause	Reasonable grounds. In the criminal context it implies that police have a sufficient reason to arrest a person or conduct a search.
Public Law 280	A federal law enacted by Congress in 1953, PL-280 gave certain states the authority to apply state criminal law within Indian country, and opened the doors of state courts to civil suits which arise in Indian country; it did not give states the authority to apply its civil laws in Indian country.
rescission	Cancelation of a law, repeal.
restricted trust allotments	allotted land, the title to which is held in trust by the federal government, giving the federal government the authority to manage the land.
right of occupancy	Often associated with Indian title, the right to occupy property includes the right to use it including the right to live upon land and to harvest or profit from its resources.
separation of powers	The principle that the different branches of government (legislative, executive, and judicial) are each given their own unique responsibility for the creation and enforcement of laws and that each branch has the ability to place a check on the other branches.
Solicitor General	The Solicitor General is the person responsible for arguing cases before the Supreme Court on behalf of the United States. The Solicitor General operates under the Attorney General in the US Department of Justice.

sovereign immunity /   Immunity is the principle that the government may
tribal immunity   not be sued without its consent. It is designed to
                           ensure government funds are spent for their
                           intended purpose, and not to defend lawsuits.

stare decisis   A Latin phrase meaning "to stand by things
                           decided," *stare decisis* is the legal principle by which
                           courts should ordinarily decide new cases the same
                           way they decided older cases.

statute of limitations A limit of time within which parties must file a claim
                           or otherwise forfeit their right to recover for an
                           injury.

subject matter jurisdiction The authority of a court to hear cases dealing with a
                           particular subject or between particular parties. For
                           example, state courts lack subject matter jurisdiction
                           to hear cases involving bankruptcy while federal
                           courts typically lack subject matter jurisdiction to hear
                           cases involving divorce, alimony, or child custody.

sui generis   A Latin phrase meaning "of its own kind," unique.

Takings Clause   Part of the Fifth Amendment to the Constitution
                           which says that private property may not be taken for
                           public use without the payment of just
                           compensation.

venire   The panel of prospective jurors from which a jury is
                           ultimately selected.

venue   The place where a lawsuit is heard.

wampum   Beads often made from shells and used by some
                           American Indians (typically in the Northeast). Often
                           the beads were kept on strings. Some wampum
                           strings were joined together as belts and were used to
                           commemorate important occasions or agreements,
                           including treaties with Europeans.

Summary of Relevant Supreme Court Cases

This Appendix includes a brief summary and complete citation of every US Supreme Court case mentioned in the sixteen excerpted readings and their corresponding notes and comments. It does not include tribal court cases, state court cases, or lower federal court cases. It is designed to provide the reader with a quick and easy-to-use summary of materials they may come across when using this text, and should be consulted if the use of a case in the text itself proves to provide insufficient context for the reader to understand the author's commentary.

Amoco Production Co. v. Southern Ute Indian Tribe, 526 U.S. 865 (1999). The United States opened western land to settlement under the Coal Lands Acts, but reserved to itself the mineral rights to the coal. In 1938 the United States restored to the Southern Ute Tribe, in trust, lands that it still owned under the Acts. The Tribe brought suit against subsequent landowners, seeking a recognition that the coalbed methane gas mined from these lands was really "coal" and therefore that the Tribe was entitled to royalties. The Supreme Court disagreed. It reasoned that at the time the Coal Lands Acts were made the gas was considered a dangerous waste product, and therefore Congress could not have intended to transfer to the Tribe the rights to the gas when it transferred rights to the coal.

Atkinson Trading Company v. Shirley, 532 U.S. 645 (2001). The Atkinson Trading Company owned a hotel and retail operation within the boundaries of the Navajo Nation but on land owned in fee by the Company. It sought a judgment that it was not subject to the Navajo Nation's hotel occupancy tax, a generally accepted form of taxation imposed by most states. In a unanimous opinion the Court relied on the *Montana* test to conclude that the Navajo Nation could not impose a tax upon a non-Indian business on non-Indian owned fee land unless it was necessary to protect tribal self-government or control internal tribal relations.

Brendale v. Confederated Bands and Tribes of the Yakima Nation, 492 U.S. 408 (1989). This case was a consolidation of several cases which asked whether the State of Washington or the Yakima Nation had the authority to impose zoning ordinances on an allotted reservation. The Court held 6-3 that the State of Washington could zone lands owned by non-Indians on the part of the reservation which had been largely opened to allotment, but the Court held 5-4 that the Tribe had the exclusive right to zone even non-Indian owned parcels of land in the portion of the reservation that had been largely closed to non-Indian settlement.

Brown v. Board of Education, 347 U.S. 483 (1954). The Supreme Court essentially overturned *Plessy v. Ferguson* and declared that the segregation of public schools by race was unconstitutional. This unanimous decision was one of the harbingers of the civil rights movement. Although *Brown* did not specify a timeline for ending desegregation, a second order in *Brown v. Board of Education* (*Brown II*), 349 U.S. 294 (1955) ordered states to desegregate "with all deliberate speed."

Bryan v. Itasca County, 426 U.S. 373 (1976). Public Law 280 allowed states to enact and enforce criminal laws on some reservations. To pay for its criminal law enforcement, Itasca County imposed a tax on the personal property of Indians living on the reservation. The Bryans had a mobile home which was assessed a $147.95 tax bill. They contested the ability of the County to tax Indian property located on Indian land. The Supreme Court held that under Public Law 280 states may impose criminal/prohibitory rules but not civil/regulatory ones. Essentially, states may have criminal law enforcement powers but may not levy taxes or otherwise regulate the non-criminal conduct of Indians on the reservation.

California v. Cabazon Band of Mission Indians, 480 U.S. 202 (1987). California attempted to shut down the high stakes bingo operation of the Cabazon Band. The Court applied a Public Law 280 analysis and held that Indian tribes could not engage in gaming activity if California prohibited gaming, but because California merely regulated gaming, the tribe as a sovereign could engage in gaming and promulgate its own regulations. The case opened the door to casino gaming on Indian reservations and led directly to the Indian Gaming Regulatory Act.

Cherokee Nation v. Georgia, 30 U.S. 1 (1831). Part of the Marshall Trilogy, *Cherokee Nation* held that Indian tribes are neither "states" of the union nor "foreign states" but are "domestic dependent nations." This meant that Indian tribes cannot take advantage of the Supreme Court's original jurisdiction, but are sovereign entities with some inherent governmental powers.

Cotton Petroleum Corp. v. New Mexico, 490 U.S. 163 (1989). Cotton Petroleum paid severance taxes to both the Jicarilla Apache Tribe and the State of New Mexico. It then challenged the ability of New Mexico to impose taxes on a non-tribal entity doing business on Indian land. The Supreme Court held that because New Mexico provided some services to the company while it was operating on the reservation, the State could levy its tax. It further held there was no proportionality requirement: so as long as the State provided some services it could impose taxes that vastly exceeded the value of the services provided.

County of Yakima v. Yakima Indian Nation, 502 U.S. 251 (1992). Tribal members who owned their land in fee on the Yakima reservation sued to stop the County from imposing an annual property tax and a tax upon the sale of this property. The Court held that state taxation on reservations must be expressly provided by Congress and that the General Allotment Act permitted states to impose a property tax on land on the reservation held by tribal members in fee, but did not authorize the tax of the sale of the land itself.

DeCoteau v. District Court, 420 U.S. 425 (1975). In 1891 the Lake Traverse Reservation was allotted with about 15 percent of its land being held by tribal members as Indian trust allotments and all remaining lands purchased by the United States for resale to non-Indian settlers. The Supreme Court held that the 1891 allotment "terminated" the reservation, so that only the Indian trust allotments remained "Indian country" and therefore the State of South Dakota had jurisdiction over events and activity on non-Indian owned land within the original boundaries of the Reservation.

Department of Taxation and Finance of New York v. Milhelm Attea & Bros., Inc., 512 U.S. 61 (1994). New York sought to prevent Indian tribes from selling untaxed cigarettes to non-Indians. It imposed quotas on the amount of untaxed cigarettes wholesalers could provide to tribes and tribal retailers. A group of wholesalers challenged the quota on the grounds that it violated the Indian Trader Statutes and was thus preempted by federal law. The Supreme Court upheld the regulations; reasoning that Indian traders were not wholly immune from state regulation, and that the regulations at issue were reasonable and necessary to ensure compliance with state law.

Dred Scott v. Sandford, 60 U.S. 393 (1857). Dred Scott was an enslaved man who sued for his freedom on the basis that he had been taken into free states and territories and that, because slavery was unlawful in those lands, he had been emancipated. In a 7-2 decision the Supreme Court disagreed. It held that a Black man whose ancestors had been imported to the country as slaves could never be a citizen, and therefore Scott had no standing in federal court to petition for his freedom. The holding was essentially overturned by the Civil Rights Act of 1866 and the Fourteenth Amendment to the US Constitution.

Duro v. Reina, 495 U.S. 676 (1990). Duro was an enrolled member of the Torres-Martinez Desert Cahuilla Indians. He was prosecuted by the Salt River Pima Maricopa Indian Community for crimes committed on its reservation. The Supreme Court held that Indian tribes lacked the inherent criminal jurisdiction over nonmember Indians. *Duro* was issued May 29, 1990, and by November 5, 1990, Congress had enacted a law overturning *Duro.* This "*Duro*-fix" was upheld by the Court in *United States v. Lara* in 2004.

Elk v. Wilkins, 112 U.S. 94 (1884). John Elk was born a Winnebago Indian. He moved to Omaha, renounced his tribal allegiance, and claimed US citizenship. The registrar of voters refused to add him to the voter roll and so Elk sued. The Court held that Indians are not eligible for birthright citizenship under the Fourteenth Amendment because, although they are born in the United States, they are not subject to the jurisdiction thereof. The Court reasoned that Indians were instead subject to the jurisdiction of their tribe. The case was effectively overturned by the Indian Citizenship Act of 1924 which extended citizenship to all Indians.

Employment Division v. Smith, 494 U.S. 872 (1990). Appellees were fired from their job at a drug rehabilitation clinic for using peyote as part of their religious practice as members of the Native American Church. They were subsequently denied unemployment benefits and they sued alleging a violation of their freedom of religion. The Court changed the test for determining whether there has been a violation of the Free Exercise Clause, ruling that neutral laws of general applicability do not and cannot violate the First Amendment. In response Congress enacted the Religious Freedom Restoration Act which required the application of strict scrutiny to cases where government attempts to interfere with religious practice. The Supreme Court upheld RFRA as applied to the federal government, but struck it down as unconstitutional as applied to state governments.

Ex Parte Crow Dog, 109 U.S. 556 (1883). Kan-gi-shun-ca (Crow Dog) killed a fellow Lakota tribal member (Spotted Tail) and was charged with murder in a federal territorial court. The Supreme Court held that no law or treaty made it illegal for an Indian to kill another Indian on Indian land and so granted Crow Dog's release. In response Congress enacted the Major Crimes Act which made it unlawful for Indians to commit several specified crimes in Indian country.

Ex Parte Young, 209 U.S. 123 (1908). Ordinarily states and the federal government cannot be sued without their permission because as governments they are entitled to sovereign immunity. In *Ex Parte Young* the Court reasoned that although a state itself might be entitled to immunity, government officials can be sued to prevent enforcement of an unconstitutional law. The Court reasoned that when a state official acts to enforce an unconstitutional law they are acting illegally because the Supremacy Clause invalidates all laws contrary to the Constitution. A state official enforcing the said unconstitutional law is thus stripped of his official title and may be sued as any other citizen.

Fletcher v. Peck, 10 U.S. 87 (1810). This case is notable because it is the first time the Supreme Court declared a state law unconstitutional. The Georgia legislature approved the sale of the Yazoo lands, which were then part of a large Indian reserve, at an artificially low price. When a subsequent legislature attempted to void the sale, the purchasers sued. The Court held the legislature's attempt to void the sale violated the Contract Clause of the Constitution and, in dicta, suggested that Indians did not own fee simple title to their lands. The issue of Indian title was more directly taken up a decade later in *Johnson v. M'Intosh*.

Idaho v. Coeur d'Alene Tribe, 521 U.S. 261 (1997). The Coeur d'Alene Tribe tried to sue the State of Idaho to secure title to the land under Lake Coeur d'Alene.

The Court held that the Tribe could not sue the State of Idaho because Idaho was entitled to sovereign immunity. The United States, as guardian for the Coeur d'Alene Tribe, subsequently brought suit on behalf of the Tribe. In a 5-4 opinion the Supreme Court found in favor of the Tribe's claim to the lake. *See Idaho v. United States*, 533 U.S. 262 (2001).

Iowa Mutual Ins. Co. v. LaPlante, 480 U.S. 9 (1987). The Blackfeet Tribal Court held it had jurisdiction over an insurance company with a dispute involving a tribal member for an accident that occurred on the reservation. Without seeking an appeal in tribal court, the Insurance Company sought a federal court order that the Tribe lacked jurisdiction. The Court held that regardless of how the federal court obtained subject matter jurisdiction, defendants in tribal court must exhaust all of their tribal court remedies, including the appellate process, to give the tribal appellate court the opportunity to correct any error.

Johnson v. M'Intosh, 21 U.S. 543 (1823). Part of the Marshall Trilogy, a quiet title action was filed between two potential owners, one who traced his claim to a purchase from Indian tribes and another who traced his claim to a purchase from the United States. The case is notable for the insertion of the Doctrine of Discovery into American law. The Court held that Indian title included the right to use and occupy but that Indians lost the right to sell the land to anyone but the United States. Therefore federal courts could not recognize or protect individuals who purchase land directly from Indians.

Kerr-McGee v. Navajo Tribe, 471 U.S. 195 (1985). Kerr-McGee argued that an Indian tribe could not tax non-Indians without authorization from the Secretary of Interior. In a unanimous opinion the Court held that Indian tribes are sovereign entities which do not need to ask permission to impose taxes on non-Indian conduct that occurs on the reservation.

Lincoln v. Vigil, 508 U.S. 182 (1993). Tribal members sued the Indian Health Service after it decided to discontinue the Indian Children's Program which provided clinical services to Indian children in the Southwest. The Court held that the program existed at the discretion of the agency using unrestricted funds and so was not reviewable by a federal court. It further held that the decision to discontinue the program was not subject to notice and comment rulemaking.

Lone Wolf v. Hitchcock, 187 U.S. 553 (1903). Lone Wolf, a Kiowa chief, brought suit against the United States arguing that the Tribe had been defrauded of its land and that the land cession at issue was in violation of the Medicine Lodge Treaty. The Court held that Congress could decide to take the land unilaterally using its plenary power. It further held that courts should presume that Congress would act in "perfect good faith" when acting toward Indians. It therefore affirmed Congress's acquisition of tribal lands in a manner which expressly violated the terms of an earlier treaty.

Lyng v. Northwest Indian Cemetery Protective Association, 485 U.S. 439 (1988). The US Forest Service proposed to build a road through the Chimney Rock area in

California. The area is sacred to the Yurok, Karuk, and Tolowa tribes, and they sued to prevent the construction of the road, arguing that it interfered with the free exercise of their religion. The Court disagreed. It held that because the construction of the road does not compel Indians to act contrary to their religious beliefs, and does not punish them for their religious practice by imposing a fine, incarceration, or depriving them of a government benefit to which they were otherwise entitled, there was no violation of their First Amendment rights. Despite its victory the Forest Service has never built the road.

Marbury v. Madison, 5 U.S. 137 (1803). Marbury had been appointed as Justice of the Peace by President John Adams, but his commission had not been delivered before Thomas Jefferson assumed the presidency. Marbury sued, seeking the delivery of his commission. The Supreme Court held that while Marbury had a right to the commission, the Judiciary Act of 1789 unconstitutionally expanded the Supreme Court's power and so was unconstitutional. Accordingly, the Court could not order the delivery of the commission as the power to issue writs of mandamus was beyond the scope of the Supreme Court's original jurisdiction as articulated in Article III of the Constitution. The case established the principle of "judicial review" whereby courts have the power to strike down laws which violate the Constitution, and is therefore one of the most foundational early Supreme Court opinions.

McCulloch v. Maryland, 17 U.S. 316 (1819). This case is notable for its explication of the Supremacy and the Necessary and Proper clauses. Maryland attempted to levy a tax on all notes of banks not chartered in Maryland; the only relevant bank being the Second Bank of the United States. The Court held that states could not tax the federal government and that the Constitution gives the federal government implied powers that are necessary to further the express powers named in the document.

Merrion v. Jicarilla Apache Tribe, 455 U.S. 130 (1982). Merrion had a lease with the Jicarilla Apache to extract oil and gas on the reservation. The Tribe then enacted a severance tax and Merrion contested the ability of the Tribe to impose tribal taxes after it had agreed to royalty payments in a lease. The Court held that Indian tribes have the inherent power to tax non-Indians on the reservation. The Court reasoned that tribes have the right to exclude non-Indians from their lands and so they may also condition the presence of non-Indians on the payment of taxes which support the tribally provided services the non-Indians use while on the reservation.

Minnesota v. Mille Lacs Band of Chippewa Indians, 526 U.S. 172 (1999). In an 1837 Treaty the Mille Lacs Band secured the right of hunting and fishing on their reservation. In an 1855 Treaty, the Tribe gave up some of the 1837 reservation lands; however, the 1855 Treaty was silent as to whether the Tribe also gave up its right to hunt and fish on these lands. The Tribe sued to force the recognition that it retained the right to hunt and fish on lands that were part of the 1837 reservation but given up in the 1855 Treaty. The Court agreed, holding that while Congress may abrogate an earlier treaty it must do so explicitly.

Montana v. Blackfeet Tribe, 471 U.S. 759 (1985). A 1924 Act authorized states to tax the production of oil and gas on Indian reservations. The Indian Mineral Leasing Act of 1938 contained no provision for state taxation, but did contain a general repeal of previous laws inconsistent with the 1938 Act. Montana wanted to tax leases issued pursuant to the 1938 Act and the Tribe opposed taxation. The Supreme Court held that the State could not tax the leases; reasoning that states may tax Indians only when Congress has manifested clearly its intent to permit the taxation. The ambiguity created by the 1938 Act demonstrated that Congress had not sufficiently clearly authorized the tax.

Montana v. Crow Tribe, 523 U.S. 696 (1998). The Crow Tribe and Montana each imposed their own severance tax on the extraction of coal by a non-tribal entity. The Tribe entered an agreement whereby the non-Indian coal miner would pay taxes only to Tribe or Montana to avoid double taxation, and then the Tribe sued to enjoin Montana from taxing coal extracted from tribal lands. The Court held that neither the Tribe nor the State have the exclusive right to tax, and so permitted Montana to impose its severance tax.

Montana v. United States, 450 U.S. 544 (1981). The Crow Tribe wanted to impose its ban on non-Indians fishing on the reservation. The Court held that the land under the Big Horn River belonged to the State of Montana and that while the Crow Tribe had the right to regulate the conduct of non-Indians on tribal land, it could not regulate the conduct of non-Indians on non-Indian owned land (even if that land was on the reservation) unless necessary to protect tribal self-government or control internal relations. The Court articulated two exceptions for when tribal regulation was proper: (1) when the parties had entered into a consensual relationship with the tribe through commercial dealings, contracts, leases, or other arrangements or (2) when the activity to be regulated would have a direct effect on the political integrity, economic security, health or welfare of the tribe.

Moragne v. States Marine Lines, 398 U.S. 375 (1970). A longshoreman was killed while working aboard a vessel in Florida waters. His wife brought a wrongful death action. Wrongful death actions were not allowed under common law, but the Supreme Court essentially overruled the common law rule against wrongful death actions, noting that all state legislatures and Congress had abandoned the rule. The Court allowed the wrongful death action to proceed.

Morton v. Mancari, 417 U.S. 535 (1974). The Bureau of Indian Affairs (BIA) established a preference for the promotion of employees which preferred American Indians over non-Indians. Non-Indian employees of the BIA challenged the preference as a violation of their right to the equal protection of laws. The Supreme Court held that the hiring preference was not a racial preference but a political one because the preference was given not to American Indians but to members enrolled in federally recognized tribes. The Court held that the BIA had a rational basis for the implementation of the preference and therefore found no constitutional violation.

National Farmers Union Ins. Co. v. Crow Tribe, 471 U.S. 845 (1985). A tribal member was injured at school and sued for damages in tribal court. The complaint was served upon school leaders but no legal action was taken and a default judgment was entered. The judgment was forwarded to the insurance company for payment and the insurance company challenged the jurisdiction of the tribal court. A unanimous Supreme Court held that while the jurisdiction of a tribal court raised a federal question and thus was suitable for resolution in federal court, all parties must exhaust their remedies in tribal court first because that will encourage tribal self-government and create a record that the federal court could review.

Neal v. Delaware, 103 U.S. 370 (1881). A Black man was charged with rape in Delaware, and in the county where he was charged no Black person had ever been called or selected for jury duty. The appellant argued that a proceeding in which no Black person could be called as a juror was a violation of his constitutional rights. The Supreme Court agreed. It held that because the civil rights amendments made Black men citizens and voters they should also be qualified jurors, and a system where only White people would serve as jurors was thus unconstitutional.

Nebraska v. Parker, 136 S. Ct. 1072, 577 U.S. ___ (2016). The Omaha Tribal Council enacted a tax on the sale of alcohol and required businesses selling alcohol to obtain a tribal license. The village of Pender, Nebraska, was within the original boundary of the Omaha Reservation but had been almost exclusively populated by non-Indians since allotment. Its businesses opposed the application of the tax. In a unanimous opinion the Court applied the three-part test from *Solem v. Bartlett* and held that the Omaha Reservation had not been diminished. It noted that while the demographics of the community have been a part of the analysis, a largely non-Indian population, without more, is not enough to diminish a reservation.

Negonsott v. Samuels, 507 U.S. 99 (1993). A Kickapoo tribal member was convicted in Kansas state court of aggravated battery for shooting another Indian on the reservation. The tribal member appealed the conviction, arguing only the federal court could prosecute Indians for crimes committed in Indian country. The Court held that Congress had conferred to the State of Kansas criminal jurisdiction over Indians in Indian country when it enacted the Kansas Act and therefore Kansas properly exercised a power delegated by Congress.

Nevada v. Hicks, 533 U.S. 353 (2001). An officer from the State of Nevada, with the permission of the tribal court, entered the reservation to serve a warrant on a tribal member who was accused of breaking Nevada law. The tribal member sued the state law enforcement officer for trespass and other torts in tribal court. The Supreme Court held that the tribal court lacked jurisdiction over state law enforcement officers who are on the reservation to execute a warrant. The case is particularly noteworthy because it is the only time the Supreme Court has concluded an Indian tribe lacks jurisdiction over an action that occurred on Indian-owned reservation land.

Nevada v. United States, 463 U.S. 110 (1983). In 1944 a federal court approved a water rights settlement to apportion water in the Truckee River to the Pyramid Lake Indian Reservation and the local water district. In 1973 the United States and the Tribe brought suit seeking additional water rights. The Supreme Court held that because the United States was representing the Tribe's interests when it entered the original settlement, both parties were precluded from relitigating the question of water rights from the river.

Obergefell v. Hodges, 576 U.S. ___, 135 S. Ct. 2584 (2015). A consolidation of six lower court cases, the Supreme Court held that states could not deny same-sex couples the right to marry. The 5-4 opinion held that limiting marriage to opposite sex couples violated the Due Process and Equal Protection guarantees of the Fourteenth Amendment, and essentially legalized same-sex marriage wherever the US Constitution is binding.

Oklahoma Tax Commission v. Chickasaw Nation, 515 U.S. 450 (1995). The Chickasaw Nation challenged the ability of Oklahoma to impose its motor vehicle fuels tax on tribal businesses and its income tax on tribal employees. The Court held that the legal incidence of the fuels tax fell on the tribal business and the state could not impose its tax on Indian tribes without the express authorization of Congress. However, the Court also held that the state may impose its income taxes on Indians who work for the tribe if they live outside of Indian country because states have the right to tax their own citizens.

Oklahoma Tax Commission v. Citizen Band Potawatomi, 498 U.S. 505 (1991). The Tribe sued Oklahoma to prevent it from enforcing its cigarette tax on sales occurring on the reservation. The State counterclaimed for back taxes owed and the Tribe raised sovereign immunity as a defense. The Court held that tribes do not waive immunity to counterclaims merely by filing a claim in federal court. The Court reasoned that while the Tribe is liable to the State to pay the cigarette taxes, the Tribe may raise immunity as a defense to a collection action.

Oklahoma Tax Commission v. Graham, 489 U.S. 838 (1989). Oklahoma filed suit to collect taxes from the Chickasaw Nation owed for its bingo games and cigarette sales. The Tribe removed the action to federal court, asserting federal question jurisdiction. The Supreme Court declared the removal improper because the possible existence of a sovereign immunity defense does not turn a claim based on state law into one arising under federal law.

Oklahoma Tax Commission v. Sac & Fox, 508 U.S. 114 (1993). Oklahoma attempted to tax the salary of tribal members who work for the tribal government. The Court held that states may not tax tribal members who work for the tribal government if they also live in Indian country without explicit authorization from Congress.

Oliphant v. Suquamish Indian Tribe, 435 U.S. 191 (1978). Two non-Indians were criminally prosecuted in tribal court for criminal activity that occurred on the

Suquamish Reservation. The Court held that Indian tribes had lost the inherent power to criminally prosecute non-Indians in tribal court because the assertion of that power had been implicitly divested by virtue of their status as domestic dependent nations.

Plessy v. Ferguson, 163 U.S. 537 (1896). Louisiana enacted the Separate Car Act which required separate accommodations for Blacks and Whites on railroads. Homer Plessy, a man of mixed race, challenged the law by sitting in the car reserved for White passengers. In a 7-1 decision the Court held that Louisiana's law was not unconstitutional and introduced the principle of "separate but equal" into American law. Widely regarded as one of the worst Supreme Court opinions ever issued, its principle of "separate but equal" was impliedly overturned by *Brown v. Board of Education* which precipitated the end of formal segregation.

Rice v. Cayetano, 528 U.S. 495 (2000). Voters in Hawaii amended the Hawaiian Constitution to create an Office of Hawaiian Affairs (OHA) to manage funds and land for Native Hawaiians. The Hawaiian Constitution limited voting for the Board which would manage the OHA to persons of Native Hawaiian descent. A non-Native citizen of Hawaii challenged the restriction. The Court held that Hawaii could not limit qualified voters in a public election solely to those persons of a certain ancestry, as ancestry in this instance was a proxy for race.

Rosebud Sioux Tribe v. Kneip, 430 U.S. 584 (1977). The 1868 Treaty with the Sioux Nation required any future land cession to be approved by a three-quarters vote of all adult male members. Congress subsequently unilaterally passed a series of Acts requiring land cessions from the reservation without the approval of tribal members. The Court held that Congress had intended to diminish the reservation through its unilateral land cessions, and that the land could be ceded without the approval of tribal members.

Santa Clara Pueblo v. Martinez, 436 U.S. 49 (1978). The Santa Clara Pueblo enacted a membership ordinance that enrolled the children of male members even when the mother was not a tribal member, but prohibited the enrollment of the children of female members whose male partners were not enrolled. Julia Martinez challenged the ordinance as denying her the equal protection of the law. The Court refused Ms. Martinez her requested relief. It reasoned that the Fourteenth Amendment does not apply to tribal government and that the only remedy a tribal member has to challenge a violation of rights guaranteed in the Indian Civil Rights Act is habeas corpus. Because Ms. Martinez was not detained, federal courts could not offer her a remedy.

Seminole Tribe v. Florida, 517 U.S. 44 (1996). The Seminole Tribe sued the State of Florida for refusing to negotiate for a gaming compact in good faith as permitted under the Indian Gaming Regulatory Act (IGRA). The Court held that the Eleventh Amendment prohibited Congress from waiving a state's claim to sovereign immunity, and therefore that Congress did not have the power to permit a tribe to sue a state under IGRA.

Seymour v. Superintendent, 368 U.S. 351 (1962). Seymour challenged his state court criminal conviction for attempted burglary because he alleged that he was an Indian, and the crime was committed on the Colville Indian Reservation, and therefore only the federal government could prosecute him. The Supreme Court agreed. It reasoned that only Congress can diminish the boundaries of a reservation, and while Congress may have opened the northern part of the Colville Indian Reservation up to settlement, the southern part remained Indian country. Because the alleged offense took place in Indian country, the State of Washington had no jurisdiction.

Solem v. Bartlett, 465 U.S. 463 (1984). South Dakota criminally prosecuted John Bartlett for an attempted rape occurring on land that was part of the Cheyenne River Sioux Reservation that had been opened to settlement. The Supreme Court applied a three-part test and concluded that the Reservation had not been diminished, and that therefore the state lacked the authority to prosecute an Indian for a crime that occurred in Indian country. The test requires an examination of the language of the allotment act which opened the land to settlement, the events and circumstances surrounding passage of the Act, and the Indian character or demographic condition of the land.

South Dakota v. Bourland, 508 U.S. 679 (1993). The question was whether Congress had abrogated the Cheyenne River Sioux Tribe's right to regulate hunting and fishing (as guaranteed in the 1868 Treaty of Fort Laramie) when it enacted the Flood Control Act and the Cheyenne River Act which collectively paid the Tribe to acquire land along the Missouri River for the construction of dams. The Court held that Congress must clearly express its intent to abrogate a treaty, but that the payment of money to purchase the land implied the loss of the power to regulate it and thus held the Treaty provision abrogated.

South Dakota v. Yankton Sioux Tribe, 522 U.S. 329 (1998). South Dakota wanted to build a landfill on land it acquired in fee within the original boundary of the Yankton Sioux Reservation. The Tribe sued to prevent construction. The Court held that the reservation had been diminished because the allotment act at issue coupled clear language of cession with an unconditional payment of a sum certain. For the Court this looked like Congress had purchased the land directly from the Tribe and had opened the lands to non-Indian settlement, thereby permitting its regulation by the State instead of the Tribe.

Strate v. A-1 Contractors, 520 U.S. 438 (1997). A traffic accident occurred on a North Dakota state highway between Gisela Fredericks, the wife of a tribal member, and a vehicle owned by a non-Indian company contracted with the Three Affiliated Tribes. Mrs. Fredericks filed a tort claim in tribal court and the non-Indian company contested the tribal court's jurisdiction. The Supreme Court held that the highway was equivalent to non-Indian owned fee land and that a single car accident constituted neither a consensual relationship nor would have a direct effect on the Tribe as required for tribal regulation by *Montana v. United States*.

Strauder v. West Virginia, 100 U.S. 303 (1880). Taylor Strauder, a former slave, was convicted of murdering his wife in West Virginia and sentenced to death by a jury in state court. Black persons were prohibited by law from serving on juries and so Strauder attempted to remove the case to federal court as permitted by the Civil Rights Act of 1866, but the removal was refused by the West Virginia Supreme Court. The US Supreme Court held that the categorical exclusion of Black persons from juries violated the defendant's rights under the Equal Protection Clause.

Tee-Hit-Ton Indians v. United States, 348 U.S. 272 (1955). A band of Tlingit Indians sought compensation from the United States for the loss of timber that was cut on their aboriginal lands. The Court concluded that Congress must recognize the Indian title before the interference with said title becomes compensable. Because the majority could find no place where Congress recognized the rights of the Tlingit Indians to the timbered lands, no compensation was owed.

United States v. Dann, 470 U.S. 39 (1985). The United States brought a trespass action against Shoshone tribal members who were grazing livestock without a permit on federal land. The tribal members claimed they had aboriginal title to the lands in question. The Court held that the aboriginal title had been extinguished through a successful claim filed by the Tribe with the Indian Claims Commission, and that the appropriation of a $26 million judgment was compensation for the loss of aboriginal title. Since the Tribe no longer had rights to the land, the trespass action was upheld.

United States v. Jicarilla Apache, 564 U.S. 162 (2011). The Jicarilla Apache Tribe sued the United States in an attempt to force the disclosure of reports the United States had commissioned regarding money held in trust for the Tribe. The Court held that the common law fiduciary exception to attorney–client privilege did not extend to the general trust relationship that exists between the United States and Indian tribes in part because the United States pays for advice not from trust assets but out of general revenues. Justice Sotomayor issued her first lone dissent, arguing that the common law rule of trusts should apply to Indian tribes.

United States v. Lara, 541 U.S. 193 (2004). Lara, a member of the Turtle Mountain Band of Chippewa Indians, was prosecuted by the Spirit Lake Tribe for striking an officer who worked for both the Tribe and the BIA. After being convicted in tribal court, Lara was prosecuted by the United States for striking the same officer in federal court. Lara challenged the second conviction as violating the Double Jeopardy Clause of the Constitution. The Court upheld the second conviction. It concluded that Congress had recognized the inherent power of tribes to criminally prosecute even nonmember Indians and so a prosecution by a tribe and by the federal government were prosecutions by separate sovereigns. The case effectively overturned the Court's earlier opinion in *Duro v. Reina*.

United States v. McBratney, 104 U.S. 621 (1881). A non-Indian murdered another non-Indian on the Ute Reservation. The Supreme Court held that the State of Colorado and not the United States had jurisdiction over a crime committed by a non-Indian against another non-Indian even on an Indian reservation because the tribe, and through its trust obligation the United States, is essentially a stranger to the crime and therefore has limited interest in its prosecution.

United States v. Rogers, 45 U.S. 567 (1846). Rogers, a White man, was indicted by a grand jury for the murder of another non-Indian in Indian territory. Rogers claimed that both he and the man he had murdered had been adopted by the Cherokee and were therefore Indians, depriving the United States of jurisdiction. The Supreme Court disagreed. It held that for purposes of criminal jurisdiction an Indian requires both a degree of Indian blood and recognition of their Indian status by the Tribe. Because Rogers had no Indian blood he could not be an Indian.

United States v. Sioux Nation, 448 U.S. 371 (1980). The Sioux Nation won the right to challenge the loss of much of its original territory. The Supreme Court held that the United States could take Indian land, or it could act as a trustee for the tribe, but it could not do both; "Congress can own two hats, but it cannot wear them both at the same time." The Court concluded that since Congress had not attempted to make a good faith effort to give the Indians the full value of the land at the time it was taken, the United States had effected a taking and ordered compensation for the loss of the land plus interest. As of this writing, the Sioux have so far declined to take the money – insisting instead that the land be returned. The original judgment was placed in an interest-bearing account and exceeded $1 billion by April 2011.

United States v. White Mountain Apache Tribe, 537 U.S. 465 (2003). Fort Apache on the White Mountain Apache Reservation was transferred to the Tribe by Congress in 1960, subject to the ability of the Department of Interior to use the Fort for administrative and school purposes. In 1999 the Tribe sued for breach of trust, arguing the United States had allowed the Fort to fall into disrepair. In a 5-4 decision the Supreme Court agreed. It held that there was a clear statute creating a trust responsibility and that the United States retained an ongoing physical presence at the Fort that came with an obligation to maintain the facility. It affirmed monetary damages.

Washington v. Confederated Bands and Tribes of the Yakima Nation, 439 U.S. 463 (1979). The Yakima Nation challenged Washington's assumption of criminal jurisdiction pursuant to Public Law 280 in eight circumstances selected by the State. A divided Supreme Court held that Washington could assume partial criminal jurisdiction because it had enacted the appropriate enabling statute as required by PL-280 and because federal laws related to Indians are not subject to strict scrutiny and therefore did not violate the Equal Protection Clause.

Washington v. Washington State Commercial Passenger Fishing Vessel Association, 443 U.S. 658 (1979). The case concerned the interpretation of the language in a series of 1854 and 1855 treaties giving tribes in the Pacific Northwest the right to take fish at their usual and accustomed grounds in common with all the citizens of the Territory. The Supreme Court held that Indian tribes were entitled to approximately half the fish, and any regulatory attempt by the State of Washington to limit the right of Indians to their half is unconstitutional by virtue of the Supremacy Clause.

Williams v. Lee, 358 U.S. 217 (1959). A non-Indian trader brought suit against two Navajo tribal members in Arizona state court to recover for monies extended them on credit to purchase goods from his on-reservation store. The Navajo challenged the jurisdiction of Arizona courts. The Supreme Court held that Arizona had no jurisdiction to hear a dispute involving tribal members and arising from the reservation. The Court held that states could not infringe on the right of reservation Indians to make their own laws and be governed by them. The case is often considered a turning point, ushering in the self-determination era in Indian law.

Worcester v. Georgia, 31 U.S. 515 (1832). Part of the Marshall Trilogy, Georgia had enacted a law requiring anyone who wanted to live among the Indians to obtain a license from the state and to swear an oath of loyalty. Georgia convicted two missionaries of living among the Cherokee without a license. The missionaries challenged the authority of Georgia to regulate their presence among the Indians. Chief Justice Marshall, writing for the majority, held that Georgia had no jurisdiction over persons located on Indian lands and ordered the missionaries released. The case articulated a strong territorial conception of jurisdiction whereby states have no power or interest on Indian lands. It also reaffirmed the inherent sovereign powers of Indian tribes.

APPENDIX 3

Master List of Additional Resources

Gregory Ablasky, *Making Indians "White": The Judicial Abolition of Native Slavery in Revolutionary Virginia and Its Racial Legacy*, 159 U. Pa. L. Rev. 1457 (2011).
The Savage Constitution, 63 Duke L.J. 999 (2014).
Kathryn Abrams, *On Reading and Using the Tenth Amendment*, 93 Yale L.J. 723 (1984).
Jane Anderson, *Indigenous/Traditional Knowledge & Intellectual Property*, Duke University Center for the Study of the Public Domain (2010).
Dennis Arrow, *Oklahoma's Tribal Courts: A Prologue, the First Fifteen Years of the Modern Era, and a Glimpse at the Road Ahead*, 19 Okla. Cty. U. L. Rev. 5 (1994).
Raymond D. Austin, *American Indian Customary Law in the Modern Courts of American Indian Nations*, 11 Wyo. L. Rev. 351 (2011).
Navajo Courts and Navajo Common Law (University of Minnesota Press 2009).
Milner Ball, *Constitution, Court, Indian Tribes*, 1987 Am. Bar. Found. Res. J. 1 (1987).
John Marshall and Indian Nations in the Beginning and Now, 33 J. Marshall L. Rev. 1183 (2000).
Joanne Barker, *Critically Sovereign: Indigenous Gender, Sexuality, and Feminist Studies* (Duke University Press 2017).
Russel Lawrence Barsh, *Putting the Tribe in Tribal Court: Possible? Desirable?*, 8 Kan. J. L. & Pub. Pol'y 74 (1998).
Bethany Berger, *Indian Policy and the Imagined Indian Woman*, 14 Kan. J.L. & Pub. Pol'y 103 (2004).
Justice and the Outsider: Jurisdiction over Nonmembers in Tribal Legal Systems, 37 Ariz. St. L.J. 1047 (2005).
Liberalism and Republicanism in Federal Indian Law, 38 U. Conn. L. Rev. 813 (2006).
"Power over this Unfortunate Race": Race, Politics and Indian Law in United States v. Rogers, 45 Wm. & Mary L. Rev. 1957 (2004).
Kenneth H. Bobroff, *Retelling Allotment: Indian Property Rights and the Myth of Common Ownership*, 54 Vanderbilt L. Rev. 1559 (2001).
John Borrows, *Drawing out Law: A Spirit's Guide* (University of Toronto Press 2010).
William Bradford, *"With a Very Great Blame in Our Hearts": Reparations, Reconciliation, and an American Indian Plea for Peace with Justice*, 27 Am. Indian L. Rev. 1 (2002).
Margery H. Brown & Brenda C. Desmond, *Montana Tribal Courts: Influencing the Development of Contemporary Indian Law*, 52 Mont. L. Rev. 211 (1991).

Christopher S. Byrne, Chilkat Indian Tribe v. Johnson *and NAGPRA: Have We Finally Recognized Communal Rights in Cultural Objects?*, 8 J. Envtl. L. & Litig. 109 (1993).

Jennifer Byrum, *Civil Rights on Reservations: The Indian Civil Rights Act and Tribal Sovereignty*, 25 Okla. Cty. U. L. Rev. 491 (2000).

Naomi Cahn, *Family Law, Federalism, and the Federal Courts*, 79 Iowa L. Rev. 1073 (1994).

Kirsten Matoy Carlson, *Congress and Indians*, 86 U. Colo. L. Rev. 77 (2015).

Kristen A. Carpenter, *A Property Rights Approach to Sacred Sites Cases: Asserting a Place for Indians as Nonowners*, 52 UCLA L. Rev. 1061 (2005).

Real Property and Peoplehood, 27 Stan. Envtl. L.J. 313 (2008).

Brenda J. Child, *Boarding School Seasons: American Indian Families, 1900–1940* (University of Nebraska Press 1998).

Grant Christensen, *Creating Bright-Line Rules for Tribal Court Jurisdiction over Non-Indians: The Case of Trespass to Real Property*, 35 Am. Indian L. Rev. 527 (2010).

Judging Indian Law: What Factors Influence Individual Justice's Votes on Indian Law in the Modern Era, 43 U. Tol. L. Rev. 267 (2012).

A View from American Courts: The Year in Indian Law 2017, 41 Seattle U. L. Rev. 805 (2018).

Carla Christofferson, *Tribal Courts' Failure to Protect Native American Women: A Reevaluation of the Indian Civil Rights Act*, 101 Yale L.J. 169 (1991).

Robert Clinton, *Redressing the Legacy of Conquest: A Vision Quest for a Decolonized Federal Indian Law*, 46 Ark. L. Rev. 77 (1993).

Tribal Courts and the Federal Union, 26 Willamette L. Rev. 841 (1990).

Donna Coker, *Restorative Justice, Navajo Peacemaking and Domestic Violence*, 10 Theoretical Criminology 1 (2006).

Richard B. Collins, *Indian Consent to American Government*, 31 Ariz. L. Rev. 365 (1989).

Elizabeth Cook-Lynn, *Who Stole Native American Studies?*, 12 Wicazo Sa Review 9 (1997).

Robert Cooter & Wolfgang Fikentscher, *American Indian Law Codes: Pragmatic Law and Tribal Identity*, 56 Am. J. Comp. L. 29 (2008).

Indian Common Law: The Role of Custom in American Indian Tribal Courts, 46 Am. J. Comp. L. 287 (1998).

Stephen Cornell & Joseph P. Kalt, *Where's the Glue? Institutional and Cultural Foundations of American Indian Economic Development*, 29 Journal of Socio-Economics 443 (2000).

Barbara Creel, *The Right to Counsel for Indians Accused of a Crime: A Tribal and Congressional Imperative*, 18 Mich. J. Race & L. 317 (2013).

Kimberle Crenshaw & Neil Gotanda, *Critical Race Theory: The Key Writings That Formed the Movement* (The New Press, 1996).

Raymond Cross, *Sovereign Bargains, Indian Takings, and the Preservation of Indian Country in the Twenty-First Century*, 40 Ariz. L. Rev. 425 (1998).

Chris Cunneen & Juan Tauri, *Indigenous Criminology* (Bristol University Press 2016).

Jered T. Davidson, *This Land Is Your Land, This Land Is My Land? Why the Cobell Settlement Will Not Resolve Indian Land Fractionation*, 35 Am. Indian L. Rev. 575 (2011).

Seth Davis, *American Colonialism and Constitutional Redemption*, 105 Calif. L. Rev. 1751 (2017).

Sarah Deer, *The Beginning and End of Rape: Confronting Sexual Violence in Native America* (University of Minnesota Press 2015).

Sarah Deer & John Jacobson, *Dakota Tribal Courts in Minnesota: Benchmarks of Self-Determination*, 39 Wm. Mitchell L. Rev. 611 (2013).

Sarah Deer & Cecilia Knapp, *Muscogee Constitutional Jurisprudence: Vhakv Em Pvtakv (The Carpet under the Law)*, 49 Tulsa L. Rev. 125 (2013).

Sarah Deer & Justin B. Richland, *Introduction to Tribal Legal Studies* (Rowman & Littlefield 3rd ed. 2015).

Philip Deloria, *Playing Indian* (Yale University Press 1999).

Vine Deloria, Jr., *Custer Died for Your Sins: An Indian Manifesto* (University of Oklahoma Press 1969).

Vine Deloria, Jr. & Clifford M. Lytle, *American Indians, American Justice* (University of Texas Press 1983).

Jennifer Rose Denetdale, *New Novel Twists Diné Teachings, Spirituality*, Navajo Times, Nov. 21, 2018.

Maura Douglas, *Sufficiently Criminal Ties: Expanding VAWA Criminal Jurisdiction for Indian Tribes*, 166 U. Pa. L. Rev. 745 (2018).

Allison Dussias, *Geographically-Based and Membership-Based Views of Indian Tribal Sovereignty: The Supreme Court's Changing Vision*, 55 U. Pitt. L. Rev. 1 (1993).

 Waging War with Words: Native Americans' Continuing Struggle against the Suppression of Their Languages, 60 Ohio St. L.J. 901 (1999).

Graham Dutfield, *TRIPS-Related Aspects of Traditional Knowledge*, 33 Case W. Res. J. Int'l L. 233 (2001).

N. Bruce Duthu, *Shadow Nations: Tribal Sovereignty and the Limits of Legal Pluralism* (Oxford University Press 2013).

 The Thurgood Marshall Papers and the Quest for a Principled Theory of Tribal Sovereignty: Fueling the Fires of Tribal/State Conflict, 21 Vt. L. Rev. 47 (1996).

Angelique EagleWoman, *Balancing between Two Worlds: A Dakota Woman's Reflections on Being a Law Professor*, 29 Berk. J. Gender L. & Just. 250 (2014).

 Tribal Nations and Tribalist Economies: The Historical and Contemporary Impacts of Intergenerational Material Property and Cultural Wealth within the United States, 49 Washburn L.J. 805 (2010).

Angelique EagleWoman & G. William Rice, *American Indian Children and US Indian Policy*, 16 Tribal L.J. 1 (2016).

Samuel Ennis, *Reaffirming Indian Tribal Court Criminal Jurisdiction over Non-Indians: An Argument for a Statutory Abrogation of Oliphant*, 57 UCLA L. Rev. 553 (2009).

Daniel Epps & William Ortman, *The Lottery Docket*, 116 Mich. L. Rev. 705 (2018).

Adam Feldman & Alexander Kappner, *Finding Certainty in Cert: An Empirical Analysis of the Factors Involved in Supreme Court Certiorari Decisions from 2001–2005*, 61 Vill. L. Rev. 795 (2016).

T.J. Ferguson, Roger Anyon, and Edmund J. Ladd, *Repatriation at the Pueblo of Zuni: Diverse Solutions to Complex Problems*, 20 Am. Indian Q. 251 (1996).

Matthew L. M. Fletcher, *American Indian Legal Scholarship and the Courts: Heeding Frickey's Call*, 4 Calif. L. Rev. Circuit 1 (2013).

 American Indian Tribal Law (Aspen Publishers 2011).

 Indian Courts and Fundamental Fairness: 'Indian Courts and the Future' Revisited, 84 U. Colo. L. Rev. 59 (2013).

 The Iron Cold of the Marshall Trilogy, 82 N.D. L. Rev. 627 (2006).

 Race and American Indian Tribal Nationhood, 11 Wyo. L. Rev. 295 (2011).

 Resisting Federal Courts on Tribal Jurisdiction, 81 U. Colo. L. Rev. 973 (2010).

 Rethinking Customary Law in Tribal Court Jurisprudence, 13 Mich. J. Race & L. 57 (2007).

 Same Sex Marriage, Indian Tribes, and the Constitution, 61 U. Miami L. Rev. 53 (2006).

 The Supreme Court and Federal Indian Policy, 85 Neb. L. Rev. 121 (2006).

 The Supreme Court's Indian Problem, 59 Hastings L.J. 579 (2008).

Carla F. Fredericks & Jesse D. Heibel, *Standing Rock, the Sioux Treaties, and the Limits of the Supremacy Clause*, 89 U. Colo. L. Rev. 477 (2018).

Philip P. Frickey, *A Common Law for Our Age of Colonialism: The Judicial Divestiture of Indian Tribal Authority over Nonmembers*, 109 Yale L.J. 1 (1999).

Doctrine, Context, Institutional Relationships, and Commentary: The Malaise of Federal Indian Law through the Lens of Lone Wolf, 38 Tulsa L. Rev. 5 (2013).

Domesticating Federal Indian Law, 81 Minn. L. Rev. 31 (1996).

Tribal Law, Tribal Context, and the Federal Courts, 18 Kan. J.L. & Pub. Pol'y 24 (2008).

Gabriel Galanda & Ryan Dreveskracht, *Curing the Tribal Disenrollment Epidemic: In Search of a Remedy*, 57 Ariz. L. Rev. 383 (2015).

Patty Gerstenblith, *Identity and Cultural Property: The Protection of Cultural Property in the United States*, 75 Boston Univ. L. Rev. 559 (1995).

David Getches, *Conquering the Cultural Frontier: The New Subjectivism of the Supreme Court in Indian Law*, 84 Cal. L. Rev. 1573 (1996).

H. Patrick Glenn, *Legal Traditions of the World* (Oxford University Press 2010).

Carole Goldberg, *Not "Strictly" Racial: A Response to Indians as Peoples*, 39 UCLA L. Rev. 169 (1991).

Overextended Borrowing: Tribal Peacemaking Applied in Non-Indian Disputes, 72 Wash. L. Rev. 1003 (1997).

L. Scott Gould, *The Consent Paradigm: Tribal Sovereignty at the Millennium*, 96 Colum. L. Rev. 809 (1996).

Kevin Gover & Robert Laurence, *Avoiding* Santa Clara Pueblo v Martinez: *The Litigation in Federal Court of Civil Actions under the Indian Civil Rights Act*, 8 Hamline L. Rev. 497 (1985).

Emily Grant, Scott A. Hendrickson, & Michael S. Lynch, *The Ideological Divide: Conflict and the Supreme Court's Certiorari Decision*, 60 Cle. St. L. Rev. 559 (2012).

James Grijalva, *Compared When? Teaching Indian Law in the Standard Curriculum*, 82 N.D. L. Rev. 697 (2006).

W.G. Guedel, *Capital, Inequality, and Self-Determination: Creating a Sovereign Financial System for Native American Nations*, 41 Am. Indian L. Rev. 1 (2016).

Richard A. Guest, *Intellectual Property Rights and Native American Tribes*, 20 Am. Indian L. Rev. 111 (1995).

Kathleen R. Guzman, *Give or Take an Acre: Property Norms and the Indian Land Consolidation Act*, 85 Iowa L. Rev. 595 (2000).

Carol Hand, Judith Hankes, & Toni House, *Restorative Justice: The Indigenous Justice System*, 15 J. Contemporary Justice Rev. 4 (2012).

Harvard Project on American Indian Economic Development, *The State of Native Nations* (Oxford University Press 2007).

Jennifer Hendry & Melissa L. Tatum, *Human Rights, Indigenous Peoples, and the Pursuit of Justice*, 34 Yale L. & Pol'y Rev. 351 (2016).

Justice for Native Nations: Insights from Legal Pluralism, 60 Ariz. L. Rev. 91 (2018).

John R. Hermann, *American Indian Interests and Supreme Court Agenda Setting: 1969–1992 October Terms*, 25 Am. Pol. Q. 241 (1997).

John R. Hermann, *American Indians in Court: The Burger and Rehnquist Years*, 37 Soc. Sci. J. 245 (2000).

John R. Hermann & Karen O'Connor, *American Indians and the Burger Court*, 77 Soc. Sci. Q. 127 (1996).

Mary Jo B. Hunter, *Tribal Court Opinions: Justice and Legitimacy*, 8 Kan. J. L. & Pub. Pol'y 142 (1998).

Robert Alexander Innes & Kim Anderson, *Indigenous Men and Masculinities* (University of Manitoba Press 2015).

Scott Jaschik, *Fake Cherokee?*, Inside HigherEd July 6, 2015.

Jennie R. Joe and Francine C. Gachupin (eds.), *Health and Social Issues of Native American Women* (Praeger 2012).

David Johnson & Scott Michaelson, *Border Theory: The Limits of Cultural Politics* (University of Minnesota Press, 1997).

Ralph W. Johnson & Berry Martinis, *Chief Justice Rehnquist and the Indian Law Cases*, 16 Pub. Land L. Rev. 1 (1997).

B.J. Jones, *Tribal Courts: Protectors of the Native Paradigm of Justice*, 10 St. Thomas L. Rev. 87 (1997).

Welcoming Tribal Courts into the Judicial Fraternity: Emerging Issues in Tribal–State and Tribal–Federal Court Relations, 24 Wm. Mitchell L. Rev. 457 (1998).

Miriam Jorgensen (ed.), *Rebuilding Native Nations* (University of Arizona Press 2007).

Eric Kades, *The Dark Side of Efficiency: Johnson v M'Intosh and the Expropriation of American Indian Lands*, 148 U. Penn. L. Rev. 1065 (2000).

Christine A. Klein, *Treaties of Conquest: Property Rights, Indian Treaties, and the Treaty of Guadalupe Hidalgo*, 26 N.M. L. Rev. 201 (1996).

Melissa L. Koehn, *Civil Jurisdiction: The Boundaries between Federal and Tribal Courts*, 29 Ariz. St. L.J. 705 (1997).

The New American Caste System: The Supreme Court and Discrimination among Civil Rights Plaintiffs, 32 Mich. J. L. Ref. 49 (1998).

Sarah Krakoff, *Inextricably Political: Race, Membership, and Tribal Sovereignty*, 87 Wash. L. Rev. 1041 (2012).

Karl J. Kramer, *The Most Dangerous Branch: An Institutional Approach to Understanding the Role of the Judiciary in American Indian Jurisdictional Determinations*, 1986 Wis. L. Rev. 989 (1986).

Nancy Kremers, *Speaking with a Forked Tongue in the Global Debate on Traditional Knowledge and Genetic Resources: Is US Intellectual Property Law and Policy Really Aimed at Meaningful Protection for Native American Cultures?*, 15 Fordham Intell. Prop. Media & Ent. L.J. 1 (2004).

Elizabeth Kronk, *The Emerging Problem of Methamphetamine: A Threat Signaling the Need to Reform Criminal Jurisdiction in Indian Country*, 82 N.D. L. Rev. 1249 (2006).

Patrice Kunesh, *Constant Governments: Tribal Resilience and Regeneration in Changing Times*, 19 Kan. J. L. & Pub. Pol'y 8 (2009).

Robert Laurence, *The Dominant Society's Judicial Reluctance to Allow Tribal Civil Law to Apply to Non-Indians: Reservation Diminishment, Modern Demography, and the Indian Civil Rights Act*, 30 U. Rich. L. Rev. 781 (1996).

Indian Law Scholarship and Tribal Survival: A Short Essay, Prompted by a Long Footnote, 27 Am. Indian L. Rev. 503 (2003).

Learning to Live with the Plenary Power of Congress over the Indian Nations: An Essay in Reaction to Professor Williams' Algebra, 30 Ariz. L. Rev. 413 (1988).

Martinez, Oliphant, and Federal Court Review of Tribal Activity under the Indian Civil Rights Act, 10 Campbell L. Rev. 411 (1988).

On Eurocentric Myopia, the Designated Hitter Rule and "The Actual State of Things," 30 Ariz. L. Rev. 459 (1988).

A Quincentennial Essay on Martinez v. Santa Clara Pueblo, 28 Idaho L. Rev. 307 (1992).

John LaVelle, *Review Essay*, 20 Am. Indian Q. 109 (1996).

Sanctioning a Tyranny: The Diminishment of Ex Parte Young, *Expansion of* Hans *Immunity, and Denial of Indian Rights in* Coeur d'Alene Tribe, 31 Ariz. St. L.J. 787 (1999).

Gary Lawson, *Territorial Governments and the Limits of Formalism*, 78 Calif. L. Rev. 853 (1990).

Edward Lazarus, *Black Hills, White Justice: The Sioux Nation versus the United States 1777 to the Present* (University Nebraska Press 1999).

Stacy L. Leeds, *The Burning of Blackacre – A Step toward Reclaiming Tribal Property Law*, 10 Kan. J. L. & Pub. Pol'y 491 (2000).

Sanford Levinson, *On Political Boundary Lines, Multiculturalism, and the Liberal State*, 72 Ind. L.J. 403 (1997).

Brian L. Lewis, *Do You Know What You Are? You Are What You Is; You Is What You Am: Indian Status for the Purpose of Federal Criminal Jurisdiction and the Current Split in the Courts of Appeals*, 26 Harv. J. Racial & Ethnic Just. 241 (2010).

Carolyn Liebler, *American Indian Ethnic Identity: Tribal Nonresponse in the 1990 Census*, 85 Soc. Sci. Q. 310 (2004).

K. Tsianina Lomawaima, Brenda J. Child, & Margaret L. Archuleta (eds.), *Away from Home: American Indian Boarding School Experiences, 1879–2000* (Heard Museum 2nd ed. 2000).

Catherine MacKinnon, *Feminism Unmodified: Discourses on Life and Law* (Harvard University Press 1987).

Kevin Noble Maillard, *The Pocahontas Exception: The Exemption of American Indian Ancestry from Racial Purity Law*, 12 Mich. J. of Race & Law, 351 (2007).

Peter Maxfield, Oliphant v. Suquamish Tribe: *The Whole Is Greater Than the Sum of Its Parts*, 19 J. Contemp. L. 391 (1993).

Robert McCarthy, *Civil Rights in Tribal Courts: The Indian Bill of Rights at Thirty Years*, 34 Idaho L. Rev. 465 (1998).

Daniel McCool, Susan M. Olson, and Jennifer L. Robinson, *Native Vote: American Indians, the Voting Rights Act, and the Right to Vote* (Cambridge University Press 2007).

Armen H. Merjin, *An Unbroken Chain of Injustice: The Dawes Act, Native American Trusts, and* Cobell v. Salazar, 46 Gonz. L. Rev. 609 (2010).

John Henry Merryman, *The Public Interest in Cultural Property*, 77 Calif. L. Rev. 339 (1989).

Jon'a F. Meyer, *History Repeats Itself: Restorative Justice in Native American Communities*, 14 J. Contemporary Crim. Just. 1 (1998).

Robert Miller, *The Doctrine of Discovery in American Indian Law*, 42 Idaho L. Rev. 1 (2006).
Reservation "Capitalism": Economic Development in Indian Country (Native America: Yesterday and Today) (Praeger 2012).

Robert Miller & Jacinta Ruru, *Discovery Indigenous Lands: The Doctrine of Discovery in the English Colonies* (Oxford University Press 2012).

David Milward, *Not Just the Peace Pipe but Also the Lance: Exploring Different Possibilities for Indigenous Control over Criminal Justice*, 43:1 Wicazo Sa Review 97 (2008).

Richard A. Monette, *Governing Private Property in Indian Country: The Double-Edged Sword of the Trust Relationship and Trust Responsibility Arising out of Early Supreme Court Opinions and the General Allotment Act*, 25 N.M. L. Rev. 35 (1995).
Indian Country Jurisdiction and the Assimilative Crimes Act, 69 Or. L. Rev. 269 (1990).

Douglas R. Nash & Cecelia E. Burke, (2006) *The Changing Landscape of Indian Estate Planning and Probate: The American Indian Probate Reform Act (AIPRA)*, 5 Seattle J. Soc. Just. 121 (2006).

Nell Jessup Newton, *Compensation, Reparations, & Restitution: Indian Property Claims in the United States*, 28 Ga. L. Rev. 453 (1994).

Federal Power over Indians: Its Sources, Scope, and Limitations, 132 U. Penn. L. Rev. 195 (1984).

Indian Claims in the Courts of the Conqueror, 41 Am. U. L. Rev. 753 (1992).

Memory and Misrepresentation: Representing Crazy Horse, 27 Conn. L. Rev. 1003 (1994–1995).

Note, *Securing Indian Voting Rights*, 129 Harv. L. Rev. 1731 (2016).

David M. O'Brien, *Join-3 Votes, the Rule of Four, the Cert. Pool, and the Supreme Court's Shrinking Plenary Docket*, 13 J.L. & Politics 779 (1997).

Sandra Day O'Connor, *Lessons from the Third Sovereign: Indian Tribal Courts*, 33 Tulsa L.J. 1 (1997).

Aliza Organick, *Tribal Law and Best Practices in Legal Education: Creating a New Path for the Study of Tribal Law*, 19 Kan. J. L. & Pub. Pol'y 63 (2009).

Barbara Palmer, *The 'Bermuda Triangle?' The Cert Pool and Its Influence over the Supreme Court's Agenda*, 18 Const. Commentary 105 (2006).

Patricia L. Parker & Thomas F. King, *Guidelines for Evaluating and Documenting Traditional Cultural Properties*, National Register Bulletin No. 38, US Dept. Interior (1998).

Jo Pascualucci, *International Indigenous Land Rights: A Critique of the Jurisprudence of the Inter-American Court of Human Rights in Light of the United Nations Declaration on the Rights of Indigenous Peoples*, 27 Wis. Int'l L.J. 51 (2009).

Wendy Collins Perdue, *Conflicts and Dependent Sovereigns: Incorporating Indian Tribes into a Conflicts Course*, 27 U. Tol. L. Rev. 675 (1996).

Stephen L. Pevar, *The Rights of Indians and Tribes* (Oxford University Press 4th ed. 2012).

Frank Pommersheim, *Braid of Feathers: American Indian Law and Contemporary Tribal Life* (University of California Press 1997).

Broken Landscape: Indians, Indian Tribes, and the Constitution (Oxford University Press 2009).

The Crazy Horse Malt Liquor Case: From Tradition to Modernity and Halfway Back, 57 S.D. L. Rev. 42 (2012).

"Our Federalism" in the Context of Federal Courts and Tribal Courts: An Open Letter to the Federal Courts Teaching and Scholarly Community, 71 U. Colo. L. Rev. 123 (2000).

A Path Near the Clearing: An Essay on Constitutional Adjudication in Tribal Courts, 27 Gonzaga L. Rev. 393 (1992).

Tribal Court Jurisprudence: A Snapshot from the Field, 21 Vt. L. Rev. 7 (1996).

Tribal Courts and Federal Courts: A Very Preliminary Set of Notes for Federal Court Teachers, 36 Ariz. St. L.J. 63 (2005).

Robert Porter, *The Inapplicability of American Law to the Indian Nations*, 89 Iowa L. Rev. 1595 (2004).

A Proposal to the Hanodaganyas to Decolonize Federal Indian Control Law, 31 U. Mich. J. L. Ref. 899 (1998).

Strengthening Tribal Sovereignty through Peacemaking: How the Anglo-American Legal Tradition Destroys Indigenous Societies, 28 Colum. Hum. Rts. L. Rev. 235 (1997).

Carla Pratt, *Tribal Kulturkampf: The Role of Race Ideology in Constructing Native American Identity*, 36 Seton Hall L. Rev. 1241 (2006).

Richard H. Pratt, *The Advantages of Mingling Indians with Whites*, in *Americanizing the American Indians: Writings by the "Friends of the Indian" 1880–1900* (Harvard University Press 1973).

Lisa R. Pruitt & Bradley E. Showman, *Law Stretched Thin: Access to Justice in Rural America*, 59 S.D. L. Rev. 466 (2014).

Renee Racette, *Tsilhqot'in Nation: Aboriginal Title in the Modern Era*, in *Indigenous Justice: New Tools, Spaces, and Approaches* (Palgrave Macmillan 2018).

Judith Resnik, *Tribes, Wars, and the Federal Courts: Applying the Myths and the Methods of Marbury v. Madison to Tribal Courts' Criminal Jurisdiction*, 36 Ariz. St. L.J. 77 (2005).

G. William Rice, *There and Back Again – An Indian Hobbit's Holiday: 'Indians Teaching Indian Law'*, 26 N.M. L. Rev. 169 (1996).

Justin B. Richland, *Arguing with Tradition: The Language of Law in Hopi Tribal Court* (University of Chicago Press 2008).

Keith Richotte, *Legal Pluralism and Tribal Constitutions*, 36 Wm. Mitchell L. Rev. 447 (2010).

Angela R. Riley, *Crime and Governance in Indian Country*, 63 UCLA L. Rev. 1564 (2016).

Good (Native) Governance, 107 Colum. L. Rev. 1049 (2007).

The History of Native American Lands and the Supreme Court, 38 J. Sup. Ct. Hist. 369 (2013).

Recovering Collectivity: Group Rights to Intellectual Property in Indigenous Communities, 18 Cardozo Arts & Ent. L.J. 175 (2000).

Straight Stealing: Towards an Indigenous System of Cultural Property Protection, 80 Wash. L. Rev. 69 (2005).

Angela R. Riley & Kristen A. Carpenter, *Owning Red: A Theory of Indian (Cultural) Appropriation*, 94 Texas L. Rev. 859 (2016).

Lindsay G. Robertson, *Conquest by Law: How the Discovery of America Dispossessed Indigenous Peoples of Their Lands* (Oxford University Press 2007).

Katherine Robillard, *Uncounseled Tribal Court Convictions: The Sixth Amendment, Tribal Sovereignty, and the Indian Civil Rights Act*, 2013 U. Ill. L. Rev. 2047 (2013).

Naomi Roht-Arriaza, *Of Seeds and Shamans: The Appropriation of the Scientific and Technical Knowledge of Indigenous and Local Communities*, 17 Mich. J. Int'l L. 919 (1996).

Addie Rolnick, *The Promise of Mancari: Indian Political Rights As Racial Remedy*, 86 N.Y.U. L. Rev. 958 (2011).

Mark Rosen, *Multiple Authoritative Interpreters of Quasi-Constitutional Federal Law: Of Tribal Courts and the Indian Civil Rights Act*, 69 Fordham L. Rev. 479 (2000).

H.D. Rosenthal, *Their Day in Court: A History of the Indian Claims Commission* (Garland Publishing 1990).

Judith V. Royster, *Stature and Scrutiny: Post-Exhaustion Review of Tribal Court Decisions*, 46 Kan. L. Rev. 241 (1998).

Elmer Rusco, *Civil Liberties Guarantees under Tribal Law: A Survey of Civil Rights Provisions in Tribal Constitutions*, 14 Am. Indian L. Rev. 269 (1989).

Natsu Taylor Saito, *The Plenary Power Doctrine: Subverting Human Rights in the Name of Sovereignty*, 51 Cath. U.L. Rev. 1115 (2002).

Race and Decolonization: Whiteness as Property in the American Settler Colonial Project, 31 Harv. J. Racial & Ethnic Just. 31 (2015).

Molly Schiffler, *Women of Color and Crime: A Critical Race Theory Perspective to Address Disparate Prosecution*, 56 Ariz. L. Rev. 1203 (2014).

Pat Sekaquaptewa, *Evolving the Hopi Common Law*, 9 Kan. J. L. & Pub. Pol'y 761 (2000).

Jill Kappus Shaw & Melissa L. Tatum, *Law, Culture & Environment* (Carolina Academic Press 2014).

Jessica Shoemaker, *Like Snow in the Spring Time: Allotment, Fractionation, and the Indian Land Tenure Problem*, 2003 Wis. L. Rev. 729 (2003).

Wenona Singel, *The First Federalists*, 62 Drake L. Rev. 775 (2014).

Wenona Singel & Matthew L. M. Fletcher, *Power, Authority, and Tribal Property*, 41 Tulsa L Rev. 21 (2005).

Joseph Singer, *Canons of Conquest: The Supreme Court's Attack on Tribal Sovereignty*, 37 New Eng. L. Rev. 641 (2003).

Alexander Tallchief Skibine, *Constitutionalism, Federal Common Law, and the Inherent Powers of Indian Tribes*, 39 Am. Indian L. Rev. 77 (2015).

Duro v. Reina *and the Legislation That Overturned It: A Power Play of Constitutional Dimensions*, 66 S. Cal. L. Rev. 767 (1992–1993).

Formalism and Judicial Supremacy in Federal Indian Law, 32 Am. Indian L. Rev. 391 (2008).

Redefining the Status of Indian Tribes within "Our Federalism": Beyond the Dependency Paradigm, 38 Conn. L. Rev. 667 (2006).

The Supreme Court's Last 30 Years of Federal Indian Law: Looking for Equilibrium or Supremacy?, 8 Colum. J. Race & L. 22 (2018).

Jenny Small, *Financing Native Nations: Access to Capital Markets*, 32 Rev. Banking & Fin. L. 463 (2012–2013).

Paul Spruhan, *Indian As Race/Indian As Political Status: Implementation of the Half-Blood Requirement under the Indian Reorganization Act, 1934–1945*, 8 Rutgers Race & L. Rev. 27 (2006).

Rennard Strickland & Gloria Valencia-Weber, *Observations on the Evolution of Indian Law in the Law Schools*, 26 N.M. L. Rev. 153 (1996).

Imre Sutton (ed.), *Irredeemable America: The Indians' Estate and Land Claims* (University of New Mexico Press 1985).

Ruth Swentzell, *Testimony of a Santa Clara Woman*, 14 Kan. J.L. & Pub. Pol'y 97 (2004).

Melissa L. Tatum, *Tribal Courts: Tensions between Efforts to Develop Tribal Common Law and Pressures to Harmonize with State and Federal Courts*, in *Harmonizing Law in an Era of Globalization: Convergence, Divergence and Resistance* (ed. Larry Backer, Carolina Academic Press 2007).

Melissa L. Tatum, Miriam Jorgensen, Mary E. Guss, & Sarah Deer, *Structuring Sovereignty: Constitutions of Native Nations* (UCLA American Indian Studies Center 2014).

Jack Trope & Walter Echo-Hawk, *The Native American Graves Protection and Repatriation Act: Background and Legislative History*, 24 Ariz. St. L.J. 35 (1992).

Rebecca Tsosie, *Land, Culture, and Community: Reflections on Native Sovereignty and Property in America*, 34 Ind. L. Rev. 1291 (2001).

Reclaiming Native Stories: An Essay on Cultural Appropriation and Cultural Rights, 34 Ariz. St. L.J. 299 (2002).

Ann Tweedy, *Connecting the Dots between the Constitution, the Marshall Trilogy, and* United States v. Lara: *Notes toward a Blueprint for the Next Legislative Restoration of Tribal Sovereignty*, 42 U. Mich. J. L. Ref. 651 (2009).

Gloria Valencia-Weber, *Racial Equality: Old and New Strains and American Indians*, 80 Notre Dame L. Rev. 333 (2005).

Santa Clara Pueblo v. Martinez: *Twenty-Five Years of Disparate Cultural Values: An Essay Introducing the Case for Reargument before the American Indian Nations Supreme Court*, 14 Kan. J. L. & Pub. Pol'y 49 (2004).

Tribal Courts: Custom and Innovative Law, 24 N.M. L. Rev. 225 (1994).

Rose Cuison Villazor, *Blood Quantum, Land Laws, and the Race versus Political Identity Dilemma*, 96 Cal. L. Rev. 801 (2004).

Artemus Ward & David L. Weiden, *Sorcerers' Apprentices: 100 Years of Law Clerks at the United States Supreme Court* (New York University Press, 2006).

Kevin Washburn, *Federal Criminal Law and Tribal Self-Determination*, 84 N.C. L. Rev. 779 (2006).

David E. Wilkins, *Hollow Justice: A History of Indigenous Claims in the United States* (Yale University Press, 2013).

The US Supreme Court's Explication of 'Federal Plenary Power': An Analysis of Case Law Affecting Tribal Sovereignty 1886–1914, 18–3 Am. Indian Q. 349 (1994).

David E. Wilkins & Sheryl Lightfoot, *Oaths of Office in Tribal Constitutions: Swearing Allegiance, but to Whom?* 32 Am. Indian Q. 389 (2008).

David E. Wilkins & Heidi Kiiwetinepinesiik Stark, *American Indian Politics and the American Political System* (Rowman & Littlefield 4th ed. 2018).

Robert A. Williams Jr., *The American Indian in Western Legal Thought* (Oxford University Press, 1990).

Columbus' Legacy: Law As an Instrument of Racial Discrimination against Indigenous Peoples' Rights of Self-Determination, 8 Ariz. J. Int'l & Comp. L. 51 (1991).

Documents of Barbarism: The Contemporary Legacy of European Racism and Colonialism in the Narrative Traditions of Federal Indian Law, 31 Ariz L Rev 237 (1989).

Learning Not to Live with Eurocentric Myopia: A Reply to Professor Laurence, 30 Ariz. L. Rev. 439 (1988).

Like a Loaded Weapon: The Rehnquist Court, Indian Rights, and the Legal History of Racism in America (University of Minnesota Press, 2005).

Mary Wood, *Indian Land and the Promise of Native Sovereignty: The Trust Doctrine Revisited*, 1994 Utah L. Rev. 1471 (1994).

Michael Yellow Bird, *The Future of American Indian Studies in the Time of Global Warming*, 23:2 Wicazo Sa Review 91 (2008).

James Zion, *Civil Rights in Navajo Common Law*, 50 Kan. L. Rev. 523 (2002).

Marcia Zug, *Traditional Problems: How Tribal Same-Sex Marriage Bans Threaten Tribal Sovereignty*, 43 Wm. Mitchell L. Rev. 761 (2017).

William P. Zuger, *A Baedeker to the Tribal Court*, 83 N.D. L. Rev. 55 (2007).

Christine Zuni, *The Southwest Intertribal Court of Appeals*, 24 N.M. L. Rev. 309 (1994).